CANCER DOESN'T CARE

We Do.

If you or someone you care about has cancer, then Chai cares too.

To find out more please call our free telephone helpline on **0808 808 4567** or **020 8202 2211** or visit **www.chaicancercare.org**

Chai's range of services are available at:

Chai Cancer Care Centre	**North West London**
Redbridge Community Centre	**Essex**
Nightingale	**South London**
Home Support Service	**Your own home**

chai cancer care
together we can cope

Chai Lifeline Cancer Care
Registered Charity No.1078956

Brick by brick
JCD is helping Jewish children build a
better quality of life
We provide worldwide support for thousands of neglected, abused, handicapped and disadvantaged children.
To help support the vital work JCD undertakes each year:
www.jcd.uk.com
info@jcd.uk.com
020 8446 8804
707 High Road London N12 0BT
Helping to make a Jewish child's day
JCD
Registered Charity No. 209266

Saving More Lives

Magen David Adom is Israel's only medical emergency and blood bank service, saving more lives every day. It responds to approximately 500,000 calls a year: from accidents, births and everyday emergencies to suicide bombings and other terror attacks – at speeds not bettered anywhere in the world.

Magen David Adom relies on voluntary donations in order to carry out this critical work – 35% of which is funded by diaspora Jewry. Every single donation received is vital in helping Magen David Adom to save more lives.

To save more lives visit **www.mdauk.org** or call **020 8201 5900**

Head Office: Shield House,
Harmony Way, London NW4 2BZ
Tel: 020 8201 5900 **Fax:** 020 8201 5901
Regional Office: Joseph Mamlock House,
142 Bury Old Road, Manchester M8 4HE
Tel: 0161 795 2999 **Fax:** 0161 929 1705
Email: info@mdauk.org

Registered Charity Number: 1113409

MAGEN DAVID ADOM UK — SAVING MORE LIVES

Supporting Israel's Medical Emergency Service

THE JEWISH YEAR BOOK
2009

The Jewish Year Book

Published in association with the
Jewish Chronicle, London

Founded 1896

2009
5769–5770

Edited by
STEPHEN W. MASSIL

VALLENTINE MITCHELL
LONDON • PORTLAND, OR

Published in 2009 by Vallentine Mitchell

Suite 314, Premier House
112–114 Station Road
Edgware, Middlesex HA8 7BJ
UK

920 NE 58th Avenue, Suite 300
Portland, Oregon,
97213-3786
USA

www.vmbooks.com
jyb@vmbooks.com

British Library Cataloguing in Publication Data

The Jewish year book 2009, 5769-5770
1. Jews - Great Britain - Periodicals 2. Judaism - Great
Britain - Periodicals
I. Massil, Stephen W. II. Jewish Chronicle
296'.0941'05

ISBN 978 0 85303 890 0
ISSN 0075-3769

Printed by Antony Rowe Ltd., Chippenham, Wiltshire

CONTENTS

PREFACE

Looking back it was the purpose of the meetings at Annapolis in December 2007 to entrench the peace-process between Israel and the Palestinian leader Mahmoud Abbas as the political business of 2008 but little has been achieved. The state of Gaza and the intransigence of Hamas still predominate in the news and while there have been cease-fires and some cessation of overt hostilities, the building of Israeli settlements has continued unabated and suicide bombing has now returned to Jerusalem and from amongst the Israeli-Arab population. While the perceived threat from Iran has been sustained, it is understood that some level of secret talks about a settlement with Syria have also been entered. Levels of Aliyah have continued to be high. In Israel the publication of the Winograd Report has finally brought Prime Minister Ehud Olmert to the point of resignation. Foreign Minister Tzipi Livni won the Kadima vote to succeed him in government but her efforts to form a new coalition have not been successful and rather than accommodate herself to unsustainable alliances with the minority (religious) parties she has called for an election (not otherwise due until 2010) in early 2009. The forthcoming campaign will see Ms Livni and Kadima confronted by Likud under Binyamin Netanyahu once more, as the major contenders, with the Israel Labour Party still in some disarray. Plainly, and as ever, and, whatever the economic situation (and no-one has apparently referred to the state of the Israeli economy in the context of the current world-wide crisis affecting so many countries) the voters' choice in Israel is between continued exploration for peace through concessions for a two-state solution and 'hawkish' policies designed to sustain 'the one-state' solution.

Israel's sixtieth anniversary has been widely celebrated by organisations across the country, and H.E. the Ambassador Ron Prosor has enjoyed a high profile throughout a particularly extensive and energetic year responding to tributes. The events included a dinner at Windsor Castle. In the Australian Parliament there was a bipartisan motion in support of Israel. The year marks also the fiftieth anniversary of the beginnings of Anglo-Jewish tourism to Israel when in the aftermath of the Suez campaign organisations not otherwise specifically associated with Zionism began to organise visits to Israel: the AJY and the Zemel Choir in particular. That Andrew Balcombe of the Zionist Federation, who was a member of such a party in 1958, has gone on Aliyah this year, and also Alan Webber of Hillel and Bnai Brith, who participated in the Young Jewish Leadership Course of 1978 which included a full tour in Israel, shows the long term effects of such initiatives.

With the resignation of David Rowan, Dr Stephen Pollard has been appointed the new editor the Jewish Chronicle in the year of William Frankel's death. James Harding became editor of the Times at the end of 2007. Daniel Finkelstein was awarded the first Chaim Bermant Prize for Journalism at an event at Jewish Book Week.

Along with continuing vigilance tracing the growing menace of antisemitic discourse and acts in the country at large, the energies of the community focus on problems over conversion, the argument with Independent Jewish Voices, and the 'Statement on Communal Collaboration' among the initiatives of the Masorti, Reform and Liberal congregations.

Holocaust Memorial Day was marked formally in Liverpool and apparently Muslim groups participated for the first time in events around the country. But Greenbank Drive Synagogue closed at its seventieth anniversary. The 'Three sisters on Hope Street', one of the highlights of the Liverpool cultural season, enjoyed a run at Hampstead in the spring balanced by Tom Stoppard's new version of Chekhov's 'Ivanov' which participated in the distinguished success of that production at the Donmar's West End season in the autumn; at the Donmar itself Arthur Miller's early play 'The man who had all the luck' proved to be well worth the revival. 'Golda's Balcony' was performed at the Shaw Theatre.

One complicated set of theatrical interconnections can be retraced through the fact that Michael Frayn's new play 'Afterlife' dealing with Max Reinhardt and his collaborations on 'Everyman' at the Salzburg Festival from 1920 was premiered in London while at the Edinburgh Festival Honegger's 'Le Roi David'was performed for the first time here, a work conceived for a rival Festival at Mézières in 1921 which had a small but dramatic role for Madeleine Milhaud who died at age 106 in January.

Both Jewish Care and the Jewish Museum are undertaking refurbishment and redevelopment of their respective buildings. The IJPR has moved premises, and London's Hillel has moved from Bloomsbury to Camden Town. Westmount has closed and the Shalom Singers in

Glasgow disbanded. The Oxford Mikveh opened in July whereas progress in the establishing of a mikveh in Cambridge has become fraught.

The strength of the BNP at the local elections has become a matter of concern. A moot point of the voting in London concerned whether Mr Livingstone lost the London mayoral vote on the strength of Jewish opposition to his record. Sir Trevor Chinn has been appointed chairman of the new Mayor of London's Fund for London. Councillor Sandra Parnell is the new Mayor of Hertsmere, Farida Turner the Mayor of Elstree, Louise Hyams the Lord Mayor of Westminster; Solomon Levy the Mayor Gibraltar; and Rabbi Gilles Bernheim was elected new Chief Rabbi of France.

Nick Cohen gave the Fifth Isaiah Berlin Lecture. Dr David Ariel was appointed the new Principal at Yarnton. Jane Eisner the new editor of 'Forward'. Matt Plen is the new director of the Assembly of Masorti Synagogues. Rabbi Shraga Zimmerman was appointed to Gateshead in succession to Rabbi Bezalel Rakow who died in 2003. Sarah Harel Hoshani was appointed curator of Judaica at the Jewish Museum. Nicole Delamere the new headteacher at Simon Marks Primary.

The gift of £20 million to the National Maritime Museum by Sammy Ofer, an Israeli nostalgic for his days in the Royal Navy, is part of a long tradition – and he consolidated his support by an additional donation to assist in the restoration of the Cutty Sark.

Sir Tom Stoppard shared the 2008 Dan David Prize with Amos Oz and Atom Egoyan; Saul Friedlander won a Pulitzer Prize; Dannie Abse the Welsh Book of the Year award; Photographer Walter Suschitsky awarded the Viennese Gold Medal; Dame Rosalyn Higgins was awarded the Balzan Prize; Trude Levi was honoured in Germany for her work in Shoah education.

The Jewish Historical Society has formally launched a digitization of all its publications on its web-site. Israel Finestein published another volume of his papers, 'Studies and profiles in Anglo-Jewish History', Geoffrey Alderman published a collection, 'Controversy and Crisis : Studies in the History of the Jews in Modern Britain', Meir Persoff published, 'Faith Against Reason: Religious Reform and the British Chief Rabbinate, 1840–1990', and Marc Saperstein published, 'Jewish Preaching in Times of War, 1800–2001' and has been in demand lecturing on this topic. While Derek Taylor and Lord Janner seized on the hundred and fiftieth anniversary of Lionel de Rothschild's formal entry into Parliament in 1858 to publish a digest of his successors, 'Jewish Parliamentarians', the Jewish Members of Parliament who have followed in his footsteps, N.M. Rothschild's ensured that visitors to Waddesdon throughout the season could see Henry Barraud's picture of the scene when Lionel was sworn in, and the Rothschild Archives web-site has featured an on-line exhibition describing the campaign whose fruition the picture celebrates: 'From Bank to Westminster'.

The Jewry of Zimbabwe is in its final crisis as the political and economic turmoil exacted by the regime grinds the country into catastrophe; the Jews of Gori apparently bore the brunt of the Russian-powered attacks on Georgia.

It has been the tenth anniversary of the Estorick Collection in Canonbury. Tate Modern has displayed Mark Rothko's late Murals. The Israel Museum can be congratulated on the irony of its contribution of major treasures for the Hadrian exhibition at the British Museum. Unexpectedly, the exhibition of the Danish painter Viktor Hammershøi at the Royal Academy included what appeared to be a conundrum in that a picture from a collection in Schleswig-Holstein and entitled in the original catalogue of his oeuvre 'Jewish School in Guilford Street' (1912) proved to be a record of Jews' College on one of its removes.

The Ben Uri exhibited 'Whitechapel at War: Isaac Rosenberg and his Circle' and one of Rosenberg's poems has been selected for the Poems on the Underground for the 90th anniversary of the Armistice. Emanuel Litvinoff was celebrated in an event in Whitechapel on the re-issue of his 'Journey Through a Small Planet' of 1972, and Rudolf Rocker at Toynbee Hall.

Deaths during the year have depleted the Who's who entries quite considerably this year. Amongst these, Rabbi Dr. Isaac Cohen, former Chief Rabbi of Ireland, while the current incumbent Rabbi Pearlman has retired. The deaths of the Rev. Leslie Olsberg and the Rev. Leslie Hardman raised perhaps the most poignant memories, as also the deaths of Lord Bethell, and in particular, Irena Sendler (at 97) and Henri Bartoli whose careers the obituarists have delved into in extraordinary detail.

I have had occasion to update Aron Owen's first notes on the original North West London Eruv with the inclusion of its counterpart in Edgware and in anticipation of others being negotiated around the country. In the aftermath of the death of Sydney Shipton, I have formalised the presence of the representative national interfaith groups so long the sole territory of the Council of Christian and Jews whose only counterpart and earliest precursor had been the London Society of Jews and Christians now at 80 years.

I record my thanks as ever to Mordaunt Cohen, Barry Hyman, Marlena Schmool and Barbara Goldstone for regular assistance in preparing this volume, as also to John Fischer for the Calendar and the many officers of organisations in London and around the country whose notices maintain the substantive content of the directory.

Two of this year's essays serve to mark Israel's 60th anniversary and indicate the abiding strengths of the country. The creation of Tel Aviv predates the Balfour Declaration and the Mandate but like many things taken for granted can be seen to have deep roots. The centenary of the City gives a sharper context to the sixtieth anniversary of the State. Professor Shindler will be celebrating this at a major conference in 2009. The recognition of the strengths and diversity of Israeli science and technology in national development needs to be coupled with its world-wide appeal and I am grateful to Professor Apeloig for his contribution from the Technion. The ZF will be holding an exhibition of Israeli science and technology at a major London venue in 2009 and I am glad to have anticipated this. The Mendelssohn Family holds a major place in the history of modern German-Jewry. The music of Felix Mendelssohn and the place he and his sister hold in the romantic imagination are a constant delight. I am grateful to David Conway for focussing on the difficult question of tracing Jewish connections and roots in the work of such a musician. The anti-semitic tendency will always dog the careers of formerly Jewish families but that is no reason not to explore what might or might not be the 'Jewish' figures in the achievement of the musician, music itself being elusive to the expression of the rational. But as we have this year taken pride in celebration of Daniel Barenboim's plaudits and achievement in performing the cycle of Beethoven's sonatas, so the anticipation of a year ahead featuring the music of Mendelssohn is worth marking in the sort of examination that Dr. Conway offers. I would add that Dr Conway and his wife have been instrumental in establishing a music festival at Levrea in Slovakia. In launching this series of essays it was not Frank Cass's intention to mark the achievements of individuals through the inclusion of specific obituary notices but I make no apology for following last year's celebration of his life, as also of Celia Rose, by including as my own contribution an essay on Ruth Winston-Fox. The fact is that like Celia Rose, she was an important figure in my own life and career and a careful reading of this volume will discover that in several different ways. But the essay is also offered in its wider intention as a starter for a consideration of the work of Jewish women in communal leadership in Jewry and at large during the twentieth century. As well as at a Memorial Service at her synagogue at Palmer's Green Ruth's memory was evoked by the launch of a DVD at Westminster on the 'Jewish Way of Life' one of her major communal initiatives which she launched in an exhibition at the Palmer's Green jubilee in 1978.

For the year ahead, as I have said, Knesset elections in Israel will be a dominant factor as the new year opens and as well as the implications for progress in any peace-process, pending the outcome the campaign will become braided with the efforts that the new American President may want to make in making an early mark with new policies and relations in the Middle East. Jewish Book Week may want to review the hundred and twenty years of publishing by the Jewish Publication Society of America. The hundred and fiftieth anniversary of the Mishkenot Sha'annanim will give the Montefiore saga a further. Hand in hand with the multiple anniversaries of the Anschluss, Kristallnacht, and the Holocaust, there follow the anniversaries of the Belsize Square Synagogue whose seventieth anniversary will be marked in 2009. Coventry is to host National Holocaust Day. There will be elections at the Board of Deputies. In February, at the Wallace Collection there is to be an exhibition of Jewish jewellery from Germany, and a Yiddish Film Festival at the Barbican. The lectures presented by the Chief Rabbi in his 'Future Tense' lecture series of 2007 are due to be published during the coming year.

**London 28th October
2008 / 29th Tishri 5769**

ISRAEL AND SCIENCE
By Yitzhak Apeloig

Israel is the 100th smallest country in the world, with less than 1/1000th of the world's population ... about the size of Wales. Yet despite its small size and the absence of any natural resources of any significance, Israel is today recognised as a world leader in science and technology and the home to the highest number of high-tech and start-up companies in the world after the U.S.

How did Israel reach this level of achievement over the last decade despite terrorist attacks, the competition and challenges of growing globalization, conflict with her neighbours, maintaining a high cost of defence, and the absorption of over one million new immigrants from the former Soviet Union?

Firstly, successive Israeli governments since 1967 have made a strategic effort to encourage foreign investment and trade and become technologically competitive, with spending on research and development one of the highest in the world. These endeavours have resulted in nearly 100 leading international companies establishing corporate R&D centres in Israel including Intel, IBM, Microsoft, Motorola and Google, and led to the development of many new technologies and products based on cutting edge technology. The close link to the private sector has led to the most innovative Israeli technology being successfully brought to market. Voice mail technology, for example, was first developed by the Israeli company Amdocs, and MSystems developed the flash memory technology used to store data in memory cards and USB flash drives. Often cited as two of the technology world's leading inventions of the 20th Century, the mobile phone was first developed at Motorola-Israel's research laboratory, and the Centrino processor for laptops was entirely designed, developed and produced at the Intel international development centre in Haifa.

Indeed, one can see Israeli innovations being used on a daily basis. From the popular 'Instant Messaging' programme developed by Israeli start-up Mirabilis; to shopping online with the help of Israeli start-up comparison shopping site, Shopping.com; to the NHS' use of a miniature camera on a pill developed by Israeli company, Given Imaging, to study diseases of the oesophagus; to soon being able to use our mobile phones on airplanes thanks to technology designed by communication experts Qualcomm Israel. Israeli technology is transforming lives across the globe. In a comprehensive study of the global marketplace published in 2006 by the National Science Board of the U.S. National Science Foundation, Israel and China received the highest scores of nations positioning themselves for future prominence as exporters of technology products in the global marketplace.

The Israel of today houses the infrastructure needed to advance a high technology, science-based economy. These include a system for the protection of intellectual property rights, readiness for the application of R&D to industry; competency in high-technology manufacturing; and the capability to train highly-qualified scientists and engineers. Israel leads the world in the number of scientists, engineers, and technicians in the workforce. This access to a large pool of skilled labour, its high number of start-up companies (second only to the U.S.), and proven management ability, are key factors behind Israel's remarkable development in the field of science and technology.

Without doubt, the creation of Israel as a world leader in science and technology could not have been achieved without the direction of the nation's research universities. It is the universities that provide the knowledge through innovative research and the highly-trained graduates that ensure a strong and innovative Israel capable of creating the technologies of tomorrow. 'Research & Development' related products comprise more than one-half of the total of Israel's industrial exports (excluding diamonds). The key sectors include electronics; optics; computer-based equipment; robotics; and aeronautics. Israel's industrial strategy rests on fostering the

Professor Apeloig is President, Technion-Israel Institute of Technology. His article under a similar title first appeared in the Canadian Jewish News.

growth of research and development in the industrial sector. And such activity is also wholly dependent on knowledge gained and personnel enlisted from the universities, particularly of graduate students, especially in the last decade, who have pursued advanced degrees.

It is the presence of world-class research universities that provide the knowledge, the highly-qualified scientists and engineers, cutting-edge research, personnel, and initiative that ensures Israel's success in the global marketplace. A prime example is Israel's young and rapidly growing life sciences industry. This sector is focused on major diseases for which existing therapies are largely ineffective. These include treatments for cardiovascular and peripheral vascular diseases, oncology, neurodegenerative disease, and age-related diseases such as ophthalmic and orthopaedic. All six of Israel's research universities offer high level studies in the life sciences, and over one-third of Israel's researchers are involved in this field.

Israeli universities are considered to have a competitive advantage due to their interdisciplinary approaches with other disciplines such as computer science, chemistry, and physics. The abilities and achievements of Israel's universities and its researchers will "make or break" Israel's position in this future-oriented, highly promising sector. Israel's economic miracle could not have been accomplished without the leadership of the nation's research universities.

Over 80% of all published Israeli research emanates from the nation's universities, and Israeli researchers publish more scientific papers per capita than any other nation, having notable influence on the world's scientific community. Relative to the size of its labour force, Israel has a significantly large number of scientists and scholars who have published in the natural sciences, engineering, agriculture and medicine as compared to other countries. Indeed, over the last five years, no fewer than three Israeli scholars have received the coveted Nobel Prize in economics and chemistry. Professor Robert Aumann from the Hebrew University of Jerusalem was awarded the Nobel Prize in Economics in 2005 for being the first to conduct a fully-fledged formal analysis of so-called infinitely repeated games. Professors Aaron Ciechanover and Avram Hershko from the Technion – Israel Institute of Technology in Haifa, received the Nobel Prize in Chemistry in 2004 for their remarkable discovery of the "Ubiquitin System" which rids cells of redundant proteins – a breakthrough in research into cancer and degenerative brain diseases.

In order to ensure Israel's place in the international academic community, Israeli institutions encourage post-doctoral research and sabbaticals abroad at the world's leading universities and research institutions as well as frequent attendance at foreign scientific conferences. The universities maintain and encourage a wide range of exchange programs and joint projects with leading institutions of higher learning around the world as well as host international scientific conferences on a regular and frequent basis.

Interdisciplinary research and testing institutes are functioning at the universities in various scientific and technological fields vital to the country's industrial capability. And a high proportion of faculty serves as advisors to industry.

The universities have established technology transfer companies for the commercial utilization of their research. The Technion-Israel Institute of Technology, Weizmann Institute of Science, and the Hebrew University of Jerusalem have established science-based industrial parks in proximity to their respective campuses to encourage interaction between scientists and the corporate sector. Indeed, it was the universities that pioneered "incubators" for developing technology allowing talented entrepreneurs to turn innovative ideas into products. The universities have also set up "spin-off" industrial firms for the commercialization of specific products based on their research, often in partnership with local and foreign firms.

The people of Israel look toward the Technion-Israel Institute of Technology in particular, to guarantee the nation's industrial strength and financial resilience. Technion graduates constitute the core and driving-force behind Israel's high-tech and science-based industries. An estimated 70% of Israel's engineers are educated at the Technion, and the market value of Israeli companies headed by Technion graduates has reached an estimated $30 billion.

Ranked by the Times of London among the world's leading universities in science and technology, Israel relies upon the Technion to provide the nation with high-quality research and personnel in all areas of national infrastructure, industrial development, new technologies, and defence. Indeed, Technion graduates are responsible for scientific advances such as the peroxide explosive pen that detects previously undetectable materials used in the 7/7 bombing, and the construction and launch of the Gurwin-TechSat microsatellite, which has been providing valuable information from space since 1998. Just a short visit of the Technion labs allows one to witness time-lapse photography through electron microscopes that disclose the secrets of cancer cells mutating; patches that allow the regeneration of bone tissue; nano robots that cruise through the body delivering medication; computerized face-recognition programs that can pick a terrorist out of a crowd; embryonic stem cells morphed into a biological patch to fix a diseased heart; and much more.

Israel's ability to remain a leader in the competitive high-tech world will continue to rely upon the nation's universities to provide innovative research and talented graduate professionals. However, the ability to maintain a modern, technologically-oriented vibrant nation is now endangered by the Israeli government's dramatic reduction in the funding of higher education.

Reduction in government support represents a real, long-term, strategic threat to Israel's ability to grow and thrive. Without world-class research universities, and without a well-trained workforce, Israel will not be able to maintain a modern, technologically oriented vibrant economy. Furthermore, if the universities cannot offer attractive, long-term careers to its young scholars and scientists, they will simply "vote with their feet" and pursue their careers elsewhere, including overseas, and other countries, mainly the United States, will benefit from their talents. And if the research universities cannot offer well-equipped teaching and research environments, academic standards will be adversely affected and Israel will not have the high level of trained manpower it requires to attract foreign investment and remain competitive in the global economy.

In speaking at the Technion in 1959, Israel's first Prime Minister David Ben-Gurion remarked, "The progress of man is built on three things: Knowledge, energy, and raw materials. Of the three, knowledge is the greatest, for on it depends the discovery and utilisation of the other two. Since the day when we began to build our new culture as an independent people in our ancient homeland, we have zealously striven to foster science, both pure and applied."

Notwithstanding the obstacles and difficulties before Israel's academic and scientific community, we remain confident that the nation's scholars and researchers will continue to provide the creativity and knowledge required to ensure Israel's place at the forefront of world science and technology.

TEL AVIV AT 100:
A SHORT WALK TO MODERNITY
By Colin Shindler

Tel Aviv was founded on 11 April 1909 (20 Nissan 5669) as a city of rebellion. It was a reaction to the misery and deprivation of the East European shtetl. It was a desire to improve living conditions for the Jews of nearby Jaffa and to liberate them from Arab slumlords. It was a break with the ultra-orthodox of Jerusalem who believed that Jews should passively await the coming of the Messiah and not force God's hand. It was an attempt to build a clean, efficient and economically sustainable European city on the shores of the Mediterranean. Not Vilna, but Vienna. For the Socialist Zionists, the model was 'Red Vienna' with its public ownership of common utilities, wide open spaces, collective responsibility and community loyalty as important. Yet Tel Aviv in 2009 with its high rise buildings, booming economic development, high tech enterprises, frenetic stock exchange and an urgency to overcome all obstacles suggest that Herzl's capitalism has triumphed over Borochov's Marxism. Yet the spirit of political dissent has not been extinguished. All mass demonstrations take place in Tel Aviv – from support for the West Bank settlements to the legalisation of marijuana. In 1982, over 400,000 Israelis demonstrated against Menachem Begin's ill-fated invasion of Lebanon. And it was here that Yitzhak Rabin was murdered by bullets from a beretta, following a Peace Now rally.

Tel Aviv is famously known as ha'ir ha'ivrit ha'rishona – the first (modern) Hebrew city. It is also, of course, where escapees from Nazi Germany propagated their belief in the Bauhaus, but the earlier streets – Berdichevsky, Bialik, Brenner – were all named after East European Jews in transition. They no longer belonged to the world of religious learning in Eastern Europe, but neither could they strip themselves of the traditions of millennia. Vladimir Jabotinsky, the liberal-conservative founder of the Revisionist movement and founder of the Jewish Legion, vigorously promoted the evolution of the 'new Jew' and the burial of the old. In 1924, he wrote:

> The ghetto despised physical manhood, the principle of male power as understood and worshipped by all free peoples in history. Physical courage and physical force were of no use, prowess of the body rather an object of ridicule. The only true heroism of the Ghetto acknowledged was that of self-suppression and dogged obedience to the Will above.[1]

Jabotinsky's political opponents, whether Ben-Gurion or Ahad Ha'am, also lauded the coming of the 'new Jew', moulded in their own image. In one sense, Tel Aviv, a city with no history, was to become the location where they should dwell and build.[2] It was a place to innovate and to rebel. On the twentieth anniversary of its founding, Jabotinsky idealised it as 'a city spoken about all over the world'.[3] The poet, Natan Alterman called it 'naughty and mischievous, joyful and daring'.[4] Its 'whiteness' and plethora of architectural styles attracted writers such as Shai Agnon and painters as Reuven Rubin.[5]

Today, Tel Aviv prides itself on its secularism, a place to disrobe religiously. Jews came to the city to shake off the past - a past, often studded by persecution, insult and humiliation. It is a city where the little Jew could disappear and the Israeli warrior could emerge. The Israeli writer, Dahn Ben-Amotz insisted for many years that he did not understand Yiddish and held the Galut in utter contempt. Yet as he revealed later on in life, he was really Moshe Tehillimzager from Rovna, Poland.

Ironically, the founders of the first districts which eventually became Tel Aviv were traditional Jews. Neve Tsedek was established primarily as the first Jewish quarter on the outskirts of Jaffa just as there were other ethnic quarters such as the Armenian and the Greek. It abutted the German colony of Valhalla.

Colin Shindler is Professor of Israeli Studies at the School of Oriental and African Studies, University of London. His 'History of Modern Israel' was published in 2008 by Cambridge University Press to mark the 60th anniversary of the founding of the State of Israel.

Prior to the first wave of immigration in the 1880s, probably 1000 – 2000 Jews lived in Jaffa. Unlike the Jews of Jerusalem, these traditional mainly Sephardi Jews earned their own living through a multitude of professions rather than relying on halukah – donations for the pious from Jews abroad .

The first aliyah after 1882 brought another 5,000 Jews who lived in squalid conditions in Jaffa. In 1884, the Rokach brothers, Eliezer and Shimon, established Ezrat Israel to help the new immigrants. Both believed in Jewish settlement beyond the holy cities of Jerusalem, Hebron, Tiberias and Safed. Eleazar was thus one of the founders of Gei Oni (Rosh Pina). Ezrat Israel initiated the building of Neve Tsedek and acquired the land from Aaron Chelouche who had settled in Jaffa in 1840. Chelouche worked in his shop in the port and with the fruit of his labour purchased land outside Jaffa's walls. It was appropriately named Neve Tsedek – 'a dwelling of righteousness' – from the Book Of Jeremiah.[6] Shimon Rokach lived in one of the first houses constructed there. It even boasted the presence of two synagogues - one for the Hasidim and one for their opponents.

Neve Shalom, the next Jewish settlement outside Jaffa was founded by Zerach Barnett, a graduate of Kovna's Slobodka yeshiva.[7] Barnett married Rachel Leah of London in 1864, settled in the British capital and developed a trade in furs.[8] He and his family travelled to the Holy Land for the first time in 1872 and reached Jerusalem after a perilous journey via Ramle and Bab-el-Wad.[9] Zerach Barnett purchased one of the first houses in Mea Shearim, the first neighbourhood outside the walls of Jerusalem.

Barnett was ultra-orthodox, yet was a Zionist before the first aliyah of 1882 and long before Pinsker and Herzl.[10] Ironically, Barnett has become part of secular Israeli folklore as one of the founders of Petah Tikva.[11] Indeed his deep desire to build in the Land of Israel was frowned upon by his fellow Jerusalemites as unseemly and unholy. His compatriots in London ridiculed him, asking if he had rebuilt Jerusalem yet. His daughter, Hannah Treger, recalled her father's attempts in the 1870s to survey land near Jaffa for purchase - and the reaction of his fellow inhabitants in Mea Shearim.

But not all the faces I saw reflected the light in my father. There were faces of old men and faces of young men, framed all alike in black caps and earlocks and all equally intent on his words, but expressing various shades of doubt and even of contempt and displeasure. I did not know then, but I know now, that those who disapproved of the whole scheme. In their eyes, the duty of a pious Jew was to study the Torah and to wait for the restoration of Palestine by miracle, and all this talk of buying land, piece by piece, and of building and farming, was little short of sinful.[12]

According to his daughter, Zerach Barnett believed that 'God helps those who helps themselves'. Yet he remained true to the traditions of his fathers. Hannah Treger wrote that he was clearly disdainful of any 'freethinkers who called themselves Jews, but in the eyes of our parents, were not.'[13] Barnett established a Talmud Torah, Sha'arei Torah in Neve Shalom in 1896 and founded the Or Zore'ah yeshiva in Jaffa.

The second aliyah after 1904 increased the number of Jaffa's Jews to 7,000. This catalysed a desire not simply to create another Jewish quarter, albeit on Jaffa's outskirts, but a separate location, removed, yet in close proximity to Jaffa and to the foreign consulates. A first meeting on 5 July 1906 at Jaffa's Yeshurun Club made a decision to move away and to establish a building society, Ahuzat Bayit, under the leadership of Akiva Weiss[14] and Meir Dizengoff, was established to look for and purchase land. They soon found Sheikh Jebali's vineyard.[15] This land was worked and occasionally lived on by local Arabs. There were also bedouin who grew vegetables there and grazed their cattle. The bedouin objected to the intentions of the Zionists, went to court and won their case. They were subsequently paid to leave the land peacefully. Since only Ottoman citizens could purchase land, two Jewish inhabitants of Jaffa actually bought the land. In return, they received a plot of land in the new neighbourhood. Yet life in these new Jewish quarters was painfully hard.

Arthur Ruppin, later the World Zionist Organisation's representative in Palestine, made his first visit to Palestine in 1907. As the archetypal yekker, he found both Neve Tsedek and Neve Shalom, dirty and neglected, while the German colonies were clean and efficient. He wrote about Jaffa:

> In the areas inhabited by Arabs and Jews, many houses were dilapidated or were still being built, and the rubbish-filled streets were unpaved or the surfaces marked with innumerable holes. There was no drainage, and therefore an unpleasant smell hung everywhere. There was no running water, and as water was obtained from draw wells or pumped up by hand from - frequently heavily contaminated - wells, every summer there were typhoid epidemics; trachoma and malaria were also widespread. The roads were lined with beggars, men and women (often holding children) whose eyes, sick with trachoma, were covered with flies.[16]

By July 1907, Ruppin was already requesting a loan of 300,000 francs from the Jewish National Fund in Cologne.[17] The loan, to be repaid over 18 years with 4% interest guaranteed on the capital, would be paid to Ahuzat Bayit to build the first houses that would become Tel Aviv. Since Arab labour was cheaper than Hebrew labour, they were employed to build the first 50 homes. These were ready by 1910.

Various names were suggested for this new settlement including Herzliya and Yefe Yafo (Oasis of Jaffa). The name, Tel Aviv, was proposed by Menachem Sheinkin after the title of Nahum Sokolov's Hebrew translation of Herzl's book, Altneuland. Set twenty years hence in 1923, its futuristic and utopian sentiment seemed appropriate. Ironically, Tel Aviv (Abib) was originally a village of Jewish exiles in Babylonia near the River Chebar, which was visited by the Prophet Ezekiel.[18]

The first public building was the Herzliya high school where its pupils studied the cultural values of Europe interspersed with Jewish history.[19] It was paid for by another British Jew, Jacob Moser, a one-time mayor of Bradford[20] and also served as a cultural centre for the growing community.

Herzl Street became the central thoroughfare of Tel Aviv. The settlement expanded at an astounding rate, amalgamating Neve Tsedek and Neve Shalom as well as other districts such as Machane Yosef , Kerem Hateimanim and Ohel Moshe. Within four years, it had increased its area sixfold and effectively blocked the expansion of Jaffa northwards. Yet despite its desire to strike out, it held close to the east European model and its Jews still worked in Jaffa. Although they did not want Tel Aviv to resemble, Whitechapel-on-sea, there were no building regulations and each built according to his taste and means. The well-to-do tended to populate the north of the city and in the south was the Hatikva quarter which was the residence of the poverty stricken. It was only when the British arrived at the end of 1917 that the city began to develop properly and Allenby Street became the main artery.

By the 1920s, there were so many different styles that such anarchy in planning not only gave Tel Aviv a distinctive character, but also its newly established municipal authorities great heartache. In 1925, Sir Patrick Geddes, the revamper of Edinburgh was asked to submit a blueprint for the city's development. Geddes fixed the main traffic routes through the city from north to south along Dizengoff and Ben-Yehuda. He stipulated that there should be no buildings more than three floors high and they should face westward.

The boundaries of the city were the Mediterranean, Jaffa and the German colony of Sarona. From these small beginnings, an ir metropolinit[21] - a modern metropolis grew. The first inhabitants were both dreamers and realists. As one of the earliest inhabitants of Tel Aviv wrote in 1910:

> Can anyone living in Europe imagine with what a sense of pride and liberation we residents of Tel Aviv draw our breath? In the eyes of the tourist who visits our city and is shown Tel Aviv as a sight worth seeing, I always read astonishment. Of course our Tel Aviv is small and has modest little houses; but it is ours, and here we are entre nous.[22]

That sense of wonder was there at the outset. It was propelled by a belief in the future and a desire to participate in a voyage of discovery. Above all, the building of Tel Aviv was an exercise in challenging history and controlling Jewish destiny.

NOTES

1. Vladmir Jabotinsky's introduction to Chaim Nachman Bialik: Poems from the Hebrew ed. by L.V. Snowman (London 1924).
2. Natan Harpaz, Shel Shanot Hashloshim be-Tel Aviv in Tel Aviv be-reshitah 1909–1934 (Jerusalem 1984) ed. Mordechai Naor pp.91–106.
3. Vladimir Jabotinsky, Tel Aviv Zu: Al Shum Mah? Doar Hayom 10 April 1929.
4. From Diana in Natan Alterman's Little Tel Aviv (Tel Aviv 1979).
5. Dalia Manor, Art in Zion: The Genesis of Modern National Art in Jewish Palestine (London 2005) pp.119–121.
6. Jeremiah 31:23 'Thus said the Lord of Hosts, the God of Israel: Yet shall they utter this word again in the land of Judah and in the cities there. When I will turn their captivity: 'The Lord bless you, o dwelling of righteousness, o mountain of holiness'.
7. Zerach Barnett, Zikhronot (Jerusalem 1929) p.1.
8. Jerusalem Post 19 September 2008.
9. Zerach Barnett Zikhronot (Jerusalem 1929) p.7.
10. Zerach Barnett was one of the two English delegates to the founding conference of Hovevei Zion in Katowice in November 1884.
11. Avraham Ya'ari wrote about Barnett and the founding of Petah Tikva in Zikhronot Eretz Yisrael (Ramat Gan 1974. Yoram Tahar-Lev utilised it to write HaBalada al Yoel Moshe Saloman which was sung by Arik Einstein as a popular song of the 1970s.
12. Hannah Treger, Stories of the First Pioneers in Palestine (London 1923) p.5.
13. Ibid. p.39.
14. Akiva Arieh Weiss, Kaysud nosud 'Ahuzat Bayit' (Tel Aviv 1934) in Tel Aviv be-reshitah 1909–1934 (Jerusalem 1984) ed. Mordechai Naor pp.2-3.
15. Karm al-Jabali in Arabic and Kerem Jebali in Hebrew.
16. Arthur Ruppin, Memoirs, Diaries, Letters ed. Alex Bein (London 1971) p.90.
17. Ibid. pp.120–121.
18. Ezekiel 3:15.
19. The Hezliya High School was demolished in 1958 and the Shalom Tower built on its site three years later.
20. Jacob Moser gave 80,000 francs towards the construction of the school in 1907. This was the largest philanthropic donation to the Zionist cause before 1914.
21. Ya'akov Shavit and Gideon Biger, ha-Historiyah shel Tel-Aviv (Tel Aviv 2001) p.23.
22. Sarah Leah, 'Tel Awiw: Der Hügel des Frühlings', in Palestina: Eine Werbeschrift fur die jüdische 24, Arbeit in Erez Israel, published by the Zionist Central Office in Cologne, 1910, quoted in Joachim Schlör's Tel Aviv : From Dream to City (London 1999) p.48.

'SHORT, DARK & JEWISH LOOKING':
FELIX MENDELSSOHN IN BRITAIN
By David Conway

The *Jewish Chronicle* has recently run a popular feature entitled *'How Jewish is…?'* in which it examines the Jewish credentials, genetic, social and behavioural, of figures in the news, and assesses a percentage 'result' of its subjects. Had this series been running in the paper's first decade in the 1840s, Felix Mendelssohn could interestingly have come under its scrutiny. In his ten visits, totalling not more than twenty months, to Britain between 1829 and 1847, the year of his death, Mendelssohn was treated as a major celebrity, and had a profound effect on the country's musical life, which will doubtless be warmly recognised during 2009, his bicentenary year.

Felix never, as far as we know, visited a synagogue; he was not circumcised; he was baptised at the age of 9 and was throughout his life a sincere, if not zealous, Lutheran. Yet right from the start his Jewish connections were noted in the British press. *The Harmonicon* of 26 April 1829 announced excitedly:

> Another arrival in London is the young Mr. Mendelssohn, son of the rich banker of Berlin, and, I believe, grandson of the celebrated Jewish philosopher and elegant writer. He is one of the first pianoforte players in Europe and though a very young man is supposed to be better acquainted with music than most professors of the art. Meyerbeer too is expected but he has so often promised to come to England, that he cannot be calculated upon until he actually arrives. The two last are amateurs only, the independence of their fortunes rendering it unnecessary for them to pursue the art with any view of profit.

Meyerbeer, whose originality as a composer is nowadays obscured by the fact that he was a principal butt of Wagner's odious *'Judaism in Music'*, was also the scion of a wealthy Jewish family, and was to become renowned as the father of Grand Opera (a genre which, by the way, Mendelssohn detested). He did not actually come to London until a few years later. It is interesting that Mendelssohn and Meyerbeer are linked by the *Harmonicon*. Clearly the two met some standard of refinement (or perhaps just wealth) that allowed the *Harmonicon* implicitly to commend them – 'amateurs' in this context means those who practice an art for love not mere lucre, unlike worldly 'professors'. This conclusion was later to be turned upside-down by Wagner who hinted that Mendelssohn and Meyerbeer, being Jews, were only in their profession for the money.

Interest in Felix may also have been stimulated by the publication in London in 1825 of a book on his grandfather Moses, who was already established as a name in Germany as a philosopher of the Enlightenment. Amateurs of psychology may ponder whether Felix's father Abraham (who is alleged to have commented resignedly 'Once I was the son of a famous father – now I am the father of a famous son') was motivated by his own father's fame to renounce his Jewish heritage. Although Abraham and his wife Lea had been married in synagogue, Abraham had thereafter decided there was no future in Judaism, had avoided circumcision for his sons, and had his children baptised in childhood. When Abraham wrote to Felix in London urging him to drop the name Mendelssohn in favour of his own adopted surname Bartholdy - arguing that 'there can no more be a Christian Mendelssohn that there can be a Jewish Confucius' – it may have been a similar obstinacy in Felix to continue to have his cards printed, and to sign his name, 'Felix Mendelssohn Bartholdy'.

David Conway received his PhD from University College London for his dissertation on the entry of Jews to the musical professions in the period 1780–1850, which he is presently rewriting as a book. His study on the Jewish ambience of Felix Mendelssohn will be published in a forthcoming anthology, "Mendelssohn in the Long Nineteenth Century".

Mendelssohn's first London visit included a rapturously received performance of his First Symphony, to conduct which he used the innovation of a baton. *The Harmonicon* commented ecstatically that 'he will in a few years be considered as the fourth of that line which has done such immortal honour to the most musical nation in Europe' thus placing him in English minds in the great line of German composers, Haydn, Mozart and Beethoven. British opinion of Mendelssohn remained at these levels throughout his life, and for some time beyond. Mendelssohn reciprocated this regard, enjoying Britain immensely (and equally disliking France). He was adopted from the start as an acceptable member of society; his 1829 engagement book reveals a constant whirlwind of invitations, concerts and dinners.

Amongst his constant companions during his visits was the Jewish pianist and composer Moscheles and his family. Moscheles (b. 1794) who had been based in London since the early 1820s, had been entrusted by Abraham with looking after Felix on his first visit. He had first encountered the 15 year old Felix at the Mendelssohn household in Berlin in 1824 when he had given the young man a piano lesson 'without losing sight for a single moment that I was sitting next to a master, not a pupil'. Their friendship grew extremely deep; Felix became godfather to Moscheles's son Felix (b. 1834), who recalled that 'Mendelssohn, and what he said and did, was […] a constant theme of conversation in our family'. Felix offered Moscheles a professorship at the Leipzig Conservatoire which he founded in 1843, and of which Moscheles became the director after Mendelssohn's early death in 1847.

Felix frequently concertized with Moscheles during his English visits, sharing the same musical tastes, and devotion to Bach and Beethoven. Amongst his own compositions Mendelssohn gave premières in England of his *Hebrides* overture (then entitled *The Isles of Fingal*) (1832) and his *Scottish* Symphony (1842) (souvenirs of his extensive travels in North Britain), his *Italian* Symphony (1833), and his Second Piano Concerto (1837). He conducted the second performance of his so-called Second Symphony (actually his last), the *Lobgesang,* at Birmingham in September 1840, with the Jewish tenor John Braham (now in his mid-sixties) as tenor soloist. Moscheles, who was present, wrote to his wife:

> [O]ne of the chorales of this glorious work told so powerfully that the whole audience rose involuntarily from their seats – a custom usually confined in England to the performance of the Hallelujah chorus.

Notably, Mendelssohn premiered his oratorio *Elijah* on his penultimate visit in 1846 at the Birmingham Festival, again with Braham amongst the soloists.

All of these works became staples of the English concert repertoire throughout the nineteenth century, and his sets of *Songs Without Words* for the piano were to be found in every musical household in the country. Mendelssohn further endeared himself to the English musical establishment by undertaking for British publishers the first scholarly editions of the organ works of Bach and the oratorios of Handel.

Mendelssohn's status was endorsed by the ultimate authorities. When Queen Victoria met him in 1842 her first comment in her journal was that 'he is short, dark and Jewish-looking', but her admiration and that of Prince Albert is indisputable. Following a visit a few days later, Mendelssohn gives a charming account of the Queen and Prince informally at home, joining in a chorus from *St Paul* with the composer at the organ. On this occasion, the Queen sang him her favourite of his songs (which he had to confess had actually been written by his sister Fanny).

The Queen and Prince continued to favour Mendelssohn. Mendelssohn's friend Moscheles was appointed as 'Pianist to the Prince Consort', a sinecure to be sure, but a prestigious one. The Royal couple were present in 1847 when Mendelssohn conducted the London premiere of *Elijah*, and at his subsequent (last) concert in London with the Philharmonic, when he played Beethoven's Fourth Piano concerto and conducted his own *Scottish* Symphony. During this final visit Mendelssohn also introduced to London his protegé, the Jewish violinist Joseph

Joachim (then only 16 years old), who played under his baton the Beethoven Concerto. This initiated, in turn, the young virtuoso's long and close relationship with England.

The musical legacy in England of Mendelssohn was significantly formative; so much so that at least for a generation Leipzig was regarded as a premier destination for any British students wishing to acquire a recognised musical training. Amongst Britons who studied there were Mendelssohn's friend Sterndale Bennett and Arthur Sullivan. Under Moscheles the Conservatory remained a bastion of Mendelssohnian musical conservatism: Edward Dannreuther, who studied there between 1859 and 1863, later wrote:

> It was whispered that the two old Grands in the pianoforte-room of the Conservatorium were wont to rehearse Mendelssohn's D minor Concerto all alone by themselves, from 12.30 on Sunday night until cock-crow! Force of habit, probably.

Efforts to demonstrate Jewishness in Mendelssohn's music are not convincing. Vague resemblance to traditional Jewish tunes here and there can only be coincidental, and there is no reference in the composer's voluminous correspondence of any interest in music of the synagogue. The German tradition in music was supreme to him, and this was natural for one whose great-aunt, Sara Levy, was a pupil and patron of JS Bach's son, Carl Philip Emmanuel, and had amassed a magnificent collection of Bach manuscripts. It was almost certainly his aunt Sara who had recommended as teacher to Felix her friend Carl Zelter (1758–1832), a conservative musician and friend of Goethe, (to whom he introduced Felix in 1821). Felix, by his revival of Bach's *St. Matthew Passion* in 1829, reawakened interest in the then-forgotten master; but although this seems a Christian enough event, it is noteworthy that he commented to his colleague the actor Eduard Devrient, who sang the part of Christ, 'To think that it should be an actor and a Jew that give back to the people the greatest of Christian works'.

For although Mendelssohn the composer was a German, in Mendelssohn the man we often find glimpses of the Jew, or rather, of *yiddishkeit*. Visiting Parliament in London he listened with interest to debates on the 'Posen statutes' limiting the rights of German Jews, and did not hesitate, in his correspondence with Fanny, to condemn those who spoke against Jewish civic rights as 'Jewhaters' and '*Rohsche*' (using the Yiddish word derived from the Hebrew wicked). Indeed his family correspondence is littered with Yiddish – his mother Lea for example writes to warn him 'to avoid *shatchanisieren*' (being married off: from Yiddish *shad-chan* = marriage broker). Nor is the Jewish ironic inflection absent: in a letter to his sister Rebecka, Felix chafes her mocking complaint about a displeasing relative: 'What do you mean by saying you are not hostile to Jews? I hope this was a joke […] It is really sweet of you that you do not despise your family, isn't it?'

This sort of family interplay disproves almost by itself the assertions of some modern academics that Abraham Mendelssohn and his offspring went out of their way to distance themselves from their Jewish origins. All the evidence is that they continued to socialise largely with Jews or *Neuchristen* (Jewish converts to Christianity). We have seen that Abraham entrusted Felix to Moscheles, who at that time still regarded himself as a Jew (he had married in synagogue in Frankfurt in 1825, and converted in London in 1832 for social reasons after the birth of his son). In Paris and in London, Felix continued to associate closely with the established Jewish banking families such as the Foulds, the d'Eichthals and the Rothschilds, and with Jewish musicians such as Ferdinand Hiller and Julius Benedict. With Meyerbeer, true, he did not get on, liking the man no more than his music. But then, they were relatives (both descended from Rabbi Moses Isserlis), which perhaps explains the *broiges* between them. When Hiller commented to Felix on his resemblance to his distant cousin, Mendelssohn was so disgusted that he rushed to get his hair cut to diminish the similarity. Even after death the Mendelssohn family were buried in a part of the Lutheran *Dreifältigkeit* Cemetery in Berlin reserved for other *Neuchristen*, where their tombs can been seen today close to those of Rahel Levin, Henrietta Herz and other notable German-Jewish converts.

In England after his death Mendelssohn's Jewish roots also became part of his enduring legend, partly due to a once highly popular but now forgotten, and almost unreadable, novel. *Charles Auchester*. Its author, Elizabeth Sara Sheppard, wrote it in 1847 at the age of seventeen. Sheppard, who, although the daughter of an English parson, had a Jewish grandmother, was enthusiastically philo-Semitic, and her book, whose hero is the noble, talented and generous Chevalier Seraphael, a very thinly disguised idealization of Mendelssohn, is embarrassingly effusive on the supposed God-given musicality of the Jewish people, expressed in the purplest of prose. Shrewdly the young authoress showed the manuscript before publication to Disraeli, who pronounced 'No greater work will ever be written upon music'. Mendelssohn's friend the critic Henry Chorley described it more accurately as 'half-crazy'. Nonetheless it sold by the thousand, and was still in print (in *Everyman's Library*) in 1928. In this eccentric but influential work Mendelssohn had somehow become both the perfect Jew and the perfect English gentleman.

So – to sum up 200 years after his birth – how Jewish is Felix Mendelssohn? Against – the absence of a *bris,* his Lutheran adherence and marriage, and, perhaps, his oratorio *St. Paul.* In favour – *halakha,* his appearance (as attested by royalty), his name, his friends, his demonstrable familiarity with Yiddish expressions, his interest in Jewish civil rights, his being attacked by Wagner, his *Elijah* and his literary transformation as Seraphael. I think we must concede at the very least 85%.

RUTH WINSTON FOX AND THE
JEWISH WAY OF LIFE
By Stephen Massil and Willow Winston

Ruth Winston Fox, née Lipson, MBE, J.P, BSc died last year at a great age. She was born in 1912.

After the obituariesi, tributes, family impressions and public memorials there is a time for placing the career of such a woman in its wider context. In trying to offer more than a personal reminiscence of her life I am conscious that the history of the women of the Anglo-Jewish community of the twentieth century has yet to be studied in depth, just as in the wider field of the social services in which she was involved, at local, national and international levels, public recognition of such women of whom Ruth was exemplary has barely been forthcoming. It is her longevity that brings the matter into focus. Her successors and their daughters have followed careers for which due recognition has come in the form of the highest honours, and some of them fill positions also at the height of the legal profession, which Ruth and her sisters, albeit of the magistracy, did not aspire to. Likewise politics with its scope for social reform was not a career that Ruth pursued, lacking scope for independence of thought and action as she perceived it, although the career and approach of a figure such as Beatrice Serota (née Katz), Baroness Serota of Hampstead (1919–2002)[2] which grew out of a position in the Civil Service offers close parallels. Of the women of Ruth's generation in social works at large only Lucy Faithfull, Baroness Faithfull of Wolvercote (1910–1996) came to be honoured with a life peerage. Lady Faithfull's papers are at St. Hilda's College, Oxford, where amongst the academic pioneers of the women's colleges and the headmistresses of the girls schools, Julia de Lacy Mann (1891–1985) might serve as another example from the field of education. Amongst the Jewish women of her time I would cite Lady Janner (née Elsie Cohen (1905–1994)[3] and Sarah Kitay (Mrs Leonard Stein) (1899–1997), herself American-born, equally long-lived, and resident to the end in chambers at the Temple[iv]. Last year these pages featured a celebration of Celia Rose née Steinberg (1912–2007) doyenne of the old club leadership.

More recent generations of women ride perhaps on the progress of overt 'feminism' since the 1960s. Ruth's generation emerged from and supplanted the generation of the ladies of the 'Cousinhood' and the era of benign patronage and ladies' committees counterparts to those of their well-placed husbands. These ladies were well-placed socially, cultured and well-read, forthright, and alert to their position and the management of educational, youth, social, and other public services relied on them for patronage, character, and direction. Someone like Hannah Rothschild, Lady Rosebery (1851–1890), political hostess and philanthropist, who at her marriage to Archibald Primrose in 1878 was probably the wealthiest woman in England, could even negotiate and wield considerable political power and influence which sustained (after her death) his credentials to succeed Gladstone as Prime Minister in 1894–5 (albeit so briefly). These credentials have largely been superseded but still, especially since of communal duty, play their part, in communal as well as civic terms. And Sarah Kitay certainly came from the same background (in its American context); but for Ruth Lipson that world came at a remove and by association. Her Shandel grandparents were associated with the household of Sir Moses Montefiore . In 1875 Sir Moses appointed Rev. Herman Shandel, Ruth's grandfather, Minister at the Ramsgate Synagogue, where he served for nearly 50 years (1875–1923)[5]. He was Minister, Reader and Shochet during the last years of Sir Moses, not entirely in his retirement so filled with public claims as it was, and Shandel, as administrator of the synagogue, the Judith Lady Montefiore College and the East Cliff Lodge Estate for the Sebag-Montefiores following Sir Moses's death in 1885, served also as an army chaplain, being appointed Senior Chaplain to HM Forces in World War I, as was his son-in-law. Ruth's mother Tilly Shandel (1875–1957) had memories of Sir Moses's tea-table and going to East

Cliff Lodge from the Shandel home Mill House on the Estate for Friday night to welcome in the Sabbath. However, the Shandels and the Lipsons of Ruth's parentage had to make their own way in the world.

Hyman Lipson, furniture dealer of Sheffield, and his wife Eve Jacobs had five sons including: Daniel Leopold Lipson (1886–1963), headmaster, councillor and Mayor of Cheltenham in the 1930s, who was elected to Parliament in 1937 as an Independent Conservative holding the seat until 1950[6]; and Ephraim Lipson (1888–1960),[7] Reader in Economic History at Oxford, who wrote, amongst other established reference works, 'The Economic History of England'. Ruth's father, the eldest son [although not the first-born; his elder sister, whom he always mourned, died shortly after her birth], was the Rev. Solomon Lipson (1877–1959), a religious Jew of remarkably broad mind and wide reading. After studying at Jews College, also gaining a Certificate in Physical Education from the London County Council, he was the first headmaster of the Notting Hill Synagogue Hebrew & Religious Classes[1900–1909]. He was then appointed Minister of the Hammersmith and West Kensington Synagogue (1909–1938)[8]; Senior Chaplain to HM Armed Forces in World War I, serving in France; and Chaplain to Friern Mental Hospital [1909–1953] where he was respected and loved for the comfort he brought to all members of the community, Jew and non-Jew, patient and staff. He was ahead of his time in his belief in the value of women going into higher education. He married Tilly Shandel, headmistress of a Ramsgate school, in 1902. Ruth's older brother was Eric Lipson (1905-1995).

No less forthright and self-assured socially than the grand ladies of the cousinhood, Ruth was more formally educated; firstly at St. Paul's Girls School under the school's first and second High Mistresses, Frances Ralph Grey, OBE (1903–27) and Ethel Strudwick CBE (1927-48), she went on to one of the early constituents of King's College, London, at Campden Hill, Kensington, taking a BSc. degree which she followed up with a Home Office Certificate in Child Care. This equipped her for a career with the London County Council to work (from 1936) in departments for child care and in mental hospitals. On her marriage to Laurence Winston in 1938 the couple set up home in Southgate, North London, and became members of the Palmer's Green & Southgate Synagogue, and Ruth lived at that address for the rest of her life. They had three children but Laurence, a diamond-cutter, died in 1949. Her degree and earlier work for the LCC as well as her voluntary work, equipped her to find work with Hertfordshire County Council as Child Care and Probation Officer shortly before her husband's death when money ran out during his illness. With this work she continued to support her single-parent family.

During the War Ruth was Deputy Organiser of the Women's Voluntary Service in Southgate under the leadership of Dr.Westlake. Organising the 1,500 members with their various abilities and talents in London under siege laid the ground plans for methods she used to inspire and include people in her later local government and voluntary work. She was elected a local councillor immediately after the War and served from 1945 until 1965. She became a J.P. in 1954, specialising in the Juvenile Bench, and Alderman of the Borough in 1955. She was one of the youngest to either of these appointments, a rare woman and even rarer Jew. She became both the first woman and the first Jewish Mayor of Southgate in 1958–59, and Deputy Mayor 1959-1961. Her retirement from the Council came after the creation of the Greater London Council and the amalgamation of the former London boroughs in a period which saw her engaged in the negotiations with the various potential partner boroughs that came together as the new borough of Enfield. She had stood in the Independent interest, never wanting to be under the thumb of a party, a standpoint swept aside in local politics by the break up of the old LCC and the inauguration of the GLC and subsequently over the whole country by the implementation of the Radcliffe Maude Report a decade later.

Following her husband's death Ruth's career as Child Care and Probation Officer soon focused on adoption work. She was Senior Adoptions Officer for Hertfordshire County Council for much of her time and was Consultant Adoptions Officer when she retired in 1975 after twenty-six years service. During that period she placed possibly the greatest number of adoptions of any Council throughout the country.

She was always keen to foster the careers of Jewish youth. In those days Ruth always convened a round-table of teenagers at the Maccabaean winter and summer dinners (and I remember one such when the guest speaker was John Yudkin, Professor at Ruth's old college, by then Queen Elizabeth College, where his nutrition programme was at the height of its fame), as also with her fellow-Jewish councillors at the Mayoral dinners held as part of the municipal 'match-making' that were part of the social programme of the GLC negotiations in 1962-3. Her Jewish life was fundamental to Ruth's conduct of life, bringing up a Jewish family and sustained locally by her parents. In the last year of his life her newly widowed father served as her Mayoral Chaplain. Ruth having imbibed that part of the tenets of the older generation of women in social work concerned with the duty of a woman in society, was no stranger to Jewish affairs and the local community. In 1956 she led one of the first British Jewish tour parties to Israel that was not promoted by one of the overtly Zionist organisations, giving lectures to local groups on the subject, which in turn led to such tours for AJY clubs and the Zemel Choir in 1958, and the years following when such parties still travelled by sea from Marseilles [In fact, Ruth's party had flown to Israel, necessitating several stops across Europe on the way].

This was a leadership based both on professional training and on long experience of professional and executive engagement in social work and civic affairs, and marked out the ways of her generation from those of her predecessors in Jewish communal service. Part of that training was in public speaking. Ruth spoke eloquently on a platform and effectively in committee.

In 1960 Ruth married Goodwin Fox, who was elected as an Independent to Southgate Council and served on it with her during the last four years of its existence. He also served for a decade on the Rent Assessment Panel, dealing with housing problems and the practical issues of fair rent. Ruth followed him onto the Panel [1975–83] after he left her widowed for a second time in 1974.

Ruth became a member of the Board of Deputies in 1960 and served as Chairman of the Board's Education Committee from 1974-80. She was active in the League of Jewish Women for which her work in the wartime WVS equipped her very well, and she served as the League's president in 1967–72. She was president of B'nai B'rith First Women's Lodge from 1972–4 and led a delegation of the League to Australia and the Far East in 1975.

Her activities in these years braided both local and Jewish engagement, also of significance for her generation of communal leadership. She was Elected Co-Chairman of the Government advisory body, the Women's National Commission, from 1979–81 and led a delegation to China for discussion of social issues including child care, womens' position in society and their education. On the one hand this engagement involved her in the reception and placing of Chinese students in Britain amongst whom she came to be their 'Mother in England' while in respect of Jewish problems it strengthened her stand on the need for improvements in the status of Jewish women, in particular in respect of divorce and agunah. She was president of Enfield Relate in 1985 extending her involvement with marriage guidance. Inspiration for Jewish teenagers and Chinese students bespeak an obvious concern for the young. Equally, Ruth immersed herself in concern for the elderly so that in her mayoralty she initiated planning and raised funding for a model day-centre for the elderly which came to fruition with the opening of Southgate's Old People's Day Centre in 1961, subsequently re-launched as Ruth Winston House in 1972 (now Ruth Winston Centre).

She was indefatigable, formidable and unabashed but also ready to learn and to seek advice coming, as I and my sisters remember, to talk of a Sunday morning to our mother on some undivulged matters, as no doubt to others of the neighbourhood.

There was never any time when Ruth did not remember her upbringing and the roots of her being and her mother's recollections of the life of East Cliff Lodge alongside the Ramsgate Synagogue, so much so that the echoes of the East Cliff Lodge Seder were maintained at her Passover Table over all the years. This remembrance of old days increasingly gained expression in her later career, starting with her commitment to the work of creating an exhibition to mark the Jubilee of the Palmers Green and Southgate Synagogue in 1978. This required a committee of activists and the delegation of tasks to furnish strands of Anglo-Jewish historical background, a survey of the history and personalities of the local synagogue itself, and, essentially and explicitly, an educational model of the 'Jewish Way of Life', mostly for the expected local non-Jewish visitors to the exhibition but also to remind visiting Jews of their heritage. The success of Ruth's efforts during 1977-78 to create this exhibition can be judged by the fact that her local cohort of volunteers and activists were sufficiently inspired to remain active in new directions, reconstituting themselves as the Jewish Research Group under the aegis of the Edmonton Hundred Historical Society. To date they have produced 6 volumes of their 'Heritage' series on the history and personalities in the Jewish life of the locality, the latest published in October 2007[9]. Ruth's success is also reflected in the fact that over many years she co-chaired the Jewish Community Exhibition Centre committed to the furbishment and display of the historical sections of the original 1978 exhibition. However, her success is shown principally by the fact that, with some support from the Board of Deputies, but largely by her own efforts and application, the 'Jewish Way of Life' Exhibition in its own right became one of her chief commitments so that she personally oversaw the transport and setting up of the exhibition in scores of venues up and down the country in museums, schools, community centres and synagogues during the ensuing decade and a half. Refurbished over recent years and presented as a touring resource for schools, it has attained a new format in the recent issue of a CDROM[10], launched at Westminster in June 2008, in tribute to her dedication to the task, and to her understanding of the content and the audience to be treated by such a project.

But that was not all. In anticipation of the bi-centenary of Sir Moses Montefiore in 1984-5 and in conjunction with a sub-committee of the JHSE, Ruth soon became involved in the practicalities of planning and installing an exhibition on what was after all one of her favourite subjects. She brought relics and exhibition material to the project from her own family resources (inherited from Herman Shandel's collections) which, without competing with some of the more majestic portraits in other hands, could match some of the contributions made by the Sebag-Montefiore family with memories[11]. But she could as well negotiate with exhibition designers and institutional lenders such as the Sun Life Assurance Company to secure their participation. Many hands contributed to the exhibition at its success in Enfield over the summer of 1984 but it was through her international connections and her tireless attendance that Ruth secured the transfer of parts of the exhibition to both New York in 1985 and to South Africa in 1986. Travel and exploration, above all an undying curiosity about the world, both of the past and present, kept Ruth active and concerned in the world about her, evinced both for her family down to a third generation, as also for her innumerable friends and associates, and in her concern to do honour to her heritage.

Of the careers and characters of the figures I posed at the outset as fit foils for such a life as Ruth's, it is also their longevity that was shared. When it comes to such a tribute the longevity of a matriarchal personality carries dangers of insufficiency of appreciation and an incapacity fully to comprehend the force of the personality and the depth of the experience that such a life carries in train. The tributes are the easy portion, the sense of history and spiritual significance what is hard.

NOTES

1. *Jewish Chronicle*, 14 December 2007
2. Oxford Dictionary of National Biography
3. Michael Freedland's obituary notice of 'Elsie Janner' in *The Independent*, 21 July 1994
4. Albert Friedlander's obituary notice of 'Kitty Stein' in *The Independent*, 15 February 1997
5. Cardozo and Goodman, 'Think and Thank : The Montefiore Synagogue and College, Ramsgate,

1833–1933; [and] The Montefiore Endowment, 1885-1933', Oxford University Press, 1933, pp.135–6

6. Without an entry in the ODNB though mentioned in that of his brother; his parliamentary career is recorded in G. Janner and D. Taylor, 'Jewish Parlamentarians', with a foreword by Gordon Brown, London, Vallentine Mitchell, 2008, pp. 91–2

7. ODNB [but the entry only mentions two of his brothers]

8. Michael Adler, 'The history of the Hammersmith Synagogue; with a memoir by Arthur Barnett, Goldston, 1950, *passim*

9. 'Heritage 6' the magazine of the Jewish Research Group of the Edmonton Hundred Historical Society, 2007

10. Jewish Way of Life : an interactive guide to learning about Judaism and the Jewish People. – Board of Deputies, 2008

11. Sir Moses Montefiore, 1784–1885 : Memorial Exhibition held at Forty Hall, Enfield, July–September 1984, prepared by S.W. Massil and Ruth Winston-Fox, including contributions by Dr. Solomon Gaon, Ruth Sebag-Montefiore and Cecil Roth. – London: Jewish Historical Society of England and the London Borough of Enfield, 1984, 48pp

ABBREVIATIONS USED

Ad. – Address
Admin. – Administrative; administration; administrator; administer
Adv. – Advisory; adviser
AJA – Anglo-Jewish Association
Ajex. – Association of Jewish Ex-Servicemen and Women
Amer. – America; American
Assn. – Association
Asst. – Assistant
Auth. – Authority; author

B. – Born
Bd. – Board
BMA – British Medical Association
BoD – Board of Deputies
Br. – Branch
Brit. – British; Britain

C. – Council
CBF-WJR – Central British Fund for World Jewish Relief
CCJ – Council of Christians and Jews
C of E – Council of Europe
Cllr. – Councillor
Coll. – College
Com. – Communal; community; commission(er)
Comp. – Company
Cttee. – Committee

Dep. – Deputy
Dept. – Department
Dev. – Development
Dir. – Director
Distr. – District

Eccl. – Ecclesiastical
Edr. – Editor, Editorial
Educ. – Education; educationist; educational
Emer. – Emeritus
Exec. – Executive

Fdr. – Founder
Fed. – Federation; federal
Fel. – Fellow; Fellowship
Fin. – Finance; financial
Form. – Former; formerly
Fr. – Friends

Gen. – General
Gov. – Governor; governing
Govt. – Government

H. – Honorary
Hist. – History; historical; historian
HM – Headmaster
HT – Head Teacher

IJPR – Institute for Jewish Policy Research
Instit. – Institute; institution(al)
Internat. – International

JBS – Jewish Blind Society
JEDT – Jewish Educational Development Trust
JMC – Jewish Memorial Council
JNF – Jewish National Fund
JWB – Jewish Welfare Board

Lab. – Labour; laboratory
Lect. – Lecturer; lecture(ship)
Libr. – Librarian; library
Lit. – Literature
LJ – Liberal Judaism

M. – Minister
Man. – Manager; management; managing
Med – Medical; medicine
Min. – Ministry; ministerial
MEP – Member of European Parliament
MP – Member of Parliament

Nat. – National; nationalist; nation(s)

Off. – Officer; office
Org. – Organiser
ORT – Organisation for Resources and Technical Training

Parl. – Parliament; parliamentary
Pol. – Political; policy
Princ. – Principal
Prof. – Professor
Publ. – Publication; public; publicity; publishing

R. – Reader
Reg. – Registrar; Register(ed); region(al)
Rel. – Religion; religious; relation; relief
Rep. – Representative
Res. – Research; Residence; Resource
Ret. – Retired
RM – Reform Movement

Sch. – School; Scholar(ship)
SDP – Social Democratic Party
Sec. – Secretary
Soc. – Society; social; sociology
Sr. – Senior
Supt. – Superintendent
Syn. – Synagogue

T. – Treasurer
TAC – Trades Advisory Council
Tech. – Technical; technology, -ical
Tr. – Trustee; trust

Univ. – University
UK – United Kingdom
US – United Synagogue

V. – Vice
Vis. – Visitation; visitor; visiting
Vol. – Voluntary; volunteer; volume

W. – Warden
WIZO – Women's International Organisation
WJC – World Jewish Congress
WZO – World Zionist Organisation

Z. – Zionist; Zionism

ANGLO-JEWISH INSTITUTIONS
REPRESENTATIVE ORGANISATIONS

BOARD OF DEPUTIES OF BRITISH JEWS
6 Bloomsbury Square, London WC1A 2LP.
☎ 020-7543 5400. Fax 020-7543 0010. Email info@bod.org.uk; Website www.bod.org.uk.
Board of Deputies Charitable Foundation (Reg. Charity No. 1058107)
Founded in 1760 as a joint committee of the Sephardi and Ashkenazi communities in London, the Board of Deputies of British Jews has flourished in its role as the elected representative body of the British Jewish community. It has been involved in all issues affecting the political and civil rights of British Jewry and in many cases at times of crisis in affairs overseas. It conveys the views of the community to Government and other public bodies on political and legislative matters which affect British Jewry, and provides information about the Jewish community and Israel to the non-Jewish world. The Board examines legislative proposals in Britain and the European Union which may affect Jews, and ensures the political defence of the community. It collects statistical and demographic information and undertakes research on and for the community. It maintains contact with and provides support for Jewish communities around the world and promotes solidarity with Israel. It counters bias in the media and ensures that Jews enjoy the full rights of all British citizens.

The Board plays a co-ordinating role in key issues affecting the Jewish community, and promotes co-operation among different groups within the community. The basis of the Board's representation is primarily synagogal, although the body itself has no religious affiliations. All properly constituted synagogues in Great Britain are entitled to representation, as are other significant communal organisations, such as the Regional Representative Councils, youth organisations and other communal bodies, including major charities. The Board meets most months in London, but holds one meeting a year in a regional community.

President Henry Grunwald, QC; *Senior Vice President* V. Wineman; *V. Presidents* Flo Kaufmann, J.P., Paul Edlin; *T.*, Clive Lewisohn J.P.; *Chief Exec.* Jon Benjamin.

The work of the Board is channelled through four Divisional Boards, each chaired by an Honorary Officer and supported by a professional Director.

International Division: *Chairman* Flo Kaufmann.
Community Issues: *Chairman* P. Edlin; *Dir.* A.Goldberg.
Finance and Organisation: *Chairman* Clive Lewisohn; *Dir.* Sandra Clark.
Defence Policy and Group Relations: *Chairman* V. Wineman; *Dir.* Mike Whine.
Regional Assembly: *Chairman* Agnes Grunwald-Spier.
Public Affairs: *Dir.* E. Harris
Community Policy Research Unit: (Est. 1965) Compiles statistical data on various aspects of the community and prepares interpretative studies of trends. *Chairman, Dir.*
Trades Advisory Council: Affiliated to the Board of Deputies, the Council seeks to combat causes of friction in industry, trade and commerce, and discrimination in the workplace, where these threaten good relations in which Jews are concerned. The TAC offers arbitration and conciliation facilities in business disputes and advice to employees who consider that they have suffered discrimination. *Dir.* Sandra Clark.
Jewish Community Information Desk, Communal Diary: Operated by volunteers, the Desk provides factual information on all aspects of Jewish home and community life and indicates access to the appropriate authorities to members of the public requiring expert advice. The Communal Diary is designed to avoid difficulties which often arise when dates and times of important meetings and functions clash. ☎ 020-7543 5421/5423. Email jci@bod.org.uk
Jewish Community Services - Ombudsman, c/o The Board of Deputies of British Jews, ☎ 020-7543 0105 (answerphone). (Reg. Charity No: 269525) The Ombudsman is available to deal with disputes or complaints concerning Jewish community services, i.e. any institutions in the Jewish community. It is an independent service, for which no fee is charged, provided for the benefit of the community; *Ombudsman* Paul Shaerf, Email info@bod.org.uk

JEWISH REPRESENTATIVE COUNCILS

Berkshire Jewish Representative Council (Est. 1995). *Chairman* D. Adelman, c/o 21 Christchurch Rd., Reading Berks RG2 7AA. ☎ 0118-9867 769. Email dizzie13@tiscali. co.uk.

Representative Council of Birmingham & West Midlands Jewry (Est. 1937). *President* Sir B. Zissman; *Chairman* Mrs R. Jacobs; *Hon. Sec.* Leonard Jacobs. ☎ 0121-236 1801; *Admin.*, Singers Hill, Ellis St., B1 1HL. ☎ 0121-643 2688. Email jewishbirmingham @talktalk.net; Website www. brijnet.org.birmingham.

Bournemouth and District Jewish Representative Council. *Chairman* B. Webb; *Hon. Sec.* P. Davidson. (The Southampton and adjacent area is also represented).

Brighton & Hove Jewish Representative Council. *President* Beryl Sharpe; *Sec.* Mrs. J. Rosenthal. *Corr.* PO Box 2178, Hove, BN3 3SZ;. ☎ 01273 206456 Email rep@jewishsussex.com. Website www.jewishsussex.com.

Bristol Representative Council. *Chairman* M. Romain, 7 College Fields, Bristol BS8 3HP ☎ 0117-973 9312. Email romain@netgates.co.uk. *Sec.* Mrs K. Balint-Kurti, 6 Ashgrove Rd., BS6 6LY. ☎ 0117-973 1150.

Glasgow Jewish Representative Council. 222 Fenwick Rd., Giffnock, Glasgow G46 6UE. ☎ 0141-577 8200. Fax 0141-577 8202. Email jrepcouncil@aol.com; Website www.glasgowjewishrepcouncil.org. *President* P. Mendelsohn; *Admin.* Mrs B. Taylor.

Hull Jewish Representative Council. *President* J. Rose (01482 655367; *H. Sec.* Prof. J. Friend, 9, Allanhall Way, Kirk Ella, HU10 7QU. ☎ 01482 658930.

Leeds Jewish Representative Council. *President* Mrs S. Dorsey; *Vice Presidents.* R. Bartfield, S. Jackson; *T.*Dr R. Addlestone; *H. Sec* K. Ackerman; *Exec. Off.* Mrs M. Jackson.

Jewish Representative Council of Greater Manchester & Region. *President* Barbara D. Goldstone, Jewish Community Centre, Bury Old Road, M7 4QY. ☎ 0161-720 8721. Email office@jewishmanchester.org; Website www.jewishmanchester.org.Vice Presidents Dr S. Baigel, D. Davis, *H. Sec* P. Langer, *H.T.* L. Jacobs, *Media Analyst* F.Baigel; *Publ.* Year Book.

Merseyside Jewish Representative Council. *President & Chairman of C.* G.S. Globe; *H. Sec.* P. Sapiro, 433 Smithdown Road, L15 3JL. ☎ 0151-733 2292. Fax 0151-734 0212. Email repcouncil@mjccsfufrin,co.uk; Website www.liverpooljewish.com. *Publ.* Year Book.

Representative Council of North East Jewry (Reg. Charity No. 1071515).*Co-Presidents* D.Van der Velde ☎ 0191 285 1253 and L. Boobis ☎ 0191 285 0190. *H. Sec.* J. Cawson, 14 Beechcroft, Newcastle NE3 4NB. ☎ 0191-285 1046. Email caro.bee@hotmail.co.uk. *H. Tr.* W. Knoblauch. Email total_accounting@hotmail.com, *Press Officer* C. Boobis

Nottingham Representative Council. 265 Wollaton Vale, Wollaton, Nottingham NG8 2PX. ☎ 0115 928 1613. Fax 0115 916 2960. Email lynnechapman@ntlworld.com. *Chairman* D. Lipman; *Sec.* Mrs L. Chapman.

Sheffield Jewish Representative Council. *President* B. Rosenberg ☎ 0114 230 8433; Immediate Past President Agnes Grunwald-Spier. ☎ 0114 236 0984.

South Wales Jewish Representative Council. *Chairman* A. Schwartz; *H. Sec.* Mrs R. Levene, 141 Carisbrooke Way, Cardiff CF23 9HU. ☎ 029-2048 8198.

Southport Jewish Representative Council. *President* Mrs S. Abrahamson ☎ 01704 540704; *H. Sec.* R. Jackson. ☎ 01704 532696.

ANGLO-JEWISH ASSOCIATION

152, West End Lane, London NW6 1SD.
☎ 020-7443 5169. Email info@anglojewish.org.uk; Website www.anglojewish.org.uk. (Est. 1871. Reg. Charity No. 256946). Membership of the Association is open to all British Jews who accept as their guiding principle loyalty to their faith and their country. Its aims are: to promote the education of Jews in the United Kingdom and elsewhere. Offers scholarships to UK university students who can demonstrate academic excellence and financial need. *President* N. Miron.

ASSOCIATION OF JEWISH FRIENDSHIP CLUBS
26 Enford Street, London W1H 1DW.
☎ 020-7724 8100. Fax 020-7724 7574.
(Est. 1948. Reg. Charity No. 211013) An umbrella organisation for a network of social clubs for men and women in the sixty-plus age group (see p. 91). *Nat. Chairman* Mrs L. Bromley; *Hon. Chaplain* Rev. G. Glausiusz.

ASSOCIATION OF JEWISH WOMEN'S ORGANISATIONS IN THE UNITED KINGDOM
6 Bloomsbury Square, London WC1A 2LP.
☎ 020-7242 8300. Fax 020-7242 8313. Website www.ajwo.org
(Est. 1965) To further communal understanding; to promote the achievement of unity among Jewish women of differing shades of opinion, belonging to autonomous organisations with different aims. *Affiliate orgs:* Agunot Campaign; Association of Masorti Women; Association of United Synagogues Women; B'nai B'rith Women; British Emunah; Friends of Hebrew University of Jerusalem Women's Group; Friends of Ort Women's Division; JNF First Ladies; Jewish Women's Aid; Jewish Women's Network; League of Jewish Women; Liberal Judaism Women; Reform Jewish Women; Sephardi Women (Lauderdale Road Synagogue Association); United Jewish Israel Appeal Women's Division; WIZO.uk; 35's Women's Campaign for Soviet Jewry; *Chairman* Linda Carr; *Vice Chairman* Louise Freedman; *H. Sec.* Rita Adler; *H.T.* Joyce Rose.

BICOM: BRITISH ISRAEL COMMUNICATIONS AND RESEARCH CENTRE
32-36 Great Portland Street, London W1W 8QX
☎ 020-7636 5500 Fax 020-7636 5600 Email info@bicom.org.uk Website www.bicom.org.uk
(Est. 2001. Reg. Charity No. 04204458) To provide a better understanding of Israel in the UK; to create a more positive environment for Israel in the UK. *Chairman* Poju Zabludowicz; *Chief Exec* Lorna Fitzsimons

COMMUNITY SECURITY TRUST (CST)
Head Office, London and Southern Region, PO Box 35501, London NW4 2FZ. ☎ 020-8457 9999. Manchester and Northern Region: PO Box 245, Manchester M7 2WY. ☎ 0161-792-6666; Email Enquiries@thecst.org.uk Website www.thecst.org.uk.
(Reg. Charity No. 1042391) CST represents British Jewry to Police, Government and Media, on antisemitism and security. CST provides physical security, training and advice for the protection of British Jews. CST assists victims of antisemitism and monitors antisemitic activities and incidents.

JEWISH LEADERSHIP COUNCIL
6 Bloomsbury Square, London WC1A 2LP.
☎ 020-7242-9734 Fax 020-7543 0101 Email email@thejlc.org wwwthewjlc.org
Northwest London Office, Shield House, Harmony Way, NW4 2BZ
(Est. 2006, formerly Jewish Community Leadership Council; Reg. Charity no. 1115343). The JLC comprises the heads of the major institutions in each sector of British Jewish life, together with significant individual leaders of British Jewry. *Publ.* The Future of Jewish schools (2008). *Chairman* Henry Grunwald; *Chief Exec.* Jeremy Newmark, MCIPR.

LEAGUE OF JEWISH WOMEN
6 Bloomsbury Square, London WC1A 2LP.
☎ 020-7242-8300. Fax 020-7242 8313. Email office@theljw.org; Website www.theljw.org.
(Est. 1943. Reg. Charity No. 1104023) Vol. service org. to unite Jewish women of every shade of opinion who are resident in the United Kingdom; to intensify in each Jewish woman her Jewish consciousness and her sense of responsibility to the Jewish community and the community generally; to stimulate her personal sense of civic duty and to encourage her to express it by increased service to the country. *President* Ella Marks; *H. Sec.* Mrs Jean Karsberg.
   Groups operate in the following centres:

Greater London
Barnet; Bushey Heath; Central; Chigwell & Hainault; Clissold; Coombe & District; Ealing; Harrow & Kenton; Hendon; Ilford; Kingston & Wimbledon; London North West; Muswell Hill & Highgate; Newbury Park Distict; North & East London; Northwood; Oakwood & Winchmore Hill; Pinner; Radlett; Southgate; Stanmore & Edgware; Streatham; Surrey; Prime Time (single women).

Outside London
Bournemouth; Cardiff; Glasgow; Leicester.

North West Region (centred at Manchester)
Bowdon & Hale; Brantwood; Bury; Cheadle & Gatley; Didsbury; Fylde; Heaton Pk. & Higher Broughton; Kingsway; Northenden; Park & Windsor; Prestwich; Sale & Altrincham; Southport; Whitefield & Ringley.

League Associate Division (LADS) (men).

ORT HOUSE CONFERENCE CENTRE
126 Albert Street, London NW1 7NE.
☎ 020-7446 8509. Fax 020-7446 8651. Email ort@pavpub.com. Website www.pavpub.com.
Est. 1996) A Jewish conference centre and IT Suite. Capacity 120. Suitable for business, community or social events. *Org.* Mrs C. Godden.

'WOMEN IN THE JEWISH COMMUNITY' REGIONAL CO-ORDINATING COUNCIL
(Est. 1994) To implement the recommendations in the Chief Rabbi's Review of Women in the Jewish Community (chaired by Rosalind Preston, OBE). Aims to support Jewish women, maximize their Jewish involvement and respond to their concerns, and works in conjunction with local rabbis and ministers. Meets in different towns two/three times a year, exchanges good practice and monitors progress. The Symposium held in Manchester in 2004 was attended by 200 women. *Sec.* Doreen Wachman, BA (Manchester). *Publ.* Facing the Future – Five Years On (1999), with 'Update 2002', and Celebrating Jewish Women: an update on progress, 2004.

WORKING PARTY ON JEWISH MONUMENTS IN THE UK & IRELAND
c/o Jewish Heritage UK pp.197–9 and Jewish Memorial Council.
(Est. 1991. Reg. Charity No. 206565) For the preservation and documentation of Jewish monuments of architectural and historical importance. (See listings pp.198-200 ☎ 020-7724 7778. Fax 020-7706 1710. *Chairman* M. Harris; *T. Sec.* Mrs K. B. Green. www.jewish-heritage-uk.org.

INTERFAITH REPRESENTATIVE BODIES

COUNCIL OF CHRISTIANS AND JEWS
Patron: Her Majesty the Queen.
1th Floor, Camelford House, 87-89 Albert Embankment, London SE1 7TP.
☎ 020-7820 0090. Fax 020-7820 0504. Email cjrelations@ccj.org.uk Website www.ccj.org.uk.
(Est. 1942. Reg. Charity No. 238005.) The Council brings together the Christian and Jewish Communities in a common effort to fight the evils of prejudice, intolerance and discrimination and to work for the betterment of human relations, based on mutual respect, understanding and goodwill. It is neither a missionary nor a political organisation. *Presidents* The Archbishop of Canterbury; The Cardinal Archbishop of Westminster; The Archbishop of Thyateira and Gt. Brit.; The Moderator of the Church of Scotland; The Free Churches' Moderator; The Chief Rabbi; Rabbi T. Bayfield; *Chairman, Bd. Trustees* Rt Revd. Nigel McCulloch, Bishop of Manchester; *C. E. O.* David Gifford, *Publ.* Common Ground.
There are 50 local Branches. A list of these is obtainable from the central office.

THE THREE FAITHS FORUM
Star House, 104-108 Grafton Road, London NW5 4BA.
☎ 020-7482 9549. Fax 020-7485 4512. Email info@threefaithsforum.org.uk. Website www.threefaithsforum.org.uk and www.3ff.org.uk

(Est. 1997. Reg. Charity No. 1092465) To encourage friendship, goodwill and understanding amongst people of the 3 monotheistic and Abrahamic faiths in the UK and elsewhere. Basis of equality and exploring and enjoying those differences where appropriate. *Patrons* H.E. Cardinal Francis Arinze, George Mallinckrodt KBE, Prof. Dr Klaus Schwab KCMG, Alderman John Stuttard, Baroness Boothroyd of Sandwell, Lord Carey of Clifton, The Rt. Hon. Baroness Hayman, Rabbi Professor Jonathan Magonet, The Rt Hon Michael Martin, Chief Rabbi M Rene-Samuel Sirat, Dr Otto Von Habsburg, HRH Dom Duarte Duke of Bragança, Lord Hameed of Hampstead CBE DL, *Hon Consult.*:The Rt Hon John Battle PC, MP, *Adv*: Imam Maulana Shahid Raza, *Founders*: Sir Sigmund Sternberg, OstJ, KCSG, JP, Sheikh Dr MA Zaki Badawi, KBE, Revd Dr Marcus Braybrooke, DD; *Exec Dir.* Mark Ebert, *Dir.* Stephen Shashoua

JOSEPH INTERFAITH FOUNDATION
1st Floor, 86, Brook Street, London W1K 5AB
(Est. 2006. Reg. Charity 1119284)
☎ 07816 814691 Email info@josephinterfaithfoundation.org. Website www josephinerfaith foundation.org
The Jewish-Muslim interfaith organisation committed to promoting a deeper understanding of both faiths and fostering engagement through dialogue between the two communities in Britain and abroad. *Tr.* The Lord Ahmed, Baroness Neuberger, Prof. M. Siddiqui, the Lord Turnberg. *Exec. Dir.* M. Niknam, MBE.

JEWISH PRESS, RADIO AND INFORMATION SERVICES
The following is a selection of the major national publications. The Representative Councils of Leeds, Manchester, Merseyside and the North East publish yearbooks. Many synagogues and communal organisations publish newsletters and magazines.

BRITISH-JEWISH PRESS

AJR Journal, Jubilee House, Merrion Avenue, Stanmore, Middx HA7 4RL. ☎ 020-8385 3070. Fax 020-8385 3080. Email editorial@ajr.org.uk; Website www. ajr.org.uk. Monthly. *Edr.*

Belfast Jewish Record (Est. 1953), 42 Glandore Ave., Belfast BT15 3FD. ☎ 028-9077 9491. Quarterly. *Edr.Bd. Hon. Sec.* Mrs N. Simon.

BIMAH: The Platform of Welsh Jewry (Est. 1994), 23 Solva Avenue, Llanishen, Cardiff CF14 0NP. ☎ 02920 750990. Quarterly. *Ed.* Alan Schwartz. *Ch.* Hanuš Weisl.

Birmingham Jewish Recorder, PO Box 10769, Birmingham B14 7ZQ. ☎ 0121-428 3347. Email admin@recorder.org.uk. Monthly. Est. 1935.

Edinburgh Star, 2 Marchhall Crescent, Edinburgh EH16 5HN. Est. 1989. 3 issues a year. *Edr.* Judy Gilbert.

Essex Jewish News, Vallentine Mitchell, Suite 314, Premier House 112-114 Station Road, Edgware, Middlesex HA8 7BJ. ☎ 020-8952 9526. Fax 020 8952 9242. *Edr.* Manny Robinson.

European Judaism, Leo Baeck College, 80 East End Rd., London N3 2SY. ☎ 020-8349 5600. Fax 020-8349 5619. Email info@lbc.ac.uk; Website www.lbc.ac.uk. Est. 1966. Two issues a year. *Edr.* Rabbi Professor J. Magonet.

Hamaor, Federation of Synagogues, 65 Watford Way, London NW4 3AQ. Est. 1962. Two issues a year. *Edr.* Mrs E. Chapper.

Jewish Book News and Reviews, now incorporated in the Jewish Quarterly.

Jewish Chronicle, 25 Furnival St., London EC4A 1JT. ☎ 020-7415 1500. Fax 020-7415-1577. Est. 1841. Weekly. *Chairman* Peter Levy OBE; *Comm. Dir.* A. Rubenstein, *Edr.* Stephen Pollard.

Jewish Community Pages (incorporating the Jewish Business Directory), Forum Publications Ltd., 2300 Northolt Rd., Harrow, Middx HA2 8DU. ☎ 020-8422 7086. Fax 020-8422 9175. *Edr.* B. King.

Jewish Journal of Sociology, 187 Gloucester Place, London NW1 6BU. ☎ 020-7262 8939. Fd. 1959. Published by Maurice Freedman Research Trust (Reg. Charity No. 326077). Annual (July) *Edr.* Judith Freedman.

Jewish Quarterly, incorporating Jewish Book News and Reviews, PO Box 35042, London NW1

7XH. ☎/Fax 020-8830 5367. Email editor@jewquart.freeserve. co.uk. Est. 1953. (Reg. Charity No. 268589.) *Edr.* Rachel Lasserson.

Jewish Renaissance: Magazine of Jewish Culture, PO Box 28849, London SW13 0WA. ☎ 020-8876 1891. Email Info@jewishrenaissance.org.uk; Website www.jewishrenaissance. org.uk. Est. 2001. Four issues a year. *Edr* Janet Levin; *Chairman* L. Gordon.

Jewish Socialist: magazine of the Jewish Socialists' Group, BM3725, London WC1N 3XX. Email jsg@jewishsocialist.org.uk; Website www.jewishsocialist. org.uk Est. 1985. Quarterly. Edr. Cttee.

Jewish Telegraph, Est 1950. www.jewishtelegraph.com. Telegraph House, 11 Park Hill, Bury Old Rd., Prestwich, Manchester M25 0HH. ☎   0161-741-2631(Newsdesk)☎ 0161-740 9321. Fax 0161-740-9325. Email manchester@jewishtelegraph.com. Weekly. (Also in Leeds leeds@jewishtelegraph.com, Liverpool liverpool@jewishtelegraph.com and Glasgow glasgow@jewishtelegraph.com.) *Edr.* P. Harris.

Jewish Travel Guide, Vallentine Mitchell, Suite 314, Premier House 112-114 Station Road, Edgware, Middlesex HA8 7BJ. ☎ 020-8952 9526. Fax 020 8952 9242. Email info@vmbooks. com. Website www.vmbooks.com. (Est. 1956. Formerly published by the Jewish Chronicle.) Annual.

Jewish Tribune, 8, Grosvenor Way, London E5 9ND. ☎ 020-8800 1978. Fax 020-880 5550. Email editor@jewishtribune,com. English & Yiddish. Est. 1962. Weekly. *Edr.* D. Levy (Agudas Yisroel of Great Britain).

Jewish Year Book, Vallentine Mitchell, Suite 314, Premier House 112-114 Station Road, Edgware, Middlesex HA8 7BJ. ☎ 020-8952 9526. Fax 020-8952 9242. Email info@vmbooks.com. Website www.vmbooks.com. (Est. 1896. Formerly published by the Jewish Chronicle.) Annual. *Edr.* S.W. Massil.

Journal of Progressive Judaism, Two issues a year. *Edr.* Rabbi Sybil Sheridan.

Leo Baeck Institute Year Book, 4 Devonshire Street, London W1W 5LB. Email info@leobaeck.co.uk Est. 1956. Ann. *Edr.* J.A.S. Grenville, R. Gross.

London Jewish News, Unit 611, Highgate Studios, 53-79 Highgate Road, London NW5 1TL. ☎ 020-7692 6929. Email newsdesk@totallyplc.com. *Edr.*

Manna: the voice of Living Judaism, Quarterly Journal of the Sternberg Centre for Judaism, 80 East End Rd., London N3 2SY. ☎ 020-8349 5645. Fax 020-8349 5699. Email manna@reformjudaism.org.uk. *Edr.* Rabbi Dr Tony Bayfield.

Mazel & Brocho, 168 Stamford Hill, 2nd Floor, N16 6QX.   ☎ 020-8211-7876, Fax: 020-8211-7874. *Edr.* Sarah Schleimer.

Menorah: a magazine for Jewish members of H.M. Forces. *Ed. Consult* Col. M. Newman ☎ 0161 766 6479. martin.newman@armymail.mod.uk.Semi-Ann. *Edr.* Rev. M. Weisman, OBE.

The Scribe: Journal of Babylonian Jewry, 4 Carlos Place, London W1K 3AW. Email scribe@dangoor Website www.scribe1.com. Est. 1971. Ann. *Edr.* N.E. Dangoor, OBE.

Sussex Jewish News, P.O. Box 2178, Hove BN3 3SZ, ☎ 01273 220461, email: editor@sussexjewishnews.com. Website www.sussexjewishnews.com. *Edr* L. Freedman.

Wessex Jewish News, PO Box 6012, Bournemouth, BH1 9AQ. ☎ Fax 01202 520671. Email edwjn@onetel.com.

JEWISH RADIO PROGRAMMES

BBC London 94.9: Contact: 'Jewish London', 35c Marylebone High St., W1A 4LG. Programmes at 19.00 hours, every Sunday evening on GLR 94.9FM. *Ed.* Gloria Abramoff ☎ 020-7224 2424, 020-7935 1026; *Prod.* Roma Felstein ☎ 020-7224 2424, 020-8446 0927 (home); *Res.* Osa Fowler ☎ 020-7224 2424, 020-7935 1696; *Presenter* Wendy Robbins ☎ 020-7224 2424.

'Jewish Night': Produced by Basil Herwald. Broadcast every Monday evening at 7.00–8.00pm. On GMR 95.1 and 104.6 FM. ☎ 0161 244-3050/3058. Write to 'It's Kosher', c/o BBC GMR, PO Box 951, New Broadcasting House, Oxford Road, Manchester M60 1SD Email basil.herwald@fieldingsporter.co.uk Website www.BBC.uk/Manchester

Tikkun Spectrum Jewish Radio, 4 Ingate Place, Battersea, London SW8 3NS. *Producer* Michael Milston, *Presenters* J. Kaye, R. Ford. Two weekly one-hour programme of news, views and discussion. See Website for programme details weekly. ☎ 020-7627 4433. Phone-In: 020-7501 1544. Fax: 020-7627 3409. Email: tikkunspectrum@spectrumradio. net. Website www.spectrumradio.net

INFORMATION SERVICES

Brijnet
11, The Lindens, Prospect Hill, Waltham Forest, London E17 3EJ.
☎ 020-8520 3531. Email info@brijnet.org.
Provider of UK Jewish communal internet services. Creates awareness of the use and benefits of the Internet in the community through training and assistance with all Internet tools. Creates and maintains a useful quality communal electronic information database. Published electronic listings including: brij-announce, daf-hashavua. Websites www.shamash.org/ejin/brijnet/; www.brijnet. org *Dir.* Rafael Salasnik.

Jewish Community Information, Board of Deputies, 6 Bloomsbury Square, London WC1A 2LP. ☎ 020-7543 5421/3. Fax 020-7543 0010. Email jci@bod.org.uk. *Prof. Off.* D. Vulkan. (Est. 1996.) 'Jewish Community Information (JCI) is a service of the Board of Deputies, providing information to the Jewish and non-Jewish public on all aspects of the Jewish community in the UK.'

RELIGIOUS ORGANISATIONS

THE CHIEF RABBINATE
The Chief Rabbinate of Britain has evolved from the position of the Rabbi of the Great Syn., London. From the early years of the 18th century until recently, he was acknowledged as the spiritual leader of the majority of the London community, a recognition also accorded by the provinces and overseas. Jonathan Sacks was inducted into office in 1991. Previous holders of the office were: Aaron Hart (1709–1756); Hart Lyon (1756–1764); David Tevele Schiff (1765–1791); Solomon Herschell (1802–1842); Nathan Marcus Adler (1845–1890); Hermann Adler (1891–1911); Joseph Herman Hertz (1913–1946); Israel Brodie (1948–1965); Immanuel Jakobovits (1967–1991).

The formal designation (1845–1953) of the office was 'Chief Rabbi of the United Hebrew Congregations of the British Commonwealth of Nations' and subsequently 'Chief Rabbi of the United Hebrew Congregations of the Commonwealth'.

Chief Rabbi Sir Jonathan Sacks, MA(Cantab), PhD. Office of the Chief Rabbi: Adler House, 735 High Road, London N12 0US. ☎ 020-8343 6301. Fax 020-8343 6310. Email info@chiefrabbi.org. Website www.chiefrabbi.org. *Exec. Dir.*: Syma Weinberg.

Chief Rabbinate Trust: *Chairman* Simon Hochhauser.

BETH DIN (COURT OF THE CHIEF RABBI)
Adler House, 735 High Road, London N12 0US.
☎ 020-8343 6270. Fax 020-8343 6257. Email info@bethdin.org.uk.
Dayanim Rabbis Menachem Gelley, Ivan Binstock, BSc., Yonason Abraham, Shmuel Simons, *Registrar* D. Frei, LLB; *Marriage Authorisations* Rabbi J. Shindler. ☎ 020-8343 6313.

The Beth Din fulfils the following functions for the orthodox community: (i) dispute arbitration and mediation; (ii) supervision of Jewish religious divorces, adoptions and conversions; (iii) certification of religious status; (iv) supervision of shechita and kashrut.

General enquiries may be made from 9.00 a.m. to 5.00 p.m. (Monday to Thursday). Enquiries on kashrut should be made to the Kashrut Division (see below). Visitors may attend the Beth Din by appointment only. Messages left on the answerphone will be dealt with as soon as possible.

Details of the Eruv in north-west London are given on p. 80.

Kashrut Division. ☎ 020-8343 6255. Fax 020-8343 6254. Website www. kosher.org.uk. *Dir.* Rabbi J. Conway, BA; *Kashrut Admin.* N. Lauer. *Publ.:* The Really Jewish Food Guide, Kosher Nosh Guide, Passover Supplement.

UNITED SYNAGOGUE

While the Act of Parliament under which it was created bears the date July 14, 1870, the United Synagogue had its origin much earlier in the history of London Jewry. Of the five Constituent Synagogues which joined to form the United Synagogue, the oldest – the Great Synagogue – had a history of more than 280 years; the Hambro dated from 1707, while the New Synagogue was founded in 1761. The Member Synagogues now number 42, and the Affiliated Synagogues 21, providing religious facilities for over 39,000 families (over 100,000 people). From the outset, the US has also taken a large share in the social and philanthropic work of the Community.

The **Community Development Department** is the interface between Head Office and the local synagogue communities. The Department provides a range of activities including US Cares, United Synagogue Volunteer Project, North West Jewish Singles and Lunch'n Learn programmes. It supports youth activities in United Synagogues and offers training for lay leaders and coordinates cross-communal events.

The **Visitation Committee** provides a caring service for all Jews who unfortunately find themselves in hospital, in prison or who are bereaved (see p.94). The Jewish Bereavement Counselling Service has a team of trained bereavement counsellors available to meet the needs of all members of the Jewish community.

Conjoint Passover Flour Committee is operated by the United Synagogue and is responsible for the distribution of Matzot and Passover provisions to the needy.

The US bears the financial responsibility for the **Beth Din** (Court of the Chief Rabbi, see above) and is the main contributor to the maintenance of the Chief Rabbinate.

The US plays a large part in the work of the **Jewish Committee for H.M. Forces**, which provides facilities for Jewish members of the Forces to maintain the practices of their faith (see below).

President Simon Hochhauser; *V. Presidents* K. Barnett, S. Pack, P. Zinkin; *Ts.* G. Hartnell, Stephen Fenton, R. Tenzer; *Chief Exec.* (Reg. Charity No. 242552).

Head Office: Adler House, 735 High Road, London N12 0US. ☎ 020-8343 8989. Fax 020-8343 6262. Website www.unitedsynagogue.org.uk. Member, Affiliated and Associated Synagogues are listed on pp.68-71.

Burial Society, *Manager Bushey Office* Marcia Wohlman.

INITIATION SOCIETY

President L. Gerber. *Medical Off.* Dr J. Spitzer. ☎ 020-8802 2002. Email j.spitzer@doctors.org.uk; *Sec.* A. Minn, 15 Sunny Hill Ct., Sunningfields Cres. NW4 4RB. ☎/Fax: 020-8203 1352. (Est. 1745; Reg. Charity No. 207404) To train Mohalim and to supply Mohalim in cases where required. For a list of Mohalim practising in the British Isles and registered with the Society, apply to the Secretary.

JEWISH COMMITTEE FOR H.M. FORCES

25 Enford Street, London W1H 1DW.
☎ 020-7414 3229. Fax 020-8203 7471. Email chaplainsclerk@bt.connect.com
The Cttee. officially recognised by the Min. of Defence to appoint Jewish chaplains and to provide for the religious needs of Jewish members of H.M. Forces.

Chairman Lt.Cdr. Alan Tyler RN; *H.T.* Alfred Dunitz, J.P; *Sen. Jewish Chaplain to H.M. Forces* Rev. Malcolm Weisman, OBE, MA (Oxon.), OCF; *Jt. H. Secs* Dr P. Wagerman, R. Wright; *Publ.* Menorah.

JEWISH MEMORIAL COUNCIL

25 Enford Street, London, W1H 2DD.
☎ 020-7724 7778 Fax 020-7706 1710. Email jmcouncil@btinternet.com; Website www.jmcouncil.org.

(Est. 1919.) To commemorate the services rendered by Jews in the UK and British Empire in the war of 1914-18 by establishing an organisation which will carry on Jewish tradition as a permanent ennobling force in the lives of Jews in this country.
Chairman E. Astaire; *Admin.*; *President* Edmund L. de Rothschild, T.D.; *V. President* Chief Rabbi; *H. Sec.* T. M. Simon; *H. T. Sec.* K. Hoodless.

Jewish Memorial Council Pensions Fund. A superannuation fund administered by the JMC, membership of which is open to all those employed by non-profit organisations working for the Jewish communitys. *Chairman* E. Astaire; *Admin.*

NATIONAL COUNCIL OF SHECHITA BOARDS
Elscot House, Arcadia Ave., London N3 2JU.
☎ 020-8349 9160. Fax 020-8346 2209.Email info@shechita.co.uk www.shechita.uk.org
Provides information on all matters relating to the performance and administration of shechita, and to act as liaison between all the shechita boards and the various Ministries and agencies affecting shechita and the kosher meat and poultry industry, throughout the UK and abroad.

The National Council registered a trade mark in 1955 and re-registered in 1995 a warranty of Kashrus testifying that the holder of this trade mark was a purveyor of kosher meat and/or poultry and is licensed by a recognised Shechita Board affiliated to the Council and under the supervision of a Rabbinical Authority. *President* S. D. Winegarten; *Jt. V. Presidents* J. Lobenstein, I. R. Singer; *Jt Ts.* A. Schwalbe;, R. Stern; *Exec. Dir.* D. J. Rose.

RABBINICAL COMMISSION FOR THE LICENSING OF SHOCHETIM
Est. under Schedule 12 of Statutory Instrument 731 of 1995 in respect of Welfare of Animals Regulations (1995), which provides for the shechita of animals and poultry by a shochet duly licensed for the purpose by the Rabbinical Com., and constitutes the Rabbinical Com. as follows: The Chief Rabbi, who shall be the permanent Chairman; one member appointed by the Spanish and Portuguese Syn. (London), who shall be a Vice-Chairman, three members appointed by the Beth Din (London); two members appointed by the Federation of Synagogues (London); one member appointed by the Union of Orthodox Hebrew Congregations (London); two members appointed by the President of the BoD to represent regional congregations. *Chairman* The Chief Rabbi. *H.Sec.* Alan Greenbat, Adler House, 735 High Rd., London N12 0US ☎ 020-8343 6301.

SINGER'S PRAYER BOOK PUBLICATION COMMITTEE
Administered by the United Syn. ☎ 020-8457 9715. *Chairman* E. D. Levy. The purpose of Singer's Prayer Book, first published in 1890, is 'to place within the reach of the Community at large a complete daily Prayer Book in Hebrew and English, equally suitable for use in syns. families, and schools.' 1st edn., 1890; 26 imp., 1891-1961; 2nd revd. edn., 6 imp., 1962-1988; 3rd revd. centenary edn., 1990; enlarged centenary edn., 1992; revd. 1998; 4th Edition, completely revised and redesigned, with new translation and commentary by Chief Rabbi Sir Jonathan Sacks, 2006, second and third impressions, 2007.

SPANISH AND PORTUGUESE JEWS' CONGREGATION
The Community of Spanish and Portuguese Jews in London was founded by Marranos in the middle of the seventeenth century. The congregation 'Sahar Asamaim', worshipped in Creechurch Lane (where a tablet records the site) from 1657 to 1701, when the Bevis Marks Synagogue was built. It is the oldest extant syn. building in Britain except for the long-forgotten medieval syn. of Lincoln. The first branch syn. of the congregation in the West End was est. in Wigmore St. in 1853, and in 1861 removed to Bryanston Street; in 1896 the existing building in Lauderdale Road, Maida Vale was opened. In 1977 another branch of the S. & P. Jews' Cong. was opened in Wembley. The cong. is run by a Board of Elders as well as a Mahamad (five members) who act as Executive. An assessment (Finta) is levied on the Yehidim and congregational affairs are regulated by laws, termed Ascamot, the first code of which was drawn up in 1663.

The congregation maintains the Medrash of Heshaim (founded in 1664). Hebrew religious instruction is given at the Communal Centre, Ashworth Road, W9.

A brotherhood Mikveh Israel (Lavadores), est. 1678, and a Burial Society, Hebrat Guemilut Hassadim (1665), attend to the last rites to the dead. A number of charitable and educational trusts exist for the benefit of Sephardim.

For the history of the Sephardi community in London see A. M. Hyamson: The Sephardim of England (reprinted 1991), L. D. Barnett: Bevis Marks Records Part I (1940), El Libro de los Acuerdos (1931); For genealogical records see Bevis Marks Records [Part II and III (marriages), IV (circumcisions), V (births), VI (burials)]. Available from the Synagogue offices. Other publications include: Treasures of a London Temple (1952), edr. R. D. Barnett, Laws and Charities of the Spanish and Portuguese Congregation, by Neville J. Laski, The Mitsvot of the Spanish & Portuguese Jews' Congregation, by G. H. Whitehill.

President of Elders A. Magnus; *V. President of Elders* D. Dangoor; *Chief Exec.* Howard Miller; *Sec., London Sephardi Trust.* Office: 2 Ashworth Road, W9 1JY. ☎ 020-7289 2573. Fax: 020-7289 2709. Email howardmiller@spsyn.org.uk.

Ecclesiastical Authority Rabbi Dr. A. Levy; *Rosh Beth Din* Dayan S. Amor. (Reg. Charity No. 212517.)

Synagogues and organisations are listed on pp. 76-78.

FEDERATION OF SYNAGOGUES
65 Watford Way, NW4 3AQ.
☎ 020-8202 2263. Fax 020-8203 0610. Email info@federationofsynagogues. com. Website www.federationofsynagogues.com.
The Federation of Synagogues, then embodying 16 small syns. in the eastern districts of London, was est. in 1887. It now comprises 11 Constituent syns. and 10 affiliated congregations situated in most parts of Greater London. The objects of the Federation include:
To provide the services of Orthodox rabbis, ministers and dayanim; the provision of a Burial Society; to assist syns. in the erection, reconstruction or redecoration of their Houses of Worship, to assist in the maintenance of Orthodox religious instruction in Talmud Torahs and Yeshivot; to obtain and maintain Kashrut; to support charitable and philanthropic works; to further the progress of Eretz Yisrael. *President* A. Finlay; *V. Presidents* B. Mire; H. Dony; *Ts.* L. Newmark, P. Westbrook; *Chief Exec.* Dr E. Kienwald

Associated Bodies
Beth Din of the Federation of Synagogues. Dayan Yisroel Yaakov Lichtenstein, Rosh Beth Din, Dayan M.D. Elzas; *Registrar* Rabbi S.Z. Unsdorfer.
Kashrus Board. *Kashrus Dir.* Dayan M. D. Elzas; *President* A. Finlay.
Federation Burial Society. ☎ 020-8202 3903. Fax 020-8203 0610. *Admin.* T. Zelmanovits; *Sexton* N. Kahler; *Ts.* Rabbi J. Cohen, M. Ezra.
Constituent and affiliated synagogues are listed on pp.71-73.

UNION OF ORTHODOX HEBREW CONGREGATIONS
140 Stamford Hill, N16 6QT. ☎ 020-8802 6226. Fax 020-8809-6509. (Est. 1926.Reg. Charity No. 249892) The Union of Orthodox Hebrew Congregations was est. by the late Rabbi Dr. V. Schonfeld to protect traditional Judaism, and serves as the umbrella organisation for Charedi synagogues and communities in the UK and Commonwealth.
Rabbinate Rabbi Ephraim Padwa (Princ. Rab. Authority), Dayan A. D. Dunner, Rabbi Z. Feldman, Dayan S. Friedman, Dayan D. Grynhaus, Rabbi Ch. Halpern, Rabbi E. Halpern, Rabbi P. Roberts, Dayan J. Padwa; *Court Registrar* J. R. Conrad, *President* Rabbi D. Frand, *Exec. Coord.* Chanoch Kesselman, *Gen. Sec.* C. Z. Schnek.

Associated Bodies
Kashrus Committee-Kedassia, address as above. ☎ 020-8800 6833. Fax 020-8809 7092. *Chairman* E. M. Hochhauser; *Admin.* T. Feldman, Y. Y. Frankel
Central Mikvaoth Board, address as above. ☎ 020-8802 6226.
Adath Yisroel Burial Society, 40 Queen Elizabeth's Walk, N16 0HH. ☎ 020-8802 6262/3. Fax 020-8800 8764. *Sec.* D. Lobenstein. Cemeteries: Carterhatch Lane, Enfield.

☎ 020-8363 3384. Silver Street, Cheshunt Herts. ☎ 01707-874220.
Constituent and affiliated synagogues are listed on pp. 73-75.
Details of the Eruv in Edgware are given on p. 80

MASORTI
ASSEMBLY OF MASORTI SYNAGOGUES
Alexander House 3, Shakespeare Rd., London N3 1XE. ☎ 020-8349 6650. Fax 020-8349 2743.
Email enquiries@masorti.org.uk   Website www.masorti.org.uk.
(Reg. Charity No. 1117590). (Est. 1985) The Assembly of Masorti Synagogues is the umbrella
body that serves all Masorti communities in Britain. It acts as a central co-ordinating body
with responsibility for developing Masorti communities, providing social, cultural and
educational opportunities for youth, students and young adults, and for promoting Masorti
ideology. Masorti Judaism accepts the binding force for Jewish law and understands that it has
developed throughout history. The Assembly of Masorti Synagogues runs leadership-training
programmes, as well as the Masorti Academy, which provides adult education, Gesher Teenage
Centre and Noam Youth Movement. *Vice Presidents* Jaclyn Chernett, Michael Rose; *Chair*
J.Kelly; *H.T.* ;*Dir.* M. Gluckman.
Constituent synagogues in London are listed on p. 75. See also: Leeds, Oxford, St Albans.

REFORM

THE MOVEMENT FOR REFORM JUDAISM
The Sternberg Centre for Judaism, 80 East End Road, London N3 2SY.
☎ 020-8349 5640. Fax 020-8349 5699. Email admin@reformjudaism.org.uk; Website
www.reformjudaism.org.uk.
The Movement for Reform Judaism was formed in 2005 as successor to the Reform Synagogues
of Great Britain, founded in 1942 with just 6 synagogues. The Movement for Reform Judaism in
Britain now consists of 42 synagogues with more than 35,000 men, women and children
(approximately 20 per cent of UK synagogue affiliations). The Movement is a major supporter of
the Leo Baeck College where its rabbis and educators are trained. Akiva Primary School is under
the auspices of the Reform and Liberal Movements and Clore Tikva and Clore Shalom Primary
Schools are under Reform, Liberal and Masorti auspices. The Movement sponsors thr RSY-Netzer
Youth Movement and supports the Jewish Cross Communal Secondary School project. The
Movement for Reform Judaism seeks to reach out to and egage with Jews 'where they are',
understand their Jewish needs and facilitate a wide range of continuing Jewish journeys. It offers
authentic, pluralist Judaism, rooted in tradition yet in dialogue with modernity.
President Sir Sigmund Sternberg; *H. of the Movement Chairman* Rabbi Dr Tony Bayfield;
Movement Chairman S. Moss; *Movement Tr.* F. Marcus, H. Lask; *Exec. Dir.* Rabbi Shoshana
Boyd Gelfand.

Constituent Synagogues: Metropolitan: Synagogues are listed on pp. 78-79.
    Regions: Cambridge Beth Shalom Syn.; Blackpool Ref. Jewish Cong.; Bournemouth Ref.
Syn.; Bradford Syn.; Brighton & Hove Reform Syn.; Cardiff Reform Syn.; Glasgow Reform Syn.;
Hull Reform Syn.; Liverpool Reform Syn.; Maidenhead Ref. Syn.; Manchester Ref Syn.; Menorah
Syn., Cheshire; Milton Keynes Ref. Syn.; Newcastle Ref Syn.; Sinai Syn., Leeds; Sha'arei Shalom
N. Manchester Reform Cong; Sheffield & Distr. Ref. Jewish Syn.; Southend & District; South
Hampshire Reform; Southport New Syn.; Thanet & Distr. Ref. Jewish Community.

   Associated Communities: Coventry Jewish Ref. Syn; Darlington Hebrew Cong.;
Swindon Jewish Com.; Totnes Jewish Com.; Cornwall Jewish Com.; Beth Shalom (Munich).
    Assembly of Rabbis: *Chairman* Rabbi Dr. J. Romain. ☎ 020-8349 5657.
    Rabbinical Court: (Beit Din). ☎ 020-8349 2568. *Convenor* Rabbi Rodney Mariner.
    Associated Schools: Akiva Finchley, Clore Shalom Shenley, Clore Tikva Redbridge (see p.95)
    RSY-Netzer (The Movement for Reform Judaism's Youth & Students) *Mazkir* D. Lichman;
Schaliach B. Jardine.

Reform Foundation Trust: *Chairman* Michael Grabiner; *T.* Stephen Moss

THE STERNBERG CENTRE FOR JUDAISM
80 East End Road, N3 2SY.
☎ 020-8349 5640. Fax 020-8349 5699.
(Manor House Trust, Est. 1982. Reg. Charity No. 283083) A major European centre for the promotion of Jewish religious, educational, intellectual and cultural matters. The Centre includes a Holocaust Memorial Garden and a mikveh; it houses the Akiva School; C. of Reform & Liberal Rabbis; Leo Baeck College – Michael Goulston Educ. Foundation; Manor House Books; Manor House Centre for Psychotherapy & Counselling; Pro-Zion; Reform and Liberal Association of Mohalim; The Movement for Reform Judaism; the Masorti New North London Synagogue.
    Chairman of Trs. Sir Sigmund Sternberg, KCSG, JP; *T.* G. Rothman; *Dir.* Rabbi Dr Tony Bayfield, MA. *Publ.:* Manna (quarterly).

LIBERAL JUDAISM
(Formerly ULPS) 21 Maple St., London W1T 4BE. ☎ 020-7580 1663. Fax 020-7631-9838. Email montagu@liberaljudaism.org; Website www.liberaljudaism.org
Est. 1902 for the advancement of Liberal Judaism and to establish and organise Congregations, Groups and Religion Schools on Liberal Jewish principles.
    Senior V. President Rabbi Dr Sidney Brichto, MA, DD; *Chairman* N. Cole; Chief Exec. Rabbi D. Rich. *Outreach Dir.* .
    Constituent Synagogues: Metropolitan: Synagogues are listed on pp. 78-80.
    Regions: Bedfordshire Progressive Syn.; Birmingham Progressive Syn.; Brighton & Hove Progressive Syn.; Bristol & West Progressive Jewish Cong.; Crawley Jewish Com; Dublin Jewish Progressive Cong.; East Anglia Progressive Jewish Com; Eastbourne Progressive Jewish Cong.; Edinburgh Liberal Jewish Com.; Gloucestershire Liberal Jewish Com.; Herefordshire Jewish Com.; Kent L. Jewish Community; Leicester Progressive Jewish Cong.; Lincolnshire Jewish Community; Manchester Liberal Jewish Community; Nottingham Progressive Syn.; Peterborough Liberal Jewish Com; Suffolk Liberal Jewish Community; Reading Liberal Jewish Com. South Bucks (Amersham) Liberal Jewish Community; Beit Ha-Chidush (Amsterdam); Or Chadash Liberal Jewish Community, (Luxembourg).
    Rabbinic Conference: *Chair* Rabbi P. Tobias
    Associate Communities: Oxford
    Liberal Judaism Youth Department LJY-Netzer.
For further information see under the respective headings.

ASSOCIATION OF REFORM AND LIBERAL MOHALIM
The Sternberg Centre for Judaism, 80 East End Road, London N3 2SY. ☎ 020-8349-4731. Fax 020-8349-5699. Email sylvia.morris@reformjudaism.org.uk.
(Est. 1988.) A full list of practitioners may be obtained from constituent synagogues, from Reform Judaism (020-8349 4731), Liberal Judaism (020-7580 1663) or by writing to the Association at the Sternberg Centre.

WELFARE ORGANISATIONS

BRITISH TAY-SACHS FOUNDATION
Now under the administration of Jewish Care (see p.13). ☎ 020-8922 2222.

CHAI CANCER CARE
144-146 Great North Way London NW4 1EH. ☎ Office: 020-8202-2211. Helpline Freephone 0808-808 4567. Fax 020-8202-2111. Email info@ chaicancercare.org; Website www.chai cancercare.org.
(Reg. Charity No. 1978956). Chai Cancer Care is the community's cancer support organisation, providing a range of services including counselling, complementary therapies, helpline, a comprehensive programme of social and physical activities, advocacy, advice and expert lectures. Its services are available to patients and their families based at its centre in

Hendon, and also at Sinclair House (Redbridge) and at Nightingale (South London), Chai Cancer Care is an independent organisation reliant on voluntary contributions. *President* The Lord Young; *Chairman* L. Hager; *Chief Exec* Eliane Kerr. For appointments *contact* Sue Heimann.

CHILDREN'S AID COMMITTEE CHARITABLE FUND
PO Box 686, Borehamwood, Herts WD6 9EQ.
(Est. 1955. Reg. Charity No. 302933) *Chair* H. Minkoff, *ViceChairman* M. Herman; *Sec.* A. Littman; *Admin* Beverley Hoffman.

FINNART HOUSE SCHOOL TRUST
PO Box 603, Edgware, HA8 4EQ
☎ 020-3209 6006. Email: info@finnart.org. Website www.finnart.org
(Est. 1901. Reg. Charity No. 220917). A charitable trust, the object of which is to relieve children of the Jewish faith who are delinquent, deprived, sick, neglected and in need of care or education. To provide scholarships and Bursaries to young people. *Jt. Chairmen of Trustees* Dame Hilary Blume, D. Fobel; *Clerk* Peter Shaw.

GET (*Religious Divorce*) *Advisory Service*, 23 Ravenshurst Ave., London NW4 4EE. ☎ 020-8203-6311. Trained negotiators to help people who have problems in obtaining a Get.

JAT (formerly Jewish AIDS Trust)
DVS House, 4 Spring Villa Road, Edgware, Middx HA8 7EB ☎ 020-8952 5253. Fax 020-8952 5303. Email admin@jat-uk.org; Website www.jat-uk.org.
(Reg. Charity No. 327936). JAT stands to counter the current epidemic of sexually-transmitted infections and enormous rate of teenage pregnancy in UK affecting the Jewish community no less than elsewhere. It provides sexual-health education based on Jewish religious and cultural sensitivities. JAT also provides support for people with HIV, across the community. *Patrons* Professor Michael Adler, CBE, Clive Lawton, Lady Morris of Kenwood, The Chief Rabbi; Rabbi Dr. M. Winer; *Chair of Tr.* Harry Rich; *Dir.* Rosalind Collin.

JEWISH ASSOCIATION FOR THE MENTALLY ILL – JAMI
16a North End Rd, Golders Green, London NW11 7PH.
☎ 020-8458 2223. Fax 020-8458 1117. Email info@jamiuk.org.
(Reg. Charity No. 1003345). JAMI provides guidance, support and advice for sufferers and carers. Principal objectives are: recognition and support for the mentally ill through education and training; to ensure the provision of efficient and effective Jewish social and welfare services.
JAMI operates day-care facilities and a therapeutic centre at JAMI House, 131 Golders Green Road, London NW11. ☎ 020-8731 7319.

JEWISH CARE
Merit House. The Hyde, 508 Edgware Rd., London NW9 5AB. For information and referrals call Jewish Care Direct on 020-8922 2222. For general enquiries call 020-8922 2000. Fax 020-8922 1998. Email info@jcare.org; Website www.jewishcare.org (Est. 1990. Reg. Charity No. 802559) Jewish Care is a charity caring for people in the Jewish community. Supporting older people, Holocaudst survivors, people with physical and sensory disabilities, and those with mental health needs. We also offer a range of support rgroups and run leadership and activity programmes for children and younger people.
Our centres and services are based in London and the south-east, and our staff and volunteers support thousands of members of the community each week. (For details of resources see p.89)
Jewish Care was formed on 1 January 1990 by the merger of the Jewish Blind Society and the Jewish Welfare Board. Jewish Care has since merged its activities with a number of other Jewish organisations. These include: Jewish Welfare Board, Jewish Blind Society, Jewish Home and Hospital at Tottenham, Food for the Jewish Poor, British Tay Sachs Foundation, Waverley Manor (Friends of the London Jewish Hospital) Brighton & Hove Jewish Home, Stepney

Jewish (B'nai Brith) Clubs and Settlements, Redbridge Jewish Youth and Community Centre (Sinclair House). *President* The Lord Levy; *Chairman* Stephen Zimmerman; *Chief Exec.* Simon Morris; *Fin. Dir.* Helen Verney.

JEWISH CHILD'S DAY (JCD)
707 High Road, London N12 0BT
☎ 020-8446 8804. Fax 020-8446 7370. Email info@jcd.uk.com; Website www.jcd.uk.com.
(Est. 1947. Reg. Charity No. 209266) Raises funds to distribute to agencies providing services to Jewish children in need of special care throughout the world. Provides equipment of all kinds and supports specific projects for children who are blind, deaf, mentally, physically or multi-handicapped, orphaned, neglected, deprived, abused, refugee or in need of medical care. *Life President*s Mrs J. Jacobs, A. Handler; *Chairman* Mrs J. Moss; *T. S. Moss*, CBE; *Exec. Dir.* Daniel Burger.

JEWISH HELPLINE LTD
39, The Metro Centre, Tolpits Lane, Watford, Herts WD18 9SB.
☎ 020-8457 5810.
Serving MIYAD (first est. 1988), JLINE (opened in 2004) (reg. Charity No. 1101612). Telephone crisis lines for Jewish children and adults, manned by professionally trained volunteers. *Trustees* R, Rosenberg, M. Stalbow, P.Caplan.

JEWISH MARRIAGE COUNCIL
23 Ravenshurst Avenue, NW4 4EE.
☎ 020-8203 6311. Fax 020-8203 8727. Email info@jmc-uk.org; Website www. jmc-uk.org.
(Est. 1946) The Council provides the following services: a counselling service for individual, marital and family problems for those with a relationship problem whether they are single, married, divorced or separated (020-8203 6311); and workshops for engaged couples; CONNECT: the Jewish Introdution Agency ☎ 020 8203 5207**JMC Manchester:** Nicky Alliance Day Centre, Middleton Rd., Crumpsall. ☎ 08457 585159; 0161-740 5764

JEWISH WOMEN'S AID (JWA)
JWA, PO Box 2670, London N12 9ZE.
☎ 020-8445 8060. Fax 020-8445 0305; Helpline 0800-591203. Email info@jwa.org.uk. www jwa.org.uk
(Est. 1992. Reg. Charity No. 1047045) JWA works to support Jewish women and children affected by domestic violence, to raise awareness of domestic violence in the Jewish community and work towards it's prevention. JWA operates a freephone confidential national heipline and a Refuge for Jewish women and their children fleeing domestic violence. *President* Judith Usiskin; *Chair* Judi Newman *Exec. Dir.* Claire Goodman.

THE MANOR HOUSE CENTRE FOR PSYCHOTHERAPY AND COUNSELLING
The Sternberg Centre, 80 East End Road, N3 2SY.
☎ 020-8371 0180. Fax 01923 855141. Email admin@manorhousecentre.org.uk.
(Reg. Charity No. 1054223) The Centre provides: Certificate in Counselling Skills; Diploma in psychodynamic counselling; short courses for continuing professional development; individually designed courses; counselling referral service.

MAZALTOV: PROGRESSIVE JEWISH MARRIAGES
c/o 28 St John's Wood Rd, London NW8 7HA. ☎ 020-7289 8591. Email mazaltov@liberal judaism.org.
(Est. 1995. Reg. Charity no. 236590) Non-profit making marriage bureau under aegis of Liberal Judaism. *Chairperson Management Team* Carole Goldberg; *Admin* Ruth Green.

NATHAN AND ADOLPHE HAENDLER CHARITY
c/o World Jewish Relief, 74-80 Camden Street, London NW1 0EG.

☎ 020-7691 1771. Fax: 020-7691 1780. Email jrc@wjr.org.uk. Website www. worldjewishrelief.org.uk.
The assets of the Fund are applicable by the Trustees (World Jewish Relief) for the purpose of assisting poor Jews who, in consequence of religious persecution or other misfortune, have come or shall come to take refuge in England..

NATIONAL NETWORK OF JEWISH SOCIAL HOUSING
c/o Harmony Close, Princes Park Avenue, London NW11 0JJ. ☎ 020-8381 4901. Fax 020-8458 1772.
Co-ordinates the work of Jewish housing associations, enabling them to share information and assess the housing needs in the Jewish community. *President* Fred Worms, OBE; *Chairman* Robert Manning.

NATIONAL TAY-SACHS AND BIOCHEMICAL GENETICS CENTRE
1st Floor, Ward 2, Booth Hall Children's Hospital, Charlestown Road, Blackley, Manchester, M9 7AA. ☎ 0161-918 5094. Website www.zyworld. com/taysachs.
(Reg. Charity No. 326403). Screening and counselling services for Tay-Sachs, Gauchers, Nieman-Pick etc. Community screening sessions in the north of England. Postal screening UK and Europe. Informative literature for students and families. Tay-Sachs Coordinator, any morning, or leave message on 24-hour answerphone. No fixed charge. Donations welcome. Medical enquiries to Dr. Sybil Simon (Research Centre).

OTTO SCHIFF HOUSING ASSOCIATION (OSHA)
The Bishop's Avenue, N2 0BG.
☎ 020-8458 1165. Fax 020-8458 4697.
(Reg. Charity No. 210396. Est. 1934.) In partnership with Jewish Care since 2000, OSHA has been the specialist provider of residential, nursing care and sheltered housing in the UK to Jewish refugees from Nazi persecution for over 60 years. Services include short-term respite care, daycare and specialist care for people with dementia. The charity makes grants to other organisations caring for the victims of Nazi persecution living in the UK. *Inquiries* ☎ 020-8922 2222; *Chairman* Ashley Mitchell; *H.T.* Frank Harding; *Hon. Sec.* Andrew Kaufman; Rosemary Lewis, Susan Grant, Paul Balcombe; *Company Sec.* Brenda Feldman.

TAY-SACHS SCREENING CENTRE
Clinical, Genetics 7th Floor, New Guy's House, Guy's Hospital, St. Thomas Street, London SE1 9RT. ☎ 020-7188 1364. Fax 020-7188 1369.
Provides information, carrier testing and genetic counselling for Tay-Sachs disease, and a walk-in clinic on Monday morning. *Sec.* Mrs R. Demant; *Genetic Counsellor* Sara Levene.

REFUGEE ORGANISATIONS

45 AID SOCIETY HOLOCAUST SURVIVORS
46 Amery Road, Harrow, Middx HA1 3UQ.
☎ 020-8422 1512.
(Est. 1963) The Society consists mainly of survivors who came to England in 1945/6 and others who have immigrated subsequently. It maintains close links with members who have emigrated to Israel, USA, Canada and other countries. The Society is active in the community, helps members as well as others in need. It furthers Holocaust education and other charitable causes. *President* Sir Martin Gilbert; *Chairman* Ben Helfgott, MBE; *V. Chairman* Z. Shipper; *T.* Krulik Wilder; *Sec.* Mick Zwirek.

ACJR (Association of Children of Jewish Refugees)
☎ 020-8427 4091. Email info@acjr.org.uk; Website www.acjr.org.uk.
Cultural and social group for people whose parents were victims of or who fled from Nazi persecution in the 1930s and 1940s. *Publ.* Monthly newsletter. *Chair* Oliver Walter.

AJR CHARITABLE TRUST (Association of Jewish Refugees in Great Britain)
Jubilee House, Merrion Avenue, Stanmore, Middx HA7 4RL.
☎ 020-8385 3070. Fax 020-8385 3080. Email enquiries@ajr.org.uk; Website www.ajr.org.uk.
(Reg. Charity No. 211239). The AJR provides social and welfare services to Holocaust survivors, their dependants and descendants. The AJR operates a network of regional groups, and the Central Office for Holocaust Claims provides advice and guidance on Holocaust restitution and compensation matters. *Dir.* Carol Rossen, Gordon Greenfield. *Publ.* AJR Journal (monthly).

ANNE FRANK TRUST UK
104-108 Grafton Rd., London NW5 4BA.
☎ 020-7284 5858. Email info@annefrank.org.uk; Website www.annefrank.org.uk.
(Est. 1990. Reg. Charity No.) A sister organisation of the Anne Frank House in Amsterdam having an educational mission inspired by the life and diary of Anne Frank, her values and integrity. The Trust aims to educate young people and inspire them to reject prejudice and to build a society founded on mutal respect and moral courage. The Trust promotes a travelling exhibition that tours the UK. The current programme includes a Prisons Exhibition, the Anne Frank Awards, the Free2Choose debating workshops and a schools programme in London.

ASSOCIATION OF JEWS FROM EGYPT (AJE)
4 Folly Close, Radlett, Herts WD7 8DR.
☎ 01923 856801. Email pmmaleh@yahoo.co.uk.
(Est. 2002) To preserve the cultural and social links of Jews from Egypt. *Chairman* Maurice Maleh; *Membership Sec.* James Levy, 114 Sunny Gardens Road, London NW4 1RY ☎ 020-8203 1325.

CLUB 1943: ANGLO-GERMAN CULTURAL FORUM
51 Belsize Square, NW3 (Synagogue)
☎ 01442-54360.
The Society's aim and purpose was to preserve and develop members' cultural standards in their countries of immigration. *Chairman* Hans Seelig, 27 Wood End Lane, Hemel Hempstead. ☎ 01442-54360; *Publ. Rel.* Julia Schwarz ☎ 020-8209 0318; *Sec.* Leni Ehrenberg. ☎ 020-7286 9698.

HOLOCAUST SURVIVORS' CENTRE (Jewish Care with support of World Jewish Relief)
Corner of Parson Street/Church Road, London NW4 1QA.
☎ 020-8202 9844. Fax 020-8202 2404. Email hsc@jcare.org. *Dir.* Judith Hassan; *Co-ord.* Rachelle Lazarus, Melanie Gotlieb.
And **SHALVATA**
Parson Street/Corner of Church Road, London NW4 1QA
☎ 020-8203 9033. Fax 020-8201 5534. Email shalvata@jcare.org.
The Holocaust Survivors' Centre is a social centre for Holocaust survivors and refugees. Testimonies are recorded. Shalvata is a counselling and social work service. It is also known as a training and consultation service for professionals working with war trauma. In conjunction with World Jewish Relief, Shalvata is currently working with a group of Bosnian refugees.

POLISH JEWISH EX-SERVICEMEN'S ASSOCIATION
12 Antrim Grove, London NW3 4XR.
(Est. 1945.) To aid and protect Polish-Jewish ex-Servicemen in the UK, look after the interests of Polish-Jewish refugees, perpetuate the memory of Jewish martyrs of Nazi persecution. *Chairman* L. Kurzer; *V. Chairman* L. Feit; *H. Sec.* L. Kleiner. *H. T.* J. Tigner.

SOCIETY OF FRIENDS OF JEWISH REFUGEES
Balfour House, 741 High Road, Finchley N12 0BQ.
☎ 020-8369 5000. Fax 020-83696 5001.
(Reg. Charity No.227889.) *Chairman* D.M. Cohen; *H.T.* S. Clarke; *Fin. Sec.* E.H. Kraines.

ORGANISATIONS CONCERNED WITH THE JEWS OF EASTERN EUROPE

EXODUS 2000
Sternberg Centre for Judaism, 80 East End Road, London N3 2SY.
☎ 020-8349 5651. Fax 020-8349 5699. Email kathrynmichael@europeanregion.org.
Campaign for Progressive Judaism in Eastern Europe, under the aegis of the European Region of the WUPJ. Exodus has a national exec. and groups in many synagogues. Its major areas of work are: (i) supporting the growth of Progressive Judaism in the former Soviet Union; (ii) twinning with new Eastern European Progressive Congregations; (iii) sending Rabbis and lay educators to teach. Exodus 2000 works closely with the World Union of Progressive Judaism in Israel and America. *Chairman* Rabbi David Soetendorp; *Admin* K. Michael; *T.*

NATIONAL COUNCIL FOR JEWS IN THE FORMER SOVIET UNION
Contact: 6 Links Drive, Elstree, Herts WD6 3PS.
☎ 020-8953 8764.
(Est. 1975) Initiates and coordinates activities on behalf of Jews in the FSU including safeguarding and promoting their human, civic, religious and cultural rights. It acts as the umbrella org. for all bodies in Britain with similar objects. The Council is the voice of the community to Government and other bodies in the UK & internationally on FSU Jewish issues. *President* H. Grunwald, QC; *Acting Chairman* Jonathan Arkush.

ZIONIST ORGANISATIONS

ISRAEL EMBASSY: 2 Palace Green, Kensington, W8 4QB.
☎ 020-7957 9500. Fax 020-7957 9555. Email info-assist@london.mfa.gov.il. Website www.israel-embassy. org.uk. Opening Hours: Mon.-Thur. 09.00-17.30 and Fri. 09.00-13.30. *Defence Sec.* 2A Palace Green, Kensington, W8 4QB; ☎ 020-7957 9548. *Consular Sec.* 15A Old Court Place, Kensington, W8 4QB. ☎ 020-7957 9516; *Ambassador* H. E. Ron Prosor; *Min. Plenipotentiary* Talya Lador-Fresher; Ronit Ben-Dor (Dir. of Public Affairs); Councellor Ran Gidor (Political Aff.); Political Councellor for Media Affairs Lior Ben-Dor; Shmulik Ben-Tovim (Economic Affairs); Gil Erez (Commercial Aff.); Councellor Liora Givon (Consular Aff.); B. Kokavi (Admin.)

JEWISH AGENCY FOR ISRAEL
London office: 741 High Road, Finchley, N12 0BQ.
☎ 020-8369 5200. Fax 020-8369 5201. Email londonoffice@JAFI.org.
The Jewish Agency for Israel in Great Britain is one of eight delegations worldwide. In partnership with the Zionist Youth Movements and Jewish Communities in the world, the Jewish Agency's main activities are focused on encouraging and nurturing Aliyah to Israel, reinforcing Jewish Zionist education and strengthening the connection between the Diaspora and the State of Israel. *Chairman of the Exec.* Zeev Bielski; *Chairman of the Bd of Gov.* Ms Carole A. Solomon; *Dir. Gen.* Moshe Vigdor.

JEWISH LABOUR MOVEMENT (incorporating Poale Zion)
PO Box 695, Harrow, HA3 0HF.
☎/Fax 020-8621 4574. Email info@jlm.org.uk Website www.jlm.org.uk
The Jewish Labour Movement, launched officially on 21st July 2004, is the successor to Poale Zion. As such it retains its Labour Zionist ideals and affiliation to the Labour Party, where it acts as a link between Labour and the Jewish community and as a campaigning organisation to promote negotiations aimed at a peaceful conclusion of the Israel-Palestinian conflict based on a two state solution. As such, the movement operates within Jewish communal organisations, such as the Board of Deputies of British Jews, the Zionist Federation and the Jewish Council for Racial Equality, and also works in the wider community within bodies such as the National Assembly against Racism and local Race Equality Councils.
Chair Louise Ellman MP; *Vice Chairs* Neil Nerva and Cllr. Jeff Rodin; *Hon. Sec.* Dr Judith Bara; *Hon. Tr.* L. Nerva; *Contact: Hon. Sec.*

JNF CHARITABLE TRUST
Head Office: JNF House, Spring Villa Park, Edgware, Middx. HA8 7ED.
☎ 020-8732 6100 Fax 020-8732 6111; 020-8732 6103 Website: www.jnf.co.uk.
President S. Hayek; *Vice-President* J. Zinkin; *H. T.* David Kibel, F.C.A.; *Chief Exec.* Simon Winters, MBA, FRSA; *Admin.* S. Epstein.
Education Department: ☎ 020-8732 6103. Email info@jnf.co.uk.*Chairman* Helen Rosen. (See p. 42).
KKL Charity Accounts
Head Office: JNF House, Spring Villa Park, Edgware, Middx. HA8 7ED. ☎ 020 8732 6102 Fax 020 8732 6111. Email giving@kkl.org.uk
KKL Executor & Trustee Co. Ltd.: ☎ 020-8732 6101. Email harvey@kkl.org.uk.*Man.* Hilary Cane; *Chairman* Jeffrey Zinkin; *Dir.* Harvey Bratt, LL.B. Objects: Bequests, advisory and covenant services for charity.

LIKUD-HERUT MOVEMENT OF THE UNITED KINGDOM
Wilberforce House, Station Rd., London NW4 4QE
☎ 020-8203 9191. Email info@Likud-Herut.org.uk, Website www.likud-Herut.org.uk.
(Est. 1970) To promote the Zionist ideology as conceived by Ze'ev Jabotinsky. Member of Likud Haolami. *Life President* E. Graus; *Chairman* Zalmi Unsdorfer.
Affiliated Organisations: Young Likud Herut; (Brit Nashim Herut Women's League); Betar-Tagar, Brit Hashmonayim.

MERETZ-YACHAD FOR A DEMOCRATIC ISRAEL
Hashomer House, 37A Broadhurst Gardens, NW6 3BN.
☎ 020-7328 5451. Fax 020-7624 6748.
An Anglo-Jewish organisation which identifies with Meretz-Yachad's world outlook and strives to vitalise Anglo-Jewry in the spirit of Jewish humanism and democracy. It seeks to promote Socialist Zionism, the unity of the Jewish people, aliya, social justice in Israel, Jewish educ., culture and peace as vital elements of Zionism, complete political, social and economic equality for all Israeli citizens, with religion left to the conscience of each individual. Affiliated to: World Union of Meretz; Z. Fed.; BoD. *Chairman* Pauline Levis; *Admin.* Avivit Caspi.

MIZRACHI FEDERATION
Maple Leaf House, 141-155 Brent St., London, NW4 4DJ.
☎ 020-8201 7120. Fax 020-8201 7130. Email office@mizrachi.org.uk; Website www.mizrachi.org.uk.
(Est. 1918) The Mizrachi Federation supports the State of Israel and its educational institutions. It is the umbrella organisation of the religious Zionist community, and focuses its efforts on educational activities and being a support for the religious Zionist youth movements in order to provide productive informal education activities for their children.
Exec *President* A. L. Handler; *Chairman* S. Taylor; *Exec. Dir.* J. Lipczer; *Exec. Cttee* Rabbi E. Mirvis, *Admin* Mrs B. Mandelsohn, *Publ.* Jewish Review.
Constituent Orgs.: British Emunah; Bnei Akiva; Bachad Fellowship.
Affiliated Orgs.: Torah Mitzion; Yavne Olami; Mifal Hatorah.
Mizrachi Charitable Trust (Reg Charity no. 1099851) provides scholarship support for school graduates at Yeshivah in Israel.

PRO-ZION: PROGRESSIVE RELIGIOUS ZIONISTS
The Sternberg Centre for Judaism, 80 East End Road, N3 2SY.
☎ 020-8349 5640. Email info@prozion.org.uk, Website www.prozion.org.uk
(Est. 1978) To work for full legal and rel. rights for Progressive Judaism in Israel, to affirm the centrality in Jewish life of the State of Israel. Affiliated to the Zionist Federation, Liberal Judaism and the Movement for Reform Judaism. Associated to the Israel Movement for Progressive Judaism. A constituent of Arzenu. *Co-Chairmen* D. Needlestone, C. Gluckman; *H. Sec.* M. Silverman; *H.T.* R. Kramer *Admin.* P. Lewis. *Publ.* Shema, Progressive Jewish News

UJIA (United Jewish Israel Appeal)
Balfour House, 741 High Road, Finchley N12 0BQ.
☎ 020-8369 5000. Fax 020-8369 5001. Email central@ujia.org. Website www.ujia.org
(Reg. Charity No. 1043047, Reg. Company 3295115) The UJIA ia an inclusive and cross-communal charity. The UJIA is committed to investing in education and young people in Israel and in the UK. It works in partnership with individuals, communities and organisations to raise funds that cover the full spectrum of Jewish life. Its work in Israel is currently dedicated to regeneration of Galil. *H. Presidents* Chief Rabbi Sir Jonathan Sacks, The Lord Levy, The Rt. Hon. The Lord Woolf; *Hon. V. Presidents* The Lord Janner QC, Sir Jack Lyons, D.M. Cohen, Gerald M. Ronson, Cyril Stein, Fred S. Worms, OBE; *Presidents* Sir Trevor Chinn, CVO, Brian Kerner; *V. Presidents* M. Bradfield, Stanley Cohen, OBE, Alan Fox, D. Hamburger, Ronald Preston, Stephen Rubin, OBE, Sir Harry Solomon, A. Spitz; *Bd. Chairman* M. Davis; *Chief Exec.* D. Krikler; *Company Sec.* Eldred Kraines, CA (SA); *Fin. Dir.* E. Samuel.

WIZO.uk
107 Gloucester Place, London W1U 6BY.
☎ 020-7486 2691. Fax 020-7486 7521. Finance Fax 020-7486 0703. Email central@wizouk.org; Website www. wizouk.org.
(Est. 1918; Reg. Charity No. 296444) WIZO.uk is the British Federation of World WIZO, the leading provider of social welfare and educational services for disadvantaged people in Israel. It has some 100 affiliated groups with over 9,000 members. Its mission is to help support and strengthen families in Israel through fundraising. *President* Michele Vogel ; *Chairman* Loraine Warren; *H. Sec.* M. Pollock; *Ts.* Helen Raisman, Hanni Seifert; *Exec. Dir.* Alison Rosen *Publ.* WIZO.uk newsletter (4 issues a year).

WORLD ZIONIST ORGANISATION
741 High Road, Finchley, N12 0BQ.
☎ 020-8343 9756. Fax 020-8446 0639. Email zion-fed@dircon.co.uk.
The WZO was established by the first Zionist Congress, which met in Basle on August 29, 1897. The aim of the Org., as defined in the programme adopted by the Basle Congress, was to secure for the Jewish people a home in Palestine guaranteed by public law. At the Congress a constitution providing for a self-governing World Organisation, with the Zionist Congress as the supreme body, was adopted.

In 1908 the Z.O. embarked upon the work of practical settlement and development in Palestine. When the Z.O. was recognised in 1922 as the Jewish Agency under the Palestine Mandate, it was already responsible for a wide field of development and settlement activities and it commanded the support of important Jewish groups throughout the world.

The aims of Zionism, as enunciated in the 'New Jerusalem Programme' adopted by the 27th World Zionist Congress in June, 1968, are:

The unity of the Jewish People and the centrality of Israel in Jewish Life;

The ingathering of the Jewish people in its historic homeland, Eretz Israel, through Aliya from all countries;

The strengthening of the State of Israel which is based on the prophetic vision of justice and peace;

The preservation of the identity of the Jewish people through the fostering of Jewish and Hebrew education and of Jewish spiritual and cultural values.

ZIONIST FEDERATION OF GT. BRITAIN AND IRELAND
Balfour House, 741 High Road, N12 0BQ.
☎ 020-8343 9756. Fax 020-8446 0639. Email zion-fed@dircon.co.uk.
(Est. 1899) The Zionist Federation is an umbrella organisation encompassing most of the Zionist organisations and individuals in the country and, as such, represents the Zionist Movement in the United Kingdom. Its function is to support, co-ordinate and facilitate the work of all its affiliates nationwide. The Zionist Federation aims to encourage the participation

of Jews in Zionist activities including education, culture, Hebrew language and Israel information, underpinned by our belief that the main goal of Zionism is Aliyah.

Executive: *Exec Chairman* Andrew Balcombe, *Vice Chairmen* David Duke-Cohan, P. Margolis; *Hon. Tr.* Harvey Rose; *President* Prof, Eric Moonman, OBE; *Hon Vice-President* Geoffrey Gelberg; *Dir.* Alan Aziz; *Asst. Dir.* Tracy Seigal; *Admin* Barbara Simia; *Finance* Nadia Nathan; *Public Affairs* Gavin Gross; *Young Leadership* Gary Sokol.

Committee Chairmen: Constitution – Jonathan Kramer; Finance – H.Rose; Fundraising – M. Plawner; Yom Ha'atzmaut – E. Gilston; Israel Connect – S. Fischer.

OTHER ORGANISATIONS CONCERNED WITH ISRAEL AND ISRAELI ORGANISATIONS

ACADEMIC STUDY GROUP ON ISRAEL AND THE MIDDLE EAST
PO Box 42763, London NW2 0YJ.
☎ 020-8444 0777. Fax 020-8444 0681. Email info@foi-asg.org.
(Reg. Charity No. 801772) An academic org. which aims at forging and expanding research contacts between academics in this country and their colleagues in Israel. Organises Anglo-Israel Research Workshops in Israel and the UK. *President* Sir Walter Bodmer, Oxford University; *T.* Aviva Petrie, Eastman Dental Institute; *Dir.* J. D. A. Levy.

AKIM
(Est. 1964. Reg. Charity No. 241458) To assist with the rehabilitation of mentally handicapped children in Israel. *President* Sir S. W. Samuelson CBE. *V. President* Judge B. Lightman; *Chairman* A. Broza; *V. Chairman* J. Samad; *H.T.* V. Cohen. *Corr. to*: 22 Golf Close, Stanmore, Middx HA7 2PP. ☎ 020-8954 2772. Fax 020-8954 2999. Email asbrosa@hotmail,com *H. Sec.* Mrs B. Kober.

ALL-PARTY-BRITISH ISRAEL PARLIAMENTARY GROUP
c/o Lord Janner of Braunstone, House of Lords, London, SWIA OPW.
☎ 020-7976 8443, Email lordj@netcomuk,co.uk. *Chairman* Lord Hogg of Cumberland; *President* Lord Weidenfeld.

ANGLO-ISRAEL ARCHAEOLOGICAL SOCIETY
126 Albert St., London NW1 7NE.
☎ 020-7691 1467. Email diana_davis@hotmail,co.uk. Website www.aias.org.uk.
(Reg. Charity No. 220367) Lectures on recent archaeological discoveries in Israel, publication of annual research bulletin and award of travel grants to students to participate in excavations in Israel. *Chairman* Prof. H.G.M. Williamson, Oriental Instit., Pusey Lane, Oxford OX1 2LE; *Admin.* Mrs D. Davis.

ANGLO-ISRAEL ASSOCIATION
PO Box 47819, London NW11 7WD.
☎ 020-8458 1284. Fax 020-8458 3484. Email info@angloisraelassocation.com. Website www.angloisraelassocation.com
(Est. 1949. Registered Charity No. 313523) The purpose of the Association is to promote wider and more positive understanding of Israel in the UK; to encourage exchanges in both directions; and generally to support activities which foster goodwill between the two countries. The AIA administers two educational Trust Funds. The Wyndham Deedes Memorial Travel Scholarship provides British Students the opportunity to study in Israel whilst the Kenneth Lindsay Scholarship Trust provides scholarships for Israeli students to study in the UK. *Founder* The late Brigadier-General Sir Wyndham Deedes, CMG, DSO; *Hon. President* The Israeli Ambassador; *Chairman of C.* The Lady Sainsbury; *Chairman Exec. Cttee* Sir Andrew Burns; *H.T.* J. Nedas; *Exec. Dir.* R. Saunders.

THE BALFOUR DIAMOND JUBILEE TRUST
67 Addison Road, London W14 8JL.

Fax 020-7371 6656.
(Est. 1977. Reg. Charity No. 276353) To consolidate and strengthen cultural relations between the UK and Israel. Provides the community with a diverse programme of topical activities throughout the year – in literature and the arts. Makes financial support available to individuals and small organisations – both in the UK and Israel – whose work will make an enduring cultural contribution.

The **Lord Goodman Fellowship Award**, a joint venture with the British Council, awards scholarships to Israeli scholars for up to a full year of study or research in a field related to the Environment (see www.britcoun.org). *Exec. Sec.*

BANK LEUMI (UK) plc.
London Office: 20 Stratford Place, London W1C 1BG.
☎ 020-7907 8000. Email info@bankleumi.co.uk
Originally established in London in 1902 as the financial instrument of the Zionist Movement under the name of Jewish Colonial Tr. Hd. office in London; Northern branch in Manchester; invoice Discounting Subsidiary in Brighton; two subsidiaries in Jersey, C.I., Bank Leumi (Jersey,) Ltd.; Leumi Overseas Trust Corp. Ltd. Incorporated in 1959 as a subsidiary of Bank Leumi Le-Israel B.M. *Chairman* E. Raff; *Dep. Chairman* Sir Bernard Schreier; *Man. Dir. & Chief Exec.* C. Cumberland and L. Secretan.

BEN-GURION UNIVERSITY FOUNDATION
ORT House, 126 Albert Street, London NW1 7NE.
☎ 020-7446 8558/4. Fax 020-7446 8557.
(Est. 1974. Reg. Charity No. 276203). To promote Ben-Gurion University of the Negev in Beer-Sheva, Israel, as an international centre for academic excellence and advanced research in medicine, science and desert agriculture – by donations, books, equipment and subscriptions. *President* The Lord Weidenfeld; *V. President* Suzanne Zlotowski; *Chairman* Harold Paisner.

BRITISH & EUROPEAN MACHAL ASSOCIATION
3 Moorcroft Court, Bibsworth Road, London N3 3RF.
☎/Fax 020-8343 3508. Email stanleymedicks@email.uk.com. Website www.machal2000.com/aboutmachal.pdf.
MACHAL (Mitnadvei Chutz L'Aretz). Volunteers from abroad in the 1948 Israel War of Independence. To collect personal stories and memorabilia. To publicise Machal's endeavour and sacrifice. To honour the 119 fallen commemorated on the Machal Memorial, Sha'ar Hagai. *Co-ordinator* Stanley Medicks. *Sec.* Sidney Lightman, FIS.

BRITISH COMMITTEE OF BNEI BRAK HOSPITAL
273 Green Lanes, N4 2EX.
☎ 020-8800 2996
European Off. 21D Devonshire Place, W1. Est. 1979 as part of communal efforts in many countries to build an Orthodox hosp. with a special cardiac dept. in Bnei Brak. Maternity and other wards are open. *Chairman* Dr. L. Freedman; *V. Chairmen* Dayan M. Fisher, V. Lucas, F.S.V.A.; *H. T.* B. Freshwater; *Med. Dir.-Gen.* Dr. M. Rothschild.

BRITISH COMMITTEE OF KEREN YALDENU
(Est. 1955.) To protect Jewish children in Israel through the opening of special centres and institutions from missionary activities and influences alien to Judaism. *Chairman* Mrs. A. Finn, 4 Cheyne Walk, NW4 3QJ ☎ 020-8202 9689. Email zalmiuk@yahoo.com

BRITISH FRIENDS OF THE ART MUSEUMS OF ISRAEL
Wizo House, Suite 3, 105–107 Gloucester Place, London W1U 6BY.
☎ 020-7935 3954. Fax 020-7224 0744. Email bfami@btconnect.com. Website www.bfami.org
(Est. 1948. Reg. Charity No. 313008) BFAMI raises funds to help maintain museums in

Israel, acquire works of art and antiquities for them, sponsor exhibitions and youth-art educational programmes. *Patrons* H.E. The Ambassador of Israel, Avigdor Arikha, Sir Anthony Caro, OM, CBE, the Duke of Devonshire, Walter Griessmann, Anish Kapoor, Sir Timothy Sainsbury P.C., Dame V. Duffield, CBE; *Chairman* Mrs W. Fisher; *Exec. Dir.* Mrs M. Hyman.

BRITISH FRIENDS OF ASSAF HAROFEH MEDICAL CENTRE
PO Box 244, Edgware, Middx HA8 8WF.
☎ 020-8905 3650. Email friendsofassaf@ukonline.co.uk.
(Est. 1980. Reg. Charity No. 281754) Committed to raise funds for Assaf Harofeh Medical Centre, Zrifin 70300, Israel, which is the third largest government hospital and is affiliated to the Sackler Faculty of Medicine, Tel-Aviv University. *President* David Elias, BEM, MWI, FINO; *Jt Chairmen* Dr Les Berger, David Pearl; *Vice-Chairman* Mayer Aron; *H.T.* Stanley Bloom; *Consult.* Y. Pre-El, MHFS, ICHT.

BRITISH FRIENDS OF BAR ILAN UNIVERSITY
87a Bell Lane, London NW4 2AS
☎ 020-8201 7666; Fax 020 8201 7444 Email admin@bfbiu.or. Website www.bfbiu.org
(Est. 1957. Reg. Charity No. 314139) To raise monies for projects at Bar-Ilan University (see p. 155) *Chairman* Conrad Morris.

BRITISH FRIENDS OF BOYS TOWN JERUSALEM
6 Bloomsbury Sq., London WC1A 2LP.
☎ 020-7404 1437.
(Est. 1963. Reg. Charity No. 110332) To organise support for secondary education and technical training for 1,000 students at Boys Town Jerusalem (Kiryat Noar, Bayit Vegan). *Chairman* J. Pinnick, F.C.A.; *Dev. Dir.* L. Stein.

BRITISH FRIENDS OF HAIFA UNIVERSITY
26 Enford St., London W1H 2DD.
☎ 020-7724 3777.
(Reg. Charity No. 270733) To further the interests and development of Haifa Univ (see p. 155) by donations, books, equipment and subscriptions. The Brit. Frs. are represented at the Bd. of Govs. of Haifa Univ. *Chairman* Lady Irene Hatter; Lord Jacobs (Chairman of Board of Govs); *Dir.* Dr Joseph Shub.

BRITISH FRIENDS OF HATZOLAH ISRAEL (formerly Hatzolah Jerusalem) c/o Joseph Kahan Associates (chartered accountants) 923 Finchley Road, London, NW11 7PE. ☎ 020-8455 9575. Email:pelsem@netvision. net.il (Reg. Charity No. 1101329)

BRITISH FRIENDS OF THE HEBREW UNIVERSITY OF JERUSALEM
126 Albert Street, London NW1 7NE.
☎ 020-7691 1500. Fax 020-7691 1501. Email friends@bfhu.org.uk. Website www. bfhu.org.uk.
(Est. 1926. Reg. Charity No. 209691) To promote the interests and development of the Hebrew University of Jerusalem, to promote opportunities to study, and to partner the University in its contribution to the improvement of people's lives around the world. *President* John Sacher CBE; *Chairman* B. Isaacs. *Exec. Dir.* Wendy Pollecoff. The Brit. & Irish Friends are represented on the Hebrew Univ. Bd. of Govs. **Groups**: Legacies/Legacy Angels; Students/Alumni; Women's Group; Legal; Medical; New Leadership; The University Library Group; British Friends of YISSUM (commercialisation of HU research); and regional groups.

BRITISH FRIENDS OF THE ISRAEL FREE LOAN ASSOCIATION
c/o K. Keller, 23 Allum Lane, Elstree, Herts WD6 3NE. ☎ 020-8953 5605; Website www.freeloan.org.il; Email ifla@freeloan.org.il.
(Reg. Charity No. 1009568). Provides interest free loans to Russian and Ethiopian immigrants in Israel and other needy Israelis, including small business loans, emergency housing, medical loans, and loans to families with handicapped children.
Established in Jerusalem, 1990, and in 1992 in London. *Chairman* Kenneth Keller; *H. T.* Mrs. A. Druce; *Patrons* Chief Rabbi Dr Sir Jonathan Sacks, The Lady Jakobovits.

THE BRITISH FRIENDS OF THE ISRAEL PHILHARMONIC ORCHESTRA FOUNDATION
c/o 10 Rainville Road, London W6 9HA.
☎ 020-7389 5648. Fax 020-7385 4320.
(Reg. Charity No. 291129)   *Contact* Oded Gera.

BRITISH FRIENDS OF ISRAEL WAR DISABLED
45 Ealing Road, Wembley, Middx. HA0 4BA.
☎ 020-8903 8746. Fax 020-8795 2240. Email info@bfiwd.org.
(Est. 1974. Reg. Charity No. 269269) BFIWD is a non-political organisation dedicated to helping disabled soldiers rebuild their lives. Aid is given in purchasing rehabilitation equipment at Beit Halochem. Working with the ZAHAL Disabled Veterans' Organisation, BFIWD brings groups of injured soldiers to the UK to stay with caring families. *Chairman* F. M. Weinberg; *Hon. Solicitor* L. Curry; *H. Sec.* G. Daniels; *H.T.* C. Niren.

BRITISH FRIENDS OF THE JERUSALEM COLLEGE OF TECHNOLOGY (BFJCT)
2a Lichfield Grove, London N3 2TN.
☎ 020-8349 5129. Fax 020-8349 5110. Email info@bfjct.co.uk
(Est. 1971. Reg. Charity No. 263003) To promote the interests of the College and to support its charitable work. To endow and contribute towards campus projects and to further the work of development and research. *Chairman* S. Bentley.

BRITISH FRIENDS OF PEACE NOW
PO Box 35583, London NW4 4QY.
☎ 020-8621 7172. Email peacenow.uk@ntlworld.com; Website www.peacenow- uk.org.
(Est. 1982. Reg. Charity No. 297295) Peace Now is a grassroots Israeli movement dedicated to Israeli–Palestinian and Israeli–Arab peace. Peace Now organises pro-peace activities and monitors Israel's settlement policy on the West Bank and Gaza Strip. The first and primary goal of Peace Now is to press the Israeli government to seek peace – through negotiations and mutual compromise – with Israel's Arab neighbours and the Palestinian people. Only peace will bring security to Israel and ensure the future of our peoples. British Friends of Peace Now mobilises support for the Israeli peace movement and the peace process among British Jews and the wider community. It is a membership organisation funded by annual membership fees and donations, and has a charitable arm. Membership expresses support for the many Israelis actively working for peace, security, justice and reconciliation in the Middle East.

BRITISH FRIENDS OF RAMBAM MEDICAL CENTRE
1 Opal Court, 120 Regents Park Road, London, N3 3HY.
☎ 020-8371 1500. Fax 020-8371 1501.
(Reg. Charity No. 028061) Voluntary organisation raising funds for the purchase of medical equipment for all hospital departments. *Dir.* Anita Alexander-Passe.

BRITISH FRIENDS OF SARAH HERZOG MEMORIAL HOSPITAL (EZRATH NASHIM), JERUSALEM
37, The Avenue, Radlett, WD7 7DQ.

☎ 01923 850100. Email info@herzoghospital.co.uk; Website www.herzoghospital. co.uk. (Reg. Charity No. 1024814) Israel's foremost centre for geriatric and mental health care, Sarah Herzog Hospital offers exceptional medical care and has outstanding research achievements. The Hospital, with over 100 years of experience, treats the effects of advancing age and mental instability with the best medical technologies. With 350 beds, the Hospital is the third largest in Jerusalem. Its Israel Centre for the Treatment of Psychotrauma and Community Mental Health Centre have leading roles in helping individuals affected by terrorist attacks. *President* The Lady Jakobovits; *Chairman* D. Halpern, QC.

BRITISH FRIENDS OF SHALVA
c/o G. M. Simmonds, Suite 3, 7 Paddington St., London W1U 5QQ.
☎ 020-7935 0823. Fax 020 7935 0843. Email info@shalva.org. Website www.shalva.org.
(Est 1990. Reg. Charity No.1081887) To support the Israel Association to assist mentally and physically handicapped children.

BRITISH FRIENDS OF SHUVU
United Fund for Russian Immigrant Children in Israel
17, Golders Court, Woodstock Road, London NW11 8QG
☎ 020-8209 3010. Fax 0870 460 4997 Email shuvuuk@aol.com
(Est. 2003, Reg. Charity No. 1100984) Shuvu/return was established in Israel in 1991 to create a network of schools for Russian immigrant children and their families. There are now 69 schools and nurseries throughout Israel educating some 15,000 Jewish Russian children and assisting families through counselling, finance, and medical assistance. *Exec. Dir* David Blachman; *Dir. Operations* D. Denton.

BRITISH FRIENDS OF ZAKA
223a Golders Green Road, London NW!! 9ES
☎ 020-8458 5391; Fax 020-8458 5398; Email info@zaka.org.uk
(Est. 2003. Reg. Charity No. 1099639). Provides support for the Israel Emergency Service Zaka ('Chessed shel Emet') whose purpose is the succour and relief of the victims of natural and unnatural disasters. *Patrons* The Chief Rabbi, The Lady Jacobovits, C. Morris; *Trustees* J. Wahnon, Mrs F. Frank, H. N. Frank; *Exec. Dir.* D. Rose.

BRITISH ISRAEL ARTS FOUNDATION
98 Belsize Lane, London NW3 5BB
☎ 020-7435 9878. Fax 020-7435 9879.
(Est. 1985) To promote forms of bilateral culture between Britain and Israel. The Foundation organises concerts, theatre, dance and literary events and exhibitions. Arts Liaison Group est. to coordinate Israeli culture activities in UK. *President* Lilian Hochhauser; *V. President* Norman Hyams; *Chairman* S. Soffair; *Dir.* Ruth Kohn-Corman.

BRITISH-ISRAEL CHAMBER OF COMMERCE
c/o Stylo Plc, Stylo House, Harrogate Road, Bradford , West Yorkshire BD10 0NW ☎ 01274 617 761 Fax 01274 893 287 Email mail@b-icc.org Website www.b-icc.org
(Est. 1950) To promote and develop trade and economic relations between the Uk and Israel. *Chairman* Michael Ziff. North-West *Regional Dir.* Gideon Klause ☎ 0161 929 8916 Fax 0161929 6277. North-East *Regional Dir.* Jane Clynes ☎/ Fax 0113 393 0200.

BRITISH TECHNION SOCIETY
62 Grosvenor Street, W1K 3JF.
☎ 020-7495 6824. Fax 020-7355 1525. Email bts62@aol.com. Website www. britishtechnionsociety.org.
(Est. 1951. Reg. Charity No. 1092207) To further the development of the Technion, Israel's

University of Science and Technology. *H. Presidents* Sidney Corob CBE, Lord Wolfson of Marylebone; *V. President* W. S. Churchill; *H. Patron* H. E. Ambassador of Israel;*Co-Chairmen* L. Peltz, M. Heller; *H.T.* M. Sorkin; *Exec. Dir.* A. Bernstein; *Sec.* S. Posner; Social Cttees. in London and Regions.

CONSERVATIVE FRIENDS OF ISRAEL
45b Westbourne Terrace, W2 3UR.
☎ 020-7262 2493. Fax 020-7224 8941. Email info@cfoi.co.uk
CFI is committed to the Conservative Party and to the welfare of the State of Israel and dedicated to establishing close links between GB and Israel. CFI distributes balanced and accurate information on events in the Middle East and through visits to Israel, gives MPs and candidates a greater understanding and insight into the Middle East. *Parliamentary Chairman* Rt. Hon. James Arbuthnot MP, *Political Dir.* R. Halfon; *Chairman Exec.*; Richard Harrington; *Exec. Dir.* Stuart Polak.

FEDERATION OF JEWISH RELIEF ORGANISATIONS
143 Brondesbury Pk., NW2 5JL.
☎ 020-8451 3425. Fax 020-8459 8059.
(Reg. Charity No. 250006) *Chairman* M. Katz, OBE;*Gen. Sec.* Mrs B. Shepherd; *Tr.* A. Garfield FCA.

FRIENDS OF ALYN
88 Ossulton Way, London N2 0LB.
☎ 020-8883 4716. Email alynuk@ip3.co.uk. Website www.alyn. org.
(Est. 1962. Reg. Charity No. 232689) To assist the work of the Alyn Pediatric and Adolescent Rehabilitation Centre in Jerusalem, *H.Sec.* Mrs Maureen Lowry.

FRIENDS OF THE BIKUR CHOLIM HOSPITAL, JERUSALEM & BRITISH AID COMMITTEE
3A Princes Parade, Golders Green Road, NW11 9PS.
☎/Fax020-8458 8649.
Bikur Cholim, Jerusalem's oldest hosp. is now the largest med. centre in the heart of the city. *President* Lady Jakobovits; *Chairman* J. Cohen, BA; British Aid Committee: *Chairman* David Godfrey, MA; *V. Chairman* Morley Franks; *Jt. H. Ts.* B.S.E. Freshwater, P. Englard.

FRIENDS OF THE ISRAEL AGED (RE'UTH)
53, Danescroft, Brent St., London NW4 2QH.
☎ 020-8203 9457.
(Est. 1950. Reg. Charity No. 278505) To assist the work of the Women's Social Service (Re'uth) in maintaining sheltered housing, old age homes and the Re'uth Medical Centre in Israel. *President* Arieh L. Handler; *H. T.* David Toledano; *Admin.* G. Fainer

FRIENDS OF THE ISRAEL CANCER ASSOCIATION
c/o Berwin Leighton Paisner, LLP, Adelaide House, London Bridge, EC4R 9HA.
☎ 020-7427 1361. Fax 020-7760 1111. Email jonathan.morris@blplaw.com
(Est. 1955. Reg. Charity No. 260710) The Charity raises funds for the Israel Cancer Association (ICA). The ICA plays a prominent role in the fields of detection, research, treatment and education, supporting oncological institutes, nationwide screening, patient care and information services. *President* V. Aaron; *V. Presidents* Dame Vivien Duffield, CBE, Lady Alliance, Stephan Wingate; *H. T.* J. Morris.

FRIENDS OF ISRAEL EDUCATIONAL FOUNDATION
PO Box 42763, London N2 0YJ.
☎ 020-8444 0777. Fax 020-8444 0681. Email info@foi-asg.org.
(Reg. Charity No. 1095303) To promote and advance the education of the public in the knowledge of the country of Israel and its citizens. F.O.I.E.F. undertakes an extensive UK

education programme and sponsors a variety of young adult and professional scholarships in Israel. *Bd.:* Jeremy Manuel, Hon. Gerard Noel, Peter Oppenheimer, David Kaye, L. Levine, M. Rebuck, M. Sayers; *Dir.* J. D. A. Levy.

FRIENDS OF ISRAEL SPORT CENTRE FOR THE DISABLED
23 Bentinck Street, London W1U 2EZ.
☎ 020-7935 5541. Fax 020-7935 6638. Email fiscd@btinternet.com.
(Est. 2001. Reg. Charity No. 1086205) Supports the work of the Sports Centre for the Disabled established in 1961 at Ramat Gan through donations. *Chairman* Brian Harris; *V. Chairman* Irwyn Yentis; *T.* Jeremy Harris; *Sec.* Jane C. Jukes.

FRIENDS OF JERUSALEM ACADEMY OF MUSIC AND DANCE
11 Radnor Mews, W2 2SA.
☎ 020-7402 3167. Fax 020-7706 3045.
To provide scholarships for talented children and to help in providing musical instruments, publications, etc. *Jt. Chairmen* Manja Leigh, Lilian Hochhauser.

FRIENDS OF LANIADO UK
Shield House, Harmony Way, London NW4 2BZ
☎ 020 8201 6111. Fax 020-8201 6222. Email info@laniado.co.uk; Website www. laniado.co.uk. (Est. 1976. Reg. Charity No. 267133). Supporting the work of the Laniado Hospital of Netanya and its locality. *Chairman* Dr M. Sinclair; *Hon. Life Ts* L. Feinerh; *Leeds Chairman* C. Evans; *Manchester Chairman* D. Hamburger; *Campaigns Dir.* JG. Blauer; *Chief Exec.* Mrs Y.S. Simon; *Exec* Y. Allalouf, S.Dayani, R. Suss: *Young Laniado Co- Chairman* A. Wolfin, *Northern Coord.* Mrs K. Dawson

FRIENDS OF THE MIDRASHIA
79 Princes Park Avenue, London NW11 0JS.
☎ 020-8459 8877. Fax 020-8459 1177.
(Reg. Charity No. 285047) The British Commonwealth and Eire Cttee. was est. in 1952 to aid the Midrashia, the boys' boarding schools at Pardess Hana and Kfar Saba with over 1,000 pupils. *Founder* The late Dr J. Braude; *Chairman* A. J. Braude.

FRIENDS OF YAD SARAH
(Reg. Charity No. 294801) Yad Sarah, a volunteer-operated home care organization, lends free, regular and hi-tech medical rehabilitative equipment and provides a spectrum of home care supportive services. Services available to tourists. *Trustee* D.S. Davis, c/o Cohen Arnold & Co., New Burlington House, 1075 Finchley Road, London NW11 0PU. ☎ 020-8731 0777. Fax 020-8731 0797.

FRIENDS OF YESHIVAT DVAR YERUSHALAYIM
(Jat: The Jerusalem Academy Trust)
Office: 1007 Finchley Road, London NW11 7HB.
☎/Fax 020-8458 8563.
(Reg. Charity No. 262716) London Cttee: *Jt. Chairmen* A. Maslo, BCom; FCA, and M.A. Sprei, MA(Cantab), MSc; *Patrons* Chief Rabbi Dr Sir Jonathan Sacks, Rabbi J. Dunner; *Principal* Rabbi B. Horovitz, MA.

FUNDING FOR PROGRESSIVE JUDAISM (FPJ)
75 Chase Road, London N14 4QY
☎ 01753 886220. Email admin@fpjie.org.uk
Formerly Friends of Progressive Judaism in Israel and Europe (Reg. Charity No. 241337). *Admin.* Neil Drapkin.

HADASSAH MEDICAL RELIEF ASSOCIATION UK
26 Enford Street, London W1H 1DW.

☎ 020-7723 1144. Fax 020-7723 1222. Email uk.office@hadassah.org. Werbsite www.hadassahuk.org
(Est. 1986. Reg. Charity No. 1040848) Committed to fund-raising and promoting the work of the Hadassah Medical Organisation (Est. 1912), at Ein Kerem and the Hadassah Univ. Hosp. on Mt. Scopus. *H. President* Lady Wolfson; *Patron* Lady Jakobovits; *Chairman* Mrs G. Shamash; *Exec . Dir.* Dr H. Stellman.

HOLYLAND PHILATELIC SOCIETY
(form. British Association of Palestine Israel Philatelists)
(Est. 1952.) For the study and encouragement of all branches of the philately of Palestine and the State of Israel, and of other countries connected with the postal history of the region. *H. Mem. Sec.* A. Tunkel, 3 Stone Buildings, Lincoln's Inn, London WC2A 3XL. ☎ 020-7242 4937. Fax 020-7405 3896. Email atunkel@3sb.law.co.uk.

ISRAEL DISCOUNT BANK LTD.
(UK Representative Office) 65 Curzon Street, London W1Y 8PE.
(☎ 020-7499 1444. Fax 020-7499 1414.
(Est. 1935) Israel Discount Bank Ltd. is one of the three largest banks in Israel. The bank in Israel offers a complete range of domestic and international banking services. The London office offers corporate and private banking facilities and is regulated by the FSA. *UK Gen. Man.* Danny Elkanati.

ISRAEL GOVERNMENT TOURIST OFFICE
UK House, 180 Oxford Street, London W1D 1NN.
☎ 020-7299 1111. Fax 020-7299 1112. Email information@igto.co.uk;
Website www. thinkisrael.com.
(Est. 1954) *Dir.* R. Shalev. The office provides information about Israel as a tourist destination, and assistance to the British and Irish travel trade wishing to promote Israel as a holiday destination.

ISRAEL–JUDAICA STAMP CLUB
(formerly Judaica Philatelic Society)
☎ 020-8886 9331. Fax 020-8886 5116. Email cliverosen@tiscali.co.uk
A committee of the JNF and a ZF affiliate. Services collectors of the Jewish theme in philately; promotes KKL/JNF labels, Jewish education through philately, commemorative covers, and production of the Journal, the Israel-Judaica Collector, including an alphabetical listing of Jews and their achievements honoured on stamps and Judaica issues world-wide. Also illustrated lectures on this theme. *Patron* Sir Martin Gilbert; *President* M. Persoff, MA, FRSA; *Chairman* C. H. Rosen, F.C. Optom.; *V. Chairman* A. Field; *Sec.* H. Wolman, Email israeljudaicaclub@stamps.gioserve.com; *T.* P. Dear. *Publ.* The Israel–Judaica Collector: C. H. Rosen, E. Sugerman (jt. eds).

ISRAEL PHILATELIC AGENCY IN GREAT BRITAIN
PO Box 2, Watford, Herts. WD24 4HX.
☎ 01923 475548. Fax 01923 475556. Email enquiries@harryallen.com
Official Agents of the Philatelic Service, Israel Postal Authority, Tel Aviv-Yafo, Israel, for the distribution and promotion of postage stamps and related products of Israel (in the United Kingdom). *New Issues Man.* Mrs Val Crowhurst on behalf of Harry Allen (International Philatelic Agencies).

THE JERUSALEM FOUNDATION
ORT House, 126 Albert Street, London NW1 7NE.
☎ 020-7482 6076. Fax 020-7482 6025.
(Est. 1969. Reg. Charity No. 258306) To support charitable projects in the city of Jerusalem embracing (*inter alia*) education, social welfare, the arts and preservation of its historic heritage. *President* Alex Bernstein; *Chairman* Martin Paisner; *Admin* Sheila Ford.

JEWISH AID COMMITTEE/ONE TO ONE PROJECT
237 Regent's Park Rd., London N3 3LF
☎ 020-8343 4156. Fax 020-8343 2119. Email admin@one-to-one.org
(Reg. Charity No. 801096). The Jewish Aid committee, (formerly the 35's), responding to the mass immigration of Soviet Jews to Israel formed the One to One project in 1991. Funds are raised through sponsored treks, individual donations and grant making trusts/ foundations *Co-Chairmen* Mrs. Rita Eker MBE, Mrs. Margaret Rigal.

JEWISH BLIND IN ISRAEL ASSOCIATION
c/o K. C. Keller F.C.A., Lynwood House, 373/375 Station Road, Harrow, Middx. HA1 2AW.
☎ 020-8357 2727. Fax 020-8357 2027. Email ken@newmanandpartners.co.uk
(Reg. Charity No. 1006756) Provides financial support and equipment to the Jewish registered blind in Israel. *Adv:* Prof. Lutza Yanko & Prof. Eliezer D. Jaffe, Dr Ben-Zion Silverstone (Jerusalem), Joseph S. Conway, F.R.C.S. (London). *Chairman* K.C. Keller.

JEWISH INSTITUTE FOR THE BLIND (British Aid Committee) 71 Eyre Court, Finchley Road,
London NW8 9TX. ☎ 020-7266 9966; Fax 020 7289 4741; Email info@jibj.org.uk; Website www.jewishblind.org
(Est 1964. Reg. Charity No. 222849). The British Aid Committee for the Jewish Institute for the Blind, Jerusalem (est. 1902) has provided aid to the Institute since 1964 and undertakes work and support through legacies and donations.

LABOUR FRIENDS OF ISRAEL
BM LFI, London, WC1N 3XX.
☎ 020-7222 4324; Fax 020-7222 4324. Email mail@lfi.org.uk, Website www. lfi.org.uk
Chairman Andrew Gwynne, MP; *Dir.* L. Berger.

LIBERAL DEMOCRAT FRIENDS OF ISRAEL
31, The Vale, London NW11 8SE. ☎ 020-8455 5140.
Open to all supporters of the Liberal Democrats in UK who recognise the right of Israel to a free, independent, permanent and prosperous existence as a member state of the United Nations. The Assoc. exists to foster good relations and understanding between Britain and state of Israel. *President* Rt. Hon. Alan Beith, MP; *Chairman* Monroe Palmer, O.B.E.; *Vice-Chairman* G. Stollar; *Sec.* M. Harris.

LIFELINE FOR THE OLD
6 Charlton Lodge, Temple Fortune Lane, London NW11 7TY.
☎ 020-8455 9059.
(Reg. Charity No. 232084) To assist the work of Lifeline for the Old in Jerusalem, which aims to help the aged in Israel by providing training in occupational skills, and improve the welfare and quality of life of Jerusalem's elderly and disabled. *H. Sec.* Miss J. Mitzman. *Leeds Branch*: *Jt. Chair* Dr M.E. Ziff, Mrs D. Cohen

MAGEN DAVID ADOM UK
Shield House, Harmony Way, off Victoria Road, London NW4 2BZ.
☎ 020-8201 5900. Fax 020-8201 5901; Email info@mdauk.org; Website www.mdauk.org
(Reg. Charity No. 1113409) To assist the work of Israel's voluntary emergency medical and national ambulance services which are responsible for supplying and maintaining first-aid posts and casualty stations, national blood services, medical wing of Israel Civil Defence, medical care of immigrants, missing persons bureaux, beach rescue stations, national responsibility for First-Aid training and all the other services usually supplied by a Red Cross Society. *Chairman* S. Glynn; *J.t H. T.* N. Posnansky, FCA, T. Shasha; *Chief Exec. Dir.* Eli Benson. Groups in many districts of London and the Regions.

MEDICAL AID COMMITTEE FOR ISRAEL

MAC-I: Reg. Charity No. 258697.
c/o 69 Hampstead Way, London NW11 7LG. Email mail@120harley.co.uk
(Est. 1969.) To provide med. and lab. equipment and offer technical and prof. advice. To assist and promote health and welfare projects in Israel. Applications from the Director Inter. Relations, Israel Min. of Health, 2 Ben Tabai Street, Jerusalem 93591. Dr Lionel P. Balfour-Lynn, MA, MD (Cambs), FRCPCH, DCH.

MIZRAHI TEFAHOT BANK LTD.

30 Old Broad Street, London EC2N 1HQ.
☎ 020-7448 0600. Fax 020-7448 0610. Email umb-main@umtb.co.uk, Website www.umtb.co.uk. Br. of Mizrahi Tefahot Bank in Israel. *Gen. Man.* Arik Bandel.

NEW ISRAEL FUND

25-26 Enford Street, London W1H 1DW.
☎ 020-7724 2266. Fax 020-7724 2299. Email info@uknif.org.
(Est. 1992. Reg. Charity No. 1060081) The New Israel Fund works to strengthen Israel's great founding vision of a free and democratic society. NIF is at the forefront of social change in Israel, providing hundreds of Israeli non-profit organisations with financial and technical support each year. NIF projects safeguard civil and human rights, cultivate Jewish–Arab coexistence and foster religious understanding in Israel. NIF also supports women's groups and environmental protection programmes. *Chair* Mark Goldberg; *Exec.Dir.* E. Goldberg.

OPERATION WHEELCHAIRS COMMITTEE

1 Opal Court, 120 Regents Park Road, London, N3 3HY.
☎ 020-8371 1500. Fax 020-8371 1501.
(Est. 1970. Reg. Charity No. 263089) Voluntary organisation providing rehabilitation and general medical equipment to hospitals in Israel treating wounded soldiers, and sports equipment for Beit Halochem. *Founder* Mrs Lily Perry; *Chairman* Mrs Anita Alexander-Passe.

POALE AGUDAT ISRAEL

Unites Orthodox religious workers to build up Eretz Yisrael in the spirit of the Torah. **World Central Off.**: 64 Frishman Street, Tel Aviv. *President* Rabbi A. Werdiger. **European Office and Great Britain**: P.A.I. Ho., 2A Alba Gardens, NW11 9NR. ☎/Fax 020-8458 5372. *Chairman* F. Wolkenfeld; *Corr.* D. Winter. *Publ.:* PAI Views.

REFORM MOVEMENT ISRAEL DESK

c/o Sternberg Centre, 80 East End Road, London N3 2SY. ☎ 020-8349 5640. Fax 020-8349 5699. Email israel@reformjudaism.org.uk. Website www.reformjudaism.org.uk.
(Est. 1989) Aims to create knowledge and love of Israel through theology, education and Israel action by raising Israel conciousness within the Reform Movement and by building links with IMPJ (Israel Movement Progressive Judaism) and its constituent communities. *Chairman* M. Reik.

SHAARE ZEDEK UK

766 Finchley Road, London NW11 7TH and PO Box 202, Salford, M7 4WS.
☎ 020-8201 8933. Fax 020-8201 8935. Email office@shaarezedek.org.uk; Website www.shaarezedekuk.com.
(Hospital est. Jerusalem 1902.) (Reg. Charity No. 262870) Raising funds by way of donations and legacies to support the hospital's programmes. *President* Lord Wolfson of Marylebone; *Chairman* M. Sorkin; *H.T.* A. Stechler, ACA; *Exec. Dir.* Mrs R. Goodman.

STATE OF ISRAEL BONDS
Development Company for Israel (UK) Ltd.

79 Wimpole Street, London W1G 9RY.

☎ 020-7224 6220. Fax 020-7224 6334. Website www.israelukbonds.com.
(Est. 1981.) Promotes and sells State of Israel Bonds (Israel's gilt-edged securities). *Managing Dir.* H. Myers. Email info@israelukbonds.com.

TEL AVIV UNIVERSITY TRUST
1 Bentinck Street, W1U 2EB.
☎ 020-7487 5280. Fax 020-7224 3908.
(Reg. Charity No. 314179) The principal aim of the Trust is to raise funds to promote the work of Tel Aviv University and to encourage support for academic projects, scholarships and campus development. The Trust also advises those who may wish to study at the University. *H. Presidents* Lord and Lady Wolfson, Dame Shirley Porter; *Chairman* D. Meller.

TRADE UNION FRIENDS OF ISRAEL
BCM TUFI, London, WC1N 3XX. Fax 020-7222 4323.

UK FRIENDS OF THE ASSOCIATION FOR THE WELLBEING OF ISRAEL'S SOLDIERS
☎ 020-8210 3060. Fax 020-8210 3075. Email ukawis@ukawis.net. Website www.ukawis.co.uk.
(Est. 2001. Reg. Charity No. 1084272). To support the work of the Association in Israel, by raising funds for the wellbeing, education and culture of Israel's soldiers. *Tr.* P. Sussmann, Julian Kemble, Zeev Remez, R. Rogoff; *Exec. Dir.* E. Hellerstein.

UK SOCIETY FOR THE PROTECTION OF NATURE IN ISRAEL
PO Box 42763, London N2 0YJ.
☎ 020-8444 0777. Fax 020-8444 0681. Email info@foi-asg.org.
(Est. 1986. Reg. Charity No. 327268) To generate interest in the beauty of Israel's natural landscapes; muster support for the conservation lobby in Israel. *Trs.* Godfrey Bradman, Edward Goldsmith, Zak Goldsmith, Arnold Kransdorff, John D. A. Levy, Bill Oddie.

WEIZMANN UK
126 Albert St, London NW1 7NE.
☎ 020-7424 6860. Fax 020-7424 6869. Email post@weizmann.org.uk; Website www.weizmann.ac.il
(Est. 1956. Reg. Charity No. 232666) To stimulate financial, scientific and cultural support in the UK for the Weizmann Institute of Science in Rehovot. *Chairman of Exec. Cttee.* Lord Mitchell; *V. Chairman* Dame Vivien Duffield, DBE; *Jt.H. Secs* J. Kropman, A. Cohen; *H.T.* R. Ohrenstein; *Dir.* S. Gould.

YAD VASHEM UK FOUNDATION
Contact Administrator 6 Bloomsbury Square, London WC1A 2LP
☎ 020-7543 5402. Fax 020-7404 1437. Email yadvashem.org.uk.
(Est 1978. Reg. Charity No. 1099659). Evolved originally as committee of the Board of Deputies, constituted as the National Yad Vashem Charitable Trust, incorporated in 2003 to represent the Yad Vashem, Jerusalem (see p. 161). *Life Presidents* Ben Helfgott, MBE, Simon Reiss; *Chairman* J. Pinnick.

YOUTH ALIYAH-CHILD RESCUE
126 Albert St., London, NW1 7NE
☎ 020 7485 8375 Fax 020 7485 8391. Email info@youthaliyah.org.uk.
Website www.youthaliyah.org.uk.
(Est. 1933. Reg. Charity No. 1077913) Object: to offer a secure home for under-privileged and deprived refugee, immigrant and native Israeli children. Five Youth Villages offer residential community care. *Jt. Chairmen* Stephen Barry, Adrienne Sussman; *Admin. Dir.* N. Ebert.

EDUCATIONAL AND CULTURAL ORGANISATIONS

Hebrew and Religion Classes are attached to most synagogues listed.
For University Centres and Institutions see pp. 37-40.

AGENCY FOR JEWISH EDUCATION
Bet Meir, 44B, Albert Road, NW4 2SG.
☎ 020-8457 9700. Fax 020-8457 9707. Email info@aje.org.uk; Website www.aje.org.uk
Training, resourcing, curriculum and servicing schools, nurseries and part-time education
organisations of the Jewish community in Britain. *Chief Exec.* Simon Goulden; *Dir. Education.*
Jeffrey Leader.

ASSOCIATION OF JEWISH TEACHERS
c/o Agency for Jewish Education, 44 Albert Road, London NW4 2SJ.
☎ 020-8906 0816. Fax 020-8457 9707.
(Est. 1986) To promote, enhance and support the welfare and professional develop-ment of
Jewish teachers in schools. *Chairman* P. Resnick; *V. Chairman* R. Marks.

BETH SHALOM HOLOCAUST CENTRE
Laxton, Newark, Notts NG22 0PA.
☎ 01623-836627. Fax 01623-836647. Email office@bethshalom.com;
Website www.beth shalom.com.
(Est. 1978 (as Beth Shalom Ltd.). Reg. Charity No. 509022) Holocaust education and
commemoration. *Officers.* Dr James M. Smith, Dr Stephen D. Smith, MBE.

BRITISH ORT
The British branch of World ORT Union (Est. 1880)
126 Albert Street, London NW1 7NE.
☎ 020-7446 8520. Fax 020-7446 8654. Email info@britishort.org; Website www.
britishort.org.
(Est. 1920. Reg. Charity No. 1105254) Education, schooling and vocational training for Jews
throughout the world; *President* The Hon. Sir David Sieff; *Chairman.* A.Goldman, *Chief Exec.* I.
Levene, OBE.

DAVAR, The Jewish Institute in Bristol and the South West
179 Whiteladies Rd., Clifton, Bristol, BS8 2AG
☎/Fax 0117-970 6594. Email davar.bristol@yahoo.co.uk. Website www.davar. com.
DAVAR provides a wide programme of cultural, educational and social activities. A regular
newsletter is available, and Jewish groups in the area advertise their own events via the
mailing list. *Chairman* Martin Weitz.

DVAR YERUSHALAYIM (London Jewish Academy)
24 Templars Avenue, NW11 0NS.
☎/Fax 020-8455 8631. Email jf@dvar.co.uk
(Est. 1978. Reg. Charity No. 284740) To provide full- and part-time courses in adult education
to enable men and women of limited Jewish knowledge and background to further their
understanding of Jewish thought and practice. *Princ.* Rabbi J. Freilich, Ph.C.

ENCOUNTER (Jewish Outreach Network)
PO Box 24046, London NW4 2ZP
☎ 020 8201 5070
(Est. 1996; Reg. Charity no. 1064674) The Jewish Outreach Network (J.O.I.N.), organised by
Encounter, provides a showcase for Orthodox Judaism. The executive comprises representatives
from Ohr Somayach, Aish, Project SEED and the United Synagogue Rabbinate. The Jewish
Outreach Network/Encounter is the impetus behind an annual winter Encounter Conference, a

day of inspiration and learning, and the Crash Courses in Judaism and Living Judaism, five-week lecture series which are offered periodically throughout the year. Encounter co-ordinates weekly explanatory services and High Holyday explanatory services throughout England, Speaker Tours and Shabbatonim. *Exec. Dir.*

HOLOCAUST EDUCATIONAL TRUST
BCM Box 7892, London WC1N 3XX.
☎ 020-7222 6822/5853. Fax 020-7233 0161. Email info@het.org.uk. Website www.het.org.uk (Est. 1988. Reg. Charity No. 1092892) To promote Holocaust education and research, not only formally but also to the wider public. The Trust works in schools and higher education, providing teacher-training workshops and lectures, as well as supplying teaching aids and resource material. New academic research on Holocaust-related issues are also produced by the Trust. *Patrons* Lord Carey of Clifton, Lord Dholakia, Lord Mackay of Clashfern, Lady Merlyn-Rees, Prof Elie Wiesel; *Board of Trustees, President* R. Stephen Rubin OBE; *V. Presidents* Rt Hon. Lord Hunt of Wirral MBE; *Chairman* Lord Janner of Braunstone QC; *V. Chairman* and *Tr.* Paul Phillips; David Gryn, Kitty Hart -Moxon, OBE, Ben Helfgott MBE, Sir Ivan Lawrence QC, Craig Leviton, Ivan Lewis MP, Jon Mendelsohn, Martin Paisner CBE, Michael Karp, Alberta Strage; *Council* James Clappison MP, Louise Ellman MP, Andrew Lansley CBE, MP, Lord Levy, Lembit Öpik MP, Sir Antony Sher; *Chief Exec.* Karen Pollock.

ISRAEL ZANGWILL MEMORIAL FUND
c/o, Sternberg Centre For Judaism, 80 East End Road, N3 2SY. ☎ 020-8349 5645. Email admin@reformjudaism.org.uk
(Est. 1929) To assist poor Jews engaged in literary, artistic, dramatic and scientific work.

ISRAELI DANCE INSTITUTE
Balfour House, 741 High Road, London N12 0JL.
Daytime ☎/fax 020-8446 6427. Evening ☎/fax 020-8445 6765. Email info@idi.org.uk; Website www.idi.org.uk
The Israeli Dance Institute uses dance as a tool to promote Jewish and Israeli culture through an annual training seminar, Machol Europa, and training and support programmes that include an annual dance festival for schools across the country. The Institute's performance troupes represent the community in inter faith and multi-cultural events.. *Chairman* M. Stone.

JEWISH BOOK COUNCIL
ORT House, 126 Albert Sreet NW1 7NE.
☎ 020-7487 3401. Fax 020-7487 4211. Email jewishbookcouncil@btopenworld. com; Website www.jewishbookweek.com. *Admin.* Pam Lewis ☎ 020-7446 8771.
(Est. 1947. Reg. Charity No. 293800) To stimulate and encourage the reading of books on Judaism and on every aspect of Jewish thought, life, history and literature; organises annual Jewish Book Week, now Europe's largest Jewish literary festival and associated events. Administers a triennial prize for Hebrew translation and an annual children's poetry prize. *Chairmen* Andrew Renton & *H. T.* G. Sandler; *H. Sec.* R. Tager, QC.

JEWISH CHRONICLE
25 Furnival Street, London EC4A 1JT.
☎ 020-7415 1500. Fax 020-7405 9040. Website www.thejc.com (Est. 1841.) The world's oldest independent Jewish weekly newspaper. *Chairman* Peter Levy; *Edr.* Stephen Pollard.

JEWISH COMMUNITY DAY SCHOOL ADVISORY BOARD
c/o Leo Baeck College, Sternberg Centre, 80 East End Road, London N3 2SY.
☎ 020-8349 5620. Fax 020-8349 5639. Email sharon@silver-myer.com
(Est. 1998) Promotion and development of Jewish cross-community day schools throughout the UK. *Chairman* Jon Epstein; *Admin.* S. Silver-Myer.

JEWISH EDUCATION AID SOCIETY

(Est. 1896.) To investigate and advise on cases of highly talented students and in certain circumstances to provide interest-free loans to enable them to train for professions or the pursuit of art. Now under the administration of Anglo-Jewish Association (see p.3).

JEWISH FILM FOUNDATION

c/o 46a Minster Road, London NW2 3RD.

The Jewish Film Foundation is an educational charity whose aim is to promote the exhibition, distribution, production and study of Jewish cinema, television and video programmes. It initiates and co-ordinates education and cultural activities involving film and video and advises those who make and use programmes on Jewish themes. Organises an annual Jewish Film Festival in London. *Bd. of Dir.* Michael Green, Dorothy Berwin, Jonathan Davis, Dominique Green, Jeremy Isaacs, Verity Lambert, Michael May, Louis Marks, Alan Yentob; *Prog. Dir.* Sam Maser.

JEWISH GENEALOGICAL SOCIETY OF GREAT BRITAIN

33, Seymour Place, London W1H 5AP. Website www.jgsgb.org.uk.

Membership: Email membership@jgsgb.org.uk.

(Est. 1992. Reg. Charity No. 1022738) To promote and encourage the study of Jewish genealogy. The Society organises lectures, seminars and family history workshops (including those at The London Museum of Jewish Life); publishes *Shemot*, and guides to study of Jewish genealogy; promotes research; and operates a library. *President* Dr Anthony Joseph; *V. Presidents* Dr S. Issroff, D. Jacobs, G. Jaffe, R. Pearlman, G. Rigal; *Chairman* L. Harris; *Membership Sec.* A. Winner; *T. D.* Glazer; *Sec.* N. J. King; *Groups:* Leeds (F. Harris, J. Williams), North Manchester (Lorna Kay), South West London (Ena Black), East London/Essex (Shirley Collier), The Chilterns (S. Rose).

JEWISH HERITAGE UK

PO. Box 193, Manchester, M13 9PL. ☎ 0161-275 3611. Email director@jewish-heritage-uk.org Website www.jewish-heritage-uk.org

(Est. 2004. Reg. Charity No. 1118174)

To care for the historic buildings and sites of Britain's Jewish community and to promote the Jewish built-heritage through education and public access. See pp. 198-200. *Dir.* Dr Sharman Kadish; *Consult. Architect* Barbara Bowman.

JEWISH HISTORICAL SOCIETY OF ENGLAND

33 Seymour Place, W1H 5AP.

☎/Fax 020-7723 5852. Email info@jhse.org. Website www.jhse.org.

(Est. 1893. Reg. Charity No. 217331) *President* Prof. M. Alpert; *H. Sec.* Dr Joanna Newman; *Admin.* D. Freeman.

Branches: Birmingham: *Chairman* Dr Anthony Joseph, 25 Westbourne Road, Edgbaston, Birmingham B15 3TX; **Essex:** *Contact* Mrs S. Lassman ☎ 020-8554 9921; **Leeds**: *Contact* Murray Winer, 21 Primley Park Ave., Leeds LS17 7HX ☎ 0113 294 0789; **Liverpool**: *Chairman* Arnold Lewis, 61 Menlove Ave., L18 2EH; **Manchester**: *Chairman* Frank Baigel. Email manchester@jhse.org **Sussex**: *Chairman* S. Gould. **Radlett**: *Chairman*.J. Winroope.

JEWISH LITERARY TRUST

PO Box 37645, London NW7 1WB.

☎ 020-8830 5367. Website www.jewishquarterly.org.

(Est. 1984. Reg. Charity No. 268589). Established on the death of Jacob Sonntag, (founding editor), to ensure the continuity of the Jewish Quarterly. *Patrons* Elizabeth and Sidney Corob, Sue Hammerson, Peter Held, Lord Kalms, Diana and Michael Lazarus, Colette Littman, Clive Marks, Ronald Wingate, Delia and Fred Worms; *Chairman* Emmanuel Grodzinski; *H.T.* Paul Filer; *Exec. Cttee* Marion Cohen, Andrew Franklin, Jeffrey Greenwood, Michael Joseph, Stephen Massil, Jonny Geller, Adam Freudenheim, Josephine Burton; *Admin.* Pam Lewis; *Ed.* Rachel Lasserson. *Publ.* Jewish Quarterly (see p.5).

JEWISH MUSIC INSTITUTE

SOAS University of London, Thornhaugh Street, Russell Square, London WC1H 0XG ☎ 020-8909 2445. Fax 020-8909 1030. Email jewishmusic@jmi.org.uk; Website www.jmi.org.uk

(Reg. Charity No. 328228) Based at the University of London, the Jewish Music Institute (JMI) is a European Centre for study, practical training and performance of Jewish music at all levels in the music of the Jewish people across the globe.

Activities include:

Practical training: JMI presents Summer schools, evening classes and workshops at London University and in outreach programmes in Yiddish song, klezmer, Sephardi and cantorial music

Joe Loss Lectureship in Jewish Music some scholarships are available to study Jewish music at SOAP.

Performance Annual Jewish Culture Day on London's SouthBank late November on different themes. (2009 the 50th anniversary of the death of Ernest Bloch)

Consultation JMI is available for consultation and advice to the media, scholars and the general public

Wedding bands JMI recommends live Jewish music for weddings, bar mitzvahs and other functions

Visiting Composer from Israel JMI appoints a visiting composer in exchange programmes with the British Music colleges

Music Suppressed by the Nazis JMI researches, performs and records music by composers banned exiled or murdered in the Third Reich

THE JEWISH TEACHERS ASSOCIATION

C/o Board of Deputies of British Jews, 6 Bloomsbury Square, London WC1A 2LP ☎ 020-7543 5400 Email info@jewishteachers.org.uk Website www.jewishteachers.org.uk

(Est. 2007) The Jewish Teachers Association exists to:

Provde a network for Jewish teachers and educators to discuss teaching, learning, and other matters. Endeavour to liaise and represent the needs of Jewish teachers and educators to outside organisations. Provide Social Networking and Professional Development opportunities. Encourage balanced teaching about Judaism and the State of Israel. The Association is open to all Jewish educationalists, educational psychologists, and youth workers. *Chairman* D. Needlestone, *Vice-Chairs* F. Hoori, M. Robinson, S. Strauss, *T.* A. Kleinman, *Manchester Branch Chair* E. Goodman

KESHER – THE LEARNING CONNECTION

933 Finchley Rd, London NW11 7PE. ☎ 020-8458 5836. Fax 020-8201 9537. Email connect@kesher.org.uk Website www.kesher.org.uk

(Est. 1997. Reg Charity no. 1061689). Jewish Education and Outreach to singles and young couples. Reconnecting Jews of all backgrounds with their heritage. *Dir.* Rabbi Rashi Simon, MA. Educational, Shabbat and Festival Services.

LEO BAECK COLLEGE

The Sternberg Centre for Judaism, 80 East End Road, London N3 2SY.. ☎ 020-8349 5600. Fax 020 8349 5619Email info@lbcac.uk; Website www.lbc.ac.uk.

(Est. 1956. Reg. Charity No. 209777): Established for the study of Judaism and the training of rabbis and teachers, under the joint auspices of the Movement for Reform Judaism and Liberal Judaism. *Principal* Rabbi Prof. M. Saperstein;*Vice. Principal* Rabbi Dr Michael Shire; *Ch. Bd. Govs.* Miriam Kramer; *Exec. Dir.* Stephen Ross; *Hd of Academic Services* G. Ruppin; *Hd Student Services* Irit Burkeman; *Hd of HR and Support Services.* Rhona Lesner.

The Department of Rabbinic Studies and Higher Jewish Studies

☎ 020 8349 5600 Fax 020 8349 5619 Email: info@lbc.ac.uk

Offers a five-year programme leading to Rabbinic Ordination, full time and part time degrees, and caters for those wishing to further their Jewish knowledge, and supports Progressive communities developing their own programmes.

The Department of Education and Professional Development
☎ 020-8349 5620. Fax 020-8349 5639. Email admin@lbc.ac.uk. This department serves the Progressive movements, providing services to part-time religion schools and primary schools; offering teacher training, community/family education, Hebrew programming, outreach projects, a purchasing service for text-books for schools, and two Resource Centres. This department also runs an MA in Jewish Education and an Advanced Diploma in Professional Development: Jewish Education. Consultants are available to visit communities and offer programmes around the country. *Dir.* .

LIMMUD
Lancaster House, Evans Business Estate, 105 Brook Road, London NW2 7BZ.
☎ 020-8438 6555. Fax 020-8438 6600. Email office@limmud.org; Website www. limmud.org
Limmud is a cross-communal, adult education organisation. Its flagship event is its 5-day residential winter conference. Limmud also organises LimmudFest in the summer, regional Day Limmuds around the country, LimmudLive, Taste of Limmud and co-sponsors the Melton programme in London. *Chair:* Elliott Goldstein; *Exec. Dir.* R. Simonson; *Exec. Consult* C. Lawton; *Admin.* Helen Lyons.

LITTMAN LIBRARY OF JEWISH CIVILIZATION
PO Box 645, Oxford OX2 0UJ. ☎ 01865 514688. Fax 01865 722964 Email info@littman.co.uk; Website www.littman.co.uk.
(Est. 1965. Reg. Charity No. 1000784) Established for the purpose of publishing scholarly works aimed at disseminating an understanding of the Jewish heritage and Jewish history and making Jewish religious thought and literary creativity accessible to the English-speaking world. *Dirs.* Mrs C. C. Littman, R. J. Littman; *Contact* Connie Webber (Editorial); *Chief Exec. Off.* Ludo Craddock.

LONDON ACADEMY OF JEWISH STUDIES
2–4 Highfield Avenue, NW11 9ET.
☎ 020-8455 5938; 020-8458 1264.
(Est. in 1975) To assist post-Yeshiva students to further their Jewish educ. and engage in advanced Talmudic research. Graduates are expected to take up rabbinical and teaching posts in the com. The Kolel also serves as a Torah-study centre for laymen. Its specialised library is open to the gen. public throughout the year incl. Shabbat and Yom Tov. *H. Princ.* Rabbi G. Hager.

LONDON JEWISH CULTURAL CENTRE
Ivy House, 94-96 North End Road, London, NW11 7SX .
☎ 020-8457 5000. Fax 020-8457 5024. Email admin@ljcc.org.uk; Website www.ljcc.org.uk
(Est 2000. Reg. Charity No. 1081014) The London Jewish Cultural Centre offers an educational, cultural and social resource including GCSE programmes in Hebrew and Jewish Studies, and an annual Ulpan. A fullcultural programme complements the curriculum. The Holocaust and Anti-Racism Department works with Holocaust survivors in outreach to schools across the UK. Ivy House provides conference and social facilities for communal and private events. *Publ.* Prospectus. *Chief Exec.* Trudy Gold; *Dir. Languages* Haggit Inbar-Littas; *Dir. Holocaust Educ.* Stephanie Rose.

LONDON SCHOOL OF JEWISH STUDIES (formerly Jews' College)
Schaller House, 44A Albert Road, London NW4 2SJ.
☎ 020-8203 6427. Fax 020-8203 6420. Ebsite www.lsjs.ac.uk.
LSJS is a modern orthodox centre of Jewish scholarship and learning. *Dep. President* Rabbi Dr Abraham Levy, BA; *Chair of the Council* Mr Howard Stanton, FCCA; *Chief Exec* Dr R. Zarum;.*Libr.*

MAROM MASORTI
Alexander House, 3 Shakespeare Rd. London N3 1XE.

☎ 020-8349 6650. Email enquiries@masorti.org.uk.
Marom is the Students and Young Adult Department of the Masorti Movement. We offer a variety of programmes, including a weekly Bet Midrash, Friday night dinners, social events and trips to Israel and Europe for 20s-30s.

POLACK'S HOUSE EDUCATIONAL TRUST CLIFTON COLLEGE
32 College Rd., Bristol BS8 3JH.
☎ 0117 3157000. Email jgreenbury@clifton-college.avon.sch.uk.
(Reg. Charity No. 1040218) The trust supports the education of Jewish pupils at Clifton College, and in so doing continues a tradition going back to 1878. Jewish Studies, Jewish Worship and kosher food for boys and girls aged 3-18. Scholarships and bursaries available. *Hd. Jewish Studies* Jonathan Greenbury.

SCOPUS JEWISH EDUCATIONAL TRUST (formerly ZFET)
52 Queen Anne St., London W1G 8HL.
(020-7935 0100. Fax 020-7935 7787.
(Est. 1953. Reg. Charity No. 313154) To raise funds by way of endowment, legacy, bequest, gift or donation in order to provide a first-class education in Jewish Studies and Hebrew throughout its national network of day schools, all of which have a Zionist ethos and emphasize the centrality of Israel in Jewish life. *H. President* Stanley S. Cohen, OBE; *Chairman* Peter Ohrenstein; *H.T.* Jonathan M. Kramer; *H. Sec.* Brenda Hyman. Schools: **London**: Harry & Abe Sherman Rosh Pinah School, Mathilda Marks-Kennedy School, Ella & Ernst Frankel Kindergarten, Simon Marks School, Simon Marks Sherman Nursery; **Leeds**: Brodetsky Primary and Nursery School; Deborah Taylor Playgroup; **Manchester**: North Cheshire Primary School.

seed
Mowbray House, 58-70 Edgware Way, Edgware,Middx, HA8 8DJ.
☎ 020-8958 0820. Fax 020-8958 0821. Email info@seed.uk.net. Website www. seed.uk.net
(Est. 1980. Reg. Charity No. 281307 Project SEED) To provide Jewish adult education through courses, weekend residential seminars and one-to-one study throughout the year. Working also with schools and parents - specialising in the interests of parents and young children. *Dir.* Rabbi J. Grunfeld; *London contact* for One to One Rabbi A. Lazarus; *Manchester* contact Rabbi A. Hassan; *Educ. London Programmes* contact Rabbi M. Herman, Manchester contacts Rabbi M. & V. Broder; *Seminars* Y. Silkin.

THE SEPHARDI CENTRE
2 Ashworth Road, Maida Vale, London W9 1JY.
☎ 020-7266 3682. Fax 020-7289 5957. Email sephardicentre@spsyn.org.uk.
(Est. 1994. Reg. Charity No. 1039937) The Centre's aim is to promote Sephardi culture. Courses, open to all, focus on Religion, History, Music, Art and Cuisine. A library and reading room specialising in Sephardi literature is open to the public (see p.51). *Dir.*

SOCIETY FOR JEWISH STUDY
(Est. 1946. Reg. Charity No. 283732) *Sec.* Rosemary Goldstein, 1A Church Mount, London N2 0RW. Website www. sjslondon.org.uk. The Society presents academic research in Jewish religion, literature and history.

THE SPIRO ARK
c/o JMC, 25/26 Enford St., London W1H 1DW.
☎ 020-7723 9991. Fax 020-7723 8191. Email education@spiroark.org.; Website www. spiroark.org
(Est. 1998 Reg. Charity No.1070926) The Spiro Ark was established to continue the work of the Spiro Institute to meet the urgent problems facing the Jewish people in the twenty-first century and uses innovative teaching methods in order to encourage a learning community:

'My People are destroyed through lack of knowledge' (*Hosea, IV, 6*). Hebrew and Yiddish are taught at all levels, together with other Jewish and related subjects. There are regular cultural events plus national and international tours. Also intensive Hebrew Ulpanim in London and in Israel at Kibbutz Lavi. Newly created departments include *Tzavta* which provides courses and events to highlight the best of Israeli achievement: arts, science, films, politics, plus regular meetings with Israeli personalities; and *Jtrails* based at Yarnton Manor, Oxford set up with English Heritage and matching funding to discover Jewish roots in Britain with a view to presenting family research on the website.*Founders and developers of both the Spiro Institute and Spiro Ark* Nitza and Robin Spiro.

SPRINGBOARD EDUCATION TRUST
32 Foscote Road, London NW4 3SD.
☎ 020-8202 7147. Fax 020-8203 8293. Email aumie@shap32.fsworld.co.uk
(Est. 1979. Reg. Charity No. 277946) Whilst specialising in reminiscence and stimulation programmes for senior citizens, Springboard has extended its range of audio-visual and film productions to cover Jewish and Zionist history, synagogue and home traditions, inter-faith projects.
Springboard also produces low-cost DVD/film programmes for other orgs. and provides seminars for teachers and welfare workers in the use of its programmes with substantial back-up materials.
Dirs. Aumie and Michael Shapiro.

UK JEWISH FILM FESTIVAL
407,Clerkenwell Workshops, 27-31 Clerkenwell Close, London EC1R 0AT
☎ 020-3176 0048. Email info@ukjff.org.uk. Website www.ukjewishfilmfestival.org.uk
(Est. 1997, Reg. Charity No. 1072914. The UK Jewish Film Festival is aimed at the diverse range of audiences throughout the UK about worldwide Jewish cultures, identity, history and issues of concern through the medium of film. Activities include an annual two-week festival in cinemas across London, an annual UK tour from January to March, the UKFF Short Film Fund Award, the UKFF Film Library and the 'Xtras' series of screenings from January to June each year. *Festival Dir.* Judy Ironside; *Artistic Dir.* Gali Gold; *Festival Prod.* Michael Etherton; *Chairman* David H. Kustow.

UNIVERSITY CENTRES AND ORGANISATIONS
(See also Organisations concerned with Jewish students on pp. 45-46, and Libraries on pp. 46-52).

BRITISH ASSOCIATION FOR JEWISH STUDIES
Email info@BAJSBulletin.org. Website www.BAJSBulletin.org.
(Est. 1975.) Membership is open to scholars concerned with the academic pursuit of Jewish studies in the British Isles. The Assoc. promotes and defends the scholarly study of Jewish culture in all its aspects and organizes an annual conference. *President (2009)* Prof. S. Kunin, Durham University, Dean's Office, South Lodge Science Laboratories, Durham, DH1 3LE, UK, *Sec.* Dr D. Langton, University of Manchester, The Centre for Jewish Studies, Dept. of Religions and Theology, Oxford Road, Manchester M13 9PL; *T.* Dr. J. Aitken, Faculty of Oriental Studies, Sidgwick Avenue, Cambridge, CB3 9DA.

CENTRE FOR GERMAN-JEWISH STUDIES
University of Sussex, Falmer, Brighton, East Sussex BN1 9QN. ☎ 01273-606755.
Dir. Dr C. Wiese, Email c.wiese@sussex.ac.uk; ☎ 01273 877344, *Admin. Liaison Off.* Diana Franklin. ☎/Fax 01273 678771, (/Fax 020-8381 4721. Email dfranklin@ sussex.ac.uk.

CENTRE FOR JEWISH STUDIES (University of Leeds)
Leeds LS2 9JT.
☎ 0113-233 5197. Fax 0113-245 1977. Email e.frojmovic@leeds.ac.uk. Website www.leeds.ac.uk/fine_art/org/cejs.html

(Est. 1995) Teaching of Jewish Studies: at post graduate level and supervision of research degrees. *Dir.* Dr Eva Frojmovic.

CENTRE FOR JEWISH STUDIES (University of London)
School of Oriental and African Studies, Thornhaugh Street, Russell Square, London WC1H 0XG.
☎ 020-7898 4358. Email cs52@soas.ac.uk; Website www.soas.ac.uk/centres/jewish. The focus of activities during 2009 will be 'Tel Aviv 1909-2009'.The Centre seeks to promote modern Jewish and Israeli studies. It seeks to foster research seminars and to collaborate with other institutions of higher education. Through public lectures and conferences, the Centre endeavours to bring areas of academic interest to the wider community. In the multi-cultural atmosphere that is unique to SOAS, it provides a forum for discussion and dialogue. *Chairman* Prof. C. Shindler;

CENTRE FOR JEWISH STUDIES (University of Manchester)
Samuel Alexander Building, University of Manchester, Oxford Road, Manchester M13 9PL.
(0161-275 3614. Fax 0161-275 3613. Email cjs@man.ac.uk; Website www. mucjs.org.
(Est. 1997) The Centre seeks to maximise the teaching, undergraduate and postgraduate, of Jewish Studies in the University of Manchester, through support of courses and student bursaries; to foster collaborative research between staff of the University of Manchester and others in the region through research seminars and research projects (including local Jewish history); to bring the results of academic work in Jewish Studies to the wider community through public lectures (including the Sherman Lectures) and conferences; and to disseminate the results of these activities on the internet, and through its on-line journal: Melilah. The Centre for Jewish Studies is also home to Bill Williams Jewish Studies library, which contains c. 300 books, focusing on anglo-Jewish history.*Co-Dirs* Prof. Philip S. Alexander, Prof. Bernard S. Jackson; *Co-ord.* Ms Penelope Junkermann.

CENTRE FOR MODERN HEBREW STUDIES
Faculty of Asian and Middle Eastern Studies, Sidgwick Avenue, Cambridge CB3 9DA.
☎ 01223-335117. Fax 01223-335110.
The Centre functions within the Faculty of Asian and Middle Eastern Studies where degree courses include options in classical, medieval and modern Hebrew studies. The Centre's principal activities include the provision of open language classes in Modern Hebrew, seminars on Israeli literature and culture, and weekly screenings of Israeli films; also, an annual ten-day summer Ulpan. *Contact* R. Williams, Dr. M. Marzanska-Mishani.

INSTITUTE OF JEWISH STUDIES
University College London, Gower Street, WC1E 6BT.
☎ 020-7679 3520. Fax 020-7209 1026. Email ijs@ucl.ac.uk; Website www. ucl.ac.uk/hebrew-jewish/ijs.
(Est. 1953. Reg. Charity No. 213114) Founded by the late Prof. Alexander Altmann, IJS is now located within the Dept. of Hebrew and Jewish Studies at Univ. College, London, while retaining its autonomous status. Funded by the private sector. Programme of activities dedicated to the academic study of all branches of Jewish history and civilisation, including series of public lectures, seminars, symposia, major internat. conferences, and publs., especially of its conference proceedings. It brings together scholars, students, academic instits. from all sections inside and outside the Univ. of London and the scholarly scene in and outside the UK, worldwide. The conference for 2008 was on 'Consumer Culture in Modern Times'. List of publications and programme mailings available on request.
Patrons The Lord Moser, The Rt. Hon. The Lord Woolf; Bd, of Govs:*Chairman* Philip L. Morgenstern, BA; *Hon. Trs.* Daniel Peltz, BA, David J. Lewis, BSc, FRICS, Edward M.Lee, BSc (Econ), Nick Ritblat, MA, J. Caplan, FCA (also *H. Sec.*); *Dir.* Prof. Mark J. Geller. The Trustees of the Institute of Jewish Studies, a non-profit making company limited by guarantee, registered in England No. 2598783.

JOE LOSS LECTURESHIP IN JEWISH MUSIC

Music Department, School of Oriental and African Studies, University of London, Thornhaugh St., Russell Sq., WC1H 0XG.

☎ 020-7898 4243. Fax 020-7898 4519. Email aw48@soas.ac.uk.

(Est. 1991) Incorporates Jewish Music Resource Centre, and the Harry Rosencweig Collection of Jewish Music (see p. 34). Sponsored by the Jewish Music Institute (see p.??). Research, lecturing, teaching, consultancy. Studies cover the liturgical, semi-religious, folk, popular and art music of Ashkenazi, Sephardi and Oriental ethnic groups, in the context of Jewish culture, society, history, geography, language, psychology, religion and tradition (within wider Christian and Islamic environments). *Lect.* Abigail Wood, Ph.D.

LEO BAECK INSTITUTE

4 Devonshire Street, W1W 5LB.

☎ 020-7580 3493. Fax 020-7436 8634. Email info@leobaeck.co.uk. Website www. leobaeck. co.uk.

(Est. 1955. Reg. Charity No. 235163) Research and publications on history of Central European German-speaking Jewry. *Chairman* Prof. Peter Pulzer; *Dir.* Dr R. Gross; *T.* Dr A. Paucker. *Publ.:* Year Book (*Edr.* Prof. J. A. S. Grenville, Dr R. Gross), symposia, lectures, etc.

OXFORD CENTRE FOR HEBREW AND JEWISH STUDIES

Yarnton Manor, Yarnton, Oxford, OX5 1PY

☎ 01865 377946. Fax 01865 375079. Email enquiries@ochjs.ac.uk; Website www.ochjs.ac.uk. uk/ochjs.

Hebrew and Jewish Studies Unit

Oriental Institute, University of Oxford, OX1 2LE.

01865 288216. Fax 01865 278190. Website www.orinst.ox.ac.uk/nme/hjs/index.shtml

The Centre, together with the Unit which it funds, is one of Europe's leading teaching and research institutions in the area of Jewish studies. Its work includes Jewish history and literature, ancient, medieval and modern; Talmudic studies, Jewish/Islamic and Jewish/Christian relationships at all periods; Hebrew and Yiddish language and literature; anthropology; sociology; law; and theology. It provides instruction in Jewish studies towards the Oxford University BA, M.st., M. Phil, M.Litt and D. Phil degrees. The Centre initiated and runs the one-year Masters of Studies (M.St.) in Jewish Studies at Oxford.

Publications: Journal of Jewish Studies (half-yearly); and numerous books and articles by Fellows past and present. The termly listing of lectures, seminars and classes, Newsletter and the Annual Report of the Centre are available on request. *President* David Ariel; *Co-Chairmen Bd. Gov.* Stanley Fink. G.Pinto (The Centre also houses the Leopold Muller Memorial Library, see p. 50).

PARKES INSTITUTE FOR THE STUDY OF JEWISH/NON-JEWISH RELATIONS

History, School of Humanities, Highfield, Southampton University of Southampton SO17 1BJ.

☎ 023 80592261. Fax 023 80593458. Website www.parkes.soton.ac.uk

The Parkes Institute is a community of scholars, curators, librarians, students, and activists, whose work is based around the resources of the Parkes library and archive, dedicated to the study of Jewish/non Jewish relations throughout the ages. Through our research, publications, teaching, conservation and outreach work, we seek to bring the vision of James Parkes, pioneer historian against antisemitism, to new generations: to provide a world-class centre for the study of Jewish/non-Jewish relations; to study the experience of minorities, refugees and outsiders; and to examine the power of prejudice from antiquity to the contemporary world. Members teach courses in Jewish history, literature and culture at undergraduate level, and the postgraduate community is connected to the MA and MRes programmes in Jewish History and Culture, and PhD studies in the broad field of Jewish/non-Jewish relations from antiquity to the present. Publications linked to the Institute include three journals (*Patterns of Prejudice, Jewish Culture and History,* and *The*

Journal of Holocaust Education), and the Parkes-Wiener Jewish Studies monograph series. *Head of Institute* Professor Tony Kushner.

SCHOOL OF ORIENTAL AND AFRICAN STUDIES (SOAS)
Dept. of the Languages and Cultures of the Near and Middle East, Thornhaugh Street, Russell Square, London WC1H OXG.
☎ 020-7898 4320. Fax 020-7898 4359. Website www.soas.ac.uk/nme.
SOAS is one of the world's greatest concentrations of expertise on Africa and Asia. The Near & Middle East Department offers a B.A. in Hebrew & Israeli Studies and degrees combining Hebrew with Law, Economics, Management, Arabic and with many other subjects – all affording a year's study at the Hebrew University of Jerusalem. The one-year MA in Israeli Studies caters for postgraduates from around the world seeking an entrée into the field. Doctorates in Israeli and Modern Jewish Studies can be researched. These programmes have the benefit of one of the largest open-stack Jewish Studies libraries in Europe. Also based at SOAS is the Centre for Jewish Studies, which hosts lecture series and symposia on a wide range of issues (see p. 38).*Contact* Professor Colin Shindler.

STANLEY BURTON CENTRE FOR HOLOCAUST STUDIES
School of History, University of Leicester, Leicester LE1 7RH.
☎ 0116-2522800 Fax 0116-2523986. Website www.le.ac.uk/hi/centres/burton)
To promote the study of and research into the Holocaust. *Dir.* C. Szejnmann. *Dep. Dir.* Dr O. Jensen

UNIVERSITY COLLEGE LONDON
Department of Hebrew and Jewish Studies, Gower Street, WC1E 6BT.
☎ 020-7679 7171. Fax 020-7209 1026. Email jewish.studies@ucl.ac.uk; Website www.ucl.ac.uk/hebrew-jewish/home/index.php.
The largest university department in the UK and Europe for obtaining honours degrees (single subject BA degrees in History; (Central and Eastern Europe) and Jewish Studies, Modern Languages or Modern Languages Plus; MA in Hebrew and Jewish Studies, Holocaust Studies or Modern Israeli Studies; MPhil or PhD). Undergraduate students spend a year of the course at the Hebrew University of Jerusalem. All degrees are available as full- or part-time programmes. The department hosts visiting staff from aboard on an annual basis. It comprises nine full-time and seven part-time members of staff and hosts the Institute of Jewish Studies (see p. 39) *Head* Dr Ada Rapoport-Albert.
Centre for Israeli Studies
(Est. 2000) *Co. Dir.* Dr Neill Lochery, Dr T. Ratner; *President, International Adv. Bd.* Sir Martin Gilbert.

WOOLF INSTITUTE OF ABRAHAMIC FAITHS
Wesley House, Jesus Lane, Cambridge CB5 8BJ
☎ 01223 741 048. Email. enquiries@woolfinstitute.cam.ac.uk Website www. woolfinstitute. cam.ac.uk (Reg. Chartiy No. 1069589). The Woolf Institute of Abrahamic Faiths is dedicated to teaching, research and dialogue in the encounter between Jews, Christians and Muslims, and is an umbrella organisation for the Centre for the Study of Jewish–Christian Relations (CJCR, founded in 1998) and the Centre for the Study of Muslim–Jewish Relations (CMJR, established in 2006). The Institute is also Associate Member of the Cambridge Theological Federation. *Exec. Dir* Dr. E. Kessler; *Acad. Dir. (CJCR)* Dr. J. Aitken; *Dir CMJR* Dr. A. Hoti; *Admin* T. Steiner *Librarian* Y. Gez.

ORGANISATIONS CONCERNED WITH JEWISH YOUTH

B'NAI B'RITH YOUTH ORGANISATION
1–2 Endsleigh Street, WC1H 0DS.
☎ 020-7387 3115. Email bbyo@bbyo.org.uk. Website www.bbyo.org.uk
BBYO is a unique, peer-led Zionist youth organisation. It promotes Zionism, Judaism, leadership, welfare and social awareness in a pluralist, open and totally youth-led environment. There are

weekly meetings in 10 chapters, national events, Israel summer tour, 'Atid' Leadership tour and a one-year programme in Israel. *Admin.* T. Seshold, *Youth Dir.* R.Rossano

JEWISH GUIDE ADVISORY COUNCIL (JGACB)
JGAC furthers girlguiding within the Jewish community. *Nat. Chairman* Mrs J. Edelman, 41, Pinegrove, London N20 8LA. ☎ 020-8445 0230; *T.* Mrs R. Holland, 28, Ashley Lane, London NW4 1HG, WD6 1UF. ☎ 020-8203 2960.

JEWISH LADS' AND GIRLS' BRIGADE
HQ: Camperdown, 3 Beechcroft Road, South Woodford, E18 1LA.
☎ 020-8989 8990. Fax 020-8530 3327. Website www.jlgb.org. Email getinvolved@jlgb.org
(Est. 1895. Reg. Charity No. 286950) The JLGB is the longest-established Jewish youth movement in the UK.
   Jewish Operating Authority for the Duke of Edinburgh's Award. The JLGB works with almost every Jewish school in the UK promoting the Award scheme,volunteering projects and active citizenship, as well as the Challenge Award for Jewish Youth, Young Citizens' Award, Millenium Volunteers Award of Excellence, the Gateway Award, and the Sir Peter E. Lazarus Debating Competition.
   Patron Edmund L. de Rothschild, CBE, TD; *President* The Lord Levy; *Commandant* B/Col Jill Attfield; *Chairman* Norman Terrett, J.P; *Chaplain* Rabbi A. Plancey; *Chief Exec.* N. S. Martin, BSc (Hons), MA.

JEWISH SCOUT ADVISORY COUNCIL
Furthers scouting in the Jewish community. *H. Sec.* R. Simmons, 103 Kenton Lane, Kenton, Harrow, Middx HA3 8UJ. ☎ 020-8907 3446. Fax 020-8907 6297.

JEWISH YOUTH FUND
PO Box 603, Edgware HA8 4EQ.
☎ 020-3209 6006. Email info@jyf.org. Website www. jewishyouthfund. ik.com
(Est. 1937. Reg. Charity No. 251902) Provides funds to promote the social education of Jewish young people through the provision of leisure time facilities to clubs, movements and other Jewish youth organisations in the United Kingdom. *Chairman of Adv. Cttee* Jonathan Gestetner; *T.* Adam Rose; *Tr.* Jonathan Gestetner, Lady Morris of Kenwood, R. McGratty, Miss Wendy Pollecoff; *Sec.* Peter Shaw.

JEWISH YOUTH ORCHESTRA OF GREAT BRITAIN
Rehearsals: Hillel House, 1-2 Endsleigh Street, WC1H 0DS.
(Est. 1970. Reg. Charity No. 294994) For young musicians (aged 13–20, Grade V and above) to give regular concerts in London and other cities. Occasional summer courses. Rehearsals Sunday mornings during term-time. *Co-founder and conductor* Sydney Fixman; *Chairman* Dr J. W. Frank, PO Box 24006, London NW4 4ZF, ☎ 0958 434999; *T.* S. Admoni.

JNF EDUCATION
JNF House, Spring Villa Park, Edgware, Middx. HA8 7ED.
☎ 020-8732 6103. Fax 020-8732 6111. Email education@jnf.co.uk. Website www. jnf.co.uk.
JNF Education provides educational services and resources relating to Israel as well as its land and ecological issues, for primary and secondary schools, youth movements, youth clubs and university campuses. Arranges Bar/Bat Mitzvahs in Israel.

JYSG – Jewish Youth Study Groups
Beit Meir, 44a Albert Rd., London NW4 2SJ.
☎ 020-8457 9709. Fax 020-8457 9707. Email info@jysg.org.uk; Website www. jysg.org.uk.
Holds weekly Sunday meetings for the 13–18 age group on a variety of Jewish and secular topics across London and in the Regions as well as annual summer and winter schools, a post-GCSE Israel Tour and a pre-university 6-month programme in Israel. *Contact* Melanie Shutz.

LJY–NETZER (Liberal Jewish Youth, Progressive Zionist Youth)
The Montagu Centre, 21 Maple Street, W1T 4BE.
☎ 020-7631 0584. Email office@ljynetzer.org; Website www.ljynetzer.org.
The Liberal Jewish youth movement, offering events, and leadership training for young people aged eight to 23 all within a Progressive Zionist framework. *Movement workers*: B. Baginsky, B. Aarons-Richardson, V. Kaufman

MACCABI GB
Shield House, Harmony Way, Hendon, London NW4 2BZ.
☎ 020-8457 2333. Fax 020-8203 3237. Email enquiries@maccabigb.org; Website www.maccabigb.org.
To promote the active participation in sports and education of Jewish men, women and children, in order to enhance their Jewish identity, values and commitment to the community. *H. Chair* S. Greenberg; *H. V. Chair* M. Stock; *Chief Exec.* Martin Berliner; *H. Sec.*
  Twenty-six affiliated clubs, eight affiliated sports leagues, and 25 affiliated schools and universities both in London and in the Regions.

NOAM (NOAR MASORTI)
Alexander House, 3, Shakespeare Rd, London N3 1XE.
☎ 020-8349 6650. Email noam@masorti.org.uk. Website www.noam .org .uk.
(Est. 1985. Reg. Charity No. 801846) NOAM is the Masorti Zionist youth movement. We run a wide variety of educational and social activities including clubs, weekends, summer camps and Israel tours for 8–16 year olds. NOAM also runs the MELTAM leadership course for Year 11s. Other activities include: Noam Israel Tour (post-GCSE); Drachim – year-in-Israel including Machon, kibbutz, volunteer work and Jewish learning; summer camps in Britain , France and Spain; weekly clubs; weekends away; social action and charity projects; and contact with Masorti youth in Israel, Europe and America. *Mazkira* L. Fleischmann. *Movement Workers* B. Russell, A. Berkley, J. Schlagman; *Dir* .

RSY-NETZER/REFORM MOVEMENT YOUTH
Sternberg Centre, 80 East End Road, N3 2SY.
☎ 020-8349 5666. Email admin@rsy-netzer.org.uk; Website www. rsy-netzer.org.uk
Northern Office Sandra Vigon. Resource & Learning Centre, Jacksons Row, Albert Square, Manchester M2 5WD.
To inculcate a love of Reform Judaism and Reform Zionism and to offer Jewish life options in an open and creative environment. The Department offers youth work development and training models of Jewish living and learning within and outside the Reform communities for youth, students and young professionals.

RSY-NETZER/REFORM MOVEMENT STUDENT AND YOUNG ADULTS
Jeneration
Sternberg Centre, 80 East End Road, N3 2SY.
☎ 020-8349 5666. Email aly@ jeneration.org Website www.jeneration.org

SIR MAX BONN MEMORIAL JEWISH YOUTH CENTRE
Leigh House, 63 Ethelbert Road, Cliftonville, Kent.
(Est. 1947) To provide a holiday centre for young people and adolescents, conferences and discussion groups among clubs and institutions. *Contact* Mrs Doris Cohen, 2 Priory Court, Sparrows Herne, Bushey, Herts WD2 1EF. ☎ 020-8950 5141.

UJIA Jewish Life Education Centre
Balfour House, 741 High Road, London N12 0BQ.
☎ 020-8369 5270. Fax 020-8369 5271. Email info@makor.org.uk
The UJIA Jewish Life Education Centre works in partnership with the Jewish Agency for Israel assiting volunteers and prfessionals in the fields of informal Jewish education and youth work.

It is the community's main centre for youth leadership training, offering seminars, conferences, and montoring. *Dir.* R. Simonson; *Senior Adv.* Eric Finestone, MA.

YOUNG JEWISH CARE (YJC)

YJC's young fundraising arm offers events and committees for 20–35 year olds ☎ 020-8922 2816. Email yjc@jcare.org), and Redbridge Jewish Youth and Community Centre at Sinclair House ☎ 020 8551 0017. Fax 020-8551 9027) offers 5–21 year olds evening and holiday schemes involving sport, education and Jewish culture.

The following groups are associated with the Zionist Movement.

BETAR-TAGAR

31 Moatfield Rd., Bushey, Herts WD23 3BP.
☎ 020-8950 0046.
(Reg. Charity No. 290571) Betar-Tagar Zionist youth and students' movement educates Jewish students and youth towards Zionism by stressing Aliya, the value of Jewish tradition and concern for Jewish people everywhere, self-defence and Jewish identity. *Shliha Mazkir*

BNEI AKIVA

2 Hallswelle Road, London NW11 0DJ.
☎ 020-8209 1319. Fax 020-8209 0107. Email office@bauk.org; Website www. bauk.org.
(Est. 1939) Bnei Akiva is the largest religious Zionist youth movement in the world. Aims to educate young people, aged between 7 and 25 years, in ideals of Religious Zionism and Torah Ve'avodah. Supports Aliya to the State of Israel as the movement objective.More than 30 local groups in UK meeting on Shabbat afternoons. Camps run in the summer and winter. Bnei Akiva organises a month touring Israel for 16 year olds and a year scheme in Israel known as Hachshara. *Mazkira* A. Broza; *Admin* Rosemary Davidson.
 Regional centres: 72 Singleton Road, Salford M7 4LU. ☎ 0161-740 1621. Fax 0161-740 8018. Email north@bauk.org.

EZRA YOUTH MOVEMENT

British and European Off.: 2a Alba Gardens, London, NW11 9NR.
☎/Fax 020-8458 5372.
Associated with Poale Agudat Israel.
Orthodox Jewish movement based in London with a branch in Manchester and branches in Israel and other parts of the world.

FEDERATION OF ZIONIST YOUTH

25 The Burroughs, Hendon, London NW4 4AR (Head Office).
☎ 020-8201 6661 (Head Office). ☎ 0161-721 4782 (Northern Office). Email office@fzy.org.uk; Website www.fzy.org.uk.
FZY is a Zionist youth movement for those aged 14 and above. It operates within a pluralist frame work and educates its members around Jewish and Zionist themes with the intention of fulfilling the four aims of FZY: Aliya, Magen (defence of Jewish rights), Tzedaka and Tarbut Jewish culture). FZY trains its members with leadership skills and encourages them to involve themselves as leaders in the wider Jewish community. The movement is part of the Atid partnership which also incorporates Young Judaea in USA and the Israeli Scouts.*President* Paul Lenga; *Mazkir* Jack Prevezer; *Dir. of Summer Programmes* M. Gaventa; *Northern Fieldworker* D. Moses; *Dir.of 14-16 Programming* J. Slavin; *Dir. of Student Programming* R. Addlestone; *Shaliach* Einav Ayalon; *Northern Shlicha* Ayelet Isaac; *Org. Sec.* Louise Jacobs; *Year Course Admin.* Vivienne Stone; *Year Course Recruiter* Ben King-Scott. *Publ.* The young Zionist.

FRIENDS OF BNEI AKIVA (BACHAD) (Formerly Bachad Fellowship)

2 Hallswelle Road, London NW11 0DJ

020 8458 9370 Fax 020 8209 0107 Email bachad@bauk.org.
(Est. 1942 Registered Charity No. 1109706).To promote and organise Jewish religious educational activities in the UK and Israel, with a view to preparing the youth of Bnei Akiva for a life in Israel. To provide scholarships for students wishing to attend Bnei Akiva's gap year programme in Israel, and grants for children wishing to go to Bnei Akiva's activities. Maintains Youth Centres in London and Manchester. *Hon Presidents* Chief Rabbi Sir Jonathan Sacks, Arieh L. Handler; *Chairman* D. Kestenbaum; *Vice Chairman* Perry Burns; *Ts.* F. Weinberg, S. Renshaw; *Admin* Suzy Richman.

HABONIM–DROR
Platinum House, Gabriel Mews, Gewys Rd., London NW2 2GD
☎ 020-8209 2111. Fax 020-8209 2110. Website www.habodror.org.uk
(Est. 1929) Habonim was founded in the East End of London, and became the leading international socialist Zionist Jewish youth movement, merging with Dror in 1979. Habonim Dror's ideology is centred around meaningful, cultural Judaism, socialism and Zionism, educating members, aged 9–23, towards strong, Jewish identities, striving for a more equal and compassionate Israeli society. Weekly activities around the UK focus on informal education. Habonim Dror's Shnat Hachshara involves living together as a community in Israel and engaging in social activism projects, intensive educational and leadership-training seminars, and tours of Israel. *President* Ruth Lady Morris of Kenwood; *Admin.* R. Daniels; *Nat. Sec.* Adam Wagner. *Publ.* Koleinu, Ma hadash, Ma Koreh.
Youth Centres
London: at London Jewish Cultural Centre, 94-96 North End Rd., NW11 7SX Email mail@habodror.org.uk
Manchester: South, Bowdon Synagogue, North, Central Northern Office, Maccabi Centre. Email manchester@habodror. org.uk
Leeds: c/o Central Northern Office. Birmingham: c/o Central Office. Bristol: Clifton College, c/o Central Office. Glasgow: c/o Central Northern Office. Oxford: c/o Central Office

HANOAR HATZIONI
The Youth Centre, 31 Tetherdown, Muswell Hill, London N10 1ND.
☎ 020-88831022/3. Fax 020-8365 2272. Email email@hanoar.co.uk; Website www. hanoar.co.uk
(Reg. Charity No. 296973) Hanoar Hatzioni are a non-political Zionist Youth Movement catering for people between the ages of 7 and 23. Groups are run all over the country. Annual events include Summer and Winter Camps, Israel Tours for 16 year olds, outings, educational and social programmes. Hanoar Hatzioni also run the Shnat Sherut Year Scheme and the Gesher 6 months Scheme in Israel.
Mazkir Greg Krieger; *Rosh Chinuch* Adam Ross.

HASHOMER HATZAIR
Hashomer House, 37A Broadhurst Gardens, NW6 3BN.
☎ 020-7328 5451.
(Est. 1940. Reg. Charity No. 269903) The British constituent of a world movement to educate its members in Socialist Zionist ideals as a basis for life in Israel especially kibbutz.

JNF FUTURE
JNF House, Spring Villa Park, Edgware, Middx. HA8 7ED.
☎ 020-8732 6118. Fax 020-8732 6111. Email jodie@jnf.co.uk.
(Est. 1998) To support the work of the JNF in Israel in afforestation, land reclamation, environmental and ecological issues by fund-raising events organised for and by young people (18–30) nationwide. *Co-Ord.* J. Norman.

KIBBUTZ REPRESENTATIVES
16 Accommodation Road, London NW11 8ED.
☎ 020-8458 9235. Fax 020-8455 7930. Email enquiries@kibbutz.org.uk. Website www.kibby.org.uk
(Reg. Charity No. 294563) Representing all the Kibbutz movements in Israel. The organisation arranges Working Visits on Kibbutz for persons aged 18–40; Enquirers are requested to send sae for information packs.

KIDMAH
c/o Hashomer House, 37a Broadhurst Gdns, London NW6 3BN.
☎ 020-7328 5451.
Left-Zionist student organisation promoting Jewish-Arab recognisation, religious pluralism, anti-racism. Educational, social, political activities; provides lecturers to Jewish and non-Jewish groups. *Fieldworker* Daniel Marcus.

YOUNG MERETZ
Hashomer House, 37A Broadhurst Gardens, London NW6 3BN.
☎ 020-7328 5451.
Anglo-Jewish youth and student group, ages 18–35, with a Socialist-Zionist outlook. Social, cultural, educ. and political programme stressing humanistic values of Judaism and progressive Zionist elements. Aliya of members encouraged. *Chairman.*

The following organisations are concerned with Jewish students

AJ6 (ASSOCIATION OF JEWISH SIXTH FORMERS)
Hillel House, 1–2 Endsleigh Street, London WC1H 0DS.
☎ 020-7387 3384. Fax 020-7387 3392. Email office@aj6.org; Website www. aj6.org.
(Est. 1977. Reg. Charity No. 1076442) Jewish youth organisation for ages 15–18 (membership 600, service outreach 2,500). AJ6's mission is to educate and develop Jewish fifth and sixthformers, enabling them to shape Jewish life at school, on campus and in the wider community. Services include the AJ6 Guide to Jewish Student Life, campus seminars and school Jewish Society meetings and assemblies. *Nat. Dir.* Matthew Granger; *Educ. and Dev. Worker* R. Saunderson; *Schoolworker* T. Sile. *Publ.* Sixth Sense.

MASORTI GESHER TEENAGE CENTRE
1097 Finchley Road, London NW11 0PU
☎ 020-8201 8772. Fax 020-8201 8917. Email office@masorti.org.uk
Gesher provides formal Jewish education for young people of secondary-school age. It offers an environment where friendships and identity develop together with the skills and knowledge to keep young people connected to Judaism throughout their teenage years. Gesher is a project of the Assembly of Masorti Synagogues. *Dir.* Cheryl Sklan.

UJS (B'NAI B'RITH HILLEL FOUNDATION)
4, Greenland Place, London NW1 0AP.
☎ 020-7388 0801. Fax 020-7380 6599. Email info@ujshillel.co.uk. Website www.ujshillel.co.uk.
(Reg. Charity No. 313503) Jewish Student Centre, devoted to social and educational activities among Jewish students at colleges and universities. Facilities include meeting rooms, student lounge, Kosher restaurant. Closed Shabbat and Festivals, other than by arrangement. *President* Fred S. Worms, OBE; *Chairman* Sir Victor Blank; *H.T.* J. Wall; *Chief Exec.* D. Marcus; *Operations Dir.* Gerry Lucas.
    Residential and social facilities available at **Hillel Houses** in the following locations:
    Birmingham: Bella Lupasco, ☎ 0121-471 4370;**Cardiff:** Lisa Gerson, ☎ 029-2075 9982; **Leeds**: Louisa Simons, ☎ 0113-268 3585; **Leicester:** ☎ Rocky. May 0116-270 4333; **Liverpool:** Gareth Jones, ☎ 0151-280 0551; **London:** *Golders Green* Rachel Lewisl, ☎ 020-7388 0801; **Manchester:** Sydney Baigel, ☎ 0161-740 2521;**Sheffield** Jeffrey Shaw, ☎ 0114

266 9936; **York:** Phil Prosser, ☎ 01904 433580.
For enquiries about **UJS Hillel Jewish Student Centres** and accommodation in the following areas:
   Brighton Doreen Lasky, ☎ 01273 551561; **Bristol** Rabbi Natan Levy ☎ 07791-292 948; **Cambridge** CUlanu Dir. ☎ 01223 307755; **London** ☎ 020 7388 0801; **Newcastle** Susan Olsburgh ☎ 0191 231 0668; **Nottingham** Rachel Lewis ☎ 020-7388 0801.

UNION OF JEWISH STUDENTS
of the United Kingdom and Ireland
(formerly: Inter-University Jewish Federation of Gt. Britain and Ireland).
Hillel House, 1/2 Endsleigh Street, WC1H 0DS.
☎ 020-7387 4644, Fax 020-7383 0390. Email ujs@ujs.org.uk; Website www.ujs. org.uk.
(Est. 1919) Co-ordinates the activities of the Jewish societies in the universities and colleges of the UK and Ireland. It stimulates an interest among Jewish students in Judaism, Zionism, Jewish history and education, and in Jewish thought. It encourages members to play their part in the religious and social life of the community. Jewish student societies are attached to many universities and colleges. See under separate towns. *Chair* A. Pike.

UNIVERSITY JEWISH CHAPLAINCY
305, Ballards Lane, London N12 8NP.
☎ 020-8343 5678. Fax 020-8492 9325. Email office@jchaplaincy.org.
Website www.jchaplaincy.org
(Reg. Charity no. 261324) Appointment of full-time chaplains to serve all Jewish students at universities in the United Kingdom, in conjunction with local boards. Chaplains available for personal counselling, practical support, as an educational resource and for spiritual guidance.
President: The Chief Rabbi; *Chairman* Ian Myers; *Sen. V. Chairman* Jeremy Jacobs; *Chief Exec.* *Rabbi* Y. Sherizen ☎ 07783 367703; *Admin. Dir. Mrs* Ruth Marriott ☎ 07970 973099
Chaplains: Scotland/Northern Region, Rabbi Dovid Cohen ☎ ; Midland Region, Rabbi Fishel Cohen ☎ 07771 653717; Cambridge/East Anglia Region, Rabbi Y. & Mrs N. Fishman ☎07916 139974; Bristol/Western Region, Rabbi M. & Mrs M. Baron ☎07791 292948; London Region, Rabbi Gavin Broder ☎ 07811 286664; Nottingham Rabbi Y. and Mrs J. Pereira ☎ 07980 955026; Yorkshire and Humberside Rabbi A. and Mrs T. Garber ☎ 07815 108260; *South East Field-worker* P. Getz ☎ 020 8343 5678; *Assoc. Chaplain* Manchester Central, Rabbi Y.Y. Rubinstein ☎ 07831 253136; Oxford, Rabbi A & Mrs S. Katchen ☎ 07717 742835 *Nat. Hillel Counsellor*, Rev. M. Weisman OBE ☎ 020-8459 4372.

WINGATE YOUTH TRUST
(Est. 1975. Reg. Charity No. 269678) To provide facilities for youth, for recreation and leisure. *Chairman* B. Myers; *T.* M. Rebak, 58 Southwood Park, Southwood Lawn Road, N6 5SQ. ☎ 020-8340 1287; *Sec.* Malcolm Davis.

LIBRARIES, MUSEUMS AND EXHIBITIONS

Anglo-Jewish Archives. An independent Registered Charity under the auspices of the Jewish Historical Society of England. The genealogical collections have been deposited at the Society of Genealogists and the main archive collection has been deposited with the Hartley Library, University of Southampton (see p. 48). *H. Sec.* (JHSE), 33 Seymour Place, London W1H 5AP. ☎/Fax 020-7723 5852. Email info@jhse.org

Hebraica Libraries Group, Website www.lib.cam/ac.uk/hebraica/hebraicam2.htm (Est. 1979) The Group brings together representatives of all the major Judaica and Hebraica collections in Great Britain and Ireland (as listed below) together with other academic libraries with an interest in the field. It holds an annual meeting and is affiliated to both the British Association of Jewish Studies and the European Association of Jewish Studies, and to the National Council on Orientalist Library Resources (NCOLR). It offers expertise in all aspects of Hebraica collections, preservation, security, conservation, cataloguing, computer systems and collection development. *Convenor* Mrs I. Tahan. Email ilana.tahan@bl.uk

Ben Uri Gallery, The London Jewish Museum of Art, 108a Boundary Road, London NW8 0RH. ☎ 020-7604 3991. Fax 020-7604 3992. Email info@benuri. org.uk; Website (for opening times and programmes) www.benuri.org.uk.
(Est. 1915. Reg. Charity No. 280389) Founded by Lazar Benson as an East End art society in support of Jewish artists outside the mainstream of British art at the time, the objectives of the Gallery serve to promote education, entertainment and outreach by celebrating the artistic achievement of Jewish artists as part of the Jewish cultural heritage. A full programme of exhibitions and interesting activities is provided for 'Friends' including lectures, visits to other galleries and the Annual Picture Fair. *Chairman* David Glasser; *V. Chairman*, S. Bentley; *H. Sec.* K. Sanig; *Chairman of Exhibitions Cttee* I. Grose; *Dir. Chairman of Permanent Collection Cttee* J. Weiner;

Biesenthal Collection, Special Libraries and Archives, King's College, Old Aberdeen. ☎ 001224 272598. Consists of some 2,000 volumes and one of Britain's finest Rabbinical collections acquired in 1872. The Special Libraries and Archives also feature the collections and papers of Malcolm Hay of Seaton which include material on Zionism and correspondence in Hebrew.

Bodleian Library, Broad Street, Oxford OX1 3BG. ☎ 01865 277000. The Hebrew and Yiddish collections comprise 3,000 manuscript volumes and 60,000 printed books, including many incunabula, fragments from the Cairo Genizah and the Oppenheimer library, the finest collection of Hebrew books and manuscripts ever assembled. Intending readers should always contact the Admissions Office in advance. Open to holders of a reader's ticket Mon. to Fri. 9–7, Sat. 10–4. *Hebrew Specialist Libr.* Dr P. van Boxel. Email piet.vanboxel@bodley.ox.ac.uk

The British Library, Asia, Pacific and African Collections – Hebrew Section, 96 Euston Road, London NW1 2DB. ☎ 020-7412/7646. Fax 020-7412 7641. Email opac-enquiries@ bl.uk. Website www.bl.uk/collections/hebrew/html The Hebrew collection comprises over 3,000 manuscript volumes and 10,000 fragments (incl. Moses Gaster's collection and many fragments from the Cairo Genizah); Hebrew printed books, about 70,000 titles, incl. some 100 incunabula, rabbinic and modern Hebrew literature; Yiddish, Ladino, Judeo-Arabic and Judeo-Persian books; some 1,000 Hebrew and Yiddish periodicals and newspapers. Oriental Reading Room open to holders of readers' passes. (Hours of opening may be subject to revision at any time. Normal opening: Mon. 10.00–5.00; Tues.-Sat. 9.30–5.00). Some Hebrew manuscripts are on permanent display in the British Library Exhibition Galleries, open (free of charge): Mon., Wed. to Fri. 9.30–6.00, Tues. 9.30–8.00, Sat. 9.30–5.00, Sun. 11.00–5.00. The Golden Haggadah and Lisbon Bible are included in the electronic 'Turning the Pages' programme on www.bl.uk. *Hebrew Specialist* Ilana Tahan, M.Phil. Email ilana.tahan@bl.uk.

Brotherton Library, University of Leeds, Leeds LS2 9JT. ☎ 0113 3435518. Fax 0113 3435561. Email special-collections@library.leeds.ac.uk; Website www.leeds. ac.uk/library. *Librarian* Margaret Coutts. Holdings include substantial materials for Hebrew and Jewish studies and the Travers Herford Collection on Judaism and Talmudic studies. The primary Judaica collection is the Roth Collection comprising the manuscripts and printed books from the library of Cecil Roth, including 350 mss., 900 printed books (pre-1850) 6,000 modern books and other archival material. Available to bona fide scholars who should write to the Librarian in the first instance enclosing an appropriate recommendation. *Asst. Libr. Publ.* Selig Brodetsky lecture series.

Cambridge University Library, West Rd, Cambridge CB3 9DR. ☎ 01223 333000. Fax 01223 333160. Email library@lib.cam.ac.uk; Website www.lib.cam.ac.uk *Dir.* Mr P. K. Fox. The Hebraica and Judaica collections comprise c. 190,000 Cairo Genizah fragments; 1,000 complete Hebrew codices (see S.C. Reif, Hebrew Manuscripts at Cambridge University Library, CUP, 1997); approximately 40,000 printed books. Available to members of the University and bona fide scholars by application, preferably in writing in advance, to the Admissions Officer. Reading rooms open 9.30–6.45; Admissions Office: 9.30–12.30, 2.00–4.15. *Hd. Genizah Res. Unit.* Dr B. M. Outhwaite; *Hebraica Libr.* Ms Y. Faghihi.

Czech Memorial Scrolls Centre (Memorial Scrolls Trust), Kent House, Rutland Gardens, London SW7 1BX. ☎ 020-7584 3741. Fax 020-7581 8012. Email czech.scrolls@virgin.net (Reg. Charity No. 278900) This permanent exhibition tells the unique story of the rescue from Prague, in 1964, of 1,564 Torah Scrolls and of their restoration and distribution on permanent loan to communities throughout the world. The exhibits include some of the scrolls, a display of Torah binders, some dating from the 18th century, and other reminders of the vanished communities of Bohemia and Moravia. The centre is open on Tuesdays and Thursdays from 10am to 4pm and other times and Sundays by arrangement.

Harry Rosencweig Collection of Jewish Music, School of Oriental & African Studies, University of London. Printed sheet music includes 17th–20th century European, American and Israeli liturgical and art music, and various anthologies of folk music. Text books on Jewish music and dance. A few LPs. Many rare items.

The Hartley Library, University of Southampton, Highfield, Southampton SO17 1BJ. Holdings of the Special Collections Division include (i) the **Parkes Library**, founded by the late Revd Dr James Parkes in 1935 to promote the study of relations between the Jewish and the non-Jewish worlds, now containing 25,000 books and periodicals; (ii) more than 750 collections of manuscripts, in excess of 3 million items, relating to Anglo-Jewry (incorporating collections of the **Anglo-Jewish Archives**) and encompassing the papers of the Anglo-Jewish Association, Records of the London Board of Shechita, archives of the Jewish Board of Guardians and the Jewish Association for the Protection of Girls, Women and Children, papers of the International Military Tribunal and the Nuremberg Military Tribunals, Zangwill family papers papers of Sir Robert Waley Cohen, Henriques family papers, archives of Leo Baeck College, of the Reform Synagogues of Great Britain and the West London Synagogue, archives of the British Section of the World Jewish Congress and of the Institute of Jewish Affairs (nw the Jewish Policy Research Centre). The holdings of the Parkes Library are listed in the Library WebCat http://www-lib.soton.ac.uk/ A guide to the archive collections is available at www.southhampton.ac.uk/archives Visits to the Archives reading room are by appointment. *Contact* ☎ 023-8059 3335 (Parkes), 023-8059 2721 (Archives). Fax 023-8059 3007. Email libenqs@soton.ac.uk (Parkes); archives@soton.ac.uk (Archives); Website www.southampton.ac.uk/archives. *Head of Special Collections* Prof.C. M. Woolgar.

The Hidden Legacy Foundation, Kent House, Rutland Gardens, London SW7 1BX. ☎ 020-7584 2754. Fax 020-7584 6896. (Est. 1988. Reg. Charity no. 326032) Devoted to promoting the awareness of provincial (English) and rural (German) Jewish history as seen through buildings and artefacts, and has become particularly identified with German Genizot. It organises exhibitions: Genizah (1992), Mappot (1997), The Jews of Devon and Cornwall (2000), and, having been active in Germany, is now working in England cataloguing Judaica. Library, slide and photo archives on rural German Jewry. *Exec. Dir.* Evelyn Friedlander.

Imperial War Museum Holocaust Exhibition, Lambeth Road, London SE1 6HZ. *Project Office* ☎ 020-7416 5204/5285. Website www. iwm.org.uk. *Project Dir.* Suzanne Bardgett; *Res. Asst* S. Batsford; *Founding Patrons* Lord Bramall, Sir Martin Gilbert, Ben Helfgott, Lord Moser, Lord Rothschild, Lord Weidenfeld, Lord Wolfson of Marylebone, Stephen Rubin; *Advisory Gp.* Professor D. Cesarani, Sir Martin Gilbert, Ben Helfgott, Antony Lerman, Martin Smith. This major national exhibition was opened by H.M. the Queen in 2000.

Jewish Military Museum, Shield House, Harmony Way, off Victoria Road, Hendon, London NW4 2BZ. ☎ 020-8202 2323. Fax 020-8202 9900. Email museum@ajex.org.uk.; Website www.ajex.org.uk. *Curator* H. Morris; *Archivist* M. Sugarman. A History of the Jewish contribution to the Armed Forces of the Crown over three centuries. Visits by appointment

The Jewish Museum – London's Museum of Jewish Life
Website www.jewishmuseum.org.
(Est. 1932. Reg. Charity No. 10098819) The Jewish Museum aims to recover, preserve and exhibit material relating to the roots and heritage of Jewish people in Britain, and to illustrate and explain Jewish religious practice with objects of rarity and beauty. It seeks to increase knowledge and understanding about Jewish life and history through its programme of education and exhibitions, and also has a programme of holocaust education. The Friends of the Jewish Museum has been established to suport the work of the museum. *Dir.* Rickie Burman, MA, MPhil; *Chairman* Robert Craig, LLM.

The Jewish Museum – Camden Town
The museum has been awarded Designated status by the Museums and Galleries Commission in recognition of its outstanding collections. History and Ceremonial Art Galleries, audio-visual programmes and a Temporary Exhibitions Gallery with changing exhibitions. Educational programmes available. Open: Mon–Thurs, 10 am–4 pm; Sundays 10am–5pm. Closed Jewish Festivals and Public Holidays. Address: Raymond Burton House, 129–131 Albert Street, NW1 7NB. ☎ 020-7284 1997. Fax 020-7267 9008. Email admin@jewishmuseum.org.uk

The Jewish Museum – Finchley
Displays relating to the history of Jewish immigration and settlement in London, including reconstructions of East End tailoring and furniture workshops. Holocaust Education Gallery with a moving exhibition on London-born Holocaust survivor, Leon Greenman. Travelling Exhibitions, Educational Programmes and Resources and Walking Tours of Jewish London. Open: Sun. 10.30 am–4.30 pm, Mon–Thurs, 10.30 am–5 pm. Closed Jewish Festivals, Public Holidays, on Sundays in August and Bank Holiday weekends. Address: 80 East End Road, N3 2SY. ☎ 020-8349 1143. Fax 020-8343 2162. Email enquiries@jewishmuseum.org.uk.

Jewish Studies Library (Incorporating the Library of the Jewish Historical Society of England), University College London, Wilkins Building, Gower Street, WC1E 6BT. ☎ 020-7679 2598. Fax 020-7679 7373. Email library@ucl.ac.uk; Website www.ucl.ac.uk/ library The Hebrew and Jewish Studies collection comprises around 16,000 volumes in the fields of Jewish history, Hebrew and Semitic languages, Bible, Rabbinic literature, mysticism, Jewish philosophy, Hebrew literature and Yiddishh language and literature. In addition there are over 185, 000 items of rare and archival material. The collection incorporates the Mocatta Library, Altmann Library, William Margulies Yiddish Library. See website for opening times and access arrangements. *Hebrew and Jewish Studies Libr.* Vanessa Freedman.

Jews' College Library London School of Jewish Studies, Schaller House, 44A Albert Road, London NW4 2SJ. ☎ 020-8203 6427. Fax 020-8203 6420. Email info@lsjs.ac.uk. One of the most extensive Judaica and Hebraica libraries in Europe. Open, free of charge: Monday 9.00am to 4.00pm, Tuesday to Thursday, 9.00am to 1.00pm. *Libr.* Mrs Erla Zimmels.

John Rylands University Library of Manchester, 150 Deansgate, Manchester M3 3EH. ☎ 0161-275 3764; Email jrul.special.collections@manchester.ac.uk; Website www.library. manchester.ac.uk/specialcollections. The John Rylands Library has recently reopened after major refurbishment and extension.Admission is free to all visitors and readers.The Library is open to readers Monday to Saturday 10.00-17.00. Those wishing to consult rare books, manuscripts or archives should provide a suitable letter of introduction as well as proof of address; advance notice of ay visit is advisable. The Hebraica and Judaica comprise over 10,500 fragments from the Cairo Genizah; manuscripts and codices from the Crawford and Gaster collections; Samaritan manuscripts from the Gaster collection; 6,600 items of printed Hebraica and talmudic literature in the Marmorstein collection; 1,000 volumes of the Haskalah collection; the Moses Gaster collection; and some 5,000 volumes in the Near Eastern collection in the Main UIniversity Library dealing with Hebrew language and literature.*Keeper of Manuscripts and Archives* Mr John Hodgson.

Keren Hatorah Library, 97 Stamford Hill, London N16 5DN. ☎ 020-8800 6688. A comprehensive collection of Torah literature for the whole family. Operates as a lending library. Open Sun., Tues., Thurs., 10.30am–12.30pm, Mon. 3.30-5.30pm. *Libr.*

Keren Hatorah Tape Library, 97 Stamford Hill, London N16. ☎ 020-8809 8549. Over ten thousand cassette recordings including the complete Talmud in English and Yiddish and a range of other Torah and Jewish topics. Open Sun 11.30–1.00, Mon to Thurs 11.00–4.30. *Man.* A. Lauer.

Leo Baeck College Library, 80 East End Road, N3 2SY. ☎ 020-8349 5610/1. Fax 020-8349 5619. Email Library@lbc.ac.uk. Est. 1956 to provide a library for Jewish Studies and research. Holdings: 50,000 vols; 85 current periodicals; 5,000 pamphlets;15,000 sound records (shiurim and public lectures); 180 rabbinic and MA theses. Range: Bible, rabbinic literature, codes, liturgy, education, literature, history, holocaust and post-holocaust studies, Israel and Zionism, Interfaith. Open to members and occasional readers from Mon.–Thurs. 9.00–5.00, Fri. 9.00–1.00. Closed on Jewish Festivals, bank holidays and during the last week of December. During July and August, visits can be made only by appointment with the librarian. For regular access to the library a yearly contribution of £30 is to be made. *Hd. Libr.* Annette M. Boeckler, PhD; *Asst. Libr.* R. Harris-Eckstein, P. Claiden.

Leopold Muller Memorial Library, Oxford Centre for Hebrew & Jewish Studies, Yarnton Manor, Yarnton, Oxford OX5 1PY. ☎ 01865-377946 (library office: ext. 117; librarian: ext. 120). Fax 01865-375079. Email muller.library@ochjs.ac.uk. Website www.ochjs.ac.uk (Reg. Charity No. 309720) The Leopold Muller Memorial Library is an open access lending library of about 90,000 volumes and 80 current periodicals, covering the full range of Hebrew and Jewish studies, with special focus on Hebrew literature of the 19th and 20th centuries, Haskalah, modern Jewish history, Zionism, Israeli and Hebrew bibliography. Special collections: the Foyle-Montefiore Library including the library of Leopold Zunz; the Louis Jacobs collection; the Coppenhagen Collection (on Dutch Jewry and Holocaust); the largest collection of *Yizkor* books in Europe; the Hugo Gryn collection; an extensive microfiche collection containing the Montefiore collection of Manuscripts, the manuscripts and rare books collections of the Jewish Theological Seminary of America and the Harvard College Library, the *Dokumentation zur jüdischen Kultur in Deutschland 1840–1940: Die Zeitungsausschnittsammlung Steiniger* and the *Jüdisches Biographisches Archiv*; an archive of 40,000 newspaper cuttings on 12,000 Jewish personalities and on the early Yishuv in Palestine, as well as representative samples of the Hebrew and Yiddish press. For opening times, access and borrowing rights see website. *Libr.* Dr Piet W. van Boxel.

London Metropolitan Archives, 40 Northampton Road, London EC1R 0HB. ☎ 020-7332 3820. Fax 020 7833 9136. Email ask.lma@cityoflondon.gov.uk; Website www.cityoflondon.gov.uk/lma. LMA is the regional archive for Greater London. The collections within it of Jewish interest include: Board of Deputies of British Jews, Office of the Chief Rabbi, United Synagogue, London Beth Din, Jews Free School, Jews Temporary Shelter, London School of Jewish Studies, World Jewish Relief and the Spanish & Portuguese Jews' Congregation. Many collections are available to researchers only with the prior permission of the depositor, so please contact LMA in advance for relevant addresses (as in this volume). **Opening Hours:** Monday, Wednesday, Friday 0930-1645; Tuesday, Thursday 0930-1930. Open selected Saturdays 0930-1645 (call for open dates or see website).

Lubavitch Lending Library, 107–115 Stamford Hill, N16 5RP. ☎ 020-8800 5823. Email library@lubavitch.co.uk. Established in 1972 to help the Jewish public study traditional Jewish culture and aid scholarship. The library contains 15,000 volumes in Hebrew, English and Yiddish. Services include a reference libr., a children's libr. and postal lending. Lectures and displays org. anywhere. Open Sun., 10am–12.30pm, 4pm–8pm; Mon.–Fri., 10am–4pm. Some weekday evgs. Other times available by appointment. *Libr.* Z. Rabin, ALA.

National Life Stories, at the British Library Sound Archive, 96 Euston Road, London, NW1 2DB. ☎ 020-7412 7404. Fax 020-7412 7441. Email nsa-nlsc@bl.uk; Website www.bl.uk. (Est. 1987. Reg. Charity No. 327571) To 'record first-hand experiences of as wide a cross-section of present-day society as possible'. As an independent charitable trust within the Oral History Section of the British Library's Sound Archive, NLSC's key focus and expertise has been oral history fieldwork.

Living Memory of the Jewish Community (C410) is a major collection with a primary focus on pre-Second World War Jewish refugees to Britain, those fleeing from Nazi persecution during the Second World War and Holocaust survivors. The collection has recently expanded to include interviews with children of survivors. The collection complements other sound archive material on Jewish life, notably the Holocaust Survivors' Centre interviews (C830), Central British Fund Kindertransport interviews (C526), Testimony: Video Interviews with British Holocaust Survivors (C533) and London Museum of Jewish Life oral history interviews (C525).

Porton Collection, Central Library, Municipal Buildings, Leeds LS1 3AB. (0113 2478282. Fax 0113 395 1833. Comprises 3,700 loan items covering all aspects of the religion and culture of the Jewish people in English, Hebrew and Yiddish.

School of Oriental and African Studies (Univ. of London), Thornhaugh Street, Russell Square, London WC1H 0XG. ☎ 020-7898 4154. Fax 020-7898 4159. Email mideastlib@soas.ac.uk; Website www.soas.ac.uk/library. Ancient Near East, Semitics and Judaica Section of SOAS Library. *Section Head* P. Salinger The Semitics and Judaica collections comprise about 15,000 Hebrew items covering the fields of modern Hebrew language and literature (one of the finest collections in Europe), biblical and intertestamental studies, Judaism, the Jewish people, and the land of Israel. There are also a considerable number of books in Western languages covering the above mentioned fields. In addition, largely owing to the acquisition of the Stencl and Leftwich collections in 1983 and some books from the Whitechapel collection in 1984, there are about 3000 books on Yiddish language and literature. Periodicals, of which the Library holds about 200 Hebrew titles, are shelved separately. The transfer of the Joe Loss Lectureship in Jewish Music from the City University to SOAS has also brought the Harry Rosencweig Collection of Jewish Music to the library (see p.49). For details of services, please refer to the Library's web pages.

Spanish & Portuguese Jews' Congregation, 2 Ashworth Road, W9 1JY. ☎ 020-7289 2573. Fax: 020-7289 2709. **Archives** The archives of the Spanish & Portuguese Jews' Congregation, London, and its institutions, which date from the mid-17th century, include Minute and Account Books, Registers of Births, Circumcisions, Marriages and Burials. Most of the Registers have now been published and copies may be purchased from the Congregation's offices. The archives are not open to the public. Queries and requests by bona fide researchers should be submitted in writing to the Hon. Archivist. Advice and help will be given to general enquirers wherever possible. A search fee may be charged. *Hon. Archivist* Miriam Rodrigues-Pereira. **Shasha Library** (Est 1936.) Designed to contain books on Jewish history, religion, literature and kindred interest from the Sephardi standpoint. The Library is intended for the use of members of the congregation. It contains over 1,200 books. These collections are available at the Sephardi Centre (see p. 36). *Libr.* .

Wiener Library and Institute of Contemporary History, 4 Devonshire Street, London W1W 5BH. ☎ 020-7636 7247. Fax 020-7436 6428. Email info@wienerlibrary.co.uk;

Website www.wienerlibrary.co.uk (Reg. Charity No. 313015) Founded by Dr A. Wiener in Amsterdam, 1933, and since 1939 in London. Research Library and Institute on contemporary European and Jewish history, especially the rise and fall of the Third Reich; survival and revival of Nazi and fascist movements; antisemitism; racism; the Middle East; post-war Germany. Holds Britain's largest collection of documents, testimonies, and books on the Holocaust. Active educ. programme of lectures, seminars and conferences. *Chairman of Bd.* A. Spiro; *Dir.* B. Barkow.

PROFESSIONAL ORGANISATIONS

AGUDAS HARABBONIM (ASSOCIATION OF RABBIS OF GREAT BRITAIN)
(in association with the Agudas Israel World Rabbinical Council) 273 Green Lanes, London N4 2EX. ☎ 020-8802 1544. (Est. 1929) *Chairman Princ.* Rabbi E. Padwa, Av Beth Din, U.O.H.C.; *H. Dir.* Rabbi Ben Zion Blau; *H. Gen. Sec.* vacant.

AGUDATH HASHOCHTIM V'HASHOMRIM OF GREAT BRITAIN
Poultry Section: *H. Sec.* S. Leaman, 25 Rostrevor Road, London N15 6LA. ☎ 07970 721930

ASSOCIATION OF MINISTERS (CHAZANIM) OF GREAT BRITAIN
Chairman Rev. S. I. Brickman, 9 Marlborough Mansions, Cannon Hill, London NW6 1JP. (020-7431 0575; *V. Chairman* Rev. A. Levin, ☎ 020-8554 0499; *Sec.* Rabbi D. A. Katanka; *T.* Rev. M. Haschel. ☎ 020-7483 1017.

ASSOCIATION OF ORTHODOX JEWISH PROFESSIONALS OF GREAT BRITAIN
53 Wentworth Road, London NW11 0RT.
(Est. 1962) To promote research in matters of common interest, and the general acceptance of Torah and Halacha as relevant and decisive in all aspects of modern life and thought. *President* Prof C. Domb; *Chairman* H. J. Adler.

GUILD OF JEWISH JOURNALISTS
Affiliated to the World Federation of Jewish Journalists. *L. President* The Lord Janner; *Chairman* D. Yadin; *H.T.* Susan Kosky, 51 Century Court, Grove End Road, London NW8 9LD. ☎ 020-7286 2791. Fax 020-7286 8958. Email ssperber@hotmail.co.uk.

JEWISH NURSES & MIDWIVES ASSOCIATION
32 Wykeham Road London NW4 2SU.
☎ 020-8203 2241. Email sara@smbarnett.com.
(Est. 1993) A social, educational and support group for all Jewish nurses, midwives and members of allied professions. *Chair* Sara Barnett.

RABBINIC CONFERENCE OF LIBERAL JUDAISM
The Montagu Centre, 21 Maple Street, London W1T 4BE.
☎ 020-7580 1663. Email montagu@liberaljudaism.org
Chairman Rabbi P. Tobias; *Admin.* A.Grant.

RABBINICAL COUNCIL OF EAST LONDON AND WEST ESSEX
8 The Lindens, Prospect Hill, Waltham Forest, E17 3EJ.
☎ 020-85201759.
(Est. 1981) To co-ordinate and enhance Jewish com. and educ. facilities within the East London and West Essex area. *Patron* The Chief Rabbi; *Chairman* Rabbi E. Salasnik; *V. Chairman* Rev. S. Black; *Sec.* Rev. S. Kreiman.

RABBINICAL COUNCIL OF THE PROVINCES
c/o 71 Upper Park Road, Salford M7.
☎ 0161-773 1978. Fax 0161-773 7015.
President Chief Rabbi Dr Jonathan Sacks; *Chairman* Rabbi Mordechai S. Ginsbury; *V. Chairman* Rabbi Ian Goodhardt; *H. T.* Rabbi Yoinosson Golomb; *H. Sec.* Rabbi Adam S. Hill, 163 Bristol

Road, Birmingham B5 7UA. Email srni@heharim.sofnet. co.uk

RABBINICAL COUNCIL OF THE UNITED SYNAGOGUE
Adler House, 735 High Road, London N12 0US.
☎ 020-8343 6313. Fax 020-8343 6310. Email rabbi.shindler@chiefrabbi.org
Chairman Rabbi Y. Schochet; *V. Chairmen* Rabbi Dr. N. Brawer, Rabbi Dr. M.Harris; *Exec. Dir.* Rabbi Dr J. Shindler, MSc; *H.T.* Rabbi Y. Grunewald, BA; *H. Sec.* Rabbi Y. Black

UNITED SYNAGOGUE ADMINISTRATORS' ASSOCIATION
☎ 020-8883 5925 or 020 8340 7655.
Chair Mr C. Loeb, Highgate Synagogue.

MISCELLANEOUS ORGANISATIONS

ALAN SENITT MEMORIAL TRUST
118, Stonegrove, Edgware, Middlesex HA8 8AB
☎ 0771 409 1502;0771 496 0212. Email admin@alansenittmemorialtrust.org Website www.alansenittmemorialtrust.org
(Est. 2006. Reg Charity No. 1117111) A Trust established to provide scholarships for 'gap year' leadership study in Israel, and for postgraduate courses in youth work, community leadership, international relations and interfaith dialogue. Provides funding for educational programmes on Israel, interfaith dialogue, and street crime awareness; emergency funding for Jewish undergraduates. *Chair* Emma Senitt; *H.T.* R. Chaplin; *H. Sec.* K. Senitt.

ASSOCIATION OF JEWISH EX-SERVICEMEN AND WOMEN (AJEX)
Shield House, Harmony Way, off Victoria Rd. London NW4 2BZ.
☎ 020-8202 2323. Fax 020-8202 9900. Email headoffice@ajex.org.uk; Website www. ajex.org.uk
(Est. 1923) *Nat. Chairman* Dr. P. Wajerman; *Gen. Sec.* J. Weisser; *H. Chaplain* Rev. Malcolm Weisman, OBE. A list of London and Provincial Branches can be obtained from the Office. For the Jewish Military Museum contact B. Goldberg; *Curator* H. Morris; *Archivist* Martin Sugarman, (see p. 49).

ASSOCIATION OF JEWISH GOLF CLUBS & SOCIETIES
Officers: *President* Mervyn Berg, 9 Oakdale, Southgate, London N14 5RA; *Sec. T.* M.J. Bartle, 10 Pinfold Court, Pinfold Lane, Whitefield, Manchester M45 7NZ; *Tournament Sec.* Clive Leveson, Apartment 4 College House, South Downs Road, Bowdon, Altrincham, Cheshire WA14 3DZ; *Assist. Tournament Secs.* J. Denton, A. Brick, S. Levy.

ASSOCIATION OF JEWISH HUMANISTS
12 Woodland Court, Woodlands, London NW11 9QQ.
☎ 020-8455 2393.
(Est. 1983) Humanistic Jews believe each Jew has the right to create a meaningful Jewish lifestyle free from supernatural authority and imposed tradition. Humanistic Jews believe the goal of life is personal dignity and self-esteem. Humanist Jews believe the secular roots of Jewish life are as important as the religious ones, and the survival of the Jewish people needs a reconciliation between science, personal autonomy and Jewish loyalty. The Association of Jewish Humanists is a constituent member of the International Institute for Secular Humanistic Judaism (Jerusalem); an Associate of the Society for Humanistic Judaism, Farmington Hills, MI, USA; an Affiliate of the British Humanist Association, London WC1R 4RH. *H. Jt. Chairmen* M. Miller, 12 Woodland Court, Woodlands, NW11 9QQ, D. Wilkes, 7 Ashley Close, Hendon, NW4; *H. Sec.* M. Miller, 12 Woodland Court, Woodlands, NW11 9QQ; *H. T.* J. Hulman, 60 Morley Crescent East, Stanmore, Middlesex.

THE BURNING BUSH
19 Patshull Road, London NW5 2JX.
☎ 020-7485 3957. Email lucieskeaping@hotmail.com;

Website www.theburningbush.co.uk.
(Est. 1990) Small musical ensemble; much in demand for private and public concerts specialising in traditional music and song across the Jewish world. *Dir.* Lucie Skeaping.

CAMPAIGN FOR THE PROTECTION OF SHECHITA
66 Townshend Court, Townshend Road, Regents Park, London NW8 6LE.
☎ 020-7722 8523.
(Est. 1985) To protect the freedom of Jews to perform Shechita; to make representations to Government on proposed legislation or other measures which may affect the proper performance of Shechita. *Nat. Co-ord. and Hon. Solicitors* Neville Kesselman; *Reg. Coord.* Chanoch Kesselman, London; *Rabbinical Adv.* Rabbi Benjamin Vorst and Rabbi Dr David Miller, MA, MSc, DPhil (Oxon).

CELEBRITIES GUILD OF GREAT BRITAIN
Knight House, 29-31 East Barnet Road, New Barnet, Herts EN4 8RN.
☎ 020-8449 1234, 020-8449 1515, weekdays 10.00–4.00. Fax 020-8449 4994.
Email ellaglazer@tiscali.com. Website www.celebritiesguild.org.uk
(Est. 1977. Reg. Charity No. 282298) A social and fund-raising Guild of prominent people in British Jewry who organise events to raise funds to provide equipment for disabled and handicapped people. *H. Exec. Guilder* Mrs Ella Glazer, MBE; *President* David Jacobs, CBE, DL; *Master Guilder* Leonard Fenton.

CENTRE FOR PSYCHOTHERAPY IN HEBREW
☎ 020-8632 1764.
(Est. 2001) A psychotherapy service for Hebrew speakers in England. *Contact* T. Schonfield.

CONNECT – THE JEWISH INTRODUCTION AGENCY
23 Ravenshurst Avenue, NW4 4EE.
☎ 020-8203 5207. Email connect@jmc-uk.org Website www.jmc-uk.org
See Jewish Marriage Council, p. 14.

FRIENDS OF JEWISH SERVICEMEN
25, Enford Street London W1H 1DW Email
(Est. 1956. Reg. Charity No. 267647) Supports the Jewish Committee for H.M. Forces (see p.8) in ministering to the religious needs of serving Jewish personnel. *Chairman* A. A. Dunitz, JP; *President* Major Edmund de Rothschild, CBE, TD; *Dir.* P. Wagerman; *H.T.* R. Wright, FCA.

HIGH SEAS SAILING CLUB
Website www.hssc.org.uk.
(Est. 1989.) The UK's only sailing club for people with a 'Jewish affinity or friendship', affiliated to the Royal Yachting Assoc. (RYA). *Publ.* Wavelength (annual). *Club Commodore* P. Sugarman; *Membership Sec.* Ipana Isserow. ☎ 0772 0772681

INDEPENDENT JEWISH VOICES (IJV)
PO Box 56912, London N10 3WW
☎ 020-8883 7063. Email info@ijv.org.uk Website www.ijv.org.uk
(Est. 2007) To promote expression of alternative Jewish voices, particularly with respect to Israel, based on commitment to universal human rights and social justice. *Sec.* Ann Jungman.

JEWISH ASSOCIATION FOR BUSINESS ETHICS
2nd Floor, Mowbray House, 58-70, Edgware Middx. HA8 8DJ
☎ 020-8905 4048 Fax 020-8905 4658. Email info@jabe.org Website www.jabe.org
(Reg. Charity No. 1038453) To encourage the highest standards of integrity in business and professional conduct by promoting the Jewish ethical approach to business. *Chairman:* M. Moses; *Exec. Dir.* Lorraine Spector.

JEWISH ASSOCIATION OF SPIRITUAL HEALERS
24 Greenacres, Hendon Lane, Finchley, London N3 3SF.
☎ 020-8349 1544.
(Est. 1966. Reg. Charity No. 275081) Aims: (1) To attempt to relieve sickness and suffering; (2) To demonstrate that Spiritual Healing is in keeping with the teachings of Judaism. *Chairman* Steve Sharpe, 22 Boldmere Road, Pinner HA5 1PS; *Sec.* Audrey Cane, 24 Greenacres, Hendon Lane, Finchley, London N3 3SF; *Healing Centre* Ruth Green, West London Synagogue, 33 Seymour Place, London W1.

THE JEWISH COUNCIL FOR RACIAL EQUALITY
P.O. Box 47864, London NW11 1AB
☎ 020-8455 0896. Fax 020-8181 7970. Email admin@jcore.org.uk
Website www.jcore.org.uk.
(Est. 1976. Reg. Charity No. 281236) To improve race relations in Britain, encourage awareness in the Jewish community of its responsibilities in a multi-racial society and join other organisations to challenge racism. JCORE produces a variety of publications for schools, youth groups and other organisations as well as delivering educational and training programmes. JCORE campaigns for the rights of asylum seekers and for changes to legislation. It provides support for unaccompanied minors and coordinates projects that help refugee doctors to requalify. Its *Connections* Exhibition explores the hidden histories of Britain's Asian, Black and Jewish communities. JCORE organises forums that bring together Black, Asian and Jewish people. *President* Dr R. Stone; *Chair* Dr. J. Strelitz; *Dir.* Dr Edie Friedman.

JEWISH FRIENDLY SOCIETIES
Grand Order of Israel and Shield of David. *Grand Sec.* R. Salasnik
11 The Lindens, Prospect Hill, Waltham Forest, London E17 3EJ.
☎ 020-8520 3531. Email info@goisd.org.uk; Website www.goisd.org.uk
(Est. 1896) The membership is contained in four Lodges in the Metropolitan area and one in Birmingham.

JEWISH GAY AND LESBIAN GROUP
BM-JGLG, London WC1N 3XX
☎ 07504 924742. Email info@jglg.org.uk. Website www.jglg.org.uk.
(Est. 1972) Social group for Jewish gay men, lesbians and bisexuals of all ages. *President* Sonia Lawrence.

JEWISH SOCIALISTS' GROUP
BM 3725, London WC1N 3XX.
Email jsg@jewishsocialist.org.uk, Website www.jewishsocialist.org.uk
(Est. 1974) Political, cultural and campaigning organisation committed to socialism, diasporism and secularism, aiming to unite the Jewish community with other oppressed/persecuted minorities. Active on local, national and international issues. National Committee (collective leadership).

JEWISH VOLUNTEERING NETWORK
The Jewish Social action Hub, 152, West End Lane, London NW6 1SD. ☎ 020-7443 5100. Website www.jvn.org.uk
(Est 2007) An organisation that helps to match volunteers with opportunities in all sectors of communal activity; it aims to provide training and support, and to raise the profile of volunteers across the UK Jewish community. *Dir* Leonie Lewis; *Co-Chairs* Susan Winton, Judy Citron.

JEWS FOR JUSTICE FOR PALESTINIANS
PO Box 46081, London W9 2ZF.
Email jfjfp@jfjfp.org. Website www.jfjfp.org.

(Est. 2002) JFJFP is a network of Jews who are British or live in Britain, practising and secular, Zionist and not. It opposes Israeli policies that undermine the livelihoods, and human, civil and political rights of the Palestinian people, while supporting the right of Israelis to live in freedom and security within Israel's 1967 borders. It is the largest group of British Jews openly critical of Israeli human-rights abuses and transgressions of international law. It draws on Jewish values of justice, tolerance and mutal respect, and is motivated by concerns to combat antisemitism and to protect the long-term future of both peoples. It rejects any routine labeling of Israel's critics as antisemitic and promotes factually-based, open discourse on the conflict within British society, cooperating with other organisations on specific issues without necessarily endorsing everything they do. It works to build world-wide Jewish opposition to the Israeli Occupation with like-minded groups and is a founding member of *European Jews for a Just Peace*. It is a member of the Jewish Human Rights Network. *Contact* Ines Newman.

NE'IMAH SINGERS
c/o 21 Holders Hill Drive, London NW4 1NL.
☎ 020-8202 2924. Fax 020-8922 0779. Email neimah@freeserve.co.uk.
(Est. 1993) Choir performing Synagogue music. *Fd and Conductor* Marc Temerlies; *Co-Fd* Jonathan Weissbart; *Ass. Chazan* Moshe Haschel.

NOAH PROJECT
PO Box 1828, London W10 5RT.
Website www.biggreenjewish.org
(Est. 1997) Through 'Jewish Education, Celebration and Action for the Earth', the Noah Project promotes awareness of environmental issues throughout the community, and demonstrates how Jewish teachings provide guidance for greener living. It provides a Jewish voice to secular and multi-faith environmental movements. *Educ. Co-ord.* Vivienne Cato.

OPERATION JUDAISM
95 Willows Road, Birmingham B12 9QF.
☎ 0121-440 6673 (24 hrs ansaphone). Fax 0121-446-4199.
(Est. 1986) Operation Judaism is the community's defence against missionary attack. It operates nationally an information and counselling service. Information and support for those involved with cults. Man. Cttee. consists of representatives from: Office of the C. Rabbi, Board of Deputies and Lubavitch Foundation.

PAVEL HAAS FOUNDATION UK
7 Roma Read Close, London SW15 4AZ.
☎ 020-8785 4772. Email: pavelhaas@victorullmann.co.uk
Website www.pavelhaasfoundation.org.
(Est. 2002) To promote the performance of the works of Pavel Haas (1899-1944) and holocaust education. *Exec. Dir.* Jacqueline Bowen Cole.

ROYAL BRITISH LEGION (MONASH BRANCH)
(Est. 1936. Reg. Charity No. 219279) *Chairman* G. J. Kaufman; *H. Sec.* G.G. Fiegel, 55, Blockley Rd., Wembley, Middx HAO 3LN. . ☎ 020-8904 7868. Fax 020-8904 2021.

SHATNEZ CENTRE TRUST
22 Bell Lane, Hendon, London NW4 2AD
☎ 020-8202 4005.
(Est. 1990. Reg. Charity No. 1013840) To provide Shatnez checking at the Shatnez Centre and promote Shatnez observance in the community. *Ts.* A. E. Bude, David Rabson.

START YOUR DAY THE TORAH WAY

Calculu Business Centre, 8–10, Timberwharf Road, Fairweather Wharf, London N16 6DB
☎ 08456-980044. Fax 020-8211 1782. Email menasche.scharf@gmail.com
(Est. 2005) Daily morning courses in Judaism. *Dir.* M. D. Salczman.

SUPPORT GROUP FOR PARENTS OF JEWISH GAYS AND LESBIANS

59 Mowbray Road, Edgware, Middx HA8 8JL.
☎ 020-8958 4827. Email kenmowbray@aol.com
(Est. 1996) To give support and help to parents of Jewish gays and lesbians. *H. Sec.* Kenneth Morris.

SZYMON LAKS FOUNDATION UK

7 Roma Road Close, London SW15 4AZ
☎ 0208785 4772 Email: szymonlaks@viktorullmann.freeserve.co.uk Website www. szymonla
ksfoundation.org and www.musiciansgallery.com
(Est. 2005) to honour and cellebrate the life and work of composer Szymon Laks (1901-1983).
Founder and Artistic Dir. Jacqueline Bowen Cole. *Hon Patron* Dr Y. Bauer. *Hon Adr., Exec Cttee*
Dr G. Fackler, F.H. Wuthenow, Prof Andre Laks.

TJSPN

PO Box 33317, London NW11 9FR.
☎ 020-8632 0216. Fax 020-8458 3261. Email jr6287@yahoo.co.uk
The Jewish Single Parent Network aims to assist single parents with a range of services
focusing on the practical difficulties of single parenting. *Patron* The Lady Jakobovits; enq. to R.
Zrihen.

TZEDEK

(Jewish Action for a Just World)
152, West End Lane, London NW6 1SD
☎ 020-7443 5121. Email info@tzedek.org.uk; Website www.tzedek.org.uk.
(Est. 1990. Reg. Charity No. 1016767) Tzedek is an overseas development and educational
charity working in some of the poorest countries in Africa and Asia. It aims to provide direct
support to small-scale, self-help, sustainable development projects and to educate people,
particularly in the Jewish community, about the causes and effects of poverty and the Jewish
obligation to respond. It also organises an Overseas Volunteer Programme in which Jewish
volunteers work for up to eight weeks during the summer at development projects in Africa,
and Asia. *Dir.* D. Berelowitz.

UNITED KINGDOM ASSOCIATION OF JEWISH LAWYERS & JURISTS

PO Box 568 Edgware, Middx HA8 4BY.
☎ 020-8958 6110. Fax 020-8905 4406. Email ukajlj@jewishlawers.co.uk
(Est. 1990) The objectives of the Association are: to contribute, alone or in co-operation with
other international or national organisations, towards the establishment of an international
legal order based on the Rule of Law in relations between all nations and states; to promote
human rights and the principles of equality of men and the right of all states and peoples
to live in peace; to act against racism and anti-semitism, whether openly expressed or
covertly exercised, *inter alia,* where necessary, by legal proceedings; to promote the study
of legal problems affecting the world's Jewish communities in the context of national and
international law; to promote, in consultation with the legal profession within the State of
Israel and its agencies, the study of legal problems of particular concern to the State of
Israel; to promote the study of Jewish law in comparison with other laws and facilitate the
exchange of any information resulting from research thereto among member groups; to
collect and disseminate information concerning the *de facto* and *de jure* status of the Jewish

communities and other minority ethnic and religious groups throughout the world and where the occasion arises, to give help and support pursuant to human rights treaties; to promote and support co-operation and communication between the Association's member groups; to concern itself with any other matter of legal interest considered of relevance by any of the member groups.

President The Rt. Hon. The Lord Woolf; *V. Presidents* The Rt. Hon. The Lord Millett, The Rt. Hon. The Lord Justice Rix, HH Israel Finestein QC; *Chairman* HH D. Levy, QC; *Admin.* Mrs Shirley March.

VIKTOR ULLMANN FOUNDATION UK

7 Roma Read Close, London SW15 4AZ.
☎ 020-8785 4772. Email office@viktorullmann.freeserve.co.uk. Website www. viktorullmannfoundation.org.uk
(Est. 2002) To remember and celebrate the genius of Viktor Ullmann, (1898–1944), and to promote his music in association with the Terezin Music Memorial Foundation, the Jewish Music Institute, the International Forum for Suppressed Music and other bodies. *Exec. Cttee* Anita Lask Wallfisch, Martin Anderson, Alexander Knapp, Gloria Tessler; *Exec. Dir.* Jacqueline Cole.

INTERNATIONAL ORGANISATIONS

JEWISH ORGANISATIONS HAVING CONSULTATIVE STATUS WITH THE ECONOMIC AND SOCIAL COUNCIL OF THE UNITED NATIONS

Agudas Israel World Org.; Coordinating Bd. of Jewish Orgs. (comprising the British BoD, the South African BoD, and the B'nai B'rith); Consultative Council of Jewish Orgs. (comprising the Anglo-Jewish Assn., the Alliance Israélite Universelle, and the Canadian Friends of the Alliance); W.J.C. Internat. Council on Jewish Social and Welfare Services (comprising American Joint Distribution Committee, World Jewish Relief, Jewish Colonization Assn., European Council of Jewish Community Services, United Hias Service, World ORT Union); Internat. Council of Jewish Women.

AGUDAS ISRAEL WORLD ORGANISATIONS

The organisation was founded in Kattowitz in 1912. Its programme was defined as being 'the solution – in the spirit of the Torah – of problems which periodically confront the Jewish people in Eretz Yisroel and the Diaspora'. This object was to be fulfilled 'by coordination of Orthodox Jewish effort throughout the world ... by the representation and protection of the interests of Torah-true Jewish communities'. The programme was formulated by our ancestors for the unconditional acceptance by all Jewish generations of the Biblical injunction 'And ye shall be unto Me a kingdom of priests and a holy nation'. The organisation seeks to implement this injunction by its endeavours. It opposes assimilation and different interpretations of Jewish nationhood. Consult. status with United Nations, New York and Geneva, and Unesco in Paris.

Agudas Israel of Gt. Britain. *Presidium* Rabbi J. H. Dunner, Rabbi Y. M. Rosenbaum, 95-99 Stamford Hill, N16 5DN. ☎ 020-8800 6688. Fax 020-8800-5000. *Publ.* Jewish Tribune (weekly).

Zeire Agudas Israel (Reg. Charity No. 253513), 95 Stamford Hill, N16; 35a Northumberland Street, Salford, 7. *Chairman* J. Schleider.

Agudas Israel Community Services, (Reg. Charity No. 287367), 97 Stamford Hill, N16 5DN. ☎ 020-8800 6688. Est. 1980 to help find suitable employment for observant Jews, including immigrants and Yiddish speakers, and other social services. *Dirs.* J. Davis, M.M. Posen.

Jewish Rescue and Relief Cttee. (Reg. Charity No. X99706ES), 215 Golders Green Rd., NW11 9BY. (020-8458 1710. *Chairman* A. Strom.

Keren Hatorah Cttee. (Reg. Charity No. 281384). (For the relief of religious, educational and social institutions, a division of Agudas Israel in Great Britain), 97 Stamford Hill, N16 5DN. ☎ 020-8800 6688, 020-8800 5000. *Exec. Dir.* Rabbi C. Y. Davis.

Russian Immigrant Aid Fund, for the material and spiritual rehabilitation of Russian immigrants in Israel; 97 Stamford Hill, N16 5DN. (020-8800 6688. *Chairman* I. M. Cymerman.

Society of Friends of the Torah (Reg. Charity No. 238230), 97 Stamford Hill, N16 5DN, and, 215 Golders Green Rd., NW11 9BY. ☎ 020-8800 6687, 020-8458 9988. Fax 020-8800 5000. *Dir.* Rabbi C.Y. Davis.

ALLIANCE ISRAELITE UNIVERSELLE

45 rue La Bruyère, Paris 75009.
☎ (01)53 328855. Fax (01) 48 745133. Email info@aiu.org Website www.aiu.org (Est. 1860.) This educative and cultural-oriented organisation essentially works through a network of schools which affects today more than 20,000 pupils and its century-old defence of human rights before governmental and international institutions all over the world. Has two publs: Les Cahiers de L'Alliance Israélite Universelle and Les Cahiers du Judaïsme and a centre for pedagogical publs: Créer-Didactique, and NADIR publishing house. Its library with more than 120,000 books in the field of Hebraica-Judaica and its College des Etudes juives make it one of the most important Jewish centres in Europe. Today the Alliance operates in Belgium, Canada, France, Israel, Morocco, Spain. *President* Prof. A. Steg; *Dir.* J. Tolédano. Library Website www.rachelnet.net

AUSTRALIA/ISRAEL AND JEWISH AFFAIRS COUNCIL (AIJAC)
Level 1, 22 Albert Rd. South Melbourne, Victoria 3205.
☎ 613 9681 6660. Fax 639681 6650. Email aijac@aijac.org.au
The organization is active in Australia, New Zealand, and South East Asia. *Exec. Dir.* Dr Colin Rubenstein, AM;*Contact* L.Kahn. *Publ.* Review (monthly) (See p. 128).

B'NAI B'RITH
(Est. 1843) B'nai B'rith is the world's largest Jewish human rights, philanthropic and community action group, active in 58 countries around the world, with its head office in Washington DC, NGO status at the United Nations in New York, an office at the European Union in Brussels, and a World Centre in Jerusalem. It brings Jews together to work in harmony for the common good, to help the poor and oppressed, and to become active in cultural and humanitarian projects. B'nai B'rith United Kingdom is a Major National Structure within B'nai B'rith Europe, which consists of 27 countries covering eastern, western and central Europe. In 2003, B'nai B'rith celebrated its 160th anniversary.

The Core Objectives of B'nai B'rith in the United Kingdom are:
• to foster friendship through social, cultural and recreational programmes;
• to support the State of Israel and World Jewry;
• to work for charitable endeavours;
• to initiate and develop community projects;
• to strengthen B'nai B'rith links across Europe.

B'nai B'rith has been instrumental in setting up and supporting:
• the B'nai B'rith Hillel Foundation (p.46);
• the B'nai B'rith Housing Association (p.89);
• the B'nai B'rith Jewish Music Festival (p.34);
• BBYO (p.40);
• Jewish Community Information (p.7).

The London Bureau of International Afairs is an associate office of the Centre for Public Policy of B'nai B'rith International in Washington DC, and of B'nai B'rith Europe in Brussels. The London Bureau of International Affairs provides information and acts as a resource centre, serving as a major activity and lobbying facility where Jewish intrests worldwide are concerned.

International HQ, 1640 Rhode Island Avenue NW, Washington DC 20036, USA. ☎ 202 857 6600. Fax 202 857 1099. Website www.bnaibrith.org

B'nai B'rith Europe, 36 rue Dautzenberg/, B-1050 Brussels, Belgium, ☎ 00 32 2 646 9298. Fax 00 32 02 646 8949. Email direction@bnaibritheurope.org; Website www.bnaibrith-europe.org. *President* G. Weinberg; *Admin. Dir.* Aline Brandon.

B'nai B'rith United Kingdom, ORT House, 126 Albert Street, London NW1 7NE. ☎ 020-7446 8660, Fax 020-8905 8102. Email bnaibrithuk@hotmail.co.uk. Website www.bbuk.org. (Reg Charity No. 1061661) *Nat. President* Martin Kudlick; *V. Nat. President* J. Etherton; *Nat. Sec.* P. Gold, *T.* Tony Etherton.

> **London Bureau of International Affairs,** ORT House, 126, Albert Street, London NW1 7NE ☎ 01895-677378, 020 8905 8102. Email Ibia2000@hotmail.com. Website www.Ibia.org.uk. *Chairman* Mark Marcus; *Dir.* H. Briskman.
>
> **Lodges**
> Abraham Lewin (Enfield) Cheshire Unity; Edgware Women; Finchley Joint; First Lodge of England; First Unity; Ilford (Golda Meir) Unity; Jerusalem (Wembley & District); Leeds Unity; Leo Baeck; Manchester; Pegasus; Phoenix; Raoul Wallenberg Unity; Shlomo Argov Unity; Spirit; Thames; Yad B'Yad Unity; Yitzchak Rabin.

CCJO. RenéCassin
Star House, 104-108 Grafton Road, London NW5 4BA
☎ 020-7485 1475; Email info@renecassin.org. Website www.renecassin.org

(Est. 2000. reg. Charity No. 1117472). RenéCassin is dedicated to the application of the Jewish experience in the promotion of the human rights of all people through education, international campaigns, events research and publication. *Dir.* Sarah Kaiser; *Co-Chairs* M. Jaffe, D. Kingsley; *International Chair* A. Goldberg.

CENTRAL REGISTRY OF INFORMATION ON LOOTED CULTURAL PROPERTY 1933–1945
76 Gloucester Place, London W1U 6HJ.
☎ 020-7487 3401. Fax 020-7487 4211. Email info@lootedart.com; Website www.lootedart. com
(Est. 2001. Reg. Charity No. 309720. IRS No. for the American Friends 13-2943469) Provides a centre of research, expertise and information on cultural objects looted between 1933 and 1945 - paintings, drawings, books, manuscripts, Judaica, silver, porcelain, etc. *Dir.* Anne Webber.

COMMISSION FOR LOOTED ART IN EUROPE
76 Gloucester Place, London W1U 6HJ.
☎ 020-7487 3401. Fax 020-7487 4211. Email info@lootedartcommission.com; Website www. lootedartcommission.com
(Est. 1999) Non-profit, expert representative body which negotiates restitution policies and procedures, and assists families, communities and institutions internationally to locate and recover Nazi-looted cultural property. Represents the European Council of Jewish Communities and the Conference of European Rabbis.
Co-chairs David Lewis, Anne Webber.

COMMITTEE FOR THE PRESERVATION OF JEWISH CEMETERIES IN EUROPE
81A Fairholt Rd., London N16 5EW.
☎ 020-8802 3917. Fax 020-8802 3756. Email cpjce@ic24.net
(Est 1991. Reg. Charity No. 1073225) Preservation of Jewish burial sites in Europe to ensure that they are maintained according to Jewish law and tradition. *President* Rabbi E. Schlesinger; *Hon. Sec.* Y. Marmorstein; *H.T.* A. Goldman. *Exec. Dir.* A. Ginsberg.

COMMONWEALTH JEWISH COUNCIL AND TRUST
BCM Box 6871, London WC1N 3XX.
☎ 020-7222 2120. Fax 020-7222 1781. Email info@cjc.org.uk; Website: www.cjc.org.uk.
(Est. 1982.) To provide links between Commonwealth Jewish communities; to provide a central representative voice for Commonwealth Jewish communities and to help preserve their religious and cultural heritage; to seek ways to strengthen Commonwealth Jewish communities in accordance with their individual needs and wishes and provide mutual help and cooperation. *President* The Lord Janner, QC; *Vice Presidents* Fl. Kaufman, Paul Secher, Jeff Durkin; *Sec.* J. Galaun, FCA; *H. T.* H.B. Lipsith; *Dir.* Maureen Gold. .
There are 38 members including those in Antigua, Australia, Bahamas, Barbados, Belize, Bermuda, Botswana, Canada, Cayman Is., Cyprus, Fiji, Gibraltar, Guernsey, India, Isle of Man, Jamaica, Jersey, Kenya, Mauritius, Namibia, New Zealand, Singapore, Sri Lanka, Trinidad & Tobago, Turks & Caicos Is., United Kingdom, Zambia and Zimbabwe.

Commonwealth Jewish Trust (Reg. Charity No. 287564). *Trs.* M. Bethlehem, Harvey Lipsith, Dorothy Reitman, Jack Galaun, Sir Jack Zunz. The Trust undertakes charitable projects in Jewish communities throughout the Commonwealth, with special emphasis on smaller communities.

CONFERENCE OF EUROPEAN RABBIS
19 Rue St Georges, Paris 75009, France.
☎ 020-8343 8989.
President Chief Rabbi J. Sitruk, Chief Rabbi of France; *Assoc. President* Chief Rabbi J. Sacks; *Chairman Standing Cttee* Chief Rabbi P. Goldschmidt; *Exec. Dir.* Cllr A.M. Dunner, 87 Hodford

Road, London NW11 8NH. ☎ 020-8455 9960. Fax 020-8455 4968.
(Est. 1957) To provide a medium for co-operation on matters of common concern to rabbis of European communities.

CONFERENCE ON JEWISH MATERIAL CLAIMS AGAINST GERMANY, Inc.
15 East 26th Street, New York, N.Y. 10010.
☎ 212-696 4944. Fax 212-679 2126. Email info@claimscon.org; Website www. claimscon.org
(Est. 1951) Represents world Jewry in negotiating for compensation and restitution for victims of Nazi persecution and their heirs. More than 500,000 Holocaust survivors in 67 countries have received payments from Germany and Austria due to the work of the Claims Conference. Administers compensation funds, recovers unclaimed Jewish property and allocates funds to institutions that provide social welfare services to Holocaust survivors and preserve the memory and lessons of the Shoah. *Chairman* Julius Berman; *Exec. V. President* Gideon Taylor.

CONSULTATIVE COUNCIL OF JEWISH ORGANISATIONS
420 Lexington Avenue, New York City, N.Y. 10170.
☎ (212) 808-5437. Fax (212) 983-0094.
Est. 1946 for the purpose of cooperating with the U.N. and other intergovernmental orgs. and agencies in the advancement of human rights and the safeguarding of Jewish interests. Constituent Orgs.: Alliance Israelite Universelle, AJA, Canadian Frs. A.I.U. *Chairmen* Prof. Ady Steg, Clemens Nathan, Gary Waxman; *Sec. Gen.* Ralph Walden.

EAST EUROPEAN JEWISH HERITAGE PROJECT
3 Keele Farmhouse, Keele, Staffs ST5 5AR
Email eejhp@voluntas.org. Website www.eejhp.netfirms.com
(Reg. Charity No. 10616229) The East European Jewish Heritage project is active in Belarus, Lithuania and Ukraine. In addition to its humanitarian assistance programmes it encourages Jewish leadership in civil society through participation in projects which benefit the broader community. The EEJHP provides travel programmes for those interested in their ancesral past as well as genealogy services. Over the past ten years the EEJHP has engaged with many western organisations and universities in the restoration of derelict Jewish cemeteries. *Exec. Dir.* F. J. Swartz; *Dirs.* D. Solomon, K. G. Cushing.

EMUNAH (Child Resettlement Fund)
Shield House, Harmony Way, off Victoria Rd., London NW4 2BZ.
☎ 020-8203 6066. Fax 020-8203 6668. Email info@emunah.org.uk Website www.emunah.org.uk
(Est. 1933. Reg. Charity No. 215398) An international charity supporting vulnerable children and families in Israel. *H. L. President* The Lady Jakobovits; *H. President Lady* Sacks; *Found President* Gertrude Landy; *Exec. Presidents* Guggy Grahame, Daphne Kaufman; *Exec. Vice Presidents* Vera Garbacz, Gertrude Compton; *Chairmen* Vivienne Kesztenbaum, Michele Stern; *Vice Ch.* Camille Compton; Rochelle Selby; *Israel Projects Chairmen* Lilian Brodie, Daphne Kaufman, Judy Cohen, *Fundraising Chairman* Mrs Rochelle Selby; *Admin. Chairman* Rosalyn Liss; *Hon. Sec.* Estelle Berest; *H. T.* Rachelle Greenwood; *Publ.* Helen Kon

EUROPEAN ASSOCIATION FOR JEWISH CULTURE
London office: 7/8 market Place, London W1W 8AG. ☎ 020-7935 8266. Fax 020-7935 3252.
Email london@jewishcultureineurope.org; Website www.jewish cultureineurope.org
Paris office: 45 rue la Bruyère, 75009 Paris. ☎ +33(0) 1 53 32 88 55. Fax +33(0) 1 48 74 51 33. Email paris@jewishcultureineurope.org; Website www.jewish cultureineurope.org
(Est. 2001) An independent grant-making body, which fosters and supports artistic creativity and encourages access to Jewish culture in Europe. *President* Peter L. Levy OBE; *Sec.* Jean-Jacques Wahl; *Dir.* Lena Stanley-Clamp.

EUROPEAN ASSOCIATION FOR JEWISH STUDIES
Secretariat: Oxford Centre for Hebrew and Jewish Studies, Yarnton Manor, Yarnton, Oxon OX5

1PY. ☎ 01865 377946 (x111), Fax 01865 375079. Email admin@eurojewishstudies.org. Website www.eurojewishstudies.org. *Admin.* G. Gilmour *Publ.* European Journal of Jewish Studies.

EUROPEAN COUNCIL OF JEWISH COMMUNITIES (ECJC)

Floor 3, The Forum 74/80 Camden St, London NW1 0EG. Email: info@ecjc.org.
Website www.ecjc.org, www.presidents-meeting.ecjc.org, www.arachim.ecjc.org, www.jewisheritage.org, www.european-encounters.ecjc.org.
ECJC is a non government organisation (NGO) established as a non-profit association in accordance with the laws of Belgium as a "Vereniging Zonder Winstoogmerk" and has its registered office at Centraal Beheer van Joods Weldadigheid, Antwerp. The first statutes were adopted on 26/5/1968 in London. ECJC represents Jewish national communal organisations from over 40 countries in Europe. The ECJC enjoys participative NGO status with the Council of Europe and has consultative NGO status recognition with the European Union.
President Jonathan Joseph; Chief Exec. Neville Kluk. Full list of board members on websites.

EUROPEAN JEWISH CONGRESS

78 Avenue des Champs-Elysées, 75008 Paris.
☎ (33)1 43 59 94 63. Fax (33)1 42 25 45 28. Email jewcong@wanadoo.fr. Website www.eurojewcong.org.
(Est. 1986, previously the European Branch of the World Jewish Congress) Federates and co-ordinates the initiatives of 38 communities in Europe and acts as their spokesman. Has consultative status with the Council of Europe, European Commission and Parliament. Current concerns are the democratic development of Eastern Europe and the problems of racism and antisemitism throughout Europe. *President* Moshe Kantor; *Sec. Gen.* Serge Cwajgenbaum.

EUROPEAN JEWISH PUBLICATION SOCIETY

P.O. Box 19948, London N3 3ZL.
☎/Fax 020-8346 1776. Email cs@ejps.org.uk; Website www. ejps.org.uk.
(Est. 1994. Reg. Charity No. 3002158) A registered charity which makes grants to publishers (but not authors) for the publication, translation and distribution of books relating to Jewish literature, history, religion, philosophy, politics, poetry and culture. *Chairman* Fred S. Worms OBE; *Ed. Dir.* Prof. Colin Shindler.

EUROPEAN UNION OF JEWISH STUDENTS

3 ave Antoine Depage, B-1000, Brussels, Belgium.
☎ 010-32-2-647 72 79. Fax 010-32-2-648 24 31. Email info@eujs.org. Website www.eujs.org.
Est. 1978 for co-ordination purposes between national unions in the 36 countries of Europe (and Turkey). It represents more than 180,000 European Jewish students in international Jewish and non-Jewish forums dealing with cultural and political matters and opposes all forms of racism and fascism. The EUJS is also a 'service organisation' for students. It helps with courses abroad, supplies material on different subjects for university students and organises visits and seminars. *H. Presidents* Mrs Simone Veil, Maram Stern; *H. Mems.* The Lord Janner, QC, David Susskind (Belgium), Suzy Jurysta (B.), Laslov Kadelburg (Yu.); *President* Lionel Schreiber; *Exec. Dir.* David Nachfolger; *Program Dir.* Adam Mouchtar.

FRIENDSHIP WITH ISRAEL (European Parliament)

51 Tavistock Court, Tavistock Square, WC1H 9HG.
☎ 020-7387 4925.
(Est. 1979) All-Party Group in European Parl. with more than 120 MEPs. Aims at promoting friendship and co-operation between the European Com. and Israel. Provides up-to-date inf. on Israeli matters and a balanced view of Middle East events. Holds regular meetings in Strasbourg at Palais de l'Europe when the Euro-Parl. sits. Recognised as an official 'Inter-Parl. Group'. *H. Patron* Mrs. Simone Veil MEP, past President, Euro-Parl.; *Chairman* Tom Normanton, MEP (UK); *V. Chairmen* Erik Blumenfeld, MEP, Hans-Joachim Seeler, MEP (West Germany), Hans Nord, MEP (Holland), John Tomlinson, MEP (UK); *H. Sec.* John Marshall, MEP (UK); *Dir.* Mrs Sylvia Sheff, JP, BA.

HEBREWARE® USER GROUP
Calculu Business Centre, London N16 6DB.
☎ 08456 9800. Fax 020-8211 1782. Email menasche.scharf@gmail.com.
The leading User Group for Hebrew, Yiddish and Judaic software users on mac and other platforms in the UK and abroad.

HEIMLER INTERNATIONAL
(formerly The Heimler Foundation)
Peter Hudson, 47 Rosebery Road, SW2 4DQ
☎ 020-8674 6999.
(Est. 1972.) Heimler International was set up to facilitate the work and ideas of Prof. Eugene Heimler. Its aims are: (1) to provide counselling and therapy for individuals and groups, using the Heimler approach; (2) to provide basic and advanced training in the Heimler Method; (3) to recognise advanced practitioners and lecturers in the Heimler Method; (4) to sanction and collect bona fide research, act as a focal point, publish books/tapes describing the Heimler Method. There are Branches in several different countries in Europe, Canada, USA.

HIAS
333 7th Avenue, New York, NY 1001, USA. ☎ 212 967-4100
(Est. 1954, through merger of the Hebrew Sheltering and Immigrant Aid Society (HIAS), United Service for New Americans (USNA) and the migration service of the American Joint Distribution Committee (AJDC).)
  Est. 1881, HIAS, the Hebrew Immigrant Aid Society, is America's oldest international migration and refugee resettlement agency.HIAS assists Jewish and other migrants and refugees to countries of freedom and security, helps newcomers to integrate into their new communities, reunites family members, and advocates for and works with government and other agencies to promote fair migration policies and increased opportunities. HIAS' activities have always mirrored world events. In the past decade alone, the organisation has worked to help refugees and immigrants from Afghanistan, Bosnia, Bulgaria, Czech Republic, Democratic Republic of the Congo, Ethiopia, Haiti, Hungary, Iran, Morocco, Nigeria, Poland, Romania, Sudan, Tunisia, Vietnam, successor states to the former Soviet Union, and other countries where persecution and absence of liberty have forced people to seek new lives in America and other welcoming nations. *President* Gideon Aronoff; *Chairman* Michael.B. Rukin**.**

INSTITUTE FOR JEWISH POLICY RESEARCH (JPR)
7-8, Market Place, London W1W 8AG.
☎ 020-7935 8266. Fax 020-7935 3252. Email jpr@jpr.org.uk. Website www. jpr.org.uk
JPR is an independent think-tank which informs and influences policy, opinion and decision-making on issues affecting Jewish life worldwide by conducting and commissioning research, developing and disseminating policy proposals and promoting public debate. JPR's public activities include lectures, policy seminars and conferences. *Hon. President* The Lord Rothschild; *President* Lord Haskel; *Chairman* Peter L. Levy OBE; *T. B.* Smouha; *Exec. Dir.* A. Lerman; *Dir. Pub. Activities* Lena Stanley-Clamp. *Publ.* JPR Reports and PR Policy Debate papers; JPR News.

INTERNATIONAL COUNCIL OF CHRISTIANS AND JEWS
Martin Buber Haus, Werlestrasse 2, Postfach 1129, D-64646, Heppenheim, Germany.
☎ 6252 93120. Fax 6252-68331. Email info@iccj-buberhouse.de; Website www.iccj.org
President Dr. Deborah Weissman; *Patron* Sir Sigmund Sternberg; *Consultant* Ruth Weyl, Northwood, Middx HA6 3NG. Email: ruth.weyl1@talktalk.net. Est.1947 to strengthen Jewish–Christian understanding on an international basis and to co-ordinate and initiate programmes and activities for this purpose. Now increasingly engaged in trilateral dialogue of Jews, Christians and Muslims.

INTERNATIONAL COUNCIL OF JEWISH WOMEN
PO Box 12130 Local 4, Montevideo 11300, Uruguay.

☎/Fax +598 (0)2 628 5874. Email icjw@montevideo.com.uy; Website www. icjw.org.uk
ICJW is made up of 43 Jewish women's organisations in 40 countries, covering between them almost the whole spectrum of the Jewish world. The core purpose of ICJW is to bring togeth-er Jewish women from all walks of life in order to create a driving force for social justice for all races and creeds. ICJW has consultative status with ECOSOC at the United Nations and is represented on many international organisations. *President* Sara Winkowski.

INTERNATIONAL COUNCIL ON JEWISH SOCIAL AND WELFARE SERVICES
The Forum, 74-80 Camden Street, London NW1 0EG. ☎ 020-7691 1771. Fax 020-7691 1780. Email info@wjr.org.uk
(Est. 1961) Member Organisations: Amer. Jt. Distribution Cttee.; WJR.; European Council of Jewish Com. Services; HIAS; World ORT Union. *Chief Exec.* P. Anticoni.

INTERNATIONAL JEWISH GENEALOGICAL RESOURCES (IJGR(UK))
25 Westbourne Road, Edgbaston, Birmingham B15 3TX.
☎ 0121-454 0408. Fax 0121-454 9758. Email josephj-2007@hotmail.co.uk.
(Est. 1988) Provides guidance on Jewish genealogy; has a library including material on Anglo-Jewry/Anglo-Australasian Jewry; microfilm of Jewish Chronicle, etc. Research undertaken. *Org.* Dr Anthony P. Joseph and Mrs Judith Joseph.

INTERNATIONAL JEWISH VEGETARIAN SOCIETY
Bet Teva, 853/855 Finchley Road, NW11 8LX.
☎ 020-8455 0692. Fax 020-8455 1465. Email jewishvegetarian@onetel.com
(Est. 1965. Reg. Charity No. 258581.) Affiliated to the International Vegetarian Union. Branches: N. and S. America, S. Africa, Israel, Australia. *H. Sec.* S. Labelda.

IRANIAN JEWISH CENTRE
First Floor, 86 Brook St., London W1K 5AY.
☎ 020-7414 0069. Fax 020-7491 4804. Email: ijc@ijc.org.uk. Website www.ijc.org.uk
(Est. 1981. Reg. Charity No. 287256) Fundraising to support Iranian Jewish communities in Britain, Iran and the USA. Promotion of Iranian/Jewish heritage and culture. *Chairman* Hamid Sabi.

JCA CHARITABLE FOUNDATION
Victoria Palace Theatre, Victoria St., SW1E 5EA.
☎ 020-7828 0600. Fax 020-7828 6882.
(Reg. Charity No. 207031) Charitable company est. in 1891 by Baron Maurice de Hirsch to assist poor and needy Jews. The JCA was instrumental in promoting the emigration from Russia of thousands of Jews who were settled in farm 'colonies' in North and South America, Palestine/Israel and elsewhere. Today JCA's main efforts are in Israel in rural areas where it supports schs., insts. of higher learning, agricultural research and helps to promote the subsistence of needy Jews. *President* Sir Stephen Waley-Cohen, Bt.; *Man.* Y. Lothan.

JEWISH AFFILIATES OF THE UNITED NATIONS ASSOCIATION
6 Bloomsbury Square, London WC1A 2LP. ☎ 020-7543 5400.
(Est. 1971) A co-ordinating group of Jewish organisations and individuals affiliated to the United Nations Association. Members of the group represent their organisations at the UNA where they have two functions. Firstly to promote the interests of Israel and the Jewish People, and secondly to present the Jewish view on general international and humanitarian issues. *Chairman* David M. Jacobs; *Hon. Sec.* E. David.

JEWISH RECONSTRUCTIONIST FEDERATION (JRF, formerly FRCH)
7804 Montgomery Ave., St. #9, Elkins Park, PA 19027, USA. ☎ (215) 782-8500. Fax (215) 782-8805. Email info@jrf.org; Website www.jrf.org
(Est. 1955) JRF is the congregational arm of the Reconstructionist movement, representing

103 affiliates in North America. Dedicated to the concept of Judaism as an evolving religious civilisation, JRF provides outreach, consulting, programmatic and educational support to its congregations and havurot. JRF is the publisher of a new Haggadah and a variety of books, magazines and the *Kol Haneshamah* prayerbook series.

MACCABI WORLD UNION
Kfar Maccabiah, Ramat Gan 52105, Israel.
(Est. 1921) The union is a co-ordinating body for the promotion and advancement of sports, educational and cultural activities among Jewish communities worldwide. *President* R. Bakalarz; *Chairman* Oudi Recanati; *Chairman, European Maccabi Confederation* Leo Dan-Bensky; *Exec. Dir.* E. Tiberger. See Maccabi Assns., p.42.

MEMORIAL FOUNDATION FOR JEWISH CULTURE
50 Broadway, 34th Floor, New York, NY 10004.
☎ (212) 425-6606. Fax (212) 425-6602. Website www.mfjc.org
(Est. 1965) Supports Jewish cultural and educational programmes all over the world in co-operation with educational research and scholarly organisations, and provides scholarship and fellowship grants. *President* Prof. I. Schorsch; *Exec. V. President* Dr J. Hochbaum.

SIMON WIESENTHAL CENTRE
European office: 64 Avenue Marceau, 75008 Paris, France. ☎ (331) 4723-7637. Fax (331) 4720-8401.
London office: Simon Wiesenthal Centre UK, 27 Old Gloucester Street, WC1N 3XX (Reg. Charity No. 1030966). *Chairman* Graham Morris. ☎ 020-7419 5014. Fax 020-7831 9489. Email csweurope@compuserve.com. Website: www.wiesenthal-europe.com
(Est. Los Angeles, 1979) To study the contemporary Jewish and general social condition in Europe by drawing lessons from the Holocaust experience. To monitor, combat and educate against anti-semitism, racism and prejudice. *Int. Dir.* Rabbi Marvin Hier; *Chairman, Board of Trustees* Samuel Belzberg; *Dir. for Int. Affairs* Dr Shimon Samuels. 400,000 members. Headquarters: Los Angeles. Offices in: New York, Chicago, Washington DC, Miami, Toronto, Jerusalem, Paris, Buenos Aires.

WORLD COUNCIL OF CONSERVATIVE/MASORTI SYNAGOGUES
Israel:Ben Yehuda 13; PO Box 2564; Jerusalem.
☎ 02-624 7106   Fax 02-624 7677. Email maill@masortiolami.org.
USA: 3080 Broadway, New York, NY 10027
☎ 212-2806039; Fax 212 678 5321. Email.worldcouncil@masortiworld.org
(Est. 1957) To build, renew and strenthen Jewish life throughout the world, focusing on Europe, LatinAmerica, the FSU, Africa, Asia and Australia, working with all arms of the Conservative/masorti movement. Emphasizing study bof Torah in the fullest sense, and its transmission from generation, the centrality of the synagogue, Israel and the Hebrew language, centrist, dynamic Jewish practice based on *halacha* and *mitzvot*, and the values of egalitarianism, pluralism and tolerence within this framework. *President* Alan H. Silberman; *Rabbi of the Council* Rabbi Benjamin Z. Kreitman; *President Masorti Europe*. Claude Machline (-2008), Gillian Caplin (2008-); *President, Masorti Amlat of Steering* David Raij. *Immediate Past President* Rabbi Alan Silverstein.

WORLD JEWISH CONGRESS
(a) To co-ordinate the efforts of its affliated orgs., in respect of the political, economic, social, religious and cultural problems of the Jewish people; (b) to secure the rights, status and interests of Jews and Jewish communities and to defend them wherever they are denied, violated or imperilled; (c) to encourage and assist the creative development of Jewish social, religious and cultural life throughout the world; (d) to represent and act on behalf of its affiliated orgs. before governmental, intergovernmental and other international authorities in respect of matters which concern the Jewish people as a whole. *Fdr President* Late Dr N. Goldmann; *President* R. Lauder; *Chairman, Exec.* Mendel Kaplan; *Chairman, Gov. Bd.* M. Bronfman; *Sec. Gen.* M. Schneider;

Chairmen of Regions: **North America**: Evelyn Sommer, **Latin America**: Jack Terpins, **Europe**: M. Kantor; **Israel**: Sh. Hermesh, MK; **Euro-Asia**: Alexander Machkevich.
   Principal Offices: New York, 501 Madison Avenue, 17th Fl., NY 10022. ☎ 755 5770; Geneva, 1 rue de Varembe. (734-13-25; Paris, 78 Av. des Champs Elysées. ☎ 4359 9463, Fax 4225 4528; Buenos Aires, Casilla 20, Suc. 53. ☎ 5411-4962-5028; Jerusalem, P.O.B. 4293, Jerusalem 91042. ☎ (02) 563-5261/4.
   Publ.: Dateline World Jewry (monthly), WJC Report (quarterly), Boletin de Información OJI (Spanish, monthly).

WORLD JEWISH RELIEF
Oscar Joseph House, 54 Crewys Rd., London NW2 2AD. ☎ 020-8736 1250. Fax 020-8736 1259. Email info@wjr.org.uk. Website www.wjr.org.uk.
(Est. 1933. Reg. Charity No. 290767 Member: Fundraising Standards Board) World Jewish Relief (WJR) is the leading UK Jewish international agency responding to the needs of Jewish communities at risk or in crisis, outside the UK and Israel. At times of major international disaster, it directs the UK Jewish community's response to others in need. *Chairman* Nigel Layton; *Chief Exec.* Paul Anticoni.

WORLD ORT
1 Rue de Varembé, 1211 Geneva 20, Switzerland.
☎ (022) 919 4234. Fax (022) 919 4232. Email ortsuisse@vtx.ch
(Est. 1880.) Organisation for educational Resources and Technological training. Over three and a half million students have been trained since 1880, and currently 300,000 students are being trained in 60 countries in different parts of the world.
   Operational Headquarters in UK: World ORT Trust, 126 Albert St., London NW1 7NE. ☎ 020-7446 8500. Email cvo@ort.org. Website www.ort.org

WORLD UNION FOR PROGRESSIVE JUDAISM
13 King David Street, 94101 Jerusalem. ☎ 972 26203 447. Fax 262 203 446
(Est. 1926.) To foster the international growth and practice of Progressive Judaism, and to co-ordinate the activities of its autonomous constituent organisations. *President* Rabbi U. Regev; *Chairman* S. Bauman.
   European Region: The Sternberg Centre, 80 East End Rd., London N3 2SY. ☎ 020-8349 5651. Fax 020-8349 5699. Email kathrynmichael@europeanregion.org
Chairman Rabbi Dr Andrew Goldstein; *Sec.* Andrew Hart.

WORLD UNION OF JEWISH STUDENTS
King George 58, Jerusalem 91070, Israel.
☎ 02625 1682. Fax 02625 1688.
Email office@wujs.org.il. Website: ww.wujs.org.il
Est. 1924 to fight antisemitism and to act as an umbrella organisation for national Jewish students' bodies; organises educational programmes, leadership training seminars, works on Israel advocacy, an annual congress. As members: 51 national unions representing over 700,000 students; youth affiliate of the World Jewish Congress; member organization of the WZO. *First President* Prof. Albert Einstein; *Chairperson* V. Dolburd. *Publs.* Heritage & History, WUJS Reports, WUJS Leads, the Jewish student activist handbook, supplement to the Pesach Haggada, MASUA – monthly educational material, etc.

ZIONIST COUNCIL OF EUROPE
741 High Road, London N2 0BQ
☎ 020-8343 9756. Fax 020-8446 0639. Email zion-fed@dircon.co.uk
(Est. 1980) An umbrella organisation, consisting of the Zionist Federations from around Europe, with the aim of co-ordinating Zionist activities and developing young leadership on the continent. *Chairman* A. Balcombe; *Dir.* Alan Aziz.

LONDON

SYNAGOGUES

(D) where shown indicates regular daily services are held.

United Synagogue

Constituent and Affiliated Synagogues of the United Synagogue, Adler House, 735 High Road, North Finchley, N12 0US. (Reg. Charity no. 242552) *Chief Exec.* Rabbi S. Zneimer. ☎ 020-8343 8989. Fax 020-8343 6262. Website www.united synagogue.org.uk.

MEMBER SYNAGOGUES

Belmont Synagogue, 101 Vernon Dr, Stanmore, Middx HA7 2BW. *M.* Rabbi D. Roselaar; *Admin.* Mrs C. Fletcher. ☎ 020-8426 0104. Fax 020-8427 2046. Email office@belmontsy-nagogue.org.uk; Website www.belmont synagogue. org. uk. (D)

Borehamwood & Elstree Synagogue, P.O. Box 47, Croxdale Road, Borehamwood, Herts WD6 4QF. ☎ 020-8386 5227. Fax 020-8386 3303. Email info@borehamwoodshul.org; Website www.borehamwoodshul.org (Est. 1955.) Mikveh on the premises. *M.* Rabbi Dr N. Brawer; *Man.* E Rosen; *Fin., Memb* B. Winterman; *Admin.* A. Finn; *Comm. Care Co-ord.* R. Brummer:*Youth Dir.* D. Lauder (D)

Brondesbury Park Synagogue, 143 Brondesbury Park, NW2 5JL. ☎ 020-8459 1083 Fax 020 8459 5927 (Est. 1934.) *R.* Rabbi B. Levin; *Admin.* Mrs S. Littner.

Bushey & District Synagogue, 177/189 Sparrows Herne, Bushey, Herts WD23 1AJ. ☎ 020-8950 7340. Email adminstrator@busheyus. org. *M.* Rabbi Z. M. Salasnik, BA, FJC, zm@salasnik.net. *Admin.* Mrs M. Chambers; *Youth & Community Dir.* Rabbi J. Spector, jonny.spector@busheyus.org (D)

Central Synagogue, (Great Portland St.), 36-40 Hallam St., W1W 6NW. ☎ 020-7580 1355. Fax 020-7636 3831. Email administrator@centralsynagogue.org.uk; Website: www.centralsynagogue.org.uk. (Consecrated 1870, destroyed by enemy action May 1941, rebuilt 1958.) *Admin. Office* 36 Hallam Street, W1W 6NW; *M.* Rabbi B. Marcus; *R.* S. Leas; *Admin.* C. Levison.

Chigwell and Hainault Synagogue, Limes Ave., Chigwell, Essex IG7 5NT. ☎ 020-8500 2451. Fax 020-8500 4345. Email chshul@btinternet.com; Website www.chigshul.net. *M.* Rabbi B. Davis; *Admin.* W. Land; *Youth Dir.* J. Levy (D)

Clayhall Synagogue, Sinclair Hse., Woodford Bridge Rd., Ilford, Essex IG4 5LN. ☎ 020-8551 6533. Fax 020-8551 9803. Email clayhallsynagogue@hotmail.com; Website www.clay-hallsynagogue.org.uk.; *M.* Rabbi N. Wilson; *Admin.* Mrs M. Mervish.

Cockfosters & N. Southgate Synagogue, Old Farm Av., Southgate, N14 5QR. ☎ 020-8886 8225. Fax 020-8886 8234. Email office@ourshul.co.uk. Website www.ourshul.co.uk. (Est. 1948. Consecrated Dec. 1954.) *M.* Rabbi Y. Fine, BA; *R.*; *Admin.* Mrs L. Brandon.

Dollis Hill Synagogue, Parkside, Dollis Hill Lane, NW2 6RJ. ☎/Fax 020-8958 6777. *M.* Rev. M. Fine; *Admin.* W. Land.

Ealing Synagogue, 15 Grange Road, Ealing, W5 5QN. ☎ 020-8579 4894. *M.* Rabbi H. Vogel, MA; *Admin.* Mrs J. M. Gilford.

Edgware Synagogue, Parnell Close, Edgware Way, Edgware, Middx HA8 8YE. ☎ 020-8958 7508. Fax 020-8905 4449. Email edgwareunited@talk21.com; Website www.edgwaresynagogue.org. *M.* Rabbi B. Rabinowitz, BA, MPhil; *R.*; *Youth Dir.* D. Solomon Email donna@ donnaandjonny.co.uk; *Admin.* L. J. Ford. (D)

Finchley Synagogue, Kinloss Gdns., N3 3DU. ☎ 020-8346 8551. Fax 020-8349 1579. Email office@kinloss.org.uk. (Consecrated 1935.) *M.* Rabbi E. Mirvis; *Admin.* D. Lobl (D)

Finsbury Park Synagogue, 220 Green Lanes, N4 2JG. ☎ 020-8802 7004. *M.* Rabbi A. Cohn; *R.* Rev. E. Krausher; *Admin.* H. Mather.

Golders Green Synagogue, 41 Dunstan Road, NW11 8AE. ☎ 020-8455 2460. Fax 020-8731 9296; office@ggshul.org.uk (Consecrated 1922.) *M.* Rabbi H. Belovski ☎ 020-8458 8824; *Admin.* Mrs N. Hill; *Youth Dir.* Y. Hanstater (D)

Hackney & East London Synagogue, Brenthouse Road, Mare Street, E9 6QG.

☎ 020-8985 4600. Fax 020-8986 9507. (Consecrated 1897; enlarged and reconsecrated 1936, amalgamated 1993.) *M.* Rev. N. Tiefenbrun; *Admin.* W. Land.

Hampstead Garden Suburb Synagogue, Norrice Lea, N2 0RE. ☎ 020-8455 8126. Fax 020-8201 9247. Email office@hgss.org.uk; Website www.hgss.org.uk. (Consecrated 1934). *M.* Rabbi R. Livingstone; *R.* Chazan A. Freilich;*Comm. Dir.* Rabbi A. Knopf; *Youth Dir.* Mrs T. Younger; *Off. Man.* Mrs S. Drucker. (D)

Hampstead Synagogue, Dennington Park Road, West Hampstead, NW6 1AX. ☎ 020-7435 1518. Fax 020-7431 8369. Email admin@hampsteadshul.org.uk; www.hampsteadshul.org.uk (Consecrated 1892.) *M.* Rabbi Dr M.J. Harris; *R.* Rev. S. R. Gerzi; *Admin.* I. Nadel; *Youth Dir.* G. Herman.

Hendon Synagogue, 18 Raleigh Close, NW4 2TA. ☎ 020-8202 6924. Fax 020-8202 1720. Email admin@hendonus.org.uk. (Consecrated 1935.) *M.* Rabbi M.S. Ginsbury; *Exec. Sec.* L. Cohen. (D)

Highgate Synagogue (Est. 1929.), Grimshaw Close, 57 North Road, Highgate, N6 4BJ. ☎/Fax 020-8340 7655. Email highgateshul@ic24.net. *M.* Rabbi N.Liss, ☎ 020-8341 1714; *Admin.* Charles Loeb.

Ilford Synagogue, 22 Beehive Lane, Ilford, Essex IG1 3RT. ☎ 020-8554 5969. Fax 020-8554 4543. Email office@ilfordsynagogue.co.uk; Website www.ilford synagogue.co.uk. (Est. 1936.) *M.* Rabbi G. Hyman; *R. ; Admin.* A. Miller. (D)

Kenton Synagogue, Shaftesbury Avenue, Kenton, Middx HA3 0RD. ☎ 020-8907 5959. Fax 020-8909 2677. Email admin@kentonsynagogue.org.uk; Website www. kentonsynagogue.org. *M.* Rabbi Y. Black; *Admin.* Mrs C. Grayson.

Kingsbury Synagogue, Hool Close, Kingsbury Green, NW9 8XR. ☎ 020-8204 8089. Email kinsyn@hotmail.com. Website www.brijnet.org/kingsyn; *M.* Rabbi Z. Cohen; *R.*; *Admin.* Mrs C. Grayson. (D)

Mill Hill Synagogue, Brockenhurst Gdns., NW7 2JY. ☎ 020-8959 1137. Fax 020-8959 6484. Email office@millhillsynagogue.co.uk; Website www.shul.co.uk. *M.* Rabbi Y.Y. Schochet; *Youth Rabbi* A. Mallerman Email rabbishenker@millhillsynagogue.co.uk; *Admin.* A. Simonsson; *Youth Dir.* A. Mallerman. (D)

Muswell Hill Synagogue, 31 Tetherdown, N10 1ND. ☎/Fax 020-8883 5925. Email office@muswellhillsynagogue.org.uk Website www.muswellhillsynagogue.org.uk. (Est. 1911.) *M.* Rabbi D. Mason; *Sec.* C. Loeb.

New Synagogue, Victoria Community Centre, Egerton Rd., Stamford Hill, N16 6UB. (Est. in Leadenhall St., 1761.) Office: 113 Crowland Rd., N15 6UR. ☎/Fax 020-8880 2731. *Admin.* L. Newmark. (D)

New West End Synagogue, St Petersburgh Place, Bayswater, W2 4JT. ☎ 020-7229 2631. Fax 020-7229 2355. Email nwes@newwestend.org.uk; Website www.newwestend.org.uk. (Consec. 1879.) *M.* Rabbi G. Shisler; *Admin.* R. Cohen.

Newbury Park Synagogue, 23 Wessex Close, off Suffolk Road, Newbury Pk., Ilford, Essex IG3 8JU. ☎ 020-8597 0958. Fax 020-8590 2919. *M.* Rev. G. Newman; *Admin.* Mrs K. Levy. Email newburypk@spitfireuk.net.

Northwood Synagogue, 21-23 Murray Road, Middx HA6 2YP. ☎ 01923 820004. Fax 01923-820020. Email northwoodus@tiscali.com. *M.* Rabbi A. Plancey; *Admin.* Mrs E. Granger.

Palmers Green and Southgate Synagogue, Brownlow Road, N11 2BN. ☎ 020-8881 0037. Email palmgrnsyn@yahoo.co.uk. *M.* Rabbi E. Levy, BA; *R. ; Admin.* Mrs F. Cohen. (D)

Pinner Synagogue, 1 Cecil Park, Pinner, Middx HA5 5HJ. ☎ 020-8868 7204. Fax 020-8868 7011. Website www.pinner synagogue.com. *M.* Rabbi Y. Grunewald, BA; *Admin.* C. Abrahams; *Fin.* Mrs Y. Salomon Email finance@pinnersynagogue.com. *Youth Dir.* J. Philips ☎ 020-8181 4493 Email pinnerjosh@googlemail.com. (D)

Radlett Synagogue, 22 Watling St., PO Box 28, Radlett, Herts WD7 7PN. ☎ 01923-856878. Fax 01923-856698. Email radlett@hotmail.com Website www.radlett-us.org. *M.* Rabbi A. Abel. *Admin.* Mrs J. Bower.

Richmond Synagogue, Lichfield Gardens, Richmond-on-Thames, Surrey TW9 1AP. ☎ 020-8940 3526. Fax. 020-8945 6586. (Est. 1916.) *M.* Rabbi Y. Ives; *Admin.* Mrs Fellows.

St John's Wood Synagogue, 37/41 Grove End Road, St John's Wood, NW8 9NG. ☎ 020-

7286 3838. Fax 020-7266 2123. Email office@shulinthewood.com; Website www.stjohnswoodsynagogue.com. (Est. in Abbey Road 1882; present building consecrated 1964.) *M.* Dayan I. Binstock, B.Sc.; *R.* Rev. M. Haschel; *Admin.* Mrs Loraine Young; *Dir. Seniors Care* Mrs Yaffa Amit. (D)

Shenley Synagogue, P.O. Box 205, Shenley, Herts WD7 9ZN c/o W. Susman. ☎ 01923 857786.

South Hampstead Synagogue, 21 Eton Villas, Eton Road, NW3 4SG. ☎ 020-7722 1807. Fax 020-7586 3459. Email rachel@southhampstead.org; Website www.southhampstead.org. *M.* Rabbi S. Levin, M. Laitner; *Admin.* R. Perez-Arwas; *Youth Dir.* E. Levin.

South London Synagogue, 45 Leigham Ct. Road, SW16 2NF. ☎ 020-8677 0234. Fax 020-8677 5107. www.slsl.org.uk *M.* Rabbi M. Lester, M.A.; *Admin.* T. Goldman.

South Tottenham Synagogue, 111-113 Crowland Road, N15 6UR. ☎ 020-8880 2731. Email admin@stsynagogue.org.uk(Est. 1938.) *M.* Rabbi C. M. Biberfeld; *R.; Admin.* Y. Revah.

Stanmore and Canons Park Synagogue, London Road, Stanmore Middx HA7 4NS. ☎ 020-8954 2210. Fax 020-8954 4369. Email mail@stanmoresynagogue.org. *M.* Rabbi M. Lew; *R.* H. Black; *Asst. M.* Rabbi A. Shaw ; *Admin.* Mrs B. S. Dresner. (D)

Sutton & District Synogogue, 14 Cedar Road, Sutton Surrey SM2 5DA. ☎ 020-8642 5419. M. Rabbi A. Groner; *Admin.* J. Hunter ☎ 01737 351774. Email suttsyn@tiscali.co.uk.

Watford Synagogue, 16 Nascot Road, Watford, Herts WD17 4YE. ☎ 01923-222755. Email secretary@watfordsynagogue.org.uk. (Est. 1946.) *M.* Rabbi E. Levine; *Admin.* Mrs C. Silverman.

Wembley Synagogue, Forty Avenue, Wembley, Middx HA9 8JW. ☎ 020-8904 6565. Fax 020-8908 2740. E.mail office@wembleysynagogue.org. Website www.wembleysynagogue.org *M.* Rabbi S.Y. Harris, BA Hons (Lnd), *R.* Rev. A. Wolfson, BEd (Hons), MA, NPQH; *Admin.* Mrs E. Weiner. (D)

Woodside Park Synagogue, Woodside Park Road, N12 8RZ. ☎ 020-8445 4236. Fax 020-8446 5515. Email admin@woodsidepark.org.uk. Website www. woodsidepark.org.uk. *M.* ; *R.* Rev. S. Robins; *Chairman* G. Simon; *Admin.* Mrs D. Bruce. *Youth Dir.* D. Angel ☎ 020 8445 4236 Email youth@woodsidepark.org.uk(D)

ASSOCIATE SYNAGOGUE

Western Marble Arch, 32 Great Cumberland Place, London, W1H 7TN. ☎ 020-7723 9333. Fax 020-7224 8065. *M.* Rabbi L. Rosenfeld; *President* P. Faiman; *Exec. Sec.* S. Garcia.

AFFILIATED SYNAGOGUES

These are syns. belonging to U.S. by means of a scheme for small and newly est. congregations.

Barking and Becontree (Affiliated) Synagogue, 200 Becontree Avenue, Dagenham, Essex RM8 2TR. ☎ 020-8590 2737. *R.; Chairman* B. J. Lazarus; *Hon. Sec.* Mrs B. Berman.

Barnet and District Affiliated Synagogue, Eversleigh Road, New Barnet, Herts EN5 1NE. ☎ 020-8449 0145. Email administrator@barnetsynagogue.org.uk; Website www.barnet-synagogue.org.uk. *M.* Rabbi B. Lerer; *Admin.* .

Catford & Bromley Affiliated Synagogue (est. 1937), 6 Crantock Road, SE6 2QS. ☎ 020-8698 9496. *M.* Rev. Z.A. Amit. Enq. P.O. Box 4724, London SE6 2YA. *Admin.* Mrs S. Simmonds ☎ 07833-375838.

Chelsea Affiliated Synagogue, Smith Terrace, Smith Street, Chelsea, SW3 4DL. (Reg. Charity No. 1101862) ☎ 020-7351 6292. Email estheratkins@btinternet.com*M.* Rabbi M. Atkins ☎ 020-7351 6292; *Admin.* Mrs E. Atkins.

Enfield & Winchmore Hill Synagogue, 53 Wellington Road, Bush Hill Park, Middx EN1 2PG ☎ 020-8363 2697. Email enfieldsynagogue@aol.com. Website www.myshul.co.uk. (Est. 1950.) *M.* ; *Chairman Bd.* A. Sless, Email alansless@aol.com

Harold Hill and District Affliliated Synagogue, Trowbridge Road, Harold Hill, Essex RM3 8YW. (Est. 1953) *T.* D. Jacobs ☎ 020-8924 8668; *H. Sec.* Miss D. Meid, 4 Portmadoc House, Brosely Road, Harold Hill, Essex RM3 9BT ☎ 01708-348904.

Hemel Hempstead and District Affiliated Synagogue, *Admin.*

High Wycombe Affiliated Synagogue. *H. Sec.* A. Abrams, 37 Beechtree Ave., Marlow Bottom, Bucks SL7 3NH. ☎ 01628 476244.

Highams Park and Chingford Affiliated Synagogue, 81a Marlborough Road, Chingford, E4 9AJ. ☎ 020- 020-8527 0937. *M.* Rabbi A. Kahan ☎ 020-8527 5581. *Sec.* Mrs E. Herbert ☎ 020-8500 5346.

Hounslow, Heathrow and District Affiliated Synagogue, 100 Staines Road, Hounslow, Middx TW3 7LF. (Est. 1944.) ☎ 020-8572 2100. *H. Admin.* L. Gilbert, 9 Park Ave., Hounslow, Middx. TW3 2NA. ☎ 020-8894 4020.

Kingston, Surbiton and District Affiliated Synagogue, 33-35 Uxbridge Road, Kingston on Thames, Surrey KT1 2LL. (Est. 1947) (020-8546 9370. *M.* Rabbi D. Mason; *H. Admin.* Mrs C. Abrahams, 15 Albany Reach, Queens Road, Thames Ditton, KT7 0QH. ☎ 020-8224 2073. Email gerry.abrahams@ntlworld. com.

Peterborough Affiliated Synagogue, 142 Cobden Avenue, Peterborough, PEI 2NU. *Admin.* C. Salamon ☎ 01733 264151.

Potters Bar and Brookmans Park District Affiliated Synagogue, Meadowcroft, Great North Road, Bell Bar (nr. Potters Bar), Hatfield, Herts AL9 6DB. ☎/Fax 01707 656202. Email office@pottersbarshul.org.uk; Website www.pottersbarshul.org.uk. *M.* Rabbi A. S. Hill.

Romford and District Affiliated Synagogue, 25 Eastern Road, Romford, Essex RM1 3NH. ☎ 01708-741690. (Est. 1929.) *M.* J.R. Rose; *Admin.*

Ruislip and District Affiliated Synagogue, 9 Shenley Avenue, Ruislip Manor, Middx HA4 6BP. ☎ 01895 622059. Fax 01895 622059. Email secretary@ruislipsynagogue.org.uk Website www.ruislipsynagogue.org.uk (Est. 1946.) *M. Emer.* Rev D. Wolfson; *M.* Rabbi S. Coten; *Admin.* Mrs B. Hutchinson.

St Albans Synagogue, Oswald Road, St Albans, Herts AL1 3AQ. ☎ 01727 854872. Email info@stalbanssynagogue.org.uk Website www.stalbanssynagogue.org.uk.

Staines and District Affiliated Synagogue, Westbrook Road, South Street, Staines, Middx TW18 4PR. ☎ 01784-462557. Email staines.synagogue@btinternet.com. Website www.btinternet.com/-staines.synagogue. *M.* Rev. M. Binstock; *Admin.* A. Lynes ☎ 01784-458283.

Wanstead and Woodford Affiliated Synagogue, 20 Churchfields, South Woodford, E18 2QZ. ☎ 020-8504 1990. Email ww@shul-ww.org. *M.* Rabbi B. Fleischer; *Admin.* Mrs L. Appleby. (D)

Welwyn Garden City Affiliated Synagogue, Barn Close, Handside Lane, Welwyn Garden City, Herts AL8 6ST. ☎ 01707-322443. *M.* Rabbi H. Gruber. *H. Sec.* R. Rosenberg.

BURIAL SOCIETY
Finchley Office: *Man.* Mrs M. Wohlman, Finchley Synagogue, P.O. Box 9537, Kinloss Gardens, N3 3DU. ☎ 020-8343 3456. Fax 020-8346 3402 (Bushey and Willesden). Ilford Office, Schaller House, Ilford Synagogue, 22 Beehive Lane, Ilford, Essex IG1 3RT. ☎ 020-8518 2868. Fax 020-8518 2926 (Waltham Abbey, East Ham, West Ham and Plashet). *Man.* Mrs C. Block.

CEMETERIES
Willesden, Beaconsfield Road, NW10 2JE. Opened 1873. ☎ 020-8459 0394. Fax 020-8830 4582; East Ham, Marlow Road, High St. South, E6 3QG. Opened 1919. ☎ 020-8472 0554. Fax 020-8471 2822; Bushey, Little Bushey Lane, Bushey, Herts, WD2 3TP. Opened 1967. ☎ 020-8950 6299. Fax 020-8420 4973; Waltham Abbey, Skillet Hill (Honey Lane), Waltham Abbey, Essex. Opened 1960. ☎ 01992 714492. Fax 01992-650 735. Plashet, High Street North, E12 6PQ. Opened 1896. West Ham, Buckingham Road, Forest Lane, E15 1SP. Opened 1857. ☎ 020-8472 0554. Alderney Road, E1. Opened for Great Syn. in 1696 (disused). Brady street, E1. Opened for the New Syn, in 1761; subsequently used also by Great Syn. (disused); Hackney, Lauriston Road, E9. Opened for Hambro' Syn. in 1788 (disused).

Federation of Synagogues

Constituent and Affiliated Synagogues of the Federation of Synagogues, 65 Watford Way, NW4 3AQ. ☎ 020-8202 2263. Fax 020-8203 0610. Email info@ federationofsynagogues.com; Website www.federationofsynagogues.com.

CONSTITUENT SYNAGOGUES

Clapton Federation Synagogue (Sha'are Shomayim). (Incorporating Yavneh Synagogue) (in association with Springfield Synagogue) 202 Upper Clapton Road, E5 9DH,. *Sec.* W. Jacobs ☎ 020-8989 5211

Croydon & District Synagogue, The Almonds, Shirley Oaks Rd. CRO 8YW.(Est. 1908; present syn. consecrated 1995) *M.* Rev. M. Daniels; *H. Secs.* Mrs B. Harris,☎ 020 8726 0179, Mrs V. Harris. ☎ 01883-348939.

East London Central Synagogue, 30/40 Nelson Street, E1 2DE. ☎ 020-7790 9809. *M.* Rabbi Y. Austin*Sec.* J. Beninson. ☎ 07983 931178.

Finchley Central Synagogue, 2, Redbourne Avenue, N3 2BS. ☎ 020-8346 1892. *Rab.* Rabbi Y.Hamer; *Sec.* Mrs B. Needleman.

Hendon Beis Hamedrash, 65 Watford Way NW4 3AQ. *M.* Dayan Y.Y Lichtenstein; *Contact* P. Ellerman ☎ 020-8203 9030.

Ilford Federation Synagogue, 14-16 Coventry Road, Ilford, Essex IG1 4QR. ☎ 020-8554 5289. Fax 020-8554 7003. Email ilfordfeds@lineone.net. Website www.ilfordfeds.org(Est. 1927). *M.* Rabbi A. Chapper; *Sec.* Mrs L. Klein.

Machzike Hadath Synagogue, 1-4, Highfield Road, NW11 9LU. ☎ 020-8455 9816. *M.* Rabbi C. Z. Pearlman; *Sec.* R. Shaw ☎ 020-8958 0499.

Netzach Israel Synagogue, 281 Golders Green Rd., NW11 9JJ. ☎ 020-8455 0097. *M.* Rabbi D. Ahiel ☎ 020-8455 4312 *Sec.*

Ohr Yisrael Synagogue, 31-33 Theobald St., Borehamwood, Herts WD6 4RN. *M.* Rabbi R. Garson ☎ 020-8953 8385. *Contact* M. Landau ☎ 07915 605837.

Shomrei Hadath Synagogue, 64 Burrard Road, NW6 1DD. *M.* Rabbi M. Fachler; *Sec.* Mrs P. Schotten ☎ 020-7435 6906.

Sinai Synagogue, 54 Woodstock Avenue, NW11 9RJ. (Est. 1935.) *Rab.* Rabbi B. Knopfler; *Sec.* E. Cohen ☎ 020-8458 8201. (D)

Yeshurun Synagogue, Fernhurst Gdns., Stonegrove, Edgware, Middx HA8 7PH. ☎ 020-8952 5167. (Est. 1946.) *Emer.Rab.* Dayan G. Lopian; *Rab.* Rabbi A. Lewis; *Sec.* D. H. Cohen. Fax 020-8905 7439. Email admin@yeshurun.org; Website www.yeshurun.org.

AFFILIATED SYNAGOGUES

Aish Community Synagogue, (Sassover) 379 Hendon Way, NW4 3LP. M. Rabbi S. Silkin; *Sec.* Y. Ehreich. ☎ 020 8457 4444.

Congregation of Jacob, 351/353 Commercial Road, E1 2PS. ☎ 020-7790 2874. Email info@congregationofjacob.org. Website www.congregationofjacob.org. (Est. 1903.) Contact D. Brandes and D. Behr.

Fieldgate Street Great Synagogue, 41 Fieldgate Street, E1 1JU. ☎ 020-7247 2644. *Sec.* Mrs F. Treep.

Finchley Road Synagogue, 4 Helenslea Avenue, NW11. (Est. 1941.) *Rab.* Rabbi S. Freshwater. ☎ 020-8455 4305. *Contact* S. Halpern ☎ 020 8455 1814

Leytonstone & Wanstead Synagogue, 2 Fillebrook Rd., E11. *Sec. Cllr.* L. Braham. ☎ 020-8539 0088. M. Rabbi Y. Aronovitz; *Sec.* Mrs M. Lewis. Email loughtonsynagogue@lineone.net

Loughton Synagogue, Borders La., Loughton, Essex IG10 1TE. *M.* Rabbi Y. Aronovitz. ☎ 020-8418 0500. *Admin.* Mrs M. Lewis. ☎ 020-8508 0303. Email loughtonsynagogue@lineone.net.

Springfield Synagogue, 202 Upper Clapton Road, E5 9DH. (Est. 1929.) ☎ 020 8806 3167. *Rab.* Dayan I. Gukovitski; *President/Hon. Sec.* L. Blackman, ☎ 01702 340 762.

Stamford Hill Beth Hamedrash, 50 Clapton Common, E5 9AL. *M.* Dayan Grynhaus; *Sec.* M. Chontow. ☎ 020-8800 7369.

Waltham Forest Hebrew Congregation, 140 Boundary Road, E17 8LA. *M.* Rev. S. Myers; *Sec.* A. Wolpert. ☎ 020-8509 0775. Fax 020-8518 8200.Email secretary@wfhc.co.uk.

West End Great Synagogue, 32 Great Cumberland Place, W1H 7TN. ☎ 020-7724 8121. Fax 020-7723 4413. *M.* Rev. Ari Cohen; *Sec.* Mrs R. Koten.

East End synagogues are served by Rev. Gingold. ☎ 020-7790 5287.

BURIAL SOCIETY

Office: 65 Watford Way, Hendon NW4 3AQ. ☎ 020-8202 3903; Fax 020-8203 0610. *Admin.* T.

Zelmanovitz; *Sexton* N. Kahler; *Ts.* Rabbi J. Cohen, M. Ezra.
CEMETERIES
Montague Rd., Angel Road, Lower Edmonton, N18. ☎ 020-8807 2268.
Upminster Road North, Rainham, Essex. *Supt.* Rev. M. Brown ☎ 01708-552825.

UNION OF ORTHODOX HEBREW CONGREGATIONS
140 Stamford Hill, N16 6QT. ☎ 020-8802 6226 Fax 020-8809 7092.
Synagogues Associated with the Union of Orthodox Hebrew Congregations or the Burial Society.
Adath Yisroel Synagogue, 40 Queen Elizabeth's Walk, N16 0HH.☎ 020-8802 6262/3.
Rabbi Josef Zvi Dunner.
Adath Yisroel Tottenham Beth Hamedrash, 55/57 Ravensdale Road, N16. ☎ 020-8800
3978. Dayan A. D. Dunner.
Beth Abraham (Goschalks) Synagogue, 46 The Ridgeway, NW11 8QS.☎ 020-8455 2848.
Rabbi C. Schmahl.
Beth Chodosh Synagogue, 51 Queen Elizabeth's Walk, N16 5UG. ☎ 020-8809 4820. Rabbi
H. Frankel.
Beth Joseph Zvi, Schonfeld Square, Lordship Road, N16 0QQ. ☎ 020 8802 7477.
Beit Knesset Chida, Rookwood Road, N16 020 8802 0103.
Beth Shmuel Synagogue, 171 Golders Green Road, NW11 9BY. ☎ 020-8458 7511. Rabbi
E. Halpern.
Beth Sholom Synagogue, 42 St. Kilda's Road, N16 5BZ. Rabbi S. Deutsch.
Beth Talmud Centre, 78 Cazenove Road, N16.
Beth Telmund Centre, 78 Cazenove Road, N16 6AA. ☎ 020 8806 8103.
Beth Yisochor Dov Beth Hamedrash, 4 Highfield Avenue, NW11 9ET. ☎ 020 8458 1264.
Rabbi G. Hager.
Biala (Chelkas Yehoshua) Beth Hamedrash, 110 Castlewood Road, N15 6BE. Rabbi B.L.
Rabinowitz.
Bridge Lane Beth Hamedrash, 44 Bridge Lane, NW11 0EG. ☎ 020 8458 8364. Rabbi S.
Winegarten.
Chasidey Alexander Me'oron Shel Yisroel Beth Hamedrash, 9 Amhurst Park, London
N16 5DH.
Chasidey Beltz Beth Hamedrash, 99 Bethune Road, N16 5ED. ☎ 020 8802 2151. Rabbi
E.D. Friedman.
Chasidey Belz Beth Hamedrash, 96 Clapton Common, E5 9AL. ☎ 020 8802 8233. Rabbi
J.D. Babad. 49 St. Kilda's Road, N16 5BS. ☎ 020 8211 0213.
Chasidey Bobov D'Ohel Naphtoli and **Yeshiva Bnei Zion Beth Hamedrash,** 87
Eagerton Road, N16 6UE. ☎ 020 8809 0476. Rabbi B.Z. Blum.
Chasidey Ryzhin Beth Hamedrash, 33 Paget Road, N16 5ND. ☎ 020 8800 7979.
Chasidey Ryzin-Sadigur Or Yisroel Beth Hamedrash, 269 Golders Green Road, NW11
9JJ. Rabbi Y.M. Friedman.
Chasidey Sanz-Klausenburg Beth Hamedrash, 124 Stamford Hill, N16 6 QT.
☎ 020 8802 1149.
Chasidey Skver Beth Hamedrash, 47 East Bank, N16 5Pz. ☎ 020 8800 8448. Rabbi Y. Friesel.
Chasidey Wiznitz Ahavat Israel Synagogue, Wiznitz House, 89 Stamford Hill, N16 5TP.
☎ 020 8800 9359. Rabbi A. Weiss.
Chasidey Wizintz-Monsey Imrei Chaim Beth Hamedrash, 121 Clapton Common,
E5 9AB. ☎ 020 8800 3741. Rabbi D. Hager.
Cheishev Sofer D'Pressburg Beth Hamedrash, 103 Clapton Common, E5 9AB.
☎ 020 8809 1700. Rabbi S. Ludmir.
Chevras Shass Zichron Shlomo Beth Hamedrash, 11 Elm Park Avenue, N15 6UE.
☎ 020 8809 7850. Rabbi S. Meisels.
Divrei Chaim Beth Hamedrash, 71 Bridge Lane, NW11 0EE. ☎ 020 8458 1161. Rabbi
Chaim A.Z. Halpern.
Edgware Adath Yisroel Congregation, 261 Hale Lane, Edgware, Middlesex, HA8 8NX.
☎ 020 8238 2491. Rabbi Z. H. Lieberman.

Etz Chaim Yeshiva, 83/85 Bridge Lane, NW11 0EE. Rabbi Z. Rabi.
Gur Beiss Hachasidim, 98 Bridge Lane, NW11 0ER. ☎ 020 8458 6243.
Gur Beiss Hachasidim, 2 Lampard Grove, N16 6UZ. ☎ 020 8806 4333.
Gur (Avreichium) Beth Hamedrash, 122 Cazenove Road, N16.
Halaser Birkath Yehuda Beth Hamedrash, 47 Mountfield Road, N16 6DT. ☎ 020 8806 4962.
Heichal Hatorah, 27 St. Kilda's Road, N16 5BS. ☎ 020 8809 4331.Rabbi L. Rakow.
Hendon Beth Hamedrash, 3 The Approach, London NW4 2HU. ☎ 020 8202 5499. Rabbi D. Halpern.
Kehal Chareidim Beth Hamedrash, 99 Clapton Common, E5 9 AB. Rabbi A.Y. Rubinfeld.
Kehal Chareidim Beth Hamedrash, 213 Golders Green Road, NW11 9 BY. ☎ 020 8731 9583. Rabbi E. Halpern.
Kehal Chasidim D'Munkatch Synagogue, 85 Cazenove Road, N16 6BB. Rabbi Sh. Gluck.
Kehillos Yaakov Beth Hamedrash, 35 Highfield Avenue, NW11 9EU. ☎ 020 8455 3066.
Kingsley Way Beth Hamedrash, 3-5 Kingsley Way, N2 0EH.
☎ 020-8458 2312. Rabbi Y. Hertz.
Knesset Yehezkel Beth Hamedrash, 187 Golders Green Road, NW11 9BY. ☎ 020 8455 4722/3591. Rabbi A. Bassous.
Knightland Road Synagogue, 50 Knightland Road, E5 9HS. ☎ 020 8806 2963. Rabbi M. Halpern.
Kol Ya'akov Beth Hamedrash, 47 Mowbray Road, Edgware HA8 8JH. ☎ 020 8905 3254. Rabbi A. Friedman.
Lieger Beth Hamedrash Torath Chaim, 37 Craven Walk, N16 6BS. ☎ 020 8800 3868. Rabbi J. Meisels.
Lieger Beth Hamedrash Torath Chaim, 145 Upper Clapton Road, E5 9DB. ☎ 020 8806 8405. Rabbi J. Meisels.
Lubavitch Synagogue, 107-115 Stamford Hill, N16 5RP. ☎ 020 8800 0022. Rabbi N. Sudak, Dayan L.Y. Raskin. (D)
Lubavitch of Edgware, 230 Hale Lane, Edgware, Middx. HA6 9PZ. ☎ 020 8905 4141. Rabbi L.Y. Sudak.
Machzikei Hadass Edgware Beth Hamedrash, 269 Hale Lane, Edgware, Middx. HA8 8NP. ☎ 020-8958 1030. Rabbi E. Schneelbag.
Mesifta Synagogue, 82-84 Cazenove Road, N16 6AB. ☎ 020 8806 1391/5912.
Nadvorna Beth Hamedrash, 45 Darenth Road, N16 6ES. ☎ 020 8806 2030. Rabbi M. Leifer.
North Hendon Adath Yisroel Synagogue, Holders Hill Road, NW4 1NA. ☎ 020 8203 0797. Rabbi D. Cohn, Emeritus Rabbi D. Cooper.
Ohel Israel (Skoler) Synagogue, 11 Brent Street, NW4 2EU.
Ohel Yaakov Beiss Hamedrash (Pshevorsk), 126 Stamford Hill, N16 6QT. Rabbi N.E. Leiser.
Sasover Finchley Road Synagogue, 1 Helenslea Avenue, NW 11 8ND. ☎ 020 8455 4305. Rabbi S.Y. Freshwater. S
Satmar Beth Hamedrash Yetev Lev, 86 Cazenove Road, N16 6AB. ☎ 020 8806 2633. 26 Clapton Common, E5 9BA. ☎ 020 8442 4510/4511. 67 Heathland Road, N16 5PQ. ☎ 020 8809 0446. 42 Craven Wk., N16 6BU. ☎ 020 8806 2932. Rabbi C. Wosner.
Sdei Chemed D'Nitra Beth Hamedrash, 113 Clapton Common, E5. ☎ 020 8806 4828. Rabbi L. Braun.
Spinke Beth Hamedrash, 36 Bergholt Crescent, N16 6JE. ☎ 020 8809 6903. Rabbi M.M. Kahana.
Stanford Hill Beth Hamedrash, 50 Clapton Common, E5 9AL. ☎ 020 8806 8070. Dayan D. Grynhaus
Stanislowa Beth Hamedrash, 93 Lordship Park, N16 5UP. ☎ 020-8800 2040. Rabbi E. Aschkenasi.
Tiferez Amrom Beth Hamedrash, 3 Northdene Gardens, N15 6LX. Rabbi A. Jungreis.
Torah Etz Chayim Beth Hamedrash, 100 Fairholt Road, N16 5HN. ☎ 020 8800 6778. Rabbi E. Schlesinger.
Yeshivas Toras Chessed, Wellbury House, Great Offley, nr. Hitchin, Herts. ☎ 01462 768 698

& 768 925. Rabbi A.S. Stern.

Yeshuath Chaim Synagogue, 45 Heathland Road, N16 5PQ. ☎ 020 8800 2332. Rabbi C. Pinter.

Yesodey Hatorah Beth Hamedrash, 2/4 Amhurst Park, N16 5AE

Yotzei Teimon Beis Hamedrash, 118 Cazenove Road, N16. ☎ 020 8806 5906. Rabbi M. Schlesinger.

Zeire Agudath Yisroel Beth Hamedrash, 69 Lordship Road, N16 0QX.

Zeire Agudath Yisroel Beth Hamedrash, 95 Stamford Hill, N16 5DN. ☎ 020 8800 8873. Rabbi M.J. Kamionka.

ADATH YISROEL CHEVRA KADISHA
40 Queen Elizabeth's Walk, London N16 0HH. ☎ 020 8802 6262. (M) 07973 622350. *Gabai.* M. Abeles, *Chairman*: E.M. Hochhauser, *Tr.*: S.B. Stern; L Wosner, *Hon.Sec.*: D. Lobenstein.

The Assembly of Masorti Synagogues

Alexander House 3, Shakespeare Rd., London N3 1XE

☎ 020-8349 6650. Fax 020-8349 2743. Email enquiries@masorti.org.uk; Website www.masorti. org.uk.

(Est. 1985. Reg. Charity No. 1117590). *Exec. Dir.* M. Gluckman; *Chairman* M. Burman.

New London Synagogue. 33 Abbey Road, NW8 0AT. ☎ 020-7328 1026. Fax 020-7372 3142. Email office@newlondon.org.uk.Website www.newlondon.org.uk (Est. 1964 by Rabbi Dr Louis Jacobs). *R.* Rabbi J. Gordon, *M.* S. Corsen ; *Chairman* A. Marks; *Exec. Dir.* R. Cohen; *Sec.* S. Koffman.

New North London Synagogue, The Manor House, 80 East End Road, N3 2SY. ☎ 020-8346 8560. Fax 020-8346 9710. Email office@nnls-masorti.org.uk. Website www.nnls-masorti.org.uk. (Est. 1974.) An independent traditional com. following the philosophy of Rabbi Dr L. Jacobs. *M.* Rabbi J. Wittenberg;. *Co-Chairpersons* N. Brill, V. Kennard; *T.* B. Manson; *Sec.*B. Shall; *Off.* C. Mandel; *Community Co-ord.* R. Gottlieb.

Edgware Masorti Synagogue. Synagogue Office/Post/Weekly entrance: Pearl Community Centre, Stream Lane, Edgware, Middx. HA8 7YA. (Reg. Charity No. 1117623.) Shabbat entrance: Bakery Path (off Station Road), Edgware, Middx. HA8 7YE. ☎ 020-8905 4096. Fax 020-8905 4333. Email admin@ edgwaremasorti.org. *M.* Rabbi Dr Jeremy Collick; *Co-Chairpersons* H. Segal, M. Sobell;. *T.* S. Arnold; *Admin.* Mrs L. Lassman.

Elstree & Borehamwood Masorti Community *Contact:* Tony DeSwarte ☎ 020-8953 3673 or via Email info@ebmc.org.uk.

Hatch End Masorti, *Chairman* D. Benson ☎ 020-8866 0320. Email office@hems.org.uk. *M.* Rabbi D. Soetendorp; *Admin.* K. Grout.

Kol Nefesh Masorti Synagogue, PO Box 204, Edgware, Middx HA8 7FQ. (Reg. Charity No. 1081444). Enq. ☎ 0776 980 7356. Email knm@kolnefeshmasorti.org.uk. Website www.kolnefeshmasorti.org.uk. *Chairman* M. Fenster; *M.* Rabbi Joel Levy.

New Essex Masorti Synagogue, Services: Roding Valley Hall, Station Way, Buckhurst Hill, Essex IG9 6LN. Office: c/o 45 Arabia Close, London E4 7DU. ☎ 07922 090180. Email nemasorti@ hotmail.com; Website www.way.2shul.org. *Chairman* G. Sasson.

New Whetstone Synagogue, Enquiries: 020-8368 3936. *Chairman* E. Slater.

St Albans Masorti Synagogue, P.O. Box 23, St Albans, Herts AL1 4PH. *M.* ; *Co-Chairs* L.Harris, Mrs L. McQuillan; *Sec.* Mrs K. Phillips ☎ 01727 860642. Email info@e-sams.org. Website www.e-sams.org.

Independent Congregations

Belsize Square Synagogue, 51 Belsize Square, London NW3 4HX. ☎ 020-7794 3949. Fax 020-7431 4559. Email office@synagogue.org.uk; Website www.synagogue. org.uk. (Est. 1939. Reg. Charity No. 233742.) An Independent Synagogue combining traditional forms of worship with progressive ideals. *M.* Rabbi Rodney J. Mariner; *Cantor* N. Cohen Falah; *Admin.* H.Levin; *Chairman*; *H. T.* Paul Burger; *H. Sec.* V. Pollins.

Golders Green Beth Hamedrash Congregation, The Riding, Golders Green Road, NW11 8HL. ☎ 020-8455 2974. (Est. 1934.) *Rab.* Rabbi Y. M. Greenberg; *R.* Rev. N. Gluck.

Hendon Adath Yisroel Synagogue, 11 Brent Street, NW4 2EU. ☎ 020 8202 9183. Rabbi P. Roberts.

Ner Yisrael, The Crest (off Brent St.), Hendon, NW4 2HY. ☎ 020-8202 6687. Fax 020-8203 5158. Website www.neryisrael.co.uk. *M.* Rabbi A.A. Kimche. ☎ 020-8455 7347. *Admin.* Mrs L. Brayam, Email secretary@neryisrael.co.uk.

Ohel Avraham, P.O. Box 48502, London NW4 2XA. ☎ 020-8202 8021. Email info@ohelavraham.org.uk. Website www.yakarkehilla.org.uk. (Est. 2002 as successor to the Yakar Kehilla). *Chairman* S. Brookes; *Vice-Chairman* R. Mankin.

Porat Yosef (Est. 1988.), Moroccan Hebrew Congregation. 9A Burroughs Gardens, Hendon, NW4 4AU. ☎ 020-8203 9989. Email levy.benarroch@gmail.com. *President* Jacques Onona; *Sec.* B. Benarroch.

Saatchi Synagogue (Est. 1998. Reg. Charity No. 289066), 37-41 Grove End Road, NW8 9NG ☎ 020-7289 2367. Fax 020-7266 2123. Email hayley@saatchishul.org; Website www.csaatchishul.org. *Admin.* Mrs H. Bartman; *Community Dir.* S. Klein.

Sandy's Row Synagogue (est. 1854), Sandy's Row, , E1 7HW. *President* I. Kingsley, *Sec.* J. Lissner, *T.* H. Freedman, *Exec. Off.* J. Harari. ☎ 07977 923118.Email sandys.row@hotmail.co.uk Website www.sandysrow.org.uk(D).

Sarah Klausner Synagogue, 10A Canfield Gardens NW6 ☎ 020-7722 6146.

Synagogue Française de Londres (La), 101 Dunsmure Road, N16 5HT. Le Grand Rabbin Henri Brand, 54 Bethune Road, N16 5BD. ☎ 020-8800 8612. *H. T.* Rabbi C. Pinter; *H. Sec.* I. Kraus.

Walford Road Synagogue, 99 Walford Road, Stoke Newington, N16 8EF. ☎ 020 7249 1599. (Reg. Charity no. 1101200) *M.* ; *Sec.* S. Raymond.

Waltham Forest Hebrew Congregation, 140 Boundary Road, E17 8LA. Email secretary@wfhc.co.uk (Est. 1902.) ☎ Off.: 020-8509 0775. Fax 020-8518 8200. *M.* Revd S. Myers; *President* R. Jacobs; *Admin.* A. Wolpert. (D)

West End Great Synagogue, 32 Great Cumberland Place, W1H 7TN. ☎ 020-7724 8121. Fax 020-7723 4413 (Est. 1880.) *M.* Ari Cohen; *Admin.* Mrs R. Koten.

  Chesed V'Emeth. Cemeteries: Rowan Road, Greyhound Lane, SW16. (020-8764 1566; Cheshunt Cemetery (Western), Bullscross Ride, Cheshunt, Herts. ☎ 01992 717820.

Affiliated Synagogues: retaining burial rights: *Commercial Road Great Syn., Teesdale Street Syn., *Great Garden Street Syn., *Cong. of Jacob, *Ezras Chaim Syn., *Nelson Street Sephardish Syn., Sandy's Row Syn., *Fieldgate St. Syn.

The synagogues marked * still have a section of members affiliated for burial rights under the Federation of Synagogues.

Western Marble Arch Synagogue, successor to the Western Synagogue (est. 1761) and the Marble Arch Synagogue, 32 Great Cumberland Place, W1H 7TN. ☎ 020-7723 9333. Fax 020-7224 8065. Email office@wma-synagogue.org. *M.* Rabbi L. Rosenfeld; *President* P. Faiman; *Exec. Sec.* Stephen Garcia. Affiliated for burial rights with Western Charitable Foundation in the following Cemeteries: Edmonton, Montague Road, N18, Bullscross Ride, Cheshunt, Herts; *Supt.* R. Ezekiel, Bullscross Ride, Cheshunt, Herts. ☎ 01992 717820.

Affiliated Orgs.: Western Charitable Foundation. *Chairman* S. Jaque, J.P.; *Vice Chairman* Mr H. Pasha; *Tr.* A.H. Yadgaroff.

Westminster Synagogue (Est. 1957), Rutland Gdns., Knightsbridge, SW7 1BX. ☎ 020-7584 3953. Fax 020-7581 8012. secretary@westminstersynagogue.org. www.westminstersynagogue.org. *M.* Rabbi T. Salamon; *Rabbi Educator* Rabbi R Qassim Birk; *President* E. Glover ; *Chairman* H.D. Leigh.

Sephardi

Spanish and Portuguese Jews' Congregation (Reg. Charity No. 212517)

2 Ashworth Rd, Maida Vale, W9 1JY. ☎ 020-7289 2573. Fax 020-7289 2709. *Admin.* H. Miller. Email howardmiller@spsyn.org.uk.

SYNAGOGUES

Bevis Marks (1701), EC3A 5DQ. ☎ 020-7626 1274. Fax 020-7283 8825. Rabbi Dr A. Levy, OBE, BA; Rabbi N. Asmoucha; *M.* Rev. H. Benarroch, BA.

Lauderdale Road Syn. (1896), Maida Vale, W9 1JY.☎ 020-7289 2573. Fax 020-7289 2709. *Rabbi & M.* Rabbi Dr A. Levy, OBE, BA; Rabbi I. Elia.

Wembley Synagogue, 46 Forty Ave., Wembley, Middx HA9 8LQ. ☎ 020-7289-2573. Fax 020-8904-9912 Email secretary@wsps.org.uk. Rabbi Dr. A. Levy OBE, BA; *M.* Rev. J. Houri.

Sir Moses Montefiore Synagogue, Honeysuckle Road, Ramsgate, Kent.

OTHER INSTITUTIONS

Burial Society, 2 Ashworth Road, W9 1JY. ☎ 020-7289 2573.

Welfare Board, 2 Ashworth Road, W9 1JY. ☎ 020-7289 2573. (Est. 1837.)

Sephardi Kashrut Authority, 2 Ashworth Road, W9 1JY. ☎ 020-7289 2573. *Chairman* E. Cohen; *Dir.* D. Steinhof.

Communal Centre, Montefiore Hall, 2 Ashworth Road, W9 1JY. ☎ 020-7289 2573.

Beth Hamedrash Heshaim (Instituted 1664), 2 Ashworth Road, W9 1JY. ☎ 020-7289 2573. *T.* Dr. J. Schonfield.

Montefiore Endowment at Ramsgate (incorporating the **Judith Lady Montefiore College Trust**), 2 Ashworth Road, W9 1JY. (☎ 020-7289 2573.) Est. by Sir Moses Montefiore 1866. The purpose of the Endowment (reviewed by the Charity Commission in 1989) 'is the maintenance of the Synagogue, the Mausoleum and the Jewish Cemetery in Ramsgate', and 'the promotion of the advanced study of the Holy Law as revealed on Sinai and expounded by the revered sages of the Mishna and Talmud' by making grants to charitable institutions for the training of Orthodox Jewish Teachers, Ministers and Rabbis and by awarding scholarships to such trainees.

The Mausoleum with the remains of Sir Moses and Lady Montefiore is situated next to the Synagogue in Ramsgate (see above). Sir Moses's seats in Bevis Marks and Ramsgate Syns. are still preserved.

Edinburgh House (Beth Holim), 36/44 Forty Avenue, Wembley. (Est. 1747.) Home for the Aged. *Hd. of Home* C. Gibson. ☎ 020-8908 4151. Email enquiries@edinburghhouse.org.uk

CEMETERIES

253 Mile End Rd., E1. (Disused.) Opened in 1657, the oldest Jewish burial ground in the United Kingdom. 329 Mile End Road, E1. (Opened 1725. Disused.) Hoop Lane, Golders Green, NW11. *Keeper* J. Crompton. ☎ 020-8455 2569. Edgwarebury Lane, Edgware. ☎ 020-8958 3388. *Keeper* J. Crompton. Dytchleys, Coxtie Green, Brentwood. (Disused.)

Independent Sephardi Synagogues

Aden Jews' Congregation, 117 Clapton Common, E5. *H. Sec.* B. Jacobs. ☎ 020-8806 1320.

David Ishag Synagogue, Neveh Shalom Community, 352-4 Preston Road, Harrow, Middx., HA3 0QJ. *H. Secs.* E. Myers ☎ 020-8346 9850 , M. Sullam. ☎ 020-8904 3009.

Eastern Jewry Community (Est. 1955.) Newbury Park Station, Newbury Park. *M.* Rabbi C. Tangy; *H. Sec.* D. Elias. ☎ 020-8809 4387.

Hekhal Leah, 62 Brent Street, NW4 2ES. ☎ 020-8203 6210. *M.* Rabbi Mordechai Nissim.

Ilford Congregation (), Newbury Park Station, Ilford. *H. Sec.* ☎ 020-8809 4387. Fax 020-8809 4441; 020-8458 1468.

Jacob Benjamin Elias Synagogue (Reg. Charity No. 291531), 140 Stamford Hill, N16 6QT. *M.* Rabbi C. Tangy; *H. Sec.* B. Abraham. ☎ 020-8809 4387. Fax 020-8809 4387.

Od Yosef Hai Synagogue, 50 Finchley Lane, NW4 1DJ. *M.* Dayan A. David ☎ 020-8202 8374; 020-8203 5701.

Ohel David Eastern Synagogue, Lincoln Institute, Broadwalk Lane, Golders Green Road, NW11. (Reg. Charity No. 243901) *M.* Rabbi Abraham Gubbay; ☎ 020-8455 8125. *H. Sec.*

Persian Hebrew Congregation, 5a East Bank, Stoke Newington, N16 5RX. (020-8802 7339.

Spanish & Portuguese Synagogue, Holland Park (Est. 1928 under Deed of Association with Spanish and Portuguese Jews' Congregation. Reg. Charity No. 248945), 8 St James's Gdns., W11 4RB. ☎ 020-7603 7961/3232. Fax 020-7603 9471. Email admin@holland parksynagogue.com. Website www.hollandparksynagogue.com. *Admin.* Samantha Hamilton.

Reform

(Constituents of the Movement for Reform Judaism), The Sternberg Centre for Judaism, 80 East End Road, N3 2SY. *Head of Movement* Rabbi Tony Bayfield. ☎ 020-8349 5640. Fax 020-8349 5699. Email admin@reformjudaism.org.uk.

West London Synagogue of British Jews (Reg. Charity No. 212143), 34 Upper Berkeley Street, W1. Office, 33 Seymour Place, W1H 5AU. ☎ 020-7723 4404. Fax 020-7224 8258. Email admin@wls.org.uk

The congregation was organised April 15, 1840, to establish a synagogue 'where a revised service may be performed at hours more suited to our habits and in a manner more calculated to inspire feelings of devotion, where religious instruction may be afforded by competent persons, and where, to effect these purposes, Jews generally may form a united congregation under the denomination of British Jews.'

Senior M. Rabbi Mark Winer, PhD, DD; *M.* Rabbi Helen Freeman, Rabbi M. Cohen; *President M.* Bentata; *Chairman* J. Lass; *Exec. Dir.* A Shapiro.

Funerals: ☎ 020-7723 4404. Fax 020-7224 8258.

Cemeteries: Golders Green, Hoop Lane, NW11; Edgwarebury, Edgwarebury Lane, Middx. *Man* J. Crompton. ☎ 020-8958 3388.

Bromley Reform Synagogue (Est. 1964. Reg. Charity No. 1098431). 28 Highland Road, Bromley, Kent BR1 4AD. ☎ 020-8460 5460. *M.* Rabbi Tony Hammond; *Admin.* J. Burlem. Email janet@bromleyshul.org.uk.

Edgware and District Reform Synagogue, (Reg. Charity No. 1038116). 118 Stonegrove, Edgware, HA8 8AB. (Est. 1934.) ☎ 020-8238 1000. Fax 020-8905 4710. Email admin@edrs.org.uk; Website www.edrs.org.uk. *M.* Rabbi A.D. Smith, MA; *Assoc. M.* Rabbi N. S. Kraft, MA; *Admin.* Mrs K. B. Senitt.

Finchley Reform Synagogue,101, Fallow Court Avenue, North Finchley, N12 0BE. ☎ 020-8446 3244. Fax 020-8446 5980. *M.* Rabbi M. Berger; *Emer. Rabbi* J. Newman; *Admin.* Email frs@frsonline.org.

Harlow Jewish Community, Harberts Road, Hare Street, Harlow, Essex CM19 4DT. ☎ 01279-432503; 01279 792926 *M.* Rabbi I. Shiller; *Sec.* C. Petar. Email admin@harlow jewish.uk.

Hendon Reform Synagogue, Danescroft Avenue, NW4 2NA (Est. 1949.) ☎ 020-8203 4168. Fax 020-8203 9385. *M.* Rabbi S. Katz; *Admin.* Mrs R. Bloom. Email office@hendon-reform.org.uk. Website www.hendonreform.org.uk. Cemeteries: Edgwarebury Lane, New Southgate Cemetery, Brunswick Park Road, N11. ☎ 020-8203 4168.

Kol Chai-Hatch End Jewish Community (Reg. Charity No. 299063), 434 Uxbridge Road, Hatch End, Middx HA5 4RG. ☎ 020-8421 5482. Fax 020-8421 5948. Email admin@kolchai.org. *M.* Rabbi M. Hilton; *Admin.* Mrs D. Levy.

Middlesex New Synagogue, 39 Bessborough Road, Harrow, HA1 3BS. ☎ 020-8864 0133. Fax 020-8864 5323. (Est. 1959.) *M.Emer* Rabbi S.J. Franses; M. Rabbi K. DE Magtige-Middleton; *Sec.* Mrs A. Simon. Email admin@mns.org.uk.

North West Surrey Synagogue (Est. 1956. Reg Charity no. 256232), Horvath Close, Rosslyn Pk., Oatlands Dr, Weybridge, Surrey KT13 9QZ. ☎/Fax 01932 855400 Email admin@nwss.org.uk; Website www.nwss.org.uk. *M.* Rabbi Jacqueline Tabick; *H. Sec.* S. Barnett; *Admin.* Ms L. Baitman.

North Western Reform Synagogue, Alyth Gdns., Finchley Road, NW11 7EN. ☎ 020-8455 6763. Fax 020-8731 8175. Email mail@alyth.org. (Est. 1933; Reg. Charity No. 247081.) *Emer M.* Rabbi C. Emanuel; *Principal M.* Rabbi M. Goldsmith, Rabbi L. Janner-Klausner, Rabbi J. Levy; *Admin.* M. Lee. (D)

Radlett & Bushey Reform Synagogue, 118 Watling Street, Radlett, Herts WD7 7AA. ☎ 01923 856110. Fax 01923-858444. Email office@rbrs.org.uk. *M.* Rabbi P. Freedman; *Admin.* Ms J. Becker.

Shir Hayim (Hampstead Reform Jewish Community), 37a, Broadhurst Gdns., NW6 3QT. Email mail@shirhayim.org.uk. *M.* Rabbi L. Tabick; *Contact* M. Teper. ☎ 020-7794 8488.

South West Essex and Settlement Reform Synagogue (Est. 1956. Reg. Charity No. 236663), Oaks Lane, Newbury Park, Essex IG2 7PL. ☎ 020-8599 0936. Fax 020-8597 9164. Email admin@swesrs.org.uk.*Emer.* Rabbi H. Goldstein, L. Rigal *M.* Rabbi M. Michaels, Rabbi M. Pertz; *Office* Mrs C. Gardiner.

Southgate and District Reform Synagogue (Reg. Charity No. 1076670), 120 Oakleigh Road North, Whetstone N20 9EZ. ☎ 020-8445 3400. Fax 020-8445 3737. *M.* Rabbi C. Eimer, Rabbi M. Plumb, Rabbi D. Kahn-Harris; *Admin.* Mrs R. Minsky. Email info@sdrs.org.uk.

Sukkat Shalom (Reg. Charity No. 283615). 1 Victory Road, Hermon Hill, Wamstead, E11 1UL. ☎ 020-8530 3345. *M.* ; *Admin.* F. Godson. Email admin@sukkatshalom.co.uk.

Wimbledon and District Synagogue, 1 Queensmere Rd., Wimbledon Parkside, SW19 5QD. ☎ 020-8946 4836 Fax 020-8944 7790. Email office@wimshul.org. Website www.wimshul.org. (Est. 1949. Reg. Charity No. 1040712) *M.* Rabbi Sylvia Rothschild, Rabbi Sybil Sheridan; *Admin.* Ms A. Wilson.

Jewish Joint Burial Society (serving Reform & Masorti communities), 1 Victory Road, Wanstead E11 1UL. ☎ 020-8989 5252. Fax 020-8989 6075.
Email funerals.jjbs@btconnect.com. (Est. 1968; Reg. Charity no. 257345). *Sexton* C.R. Joseph, *Asst. Sexton* Ms M. Kalinsky

Liberal Judaism

(Former ULPS), The Montagu Centre, 21 Maple St., London W1T 4BE. *Chairman* N. Cole; *Chief Exec.* Rabbi D. Rich *Outreach Dir.* Rabbi A. Goldstein. ☎ 020-7580 1663. Fax 020-7631 9838. Email montagu@liberal judaism.org Website www.liberaljudaism.org.

Bedfordshire Progressive Synagogue (Rodef Shalom) c/o Liberal Judaism, The Montagu Centre, 21 Maple St., W1T 4BE. ☎ 01234 218387. Email bedsps@liberaljudaism.org.Website www.bedfordshire-ps.org.uk

Beit Klal Yisrael, PO Box 1828, London W10 5RT. *M Emer* Rabbi S. Shulman. *Sec* J. Burden.. ☎ 07505 477459. Email info@beit-klal-yisrael.org.uk. Website www.beit-klal-yisrael.org.uk

Bet Tikvah Synagogue (Barkingside) (Reg. Charity No. 283547), 129 Perrymans Farm Road, Barkingside, Ilford, Essex IG2 7LX. *Sec.* S. Spivack. ☎ 020-8554 9682. Email bettikvah@talk-talkbusiness.net.. *M.* Rabbi D. Hulbert.

Ealing Liberal Synagogue, Lynton Av., Drayton Green, Ealing, W13 0EB. ☎ 020-8997 0528. Email office@ealingsynagogue.org.uk (Est. 1943. Reg. Charity No. 1037099) *M.* Rabbi J. Burden; *Admin.* P. Spencer.

Finchley Progressive Synagogue (Reg. Charity no. 1071040), 54 Hutton Gro., N12 8DR (Est. 1953.) ☎ 020-8446 4063. Email fps@liberaljudaism.org. *M.* Rabbi N. Janes; *Admin.* Mrs R. Lester.

Harrow & Wembley Progressive Synagogue, 326 Preston Road, Harrow, HA3 0QH. (Reg. Charity No. 251172) ☎ 020-8904 8581. Fax 020-8904 6540. Email hwps@liberaljudaism.org Website www.hwps.org (Est. 1947.) *M.* Rabbi Frank Dabba Smith; *Admin.* W. Farrell Email wendy-farrell@hwps.org.

Kingston Liberal Synagogue, Rushett Road, Long Ditton, Surrey, KT7 0UX., Reg. Charity No. 270792. ☎ 020-8398 7400. Fax 020-8873 2405. Email kls@liberaljudaism.org. *M.* Rabbi C. Baginsky; *Chair* P. Levene; *Admin.* M. McHale.

The Liberal Jewish Synagogue (Reg. Charity No. 235668), 28 St. John's Wood Road, London, NW8 7HA. ☎ 020-7286 5181. Fax 020-7266 3591. Email ljs@liberaljudaism.org. Website www.ljs.org. Est. 1910 by the Jewish Religious Union, the LJS, as it is known, was the first Liberal synagogue in the UK. Syn. rebuilt 1991. *Chairman* R. Adler; *Rabbi Emeritus* Dr J. D. J. Goldberg OBE; *Senior Rabbi* Rabbi A. Wright; *M.* Rabbi M. Solomon; *Admin. Dir.* M. A. Burman.

Liberal Synagogue Elstree, High Street, Elstree, Herts. WD6 3EY. ☎ 020-8953 8889. *M.* Rabbi P. Tobias; *H. Sec.* R. Elman ☎ 020-8953 8889. Email office@tlse.org.uk Website www.tlse.org.uk.

North London Progressive Jewish Community (Est. 1921), PO Box 42702, N19 5WR. ☎ 020-7403 3779. M. Rabbi Shulamit Ambalu *Admin* J. Chalfen. Email nlpjc@liberaljudaism.org. Website www.nlpjc.org.uk.

Northwood and Pinner Liberal Synagogue, Oaklands Gate, Green La., Northwood HA6 3AA. Email npls@liberaljudaism.org (Est. 1964. Reg. Charity No. 243618) *M. Emer* Rabbi Dr A. Goldstein; *Sen. Rabbi* A. Goldstein; *Asst* Rabbi H. Athias-Robles; *H. Sec.* S. Frais. ☎ 01923 822592. Fax 01923-824454. Email admin@npls.org. uk.

South London Liberal Synagogue, (Reg. Charity No. 2367711), 1 Prentis Rd., Streatham, SW16 1QB (PO Box 14475, SW16 1ZW). (Est. 1929.) ☎ 020-8769 4787. Fax 020-8664 6439. Email slls@liberaljudaism.org. Website www.southlondon.org. *Student Rabbi* Janet Darley; *Admin.* Mrs R. Edwards.

Southgate Progressive Synagogue, 75 Chase Road, N14 4QY. (Reg. Charity No. 239096). ☎020-8886 0977. Fax 020-8886 0977. Email sps@liberaljudaism.org. Website www.sps.uk.com. (Est. 1943.) *M.* Rabbi S. Howard; *Sec.* Mrs B. Martin.

West Central Liberal Synagogue, The Montagu Centre, 21, Maple St., W1T 4BE. ☎ 020-7636 7627. Fax 020-7631 9838. Email wcls@liberaljudaism.org.
Website www. wcls.org.uk. (Cong. est. 1928; present syn. opened 1954.) *M.* Rabbi Janet Burden; *Cantor* Rev. A. Harman ALCM; *Chairman*: Dr L. Hepner; *H. Sec.* D. Mendez.

Woodford Progressive Synagogue, Marlborough Road, South Woodford, E18 1AR. (Est. 1960. Reg. Charity No. 232980). *M.* Rabbi R. Jacobi; *Chair* D. Janoff; *Hon.Sec.* J. Toffell; *H.Ts* M. Millenbach, J. Rabin. ☎/Fax 020-8989 7619. Email info@woodfordliberal.org.uk. Website www.woodfordliberal.org.uk.

CEMETERIES
Funeral-Dir. Martin Broad and Son. ☎ 020-8445 2797. Fax 020-8343 9463.
Edgwarebury Lane, Edgware, Middx. ☎ 020-8958 3388. *Supt.* T. Zelmanovits.
Liberal Jewish Cemetery, Pound Lane, Willesden, NW10. *Supt.* A. O'Brian. ☎ 020-8459 1635.
Western Cemetery, Bulls Cross Ride, Cheshunt, Herts. EN7 5HT. ☎ 01992 717820. *Supt.* A. Harris.

Religious Organisations
The London Eruvim
The North West London Eruv. was inaugurated in February 2003, The area covered by the eruv includes virtually all of NW4 and NW11, most of N2 and N3; and small parts of NW2, NW3 and NW7. This Eruv is under the supervision of Dayan Chanoch Ehrentreu
Contact: North West London Eruv Committee, 34, Fairholme Gardens, N3 3EB Website www.nwlondoneruv.org. ☎ 020-8202 ERUV/ 0202-8202 3788
The **Edgware Eruv** was inaugurated in 2006. The area covered by the eruv includes parts of HA8 and NW7. This eruv is under the supervision of Rabbi Zvi Lieberman of the Edgware Adath Yisroel Congregation and with the support and approval of Dayan Chanoch Ehrentreu
Contact: Edgware Eruv Committee, PO Box 594, Edgware, Middlesex HA8 4EE. Email info@edgware.eruv.org (Reg. Charity No. 1111850) Website www.edgwareeruv.org.
Both websites offer detailed maps of their jurisidictions. The Eruvim are inspected every week to check they are intact. This can be ascertained by visiting the respective websites after 12 noon on Friday. Observers of the Eruvim are invited to subscribe to the respective services maintained.

Association of United Synagogue Women. (Est. 1968.) The Association promotes the interests and involvement of women as an integral part of the United Synagogue. It aims to promote and facilitate Jewish cultural and educational schemes that strengthen Orthodox traditional Jewish values. It represents women in Synagogue and communal affairs and also acts in an advisory capacity to Ladies Groups. *Hon. L. President* Lady Jakobovits; *Life President* Lady Sacks; *Chair* Mrs I. Leeman; *Corr. Sec.* Mrs P. Evans, c/o United Synagogue, Adler House, 735 High Rd., N12 0US. ☎ 020-8343 8989. Fax 020-

8343 6262.
London Board for Shechita (Reg. Charity No. 233467), 1st Floor, Elscot House, Arcadia Ave, N3 2JU. ☎ 020-8349 9160. Fax 020-8346 2209. Email info@shechita.co.uk. (Est. 1804.) To administer the affairs of Shechita in London having an elected membership from the United Synagogue, the Federation of Synagogues and the Spanish and Portuguese Jews' Congregation. *President* S.D. Winegarten; *V. Presidents* M. Brodie, O. Samuel; *H. T. L.* Winter; *Exec. Dir.* D. J. Rose. Website www. shechita.org
Sabbath Observance Employment Bureau (Est. 1909. Reg. Charity No. 209451), Unit 2, 107 Gloucester Place, W1U 6BY. ☎ 020-7224 3433. To obtain employ-ment for those desirous of observing the Sabbath and Holy-days. *Trs* I.M. Katz, S.D. Winegarten; *Man.* Mrs E. Statham; *Chairman.* D. Winter, FCA.

Ritual Baths (Mikvaot)

Central Mikvaot Board, 140 Stamford Hill, N16 6QT. ☎ 020-8802 6226.
Borehamwood & Elstree Mikvah, Croxdale Rd., Borehamwood, WD6 4QF. ☎ 07504 927066;. ☎ 020-8387 1945. Email mikveh@borehamwoodshul.org. Website www.boreham-woodshul.org
Edgware & District Communal Mikvah, Edgware United Synagogue, Edgware Way, Edgware, Middlesex. (Reg. Charity No. 281586). ☎ 020-8958 3233. Fax 020-8958 4004. Email mikveh@estrin.co.uk. Gen. enquiries: Mrs Mandy Estrin ☎ 020-8958 4488, 020-8621 4488, 0780 1332508.
Ilford Mikveh, 463 Cranbrook Road, Ilford, IG2 6EW Appointments and corr. 367 Cranbrook Rd., Ilford, IG1 4UQ. ☎ 020-8554 8532.
Kingsbury Mikvah, see below. United Synagogue Mikvah.
Lordship Park Mikvah, 55 Lordship Park, N16 (entrance in Queen Elizabeth's Walk). ☎ 020-8800 9621 (day) 020-8800 5801 (evening).
Mikveh of the Movement for Reform Judaism, Sternberg Centre, 80 East End Rd., N3 2SY. Appointments essential. ☎ 020-8349 2568. Email sylvia.morris @reformjudaism. org. uk
New Central London Mikveh, 21 Andover Place, NW6 5ED. Appointments ☎ 07870 696 570, 07989 858 615.
North London Mikvah, adjoining 40 Queen Elizabeth's Walk, N16 (entrance, Grazebrook Road). ☎ 020-8802 2554. Fax 020-8800 8764. *H. Sec.* M. Mannes.
North West London Communal Mikvah, 40/42 Golders Green Crescent, NW11 8PD. ☎ 020 8457 5900, 020-8731 9494. 10a Shirehall Lane, Hendon, NW4, by appointment. (Yomtov and Fridays only) ☎ 020-8202 1427.
Satmar Mikvah, 62 Filey Avenue, N16. ☎ 020-8806 3961.
South London Mikvah, 42 St. George's Rd., Wimbledon SW19 4ED. (Reg. Charity No. 1009208) ☎ 020-8944 7149. Email sarah@dubov.org. *Hon. Sec.* L. Cohen. *Contact:* Mrs S. Dubov.
Stamford Hill Mikvah, 26 Lampard Grove, N16 (entrance in Margaret Road). ☎ 020-8806 3880.
United Synagogue Mikvah, Kingsbury United Synagogue, Kingsbury Green, NW9 8XR. ☎ 020-8204 6390. *Chairman* Mrs F. Frank. *General Enq.* ☎ 020-8958 4121 (See also Friends Group, p.88.)

Memorials

Holocaust Memorial and Garden, Hyde Park, near Hyde Park Corner. Opened in July 1983, on a site given to the Board of Deputies by the British Government.
Holocaust Memorial, Waltham Abbey Cemetery, Skillet Hill, Honey La., Waltham Abbey, Essex. Consecrated 1985 under U.S. auspices.
Holocaust Memorial, Rainham Cemetery, Upminster Road North, Rainham, Essex.
Holocaust Memorial, Sternberg Centre, 80 East End Road, Finchley N3.
Kindertransport, plaque at the House of Commons.
Memorial in Willesden Jewish Cemetery, Beaconsfield Road, NW10, to Jewish Servicemen and Women in the British Armed Forces who died in the two World Wars and

have no known graves. Annual service organised by Ajex.

Prisoners' Memorial, Gladstone Park, Dollis Hill Lane, NW2, to those who died in prisoner-of-war camps and concentration camps during the Second World War. Annual service jointly org. by Ajex and the Royal Brit. Legion.

RAF Church, crypt of St Clements Danes, Strand. Memorial plaque with 12 tribes emblems to British and Israeli RAF personnel in the Second World War.

Raoul Wallenberg statue in Great Cumberland Place.

Royal Fusiliers, City of London Regiment Memorial, High Holborn, by City boundary. The names of the 38th, 39th and 40th Battalions are inscribed on the monument, together with all other battalions which served in the First World War. Ajex is represented at the annual service.

Cemeteries

US = United Synagogue. F = Federation of Synagogues. UO = Union of Orthodox Hebrew Congregations. SP = Spanish and Portuguese Synagogue. W = Western Marble Arch Synagogue. WG = West End Great Synagogue. R = Reform. L = Liberal.

Alderney Road Cemetery (disused), E1. ☎ 020-8790 1445. (US).

Brady Street Cemetery, E1. (US).

Bullscross Ride Cemetery, Cheshunt, Herts. ☎ 01992 717820 (W, L and WG)

Bushey Cemetery, Little Bushey Lane, Bushey, Herts. ☎ 020-8950 6299. (US).

East Ham Cemetery, Marlow Road, High St. South, E6. (US). ☎ 020-8472 0554.

Edgwarebury Cemetery, Edgwarebury Lane, Edgware, Middx. ☎ 020-8958 3388. (SP, R and L.).

Edmonton Federation Cemetery, Montagu Road, Angel Road, Lower Edmonton, N18. ☎ 020-8807 2268. (F).

Enfield Cemetery, Carterhatch Lane, Enfield, Middx. ☎ 020-8363 3384. (UO).

Hackney Cemetery (disused), Lauriston Road, E9. ☎ 020-8985 1527. (US).

Hoop Lane Cemetery, Golders Green, NW11. ☎ 020-8455 2569. (SP and R).

Kingsbury Road Cemetery, Balls Pond Road, N1. (R).

Liberal Jewish Cemetery, Pound Lane and Harlesden Road, NW10. (L).

Mile End Road (disused), E1. (SP).

Plashet Cemetery, High St. North E12. ☎ 020-8472 0554. (US). [Closed except prior to New Year].

Queen's Elm Parade Cemetery (disused), Fulham Road, SW3. (W).

Rainham Cemetery, Upminster Road North, Rainham, Essex. ☎ 017085-52825. (F).

Rowan Road Cemetery, Greyhound Lane, SW16. ☎ 020-8764 1566. (WG).

Silver Street Cemetery, Cheshunt, Herts. ☎ 020-8802 6262, 01707 874220 (UO).

Waltham Abbey Cemetery, Skillet Hill (Honey Lane), Waltham Abbey, Essex. ☎ 01992 714492. (US).

West Ham Cemetery, Buckingham Road, Forest Lane, E15. ☎ 020-8472 0554. (US).

Western Synagogue Cemetery, Montagu Road, N18. ☎ 020-8971 7820. (W).

Willesden Cemetery, Beaconsfield Road, NW10. ☎ 020-8459 0394. (US).

Educational Organisations

Withdrawal on Friday Afternoons:

When the Sabbath begins at 5 p.m. or earlier, parents of Jewish children attending either State or State-aided schools can request that their children be withdrawn at such time as to reach their homes before the commencement of the Sabbath. Such requests should be submitted to the Head Teacher in writing. Hebrew and Religion Classes are attached to nearly all the syns. listed.

GENERAL

Agency for Jewish Education. (See p. 31).

Ackerman Resource Centre, Redbridge JCC, Woodford Bridge Road, Ilford, Essex, IG5 4LN.

☎ 020-8551 0017. Fax 020-8551 9027. The Resource Centre is a centre for informal Jewish and Israel education. The Centre has operated in the community for 20 years as a resource for educators who require support and advice in this field. The Resource Centre is a focus for leadership training in the community. *Comm. Res. Worker* H. Ashleigh.

Aish UK, 379 Hendon Way, NW4 3LP. ☎ 020-8457 4444. Fax 020-8457 4445. Email info@aish.org.uk. (Est 1992; Reg. Charity no. 1069048.) Social and educational programmes for 17–35 years. *Dir.* Rabbi N. Schiff; *Chairman* J. Faith.

Binoh: Norwood's Specialist Education and Therapy Service. The Kennedy Leigh Centre, Edgeworth Close, Hendon, London, NW4 4HJ, ☎ 020-8457 4457, Fax 020-8203 8233, Email binoh@norwood.org. uk (Reg. Charity No. 291978.) Binoh is part of Norwood and is a multi-disciplinary support service for Jewish children. Professional support is provided to children up to the age of eighteen who have additional or special educational needs including learning and development, language and communication, motor impairment and emotional, social and behavioural difficulties. Services can also be offered at schools and at Norwood's other Family Centre in Hackney. *Hd. of Service* G. Lebrett.

Interlink Foundation, Lower Ground Offices, 124 Stamford Hill, N16 6QT. ☎ 020-8802 2469. Fax 020-8800 5153. Email director@interlink-foundation.org.uk. (Est. 1993. Reg. Charity No. 1079311) Umbrella development agency for the Orthodox Jewish voluntary sector. Services include: capacity-building (including training) with groups, information/quarterly newsletter plus regular mailings, policy and regeneration work. *Dir.* Mrs E. Sterngold.

Jewish Learning Exchange (JLE), 152-154 Golders Green Road, NW11 8HE.
☎ 020 8458 4588, Fax 020 8458 4587. Email: jle@jle.org.uk, www.jle.org.uk. (Est. 1988.Reg. Charity No. 292886). The JLE is the largest educational and social centre of its kind in Europe. Its aim is to inspire 21st century Jews, demonstrating the relevance and deeper meaning of Judaism and enabling them to make informed life decisions by providing the highest quality Jewish education. The JLE is a service of Ohr Somayach Institutions. *Dir.* Rabbi Danny Kirsch.

Jewish Resource Centre (JRC at CRREDE), Centre for Research in Religious Education and Development, Roehampton University, Digby Stuart College, Roehampton Lane, SW15 5PH. ☎/Fax 020-8392 3349. Email a.clark@ roehampton.ac.uk. (Est. 1996) Serves as a resource for all sections of the Jewish community in South London, as well as for the non-Jewish teaching community. The Centre houses a collection of books and Judaica for purchase, loan and consultation, and hosts educational and cultural activities. Staff are available to visit synagogues, religion schools/chadarim and teachers' centres in the area to run book sales and other events. Open Wednesday afternoons during term-time from 2.00 to 5.00 p.m., and at other times by appointment. *Dir.* Anne Clark, BA (Hons), MA, Dip. Couns., UJIA Ashdown Fellow.

SAJE-Strategic Alliance for Jewish Education, 152-154, Coles Green Road, London NW2 7HD, ☎ 020-8438 6342. Fax 020-8438 6441. Email enquiries@saj.org.uk Website www.saje.org.uk. *Dir.* J. Faith; *Chief Exec.* Rabbi Ch. Silverman, BSc., MA. *Company Sec.* H. Morris, FCA

Schools' J-Link, Unit 23, Dollis Hill Estate, 105 Brook Rd., NW2 7BZ. ☎ 020-8208 2333. Fax 020-8208 0506. Email info@jlink.org.uk. (Est. 1993; Reg. Charity No. 1062551). Schools' J–Link aims to raise the sense of identity and commitment of Jewish pupils in non-Jewish secondary schools. It runs school assemblies and classes, less formal Jewish society meetings and lunch and learn sessions, and totally informal parties at Succot, Purim and other occasions, offering a broad Jewish input by co-opting rabbis, youth workers, representatives of Jewish organisations and visiting speakers from abroad. It also runs training programmes for non-Jewish teachers who are teaching Judaism. Schools' J-Link operates in 60 schools in the London area and several provincial towns, and communicates with upwards of 6,000 Jewish youngsters each year. *Dir.* Rabbi Arye Forta, BA; *Dir. of Dev.* Rabbi Dr S. Gaffin; *Admin.* Mrs R. Stemmer.

SCHOOLS

Akiva School, Levy House, The Sternberg Centre, 80 East End Road, N3 2SY. ☎ 020-8349 4980. Fax 020-8349 4959. Email admin@akivaschool.org. (Est. 1981.) Primary educ. for pupils, aged 4-11 years, under Reform & Liberal Synagogue auspices. *Head*

Teacher S. Stone; *Admin.*

Avigdor Hirsch Torah Temimah Primary School, Parkside, Dollis Hill, NW2 6RJ. ☎ 020-8450 4377. Fax 020-8830 6202. Email admin@torahtemimah.brent.sch.uk. Voluntary-aided (London Borough of Brent) Orthodox Jewish primary school and nursery for boys aged 3-11. (Est. 1989. Reg. Charity No. 1000146). *Princ.* Rabbi E. Klyne, MA (Ed); *H.T.* A. Wolfson, BEd (Hons), MA, MEd. NPQH; *Chairman of Govs.* M. Wulnick.

Beth Jacob Seminary of London, 196–198 Lordship Road, N16 5ES. Teacher Training College and finishing school for Hebrew Studies and vocational qualifications. *Fnd. Princ.* Rabbi J. H. Dunner; *Princ.* Rabbi B. Dunner. ☎ 020-8800 4719. Fax 020-8800 6067. (Reg. Charity No. 312913).

Bushey Ganim Lower & Upper School, Bushey & District Synagogue, 177–189, Sparrows Herne, Bushey, Herts., WD23 1AJ. ☎ 020-8386 1515/1616. ☎ 07733 068358; Email ganim-lower@busheyus.org. ganim-upper@busheyus.org. (For children 2½-5). *H. Princ.* Rabbi Z. M. Salasnik BA; *Jt. H. M.* Mrs D. Spector BA(Hons), QTS, Ms D. Boder-Cohn.

Clore Shalom School, Hugo Gryn Way, Shenley, Herts WD7 9BL. ☎ 01923 855631; Fax 01923 853722; Email admin@cloreshalom.herts.sch.uk. (Est. 1999) Voluntary-aided primary school (3-11). *H.T.* Irene Kay; *Admin.* Angela Peters.

Clore Tikva School Redbridge, 115 Fullwell Ave., Ilford, Essex IG6 2JN. ☎ 020-8551 1097; Fax 020-8551 2070. Email cloretikva@redbridge.gov.uk. (Est. 1999). Community, state-aided primary school (4-11), under Reform, Masorti and Liberal auspices. *Hd.* Mrs L. Rosenberg; *Admin.* Mrs Valerie Garnelas.

Hasmonean High School:
Boys, 11/18, Holders Hill Road, NW4 1NA. (020-8203 1411. Fax 020-8202 4526. **Girls**, 2/4, Page Street, NW7 2EU. ☎ 020-8203 4294. Fax 020-8202 4527. Recognised by Dept. of Education. Voluntary Aided, London Borough of Barnet. *Exec H. T..* Mr D. H. Fuller, BEd. (Hons); *H of Boys'* Rabbi D. Meyer, BA, MBA, NPQH; *H. of Girls'* Mrs B. Perin BA, NPQH.

Hasmonean Pre-Nursery, 8-10 Shirehall Lane, NW4 2PD. ☎ 020-8201 6252. Fax 020-8202 1605 (children 2-3). *Man.* Mrs J. Truman.

Hasmonean Primary School, 8-10 Shirehall Lane, NW4 2PD. ☎ 020-8202 7704. Fax 020-8202 1605. (Boys and Girls 3-11.) *Princ.* Rabbi M. Ginsbury; *Hd.* Mrs J. Rodin, MSc (Ed.Mang.), Cert Ed. Premier Degré (Paris). Rabbi M. Beaton, Rav of the School. Email head@[or]admin@hasmonean-pri.barnet.sch.uk.

Hertsmere Jewish Primary School, Watling Street, Radlett, Herts WD7 7LQ. ☎ 01923 855857. Fax 01923 853399. Email admin@hjps.herts.sch.uk. *H.T.* Mrs Michèle Bazak; *Admin.* Mrs K. Thomas. Voluntary-aided primary school for ages 3-11.

Ilford Jewish Primary School, Carlton Dr, Ilford, Essex IG6 1LZ. ☎ 020-8551 4294. Fax 020-8551 4295. Email admin.ilfordjewish@redbridge.gov.uk. Website www.ilford jewish.redbridge.sch.uk. *H.T.* Mrs R. Levin.

Immanuel College (The Charles Kalms, Henry Ronson Immanuel College), 87/91 Elstree Road, Bushey, Herts., WD23 4EB. ☎ 020-8950 0604. Fax: 020-8950 8687. Email enquiries@immanuel.herts.sch.uk; Website www.immanuelcollege. co.uk. (Reg Charity No. 803179) Independent mixed selective school. *H.* Philip Skelker, MA, PGCE; *Dep. H.* Richard Felsenstein BA(Hons), Cert Ed.

Independent Jewish Day School, 46 Green Lane, NW4 2AH. ☎ 020-8203 2299. Email office.ijds.barnet@lgfl.net. Orthodox Primary Sch. & Kindergarten (est. 1979). *Chairman* Ms D. Meyer; *Princ.* A.A. Kimche, BA; *H.T.* Miss A. Lando.

Jewish Secondary Schools Movement, Holders Hill Road, NW4 1NA. ☎ 020-8203 1411. Fax 020-8202 4526. (Est. 1929.)

J.F.S. School, The Mall, Kenton HA3 9TE. ☎ 020-8206 3100. (Est. 1732.) *H.T.* J. Miller, BSc (Hons), MA, NPQA; *Clerk to Govs.* K. Jones.

Kerem House, 18 Kingsley Way, N2 0ER. ☎ 020-8455 7524. (Boys and Girls 2½-5.) *H.T.* Mrs D. Rose, MA, Cert. Ed. Email keremhouse@kerem.org.uk

Kerem School, Norrice Lea, N2 0RE. ☎ 020-8455 0909. (Boys and Girls 4-11.) *H. Princ.* Rabbi R. Livingstone; *H.T.* Mrs R. Goulden, M. Ed.

King Solomon High School, Forest Road, Barkingside, Ilford, Essex IG6 3HB.

☎ 020-8498-1300. Fax 020-8498-1333. Email info@kshsonline.com *H.M.* S. Lewis; *Chairman of Govs.* Mrs D. Lazarus; *Denominational Body:* United Synagogue; *Auth.* London Borough of Redbridge.

Kisharon, 1011, Finchley Rd., NW11 7HB ☎ 020-8731 7009. Fax 020-8731 7005. Email info@Kisharon.org.uk. (Reg. Charity No. 271519). *Exec. Dir.* David Goodman; *Chairman of Tr.* P. Klein; *Chairman of Govs.* P. Goldberg.

Tuffkid Nursery, 3 Western Avenue, NW11 9HG. ☎ 020-8201 8488 Fax 020-8458 5465. An integrated nursery for children between the ages of two and five years, providing pre-school education to mainstream and special needs children. Email jofraser@kisharon.org.uk.

Kisharon Day School,1011 Finchley Road, Golders Green, NW11 7HB. ☎ 020-8455 7483. Email kisharondayschool@kisharon.org.uk.

Kisharon College, 54 Parson Street, NW4 1TP. ☎ 020-8457 2525. Fax 020-8457 2535. Email college@kisharon.org.uk.

Law of Truth Talmudical College (Reg. Charity No.: 312845), 50 Knightland Road, E5 9HS. *Corr.* 27 Warwick Grove, E5 9HX. ☎ 020-8806 2963. Fax 020-8806 9318. Students: 020-8806 6642. Email schneidersyeshiva@mail.com (Est. by Rabbi M. Szneider in Memel, 1911, Frankfurt 1918, London 1938.) *Princ.* Rabbi M. Halpern.

Lubavitch Foundation, 107-115 Stamford Hill, N16 5RP. ☎ 020-8800 0022. Fax 020-8809 7324. (Est. 1959.) To further Jewish religious education, identity and commitment. Separate depts. for adult education, summer and day camps, youth clubs and training, univ. counsellors, publications, welfare, and orgs. concerned with Israel. *Princ.* Rabbi N. Sudak, OBE; *Dir.* Rabbi S. F. Vogel; *Admin.* Rabbi I. H. Sufrin. Lubavitch House School–Boys' Senior, 133 Clapton Common, E5. ☎ 020-8809 7476. Girls' Senior, 107 Stamford Hill, N16. ☎ 020-8800 0022. *H. M.* Rabbi S. Lew. Boys' Primary, 135 Clapton Common E5. ☎ 020-8800 1044. *H. M.* Rabbi D. Karnowsky. Girls' Primary, 113-115 Stamford Hill, N16 5RP. ☎ 020-8800 0022. Fax 020-8809 7324; *Admin.* Mrs S. Sudak. Kindergarten, 107 Stamford Hill, N16. ☎ 020-8800 0022. *H.T.* Mrs F. Sudak. *Librarian* Zvi Rabin, ALA. ☎ 020-8800 5823. Vista Vocational Training, 107 Stamford Hill, N16 5RP. (020-8802 8772. *Man.* Mrs H. Lew. Women's Centre, 19 Northfield Rd, N16 5RL. (020-8809 6508. *Admin.* Mrs R. Bernstein. *Publ.* Lubavitch Direct.

Menorah Foundation School, Abbots Road, Edgware, Middx. HA8 0QS. ☎ 020-8906 9992. Fax 020-8906 9993. Email office.menorahfoundation.barnet@lgfl.net *H.T.* Mrs C. Neuberger, BSc, PGCE, NPQH; *Principal* Rabbi H.I. Feldman; *Chairman* Adrian Jacobs.

Menorah Primary School (and Menorah Nursery), Woodstock Avenue, NW11. ☎ 020-8458 1276. Vol. Aided (Lond. Borough of Barnet) for Boys & Girls 3-11. (Est. 1944.) *Princ.* Rabbi Y. M. Greenberg; *Hd.* Mrs J. Menczer.

Michael Sobell Sinai School, Shakespeare Dr, Kenton, Harrow, Middx HA3 9UD. ☎ 020-8204 1550. Email admin@sinai.brent.sch.uk (Est. 1981.) Vol. aided primary sch. for boys & girls, aged 3-11. *Chairman Govs.* C. Goodman; *H.T.* Mrs V. Orloff; *Denominational body* Bd. of Rel. Educ.; *Auth.* Lond. Borough of Brent.

MST College, 240-242 Hendon Way, NW4 3NL. ☎ 020-8202 2212. Fax 020-8203 2212. Email admin@mstcollege.org. Orthodox teacher training college offering a range of accredited Degree courses leading to Qualified Teacher Status. *Principal* Michael Cohen BA, M.Phil, PGCE; *Reg.* Dr Abbott Katz MA Ph.D; *College Man.* Miss Bernice Black.

Naima Jewish Preparatory School (Reg. Charity no. 289066), 21 Andover Place, NW6 5ED. ☎ 020-7328 2802 Fax 020-7624 0161. School for children aged 3-11 years offering a broad secular curriculum together with rich programme of Orthodox Jewish studies. Catering for children of all abilities through flexible learning programme. *H. Princ.* Rabbi Dr A. Levy; *Hd. T.* M. Cohen.

Nancy Reuben Primary School, 48 Finchley Lane, Hendon NW4 1DJ. ☎ 020-8202 5646. Email office@nrps.co.uk. *P.* Mrs A. Haye.

North West London Jewish Day School, 180 Willesden Lane, NW6 7PP. ☎ 020-8459 3378. Fax 020-8451 7298. Website www.nwljds.org.uk. Email admin @nwljds.org.uk. Voluntary Aided. Orthodox Primary sch. and nursery for boys and girls, 3-11 (Est. 1945).

Principal Dayan I. Binstock; *H. M.* Rabbi D.S. Kerbel, MA, NPQH.

Pardes House Primary School, Hendon Lane, N3 1SA. ☎ 020-8343 3568. *H. Princ.* Rabbi E. Halpern. *Menahel* Rabbi N. Lieberman. Kindergarten: Hendon Lane, N3 1SA. ☎ 020-8371 8292.

Pardes House Grammar School, Hendon Lane, N3 1SA. ☎ 020-8349 4222. *H. Princ.* Rabbi E. Halpern; *Head M.* Rabbi D. Dunner.

Rosh Pinah Primary School, Glengall Rd., Edgware, Middx HA8 8TE. ☎ 020-8958 8599. Fax 020-8905 4853 Website www.roshpinahschool.org.uk *H. Princ.*: Rabbi Y. Schochet; *H. T.* Mrs A. Abery, MA, NPQH

Sharon Kindergarten, Finchley Synagogue, Kinloss Gdns., N3 3DU. ☎ 020-8346 2039. (For children 2½-5.) *H.T.* Mrs E. Elek.

Side by Side Kids Ltd, 9 Big Hill, E5 9HH ☎ 020-8880 8300. Fax 020-8880 8341. Email: rebecca@sidebysidekids.org.uk. Side by Side is an integrated nursery and special needs school providing therapy and education for children and a support network for their families. *Dir.* Mrs R. Rumpler.

Torah Centre Trust, 84 Leadale Road, N15 6BH. ☎ 020-8802 3586. (Est. 1975.) To provide full or part-time facilities for children, in particular those from 'uncommitted' families, to enable them to further their secular and Hebrew educ. *Chairman* Rabbi J. Dunner; *Educ. Dir.* Rabbi M. Bernstein, B.Ed.

Wolfson Hillel Primary School, 154 Chase Road, Southgate, N14 4LG. ☎ 020-8882 6487. Fax 020-8882 7965. (Est. 1992) Email schooloffice@wolfsonhillel. enfield.sch.uk. Website www.wolfsonhillel.enfield.sch.uk. Vol. aided primary school for boys & girls aged 3-11. *Chairman Govs.* H. Rosen; *H.T.* Mrs S. Margolis. (*Auth.* London Borough of Enfield.)

Yeshiva Gedola, 3/5 Kingsley Way, N2. ☎ 020-8455 3262. *Rosh Yeshiva* Rabbi I. M. Hertz.

Yeshivah Ohel Moshe Etz Chaim, 85 Bridge Lane, NW11.(Reg. Charity No. 312232) ☎ 020-8458 5149. *Princ.* Rabbi Z. Rabi.

Yesodey Hatorah Schools, 2 and 4 Amhurst Park, N16 5AE. ☎ 020-8800 8612. (Est. 1943.) *Princ.* Rabbi A. Pinter; *V. President* Rabbi C. Pinter.

Yesodey Hatorah Nursery, 2 Amhurst Pk., N16 5AE. ☎ 020-8800 9221. *Hd.* Mrs Shine

Yesodey Hatorah Kindergarten, 2 Amhurst Pk., N16 5AE. (020-8800 8612. *Matron* Mrs Shine.

Yesodey Hatorah Primary School (Boys), 2 Amhurst Pk., N16 5AE. ☎ 020-8800 8612. *Princ* Rabbi A. Pinter; *Menahel* Rabbi P. Rosenberg.

Yesodey Hatorah Senior School (Boys), 4 Amhurst Pk., N16 5AE. ☎ 020-8800 8612. *Princ.* Rabbi A. Pinter; *Menahel* Rabbi D. Weiler.

Yesodey Hatorah Primary School (Girls), 153 Stamford Hill, N16 5LG. ☎ 020-8800 8612. *Princ.* Rabbi A. Pinter; *H. M.* Mrs D. Luria.

Yesodey Hatorah Senior School (Girls), Egerton Rd, N16 6UB. ☎ 020-8826 5500. *Princ.* Rabbi A. Pinter; *H. M.* Mrs R. Pinter

Welfare Organisations

Abbeyfield Camden (Jewish) Society, 59 Belmont Rd., Bushey, Herts. WD23 2JR. ☎ 01923 213964. The Society runs two small residential homes for the able-bodied elderly, with facilities for short-stay visitors. *Admin.* Mrs G. Benson. ☎ 020-8423 1351. Email gill@annie-b.co.uk. Houses: Lily Montagu House, 36–38 Orchard Drive, Stanmore, Middx. HA8 7SD; Belmont Lodge, 59 Belmont Road, Bushey, Herts. WD23 2JR.

Agudas Israel Housing Association Ltd, 206 Lordship Rd., N16 5ES. ☎ 020-8802 3819. Fax 020-8809 6206. Email info@aihaltd.co.uk. (Reg. Charity No. 23535). *Chief Exec.* Mrs Ita Symons, MBE.

Schonfeld Square Foundation, 1 Schonfeld Square, Lordship Road, N16 0QQ. ☎ 020-8802 3819. Fax 020-8809 6206. Email info@aihaltd.co.uk. (Reg. Charity No. 1049179). *Co.ord.* Mrs Symons.

Includes ownership of: **Beenstock Home** (Home for the Frail and Elderly), 19–21 Northumberland Street, Salford, M7 4RP. (0161-792 1515. Fax 0161-792 1616. *Care Man.* Mrs V. Begal.

Beis Brucha (Mother and Baby Home), 208 Lordship Road, N16 5ES. ☎/Fax 020-8211 8081. *Man.* L. Hirschler.

Beis Pinchos (Residential and Nursing Home for the Frail and Elderly), and **Fradel Lodge** (Sheltered Accommodation for the Frail and Elderly), Schonfeld Square, Lordship Road, N16 0QQ. ☎ 020-8802 7477. Fax 020-8809 7000. Email schonfeld@aihaltd.co.uk. *Care Man.* Mrs E. Gebb; *Social Man.* Mrs H. Pesach.

Beis Rochel (Supported Housing for Vulnerable Women), 52 Lordship Park, N16 5UD. ☎ (Office) 020-8802 2160, (Residents) 020-8802 2909. Email info@aihaltd.co.uk. *Man.*

30 Dunsmure Road (Supported Housing for Vulnerable Men), N16 5PW. ☎ (Office) 020-8800 2860, (Residents) 020-8802 0073. Email info@aihaltd.co. uk. *Man.*

Ajex Housing Association Ltd. ☎/Fax 020-8802 3348 *Scheme Man.* Mrs N. McAuliffe, Mrs J. Dalziel Email ajexhousing@btopenworld.com. Website www.ajex.org.uk (I.R. Charity Ref. 914/A5110; Friendly Society Reg. 17760DR; Housing Corporation: Registered Housing Association L0669). Provides flatlets for elderly and disabled ex-servicemen and women and their dependants. *Chairman* H. Newman; *H. Sec.* A. Lawson; *Admin.* Ajex House, East Bank, N16 5RT.

Arbib Lucas Charity (Reg. Charity No. 208666). Provides financial assistance to women in reduced circumstances. *H. Sec.* Mrs Anita Kafton, 16 Sunny Hill, NW4 4LL.

Brenner Community Centre, at Raine House, 91-93, Stamford Hill, N16 5TP. ☎ 020-8442 7750 (Reg. Charity No. 802559). Administered by Jewish Care. Community Centre for the local Jewish community. *Centre Man.* L. M. Harris.

Camp Simcha, 746, Finchley Road, NW11 7TH. ☎ 020-8731 6788. Fax 020-8458 6819. Email admin@campsimcha.org.uk. www.campsimcha.org.uk. (Est. 1995. Reg. Charity No. 1044685) Charity to help improve the quality of life for children with cancer and life threatening conditions. *Chief Exec.* N. Goldschneider.

Drugsline Chabad (Reg. Charity No. 1067573), 395 Eastern Avenue, Gants Hill, Ilford, Essex IG2 6LR. Crisis Helpline: Freephone 0808 1606 606. Office: 020-8554 3220. Fax: 020-8518 2126. Website www. drugsline.org. Drop in service for those people with drug-related problems, their families and friends. Drug and alcohol education services offered to schools, youth clubs and other organisations. *Exec. Dir.* Rabbi Aryeh Sufrin.

Employment Resource Centre Fairacres, 164 East End Road, N2 0PR. ☎ 020-8883 1000. Fax 020-8883 109. Email office@ercentre.org.Website www.ercentre.org. (Reg. Charity No. 1106331) A service for the Jewish community, the ERC offers opportunities to the unemployed to gain skills and training for the labour market. *Chairman, Exec. Cttee.* P. Ward; *Centre Man* M. Kanter.

Finchley Kosher Lunch Service, (Meals-on-Wheels for the housebound and disabled), Covers Edgware, Finchley, Golders Green, Hampstead Garden Suburb, Hendon, Mill Hill. *H.T.* Mrs Ruth Freed, ☎ 020-8202 8129. Admin. by the League of Jewish Women. (See p.4)

Food for the Jewish Poor, To provide (a) food throughout the year; (b) grocery during Passover; (c) special relief for approved emergency cases. (See Jewish Care).

Friends of the Kingsbury Mikveh – Educational and Support Group (Reg. Charity No. 1041629), Kingsbury United Synagogue, Kingsbury Green, NW9 8XR. ☎ 020-8204 6390. *H.T.* Helene Leigh, 474 Kenton Road, Kenton, HA3 9DN. ☎ 020-8206 1512.

Friends of the Sick (Chevrat Bikkur Cholim), (Reg. Charity No. 91468A), 463a Finchley Road, NW3 6HN. ☎ 020-7435 0836. Email info@friends-of-the-sick.org.co.uk. (Est. 1947.) To nurse sick and aged needy persons in their own homes. *President* Mr S. Sackman; *H.T.* M. Wechsler; *Gen. Sec.* Mrs E. Weitzman.

Hagadolim Charitable Organisation (Est. 1950) To provide financial assistance to Homes and charities in England and Israel, and to visit and provide comforts in private homes in the Home Counties. *Chairman* L. Dunitz; *Jt. Ts.* B. Wallach, Mrs R. J. Dunitz; *Sec.* Mrs S. Levy, 4 Edgwarebury Ct., Edgwarebury La., Edgware, Middx. HA8 8LP. ☎ 020-8958 8558.

Hanna Schwalbe Residential Home, 48 Leeside Crescent, NW11 0LA. ☎ 020-8458 3810. Fax 020-8922 7454. Email judymkisharon@hotmail.com.

Haven Foundation (Regd. Charity No. 264029), Alfred House, 1 Holly Park, Crouch Hill, N4 4BN. ☎ 020-7272 1345 (Admin. by Ravenswood Foundation). Est. 1971. To provide permanent residential care and development training for Jewish mildly mentally handicapped adults in its hostel, group homes and soc. development unit. *L. President* Eve Alfred; *Chairman* N. Freeder; *Jt. V. Chairman* R. Rosenberg, ACA.

Hospital Kosher Meals Service (Reg. Charity No. 1025601), Lanmor House, 370/386 High Road, Wembley, Middx. HA9 6AX. ☎ 020-8795 2058. Fax 020-8900 2462. Email hkms@btconnect.com. Provides supervised kosher meals to patients in hospitals throughout Greater London. *Chairman* M.G. Freedman, MBA, FCA; *V. Chairman* H. Glyn, BSc, FRICS; *Sec.* G. Calvert; *Admin.* Mrs E. Stone; *Hospital Liaison Off.* Mrs S. Patashnik.

Jewish Aged Needy Pension Society (Est. 1829. Reg. Charity no. 206262) Provides pensions for members of the Jewish community aged 60 or over, who have known better times and who, in their old age, find themselves in reduced circumstances. Also supplements income provided from statutory sources. Services to the middle-class of society who find themselves in greater financial need and who do not seem to fall within the purview of any other charitable organisations. *President* M.E.G. Prince; *Ts.* A.H.E. Prince; *H. Sec.* Mrs G. B. Rigal; *Sec./Admin.* Mrs Sheila A. Taylor, 34 Dalkeith Grove, Stanmore, Middx HA5 4EG. ☎ 020-8958 5390 Fax 020-8958 8046.

Jewish Bereavement Counselling Service (Est. 1980. Reg. Charity No. 1047473), 44B Albert Rd., NW4 2SG. ☎ 020-8457 9710. Fax 020-8457 9707. Email jbcs@jvisit.org.uk. Offers bereavement counselling for children, families and individuals provided by trained voluntary counsellors under supervision and support to members of the Jewish community. Covers North and NW London and Hertfordshire. *Chairman* Keith Simmons; *Co-ord.* Trisha Curtis; *Consult.* Rae Adler.

Jewish Blind & Disabled 35 Langstone Way, Mill Hill East, NW7 1GT. ☎ 020-8371 6611. Fax 020-8371 4225. Email info@jbd.org; Website www.jbd.org. (Est. 1969. Reg. Charity No. 259480).Jewish Blind & Disabled is the community's only independent charity providing care and assisted living for people with physical disabilities or vision impairment. It currently cares for some 350 tenants and their families at its seven sites in north London, with plans to open an eighth to meet the demand.*Chairman* John Joseph; *President* Malcolm Ozin; *Chief Exec.* Hazel. Kaye.

JBD Projects: *Assisted Living Schemes*: Fairacres, 164 East End Road, Finchley, N2; Cherry Tree Court, Roe Green, Kingsbury, NW9; Cecil Rosen Court, East Lane, North Wembley, Middx; Milne Court, (including the Pears Wing) Churchfields, South Woodford, E18; Hilary Dennis Court, Sylvan Road, Wanstead, E11; Aztec House, Redbridge; Frances and Dick James Court, Mill Hill, NW7.

Jewish Blind & Physically Handicapped Society,(See Jewish Blind & Disabled).

Jewish Blind Society (incorporating Jewish Assn. for the Physically Handicapped). See below: Jewish Care.

Jewish Care, Merit House, The Hyde, 508 Edgware Rd., Colindale, NW9 5AB ☎ 020-8922 2000. Jewish Care Direct (helpline) ☎ 020-8922 2222. Fax 020-8922 1998. Email info@jcare.org; Website www.jewishcare.org. (Reg. Charity No. 802559. Est. 1990).

Services managed by Jewish Care:

Community Services – Family Carer's Service; Kennedy Leigh Home Care Service; Social Work Services.

Care Homes – BClore Manor, NW4; Ella & Ridley Jacobs House, NW4; Hyman Fine House , Brighton; Kay Court, NW3; Lady Sarah Cohen House, N11; Leo Baeck House (Otto Schiff), N2; Osmond House (Otto Schiff) N2; The Princess Alexandra Home, Stanmore; Raymond House, Southend on Sea; Rela Goldhill Lodge, NW11; Rosetrees, N11; Rubens House, N3; Vi & John Rubens House, Ilford.

Communiy Centres – BBrenner Community Centre at Raine House, Stamford Hill; Redbridge Jewish Youth & Community Centre at Sinclair House; Southend and Westcliff Community Centre.

Connect@centres – connect@kenton (Monday); connect@southgate (Tuesday); connect@hendon (Wednesday); connect@stjohnswood (Wednesday); connect@jcc, NW11 (Thursday).

Day Centres – Edgware & Harrow Jewish Day Centre; The Sobell Centre in Hampstead;

Stepney Day Care Centre.

Dementia Day Care Centre– The Dennis Special Day Care Centre, IG4; Leonard Sainer Special Day Care Centre, HA8; Sam Beckman Special Day Care Centre, NW4.

Mental Health Wellbeing Centres – Kadimah Centre for Wellbeing, N16; Mitkadem Centre for Wellbeing, IG2; Shalom Centre.for Wellbeing, NW11 (including education & development, employment projects, outreach & social work service).

Mental Health Residential Homes – Jack gardener House (18-50), NW11; Mapesbury Road (50+), NW2.

Mental Health Supported Housing – Caddington Road; gillingham Road; Melrose Avenue; Montpelier Rise; Station Road.

Specialist Services – Burr Day centre, IG6; Holocaust Survivors Centre & Shalvata, NW4; Support groups, The Karten CTEC Centre, NW11 & N16; The KC Shasha Centre for Talking News & Books; Tay Sachs Screening.

Sheltered Housing – Shebson Lodge, Westcliff on Sea.

Youth Services – Redbridge Jewish Youth and Community Centre at Sinclair House.

Jewish Children's Holidays Fund (formerly the Jewish Branch of the Children's Country Holidays Fund). (Est. 1888. Reg. Charity No. 295361) *President* Mrs Joyce Kemble, JP; *Chairman* Ian Donoff; *Sec.* Mrs F. Warshawsky, 60 Oundle Ave., Bushey, Herts WD23 4QQ. ☎ 020-8950 3383.

Jewish Community Housing Association, Harmony Close, Princes Park Ave. NW11 0JJ. ☎ 020-8381 4901. Fax 020-8458 1772. *Chairman* E. Shapiro; *T.* ; *Chief Exec.* S. Clarke. The Association owns and manages sheltered housing in London, Hertfordshire and Kent. Supported housing for people with special needs is managed on the Association's behalf by Jewish Care and Norwood. Short-term accommodation for students is located in Golders Green.

Jewish Crisis Help Line, Miyad. (0800 6529249. Confidential listening service for those experiencing stress in their lives.

Jewish Deaf Association, Julius Newman House, Woodside Park Rd., London N12 8RP. ☎ 020-8446 0502 (voice), 020-8446 4037 (text). Fax 020-8445 7451; Email jda@dircon.co.uk. Website www.jewishdeaf.org.uk. (Reg. Charity No. 1105845). Support and information services and programmes for people with all levels of hearing loss, and hearing people living with deaf and hard of hearing people. Technology and Information Centre displaying specialised equipment for independent living. (☎ 020-8446 0214 for appoinments). *President* G.M. Gee, JP; *Chairman* Mrs E. Gee; *Exec. Dir.* Susan Cipin.

Jewish Society for the Mentally Handicapped, now merged with Norwood Ravenswood (see below).

Jewish Welfare Board (incorporating the Jewish Bread, Meat and Coal Society, est. 1779), see Jewish Care, (p.15).

Jews' Temporary Shelter (Reg. Charity No. 098798), 4, Greenland Place, NW1 0AP. ☎/Fax 020-7387 7447. *Admin.* Mrs R. Lewis.

Kinneret Trust, 127-129 Clapton Common, E5 9AB ☎ 020 8809 4844. Email ginaabrahams@hotmail.com. Supporting the Aden Jews community of the Stamford Hill area. *Chair* G. Abrahams; *Cttee* G. Mahalla, G. Nissim, N. Mansoor

Kisharon (For Head Office and Administration see p. 85)

Asher Loftus Business Centre 27-31 Church Road, Hendon NW4 4EB ☎ 020-8202 3936 Fax 020-8203 6071; Email jeffrey@kisharon-be.co.uk

Hackney Community Inclusion Women's site 48 Warwick Grove Stamford Hill E5 9HU ☎ 020-8880 8542; Email jeffrey@kisharon-be.co.uk. **Men's site** 13 Paget Road, N16 5NQ ☎ 020-8880 8542; Email jeffrey@kisharon-be.co.uk.

Residential Services **Supported Living Projects** 54 Parson Street Hendon NW4 1TP ☎ 020-8457 2553 Fax 020-8457 2535

Hanna Schwalbe Residential Home 48 Leeside Crescent Golders Green NW11 0LA ☎ 020-8458 3810 Fax 020 8922 7454; Email judymkisharon@hotmasil.com

Lewis W. Hammerson Memorial Home, Hammerson House, 50A, The Bishop's Avenue, N2 0BE. ☎ 020-8458 4523. Fax 020-8458 2537. Email info@hammersonhouse.org.uk. (Est.

1962, Reg. Charity No. 286002.) *President* Mrs S. Hammerson, OBE; *Chairman* T. Michaels. Applications for admission: 020-8458 4523.

MIYAD: Jewish Telephone Crisis Line, ☎ 020-8203 6211, 0345 581999. Sponsored by the Jewish Marriage Council. Confidential telephone line offered to the Jewish community for people needing help in crisis situations.

Necessitous Ladies' Fund, incorporating Delissa Joseph Memorial Fund (both funds founded by Union of Jewish Women). For the relief of Jewish women who are in need, hardship or distress (Reg. Charity No. 266921 A3L1). *Chairman* Mrs J. Nathan; *H. Admin.* Mrs H. Davis, c/o Baker Tilly, 46 Clarendon Rd., Watford WD17 1JJ. Email admin@nelf.wanadoo.co.uk.

Nightingale House, 105 Nightingale Lane, SW12 8NB. (020-8673 3495. Fax 020-8675 2258. Est. 1840, Reg. Charity No. 207316) Life Patron Dame Vivien Duffield DBE; President G. Lipton MBE; Chairman H. Rosenblatt; Jt Ts. K. Goodman, FCA, D. Tyler, D. Winton; *Chief Exec.* Leon Smith. Aid Societies: NW London; SW London; Literary Lunch Cttee; The Young Nightingales; HA7.

Norwood, Broadway House, 80/82, The Broadway, Stanmore, HA7 4HB. ☎ 020-8954 4555. Fax 020-8420 6800. Email info@norwood.org.uk. Website www.norwood.org.uk. Est. 1795 (Reg. Charity No.1059050.) Norwood is the UK's leading Jewish charity supporting children,families and adults living with learning disabilities or coping with social difficulties. Norwood's 1200 staff and 800 volunteers offer services to children and adults with a wide range of learning disabilities by providing housing, special education, employment and leisure opportunities. Norwood also supports families that are in crisis, those facing social disadvantage and children who require fostering and adoption services, both in the UK and internationally. Norwood has Children & Family Centres in Hackney, N16 ☎ 020-8880 2777, North West London, NW4 ☎ 020 8457 4745 and Redbridge, IG6 ☎ 020 8559 6200. *Patron* Her Majesty The Queen; *President* Richard Desmond; *Chairman* Michael Teacher; *Chief Exec. Dir.* Norma Brier, MSc.

Raphael Jewish Counselling Service (Reg. Charity No. 278522), PO Box 172, Stanmore HA7 3WB. ☎ 0800 234 6236 (24 hour). Email info@raphaeljewishcounselling.org. Website www.raphaeljewishgcounselling.org. Qualified Jewish Counsellors provide confidential counselling for individuals and couples. Donations, grants and bequests enable us to continue this important work in the community and to further professional training.*Patrons:* The Chief Rabbi; Rabbi Tony Bayfield and Rabbi Dr Abraham Levy.

Rishon Multiple Sclerosis Aid Group, (Est. 1966. Reg. Charity No. 252359) Affiliated to the Multiple Sclerosis Society of Great Britain. Provides social and cultural activities, help and welfare, for Multiple Sclerosis sufferers and raises funds for this and the encouragement of research into the causes and cure of the disease. *Life President* H. Bibring ☎ 020 8950 9212. bibrings@onetel.com; *H. Sec.* .

Sunridge Housing Association Ltd., 76 The Ridgeway, NW11 8PT. ☎ 020-8458 3389; *Chairman* Brian Levy; *H. Sec.* Robin Michaelson. *Man.* Mrs P. Darroux.

Westlon Housing Association. 850 Finchley Road, NW11 6BB. ☎ 020-8201 8484. Fax 020-8731 8847 *H. L. President* His Hon. Alan King-Hamilton, QC; *Chairman* Mrs Joan Ansell; *Admin.* J.W. Silverman. **Annette White Lodge,** 287/289 High Road, N2 8HB. **Deborah Rayne House,** 33b Sunningfields Road, NW4 4QX. **The Woodville,** Woodville Road, W5 2SE. Applications to 020-8201 8484.

Yad Voezer, 90 Queen Elizabeth's Walk, N16 5UQ. ☎ 020-8809 4303 Fax 020-8809 5420. Email yadvoezer@btconnect.com. Website www.ldb.co.uk/yadvoezer. (Est. 1975, Reg. Charity No. 1032490) Residential care and support for people with learning disabilities and mental health problems. *Chairman* Rabbi E. Landau; *Chief Exec.* Mrs Z. Landau.

Clubs and Cultural Societies

See also under Synagogues (pp.68–80); Organisations concerned with Jewish Youth (pp.40–46).
London Jewish Forum, PO Box 49746, WC1A 2WY. ☎ 020-8236 9453 Email info@london-jewishforum.org.uk. (Est. 2005). The London Jewish Forum is dedicated to the promotion of Jewish life in London, and provides a platform for engagement between London Jewry

and the GLA. It aims to represent Jewish interests within the GLA, London Boroughs, Local Government institutions, and to London's MPs. *Chairman* Adrian Cohn

Jewish News Unit 611 Highgate studios 53-79 Highgate Road, London NW5 1TL. ☎ 020-7692 6929. Email thejewishnews@totallyplc.com. And website www.totallyjewish.com, contactus@totallyjewish .com

Alyth Choral Society, North Western Reform Synagogue, Alyth Gdns., NW11 7EN. (020-8455 6763 (Est. 1983.) *Musical Dir.* Vivienne Bellos; *Chairman* M. Cohen; *Sec.* Ms L. Perez.

Association of Jewish Friendship Clubs, 26 Enford St., W1H 1DW. ☎ 020-7724 8100. Fax 020-7724 7574 (Head Office). An umbrella organisation for men and women in the 60-plus age group, providing companionship through clubs in London and the Provinces. A network of social clubs joining together for activities on a national basis, e.g. group holidays and central London based functions. *Jt Hon. Life Presidents* Lady Jakobovits and Lady Sacks; *Nat. Chairman* Mrs L. Bromley; *Hon. Chaplain* Rev. G. Glausiusz.

Brady-Maccabi, Youth and Community Centre, 4 Manor Pk. Crescent, Edgware, Middx. HA8 7NN. ☎ 020-8952 2948. Fax 020-8952 2393. Email office@bradymaccabi.org.uk; Website www.bradymaccabi.org.uk. (Est. 1979.) Open Sun. to Thurs. Seniority clubs meet Tues. and Thurs. pm. *President* John Cutner J.P., F.C.A.

Centre or Jewish Life, Media House, 4 Stratford Place, W1C 1AT, ☎ 020- 7495 6089 Fax 020-7495 6099. Email info@the cjl.org. website www.the cjl.org (Est. 2007) The CLJ provides opportunities for young Jews to connect with each other and our Jewish heritage. *Hon. President* Dr S. Pelz; *Chairman* Rabbi F. Vogel.

Chabad Lubavitch Centre (Reg. Charity No. 1123001), 395 Eastern Avenue, Ilford, Essex IG2 6LR. ☎ 020-8554 1624. Fax 020-8518 2126. (Est. 1986). *Exec. Dir.* Rabbi A.M. Sufrin; *Asst. Dir.* Rabbi M. Muller.

Friends of Jewish Youth, formerly Old Boys' Association. Martin Shaw, c/o A. J. Y., 128 East Lane, Wembley, Middx. ☎ 020-8908 4747. Fax 020-8904 4323.

Friends of Yiddish *Contact* Chaim Neslen, 232 Cranbrook Road, Ilford, Essex IG1 4UT. ☎ 020-8554 6112. We meet every Saturday afternoon at Toynbee Hall, nr Aldgate East Tube Station. The programme is entirely in Yiddish, and includes readings, live music and some discussion. Special events are advertised in the Jewish press.

Institute for Jewish Music Studies and Performance, 33 Seymour Pl., W1H 6AT. ☎ 020-7723 4404. (Est. 1982) To further the study and knowledge of Jewish music, both liturgical and secular, at the highest academic and performing level. *Dir.* S. Fixman.

Jewish Appreciation Group Tours, 32 Anworth Close, Woodford Green, Essex IG8 0DR ☎ 020-8504 9159. (Est. 1960.) Full history tours of the Jewish East End and the Jews in England from 1066. Historic walks and tours throughout the year. *Tours Org.* Adam Joseph.

Jewish Association of Cultural Societies (J.A.C.S.), Edgware Synagogue, Parnell Close, Edgware, Middx. HA8 9YE. ☎ 020-8444 9121. (Est. 1978.) Twenty-seven clubs located throughout the Greater London area, with two in Surrey, one in Brighton, one in Westcliff-on-Sea and one in Cardiff, providing weekly meetings for the 55+, embracing cultural and social programmes. *H. President* Mrs Annette Pearlman; *H. Nat. Chairman* C. Gordon; *H. Sec.* Mrs S. Pizer.

Jewish Community Centre for London, (Reg. Charity No. 1105622) 6, Park End, NW3 2SE. ☎ 020-7431 9866. Fax 020-7431 6483. Email info@jcclondon.org.uk. Website www.jcclondon.org.uk *Chairman* Andrew Franklin.

JHSE Essex Branch. *Contact* Mrs S. Lassman ☎ 020-8554 9921. (see also p. 33.)

Jewish Research Group, c/o Flat 4, Fernwood, 55, Clarence Rd., N22 8QE. ☎ 020-8889 8875. Email anitashapiro@dsl.pipex.com. The Jewish Research Group is an autonomous part of the Edmonton Hundred Historical Society and was established in 1978 when the Committee of the 1st Jewish Way of Life Exhibition, held to mark the 50th Anniversary of the Palmers Green and Southgate Synagogue, decided not to disband. The main aim of the J.R.G. is to research Jewish history in the 'Edmonton Hundred', which corresponds approximately to the boundaries of the London Boroughs of Enfield and Haringey, and to publish its findings. Current membership: 100. Monthly meetings are held. Six publications have been issued under the title of 'Heritage'. Heritage No. 6 published 2007. *President* Mrs Marjorie Glick, BA; *V. President* R.E. Landau, BSc; *Chairman* A. Shapiro; *V. Chairman* Mrs J. Goldman

KabbalahUK.com, 42, St George's Road Wimbledon SW19 4ED. ☎ 020 8944 7770. Email: rabbi@dubov.org. (Est. 2005) To disseminate Kabbalistic and Chassidic teaching in the UK. *Dir.* Rabbi N.D. Dubov.

Kadimah Youth Club (Reg. Charity No.: 299323), 127/129 Clapton Common, E5 9AB. ☎ 020-8809 4844. Catering for the Adeni and Sephardi youth in the Stamford Hill area. *Youth Leaders* G. Nissim, N. Mansoor.

London Jewish Male Choir. *Contact* john.mitchell@ljmc.org.uk. Rehearsals Thursday evenings, Hendon Synagogue.

Lubavitch of Edgware, 230 Hale Lane, Edgware, Middx HA8 9PZ. ☎ 020-8905 4141; Fax 020-8958 1169. Website www.lubavitchofedgware.com. (Est. 1986). Pioneers in Street Youth Work programmes: Kindergarten, Synagogue (affiliated to the Union of Orthodox Hebrew Congregations), Gan Israel Day Camp, Library, Tel Torah: telephone learning service. *Dir* Rabbi L. and Mrs F. Sudak; *Librarian* Mrs R. Brackman; *Publ.* Central, *Edr.* Mrs F. Sudak

Lubavitch of South London (Reg. Charity No. 227638), 42 St. George's Road, Wimbledon, SW19 4ED. ☎ 020-8944 7770. Email rabbi@dubov.org. Website www.chabadwimble don.com. (Est. 1988) Adult Jewish educ., library, food and bookshop, mailings, assemblies, tuition, Mitzva campaigns, youth activities. *Dir.* Rabbi Nissan Dubov.

The Maccabaeans (Est. 1891). Consisting primarily of those engaged in professional pursuits, its aims being to provide 'social intercourse and co-operation among its members with a view to the promotion of the interests of Jews, including the support of any professional or learned bodies and charities'. *President* Prof. D. Latchman; *H.T.* R. Michaelson; *H. Sec.* L. Slowe, 4 Corringway, NW11 7ED.

Museum of Immigration and Diversity, 19 Princelet Street, E1 6QH. ☎ 020-7247 5352. Email office@19princeletstreet.org.uk Website.19princeletstreet.org.uk. (Reg. Charity 287279). Grade II* heritage building incorporating a Victorian synagogue. Occasional public openings in celebration of immigration and diversity; private tours for educational groups by advance arrangement.

Oxford & St. George's (Reg. Charity No. 207191), 120 Oakleigh Road North, N20 9EZ. ☎ 020-8446 3101. Communal provision and youth clubs.

Redbridge Jewish Cultural Society (Est.1965) Meetings held at South West Essex & Settlement Reform Synagogue Oaks Lane, Newbury Park. *Contact* D. Sames, 12 Elm Walk, Gidea Park, Romford, Essex RM2 5NR. ☎ 01708 763 102. Email: david.sames @btinternet. com. Isabel Morris ☎ 020-8599 1746.

Redbridge Jewish Community Centre (Reg. Charity No.: 3013185), Sinclair House, Woodford Bridge Road, Ilford, Essex, IG4 5LN. ☎ 020-8551 0017. Fax 020-8551 9027. *Chairman* P. Leigh; *Centre Man.* R. Shone. Redbridge JCC, home of the Redbridge Jewish Youth and Community Centre, meets the social, educational and welfare needs of all sections of the Redbridge and District Jewish Community. More than 2,500 people make use of the Centre's facilities each week. The Redbridge Jewish Day Centre provides a high level of essential care for over 350 elderly and disabled people. There are programmes and services for young people, including those with special needs, and social, educational, welfare and active sports programmes for the young and adults alike. The Centre is also the base for the Community Shlicha, Clayhall Synagogue, Ackerman Resource Centre, the Redbridge Jewish Youth Council and many communal events and activities. The Redbridge Jewish Youth and Community Centre is part of Jewish Care.

Spec Jewish Youth and Community Centre (Reg. Charity No. 302921), 87 Brookside South, East Barnet, Herts EN4 8LL.. ☎ 020-8368 5117. Fax 020-8368 0891. Email info@speconline.co.uk. Est. 1962 to enable Jewish young people to meet in a secure environment and offer opportunities for personal growth. Activities include youth clubs for 5½-16 age grps. *Vice-Chairman* S. Lee; *T.* S. Pollins; *Hon. Sec.* S. Jacobs; *Sec.* Linda Rich.

Stepney Jewish Community Centre, 2-8 Beaumont Grove, E1 4NQ. ☎ 020-7790 6441. Fax 020-7265 8342. Administered by **Jewish Care.** Community Centre for the Elderly; Special care centre for physically and Mentally Frail; Kosher Meals on Wheels; outreach and support services; and Friendship Clubs. *Centre Man.* Philippa Paine.

Tribe (Young United Synagogue), Freepost, Solar House, 305 Ballards Lane N12 8NP. ☎ 020-

8343 5656. Fax 020-8905 7559. Email info@tribeuk.com. *Exec.Dir.* Rabbi A. Shaw.
Western Charitable Foundation, 32 Gt. Cumberland Place, W1H 7TN. ☎ 020-7724 7702. *Chairman* Sidney Jaque, JP; *V. Chairman* Harold Pasha; *Tr.* A.H. Yadgaroff; *Exec.Sec.* S. Garcia.
Zemel Choir (Reg. Charity No. 252572/ACL), Britain's leading mixed Jewish Choir performing a varied repertoire, with an emphasis on Hebrew, Yiddish, Israeli and liturgical music, and contemporary compositions of Jewish interest. Overseas tours, prestige concerts in London and provinces, recordings, social events. Zemel welcomes enthusiastic and committed singers who read music fairly fluently. Rehearsals most Mondays 8-10.30 p.m. North London. *Musical Dir.* B. Wolf. *Contact:* Michael Morris, 4 Mandeville Rd, N14 7NH. ☎ 020-8368 6289. Email syl.mike@btinternet.com.

Miscellaneous Organisations

ALL ABOARD SHOPS LIMITED
(Reg. Charity No. 1125462) All Aboard operate Charity Shops for the benefit of UK-based Jewish Charities. All Aboard welcome donations of clothing, bric-a-brac, etc, and welcome volunteers to assist in the shops and at Head Office. *Exec. Bd.* Stella Lucas, Monique Landau, Jeffrey Pinnick; *Exec. Dir.* Carol Marks. ☎ 020-8381 1717. Fax 020-8381 1718. Website www.allaboardshops.com; Email admin@allaboardshops.com.

Head Office 1–3 Boot Parade, 92 High Street, Edgware, Middlesex HA8 7HE.

Shops located at **Borehamwood**, 120 Shenley Road WD6 1EF, **East Finchley**, 124 High Road, N2 9ED, **Finchley Road**, 150 Finchley Road NW3 5HS, **Golders Green**, 616 Finchley Road NW11 7RR *and* 125 Golders Green Road NW11 8HR, **Hendon**, 98 Brent Street NW4 2HH, **Manchester**, Unit 10, The Longfield Centre, Prestwich MA25 5AY, **Mill Hill**, 53 The Broadway NW7 3DA, **Paddington**, 12 Spring Street W2 3RA, **Stamford Hill**, 2a Regent Parade, Amhurst Park N16 5LP, **Streatham**, 83 High Road SW16 1PH, **Temple Fortune**, 1111 Finchley Road NW11 0QB, **West Hampstead**, 224 West End Lane NW6 1UU.

JEWISH POLICE ASSOCIATION
Golders Green Police Station, 1069 Finchley Road, London NW11 0QE.
☎ 020-8733 5558 (45558 Metline). Fax 020-8733 5557 (45557 Metline). Email info@jewish-policeassociation.org.uk. Website www.jewishpoliceassociation.org.uk.
(Est. 2001) Provides a network for support and advice of Jewish staff within the Metropolitan Police Service; to promote understanding of the Jewish faith within the Police Service; and to act as a resource reference for Police Services regarding religious and cultural issues, in particular those that affect front-line policing. *Chair* Jo Poole; *Deputy Chair* Paul Vogler; *T.* Peter Russell, MBE; *Sec.* D. Phillips; *Exec.* Andrew Gee; *Hon. Chaplain* Rabbi Alan Plancey.

LONDON JEWISH MEDICAL SOCIETY
The Medical Society of London, PO Box 382, Wembley, Middx. HA9 9FA. ☎ 07929 633108. Email: admin@ljms.org.uk.
(Est. 1928.) A learned society for doctors, senior medical students and members of allied professions. *President* Prof. L. Spitz; *H. Sec.* B. Jacobs.

LONDON SOCIETY OF JEWS AND CHRISTIANS
28 St John's Wood Road, NW8 7HA.
☎ 020-7286 5181. Fax 020-7266 3591. Email a.bloom@ljs.org
(Est. 1927.) The oldest interfaith organisation of its kind in the UK, established to give an opportunity to Jews and Christians to confer together on the basis of their common ideals and with mutual respect for differences of religion. *Jt, Presidents* Rabbi Dr. D.J. Goldberg OBE, Revd. Dr. A. Harvey; *Jt. Chairmen* Rabbi M. L. Solomon, Rev. Dr N. Sagovsky; *Memb. Sec.* Margaret Rigal.

VISITATION COMMITTEE
The Visitation Committee, while under the administration of the United Synagogue, includes Hospital Visiting, Prison Visiting and Bereavement Counselling and services to all those who claim

to be Jewish, irrespective of any synagogue affiliation. The Committee is recognised by the National Health Service as the provider of hospital chaplaincy for Jewish patients, servicing hospitals throughout England. Visits by chaplains and lay visitors are made in those hospitals where there is a regular intake of Jewish patients, and information is given to other hospitals for emergency requirement and occasional visits. The Prison section, officially recognised by HM Prison Service, provides chaplaincy for prisons in England and advises Jewish chaplains in other parts of the country. *Admin* Sue Soloway, United Synagogue Visitation Committee Bet Meir, 44B, Albert Road, NW4 2SG. ☎ 020-8457 9709. Fax 020-8457 9707. Email sue.soloway@jvisit.org.uk.

Bereavement Counselling Service (see p.88).

THE REGIONS

Figures in brackets after place names indicate estimated Jewish population (see pp. 185, 189-90).

There are Zionist societies in almost every Jewish regional centre, and Women's Zionist societies in most of them.
Details of current burial arrangements have been listed where forthcoming.

Disused cemeteries are maintained by the Board of Deputies of British Jews at a number of towns in the British Isles. General enquiries about these and other locations should be addressed to the Board's Community Issues Division. **Bath:** Bradford Road, cnr of Greendown Place, abt. 2 miles from town centre. Keys held by City of Bath Probation Office. **Canterbury:** Entrance at end of passageway between 26 and 28 Whitstable Road. **Dover:** (maintained by the US) On Old Charlton Road, overlooking the harbour at Copt Hill. **Falmouth:** On main Penryn Road, Ponsharden. Keys from Vospers Garage (adjacent) ☎ 01326-372011. **Ipswich:** In Star Lane, premises of BOCM Pauls Ltd., and Jewish section of municipal cemetery. **King's Lynn:** In Millfleet (pedestrian precinct). Keys from Mr. C.J. Hilton, West Norfolk District Council, Hardwick Narrows Estate, King's Lynn. **Penzance:** Historic walled Georgian Cemetery (Grade II* listed); approx. 50 headstones. Passage between 19 and 20 Leskinnick Ter., right at end of arch, cemetery on left. (Access road unsuitable for cars.) Accompanied visits by appointment only. Contact the Custodian through the Penlee Museum, ☎ 01736-363625 or Town Clerk's Office ☎ 01736-363405. **Sheerness:** Jewish enclosure in municipal cemetery. Another site is behind shops at cnr. Hope St./High St. **Yarmouth:** On Blackfriars Road, Alma Road, on perimeter of old city walls. Key from Dept. of Technical Services, Gt. Yarmouth Town Hall.
(See also **Listed Synagogues and Other Jewish Monuments in the UK**, pp.198–200).

Mikvaot are maintained in the following centres: Birmingham, Bournemouth, Brighton, Cardiff, Edinburgh, Gateshead, Leeds, Leicester, Liverpool, Manchester, Newcastle, Sheffield, Southend, Southport, Sunderland and Glasgow.

Memorials: Large stone/slate memorial in Aberdovey Town Centre Park, West Wales, to No.3 Jewish Troop, No.10 Commando – plaque opposite on sea wall explains the Jewish refugee make-up of the troop; Clifford's Tower, York; Lincoln Cathedral.

Menorah: a magazine for Jewish members of H.M. Forces. *Edr.* Rev. M. Weisman, OBE, *Editorial Consult* Col. M. Newman ☎ 0161 766 6479. Email martin.newman@armymail.mod.uk.

BASILDON (Essex) (8)
Merged with Southend.
Burials arranged through Southend & Westcliff Hebrew Congregation at their cemetery in Southend.

BATH
The last synagogue closed in 1910. Services are currently being revived under the auspices of the Bristol and West Progressive Jewish Congregation (see p.100) at The Friends' Meeting House, York St.

BEDFORD (45)
In medieval times Bedford was one of the centres of English Jewry. A number of congregations existed at various times from 1803 onwards. The present com. originated during the 1939–45 war.
Hebrew Congregation. *Sec.* R. Berman. ☎ 01234 364723.
See also under Luton for Bedfordshire Progressive Synagogue.

BEXHILL-ON-SEA
Bexhill and District Jewish Friends, PO Box 198, TN40 9BG. Email bdjf@talktalk.co.uk. *Chairman* G. Lee; *T.* R. Caidan; *Sec* J. Caidan; *Asst. Sec.* M. Phillips. See also under Hastings

BIRMINGHAM (2,343)
This Jewish community is one of the oldest in the provinces, dating from 1730, if not earlier. Birmingham manufacturing attracted early Jewish settlers. In the Anglo-Jewish economy Birmingham's position was similar to a port, a centre from which Jewish pedlars covered the surrounding country week by week, returning to their homes for the Sabbath. The first synagogue of which there is any record was in The Froggery in 1780. But there was a Jewish cemetery in the same neighbourhood in 1730, and Moses Aaron is said to have been born in Birmingham in 1718. The history of the Birmingham community has been investigated by the Birmingham Jewish History Research Group under the leadership of the late Zoë Josephs.
Representative Council of Birmingham and West Midland Jewry. (Est. 1937.) *President* Sir Bernard Zissman; *Chairman* Mrs R. Jacobs; *H. Sec.* L. Jacobs. ☎ 0121-236 1801; *Admin.* Singers Hill, Ellis St., B1 1HL. ☎/Fax 0121-643 2688. Email jewishbirmingham@talktalk.net. Website www.brijnet.org/birmingham.
Board of Shechita, c/o Hebrew Cong., Singers Hill, Ellis Street, B1 1HL; *Sec.* B. Gingold.

SYNAGOGUES
Hebrew Congregation, Singers Hill, Ellis Street, B1 1HL. ☎ 0121-643 0884. The present syn. was consecrated on September 24, 1856 and celebrated its 150th anniversary in 2006. *M.* Rabbi Y. Jacobs; *Admin.* B. Gingold.
Central Synagogue, 133 Pershore Road, B5 7PA. (/Fax 0121-440 4044. office@central-shul.com. *M.* Rabbi S. Odze; *Sec.* C. Jennings.
Progressive Synagogue (LJ), Bishopsgate St., Roseland Way, B15 1HD. ☎ 0121-643 5640 *H. Sec.* F. Maxwell, ☎ 0167-653 3001 Email bps@liberaljudaism.org Website www. bps-liberaljudaism.org; *M.* Rabbi Dr Margaret Jacobi.

OTHER INSTITUTIONS
Birmingham Community Jewish Care, 19 Silverstone Ct., Riverbrook Dr., B30 2SH. ☎ 0121-459 3418. Fax 0121-459 3437. Email admin@bhamjha.co.uk. *President* Dr B. Roseman; *Dir.* I. Myers.
Birmingham Rabbinic Board. *Chairman* Rabbi Y.Pink ☎ 0121-706 8736.
Birmingham Union of Jewish Students, c/o Hillel House, 26 Somerset Road, Edgbaston, B15 2QD. ☎ 0121-454 5684. Mrs B. Lupasco ☎ 0121-471 4370 Email birminghamhillel @hotmail.co.uk
Hillel House, 26 Somerset Road, Edgbaston, B15 2QD. ☎ 0121-454 5684. Website www. ujshillel.co.uk/hillel-. Applications for admission to Mrs P. Harris, 4 High Trees Rd., Knowle, Solihull, B93 9PR. ☎ 01564-778710. Email birminghamhillel@hotmail.
Home for Aged, Andrew Cohen House, Riverbrook Drive, Stirchley, B30 2SH. ☎ 0121-458 5000.
Jewish Graduates Association. *Sec.* Prof. A. Travis ☎ 0121-454 1215. Email tony@ e-w-tourism.demon.co.uk.
Jewish Historical Society, (Branch est. 1968) *Chairman* Dr A. P. Joseph (see p. 34).
King David School, 244 Alcester Road, B13 8EY. ☎ 0121-499 3364. *H.T.* S. Langford. office@kingdavid.bham.sch.uk.
Lubavitch Centre & Bookshop, 95 Willows Road, B12 9QF. ☎ 0121-440 6673. Fax 0121-446 4299. *M.* Rabbi S. Arkush. Also at this address: Operation Judaism (see p.57).
Midlands Centre for Liberal Judaism, c/o Birmingham Progressive Synagogue
Mikva at Central Synagogue, For appointments ☎ 0794-664 2265.
Israel Information Centre, Bookshop and Reference Library, Singers Hill, Ellis St., B1 1HL. *Dir.* Mrs R. Jacobs (0121-643 2688. Email iicmids@talktalk.net.
Jewish Education Board. *Chairman* A. Gremson, c/o Hebrew Congregation. ☎ 0121-643 0884.

CEMETERIES
Brandwood End Cemetery, Kings Heath 14. Enqs. to Hebrew Congregation (☎ 0121-643 0884).
Witton Cemetery, The Ridgeway, College Road, Erdington 23. ☎ 0121-356 4615.

BLACKPOOL (302)
United Hebrew Congregation, Leamington Road. (Consecrated 1916.) Services were first held in the 1890s in a private house. Later a syn. was built in Springfield Road. *M.* Rev. D. Braunold. ☎ 01253 392382; *President* F. H. Freeman. ☎ 01253 393767.
Reform Synagogue, 40 Raikes Parade, FY1 4EX. (A constituent of Reform Movement.) ☎ 01253 623687. *M.* Rabbi N. Zalud; *H.T.* Mrs E. R. Ballan, 177 Hornby Road, Blackpool, FY2 4JA. ☎ 01253 625839.
Blackpool Council of Christians and Jews. Rev D. Braunold, 31 Marlborough Road, Blackpool North. (01253 392382. *H. Sec.*
Blackpool and Fylde Ajex. *H. Sec.* S. Tomlinson. ☎ 01253 728659.
Blackpool and Fylde Jewish Welfare Society. *President; H.T.* D. Lewis (01253 295608.
Fylde League of Jewish Women. *H. Sec.* Mrs A. Poston, Flat 16, The Royals, 11 Links Gate, Lytham St Annes, Lancs. FY8 3LJ. ☎ 01253 711078.

BOGNOR REGIS (30)
Hebrew Congregation. *H. Sec.* J. S. Jacobs, Elm Lodge, Sylvan Way, PO21 2RS. ☎01243 823006. Email jackneve@talktalk.net.

BOURNEMOUTH (2,100)
The Bournemouth Hebrew Cong. was est. in 1905 and met in the Assembly Rooms, where the Bournemouth Pavilion now stands. A syn., built in Wootton Gdns. in 1911, was rebuilt in 1961 to seat some 950 congregants. The Menorah suite was added in 1974, and a mikva in 1976.

Bournemouth Reform Synagogue was started by a small band of enthusiasts in 1947. Ten years later the congregation was large enough to build the present synagogue building at 53 Christchurch Road. It was extended in 1980 and now has a membership of over 700 persons, with a voluntary mixed choir, active Cheder, and many social activities, and is host to the Jewish Day Centre every Monday.

Bournemouth is the religious and social centre for the fast growing community in Dorset, West Hampshire and Wiltshire.
Bournemouth & District Jewish Representative Council (incorp. Southampton). *Chairman* B. Webb ☎ 01202-520671; *Hon. Sec.* D. Davidson; ☎ 01202-701011.
Wessex Jewish News (community newsletter), P.O. Box 2287, BH3 7ZD.
Hebrew Congregation, Wootton Gdns. BH1 1PW. ☎ 01202 557433. *President* B. Lassman; *M.* Rev M. Lev.
Mikva, Gertrude Preston Hall, Wootton Gdns. ☎ 01202 557433.
Yavneh Kindergarten, Gertrude Preston Hall, Wootton Gdns. BH1 3PW. ☎ 01202 295414. *Princ.* Mrs R. Nash.
Reform Syngagogue, 53 Christchurch Road, P.O. Box 8, BH1 3PN. (Est. 1947.) (A Constituent of the Reform Movement) ☎ 01202-557736. *M.* Rabbi N, Amswych *Chairman* R. Rosenfeld; *H. Sec.* M.Smith. Website www. bournemouthreform.org
Day Centre, *Co-ordinator* Mrs R. Lesser, 40A East Avenue, BH3 7DA. ☎ 01202 766039.
Bournemouth Sephardi Association, 69 Orchard Avenue, Poole, Dorset BH14 8AH. ☎ 01202-745168 after 8p.m. *Chairman* Simon Tammam; *Sec.* ; *T.* David Kalfon
Bournemouth University Jewish Society, Wallisdown Road, Poole. ☎ 01202 524111.
Home for Aged: Hannah Levy House, 15 Poole Road, Bournemouth. ☎ 01202 765361.
Lubavitch Centre, Chabad House, 9 Boscombe Spa Rd., Boscombe, BH5 1AW. ☎ 01202 396615.
Cemeteries: Kinson Cemetery (used by both Hebrew Cong. and Reform Syn.); Boscombe Cemetery (used by old established mems. Hebrew Cong.); Throop Cemetery (Hebrew Cong.)

BRADFORD (356)

Jews of German birth, who began settling in Bradford in the first half of the nineteenth century, were in a large measure responsible for the development of its wool yarns and fabrics exports to all parts of the world. Jewish services, first held in the 1830s in private houses, were held in 1873, on Reform lines, in a public hall. About the same period saw the beginnings of the Orthodox community.

Hebrew Congregation (Orthodox), Springhurst Road, Shipley, West Yorks. BD18 3DN. (Cong. est. 1886, Syn. erected 1970.) *President* A. A. Waxman; *H. Sec.* Mrs A.E. Dye, Brookfield, Hebden Hall Park, Hebden, Grassington, BD23 5DX. ☎ 01756-752012.

Synagogue, Bowland Street, Bradford, BD1 3BW. (Est. 1880.) (A constituent of Reform Movement) *Chairmen* R. Stroud, R. Leavor, 76 Heaton Park Drive, BD9 5QE. s☎ 01274 544198; *H. Sec.* D. Solomon, 19 Rockwood Road, Leeds LS28 5AB. ☎ 0113-2562344.

Jewish Benevolent Society. *President* A.A. Waxman; *H.T.* W. Behrend.

Cemetery (both Orthodox and Reform), Scholemoor, Necropolis Road, Cemetery Road, Bradford.

BRIGHTON & HOVE (3,358)

There were Jews resident in Brighton in the second half of the eighteenth century, and by the beginning of the nineteenth century there was an organised community. (The earliest syn. was founded in Jew Street in 1792.)

Brighton and Hove Jewish Representative Council. Nearly every synagogue, charitable organisation, social and cultural institution, as well as the communities in Eastbourne, Hastings, Bexhill and Worthing are affiliated to this Council and meetings are held quarterly *President* Beryl Sharpe. Website www.jewishsussex.com,. *Sec.* Jessica Rosenthal, PO Box 2178, Hove, BN3 3SZ, ☎ 01273 206456, Email: rep@jewishsussex.com

SYNAGOGUES

Brighton & Hove Hebrew Congregation (Reg. Charity No. 233221).
Synagogue: 31 New Church Road, Hove BN3 4AD and 66 Middle Street, BN1 1AL. (open monthly Sundays for viewing contact Admin for details) *M.* Rabbi P. Efune; *Admin.* Mrs L. Shaw. ☎ 01273 888855. Fax 01273 888810. Email shul@bhhc.fsnet.co.uk

Hove Hebrew Congregation, 79 Holland Road, Hove, BN1 3JN. *M.* Rabbi V. Silverman. ☎ 01273 732035. Email: hovehc@btinternet.com. *Chairman* Stanley. Cohen. *T.* Michele Cohen. Delgate to be advised

Brighton & Hove Reform Synagogue (Est. 1955) Palmeira Avenue, Hove, BN3 3GE. ☎ 01273 735343. *Admin* Mrs C. Sweid. Email: office@bh-rs.org

Brighton & Hove Progressive Synagogue (LJ) (Est. 1935), 6 Lansdowne Road, Hove, BN3 1FF. ☎ 01273 737223. *M.* Rabbi Elizabeth Tikvah Sarah; *Admin* Linda Gocher. Email: bhps@liberaljudaism.org

RELIGIOUS

Cemetery (Orthodox), Meadowview Cemetery, Bear Road. *Contact* Rabbi P. Efune ☎ 01273 888855.

Cemetery (Non-Orthodox), Old Shoreham Road, Hove. Contact either Reform or Progressive Synagogues.

Mikvah, *Contact* Mrs P Efune ☎ 01273 321919.

Joint Kashrut Board, *Contact* Rabbi P. Efune ☎ 01273 888855 or Rabbi V. Silverman ☎ 01273 732035.

Lubavitch Foundation (Lubavitch of Brighton), Rabbi P. Efune, 15 The Upper Drive, East Sussex BN3 6GR. ☎ 01273 321919.

WELFARE

Brighton & Hove Jewish Day Centre - See Brighton & Hove Jewish Centre at Ralli Halll

Brighton & Hove Jewish Housing Association *Ch.* Mrs. Marion. Davids, 19 Warnham Court, Hove ☎ 01273 735740. No delegate at present. *Tr* Mr S. E. Lawrence, Maycroft, London Road, Patcham, Brigton ☎ 01273 558239

Brighton & Hove Jewish Welfare Board, *Chairman* Edwin Prince, 61 Furze Croft, Furze

Hill,Hove BN3 1PD. ☎ 01273 738463. *Delegate* Stanley Jackson, 10½ Preston Park Avenue, Brighton BN1 6HJ ☎ 01273 502497. *T.* Alan Style, Bank House, Southwick Square, Southwick W.Sx BN42 4FN ☎ 01273 597343.

Helping Hands ☎ 01273 747722, Email helping-hands@ntlworld.com Email: helping-hands@ntlworld.com

Hyman Fine House (Jewish Care residential home), 20 Burlington Street Brighton,BN2 1AU (Hd of Home: Margaret Stanbridge) ☎ 01273 688226.

Sussex Tikvah (Home for Jewish adults with learning difficulties), 25 Chatsworth Road BN1 5DB. ☎ 01273 564021. *Man.* Joanne Osbaldiston. *Chairman* Peter Senker,17 Varndean Gardens, Brighton BN1 6WJ ☎ 01273 884132.Email psenker@ipra.co.uk. *Tr.* Jacqueline Senker, Email jacky@ipra.u-net.com. *Delegate* JackMazzier, 14F Bedford Towers, Kings Road Brighton BN1 2JG. ☎ 01273 202808.Email jmazzier@onetel.com.

EDUCATION
Torah Academy. 31 New Church Road, Hove, ☎ 01273 328675.

Hillel House, 18 Harrington Road, Brighton BN1 6RE. ☎ 01273 503450. *Chairman & Delegate* Aileen Hill. 2/9 Adelaide Crescent , Hove ☎ 01273 727979.

Jewish Students' Society c/o Hillel House

Centre for German-Jewish Studies, University of Sussex.

Youth Groups

AHA Group –see Reform Synagogue.

Sunday Football Club (18–15 years). *Contact* ivan.lyons@ntlworld.com.

OTHER ORGANISATIONS
AJEX. *Chairman* Aubrey Cole, 61 Langdale Road, Hove BN3 4HR. ☎ 01273 737417.

Ben Gurion University Foundation. *Chairman & Delegate* Sam Barsam 47 Woodruff Avenue, Hove BN£ 6LH *Contact* ☎ 01273 508323. Email sambarsam@hotmail.com

Brighton & Hove Interfaith Contact Group IFCG, *Contact* Arnold Lewis ☎ 01273 732177 Email admin@ifcg.co.uk, Website www.ifcg.co.uk.

Brighton & Hove Jewish Historical Society. *Chairman* Bernard Fox. ☎ 01273 248535. Email berniefox@onetel.com

Brighton & Hove Jewish Centre (Reg. Charity No. 269474) (incorporating Brighton & Hove Jewish Day Centre, Jewish Arts Society, SARID (Holocaust Survivors Group). Ralli Hall, 81 Denmark Villas, Hove BN3 3TH. ☎ 01273 202254.Email rallihall@tiscali.co.uk, *Admin*. Norina Duke; *Chairman* Roger Abrahams. Meeting centre for various citizens clubs, mother & baby club, youth clubs. Facilities include committee rooms, theatre facilities, snooker room, work-out gym, library/reading room, cafeteria, etc. Kosher kitchen (lunch available on Wednesdays and Thursdays)

Youth Aliyah. *Chairman* Elizabeth Posner, 18 Baltimore Court, 74 The Drive, Hove BN3 3PR ☎ 01273 776671. Email liz.posner@orchidserve.com. *Tr.* Laurel Woolfe 47 Woodruff Avenue, Hove BN3 6PH. ☎ 01273 559511. Email julianand laurel@amserve.com.

JACS (Jewish Association of Cultural Societies) *Co-Chair* Mrs S. Beckerman 2/41 Selborne Road Hove BN3 3AL ☎ 01273 77802, Co-Chair Mrs June Faull, 26/15 Grand Avenue, Hove BN3 2NG. ☎ 01273 723528. *Delegate* Mrs Joan Levene, 11 Gainsborough House, Eaton Gardens, Hove BN3 3UA. ☎ 01273 722926. *Tr.* Mr Stuart Bennis, 27 Carmel House, Westbourne Street, Hove BN3 3PR. ☎ 01273 779967

JAS - Jewish Arts Society. *Chairman* Rochelle Oberman, 23 Hove Park Road, Hove *Contact* ☎ 01273 50378

Jewish Woman Friends in Sussex. – Maxine Toff ☎ 01273 822742

JNF Committee. *Contact* Email: Sjoory@aol.com

Sarid. (Holocaust Survivors Group) *Contact* ☎ 01273 734648 or Email fausta@fshelton. fsnet.co.uk

Sussex Jewish Golfing Society. *Present President* Mef Sharpe ☎ 01273 734300. Tr. Michael Marks, 9 Woodlands, Hove BN3 6TJ ☎ 01273 541299 Email michael@marksand.co.uk

Sussex WIZO-Ziona. *Chairman & Delegate* Claire Barsam 47 Hove Park Road, Hove BN3 6LH *Contact* ☎ 01273 508323. Email sambarsam@hotmail.com.

BRISTOL (823)

Bristol was one of the principal Jewish centres of medieval England. Even after the Expulsion from England in 1290 there were occasional Jewish residents or visitors. A community of Marranos lived here during the Tudor period. There had been a Jewish community in the City before 1754 and the original Synagogue opened in 1786. The present building dates from 1871 and was renovated in 1981-83. Polack's House (Clifton College) was founded in 1878. The Progressive Synagogue was founded in 1961 and the present building was consecrated in 1971.

Bristol Jewish Representative Council, *Chairman* M. Romain, 7 College Fields, BS8 3HP. ☎ 0117-973 9312. Email romain@netgates.co.uk. *Sec.* Mrs K. Balint-Kurti, P.O. Box 327, BS9 1NX. ☎ 0117-973 1150.

Synagogues:

Bristol Hebrew Congregation, 9 Park Row BS1 5LP. *Sec.* B. Bermange. Email benedict@bermange.com. *H.T.* Arnold Greenwood.

Bristol & West Progressive Jewish Cong (LJ). (Reg. Charity No. 73879), 43-47, Bannerman Road, Easton BS5 0RR. *M.* . ☎ 0117-954 1937. Email bpjc@liberaljudaism,org, bwpjc@liberaljudaism.org, Website www.bwpjc.org

Bristol University Jewish & Israel Soc., c/o Hillel House.

Hillel House, 45 Oakfield Road, Clifton, BS8 2BA. ☎ 0117-946 6589. Accommodation enquiries: Mrs S. Tobias, (01454 412831.

Davar, The Jewish Institute in Bristol, cultural and educational organisation aims to encourage Jewish identity with the widest possible spectrum. ☎ 0117-970 6594. 179, Whiteladies Rd., Clifton BS8 2AG. *Admin.*

Cemetery: Oakdene Avenue, Fishponds, Bristol BS5 6QQ.

CAMBRIDGE (resident Jewish pop. approx 850, students 500)

The present congregation was founded in 1888 but an organised community was present from 1774. The synagogue in Thompson's Lane was opened in 1937. Services held there are traditionally orthodox; the building serves also as a student centre.

Cambridge Traditional Jewish Congregation (Est. 1937. Reg. Charity No. 282849), 3 Thompson's Lane, CB5 8AQ. ☎ 01223-501916. *Chairman* Prof. S. Goldhill sdg1001@cam.ac.uk; www.ctjc.org.uk

Mikvah Committee (Reg. Charity No. 1067075). Enquiries to Mrs C. Klein, c/o The Synagogue.

Beth Shalom Reform Synagogue (RM), services and cheder and adult education programme. *Chairman* O. Meir-Stacey 07798 721577. Email info@beth-shalom.org.uk; Website www.beth-shalom.org.uk.

Cambridge & Suffolk Jewish Community (Hama'ayan) (Reg. charity No. 1111197) Mikvah and children's nursery under construction at 268 Milton Road CB4 1LQ. Corr: 101, Perseway CB4 3SB.*Sec.* D. Gilinsky ☎ 01223 354825. Email info@jewishcambridge.org.uk. Website www.jewishcambridge.org.uk.

Cambridge Commmunity Mikvah Ch. Trust (CCMC) (Reg. Charity No. 1067075). *Enquiries* D. Gilinsky.

Cambridge Chabad. Rabbi R. Leigh ☎ 01223 354603; Email: info@cuchabad.org.uk

Cambridge Jewish Residents' Association (Est. 1940). ☎ 01223-352963. Provides religious, cultural, educational and welfare facilities for its members.

Cambridge University Jewish Society (Est. 1937). ☎ 01223-701646. Email soccujs@lists.com.ac.uk. Website www.cam.ac.uk/societies/cujs/. Organises orthodox services at the synagogue during term time. Kosher meals available. *Student Chaplain*

CANTERBURY & DISTRICT (210)

The history of the Canterbury community, 'The Jews of Canterbury, 1760–1931' by Dan Cohn-Sherbok, was published in 1984.

Jewish Community includes members in the whole of East Kent.

CHATHAM (ca. 50)

There was an organised Jewish community in Chatham from the first half of the eighteenth century. The present syn., erected in 1869 in memory of Captain Lazarus Simon Magnus, by his father, Simon Magnus, is on the site of its predecessor, erected about 1740. It is an indendent traditional congregation holding regular services and events. A Centenary Hall and Mid-Kent Jewish Youth Centre was consecrated in 1972. The old cemetery, dating back to about 1790, is behind the syn.

Chatham Memorial Synagogue, 366 High Street, Rochester. Website www.chathamshul. org.uk fsnet.co.uk. Inquiries: David Herling, 24 Maidstone Rd., Rochester, ME1 1RJ. ☎ 01634 831998. Email d.a.herling@city.ac.uk

CHELMSFORD (145)

Jewish Community (Reg. Charity No. 281498), Suite 6, Springfield Lyons House Springfield Lyon Approach CM2 5LB. ☎ 01245-475444. Email info@jewish communitychelmsford.co.uk; Website www.jewishcommunitychelmsford.co.uk. The community, est. in 1974, holds regular services, religion classes and social activities. It has burial arrangements through the Jewish Joint Burial Society.

CHELTENHAM (98)

The congregation was est. in 1823 and the present syn. in St. James's Sq. opened in 1839, furnished with fittings from the New Synagogue, Leadenhall Street (1761), which relocated to Great St Helen's in 1837, thus endowing the Cheltenham community with the oldest extant Ashkenazi furniture in the country. 'The History of the Hebrew Community of Cheltenham, Gloucester and Stroud', by Brian Torode, was reprinted in 1999. After two generations, the cong. dwindled and the syn. closed in 1903. Refugees from Central Europe and evacuated children and others from Jewish centres in England, however, re-established the community and a cong. was re-formed in 1939 and the old syn. reopened. The cemetery, dating from 1824, is in Elm St.

Hebrew Congregation, St. James's Sq. (Reg. Charity No. 261470-R). *H. Sec.* Christine Dyer, Bramble Cottage, Dog Lane, Witcombe, Glos GL3 4UG. ☎ 01452 862399.

CHESHAM (70)

South Bucks. Jewish Community (LJ).

PO Box 391, Chesham, Bucks. HP5 1WB. ☎ 0845 644 2370. Email sbjc@liberaljudaism.org. Website www.sbjc.org.uk. M. Rabbi R. Benjamin **Cemetery:** See Edgwarebury Cemetery (p.83).

CHESTER (132)

Jewish Congregation, Ian and Lesley Daniels, Porthouse, 6 South Crescent Rd, Queens Park, CH4 7AU. ☎ 01244 677776.

COLCHESTER (100)

Colchester and District Jewish Community (Reg. Charity No. 237240), Synagogue, Fennings Chase, Priory St., CO1 2QG. The community has close links with the University of Essex at Colchester. For information about services, Cheder and social events please contact the Hon. Secretary, J.M. Gottesman, ☎ 01206 866553.

CORNWALL

Kehillat Kernow Jewish Community (Movement for Reform). *Contact* ☎ 01209 719672/ 01872 240086.

COVENTRY (140)

There were Jews settled in and around Coventry from at least 1775. The watch making industry was instrumental in the growth of the community in the late 1800's.
The synagogue was built in 1870 and has been in (almost) continual use to the present day. The Reform community started in 1993.

Synagogue, Barras Lane, *President* Russel Starr; *Tr.* Adrian Berger

Reform Community, *Chairman* Ian Cohen; *Sec.* Ros Johnson, Email: RosAriel@aol.com; *President* Martin Been, Email: Martinbeen@aol.com ☎ 024 7662027.

CRAWLEY (ca. 50)
Jewish Community (LJ). (Est. 1959.) ☎ 01293 534294*H. Sec.* Mrs L. Bloom, c/o Tanyard Farmhouse, Lansholt, Horley, Surrey RH6 9LN.

DARLINGTON (40)
Hebrew Congregation (Movement for Reform), 15, Bloomfield Road, DL36 6RZ. (Est. 1904.) *Sec.* M. Finn, 17 Thornbury Rise, DL3 9NE; *Chairman* P. Freitag, 237 Parkside, DL1 5TG. ☎ 01325-468812.
Cemetery: Contained in a consecrated section of: The West Cemetery, Carmel Road, Darlington.

EAST GRINSTEAD AND DISTRICT (35)
Jewish Community (Reg. Charity No. 288189). (Est. 1978). *H. M.* Rev. M. Weisman, M.A.; *Warden* E. Godfrey, 7 Jefferies Way, Crowborough, Sussex TN6 2UH. ☎ 01892 653949. Corr: Mrs M. Beevor, 6 Court Close, East Grinstead, West Sussex RH19 3YQ. ☎ 01342 312148.

EASTBOURNE (63)
Hebrew Congregation, 22 Susans Road, BN21 3TJ; *H. Sec.* ☎ 01323 484135.
Eastbourne Progressive Jewish Community (LJ). *Enquiries* ☎ 01323 725650 Email epjc@liberaljudaism.org. Website www.epjcong.org.uk
Cemetery: Eastbourne Borough Cemetery has a part set aside for the comm. in conjunction with the Brighton Chevra Kedusha.

EXETER (150)
Before the expulsion, Exeter was an important Jewish centre. The syn. off Mary Arches St. was built in 1763, and the cemetery in Magdalen Road dates from 1757, but Jews are known to have lived in Exeter 30 years earlier and the com. is said to have been founded as early as 1728. The community greatly decreased during the 19th century, but has revived in recent years. Regular Progressive and Traditional services. Synagogue ☎ 01392 251529.
Hebrew Congregation Synagogue, Synagogue Place, Mary Arches St., EX4 3BA. ☎ 01392 251529. Email mail@exetersynagogue.org.uk; Website www.exetersynagogue.org.uk. *President* Paul Newgass. ☎ 01803 834486.

GATESHEAD (1,564)
Synagogue, 180 Bewick Road, NE8. ☎ (Mikva. ☎ 0191-477 3552). Rab. Rabbi S. Zimmerman
Kolel Synagogue, 22 Claremont Place, NE8 1TL. (Constituent of the Union of Orthodox Hebrew Congregations.) *Sec.* S. Ehrentreu. ☎ 0191-477 2189.
Beis Hatalmud, 1 Ashgrove Tce., NE8. *Princ.* Rabbi S. Steinhouse. ☎ 0191-478 4352.
Institute for Higher Rabbinical Studies (Kolel Harabbonim), 22 Claremont Place, NE8 ITL. ☎ 0191-477 2189. *Sec.* S. Ehrentreu.
Sunderland Talmudical College and Yeshiva, Prince Consort Road, NE8 4DS. ☎ 0191-490 0195 (Off.); 0191-490 0193 (Students). *Princ.* Rabbi J. Ehrentreu.
Sunderland Kolel – Centre for Advanced Rabbinical Studies, 139 Prince Consort Rd., NE8 1LR. (0191-477 5690. *Princ.* Dayan Ch. Ehrentreu.
Yeshiva, 88 Windermere Street, NE8 1UB. ☎ 0191-477 2616. Fax 0191-490 0480. Students, 179 Bewick Road ☎ 0191-478 3048/1351. *Sec.* S. Esofsky. Email talmudical@btopenworld.com
Yeshive Lezeirim, 36 Gladstone Tce., NE8 4EF. (Reg. Charity No. 514963). *Princ.* Rabbi E. Jaffe. (0191-477 0744. Email yltyuk@yahoo.co.uk.
Gateshead Girls High School, 6 Gladstone Tce., NE8 4DY. ☎ 0191-477 3471. *Princ.* Rabbi D. Bowden; *Sec.* Mrs R. Dunner.
Jewish Primary School, 18 Gladstone Terr., NE8 4EA. (Reg. Charity No. 527372). ☎ 0191-477 2154. Fax 0191-478 7554. *H. Sec.* Mrs C. Rabinowitz.

Ohel Rivka Kindergarten, Alexandra Road, NE8. ☎ 0191-478 3723; *H. Sec.* Mrs Esofsky, 13 Grasmere St. ☎ 0191-477 4102.

GLOUCESTER
Gloucestershire Liberal Jewish Community. ☎ 01242 521 468, Email gljc@btinternet.com

GRIMSBY (35)
There are records of Jews living here prior to 1290 and a community of sorts existed in the early 1800s. Mass immigration from eastern Europe, when Grimsby, like so many east coast ports, was the first landfall for these 'escapees' from persecution, saw many passing through *en route* for the larger northern cities and even further onward to Canada and the United States but a fair number remained, and a proper community was created. The synagogue and cemetery were consecrated in 1885. The community reached its numerical peak in the 1930s, when it numbered between 450/500, but its gradual decline began in the immediate post-war years. The history of the community has been published: D. and L. Gerlis, 'The Story of the Grimsby Jewish Community', 1986. Regular services are held every Friday evening at 7.00pm, and also on all the major festivals and holidays.

Sir Moses Montefiore Synagogue, Holme Hill, Heneage Road, DN32 9DZ. *President* L. Solomon ☎ 01472 824 463; *T.* H. S. Kalson; *H. Sec.* M. Saunders, 29 Manor Drive, Waltham DN37 ONS.

Cemetery: (Chevra Kadisha) First Avenue, Nunsthorpe, Grimsby. *Sec.* R. Resner, 14 Welholme Ave., DN32 OEA. ☎ 01472 342521; *T.* H. Kalson, 12A Welholme Avenue, DN32 OHP.

GUILDFORD (383)
Synagogue (1979), York Road, GU1 4DR. The community has grown up since the Second World War. Regular services; Cheder and social activities. *Chairman* Prof. R. Spier. ☎ 01483 259265; *Sec.* Mrs B. Gould. ☎ 01483 576470.

University of Surrey Jewish Society, c/o Professor R. Spier. ☎ 01483 259265.

Cemetery: Consecrated section of municipal cemetery.

HARLOW (190)
Jewish Community, Harberts Road, Hare St, Essex CM19 4DT. (01279-432503. (Movement for Reform.) *President* E. Clayman; *Vice-President* C. Jackson; *Chairman* Mrs H. Garnelas ☎ 020-8503 9809; *M.* Rabbi M. Pertz; *Sec.* Mrs E. Robbins.

HARROGATE (327)
'The History of the Harrogate Jewish Community' by Rosalyn Livshin was published in 1995.

Hebrew Congregation, St. Mary's Walk, HG2 OLW. (Est. 1918.) *President* Leslie Fox ☎ 01423 523439. Email miznerfox@ntlworld.com; *Sec.* P.E. Morris. ☎ 01423 871713. Email philip.morris@ukgateway.net.

Zionist Group. *Chairman* Anita Royston. ☎ 01423 561188. Email anitasandy@tiscali.co.uk.

HASTINGS (33)
Hastings and District Jewish Society (Reg. Charity No. 273806). Regular meetings of the Society including a short service are held on the first Friday of the month in Bexhill, at 7 p.m. P.O. Box 74, Bexhill-on-Sea, East Sussex TN39 4ZZ. ☎ 077 4399 2295.

HEMEL HEMPSTEAD (270)
Hebrew Congregation (affiliated to US) Est. 1956. Synagogue, Lady Sarah Cohen Community Centre, Midland Road, Hemel Hempstead, Herts. HD1 1RP. *H. Sec.* H. Nathan. ☎ 01923 32007.

Morton House, Midland Road, HP2 5BH (Jewish Care residential home).

HEREFORD
Herefordshire Jewish Community (Associate Community of Liberal Judaism). Enquiries ☎ 07789 218823.

HIGH WYCOMBE (35)
Hebrew Congregation (affiliated to U.S.). *H. Sec.* A. Abrams, 37 Beechtree Ave., Marlow Bottom, Bucks SL7 3NH. ☎ 01628 476244.

HITCHIN
Yeshivas Toras Chessed, Wellbury House, Great Offley, Hitchin, Herts. *Rab.* A. S. Stern. ☎ 01462 768698.

HOVE (see Brighton & Hove)

HULL (670)
In Hull, as in many English port towns, a community was formed earlier than in inland areas. The first recorded resident was in 1766. The first synagogue was used in 1780, which is about when the first cemetery was acquired. After London, Hull was the principal port of entry for Jews from Continental Europe. Of the 2.2 million immigrants who came through Hull between 1850 and 1914, 0.5 million were Jews. Today there are 160 souls in the orthodox congregation and 70 in the reform.
Jewish Representative Council. *President* Judah Rose ☎ 01482 655367; *H. Sec.* Prof. J. Friend, 9 Allanhall Way, Kirk Ella, HU10 7QU. ☎ 01482 658930.

SYNAGOGUES
Hull Hebrew Congregation, 30 Pryme Street, Anlaby HU10 6SH. (Reg. Charity No. 1035451). *H. Sec.* D. Lewis. ☎ 01482 653242. Fax 01482 650282, Email Shalom.osdoba@gmail.com
Reform Synagogue (Constituent of RM.), Great Gutter Lane, Willerby HU10 7JT. *H. Sec.* Mrs G. Barker, The Cherries, Temple Close, Welton, Brough, East Yorks HU15 1NX. ☎ 01482 665375.

OTHER INSTITUTIONS
Hull Jewish Community Care. (Est. 1880.) Menorah House, 335 Anlaby Rd., HU3 2SA. ☎ 01482 328227. *Chairman* S. Silver. ☎ 01482 651043
Board of Shechita, **Jewish Archive, Mikveh** c/o Hebrew Congregation.

KENT
Kent Liberal Jewish (Reg. Charity no. 1109044) ☎ 07952 242 432. Website www.jewishkent.org.uk.

LEAMINGTON & DISTRICT (132)
Progressive Jewish Group. (A branch of the Birmingham Progressive Synagogue LJ) Inq. ☎ 01926 421300.

LEEDS (8,267)
Leeds has the third largest Jewish community in Britain. Jews have lived in Leeds at least from the middle of the eighteenth century, but it was only in 1840 that a Jewish cemetery was acquired. The first so-called synagogue was a converted room in Bridge Street, where services were held up to 1846. Thereafter the place of worship was transferred to the Back Rockingham Street Synagogue, which was replaced by the Belgrave Street Synagogue built in 1860. Another syn. was built in 1877, but this closed in 1983.

The Leeds Jewish community is mainly the product of the persecution of Russian Jewry in the latter half of the nineteenth century. The bulk of immigration settled in Leeds between 1881 and 1905, enhancing the growth of the clothing industry which developed from the woollen and worsted manufacturing in the West Riding of Yorkshire. This industry was made world famous by John Barran, a non-Jew, and his Jewish associate Herman Friend, who was responsible for introducing division of labour into the clothing industry. While the sweating system existed in Leeds, both wages and working conditions were better than in London or Manchester. Trade unionism was successful and the first recorded strike by Jewish industrial workers took place spontaneously in Leeds in 1885.

During the early decades of this century the old Leylands ghetto, where most of the immigrants lived, began to break up. The main move of the Jewish people was to northern districts of Leeds, first to Chapeltown, which flourished in the 1940s, and then to the Moortown and Alwoodley suburbs. The Leeds Rep. C. republished in 1985 the late Louis Saipe's 'A History of the Jews of Leeds'.

Today, this well-organised, strong community of over 8,000 provides for Leeds Jews with over 100 organisations which are affiliated to the Leeds Jewish Representative Council, the official spokesman of the Leeds Jewish community.

GENERAL ORGANISATIONS

Jewish Representative Council, Marjorie & Arnold Ziff Community Centre, 311 Stonegate Rd., LS17 6AZ ☎ 0113 2697520. Email info@ljrc.org, Website www.ljrc.org. Nearly every synagogue, charitable organisation, social and cultural instititution and Zionist Soc. is affiliated to this council and on its exec. cttee. serve ex-officio all local Jewish magistrates, public reps. and BoD members. *President* Sue Dorsey; *V. Presidents* R. Bartfield; S. Jackson; *T.* K. Ackerman. *Hon Sec.* Dr R. Addlestone.

A.J.E.X. *Chairman* Stanley Graham; *H. Sec.* Leonard Cohen, 72 High Ash Drive, LS17 8RB.

Beth Din, *M.* Dayan Y. Refson; Rev. A. Gilbert, B.A.

Community Shaliach, 311, Stonegate Rd., ☎ 0113 2680899. Fax 0113 2668419.

JNF and Zionist Council, 311 Stonegate Rd., LS17 6AZ. ☎ 0113 2185865. Fax 0113 2185880. *District org.* S. Cohen.

Kashrut Authority, Barbara Cline ☎ 0113 2888151.

Leeds Emunah Council. *Co-ordinator* Mrs M. Gay, 4 Belvedere Court, LS17 8NF. ☎ 0113 266 1902.

Mikvah, 411 Harrogate Road, LS17 7BY. Mrs S. Cohen.☎ 0113 2693815, Mrs M. Morris ☎ 0113 2694377

UJIA Office, Balfour House, 299 Street La., LS17 6HQ. ☎ 0113 2693136. Fax 0113 2693961.

Women's Zionist Council (Wizo), 411 Harrogate Rd., LS17 7BY. ☎ 0113 2684773. *Chairman* Mrs L. Jacoby.

Yorkshire Israel Office, 311 Stonegate Rd., LS17 6AZ. ☎ 0113 2680899. Fax 0113 2688419.

SYNAGOGUES

Beth Hamidrash Hagadol Synagogue, 399 Street Lane, LS17 6HQ. (Est. 1874.) *M.* Rabbi M. Kleiman; *R.* D. Apfel; *Exec. Off.* Mrs W. Tobias. ☎ 0113 2692181.

Chassidishe Synagogue (Est. 1897), Mrs M. Silberg, 2 High Moor Grove, LS176 6DY ☎ 0113 2933634.

Etz Chaim Synagogue, 411 Harrogate Road, LS17 7TT. *Rab.* Rabbi S. Kuperman; *R.* Rev. A. Gilbert; *Sec.* Sandhill Pde., 584 Harrogate Road, LS17 7DP ☎ 0113 2662214. Fax 0113 2371183.

Masorti, *Contact* E. Frojmovic ☎ 0113 294 5112, B. Kunin ☎ 0113 266 2891

Queenshill Synagogue, *Contact H. Sec.* 311 Stonegate Rd., LS17 6AZ.

Shomrei Hadass Congregation, 368 Harrogate Road, LS17 6QB. ☎ 0113 2681461. *M.* Dayan Y. Refson.

Sinai Synagogue, Roman Avenue, Street Lane, LS8 2AN. ☎ 0113 2665256. Email info@sinaisynagogue.org.uk (Reform Judaism) (Est. 1944.) *M.* Rabbi I. Morris; *H. Sec.* R. Nysenbaum. Mon-Fri 9.30am-2pm.

United Hebrew Congregation (Reg. Charity No. 515316) 151 Shadwell La., LS17 8DW. ☎ 0113-269 4772 Fax 0113-269 6141. *M.* Rabbi D. Levy. ☎ 0113-237 0852; *R. ; Admin.* S. Rudette.

Cemeteries: For information refer to the Representative Council as above.

CULTURAL AND EDUCATIONAL ORGANISATIONS
B'nai B'rith Lodge of Leeds. *President* D. Levy. ☎ 0113 2686247.
Brodetsky Jewish Primary School, Wentworth Avenue, LS17 7TN. *H.T.* S. Camby, School ☎ 01132 930578; Deborah Taylor Nursery. ☎ 0113 2930579.
Jewish Historical Society (Branch). *President*; N. Grizzard; *H. Sec.* Mrs A. Buxbaum, 17 Pepper Hills, Harrogate Rd., LS17 8EJ. ☎ 0113 2665641.
Jewish Students' Association, Hillel House, 2 Springfield Mount, LS2 9NE. ☎ 0113 2433211. (Est. 1912.) *Sec.,* c/o Leeds University Union, LS2.
Jewish Telegraph, 1 Shaftesbury avenue, LS8 1DR. ☎ 0113 295 6000, Fax 0113 2956006. Email: leeds@jewishtelegraph.com
Leeds Council of Christians and Jews (Reg. Charity No. 238005), *Chairman* A.M. Conway, ☎ 0113 2680444; *H. Secs* Rabbi Morris, Mrs S. Crowther ☎ 0113 2561407.
Leeds Jewish Dental Society. *Sec.* Dr T Black, 1, St Michaels Lane, LS6 3AN. ☎ 0113 2788998.
Leeds Jewish Education Board (Talmud Torah), 2 Sandhill La., LS17 6AQ. (Est. 1879.) Houses the Talmud Torah classes. Administers Jewish Assemblies for pupils attending State schools. ☎ 0113 2172533. *H.T.* Mrs S. Angyalfi.
Leeds Jewish Youth Service, 2 Sand Hill Lane, LS17 6AQ. (0113 2172531.
Leeds University Library, Judaica collections (see p.55).
Limelight Drama Group. *Chairman* Harry Venet. (0113 2250651.
Makor–Jewish Resource Centre and Israel Information Centre (JPMP), 311 Stonegate Rd., LS17 6AZ. ☎ 0113 2680899. *Sec.*
Menorah School, 2 Sandhill Lane, Leeds LS17 6AQW.
Porton Collection, Central Library, LS1 3AB (see p.51). ☎ 0113 2462016
Reform Hebrew Classes, Sinai Synagogue, 22 Roman Avenue, LS8 2AN. ☎ 0113 2665256.
S.E.E.D. Project. Contact: Rabbi Y. Angyalfi, ☎ 0113 2663311.

WELFARE ORGANISATIONS
Chaplaincy Board–Yorkshire & Humberside, 17 Queens Road, LS6 1NY. ☎ 0113 2789597. *Hon. Chairman* Ivan Green. ☎ 0113-2696610.
Chevra Kadisha. Leeds *Jt Chair.* L. Burton, M. Ruddick; *Admin* Mrs L. Schulman, 21 Linton Rise, LS17 8QW ☎ 0113 237 0159.
Chevra Kadisha: Reform. Convenors Rabbi Morris, Maxine Brown ☎ 0113 268 5256
The Hub Jewish Day Centre, Marjorie & Arnold Ziff Community Centre, 311 Stonegate Rd., LS17 6AZ . ☎ 0113 2185888 *Man.* N. Caplin.
Jewish Welfare Board, Marjorie & Arnold Ziff Community Centre 311 Stonegate Rd., LS17 6AZ. ☎ 0113 268 4211. *Man.* ; *President* E. Ziff; *Chief Exec.* R. Weinberg.
Housing Association. *Admin* Mrs L. Miller. ☎ 0113 203 4910.
Miyad Helpline. ☎ 08457 581999.
Residential Nursing Home for the Jewish Elderly, Donisthorpe Hall, Shadwell Lane, LS17 6AW. (Est. 1923.) ☎ 0113 2684248. *Gen. Man.* Carol Whitehead.
Chessed, hospital meals and visitation. *Co-ord.* S. Saffman ☎ 0113 2370269.

LEICESTER (417)
There have been Jewish communities in Leicester since the Middle Ages, but the first record of a Jews' Synagogue appears in the 1861 Leicester Directory and the first marriages were consecrated in 1875. The present syn. dates from 1897.
Synagogue, Highfield St., P.O. Box 6836, LE2 1WZ. *M.* Rabbi S. Pink. ☎ 0116 2706622. *H. Sec.* G. D. Kramer ☎ 01858 440022.
Mikva, Synagogue building, Highfield St.
Communal Centre, Highfield St. ☎ 0116 2540477.
Shalom Club for Sr. Citizens. ☎ 0116 2540477.
Jewish Library, Communal Centre, Highfield St.
Ladies' Guild. *Chairman* Mrs H. Reggel, 22 Sackville Gardens, ☎ 0116 270 9687.
Jewish Students' Society, c/o The Union, Leicester University.
Maccabi Association, Communal Centre, Highfield St. ☎ 0116 2540477.
Leicester Progressive Jewish Synagogue (LJ). (Est. 1950) 24 Avenue Rd., LE2 3EA. *M.;* *H. Sec.* C. Salinger, ☎ 0116-241 2242. email lpjc@liberaljudaism.org.

Cemeteries: Leicester Hebrew Cong. uses a section of the Gilroes Cemetery, Groby Road. The Progressive congregation uses a section of the Loughborough Municipal C.

LINCOLN
Lincolnshire Jewish Community (Affiliated to LJ). ☎ 01427 628 958. Email ljc@liberalju daism.org. *Sec.* Dr K. Gennard ☎ 01522 851439

LIVERPOOL (2,698)
Liverpool, for centuries an important port, first for Ireland, later also for America, had a natural attraction for Jews looking for a place in which to start their new lives. There is evidence of an organised community before 1750. It appears to have had a burial ground attached. Little is known of this early community. It declined but about 1770 was reinforced by a new wave of settlers chiefly from Europe, who worshipped in a house in Frederick Street, near the river front, with a Mikva and a cemetery. In 1807 a synagogue of some size was built in Seel Street, the parent of the present syn. in Princes Road, one of the handsomest in the country. At this time Liverpool was already one of the four leading regional coms. The site for the Seel St. Synagogue was a gift of the Liverpool Corporation.
Merseyside Jewish Representative Council (Reg. Charity No. 1039809). *President & Chairman* G. S. Globe; *H. Sec.* P. Sapiro. Shifrin House, 433 Smithdown Road, L15 3JL. ☎ 0151-733 2292. Fax 0151-734 0212. Email repcouncil@mjccshifrin.co.uk. Website www.liverpooljewish.com. *Communal Archivist* A. Lewis.
Liverpool Kashrut Commission, c/o 433 Smithdown Road, L15 3JL. ☎ 0151-733 2292. Fax 0151-734 0212. *Rab.* Rabbi L. Cofnas.
Mikva. Childwall Synagogue. *Chairman* Rabbi L. Cofnas. ☎ 0151-722 2079.

SYNAGOGUES
Old Hebrew Congregation, Princes Road, L8 1TG. (0151-709 3431. Fax 0151-709 4187. (Congregation founded c. 1740; Synagogue consecrated 1874.) *M.* ; *Sec.* Mrs P. Nevitt.
Allerton Hebrew Congregation, 207, Mather Avenue, L18 9UB. ☎ 0151-427 4811. *Emer. Rabbi* Dr M.H. Malits, MA, MBE; *M.* ; *Admin.* P. Fisher.
Childwall Synagogue, Dunbabin Road, L15 6XL. ☎ 0151-722 2079. (Est. 1935; consecrated 1938.) *M.* Rabbi L. Cofnas; *Admin.* D. A.Coleman.
Reform Synagogue, 28 Church Road North, L15 6TF. ☎ 0151-733 5871. (Est. 1928. Affiliated to the Movement for Reform Judaism) *M. Emer* Rabbi N. Zalud; *H. Sec.* Mrs J. Doft.
Cemeteries: Liverpool Jewish Cemeteries: Springwood; Lowerhouse Lane; Broad Green; Long Lane.

CULTURAL AND EDUCATIONAL ORGANISATIONS
Community Centre (Harold House), Dunbabin Road, L15 6XL. ☎ 0151-475 5825.
Crosby Jewish Literary Society. *H. Secs.* Mrs C. Hoddes, Mrs Y. Mendick. ☎ 0151 924 1795.
Hillel House, 101 Ullet Rd. Ll7 2AB. Applications to: ☎ 0151- 280 0551; *Chaplain* Rabbi Y.Y. Rubinstein. ☎ 0161-721 4066.
Jewish Bookshop, *Chairman* M. Turner. Open at Youth and Community Centre, Sundays 11-1.
Jewish Historical Society (Branch). *Chairman* A. Lewis, 61 Menlove Ave., L18 2EH.
Jewish Telegraph, Harold House, Dunbabin Road, L15 6XL. ☎ 0151 475 6666, Fax 0151 475 2222. Email: liverpool@jewishtelegraph.com
Jewish Youth Centre, Dunbabin Road, L15 6XL. ☎ 0151-722 3303.
King David Foundation, 120 Childwall Rd., Ll5 6WU. ☎ 0151-737 1214. Fax 0151-722 9375. *Act. President* B. Michaelson; *Clerk* Mrs N. Sneeden.
King David High School, Childwall Road, L15 6UZ. ☎ 0151-722 7496. Clerk to Govs., King David Foundation. *H.T.* Mrs B. Smith, BA(Hons), PGCE, NPQH.
King David Kindergarten, Community Centre, Dunbabin Road, L15 6XL. *Teacher-in-charge*

Mrs R. Shiffman, ☎ 0151-475 5661.
King David Primary School, Beauclair Drive, L15 6XH. ☎ 0151-722 3372. Clerk to Govs. , King David Foundation, Harold House, ☎ 0151-737 1214. Fax 0151-722 9375; *H.T.* Rachel Rick, MA (Ed), NPQH.
Liverpool Jewish Resource Centre, Harold House, Dunbabin Road L15 6XL. ☎ 0151-722 3514. Fax 0151-475 2212. Sundays 11-1, Mon.-Thurs. 1-5pm. *Admin.* Mrs A. Lewis.
Liverpool Yeshivah, Childwall Synagogue, Dunbabin Road, L15. *Rosh Yeshiva* Rabbi M. L. Cofnas.
Merseyside Amalgamated Talmud Torah, Cheder etz Chayim, Harold House. *Chairman* M. Levitt.
Midrasha for Girls, c/o Childwall Synagogue, Dunbabin Road, L15.
University Jewish Students' Society, 101, Ullet Rd, L17 2AB.

WELFARE ORGANISATIONS
Jewish Community Care. (Est. 1875.) *Chief Exec.* Mrs L. Dolan, 433 Smithdown Road, L15 3JL. ☎ 0151-733 2292. Fax 0151-734 0212.
Jewish Women's Welfare Society. *H. Sec.* Mrs S. Gore, 433 Smithdown Road, L15 3JL.
Stapely Jewish Residential and Nursing Home, North Mossley Hill Road, L18. *Admin.* (0151-724 3260, 0151-724 4548 (Hosp. wing).

LUTON & DUNSTABLE & DISTRICT (534)
Luton Hebrew Congregation Synagogue, Postal address: P.O. Box No. 215, LU1 9ZJ. Email info@lutonhebrew.co.uk. Website.lutonhebrew.co.uk
Bedfordshire Progressive Synagogue (LJ), ☎ 01234 218 387. Email bedsps@liberaljudaism; Website www.bedfordshire-ps.org.uk. *Sec.* Hilary Fox.

MAIDENHEAD (1,035)
Maidenhead started in 1940 as an evacuee congregation during the Blitz. It experienced a rapid growth in the 1980s as younger families moved out of London, obliging it to move into larger premises in 2001. Its membership now covers a wide area of Berks and Bucks.
Synagogue, Grenfell Lodge, Ray Park Rd., SL6 8QX. ☎ 01628 673012. (Reform). *M.* Rabbi Dr J. A. Romain. ☎ 01628 671058. Website www.maidenheadsynagogue.org.uk
Cemetery: Braywick Cemetery, Maidenhead.

MANCHESTER (30,000)
The Manchester community of nearly 30,000 Jews is the second largest in the UK and, in contrast to other communities outside London, is still growing. In 1865 there were 4,500. The rapid and great increase came between 1883 and 1905, a consequence of the intensified persecution of the Jews in Russia.

Newcomers to England in the eighteenth century were encouraged by their co-religionists in London to go farther afield. This they did, generally financed by their longer-settled fellow-Jews in London, as pedlars along the countryside. As these newcomers prospered they settled in the ports, on their part sending out a wave of later arrivals similarly supplied with small stocks to peddle them in the inland towns and villages. This new wave also ultimately settled down, but for the most part in the interior of the country. Thus was laid the foundation of the Jewish community of Manchester.

The middle of the 1780s saw the first signs of an organized community, when two pedlar brothers, Jacob and Lemon Nathan, opened small shops in the centre of Manchester. In 1794 a plot for Jewish burials was rented just outside the city, and in 1796 a large warehouse was hired for public worship. This period coincided with Manchester's development as a major centre of industry and commerce, and Manchester Jewry steadily increased in number, attracting many enterprising settlers, including merchants and men of substance from the European mainland.

Among these was Nathan Mayer Rothschild, the first of that family to settle in England.

A later influx was from North Africa and the Levant, lands closely connected with the cotton industry of which Manchester was then the centre. This was the origin of the Sephardi community still prominent in Manchester. The last two decades of the nineteenth century saw the mass immigration to Manchester of eastern European Jews, fleeing from poverty and persecution. By the end of the century Manchester had the largest Jewish population in the provinces, reaching a peak of 35,000 just before the First World War. (Acknowledgement to Bill Williams, 'The Making of Manchester Jewry, 1740–1875' (1976).)

GENERAL ORGANISATIONS

Jewish Representative Council of Greater Manchester and Region. (Incorporating the Trades Advisory Council). The representative body for the Jewish community of Manchester, Salford and the surrounding region including Stoke, Blackpool and St Annes. Constituted of reps from all syns and other orgs, local Jewish MPs and MEPs, local members of the Board of Deputies, magistrates and town councillors. **Offices:** Jewish Community Centre, Bury Old Road, M7 4QY. ☎/Fax 0161-720 8721. Email office@jewishmanchester.org. Website www.jewishmanchester.org. *President* Mrs. B. D. Goldstone. ☎ 0161-792 1305; *V. Presidents* Dr S. Baigel; D. Davis; *H. Sec.* P. Lange; *H.T.* L. Jacobs; *Media Analyst* F. R. Baigel; *Project Officer* J. Wineberg; *Publ.* Year Book; newsletter (RepPresents).

Joseph Mamlock House, 142 Bury Old Road, M8 4HE. ☎ 0161-740 1825. Organisations at this address include:

    Zionist Central Council of Greater Manchester. *President* D. Berkley, Q.C., ☎ 0161-740 8835

    Jewish Agency Aliyah Dept. ☎ 0161-740 2864.

    Jewish National Fund. *Campaign Exec.* Lorraine Palastrand. ☎ 0161-795 7565.

    UJIA. *Reg. Dir.* I. Ray. ☎ 0161-740 1825.

    WIZO. *Chairman* Mrs. M. Fink,. ☎ 0161-740 3367.

Council of Synagogues (Orthodox). *Chairman* S. Lopian; *Sec.* M. Green, c/o Central-North Manch. Syn., Stenecourt, Holden Rd., Salford M7 4LN.

Beth Din, Jewish Community Centre. ☎ 0161-740 9711. Fax 0161-721 4249. Dayan I. Berger; Dayan G. Krausz; Dayan Y.O. Steiner. *Registrar* Rabbi Y. Brodie, BA (Hons).

Kashrus Authority, Jewish Community Centre. ☎ 0161-740 9711. Fax 0161-721 4249. *President* D. Pine; *Chief Exec.* Rabbi Y. Brodie.

Communal Mikva (under Beth Din authority), Broom Holme, Tetlow La., Salford, M7 0BU. ☎ 0161-792 3970.

(Naomi Greenberg) South Manchester Mikva (under Beth Din Authority), Shay Lane, Hale Barns, Altrincham, Cheshire. ☎ 0161-904 8296.

Whitefield Mikveh, Telephone for appointments 0161-796 1054.

SYNAGOGUES

Adass Yeshurun Synagogue, Cheltenham Cres., Salford, M7 4FE. ☎ 0161-792 0795. *M.* Rabbi Y Cohen; *H. Sec.* M.R. Goldman. ☎/Fax 0161-740 3935.

Adath Israel Synagogue, Upper Park Road, Salford M7 0HL. (Form. Kahal Chassidim Syn., present building opened in 1957). Inq.: 105 Leicester Road, Salford 7. *Sec.* Rev. S. Simon. ☎ 0161-740 3905.

Bury Hebrew Congregation. Sunnybank Road, Bury, BL9 8ET. ☎ 0161-796 5062. Email: mirrelbhc@hotmail.co.uk. *M.* Rabbi B. Singer; *Admin.* Mrs M. Wilson.. ☎ 0161-740 4830.

Cheetham Hebrew Congregation, Jewish Cultural Centre, Bury Old Road M7 4QY. ☎ 0161-740 7788. *President* B. M. Stone. *M.* Rabbi Y. Abenson.

Cheshire Reform Congregation, (Reg. Charity No. 234762), Menorah Synagogue, 198 Altrincham Road, M22 4RZ. ☎ 0161-428 7746. (Est. 1964.) (Movement for Reform). *M.* Rabbi B. Fox, AM, DD; *H. Sec.* R. Garson.

Damesek Eliezer Synagogue, Prestwich Beth Hamedrash, 74 Kings Road, Prestwich M25 0JG *M.* Rabbi S. Goldberg. ☎ 0161-798 9298.

Hale and District Hebrew Congregation, Shay Lane, Hale Barns, Cheshire WA15 8PA. ☎

0161-980 8846. (Est. 1976.) *M.* Rabbi J. Portnoy; *H. Sec.* J. Steinberg.

Heaton Park Hebrew Congregation, Ashdown, Middleton Road M8 4JX. *M.* Rabbi D. Walker; *Sec.* F. Kaye. ☎ 0161-740 4766. Email hillock.shul@ntlworld.com

Higher Crumpsall and Higher Broughton Hebrew Congregation, Bury Old Road, Salford, M7 4PX. ☎ 0161-740 1210. *M.* Emer. Rabbi A. Saunders, Rev. A. Hillman. ☎ 0161-740 4179; *Admin.* Mrs E. Somers. ☎ 0161-740 8155.

Higher Prestwich Hebrew Congregation, 445 Bury Old Road, Prestwich M25 1QP. ☎ 0161-773 4800. *M.* Rabbi A. Z. Herman; *President* P. W. Reed; *Sec.* Mrs B. Task.

Hillock Hebrew Congregation, Beverley Close, Ribble Drive, Whitefield, M45 8LB *H. Sec.* R. Walker, 13 Mersey Close, Whitefield, M45 8LB. ☎ 0161-959 5663.

Holy Law South Broughton Congregation, Bury Old Road, Prestwich M25 0EX. ☎ 0161-740 1634. Fax 0161-720 6623. Email office@holylaw.org.uk. (Est. 1865, present building opened 1935, merged with South Broughton Syn., 1978). *M.* Rabbi Y. Chazan. ☎ 0161-792 6349 (Study 0161-721 4705); *Admin.* A.Rodrigues Pereira *Burial Bd.* ☎0161-740 1634. (D)

Kahal Chassidim Synagogue (Lubavitch), 62 Singleton Road, Salford M7 4LU. *M.* Rabbi A. Jaffe ☎ 0161-740 3632; *Sec.* D. Lipsidge ☎ 0161-740 1629

Lubavitch Foundation (Reg. Charity No. 1101651), 62 Singleton Road, Salford M7 4LU. ☎/Fax 0161-720 9514. *M.* Rabbi L. Wineberg.

Machzikei Hadass Communities, 17 Northumberland Street, Salford M7 0FE. ☎ 0161-792 1313. *Rav.* Rav. M. Schneebalg. ☎ 0161-792 3063. *Sec.* A. Vogel. ☎ 0161-792 1313.

   Constituent Syn.: Machzikei Hadass. **Mikva**: Sedgley Park Road, Prestwich, M25 ☎ 0161-773 1537/0161-721 4341.

Manchester Great and New Synagogue (and Community Centre) (Est. 1740), 'Stenecourt', Holden Road, Salford, M7 4LN. *M.* Rev. G. Brodie, 43 Stanley Road, Salford M7 4FR. ☎ 0161-740 2506. Fax 0161-792 1991; *President* B. Steinberg ☎ 0161-792 8399 (Mon-Fri. 09.00am-12.00pm; Sun 10-12pm). Email office@stenecourt.force9.co.uk.

Manchester Liberal Jewish Community (LJ). *Chair* Mrs P. Alden ☎ 0870-991 7327. Email mljc@liberaljudaism.org Website www.mljcliberaljudaism.org.uk

Manchester Reform Synagogue, Jackson's Row, M2 5NH. ☎ 0161-834 0415. (Est. 1856). (Reform). The former syn. in Park Pl. was destroyed by enemy action in 1941; present premises occupied since 1953. *M.* Rabbi Dr. R. Silverman; *Sec.* Mrs F. Morris. ☎ 0161-834 0415. Email: admin@jacksonsrow.org.

North Salford Synagogue, 2 Vine St., Kersal, Salford M7 0NX. *M.* Rabbi E. Stefansky ☎ 0161-792-3278.

Ohel Torah Congregation, 132 Leicester Road, Salford M7 0ES. (Constituent of the Union of Orthodox Hebrew Congregations.) *M.*Rabbi S. Z. Hoff; *Sec.* Z. Cope. ☎ 0161-792 3442.

Prestwich Hebrew Congregation, Bury New Road, Prestwich M25 9WN ☎ 0161-773 1978. *M.* Rabbi Y. Landes; *Admin.* Mrs W. Cohen-Wilks, Mrs I. Goldstone.

Sale and District Hebrew Congregation, Hesketh Road, Sale, Cheshire M33 5AA. ☎ 0161-973 3013. *M.* Rabbi A. Lipsey; *Sec.* M. Clyne ☎ 0161-973 4565.

Sedgley Park Synagogue (Shomrei Hadass), Parkview Road, Prestwich M25 5FA. *Jt.H. Secs.* D. Gordon, S. Jeffay. ☎ 0161-740 0677.

Sephardi Congregation of South Manchester, Shaare Hayim (Reg. Charity No. 1067759), 8 Queenston Road, West Didsbury M20 2WZ. ☎ 0161-445 1943. Fax 0161-438 0571. Email shaarehayim@clara.co.uk. *M.* Rabbi S. Ellituv. ☎ 0161-434 6903. Amalgamated with the former Sha'are Sedek Synagogue.

Sha'arei Shalom, North Manchester Reform Congregation, (Reg. Charity No. 506117), Elms Street, Whitefield, M45 8GQ. (Est. 1977). (A Constituent of Movement for Reform Judaism). ☎ 0161-796 6736. Email office@shaareishalom.org.uk. Website www.shaarei-shalom.org.uk. *M.* Rabbi N. Zalud. *H. Sec.* L. Weiner.

South Manchester Synagogue (Est. 1872. Reg. Charity No. 231976), The Firs, Bowdon, Altrincham, WA14 2TE. ☎ 0161-928 2050. Fax 0161-924 0344. Email info@southman-

chestersynagogue.org.uk; *M.* Rabbi Y. Rubin; *Admin.* Mrs T. Hyams.
Spanish & Portuguese Synagogue, Shaare Tephillah (Est. 1873), 18 Moor La., Salford M74WX. ☎/Fax 0161-795 1212. *H. Sec.*
Talmud Torah Chinuch N'orim Synagogue, 11 Wellington Street, East, Salford M7 9AU. ☎ 0161-792 9292. (Constituent of the Union of Orthodox Hebrew Congregations.) *Ms.* Rev. N. Friedman, Rev. P. Koppenheim; *H. Sec.* S. Kornbluh.
United Synagogue, Meade Hill Road, M8 6LS. ☎ 0161-740 9586. *President* Sidney Huller; *Sec.* Reuben Wilner. ☎ 0161-740 9586.
Whitefield Hebrew Congregation, Park Lane, M45 7PB. ☎ 0161-766 3732. Fax 0161-767 9453. (Est. 1959). *M.* Rabbi J. Guttentag, (B.A. Hons.); *C.* Chazan Y. Muller; *Admin.* Mrs P.M. Deach.
Yeshurun Hebrew Congregation, Coniston Road, Gatley, Cheshire SK8 4AP (Reg. Charity No. XN10469A). ☎ 0161-428 8242. Fax 0161-491 5265. Email office@yeshurun.org.uk. *M.* Rabbi Ch. Kanterovitz, ☎ 0161-490 6050; *Admin.* L. Kaufmann.
Zerei Agudas Israel Synagogue, 35 Northumberland Street, Salford M7 0DQ. *M.* Dayan O. Westheim.
Zichron Yitzchak (Sephardi Congregation), 2 New Hall Road, Salford M7 4EL. *Emer. R.* Rabbi S. Amor; *Sec.* A. J. Tesciuba. ☎ 0161-795 0822.

CULTURAL ORGANISATIONS
Israel Information Centre, 142 Bury Old Road, M8 6HD. ☎ 0161-721 4344. Fax 0161-795 3387. Email iicmcr@clara.co.uk. Information and presentation of Israel's culture. *Dir.* Mrs D. Gerson
Jewish Historical Society of England (Branch), *Chairman* F.Baigel, 25 Ravensway, Prestwich M25 0EU. ☎ 0161 740 6403. Email manchester@jhse.org
Jewish Library, Central Library. ☎ 0161-236 9422. Stock now absorbed into main Social Sciences Library collection.
Jewish Museum, 190 Cheetham Hill Road, M8 8LW. ☎ 0161-834 9879 and 0161-832 7353. Fax 0161-834 9801. Email info@manchesterjewishmuseum.com. Website www.manchesterjewishmuseum.com. Mon.-Thurs., 10.30 a.m. to 4 p.m. Sun., 10.30 a.m. to 5 p.m. (Reg. Charity No. 508278). Admission charge. Exhibitions, heritage trails, demonstrations and talks. Educational visits for schools and adult groups must be booked in advance with the Administrator. *Contact* . D. Rainger
Jewish Male Voice Choir. *Cond.* A. Isaacs. ☎ 0161-740 1210.
Jewish Telegraph, 11 Park Hill, Bury Old Road, Prestwich M25 0HH. ☎ 0161 740 9321. ☎ 0161 741 2631 (Newsdesk). Fax 0161 740 9325. Email: manchester@jewishtelegraph.com,. Website www.jewishtelegraph.com
Manchester Jewish Community Centre, Jubilee School, Bury Old Road, M7 4QY. ☎ 0161-795 4000. Fax 0161-720 6222. (Reg. Charity No. 1089467); *Dir.* Rabbi Chaim Farro; *Admin.* Mrs M. Allweis.

EDUCATIONAL ORGANISATIONS
Academy for Rabbinical Research (Kolel), (Reg. Charity No. 526665), 134 Leicester Road, Salford M7 4DA. ☎ 0161-740 1960. *Princ.* Rabbi W. Kaufman; *Sec.* Rev. J. Freedman.
Beis Yaakov HighSchool, Hubert Jewish High School for Girls, 69, Broom Lane, Salford, M7 4FF. *Princ.* Rabbi Y. Goldblatt, MA (Oxon), PGCE.☎ 0161 7088220 Fax 0161 7089968
Bnos Yisroel School, Leicester Road, Salford, M7 0AH. ☎ 0161-792 3896.
Broughton Jewish Cassel Fox Primary School, Legh Road, Salford M7 4RT. ☎ 0161-792 7773 (school), ☎ 0161-792 2588 (nursery), 0161-792 7738 (kindergarten). Fax 0161-792 7768. *Act. Hd.* Mrs. S. Caplan
Bury & Whitefield Jewish Primary School, Parr La., Bury, Lancs. BL9 8JT. ☎ 0161-766 2888. Fax 0161-766 3231. *H.T.* Miss C. Potter; *Chairman of Govs.* Rabbi A.J. Jaffe. Nursery School, Parr La., Bury, Lancs. ☎ 0161-767 9390. (Children 2 yrs. plus). *Hd. J. Studies* Rabbi B. Z. Lewis. ☎ 0161-746 3341.
Delamere Forest School, Blakemere Lane, Norley, Nr. Frodsham, Cheshire WA6 6NP. ☎

01928 788263. Fax 01928 788263. Email info@delamereschool.org.uk. (Reg Charity No. 1117339). For Jewish children with special needs. *Chairman of Gov.* A. Thwaites; *H.T.* H. Burman.

Hillel House, Greenheys La., M15 6LR. ☎ 0161-226 1973; Accommodation etc: Dr S. Baigel ☎.0161 740 2521

Jerusalem Academy Study Groups. *Chairman* Rev. G. Brodie, 43 Stanley Road, Salford M7 4FR. ☎ 0161-740 2506.

Jewish Senior Boys School - Kesser Torah, Hubert House, 4 New Hall Road, Salford M7 4EL. ☎ 0161-708 9175.

Jewish Youth Project (Reg. Charity No. 1050928), Whitefield Jewish Youth Centre, Park Lane M45 7PB ☎ 0161-766 7744. Email theproject@nmjyp.f9.co.uk. (Est. 1994). The Project aims to provide an overall youth service for 13-18 year olds. *Chair* P. Broude; *Sec.* Helena Broude.

King David Schools. (Est. 1838. Reg. Charity No. 526631)

   King David Schools, Administration Centre, Eaton Road, Crumpsall, M8 5DY. *Financial Adv.* Mr D. Rose. ☎ 0161 740 3181. Fax 0161 741 5081. Email admin@kingdavidhigh. manchester.sch.uk

   King David High School, Eaton Road, Crumpsall, M8 5DY. ☎ 0161-740 7248. Fax 0161-740 0790. *H.T.* B. N. Levy, BEd; *H. of Sixth Form* J. Pitt, BA (Hon), PGCE; *H. Yavneh Girls* Rabbi T. Bodenheimer; *Yavneh Boys* Rabbi A. Ben-Shushan.

   King David Junior School, Wilton Polygon,Bury Old Road, Crumpsall, M8 6DJ. ☎ 0161-740 5090. *H.T.* P.L. Parker, BEd (Hons), ALAM.

   King David Infant School, Wilton Polygon, Bury Old Road, Crumpsall, M8 6DR. (0161-740 4110. *H.T.* Mrs J. Rich, BA (Hons)..

   King David Nursery & Crèche, Eaton Road, M8 5DY. ☎ 0161-740 3481. *Nursery Man.* Mrs S. Isaacs; *Crèche Man.* Mrs L. Crawshaw NNEB. *Governors' Admin.* Mr D. Rose.. ☎ 0161-740 3181. Fax 0161-740 3182.

Lubavitch Yeshiva, Lubavitch House, 62 Singleton Road, Salford M7 4LU. ☎ 0161-792 7649. *Dean* Rabbi A. Cohen. *Admin.* S. Weiss, ☎ 0161-740 4243.

Manchester Jewish Grammar School (Reg. Charity No. 526607), Camp Street, Salford M7 12T ☎ 0161-792 1368. Fax 0161-792 4571. *Princ.* Rabbi D. Kestenbaum; *H. M.* P. Pink, BSc(Econ), DipEd.

Manchester Mesivta, Beechwood, Charlton Avenue, Prestwich M25 0PH. ☎ 0161 7731789. *Principal* Rabbi Y. L.. Lewis. *HM.* P. Pink, BSc (Econ), DipEd.

Mechinah L'Yeshiva, 13 Upper Park Road, Salford M7 0HY. ☎ 0161-795 9275.

Moriah Institute for Further Education, Y. Y. Rubinstein, 97 Singleton Road, Salford M7 4LX. ☎ 0161 721 4066

North Cheshire Jewish Primary School, St. Anns Road North, Heald Green, Cheadle, Cheshire SK8 4RZ. ☎ 0161-282 4500. Fax 0161-282 4501. *H.* Mrs N. Massel, BEd (Hons).

North Manchester Jewish Teenage Centre (Reg. Charity No. 1009785), at the Bnei Akiva Bayit, 72 Singleton Road, Salford M7 4LU. ☎ 0161-740 1621. Website www.bauk.org *Corres.* D. & S. Gillis. Open Sunday morning only. Under the auspices of the Manchester Centre Hebrew Board, 57 Leicester Road, Salford M7 4DA. ☎/Fax 0161-798 5577. *Corres.* D. Finkelstein.

Reshet Torah Education Network, Rabbi S.M. Kupetz, 4 Hanover Gdns., Salford M7 4FQ. ☎ 0161-740 5735.

seed (Reg. Charity No. 281307), 16 Moor Lane, Salford M7 3WX. ☎ 0161-792 2709. Website www.seed.uk.net. Rabbi A. Hassan.

Talmud Torah Chinuch N'orim, 11 Wellington Street, East, Salford M7 9AU. ☎ 0161-792 4522. *Chairman, Bd. of Govs.* B. Waldman.

Whitefield Community Kollel, c/o Whitefield Hebrew Congregation, Park Lane, Whitefield, M45 7PB. *Admin. Mrs.* B. Woolfstein. ☎ 0161-766 2150.
The forum runs a wide selection of programmes for adults and youth.

Whitefield Jewish Youth Centre. *Co-ord.* Mrs R. Feldman. ☎ 0161-796 8564. Email wjyc@hotmail.co.uk

Yeshiva Kollel, Saul Rosenberg House, Seymour Road, Higher Crumpsall, M8 5BQ. (Est. 1911). ☎ 0161-740 0214. *Princ.* Rabbi Y. Ehrentreu; *Sec.* Rev. G. Brodie.

Yesoiday HaTorah School, Sedgley Park Rd., off Bury New Rd., Prestwich M25 0JW. ☎ 0161-773 6364. Fax 0161-773 3914.
Yocheved Segal Kindergarten, Sedgley Pk. Road, Prestwich M25 0JW. ☎ 0161-773 6364.

WELFARE ORGANISATIONS
Manchester Jewish Federation (The Fed). Head Office: 12 Holland Road, Higher Crumpsall, M8 4NP. ☎ 0161-795 0024. Fax 0161 795 3688. Email info@thefed.org.uk. South Manchester Branch Suite 1, Urban House, 34 Ashley Road, Altrincham, WA14 2DW. ☎ 0161 941 4442. Fax 0161 941 5039. Email southside@thefed.org.uk. *President* Lord Steinberg; *Chief Exec.* Mrs K. Phillips. *Chairman* Mr M. Adlestone. The Fed provides a range of social welfare support to the Jewish community of Greater Manchester and offers professional assistance to people of all ages and backgrounds..
Aguda Community Services, 35 Northumberland Street, Salford M7 4DQ. (Reg. Charity No. 287367). ☎ 0161-792 6265. Fax 0161-708 9177. Advice Centre for training and employment. *Sec.*
Brookvale, Caring for People with Special Needs (Reg. Charity No. 526086), Simister Lane, Prestwich, M25 2SF. ☎ 0161-653 1767. Fax 0161-655 3635. *Exec. Dir.* Mrs L. Richmond; *Fin. Dir.* M. Walters. Email admin@brookvale.org
Heathlands Village (Reg. Charity No. 1117126), Heathlands Dr., Prestwich, M25 9SB. ☎ 0161-772 4800. Fax 0161-772 4934. (Care Home with nursing input). *President* R. Berkeley. *Chief Exec.* Ms J. Lewis. Website www.heathlandsvillage.co.uk.
Jewish Marriage Council, Manchester Branch, 85 Middleton Road, Crumpsall, M8 4JY. Appointments: ☎ 0161-740 5764, 08457-585159 Offers: Confidential family and marriage counselling, assisting couples and individuals.
Jewish Soup Kitchen (Meals-on-Wheels Service), (Reg. Charity No. 226424), Rita Glickman House, Ravensway, Prestwich M25 0EX. ☎ 0161-795 4930. *H. Sec.* Mrs H. Amdurer. ☎ 0161-773 5229.
Manchester Jewish Community Care (formerly Manchester Jewish Blind Society), (Reg. Charity No. 257238), Nicky Alliance Day Centre, 85 Middleton Road M8 4JY. ☎ 0161-740 0111. Fax 0161-721 4273. Email info@mjcc.org.uk. Day Centre and social work support for the visually and physically disabled, the elderly and those suffering from dementia. *Chairman* B. White; *Chief Exec.* M. Wiseman
Manchester Jewish Visitation Board. (Est. 1903.) *Convenor* Y. Brodie; *Chairman* Rev. L. Olsberg. ☎ 0161-740 9711.
Morris Feinmann Home (Care Home for older people), 178 Palatine Road, Didsbury, M20 2YW. ☎ 0161-445 3533. Website www. morrisfeinmannhome. com. *Chairman* Mrs H. Lister; *Gen. Man.* Mrs H. Naylor.
Outreach Community & Residential Services (Reg. Charity No. 509119), 3 Middleton Road, Crumpsall, M8 5DT. ☎ 0161-740 3456. Fax 0161-740 5678. Email info@outreach.co.uk Website www.outreach.co.uk. *Chief Exec.* A. Akinola; *Dir.* P. Lismore.

MARGATE (200)
Margate Hebrew Congregation. Synagogue, Albion Road, Cliftonville, CT9 2HP. (Est. 1904; new syn. consecrated 1929; Reg. Charity No. 273506) *President* Dr N. Jacobs. ☎ 01843 831587. Enquiries to *Hon. Admin.* D.A. Coberman ☎ 01843 228550.
Thanet and District Reform Synagogue, 293A Margate Road, Ramsgate, Kent CT12 6TE. ☎ 01843 851164.
Cemetery: For Margate Hebrew Congregation & Thanet Reform at Manston Road, Margate.

MIDDLESBROUGH (65)
(Incorporating Stockton and Hartlepool.) Synagogue reported closed during 1999.
Synagogue, Park Road South. (Est. 1873.) *H. Sec.* L. Simons. ☎ 01642 819034 (for details of services and Chevra Kaddisha). J. Bloom. ☎ 01609 8832272.
Cemetery: Ayresome Green Lane, Middlesbrough.

MILTON KEYNES & DISTRICT (466)
Reform Synagogue (Beit Echud) (Est. 1978. Reg. Charity No. 1058193). (Movement for

Reform) 1 Hainault Ave., Giffard Park, MK14 5PQ. ☎ 01908 617790 Inq: S. Friedman ☎ 01908 560714 Website www.mkdrs.org.

NEWARK
Beth Shalom Holocaust Centre, Laxton, Newark NG22 0PA. ☎ 01623 836627. Fax 01623 836647. Email office@bethshalom.com; Website www. holocaustcentre.officersnet. *Dirs* Dr J. M. Smith, M. Saunders.

NEWCASTLE UPON TYNE (550)
The community was est. in the 1820s, when services were held and a Shochet employed. A cemetery was acquired in 1831. Jews, however, had been resident in Newcastle since before 1775. In the Middle Ages Jews are known to have been est. in Newcastle in 1176. The population figure quoted is that of the community's recent census.

Representative Council of North-East Jewry. (Reg. Charity No. 1071515).*Co-Presidents* D. Vander Velde. ☎ 0191 285 1253 and L. Boobis ☎ 0191 285 0190. Email repcouncil-president@northeastjewish.co.uk. *H. Sec.* J. Cawson, 14 Beechcroft, NE3 4NB. ☎ 0191 285 1046; *H.T.* W. Knoblauch; *Press and Public Rel.* C.Boobis. Email caro.bee@hotmail.co.uk

North East Jewish Recorder (communal journal published by the Representative Council). Email recorderofficers@northeastjewish.co.uk

SYNAGOGUES
United Hebrew Congregation (Est. 1973). The Synagogue, Graham Park Road, Gosforth NE3 4BH. ☎ 0191-284 0959. *President* Dr. F. Lustman; *M.* Rabbi D. Lewis; *Sec.* Mrs B. Levinson. Mikva on premises. **Burial Cttee:** *Chairman* N. Sterrie ☎ 0191-285 2735, and P. Gold ☎ 0191-285 1680

Reform Synagogue, The Croft, off Kenton Road, Gosforth, NE3 4RF. ☎ 0191-284 8621. Email info@nertamid.org.uk Website www. nertamid.org.uk (Est. 1963.) (A Constituent of Movement for Reform) *Chairman* Mrs. B. Dinsdale; *M.* Rabbi B. Borts; **Burial Cttee** ☎ 0191-284 8621.

Cemeteries: Hazelrigg and Heaton (UHC); North Shields (Reform).

WELFARE ORGANISATIONS
North East Jewish Community Services. *Chairman* H. Ross, *Community Care. Off.* Pam Muscat, Lionel Jacobson House, Graham Park Road, Gosforth NE3 4BH. ☎ 0191-285 1968. **Community Transport** ☎ 0191-285 1968.

Newcastle Jewish Housing Association Ltd., *Chairman* S. Doberman, c/o Lionel Jacobson House. ☎ 0191-284 0959.

Philip Cussins House (Residential Care for Jewish Aged in the North East), 33/35 Linden Road, Gosforth NE3 4EY. ☎ 0191 213 5353. Fax 0191 213 5354. Residents ☎ 0191 213 5355.

OTHER ORGANISATIONS
AJEX, *Chairman* J. Fox. ☎ 01661 824819.

Association of Jewish Refugees (AJR) *Contact* Walter Knoblauch ☎ 0191 285 5339

Bridge Club *Contact* David Gold, ☎ 0191 285 8013

Education and Youth Cttee., c/o United Hebrew Cong. *Chairman* D. Sadlick.

Jewish Students' Society and Hillel House, Ilford Road, Gosforth. *Contact* Susan Olsburgh ☎ 0191-213 0919. Email hillel@newcastlejsoc.org

Jewish Literary Society. *Contact* Freddie Ingram ☎ 0191-284 8118.

Newcastle Jewish Leisure Group *Co-Chairmen* S. Hymes, M. Black

Newcastle Jewish Players. *Co-Chairmen* V. Collins ☎ 0191-285 6462, M. Josephs ☎ 0191-285 7173.

North East Council Of Christians and Jews *Contact* D. Van der Velde ☎ 0191 285 1253

North East Jewish Golfing Society. *Contact* Paul Netts. ☎ 0191 285 6482. **The Swingers** (Ladies' Section). *Contact* Faga Speker. ☎ 0191 285 3110.

UJIA, *Jt Chairmen* F. Ingram ☎ 0191 284 8118, and W. Maier ☎ 0191 285 5456
WIZO: *Co-Chairmen* Pam Peterson ☎ 0191 285 4302 and Monica Stern, ☎ 0191-284 2502
UHC (Kosher meats and delicatessen), Lionel Jacobson House, NE3 4BH. ☎ 0191-284 2502.

NORTHAMPTON (322)
The community marked its centenary in 1988. For a history of the medieval and modern settlement in the town see 'A Short History of the Jews of Northampton, 1159–1996' (1996), by M. Jolles.
Hebrew Congregation, Overstone Road, Northampton, NN1 3JW. *M.; Sec.* G. Goldcrown ☎ 01604-633345. Website www.northantshc.org.
Cemetery: Towcester Road.

NORWICH (239)
The present community was founded in 1813, Jews having been resident in Norwich during the Middle Ages, and connected with the woollen and worsted trade, for which the city was at that time famous. A resettlement of Jews is believed to have been completed by the middle of the eighteenth century. A synagogue was built in 1848 and destroyed in an air raid in 1942. A temporary synagogue opened in 1948 and the present building was consecrated by the Chief Rabbi in 1969. The congregation serves a large area, having members in Gt. Yarmouth, Lowestoft and Cromer.
Norwich Hebrew Congregation Synagogue, 3a Earlham Road, NR2 3RA. ☎ 01603 623948. *M.* A. Bennett ☎ 01263 710726; *President* C. Roffe; *H. Sec.* G. Willson, ☎ 01603 616129.
Chevra Kadisha, 3a Earlham Road, Norwich. *President* B. C. Leveton. ☎ 01603 749706.
Progressive Jewish Community of East Anglia (Norwich). Affiliated to the LJ. Regular services at The Old Meeting House, Colegate, Norwich. Enquiries to *H. Sec.. Publ.* PJCEA Newsletter.
Jewish Ladies' Society, 3a Earlham Road. *President* Mrs. S. J. Bennett; *H. Sec.* Mrs P. Young.
Norfolk and Norwich Branch of the Council of Christians and Jews (Est. 1991). *Sec.* V. J. Warner ☎ 01508 537123. *H. T.* A. S. Bennett ☎ 01263 7107260
Norwich Israel Social Society (NISS), *Chairman* P. Prinsley. ☎ 01603 506482.

NOTTINGHAM (627)
A small community has lived in Nottingham since the early 19th century, and in 1890, with a com. increased by immigrants to some 100 families, the Hebrew Congregation built its first synagogue in Chaucer St. During the Second World War, there was a sharp growth in the community, and the congregation acquired its present synagogue in 1954. With the closure of the Derby syn. in 1986, many of its members joined the Nottingham Hebrew Cong. The Progressive Jewish Cong. was est. in 1959.
Nottingham Representative Council, 265 Wollaton Vale, Wollaton NG8 2PX. ☎ 0115 928 1613. Fax 0115 916 2960. Email lynnechapman@ntlworld.com. *Chairman* D. Lipman. ☎ 0115 966 4690. *Sec.* L. Chapman.
Hebrew Congregation, Shakespeare Villas, NG1 4FQ. ☎ 0115 9472004. Email OfficeNHC@aol.com. *President* M. Kirsch.
Progressive Jewish Congregation (LJ), Lloyd Street, NG5 4BP. ☎ 0115 962 4761. *Chairman* D. Lipman ☎ 0115 924 5660. Email npjc@liberaljudaism.org. Website www.npjc@org.uk. *M.; H. Sec.* R. Bott. ☎ 0115 945 2170.
Federation of Women Zionists. *H.T.* Mrs S. Cresswell.
Jewish Welfare Board. *Chairman* Dr M. Caplan. ☎ 0115 260245. *Hon. Sec.* P. Seymour, 115 Selby Rd., West Bridgford, NG2 7BB. ☎ 0115 452895.
Miriam Kaplowitch House, Jewish rest home, 470 Mansfield Road, NG5 2DR ☎ 0115 624274 (Residents) and 0115 9622038 (Matron & Admin.) (Est. 1986).
University of Nottingham Jewish and Israel Society, c/o The University of Nottingham, NG7 2RD.
Women's Benevolent Society. *Chairman* Mrs S. Besbrode. ☎ 0115 9373620.

OXFORD (500 and approx. 500 students)
An important centre in the medieval period. The modern community was est. in 1842. In 1974 the Oxford Synagogue and Jewish Centre was built on the site of the earlier synagogue. It serves the resident community and a fluctuating number of university students, and is available for all forms of Jewish worship.
Jewish Congregation, The Synagogue, 21 Richmond Road, OX1 2JL. ☎ 01865 514356. Email connectio@oje-online.org *President* K. Shock. Website www.oxford-synagogue.org.uk.
Oxford Masorti (Services held the last Shabbat each month). *Contact* Ros Abramsky.
The Progressive Jewish Group of Oxford. Inq: Katherine Shock, ☎/Fax 01865 515584, or Ruth Cohen ☎ 01865 779220. Email progressive@oxford-synagogue.org.uk
University Jewish Society. (Est. 1903). *Senior Member* J. Getzler, St. Hugh's. ☎ 01865 274932; *Sec.; Chaplain* Rev. M. Weisman, M.A. (Oxon.). ☎ 020-8459 4372. *Student Chaplains* A. and S. Katchen, Email aaron@chaplaincy.org and shira@chaplaincy.org

PETERBOROUGH (147)
Hebrew Congregation, 142 Cobden Avenue, PE1 2NU. ☎ 01733 264151. (Congregation est. 1940. Syn. opened 1954. Affiliated to the U.S.) *Admin.* C. Salmon. Services Kabbalat Shabbat 7pm.
Liberal Jewish Community (LJ). Enquiries to Elisabeth Walker. ☎ 01733 358605.☎ 020 7631 9826

PLYMOUTH (181)
The Plymouth community was founded in 1745, when a cemetery was opened. Jews lived in the city even earlier. The syn., built in 1762, is the oldest Ashkenazi house of worship still standing in the English-speaking world. Its 225th anniversary in 1987 was marked by a service attended by representatives of the United Synagogue, the Board of Deputies and the Civic Authorities. In the early 19th century, Plymouth was one of the four most important provincial centres of Anglo-Jewry. The history of the community, 'The Plymouth Synagogue 1761–1961' by Doris Black, was published in 1961.
Hebrew Congregation (Reg. Charity 220010), Catherine Street, PL1 2AD. ☎ 01752 263 162. (Est. 1761.) *H. Sec.* A. Kelly ☎ 01822 614 203. Email imannahi@aol.com; Website www.plymouthsynagogue.com

PORTSMOUTH (235)
The com. was est. in 1746 and opened a syn. in Oyster Row, later to move to a building in White's Row, off Queen St. which was occupied for over 150 years. The present syn. was built in 1936. The cemetery was acquired in 1749 and is the oldest in the Regions still in use. It is situated in Fawcett Road, which has been known for more than 200 years as Jews' Lane. By 1815 Portsmouth was one of the four main Jewish centres outside London, the others being Plymouth, Liverpool and Birmingham. Portsmouth's prosperity declined after the Napoleonic Wars. For South Hampshire Reform Jewish Community see under Southampton.
Portsmouth & Southsea Hebrew Congregation. Synagogue, The Thicket, Elm Grove, Southsea PO5 2AA. ☎ 023-92821494. (Reg. Charity No.: X50585) *M.* Rabbi D. Katanka.
Officers of the Board of Guardians (Est. 1804), the Chevra Kadisha, **Friendship Club, and the Jewish Ladies' Benevolent Society** (Est. 1770) may be contacted through the synagogue.
Cemeteries: Fawcett Road, Kingston, New Road; Catherington.

POTTERS BAR (250)
Est. in the 1940s, the com. met at members homes until 1983 when the current synagogue was purchased.
Synagogue (affiliated to the United Synagogue), Meadowcroft, Great North Road, Bell Bar (nr Potters Bar), Hatfield, Herts AL9 6DB. ☎/Fax 01707 656202. Email office@potters-barshul.org.uk. *M.* Rabbi A. S. Hill.

PRESTON (25)
Synagogue, est. 1882, now closed. *H. Sec.* Dr C. E. Nelson, 31 Avondale Road, Southport PR9 0NH. ☎ 01704 538276.

RADLETT (750)
Radlett, with Bushey and Elstree, has become the new frontier of Anglo-Jewish suburbia in North-West Herts, outdoing London NW11 of eighty years ago. At the last censis the Jewish population was calculated at over 30% amnd the number of synagogues reflects this. Radlett & Bushey Reform (originally Bushey & District Reform) and Bushey U.S. date back to the early 70's. Hertsmere Progressive (now the Liberal Synagogue Elstree) followed soon after, and Radlett U.S. branched off a decade or so back from Borehamwood & Elstree in 1995. In addition new U.S., Federation, and Masorti communities are springing up in neighbouring Shenley. Radlett U.S. and Radlett & Bushey Reform are prominent on Watling Street, which once rang to the march of Roman centurions, and now sways under the kippah. They co-operate on action for the communities of the former Soviet Union, and in interfaith work.

Synagogues:

The Liberal Synagogue Elstree (Liberal Judaism) (formerly Hertsmere Progressive), High Street, Elstree, Herts WD6 3EY. *M.* Rabbi P. Tobias; *Hon. Sec.*; R. Elman. ☎ 020 8953 8889 Email office@tlse.org.uk. Website www.tlse.org.uk.

Radlett (U.S.), 22 Watling St., P.O. Box 28, Herts. WD7 7PN. *M.* Rabbi A. Abel ☎ 01923-856878; Email: radlettus@hotmail.com *Admin.* Mrs J. Bower and Mrs A. Primhak.

Radlett & Bushey Reform Synagogue, 118 Watling St., Herts. WD7 7AA. ☎ 01923 856110. Fax 01923 858444. Email office@rbrs.org.uk Website www.rbrs.org.uk. *M.* Rabbi P. Freedman.

READING (415)
The community began in 1886 with the settlement of a number of tailors from London. They attracted the help of such personages as Samuel Montagu, Claude Montefiore, Sir Hermann Gollancz and Lady Lucas to build and support a synagogue in 1900, and the syn. has been in continuous use ever since. This flourishes today as the centre of the Reading Hebrew Cong., and is the only Orthodox cong. in Berkshire. The Sir Hermann Gollancz Hall next to the syn. is the venue of many social groups. The Progressive Community was founded in 1979 and attracts membership from across the Thames Valley. (See also under Maidenhead)

Berkshire Jewish Representative Council (Est. 1995). *Chair* D. Adelman c/o 21 Christchurch Road, RG2 7AA ☎ 0118-9867769. Email dizzie13@tiscali.co.uk.

Reading Hebrew Congregation. Synagogue (Reg. Charity No. 220098), Goldsmid Road, RG1 7YB. ☎ 0118-957 3954. Website www.rhc.org.uk; Email secretary@rhc.datanet. co.uk. *M.* Rabbi Z, Solomons.

WIZO & Judaica Shop. Mrs Pamela Kay ☎ 0118 9573680.

Food Shop. Kosher meat and provisions. Mrs Carol Kay (0118 575069.

Reading Liberal Jewish Community (Est. 1979. LJ), 2, Church Street, Reading. For details of services, religious and social events, contact ☎ 0118 375 3422. Email rljcl@liberaljudaism Website www.rljc.org *M.* Rabbi Hadassah Davis.

University Jewish Society, c/o Hebrew Congregation.

REIGATE AND REDHILL (45)
Jewish Community. (Est. 1968.) *Chairman* M. J. Kemper, 59 Gatton Road, Reigate, Surrey. ☎ 017372 42076.

ST. ALBANS (200)
St. Albans Masorti Synagogue, P.O. Box 23, AL1 4PH. *Co-Chair* L. Harris, Mrs L. McQuillan; *T.* P. Hoffbrand; *M.* ; *Sec.* Mrs K. Phillips ☎ 01727 860642. Email info@e-sams.org. Website www.e-sams.org.

St. Albans United Synagogue, Oswald Road, Herts AL1 3AQ. ☎ 01727 854872. Email info@stalbanssynagogue.org.uk. Website www.stalbanssynagogue.org.uk.

ST. ANNE'S ON SEA (500)
Hebrew Congregation, Orchard Road, FY8 1PJ. (Reg. Charity no. 66492) ☎ 01253 721831. *Chairman* L.S. Jackson; *H. T.* L.H. Caro; *H. Sec.* S. Tomlinson; *M.* Rabbi L. Book. ☎ 01253-781815.
Ladies Guild, *Chairman* J. Kendall ☎ 01253 723088.
Cemetery: Consecrated section of municipal cemetery at Regents Avenue, Lytham.

SHEFFIELD (763)
The earliest records of an organised Jewish community in Sheffield date from 1850, but the congregation had already been in existence for some time and Jews are known to have been living in the city from the eighteenth century. At its peak in the 1960s, the community numbered over 2,000. A study of the community, 'Sheffield Jewry' by Armin Krausz, was published in 1980. In 2000, the Orthodox congregation moved from the large Wilson Road synagogue (built 1929) into a new and smaller synagogue within the grounds of the Jewish Centre which was consecrated by the Chief Rabbi in 2000. The Reform congregation was founded in 1989 and was admitted as a full constituent member of the RSGB in 2000. Though now a smaller community, Sheffield has an exceptional range of societies and groups, covering all varieties of Jewish interests.
Sheffield Jewish Congregation and Centre (Orthodox). (Reg. Charity No. 250281). Kingfield Synagogue, Brincliffe Crescent, S11 8UX. ☎ 0114 281 7459 (home), or 0114 258 8855 (office). Email rabbijgolomb@tiscali.co.uk. *M.* Rabbi Y. Golomb; *President* M. Moore. Mikvah on premises.
Sheffield Jewish Burial Association (Chevra Kaddisha). *President* G. Sverdloff ☎ 0114 236 6259.
Sheffield Jewish Education Organization (Reg. Charity No. 529362). *Chairman* Dr A. Anderson ☎ 0114 235 1041.
Sheffield Hillel Association (Reg. Charity No. 529385), 1 Guest Road, S11 8UJ.*Chairman* J. Shaw ☎ 0114 230 9111.
Sheffield Jewish Welfare Organisation in association with SJCC (Inland Reg. Charity No. X75608). *President* A. Kaddish ☎ 0114 236 7958.
Sheffield & District Reform Jewish Congregation. *Chair* B.C. Rosenberg, TD. For information contact PO Box 675, S11 8SP or Website www.shef-ref.co.uk.

SOLIHULL (389)
The community began in 1962. The synagogue was built in 1977. Its close proximity to Birmingham means that many of the facilities of the Birmingham community are shared by Solihull.
Solihull & District Hebrew Congregation, Solihull Jewish Community Centre, 3 Monastery Drive, Solihull, West Midlands, B91 1DW. ☎/Fax 0121 706 8736. Website www.solihull-shul.org; Email rabbi@solihullshul.org. *M.* Rabbi Y. Pink ☎ 0121-706 8736; *President* S. Fisher; *Admin.* Mrs H. Woolf.
Solihull Jewish Social & Cultural Society. *Chairman* H. Kay ☎ 0121-705 3870; *H.Sec.* Mrs M. Leveson, 19 Bishopton Close, B90 4AH. ☎ 0121-744 8391.
Solihull & District Cheder. *H.T.* Rabbi Y. Pink ☎ 0121-706 8736. Email cheder@ solihull-shul.org.
The Thursday Club, Solihull Jewish Community Centre, Email shul@solihullshul.org, *Co-ord* Mrs Ruth Abrahams ☎ 0121-705 5287. For the over 60's
Mother and Toddler's Group, Mrs Dina Pink, ☎ 0121-706 8736. Email dina@solihulshul.org
Stanley Middleburgh Library, 3 Monastery Drive, B91 1DW. Email library@ solihullshul.org. Open Sunday 9.30am–1.00pm or by appointment.
Hakol – Community Magazine, 3 Monastery Drive, B91 1DW. Email hakol@ solihullshul.org.

SOUTH SHIELDS (9)
Hebrew Congregation, Contact: Mr H. Tavroges. ☎ 0191-285 4834. The synagogue is now closed.

Cemetery: Consecrated section of the municipal cemetery.

SOUTHAMPTON (293)
The orthodox congregation dates from 1833 when the first synagogue in East Street was founded. The synagogue built in 1864 in Albion Place was demolished in 1963, when the present one was consecrated. There were Jewish residents in Southampton in 1786. Since 1838, when Abraham Abraham was elected to the Town Council, they have shared in civic affairs. The South Hampshire Reform Jewish Community was formed in 1983.

Orthodox Synagogue, Mordaunt Road, Inner Ave. ☎ 023-80220129. *President* M. Rose. *H. Sec.*
South Hampshire Reform Jewish Community (Est. 1983; Reg. Charity no. 1040109), for Hampshire and the Isle of Wight. *Chair* R. Pell ☎ 0709 2373918, Email rdpell@yahoo.co.uk; *Sec.* Ruth Goodman, 36 Woodman Close, Sparsholt, Winchester, SO21 2NT.
Hartley Library, University of Southampton, Highfield, houses the Anglo-Jewish Archives and Parkes Library (see p. 48).
Hillel House, 2 Denbigh Gardens, Bassett. ☎ 023-80768070.
Cemetery: Consecrated section at the municipal Hollybrook cemetery.

SOUTHEND, WESTCLIFF & LEIGH-ON-SEA (2,721)
Jewish families settled in the Southend area in the late nineteenth century, mainly from London's East End. In 1906 the first temporary synagogue was built in wood in Station Road, Westcliff. In 1912 a synagogue was built in Alexandra Road, which served the community until February 2001 when it was sold. A second synagogue was built in Ceylon Road, Westcliff, in 1928, but when a new synagogue was built in Finchley Road, the Ceylon Road premises were converted into a youth centre. The Ceylon Road premises have now been sold and a new youth centre has been opened at the Talmud Torah premises.

Southend and Westcliff Hebrew Congregation, Finchley Rd., Westcliff-on-Sea, Essex SS0 8AD. *President* A. Gershlick; *M.* Rabbi Bar. ☎ 01702 344900. Fax 01702 391131. Email swhc@btclick.com. Website www.swhc. org.uk; *Gen.Man.* Mrs Janice Steel; *Admin.* Mrs Pamela Freedman, Mrs S. Symons.
Southend and District Reform Synagogue, 851 London Road, Westcliff-on-Sea. ☎ 01702 475809. Email mail@southendreform.co.uk. *M.* Rabbi W. Elf; *Chairman* L. Miller; *V. Chair* Mrs S. Levitas; *H.T.* J. Kinn; *Hon. Sec.*
Mikva, 44 Genesta Road, Westcliff-on-Sea. ☎ 01702 344900. *Supt.* Mrs R. Samuel.
Orthodox Jewish Cemetery, Sutton Road, Southend. (Entr. Stock Road). ☎ 01702 344900.
Reform Jewish Cemetery, Sutton Road, Southend. (Entr. Stock Road).
Myers Communal Hall, Finchley Road, Westcliff. ☎ 01702 344900.
Kashrut Commission, *Chair* M.Nelkin.
Ladies' Guild (Orthodox). *Chair* Mrs G. Jay ☎ 01702 715105.
Ladies' Guild (Reform). *Chair* Mrs D. Phillips. ☎ 01702 432477.

EDUCATIONAL AND YOUTH ORGANISATIONS
Coleman & Lilian Levene Talmud Torah (Orthodox), Finchley Road, Westcliff. (01702 344900. *Princ.* Rabbi B. Bar.
Hebrew Education Board. *Chairman* D. Silverstone. ☎ 01702 344900.
Jewish Lads' & Girls' Brigade. *Chairman* R. Cirsch. ☎ 020-8989 8990.
Lecture Board. Mrs S. Greenstein. ☎ 01702 477617.
Talmud Torah (Reform), 851 London Road, Westcliff. *Princ.* Mrs B. Barber. ☎ 01702 297238.
Youth Centre (Orthodox), Finchley Road, Westcliff. ☎ 01702 432067. *Chair.* L. Neidus.

SOCIAL, CULTURAL & WELFARE ORGANISATIONS
AJEX Social Club, Communal Hall, Finchley Road Synagogue, Westcliff. *Chairperson* Mrs B. Feldman. ☎ 01702 584871.
Council of Christians and Jews. *Hon. Sec.* G. Demetz. ☎ 01702 391535.
Emunah Ladies' Society. *Chairman* Mrs Fay Sober. ☎ 01702 330440. *Sec.* Mrs S. Symons.

Friendship Club. *Chairperson* Mrs Minn Rose ☎ 01702 390230.

JNF Impact. *Chairman* A. Larholt; *Sec.* Mrs Laraine Barnes.

Kosher Meals-on-Wheels Service. *Chairperson.* Anthony Rubin. ☎ 01702 345568.

Raymond House (a Jewish Care residential home), 5 Clifton Terrace, SS1 1DT. *Man.* ☎ 01702 352956; *Residents* ☎ 01702 340054; *Matron* 01702 341687.

Southend Aid Society. *Chair* Mrs S. Greenstein; *Sec.* Audrey Barcan. ☎ 01702 343192.

Southend & District AJEX. *President* ; *Chairman* S. Barnett; *H. Sec.* J. Barcan. ☎ 01702 343192.

Southend District Social Committee (Reform). *Chairman* Mrs S. Kaye ☎ 01702 475809.

Southend & Westcliff Community Centre, 1 Cobham Road, Westcliff-on-Sea, SSO 8EG (a Jewish Care day centre). ☎ 01702 334655. *Man.* G. Freeman

Tuesday Nighters. *Chairman* Lewis Herlitz. ☎ 01702 715676.

UJIA. *Chairman* S. Salt ☎ 01702 476349.

WIZO. *Chairperson* Mrs Jackie Kalms; *H. Sec.* Mrs Jane Barnett. ☎ 01702 340731.

SOUTHPORT (699)

The first Synagogue was consecrated in 1893 and the congregation moved to Arnside Road, in 1924. The New Synagogue (Reform) was est. in 1948. The community grew between and during the First and Second World Wars, but is now decreasing.

Jewish Representative Council. *President* Mrs Sonia Abrahamson, 65 Beach Priory Gardens, PR8 2SA. ☎ 01704 540704; *H. Sec.* R. Jackson, 33, The Chesters, 17-19 Argyle Rd. PR9 9LG. ☎ 01704 532696

Synagogue, Arnside Road, PR9 0QX. ☎ 01704 532964. *M.* ; *Senior Warden* Dr Cyril Nelson; *Sec.* Mrs S. Roukin.

Mikveh, Arnside Road. (01704 532964.

New Synagogue, Portland St., PR8 1LR. ☎ 01704 535950. *M.* ; *Emer. Rabbi* Rabbi S. Kay; *Sec.* Mrs E. Lippa.

Jewish Convalescent and Aged Home, 81 Albert Road. ☎ 01704 531975 (office); 01704 530207 (visitors). *Chairman* Mrs J. Bennett.

Manchester House, 83 Albert Road. ☎ 01704 534920 (office); 01704 530436 (visitors).

STAINES & DISTRICT (390)

(Incorporating Slough & Windsor)

Synagogue (affiliated to the U.S.), Westbrook Road, South Street, Middx. TW18 4PR. *M.* Rev. M. Binstock. *Admin.* S. A. Conway. ☎ 01784 455615. Website www.btinternet.com/-staines.synagogue.

STOKE-ON-TRENT AND NORTH STAFFORDSHIRE (26)

Hebrew Congregation, London Road, Newcastle, Staffs, ST5 1LZ (Est. 1873. Reg. Charity No. 232104) *President* H. S. Morris, MBE, 27 The Avenue, Basford, Newcastle, Staffs. ST5 0ND. ☎ 01782 616417; *Jt. T.* H.S. Morris, R. Elias. ☎ 01782 318110. Emailmartin@mmorriso1wanadoo.co.uk

SUFFOLK

Suffolk Jewish Community (LJ) Enquiries ☎ 020 7631 9821 Email sjc@liberaljudaism. org

SUNDERLAND (32)

The first Jewish settlement was in 1755. The first congregation was est. about 1768; and was the first regional community to be represented at the BoD. A syn. was erected in Moor St. in 1862; rebuilt in 1900; and in 1928 the cong. moved to Ryhope Road, The Beth Hamedrash, which was est. in Villiers St. in 1899, and moved to Mowbray Road in 1938, closed in December 1984. Arnold Levy published a 'History of the Sunderland Jewish Community' in 1956.

Hebrew Congregation, incorporating Sunderland Beth Hamedrash, Ryhope Road, SR2 7EQ. ☎ 0191-5658093. (Reg. Charity No. 1078345). Closed in March 2006 *Contact* Ivor

Saville, ☎ 0191-522 9710.
Chevra Kadisha. *Contact* Ivor Saville.
Hebrew Board of Guardians. (Est. 1869). *Contact* Ivor Saville.
Talmudical College and Yeshiva. ☎ 0191 490 1606. (See Gateshead p. 102). *Princ.*
Cemetery: Bishopwearmouth Cemetery, Hylton Road, Sunderland.

SWINDON (127)

The community formed by Second World War evacuees has dispersed, but a community was re-formed in 1983.
Jewish Community. (Associated Community of the Movement for Reform Judaism) C/o Reform Judaism, Sternberg Centre, 80, East End Road, London N3 2SY. *Contact* ☎ 01793-831335. Est.1983.

TORQUAY (TORBAY) (159)

Synagogue, Old Town Hall, Abbey Road. The synagogue was closed at the end of 2000 and the congregation dissolved. Inq.: E. Freed, 11 Kestor Dr., Paignton TQ3 1AP ☎ 01803 553781

Chevra Kadisha: Cemetery, Colley End Road, Paignton, Torbay. *Chairman* E. Freed.

TOTNES

Totnes Jewish Community (Movement for Reform). *Contact* ☎ 01803 867461; Email: thk-endall@phonecoop.coop

WALLASEY (50)

Hebrew Congregation, (Est. 1911.) *President* D. Daniels; *T.* D. J. Waldman; *H. Sec.* L. S. Goldman, 28 Grant Road, Wirral, Merseyside, L46 2RY. ☎ 0151-638 6945.

WELWYN GARDEN CITY (290)

Synagogue (Affiliated to U.S.), Barn Close, Handside Lane, Herts AL8 6ST. ☎ 01707 322443. *M.* Rabbi H.Gruber; *H. Sec.* R.Rosenberg.

WOLVERHAMPTON (15)

Synagogue, Fryer St. (Est. 1850.) Closure of the synagogue was reported in 1999. Contact .
Cemetery: Consecrated section at Jeffcock Road Corporation Cemetery, Wolverhampton.

WORTHING

Worthing & District Jewish Community. *Chairman* Mrs B. Gordon ☎ 01273 779720 who meet for social and cultural events at The Friends Meeting House, Mill Hill Road, Worthing. Outreach services held by visiting Chaplain the Rev. Malcolm Weisman.

YORK (191)

A memorial stone was consecrated at Clifford's Tower, York Castle, in 1978 in memory of the York Jewish community massacred there in 1190. A small community resettled and continued to live in York until the 1290 expulsion. There is now a small com. in the city and a Jewish Soc. at York Univ.
York Hebrew Congregation. *Contact* A. S. Burton ☎ 01423 330537.

WALES

CARDIFF (941)

Jews settled in Cardiff about the year 1787. The present community was founded in 1840.
Jewish Representative Council. *Chairman* A. Schwartz; *H. Sec.* Mrs R. Levene. ☎ 029-2048 8198. Email ruthandpaullevene@tiscali.co.uk.
Israel Information Centre Wales & the West of England, P.O.B. 98, CF2 6XN. ☎/Fax 02920-461780. *Dir.* Jean A. Evans.
Cardiff United Synagogue, Cyncoed Gardens, Cyncoed Rd., Penylan, CF23 5SL.

☎ 029-2047 3728. *M.* Rabbi M. Wollenberg. ☎ 029-2048 3177. Website www.cardiff-shul.org. Email Wollenberg@usa.net. **Mikveh**. Appointments (029-2048 3177
New Synagogue, Moira Terrace, CF2 1EJ. (opp. Howard Gardens.). (Movement for Reform) ☎ 029-2049 1689. Email info@cardiffnewsyn.org. *Chairman* S. Masters; *Sec.* Mrs J. Galten.
Hillel House, 89 Crwys Rd. ☎ 029-2023 1114. Applications for admission: Mrs L. Gerson. ☎ 029-2075 9982. Email lisa@gersonfamily.freeserve.co.uk.
Cardiff Jewish Helpline (formerly Cardiff Jewish Board of Guardians). *Chairman* Mr A. Schwartz (029-2075 0990.
Kashrus Commission. Penylan Synagogue Office. ☎ 029-2047 3728.
Penylan House, Jewish Residential and Nursing Home, Penylan Road, CF23 5YG. ☎ 029-2048 5327. Fax 029-2045 8409. Nursing Office 029-2049 2574. Email penyla house@aol.com. *Dir.* Paul Evans; *Matron/Nursing Man.* Geraldine Bassett; *President* Judy Cotsen.
Union of Jewish Students, c/o Hillel House. (029-2023 1114.
Bimah. South Wales Jewish Communal magazine. *Edr.* A. Schwartz. Email editor@ bimah.org.uk.
Cemeteries: Old Cemetery – High Fields Road, Roath Park; New Cemetery – Greenfarm Road, Ely; Reform: at Cowbridge Road Entrance, Ely Cemetery.

LLANDUDNO AND COLWYN BAY (15)
Hebrew Congregation, 28 Church Walks, Llandudno LL30 2HL. (Est. 1905). *Sec.* . Llandudno serves as the centre for the dwindling coms. of North Wales, including Bangor, Rhyl, Colwyn Bay and Caernarvon.

MERTHYR TYDFIL
Synagogue now closed. The com. was est. before 1850. The cemetery is still being maintained. Apply to the Cardiff Jewish Rep. C. (see above).

NEWPORT (Gwent) (39)
Synagogue (opened 1871), now closed. ☎ 01633 810013. *Chairman* A. Davidson. Email abd321@onetel.com
Burial Society, c/o Cardiff United Synagogue, Penylan, Cardiff.
Cemetery: Risca Road, Newport.

SWANSEA (170)
The Jewish community dates at the latest from 1768, when the Corporation granted a plot of land for use as a cemetery. In 1780 a syn. was built. Probably its history is even older, for Jews are known to have been living in the town from about 1730. The syn. in Goat St. was destroyed in an air raid in Feb. 1941, but another was erected in the Ffynone district. The former Llanelli cong. is now part of the Swansea com.
Hebrew Congregation. (Est. 1780.) Synagogue, Ffynone. *Chairman* H. M. Sherman, 17 Mayals Green, Mayals, Swansea SA3 5JR. ☎ 01792 401205.
Chevra Kadisha. *Chairman* D. Sandler. ☎ 01792 206285.
Cemeteries at Oystermouth and Townhill.

WELSHPOOL
Welshpool Jewish Group, c/o M. and S. Michaels, 10, Corndon Dr., Montgomery, Powys. ☎ 01686 668977. Email markjmichaels@aol.com.

SCOTLAND
Scottish Council of Jewish Communities (SCoJeC), Jewish Community Centre, 222 Fenwick Rd., Giffnock, Glasgow G46 6UE. ☎ 0141-638 6411. Fax 0141-577 8208. Email sco-jec@scojec.org Website www.scojec.org (Est. 1987 as Standing Committee of Scottish Jewry. Charity SCO 29438) Democratic umbrella body representing all the Jewish Communities in Scotland to the Scottish Parliament and Executive, churches and other faith

communities, educational, health and welfare Organisations. An educational charity to promote understanding of the Jewish religion and community. *Chairman* W. Sneader; *V. Chair* H.Rifkind (Edinburgh), P. Mendelsohn (Glasgow); F. House (Highlands) *Dir.* E. Borowski; *Public Affairs Off.* L. Granat, ☎ 07887-488 100

The Scottish Jewish Archives Centre. Garnethill Synagogue, 129 Hill Street, Glasgow G3 6UB. ☎/Fax 0141 332 4911. Email info@sjac.org.uk; Website www.sjac.org.uk. (Est. 1987) To collect, catalogue, preserve and exhibit records of communal interest. To stimulate study in the history of the Jews of Scotland. To heighten awareness in the Jewish communities of Scotland of their cultural and religious heritages. *H. Life President* Dr Jack E. Miller, OBE, JP; *Chairman* Dr Kenneth Collins, PhD; *H.T.* F. Brodie; *Dir.* Harvey L. Kaplan, MA; *H. Sec* D. Wolfson

ABERDEEN (30)
Refurbished synagogue and community centre opened 1983.
Hebrew Congregation, 74 Dee Street, AB11 6DS. ☎ 01224 582135; www.aberdeenhebrew.org.uk (Est. 1893. Reg. Charity No. SC002901) *H. Sec.* Esther Shoshan. ☎ 01224 642749.

DUNDEE (22)
Hebrew Congregation, 9 St. Mary Place. (Est. 1874. New synagogue opened 1978.) *Chairman* H. King, 1 Duntrune House, Duntrune DD4 0PJ ☎/Fax 01382 350244 Email hennyking1@btinternet.com
Dundee Univ. Jewish Society is centred at the synagogue.

EDINBURGH (763)
The Edinburgh Town Council and Burgess Roll, Minutes of 1691 and 1717, record applications by Jews for permission to reside and trade in Edinburgh. Local directories of the eighteenth century contain Jewish names. There is some reason to believe that there was an organised Jewish community in 1780 but no cemetery, and in 1817 it removed to Richmond Ct. where there was also for a time a rival congregation. In 1795, the Town Council sold a plot of ground on the CaltonHill to Herman Lyon, a Jewish dentist, to provide a burying place for himself and members of his family. In 1816, when a syn. was opened a cemetery was also acquired. The present syn. in Salisbury Road was consecrated in 1932 and renovated in 1980.
Hebrew Congregation, 4 Salisbury Road. ☎ 0131-667 3144. (Est. 1816, New Synagogue built 1932.) *Chairman* Mrs H. Rifkind ☎ 0131-667 5500. *M.* Rabbi D. Rose; *H. Sec* Mrs J. Taylor.
Board of Guardians. *H. Sec.* I. Shein (as above).
Chevra Kadisha. *H.T.* M. Cowan. ☎ 0131-667 6312 Email mcowenedin@blueyonder.co.uk
Edinburgh Liberal Jewish Community-Sukkat Shalom (LJ) Enquiries ☎ 0131 777 8024 Email eljc@liberaljudaism.org. Website www.eljc.org.
Jewish Literary Society. *President* A. Meiksin, c/o Hebrew Congregation ☎ 0131-229 5541. *H. Sec.* S. Engleman ☎ 0131-447 0911.
Jewish Old Age Home for Scotland (Edinburgh Cttee). *President* J. S. Caplan; *H. Sec.* Miss A. Lurie, 26 South Lauder Road, 9. ☎ 0131-667 5500.
Ladies' Guild. *President* Mrs H. Rifkind, 37 Cluny Drive, Edinburgh EH10 6DU. ☎ 0131-447 7386.
The Edinburgh Star. Community Journal. Published 3 times a year. *Ed.* J. Gilbert, 2 Marchhall Crescent, EH16 5HN Email judyemmi.gilbert@gmail.com.
Scottish Friends of Alyn *President* H. Cosgrove, *Chairman* C. Osborne
University Jewish Society. *President* S. Hyman, c/o Societies' Centre, Room 6, 21 Hill Place.
Wizo *Co-Chairmen* K. Goodwin, S. Donne

GLASGOW AND WEST OF SCOTLAND (5,000)
The Glasgow Jewish community was founded in 1823 although there are records of Jewish activity in the city for many years prior to that. The first Jewish cemetery was opened in the prestigious Glasgow Necropolis in 1831 and the community was housed in a variety of syna-

gogues in the city centre for many years. The community grew in the 1870s and the Garnethill Synagogue, the oldest Jewish building in Scotland and home of the Scottish Jewish Archives Centre, was opened in 1879. At the same time Jews began settling in the Gorbals district just south of the River Clyde where there was a substantial Jewish community with many synagogues and Jewish shops and communal institutions until the 1950s. None of these now remains. In more recent years the community has been centred in the southern suburbs such as Giffnock and Newton Mearns where most Jewish institutions are now situated.

Details of Jewish history in Glasgow in the early days (1790–1919) can be found in 'Second City Jewry' and 'Scotland's Jews' by Dr Kenneth Collins, available from the Glasgow Jewish Representative Council.

Jewish Representative Council, 222 Fenwick Rd., Giffnock, G46 6UE. ☎ 0141-577 8200. Email jrepcouncil@aol.com. Website www.glasgowjewishrepcouncil.org. (Est. 1914. Reg. Charity No. SCO16626.) *President* P. Mendelsohn; *Admin.* Mrs B. Taylor. Information Desk ☎ 0141-577 8228. Fax 0141-577 8202. Website www.glasgowjewishrepcouncil.org

West Scotland Kashrut Commission, *Chairman* M. Livingstone; *M.* Rabbi P. Hachenbroch; *H. Sec.* H. Tankel. ☎ 0141-423 5830.

Hebrew Burial Society (as Rep. Council), ☎ 0141-577 8226. *Chairman* S. Shenkin. *Enquiries* W. Solansky.

Mikvah, Giffnock & Newlands Syn., Maryville Avenue, Giffnock. *Enquiries* Mrs Borowski ☎ 07831 104110.

Scottish Council of Synagogues. Email s.c.synagogues@gla.ac.uk.

SYNAGOGUES

Garnethill Synagogue, 129 Hill Street, G3 6UG. ☎ 0141-332 4151. (Est. 1875.) *M.* A. Soudry; *Chairman* G. Levin; *H. Sec.* Mrs R. Livingston.

Giffnock and Newlands Synagogue, Maryville Avenue, Giffnock G46. ☎ 0141-577 8250. *M.* Rabbi A.M. Rubin; *R.*; *Chairman* E. Leviten; *Sec.* Mrs G. Gardner.

Glasgow Reform Synagogue, 147 Ayr Road, Newton Mearns G77 6RE. *Chairman* S. Woolfson; *M.*; *T.* ☎ 0141-639 4083.

Langside Hebrew Congregation, 125 Niddrie Road, G42. ☎ 0141-423 4062. *M. Chairman* J. Levingstone; *H. Sec.* N. Barnes.

Netherlee and Clarkston Hebrew Congregation, Clarkston Road, Clarkston. *M.* Rabbi R. Bokow; *Chairman* O. Lovat. ☎ 0141-637 8206.

Newton Mearns Synagogue, 14 Larchfield Court, G77 6RE. ☎ 0141-639 4000. *M.* Rabbi P. Hackenbroch; *Chairman* H. Beach; *Hon. Sec.* ☎ 0141-639 4000.

EDUCATIONAL AND COMMUNAL ORGANISATIONS

Calderwood Board of Jewish Education, 28 Calderwood Road, G43 2RU. ☎ 0141-637 7409. *Chairman* Dr M. Granach; *H. Sec..*

Calderwood Lodge Jewish Primary School, 28 Calderwood Road, G43 2RU. ☎ 0141-637 5654. *H.M.* Mrs C. Haughney.

Chaim Bermant Library, 222 Fenwick Rd., Giffnock G46 6UE. ☎.

Glasgow Kollel. *Dir.* Rabbi M. Bamberger. ☎ 0141-638 6664/0141-577 8260.

Glasgow Maccabi, May Terrace, Giffnock, G46 6DL. ☎ 0141-638 7655. *Chairman* D. Shenkin.

Glasgow Zionist Federation, 222 Fenwick Rd., Giffnock G46 6UE.

Israel Scottish Information Service, Jewish Community Centre. (0141-577 8240.

Jewish Community Centre. ☎ 0141-577 8222.

Jewish Telegraph, May Terrace, Giffnock G46 6LD. ☎ 0141 621 4422; ☎ 0141 621 4433 (Newsdesk). Fax 0141 6214333, Email: glasgow@jewishtelegraph.com

Jewish Youth Forum. ☎ 0141-577 8220.

Lubavitch Foundation, 8 Orchard Dr, Giffnock. ☎0141-638 6116. Fax 0141 638 6478. Email lubofscot@aol.com *Dir.* Rabbi Chaim Jacobs.

Northern Region Chaplaincy. *Chairman*; *H. Sec.* ☎ 0141-639 4497; *Chaplain* Rabbi D. Cohen.

Shalom Singers. *Chairman* Mrs D. Shenkin, *H. Sec.* Mrs A. Sakol. ☎ 0141-639 1756.

UJIA (incorporating Glasgow Jewish Continuity), Jewish Community Centre, 222 Fenwick Rd., Giffnock, G46 6UE. ☎ 0141-577 8210. Renewal ☎ 0141-577 8220. Fax 0141-577 8212. *Dir.* Alex Steen; *Renewal Dir.* Mrs A. Masson.
Yeshivah, Giffnock Syn., Maryville Avenue. *Chairman* Dr K. Collins. ☎ 0141-577 8260. *H. M.* Rabbi H. Bamberger.
WELFARE ORGANISATIONS
Cosgrove Care, May Terrace, Giffnock, G46 6LD. *Chairman* Mr J. Dover; *Exec. Off.* W. Hecht; *H. Sec.* Mrs M. Goldman. ☎ 0141-620 2500. Fax 0141-620 2501.
Arklet Housing Association, Barrland Court, Barrland Drive, Giffnock, G46 7QD. *Dir.* Mrs Joan Leifer. ☎ 0141-620 1890. Fax 0141-620 3044.
Jewish Blind Society Centre (Reg. Charity No. SCO11789), Walton Community Care Centre, May Terrace, Giffnock, G46 6DL. ☎ 0141-620 3339. Fax 0141-620 2409. *Chairman* D. Strang; *Sec.* Mrs C. Blake.
Jewish Care Scotland (Est. 1868. Reg. Charity No. SCO05267), May Terrace Giffnock, G46 6DL. ☎ 0141-620 1800. Fax 0141-620 1088. *Chairman* M. Solomons. *Chief Exec.* Mrs E. Woldman.
Jewish Hospital and Sick Visiting Association. ☎ 0141-638 6048. *Chairman* H. Cowen.
Newark Care, 32 Burnfield Road, Gifford, G46. *Chairmen* A. Jacobson, M. Jackson; *Chief Exec.* M. Maddox.

HIGHLANDS
Jewish Network of Argyll and The Highlands (JNAH)
Contact Frank House, Horisdale House, Strath, Gairloch, IV21 2DA. ☎ 01445 712151. Email frank.house@onetel.com.

NORTHERN IRELAND
BELFAST (130)
There was a Jewish community in Belfast about the year 1771, but the present community was founded in 1865.
Hebrew Congregation, 49 Somerton Rd. (Est. 1872; Syn. erected at Carlisle Circus, 1904, present building consecrated, 1964.) *President* ; *Chairman* E. Coppel; *M.* Rabbi M. Brackman, ☎ 028-9077 5013; *H. Sec.* G. Golstone, Apt 3, 1 Deramore Park, BT9 5JY ☎ 028-9068 7507. Email bjcinfo@yahoo.co.uk.
Jewish Community Centre, 49 Somerton Rd. ☎ 028-9077 7974.
Wizo. *Chairperson* Mrs M. Black; *H. Secs.* Mrs N. Simon, Mrs Danker.
Belfast Jewish Record. *H. Sec.* Mrs N. Simon, 42 Glandore Ave., BT15 3FD.

ISLE OF MAN (ca. 35)
Hebrew Congregation. *Contact* Carol Jempson, 8 Mountain View, Douglas IM2 5HU; *Visiting M.* Rev. M. Weisman, OBE, M.A. (Oxon.).
Cemetery: Consecrated section of the Douglas Cemetery, Glencrutchery Rd.

CHANNEL ISLANDS
JERSEY (120)
A syn. existed in St. Helier, the capital of the island, from 1843 until about 1870. The present com. was founded in 1962.
Jersey Jewish Congregation, La Petite Route des Mielles, St Brelade, JE3 8FY. ☎ 01534 44946. *President* S.J. Regal; *H. Sec.* M. Morton, 16 La Rocquaise, La Route des Genets, St Brelade, JE3 8HY. ☎ 01534 742819; *H.T.* M. Kalman; *Visiting M.* Rev. M. Weisman, OBE, MA. Seven families of the Jersey cong. live in Guernsey.

REPUBLIC OF IRELAND (1,500)
Jews lived in Ireland in the Middle Ages, and a Sephardi community was established in Dublin in 1660, four years after the Resettlement in England. In the eighteenth century there was a community also at Cork. The Dublin congregation declined in the reign of George III, and was dissolved in 1791, but was revived in 1822. The community received its largest influx of mem-

bers around 1900, the immigrants coming from Eastern Europe, Lithuania in particular. There are now some 1,300 Jews in the country. (See Hyman: The Jews of Ireland, 1972, repr. 1996.)
Chief Rabbi: Office: Herzog House, Zion Rd., Dublin, 6. ☎ 353-1-492-3751. *Sec.* Stewart Barling.
Jewish Community Office, Herzog House, 1, Zion Road, Dublin, 6. ☎ 492-3751. Fax 492-4680. Email irishcom@iol.ie; Website jewishireland.org. *Sec.* Stewart Barling.
Also located at **Herzog House:**
> **Jewish Representative Council of Ireland.** *Chairman* Leonard Abrahamson; *President* Mrs Estelle Menton; *H. Sec.*. Email jrcisec@gmail.com.
> **Chief Rabbi's Office.** . ☎ 492-3751.
> **General Board of Shechita & Kashrut Commission** (Est. 1915.).
> **Jewish National Fund.** ☎ 492-2318. *H. Sec.* Mrs Linda White.
> **Joint Israel Appeal.** ☎ 492-2318. *H. Sec.* L. Bloomfield.
Irish-Jewish Museum (Est. 1984), 3-4 Walworth Road, Portobello, Dublin 8. ☎ 453-1797. *Curator* R. Siev. The Museum contains memorabilia of the Irish-Jewish Community and houses a former synagogue.
Irish-Jewish Genealogical Society (Est. 1998). *Contact* Stuart Rosenblatt, c/o Irish-Jewish Museum.
Jewish Board of Guardians (Est. 1889), 10, Glendoher Dr., Rathfarnham, Dublin 16 ☎ 493 4422. *Admin.* Mrs L. Levine.
Jewish Home of Ireland, Stocking Lane, Rathfarnham, Dublin 14. *Admin.* ☎ 495-0021.

CORK (30)
Hebrew Congregation, 10 South Terrace. (Est. 1880). *Chairman of Trustees.* F. Rosehill, 7 Beverly, Ovens, Co. Cork. ☎ 021-4870413. Fax 021-4876537. Email rosehill@iol.ie.

DUBLIN (1,500)
Rabbi Zalman Lent; *M.* Alwyn Shulman.

SYNAGOGUES
Dublin Hebrew Congregation, (Est. 1836. Syn. opened 1892;. enlarged 1925. Closed in 1999). Merged with Terenure Hebrew Congregation in 2004). Rathfarnham Road, Terenure, 6. ☎ 490-8037. *H. President* M. Gilbert; *Chairman* Dr. H. Gross; *H. Sec.* Dr M. Levine ☎ 493-4422
Synagogue Machzikei Hadass, 77 Terenure Road North, 6. (Est. *c.* 1890). ☎ 493-8991.*President* M. Milofsky; *H. Sec.* R. Godfrey.
Knessett Orach Chayim (Dublin Jewish Progressive Congregation), 7 Leicester Ave., Rathgar, 6. Corr. PO Box 3059, Rathgar, 6. ☎ 285 6241, Email djpc@liberaljudaism.org. (Est. 1946). *M.* Rabbi C. Middleburgh; *H. Sec.* Mrs J. Solomon ☎ 285-6241.
Talmud Torah, Stratford Schools, Zion Road, Rathgar, 6. ☎ 492-2315. Fax 492-4680. *H. Sec.* Mrs M. Adler.
Cemeteries: Dublin Holy Burial Society, Aughnavannagh Road, Dolphin's Barn, Dublin 8. Enquiries to Cantor A. Shulman ☎ 492-6843. The 'old' Jewish Cemetery at Ballybough may be visited on application to the caretaker ☎ 836-9756. The Progressive Cemetery is at Woodtown, Co. Dublin.

OTHER COUNTRIES

*Denotes the organisation(s) from which further information about the Jewish community in that country can be obtained. For more detailed information about Jewish communities overseas consult **The Jewish Travel Guide** (Vallentine Mitchell). Population figures taken from 'The Jewish communities handbook 1991' (IJPR and WJC).

AFGHANISTAN

Jews have lived in Afghanistan since antiquity. Just over 100 years ago they reportedly numbered 40,000. Since 1948 there has been a mass emigration to Israel..

ALBANIA

After the recent emigration to Israel very few Albanian Jews remain in the country.

ALGERIA (30)

It is believed that there were Jews in Algeria as early as the fourth century, BCE. The fortunes of the community varied under the Turkish regime, which began in 1519. After the French conquered Algeria the community was reorganised and in 1870 most Jews were granted French citizenship. However, there have been anti-Jewish excesses even in the present century. After Algeria's bitter fight for independence, the Jews, like other French nationals, lost their possessions when they left the country. About 120,000 at independence in 1962, they remain less than 50 today: almost all fled to France. *Contact* Mme L. Meller-Saïd, 12, Ave Louis Pasteur, 922220 Bagneux France. Email linemeller@wanadoo.fr.
Communal Centre and Synagogue: 6 Rue Hassena Ahmed, Algiers.

ANTIGUA AND BARBUDA (West Indies)

A few Jewish residents live permanently on the island. *Corr.*: B. Rabinowitz, Cedar Valley P.O.B. 399. ☎ 461 4150.

ARGENTINA (240,000)

The early Jewish settlers in Argentina were Marranos, who were gradually absorbed in the general population. The present community grew through immigration (beginning in 1862) from Germany, the Balkans, and North Africa. From Eastern Europe immigrants began to arrive in 1889, many of them going to the agricultural settlements est. by the Jewish Colonization Assn. (see p.??). The com. is est. to number 300,000, incl. 60,000 Sephardim, who have their own separate institutions, according to D.A.I.A., the representative org. of Argentine Jews. The Jewish pop. of Greater Buenos Aires is estimated at 220,000. A survey conducted by the Hebrew Univ. of Jerusalem estimates the Jewish pop. at 240,000, of whom 210,000 are Ashkenazim and 30,000 are Sephardim. This source estimates 180,000 Jews live in Gtr. Buenos Aires.

There are nine other major coms. in Parana, Rosario, Cordoba, Bahia Blanca, Posadas, Resistencia, Tucuman, Mendoza and La Plata. There is a small but very active community in Mar del Plata, south of Buenos Aires. Very few Jewish families remain on the former J.C.A. settlements. There are about 100 syns. (80 Orthodox, one Reform, the rest Conservative or Liberal), and a well-organised network of communal and educ. instits. There are communal offices in **Cordoba** at Alvear 254, and in **Rosario** at Paraguay 1152.

BUENOS AIRES
Congreso Judio Latinoamericano, Larrea 744, 1030. ☎ 961-44532. Fax 963-7056.
Representative Organisation of Argentine Jews: DAIA, Pasteur 633, 5th floor.
Argentine Jewish Community (AMIA), Pasteur 633 C1028AAM ☎ 4959 8800 Email amia@amia.org.ar. webamia@amia.org.ar. (Est. 1894) Victim of terrorism in 1994, the reconstructed Community Centre has now re-opened in the service of the life and culture of the Jewish community of Argentina
Central Sephardi Community: FESERA, Las Heras 1646.
Latin American Rabbinical Seminary (Conservative), Jose Hernandez 1750.

Argentine Zionist Organisation & Jewish Agency (Sochnut), Pasteur 633.

ARMENIA (500)

Jews have lived in Armenia for many hundreds of years and the various communities were spread around different parts of the country. There was a synagogue in Yerevan, but in the 1930s it was destroyed. Nowadays, nearly all the Armenian Jews live in Yerevan, with only a few families living in Vanadzor (Kirovakan) and Gjumri (Leninakan), while others are scattered in other small towns and villages. When 'perestroyka' was introduced in 1989, the Jewish community organised itself and in 1991 was registered as a non-formal organisation. Perestroyka opened the doors, so that a large number of the population emigrated to Israel. In 1991 a Jewish Sunday school was opened both for children and adults. In 1992 the Israeli embassy in Moscow financed the school. Over 60 per cent of the population is over 60 years of age and there are about 40 children below the age of 16 years.

President: Mr Willi Weiner, ☎ (7-8852) 525882; *Dir. of Education:* Dr George Fajvush, ☎ (7-8852) 735852; *Rabbi:* Gersh Bourstein, ☎ (7-8852) 271115.

ARUBA (50)

Beth Israel Synagogue. Dedicated in 1962, this syn. serves the needs of the com. in this island formerly one of the Netherlands Antilles in the Caribbean, of some 35 Jewish families. Jews from Curaçao settled in Aruba early in the nineteenth century, but did not stay there long, and the present com. dates from 1924.

AUSTRALIA (110,000)

The earliest org. of Jews in Australia was in 1817 when 20 Jews in New South Wales formed a burial society. In 1828 a congregation was formed in Sydney and the first specially erected syn. was opened in 1844. The first Jewish service was held in Melbourne in 1839, four years after the beginning of the colonisation on the banks of the River Yarra, and a syn. was opened in 1847. Congregations were est. at Ballarat (1853) and Geelong (1854). In South Australia, a permanent congregation was formed in Adelaide in 1848. A congregation in Brisbane was est. in 1865. In Western Australia the first congregation (now ended) was formed at Fremantle in 1887, and the present Perth congregation est. in 1892, with Kalgoorlie in 1895. In Tasmania a syn. was opened in Hobart in 1845 and another at Launceston in 1846. Organised Jewish coms. were est. in other States a few years later.

In Australia's public life Jews have played a distinguished part, many having risen to high office in the Federal and State Parliaments or on the Judicial bench. Two Governors-General of Australia have been Jews, Sir Zelman Cowen and the late Sir Isaac Isaacs. Sir John Monash, the Commander of the Australian Expeditionary Forces in the First World War, was a Jew. The Executive Council of Australian Jewry represents the central Jewish organisations in each State. The Australian census has an optional question on religious affiliation. In 2001, 88,993 people declared themselves Jews by religion. If a proportionate number of 'no religion/religion not stated' replies are regarded as Jewish, the number of Jews rises to 105,000. Recent demographic res. indicated that there are probably about 92,000 people in Australia who are religiously or ethnically Jewish. The main Jewish coms. are in Melbourne (50,000); Sydney (40,000); Perth (4,870); Brisbane (1,500); Adelaide (1,250); The Gold Coast, Queensland (1,000); Canberra (500); Hobart (100).

MAIN JEWISH ORGANISATIONS
Executive Council of Australian Jewry, 146 Darlinghurst Rd, Darlinghurst, NSW 2010. ☎ (02) 9360 5415. Fax (02) 9360 5416. *President* Graham Leonard.
*N.S.W. Jewish Board of Deputies, 146 Darlinghurst Rd., Darlinghurst, NSW, 2010. ☎ 2-9360-1600. Fax 2-9331-4712. *Exec. Dir.* Ms J. Wilkenfeld.
Jewish Community Council of Victoria, 306 Hawthorn Rd., South Caulfield, Victoria 3162. *President* ; *Exec. Off.* Mrs H. McMahon. ☎ 3-92725566.
Email community@jccv.org.au. Website www.jccv.org.au.
Australia/Israel and Jewish Affairs Council (AIJAC), Level 1, 22 Albert Rd., South, Melbourne, Victoria 3205. ☎ 613-9681 6660. Fax 613-9681 6650. Email aijac@aijac.org.au.

The Australia/Israel and Jewish Affairs Council (AIJAC) is the premier public affairs organization for the Australian Jewish Community. Through research, commentary, analysis and representation, AIJAC promotes the interests of the Australian Jewish Community to Government and other community groups and organizations. It has professionals dedicated to analysis and monitoring developments in the Middle East, Asia and Australia. AIJAC is associated with theAmerican Jewish Committee in a global partnership designed to bring about a graeter understanding of the issues and challenges lying ahead for Jewry. The former Australian Institute of Jewish Affairs, now operating as a division of IAJAC, maintains its program, social and cultural actinvities, and holds important public functions and briefings throughout Australia, and retains a role in South East Asia. *Pub.* Australia/Israel Review (monthly); *Exec. Dir.* Dr Colin Rubenstein.AM; *Contact* L. Kahn

Jewish Museum of Australia, 26 Alma Rd., St. Kilda, Victoria 3182. ☎ (03) 9534 0083. Email info@jewishmuseum.com.au. Website www.jewishmuseum.com.au.

JNF Federal Office, 1402, Westfield Tower, 500 Oxford Street, Bondi Junction, NSW 2022. ☎ 02-9386-9559. Fax 02-9386-9828. Email federalO@infaustralia.com.au. Website www.jnfaustralia.com.au. *President* M. Naphtali; *Chief Exec.* R.P. Schneider.

Kadimah – Jewish Cultural Centre and Jewish National Library (Est. 1911), 7 Selwyn Street, Elsternwick, Victoria 3185. ☎ 03 9523 9817. Fax 03 9523 6161. Email jlibrary@vic net.net.au.

Zionist Federation of Australia, 306 Hawthorn Road, Caulfield South, Victoria 3162. ☎ 3-9272-5644. Fax 3-9272-5640. *President* Dr R. Weiser; *Exec. Dir.* Mrs L. Abraham. Email zfa@zfa.com.au. Website www.zfa.com.au.

Union for Progressive Judaism (Australia, New Zealand, Asia), POBox 128, St Kilda, Victoria 3182. ☎ (03) 9533 8587. Fax (03) 9529 1229. Email upj@bypond.com. *Admin.* K. Hall.

Sephardi Federation of Australian Jewry, 40-42 Fletcher St., Bondi Junction, NSW, 2022. ☎ 2-9389-3355. Fax 2-9369-2143. *President* A. Gubbay.

Victoria Union for Progressive Judaism, 78-82 Alma Rd., St Kilda, Victoria 3182. ☎ 3-9510-1488. Fax 3-9521-1229.

Federation of Australian Jewish Welfare Societies, P.O.Box 500, St Kilda, Victoria 3182. ☎ (3) 9525 4000. Fax (03) 9525 3737.

National Council of Jewish Women of Australia, 133 Hawthorn Road, Caulfield, Victoria 3161. ☎ (03) 9523 0535. Fax (03) 9523 0156. *President* Mrs R. Lenn.

B'nai B'rith Australia/New Zealand, PO Box 443, Kings Cross, Sydney, NSW 1340. ☎ (02) 9361 3875. Fax (02) 9331 3131. Email bbozdist@ozemail.com.au. *President* James Altman.

Australasian Union of Jewish Students, 306 Hawthorn Road, Caulfield, Victoria 3162. ☎ (03) 9272 5622. Fax (03) 9272 5620.

WIZO Australia, 53 Edgecliff Road, Woollahra, NSW 2025. ☎ (02) 9386 4444. Fax (02) 9387 5373.

MAIN SYNAGOGUES AND COMMUNAL CENTRES

SYDNEY

New South Wales Jewish Board of Deputies, 146 Darlinghurst Rd, Darlinghurst, NSW 2010. ☎2-9360 1600. Fax 2-9331 4712.

The Great Synagogue (Ashk. Orth.), Elizabeth St. (Office: 166 Castlereagh St.), NSW 2000. ☎2-9267 2477. Fax 2-9264 8871.

Central Synagogue (Orth.), 15 Bon Accord Ave, Bondi Junction, NSW 2022. ☎2-9389 5622. Fax 2-9389 5418.

North Shore Synagogue (Orth.), 15 Treatts Rd, Lindfield, NSW 2070. (2-9416 3710. Fax 2-9416 7659.

North Shore Temple Emanuel (Lib.), 28 Chatswood Ave., Chatswood, NSW 2067. ☎2-9419 7011. Fax 2-9413 1474. Email nste@nste.or.au.

Sephardi Synagogue (Orth.), 40-42 Fletcher St, Bondi Junction, NSW 2025. ☎2-9389 3355. Fax 2-9365 3856.

Temple Emanuel (Lib.), 7 Ocean St, Woollahra, NSW 2025. ☎ 2-9328 7833. Fax 2-9327 8715. Email emanuel@ozmail.com.au.

Yeshiva Synagogue (Orth.), 36 Flood St, Bondi NSW 2026. ☎ 2-9387 3822. Fax 2-9389 7652.

MELBOURNE
Melbourne Hebrew Congregation (Orth.), One Toorak Rd., South Yarra, Victoria 3141. ☎ 3-9866-2255.
St. Kilda Hebrew Congregation, 12 Charnwood Gr., St. Kilda, Victoria 3182. ☎ 3-9537-1433.
Temple Beth Israel (Lib.), 76 Alma Rd., St. Kilda, Victoria 3182. ☎ 3-9510-1488. Fax 3-9521-1229. Email info@tbi.org.au.
Beth Weizmann Community Centre, 306 Hawthorn Rd., Caulfield South, Victoria 3162. ☎ 3-9272-5555.
Caulfield Hebrew Congregation, 572 Inkerman Rd., Caulfield, Victoria 3161. ☎ 3-9525-9492.

PERTH
Perth Hebrew Congregation, Cnr. Plantation St. and Freedman Rd., Menora, WA 6050. ☎ 9-271-0539. *President* K. Blitz; *M.* Rabbi D. Freilich. Mikvah on premises. Email phc@theperthshule.asu.au; Website www.theperthshule.asn.au
Temple David Congregation (Prog.), 34 Clifton Crescent, Mt. Lawley, 6050. ☎ 9-271-1458. Fax 9-272-2827. Email temdavid@iinet.net.au.
Beit Midrash of WA (Inc) – Dianella Shule (Orth.), 68 Woodrow Ave., Yorkine, WA 6060. *President* Marcel Goodman; *Sec.* Peter Katz; *M.* Rabbi Marcus Solomon. ☎ 9375 8985/1276/1664. Website www.dianella.com.au.
Chabad of Western Australia (Inc.) (Orth.), 395 Alexander Drive, Noranda, WA 6062. *M.* Rabbi Mordi Gutnick; *Contact* Max Green ☎ 9375 1078.
Northern Suburbs Hebrew Congregation (Orth.), Garson Court, Noranda, WA 6062. *M.* Rabbi Moshe Rothchild ☎ 9275 3500. Fax 9275 3424. Email shul@ iinet.net.au. Website www.shul.iinet.net.au.
Jewish Centre, 61 Woodrow Ave., Mt. Yokine, WA 6060. ☎ 9-276-8572.

ADELAIDE
See B.K. Hyams, 'Surviving: A History of The Institutions and Organisations of the Adelaide Jewish Community' (1998).
Hebrew Congregation, 13 Flemington St., PO Box 320, Glenside, SA 5065. ☎ 8-8338-2922. Fax 8-9379-0142.
Beit Shalom Synagogue, 41 Hackney Rd., PO Box 47, Stepney, SA 5069. ☎ 8-362-8281. Fax 8-362-4406. Email bshalom@senet.com.au. *Admin.* L. Willis.
Jewish Community Council, 13 Flemington St. *President* Norman Schueler. ☎ 8-240-0066. Fax 8-447-6668.

BRISBANE
Brisbane Hebrew Congregation (Orth.), 98 Margaret St., Brisbane, Qld. 4000. ☎ 7-3229-3412. Fax 7-3366-8311. Email pgt_levy@world.net.
Temple Shalom (Lib.), 15 Koolatah St., Camp Hill, Qld. 4152. ☎ 7-398-8843.

CANBERRA
National Jewish Memorial Centre (A.C.T. Jewish Community Centre), Canberra Ave. and National Circuit, Forrest, P.O. Box 3105, Manuka, ACT 2603. ☎ (02) 6295 1052. Website www.actjewish.org.uk.

TASMANIA
Hobart Hebrew Congregation, PO Box 128, 7001. ☎ 3-6234-4720. Email shule@hobart.org. Website www.hobartsynagogue.org. The synagogue is the oldest in

Australia, having been consecrated in July 1845. See H. Fixel, 'Hobart Hebrew Congregation: 150 Years of Survival Against All Odds' (1999); P. and A. Elias, 'A Few from Afar: Jewish Lives in Tasmania from 1804' (2003).

Jewish Centre, Chabad House, 93 Lord Street, Sandy Bay, 7005. ☎ /Fax 3-6223-7116.

Hobart Hebrew Congregation (Progressive), 59 Argyle Street, 7000. (3-6234-4720. Email shule@hobart.org.

Launceston Synagogue, PO Box 66, St John Street, 7250. ☎ 3-6343-1143. This is the second oldest synagogue in Australia, founded in 1846.

AUSTRIA (12,000)

The story of Austrian Jewry is punctuated by accounts of expulsion and re-immigration, of persecution on false accusations of ritual murder and other pretexts and recovery. After the 1848 Revolution the Jews gained equality, and their economic and cultural importance grew. But antisemitism had not ended; it culminated in the violence of the years preceding the Second World War. Austria's Jewish population in 1934 was 191,481 (with 176,034 in Vienna), the number today is about 12,000, almost all of them in Vienna. Other coms. are in Graz, Innsbruck, Linz and Salzburg.

*Jewish Community Centre, Israelitische Kulturgemeinde, Seitenstettengasse 4, 1010 Vienna. ☎ 531 040. Fax 531-04108. *President* Dr A. Muzicant; *Sec. Gen.* R. Fastenbauer, F. Herzog

Main Syns. Stadttempel, Seitenstettengasse 4 (Trad.); Machsike Hadass, Grosse Mohrengasse 19, 1020 (Orth.); Khal Israel, Tempelgasse 3, 1020 (Orth.); Ohel Moshe, Lilienbrunngasse 19, 1020 (Orth.); Or Chaddasch Cong. (Prog.), Robertgasse 2, 1020.

Chief Rabbi: Rabbi Paul Chaim Eisenberg. ☎ 53 104-111.

Jewish Welcome Service, A-1010 Vienna, Stephansplatz 10. ☎ 533 2730. Fax 533 4098. *Dir.* Dr L. Zelman.

BAHAMAS (200)

Freeport Hebrew Congregation. 15 families.

Luis de Torres Synagogue, East Sunrise Highway, P.O. Box F-41761, Freeport. Grand Bahama ☎ (242) 373 2008. *President* Anthony Gee. ☎ (242) 373-8994. Email goldylocks@coralwaveo.com. *Sec.* Jean Berlind ☎ (242) 373-9457. Email jberlind@coralwave.com. Please contact for times of services.

BARBADOS (55)

A Jewish com. was formed in Barbados by refugees from Recife (Brazil) after its reconquest by the Portuguese about the year 1650. In 1802 by Local Govt. Act, all political disabilities of the Jews were removed, but were not confirmed by Westminster until 1820. Barbados was the first British possession to grant full political emancipation to its Jews; Gt. Britain herself doing so more than 50 years later. With the economic decline of the West Indies the fortunes of their Jewish inhabitants also declined. In 1929, only one practising Jew remained, but in 1932 a gp. of Jews settled on the island from Europe. In December, 1987, the Old Synagogue in Bridgetown, one of the two oldest houses of worship in the Western Hemisphere (the other is in Curaçao), reopened for services for the first time in nearly 60 years, following restoration with the island community's support. An appeal fund was launched with Sir Hugh Springer, the Governor-General, as patron. There is a Jewish cemetery by the syn. In 1985, the Barbadian Govt. vested the syn. in the Barbadian Nat. Trust A Jewish Museum is currently under construction in a building adjacent to the synagogue to be opened in 2007.

*Jewish Community Council, P.O.B. 256, Bridgetown. ☎ 426 4764. Fax 426 4768. *Contact* Benny Gilbert.

BELARUS (28,000)

GOMMEL
Syn.: 13 Sennaya St.
Jewish Cultural Society, 1A Krasnoarmeyska St., 24600. *Chairman* V. F. Iofedov.

GRODNO
Menorah Jewish Community, Blk 43, Flat 37, 230009. Email sh10@grsu.grod no.by. *Chair* Ludmilla Pobolowska.

MINSK
Syn.: 22 Kropotkin St. ☎ (017-2) 55-82-70.
Religious Union for Progressive Judaism in Belarus, Internationalnya 16, 220050 Minsk. Rabbi Grisha Abramovich ☎ 00375 17 206 5850. Email roopi@mail.ru.

ORSHA
Syn.: Nogrin St.

RECHITSA
Syn.: 120 Lunacharsky St.
There are also Jewish communities in Bobruisk, Mozyr, Pinsk, Brest, Grodno, Mogilev, Vitebsk and Borisov.

BELGIUM (30,000)

Jews have lived in Belgium since Roman times. After the fall of Napoleon the Belgian provinces were annexed by Holland. In 1816 a decree by the Dutch King ordered the erection of two syns. in Maastricht and Brussels. But Belgian Jews had to wait until 1830, when Belgium became independent, to see their status formally recognised. The Constitution accorded freedom of religion in 1831. Before the Second World War the Jewish population was 80,000. Today there are flourishing communities in Antwerp, Brussels, Ostend, Liège, Charleroi and Waterloo totalling (together with the smaller communities) about 30,000 Jews.

ANTWERP
Synagogues and rel. orgs.: Shomre Hadass (Israelitische Gemeente), Terlistr 35, 2018. ☎ 226.05.54. Rabbi D. Lieberman. Syns.: Bouwmeesterstr., Romi Goldmuntz, Van den Nestlei.
Machsike Hadass (Orth.) Jacob Jacobstr. 22. *Rab.* Main syn.: Oostenstr. 42-44.
Sephardi Syn.: Hovenierstr. 31.
Central Jewish Welfare Organisation, Jacob Jacobsstr. 2. ☎ 232 3890.
Home for the Aged and Nursing Home, Marialei 6-8.
Residentie Apfelbaum-Laub., Marialei 2-4. ☎ 218.9399.
Holiday camp, Villa Altol, Coxyde-on-Sea, Damesweg 10. ☎ 058 512661.
Other orgs.: Zionist Fed., Pelikaanstr. 108; Mizrachi, Isabellalei 65; Romi Goldmuntz Centre, Nervierstr. 12; B'nai B'rith–Nervierstr 12AAT 14.

BRUSSELS
***Comité de Coordination des Organisations Juives de Belgique** (C.C.O.J.B.). Av. Ducpétiaux 68, 1060 Brussels. ☎ 537 1691. Fax 539 2295. Email ccojb@scarlet.be.
Consistoire Central Israélite de Belgique, 2 rue Joseph Dupont, 1000 Brussels. ☎ 02 512 21 90.
Cercle Ben-Gurion, 89 Chausée de Vleurgat, 1050 Brussels.
Centre Communautaire Laic Juif, 52 Rue Hotel des Monnaies, 1060 Brussels.
Zionist Offices, 66-68 Avenue Ducpétiaux, 1060 Brussels.
Synagogues: 32 rue de la Régence; 67a rue de la Clinique; 73 rue de Thy; 126 rue Rogier; 11 Ave. Messidor; 47 rue Pavillon (Sephardi); Beth Hillel (Lib.) 96 Ave. de Kersbeek; Brussels airport, Zaventem.

MONS
SHAPE International Jewish Community, c/o SHAPE Chaplains' Office, B-7010 SHAPE, Belgium. ☎ /Fax (065) 6572 8769. (Est. 1967) To meet the spiritual, social and educational needs of Jewish military and civilian personnel and their families serving at or temporarily assigned to SHAPE, Mons, Belgium. *Lay Leader* Wing Commander Stephen Griffiths, MBE, RAF. *Liaison* Lisa Arbeiter ☎ (065) 44 49 38. Fax (065) 44 34 37.

BERMUDA (125)
The small community drawn from a dozen countries has never had a synagogue or communal building. A lay leader conducts a Friday service each month at the Chamber of Commerce, Albouys Point, Hamilton; a visiting Rabbi conducts High Holy day services and children's classes are held regularly.
Jewish Community of Bermuda, P.O. Box HM 1793, Hamilton, HMHX Bermuda. ☎ 441-291 1785. Website www.jcb.bm.

BOLIVIA (640)
Although there have been Jews in Latin America for many centuries, they are comparative newcomers to Bolivia, which received its first Jewish immigrants only in 1905. They remained a mere handful until the 1920s, when some Russian Jews made their way to the country. After 1935, German Jewish refugees, began to arrived in Bolivia. Also from Rumania and mostly from Poland. Today some 640 Jews live there, mostly in the capital of La Paz (about 300), Cochambamba (135) and Santa Cruz (200), Tarija and other cities (5).

COCHABAMBA
Syn.: Calle Junin y Calle Colombia, Casilla 349.
Asociación Israelita de Cochabamba, P.O.B. 349, Calle Valdivieso. *President* Ronald Golan.

LA PAZ
Syns.: Circulo Israelita de Bolivia, Casilla 1545, ☎ (591) 22785083. Calle Landaeta 346, P.O.B. 1545. Services Sat. morn. only. *President* Dr Miguel.
Comunidad Israelita Synagogue, Calle Canada Stronguest 1846, P.O.B. 2198. ☎ 313602, is affiliated to the Circulo. Fri. evening services are held. There is a Jewish sch. at this address. Circulo Israelita, P.O.B. 1545 is the representative body of Bolivian Jewry. All La Paz organisations are affiliated to it.
Two Homes for Aged: Calle Rosendo Gutierrez 307, and Calle Diaz Romero 1765.
Israel Tourist Information Office: Centro Shalom, Calle Canada Stronguest 1846, La Paz Country Club, Quinta J.K.G. Obrajes. Calle 1, esquina calle Hector Ormachea Casilla 1545, La Paz.

SANTA CRUZ
Circulo Israelita de Santa Cruz P.O.B. 7087, WIZO, Casilla 3409 ☎ (591) 33435848. *President* Sra Guicha Schwartz.

BOSNIA HERCEGOVINA (1,100)
Sarajevo Jewish Community, Hamdije Kreševlijakovica 59. ☎ 38733 663 472. Fax 38733 663473. *President* J. Finci. Email la_bene@open.net.ba.

BRAZIL (250,000)
The early history of Brazilian Jewry was affected by the struggles for power between the Portuguese and Dutch. The Inquisition, revived in Brazil, increased the number of Marrano Jews. The Dutch, after their victory in 1624, granted full religious freedom to the Jews, but 30 years afterwards the Portuguese reconquered the land and reintroduced the Inquisition. In 1822 Brazil declared its independence and liberty of worship was proclaimed. It is believed that about 250,000 Jews are living in Brazil, distributed as follows: Sao Paulo State, 90,000; Rio de Janeiro State, 80,000; Rio Grande do Sul (Porto Alegre) 25,000; Parana State (Curitiba) 2,408; Minas Gerais State (Bel Horizonte) 1,656; Pernambuco State (Recife) 1,276.

RIO DE JANEIRO
*Federacão Israelita, R. Buenos Aires 68, AN15.
Fundo Communitario, R. Buenos Aires 68, AN15.
Orthodox Rabbinate, R. Pompeu Loureiro No.40. ☎ /Fax 2360249.
Chevre Kedishe, Rua Barao de Iguatemi 306 (Orthodox).
Congrecão Beth El, Rua Barata Ribeiro 489 (Sephardi).
Associacão Religiosa Israelita, Rua Gen. Severiano 170 (Liberal). ☎ 295 6599. Fax 542 6499.
Synagogues: Agudat Israel, Rua Nascimento Silva, 109, Beth Aron, Rua Gado Coutinho, 63, Kehilat Yaacov Copacabana, Rua Capelao Alvares da Silva 15; Templo Uniao Israel, Rua Jose Higino, 375-381.
Associacão Feminina Israelita, Av. Almte. Barroso, 6/14°.
Organizacão Sionista Unificada, Rua Decio Vilares, 258.
Museu Judaico, Rua Mexico, 90/1° andar-Castelo.

SÃO PAULO
Federacao Israelita do Estado de São Paulo, Av. Paulista 726, 2nd floor. ☎ 288 6411.
Morashá (magazine) Rua Dr. Veiga Filho, 547 Cep 01229-000 São Paulo SP ☎/Fax (5511) 3662-215
Syngogues and religious centres: Centro Judaico Religioso de Sao Paulo (Orthodox). ☎ 220 5642; Beit Chabad, Rua Chabad 56/60; Communidade Israelita Sefaradi, Rua da Abolicao 457; Congregacão Israelita Paulista, "Einheitsgemeinde" (Liberal), Rua Antonico Carlos 653. Sinagoga Beit Yaacov (Congregação e Beneficência Sefardi Paulista) Rua Dr. Veiga Filho, 547 Cep 01229-000 São Paulo ☎ (5511) 3662-215.
Escola Beit Yaacov Av Marques de São Vicente, 1748 Cep 01139-002 ☎ (5511) 3611-0600
Zionist Offices, Rua Correa Mello 75.

BULGARIA (6,500)
Bulgarian Jewry dates from the second century C.E. Before the Second World War there were 50,000 Jews in Bulgaria. From 1948-49 to about 1954/55, 45,000 emigrated to Israel. Today the number is about 6,500 of whom about 3,000 live in Sofia.
Central Jewish Religious Council and Synagogue, 16 Exarch Joseph St., Sofia 1000. ☎ 359-2/983-273. *President* Robat Djerassi.
Organization of the Jews in Bulgaria "Shalom", 50 Al. Stambolijski St., Sofia 130. ☎ /Fax 359-2/4006 301. *President* Dr. Maxim Benvenisti. Publishes newspaper "Evrejski Vesti" and research compendium "Annual". Jewish museum in the Synagogue: Sofia, 16 Exarch Joseph St. Joseph Caro permanent exhibition in the city Museum and a memorial stone in the town of Nikopol. Publishing house "Shalom", Jewish Sunday School, Jewish Resource Centre, Memorial stone dedicated to the Salvation of the Bulgarian Jews near the Parliament. B'nai Brith, Maccabi and other Jewish organizations.

BURMA (Myanmar)
About 25 Burmese Jews live in Rangoon (Yangon), the capital.
Musmeah Yeshua Synagogue (est. 1896), 85 26th St., P.O. Box 45, Yangon. *Man. Tr.* Moses Samuels. ☎ 951-252814. Email samuels@mptmail.net.mm.
Israel Embassy, 15 KhaBaung Street, Hlaing Township, Yangon. ☎ 951 515115. Fax 951-515116. Email info@yangon.mfa.gov.il.

CANADA (348,605)
Jews were prohibited by law from living in Canada so long as it remained a French possession. Nevertheless, Jews from Bordeaux – David Gradis, a wealthy merchant and shipowner, and his son Abraham Gradis, in particular – had a large share in the commercial development of the colony.
  Jews played some part in the British occupation of Canada. Half a dozen Jewish officers, including Aaron Hart, whose descendants played important roles in Jewish and Canadian life for several generations, were suppliers to the expeditionary force which occupied Quebec.
  A number of Jews settled at an early date in Montreal, where the Spanish and Portuguese

Synagogue, Shearith Israel (still flourishing), was established in the 1770s and a cong. of 'German, Polish and English' Jews was granted a charter in 1846. A burial society was formed in Toronto in 1849. Montreal Jews were also among the fur traders in the Indian territories.

In the 19th century, Jewish immigrants arrived in Canada in some numbers, and in 1832 – a quarter of a century earlier than in Britain – the Lower Canada Jews received full civil rights.

A fresh era in the history of Canadian Jewry opened at the close of the century, when emigration on a large scale from Eastern Europe began. Montreal, Toronto, and, to a lesser degree, Winnipeg became the seats of Jewish coms. of some importance.

On the history of the Jews in Canada generally, see A. D. Hart, *The Jew in Canada*, 1926; L. Rosenberg, *Canada's Jews*, 1939; B. G. Sack, *The History of the Jews in Canada*, 1945; and I.M. Abella, *A Coat of Many Colours: Two Centuries of Jewish Life in Canada*, 1990. The early colonial period in North America is covered in Sheldon and Judith Godfrey, *Search Out the Land*, 1995.

NATIONAL INSTITUTIONS

*Canadian Jewish Congress. (Est. 1919, reorganised 1934.)
National Office: 100 Sparks Street, Suite 650, Ottawa, Ontario K1P 5B7. ☎ (613) 233-8703. Fax (613) 233-8748. Email canadianjewishcongress@cjc.ca; Website www.cjc.ca. *National Co-President* Rabbi Dr. Reuven Bulka and Sylvain Abitobol
Chief Exec. Bernie M.Farher ☎ (416) 635-2883 -2883 ext. 5186 Fax: (416) 635-1408 4600 Bathurst Street. Fourth Floor, Toronto. Ontario M2R 3V2, Email bfarber@on.cjc.ca *Dir. of Operations* Joshua Rotblatt ☎ (613) 233-8703 Fax (613) 233-8748. 100 Sparks Street. Ottawa, Ontario K1P 5B7. Email joshr@cjc.c
National General Counsel Jonathan Schwartz ☎ (416) 635-2883 ext. 5265 Fax (416) 635-1408; 4600 Bathurst Street, Fourth Floor, Toronto Ontario M2R 3V2 Email jschwartz@on.cjc.ca
National Archives: Janice Rosen. Archives Director, Canadian Jewish Congress Charities Committee. 1590. Avenue Doctor Penfield. Montreal, Quebec H3G 1C5 ☎ 514-931-7531 ext.27l Fax (514) 931-0548; Email janicer@cjccc,ca

CJC Atlantic Region: *Reg. Dir* Jon M. Goldberg, 5670 Spring Garden Road. Suite 508, Halifax, Nova Scotia B3J 1 H6; ☎ (902) 422-7491 Fax: (902) 422-73722 Email jgoldberg@theajc.ns.ca
CJC Quebec Region: Reg. *Dir.* Daniel Amar, 1 Cummings Square,. Montreal Québec H3W 1M6; ☎ (514) 345-6411 1Fax: (514) 345-6412; Email damar@cjc.ca
CJC Ontario Region: *Reg. Dir* Len Rudner 4600 Bathurst Street, Toronto, Ontario M2R 3V2; l☎ (416) 635-2883 ext. 5 147 Fax (416) 635-1408; Email lrudner@on.cjc.ca
Jewish Federation of Ottawa: *Exec. Dir.* Mitchell Bellman, 21 Nadolny Sachs Private. Ottawa Ontario K2A 1R9; ☎ (613) 798-4696 Fax (613) 798-4695 Email mbellman@jewishottawa.com
CJC Manitoba Region: *Community Relations Dir.* Shelley Faintuch. Jewish Federation of Winnipeg. C300-123 Doncaster St. Winnipeg Manitoba R3N 2B2; ☎ (204) 447-7423 Fax (204) 477-7405; Email sfaintuch@aspercampus.mb.ca
CJC Saskatchewan Region - North: June Aviva. c/o Congregation Agudas Israel 715 McKinnon Avenue, Saskatoon, Saskatchewan S7H 2G2; ☎ (306) 343-7023 Fax: (306) 343-1244 Email ajavivi@ shaw.ca
CJC Saskatchewan Region-South
c/o Beth Jacob Synagogue. 4715 McTavish Street. Regina, Saskatchewan S4S 6H2 ☎ (306) 569-8166 Fax (306) 569-8166
CJC Alberta -Calgary:
Calgary Jewish Community Council ; 1607 - 90th Avenue S. W. Calgary, Alberta -T2V ☎ (403) 253-8600 Fax (4031 253-7915 Email cjcc@jewish-calgary.com
Jewish Federation of Edmonton
7200 - 156th Street. Edmonton. Alberta T5R 1X3, ☎ (780) 487-5120 Fax: (780) 481 1854 Email edjfed@attcanada.ca
CJC Pacific Region: *Reg. Dir.* Rommy Ritter. Suite 801 - 1166 Alberta St., Vancouver, British Columbia V6E 3Z3; ☎ (604) 622-4240 Fax: (604) 622-4244; Email romyr@ cjc.ca
Association for Canadian Jewish Studies, c/o Dept of Religion, Concordia University, 1455 De Maisonneuve Boulevard West, Montreal H3G 1MP ☎ (514) 848 2424 2074; Fax

(514) 848 4541. *Contact* Dr I. Robinson Email robinson@alcor.concordia.ca Website www
www.acjs-aejc.ca
Canada-Israel Committee, 130 Slater St., Suite 630, Ottawa K1P 6E2. *Exec. Dir.* Shimon
Fogel. ☎ (613) 234 8271. Ontario Office: 2221 Yonge St. #502, Toronto M4S 2B4. ☎ (416)
489 8889.
Canadian Association for Labour Israel. (Est. 1939) 7005 Kildare Rd., #14 Côte St. Luc,
Quebec H4W 1C1.
Canadian ORT, 3101 Bathurst St #604, Toronto, Ontario M6A 2A6.
Canadian Zionist Federation (Est. 1967), 5250 Decarie Blvd., #550, Montreal, H3X 2H9.
☎ (514) 486 9526.
Emunah Women of Canada. Nat. *President* R. Schneidman, 7005 Kildare Rd, #18 Montreal
H3W 3C3. ☎ (514) 485 2397.
Hadassah-Wizo of Canada, 1310 Greene Av. #650, Montreal H3Z 2B8. (Est. 1917.) *Exec.
V. President* Mrs L. Frank. Chapters: 220, in most Jewish centres. Toronto office: 638A
Sheppard Ave W, #209, M3H 2S1. ☎ (416) 630 8373.
Jewish Immigrant Aid Services of Canada. (Est. 1919.) 4600 Bathurst St., Willowdale,
Ont., M2R 3V3. *Exec. Dir.* ☎ (416) 630 9051.
Jewish National Fund. 1980 Sherbrooke St. W., Montreal, H3H 1E8. ((514) 934 0313.
Labour Zionist Movement (Est. 1939), 272 Codsell Ave., Downsview, Ont. M3H 3X2.
Mizrachi Organization of Canada. *Nat. Exec. Dir.* Rabbi M. Gopin, 159 Almore Ave.,
Downsview, Ont. M3H 2H9. ☎ (416) 630 7575.
National Council of Jewish Women of Canada, 1588 Main St., #118, Winnipeg, Manitoba
R2V 1Y3. ☎ (204) 339 9700.
United Israel Appeal Federations Canada. *Exec. V. President* Ms M. Finkelstein, 4600
Bathurst St., Willowdale, Ont. M2R 3V3. ☎ (416) 636 7655. Fax (416) 635-5806.

CAYMAN ISLANDS (60)
There are approx. 60 Jewish residents in the 3 Cayman Islands, nearly all living on Grand
Cayman. They are joined by about 40 others who are regular visitors. Services in private homes.
*Contact:*Harvey De Souza, P.O. Box 72, Grand Cayman, KY1 1102 Cayman Islands.

CHILE (25,000)
The number of Jews in Chile is about 25,000. The great majority live in the Santiago area.
Communities also in Arica, Chillan, Chuquicamata, Concepción, Iquique, La Serena, Puerto Montt,
Punta Arenas, Rancagua, San Fernando, Santa Cruz, Temuco, Valdivia, Vina del Mar/Valparaiso.

SANTIAGO
*Comité Representativo de las Entidades Judias de Chile (CREJ), Miguel Claro 196.
☎ 235 8669. Fax 235 0754.
Comunidad Israelita de Santiago, Tarapaca 870. (Ashkenazi). ☎ 633 1436. Fax 638
2076.
Comunidad Israelita de Santiago Congregacion Jafetz Jayim (Orthodox) Miguel
Claro 196. ☎ 274 5389.
Comunidad Israelita Sefaradi de Chile, R. Lyon 812. ☎ 209 8086. Fax 204 7382.
Sociedad Cultural, Bne Jisroel, Mar Jónico 8860, Vitacura. ☎ /Fax 201 1623 (German).
MAZsE, (Hungarian) Pedro Bannen 0166. ☎ 2742536.
B'nai Brith, Ricardo Lyon 1933. ☎ 274 2006. Fax 225 2039.
Zionist Federation Offices, Rafael Cañas 246. ☎ 251 8821. Fax 251 0961.
Estadio Israelita Maccabi, Club, Las Condes 8361. ☎ 235 9096. Fax 251 0105.
Wizo Chile, M. Montt 207. ☎ 235 9096. Fax 251 105.

CHINA (3,100)
In recent years, Jewish tourists from a number of countries, including Britain and the U.S., have
visited the ancient city of Kaifeng, 300 miles south of Peking, and met people who claim descent
from a sizeable com. which lived there for centuries and dispersed in the 19th century. Some

experts believe the Kaifeng Jews to have originated from Persia or Yemen. Few are left of the coms. formed by other immigrants from Asia at the end of the 19th century and by the Russian and German refugees of the First and Second World Wars.

A comprehensive bibliography on the Jews of China was published in 1998: *Jews and Judaism in Traditional China: A Comprehensive Bibliography*, Donald Daniel Leslie (Sankt Petersburg: Steyler Verlag, 1998) (Monumenta serica, XLIV).

HONG KONG (3,000)

The Hong Kong com. dates from about 1857. The Ohel Leah synagogue, built in 1901, has recently been restored. The history of the community is published in A Social History of the Jews of Hong Kong: A Resource Guide by Dr Caroline B. Pluss.

The Jewish Community Centre, One Robinson Place, 70 Robinson Road, Mid-levels. ((852) 2868-0828. *Information* ☎ (852) 2801-5440. Fax 2877-0917. Website www.jcc.org.hk. *Gen. Man.* Michael Sheppard.

Synagogues:

Ohel Leah Syn., One Robinson Place, 70 Robinson Rd. ☎ (852) 2589-2621. Fax 852 2548 4200. Email pauline@ohelleah.org. Website www.ohelleah.org. *M.* Rabbi M. van den Bergh.

Mikvah *Contact* Revital Ben Yishai. ☎ (852) 2140 6475.

Chabad-Lubavitch in the Far East. Email chabadhk@netvigator.com. Website www.chabadhk.org.

The United Jewish Congregation of Hong Kong (Liberal/Reform) (Est. 1991). One Robinson Place, 70 Robinson Road. Rabbi L. Diamond. ☎ (852) 2523-2985. Fax (852) 2523-3961. Email ujc@ujc.org.hk. Website www.ujc.org.hk.

Kehilat Zion (Orth), Synagogue of Kowloon, 4/F, 21 Chatham Road, Tsim Sha Tsui, Kowloon. Rabbi N. Meoded. ☎ /Fax (852) 2366-6364.

Shuva Israel Beit Medrash and Community Centre and **Shuva Israel Synagogue** (Seph), 2/F, Fortune House, 61 Connaught Road Central. ☎ (852) 2851-6218/6300. Fax (952) 2851-7482.

Israel Consulate-General, Admiralty Centre, Tower II, Room 701, 18 Harcourt Road. ☎ (852) 2529-6091. Fax 2865-0220.

The Jewish Historical Society. Publishes monographs on subjects of Sino-Judaic interest. Information from Mrs J. Green. ☎ (852) 2807-9400. Fax (852) 2887-5235.

The **Jewish cemetery** is situated at 13 Shan Kwong Road, Happy Valley. ☎ (852) 2589-2621. Fax (852) 2548-4200.

The Jewish Women's Assn. is affiliated to WIZO and ICJW. *Chair*

United Israel Appeal is affiliated to Keren Hayesod. *Information* Dr J. Diestel. ☎ (852) 2522-2099. Fax (852) 2868-5336.

COLOMBIA (5,000)

The Jewish population is about 5,000 with the majority living in Bogotá. There are also coms. in Barranquilla, Cali and Medellin.

Confesion Comunidad Religiosa Centro Israelita de Bogotá, Carrera 20/127-55 Bogotá, PBx 6254377. Fax 274 9069. *M.* Rabbi A. Goldschmidt ☎ 611 2170. Fax 611 2160.

CONGO, DEMOCRATIC REPUBLIC (formerly Zaire)(100)

Before the Congo obtained independence from Belgian rule in 1960, there were about 2,500 Jews, with eight communities affiliated with the central community in Elisabethville. Now these are about 80 in Kinshasa (formerly Leopoldville), 2 in Lubumbashi (formerly Elisabethville), and six others in Likasi, Kannga and Kisangani. There are also some temporary Israeli residents.

Chief Rabbi of Zaire: Rabbi Moishe Levy. 50, W. Churchill Ave., Box 15, 1180 Brussels, Belgium.

COSTA RICA (2,500)

Most of the Jewish population of 2,500 live in San José, the capital, where there are a synagogue, mikveh and a Jewish primary and secondary school. There is also a country club.

*Centro Israelita Sionista de Costa Rica, Orthodox Commmunity Carretera a Pavas Frente a Acueductos y Alcantarillado P.O. Box 1473-1000. ☎ (506) 2520-1013. Fax (506) 220-1951. *President* S. Aizenman; *Sec.* M. Froimzon; *Exec. Dir.* Guita Grynspan; *Chief Rabbi* Gershon Miletski; Email ggrynspan@centroisraelita.com; Website www.centroisraelita.com.

CROATIA (2,500)
(Former constituent republic of Yugoslavia)
There are nine Jewish coms. in Croatia with a total Jewish population of 2,500 affiliated members.

ZAGREB
Jewish Com. and Synagogue. *President* Prof. Dr Ognjen Kraus; *Sec. Gen.* Dean Friedrich; Palmoticeva St. 16., P.O.B. 986; ☎ 385-1 492 2692 Email jcz@zg.t-com,hr Website www.zoz.hr. The Com. Centre was rebuilt in 1992 after being seriously damaged in an explosion. Services are held on Friday eves and holy days. It houses a Jewish kindergarten, Judaica and Hebraica Library, art gallery, auditorium with daily progammes and other facilities. Here are the headquarters of the Fed. of Jewish Coms. in Croatia, Maccabi Sports Club, Jewish Ladies Assn., the Cultural Society and Union of Jewish Students in Croatia.
The com. publishes an occasional newspaper ha-Kol.
There is an impressive monument to Jewish victims of Holocaust in the Jewish cemetery of Mirogoj and a monument to Jewish soliders fallen in the First World War.
There is a plaque in Praška St. 7 on the site of the pre-war Central Syn. of Zagreb.
Before 1941 the com. numbered over 12,000 Jews. Today there are 1,500 members.
Lavoslav Shwartz Old People's Home. *President* Dr Branko Breyer; *Man.* Paula Novak, Bukovacka c. 55; ☎ 210 026; 219 922.

DUBROVNIK
Jewish Com. and Syn., Zudioska St. 3 (Jewish Street). ☎ 020 321-028 *President* S. Horovic This is the second oldest syn. in Europe, dating back to the 14th century damaged in the 1991-2 war. There are 47 Jews in the city and services are held on Jewish holidays.

OSIJEK
Jewish Com. and Syn. *President* Ing. D. Lajos. B. Radica 13,1000 ☎/Fax 031 211-407 Email zidovska-opcina-osijek@inetnet.hr.
There are 150 Jews in the city and the com. is quite active. It suffered some damage during the 1991-92 war.

RIJEKA
Jewish Com. and Syn.: *President* V. Kon; I. Filipovica St. 9; P.O.B. 65. ☎ 051 211160 Email vlado@abc-infoservis.hr
There are 80 Jews in Rijeka. Services are held on Jewish holidays.

SPLIT
Jewish Com. and Syn.: *President* Z. Morpurgo, Zidovski prolaz 1 (Jewish Passage). ☎ 021 345-672 Email zidovska-opcina.split@st.hrnet.hr
There are 200 Jews in Split and the com. is very active, with daily meetings. The syn. is over 350 years old and services are held on Jewish holidays. There is an impressive cemetery dating back to the 16th century.
There are smaller Jewish coms. in Cakovec, Koprivnica, Virovitica, Slavonski Brod and Daruvar. In many towns in north Croatia there are old Jewish cemeteries and former syn. buildings.

CUBA (1,500)
Marranos from Spain settled in Cuba in the sixteenth century, but a real immigration of Jews did not start until the end of the nineteenth century. The majority of the 1,000 Jews live in Havana.

*Comission Coordinadora de las Sociedades Hebreas de Cuba, Calle Bel Vedado, Havana. ☎ 32-8953.

CYPRUS (50)

At the beginning of the present era and earlier, Cyprus was an important and large Jewish centre. An unsuccessful revolt against the Romans in 117, however, was followed by a ruthless suppression and the end of the great period of Jewish history in Cyprus. A new period of prosperity and immigration started in the 12th century but came to an end with the coming of the Genoese and later the Venetians as the island's rulers. By 1560 only 25 families remained in Famagusta, mostly physicians. Attempts at agricultural settlement in the 19th century were unsuccessful. The Jewish population now numbers about 50. The cemetery is at Larnaca.

Jewish Committee has offices in Nicosia c/o S. Ammar, PO Box 23807 Nicosia. ☎ 996 35408.

CZECH REPUBLIC (10,000)

Records show that Jews were settled in Bohemia in the 11th century and in Moravia as early as the 9th cent. There were flourishing Jewish coms. in the Middle Ages. The Jewish pop. of Czechoslovakia in 1930 was 356,830. The coms. were decimated in the Holocaust.

Today the Jewish population of the Czech Republic is est. at 10,000. Of these 3,000 are registered as members of the Jewish com., with some 1,500 in Prague. There are today 10 Jewish coms. in Bohemia and Moravia in the regional cities of Prague, Plzen, Decin, Usti nad Labem, Karlovy Vary, Liberec, Teplice, Brno, Ostrava, Olomouc. There are regular Shabbat and holiday services held in all these places. There is a kosher kitchen and restaurant in Prague with rabbinical supervision of the chief rabbi of Prague and Bohemia and Moravia (Rav. E. K. Sidon).

Federation of Jewish Communities in the Czech Republic. Maiselova 18, 11001, Prague, 1 ☎ 22480-0824. Fax 22481-0912. Email sekretariat@fzo,cz. Website www.fzo.cz. *President* Jan Munk; *Exec. Dir.* JuDr Tomas Kraus.

PRAGUE

Jewish Community of Prague, Maiselova 18, 11001. ☎ 4800812 Fax 2318-664. Email sekretariat@kehilaprag.cz. *Chairman* Ing. F. Bányai. M. Rabbi E. K. Sidon
B'nai B'rith Lodge, Maiselova 18, 11001.
Old-New Synagogue (Altneu), Cervena ul. 1, Praha 1 - Stare Mesto.
Jubilee Synagogue, Jeruzalemska 7, Praha 1 - Nove Mesto.
Bejt Simcha, Mánesova 8, Praha 2. ☎ 222 52472. *Co-ord* Katerina Weberova. www.bejtsimcha.cz.

DĚČIN

Žižkova 4, 405 02 Děčin, CR, ☎ +420 412 531 095. Email zidovska.obec.decin@volny.cz. *Chairman* Vladimar Poskocil
KARLOVY VARY Bezrucova 8 - P.O.B. 160, 360 21, ☎ +420 353 230 658 Email jewishky@volny.cz. *Chairman* Alexander Gajdos
LIBEREC Rumjancevova 1362, 460 01, ☎ +420 485 103 340 Fax +420 482 412 530. Email zolbc@tiscali.cz. *Chairman* RNDr. Michal Hron
OLOMOUC Komenského 7, 772 00, ☎ +420 585 223 119. Email kehila@kehila-olomouc.cz. *Chairman* Petr Papousek
CSTRAVA Tovární 15, 709 00, ☎ +420 596 621 354. Email zobec@volny.cz. *Chairman* Jirina Garajová
PLZEN Smetanovy sady 5, 301 37, ☎ +420 377 235 749. Email zoplzen@volny.cz. *Chairman* Eva Stixová
TEPLICE Lípová 25, 415, 01 ☎ +420 417 538 209. Email kehila@volny.cz, Website www.kehila-teplice.cz. *Chairman* Oldrich Látal
ÚSTÍ NAD LABEM Moskevská 26, 400 00, ☎ +420 475 208 082. Email hellerb@quick.cz. *Chairman* Bedrich Heller

DENMARK (7,000)

The history of the Jews in Denmark goes back to the early years of the seventeenth century. Nearly all of Denmark's 7,000 Jews today live in Copenhagen. Jews have had full civic equality since 1814.

COPENHAGEN

Chief Rabbi: Rabbi Bent Lexner, Bomhusvej, 18, DK 2100. ☎ 39 299520. Fax 39 292517. Email bent@lexner.dk Private: Oestbanegade 9, DK 2100. ☎ 3526 3540.
*Det Mosaiske Troessamfund i Kobenhavn (Jewish Congregation of Copenhagen), Ny Kongensgade 6, DK 1472. ☎ (33)-128-868. Fax (33) 123-357. Email mt@mosaiske.dk. Website www.mosaiske.dk.
Synagogues: Krystalgade 12, DK 1172.
Community Centre, Ny Kongensgade 6, DK 1472.

DOMINICAN REPUBLIC

The Jewish community which settled in Santo Domingo in the sixteenth century has completely disappeared. The present Jewish community, formed shortly before the Second World War, numbers about 150 in Santo Domingo and Sosua.

SANTO DOMINGO

Synagogue, Avenida Ciudad de Sarasota, 5. ☎ 533-1675.

ECUADOR (1,000)

The Jewish population in Ecuador is about 1,000, mainly resident in Quito and Guayaquil.
Comunidad Judia del Ecuador, Calle Roberto Andrade OE3-580 y Jaime Roldos, Urbanizacion Einstein (Carcelen), POBox 17-03-800. ☎ 483-800/927 – 486-749/750/751/ 752. Fax 593 2 486-755. Email aiq@cje-ec.com.
*Comunidad de Culto Israelita, Cnr. Calle Paradiso and El Bosque, Guayaquil.

EGYPT (240)

The history of the Jewish community in Egypt goes back to Biblical times. Following the establishment of the State of Israel in 1948 and the subsequent wars, only about 200 Jews remain, about 150 in Cairo and 50 in Alexandria. Services are conducted in Shaar Hashamayim Synagogue during the High Holy Days.

CAIRO

*Jewish Community Headquarters, 13 rue Sebil el Khazendar, Midan el Gueish, Abbasiya. ☎ 0202-24824613. Email bassatine@yahoo.com. Website www.bassatine.news *President* Mrs C. Weinstein. ☎ 0202-23935896.
Great Synagogue Shaar Hashamayim, 17 Adly Pasha St. ☎ 0202-23929025.
Ben-Ezra Synagogue, 6 Haret il-Sitt Barbara, Old Cairo.
Heliopolis Synagogue "Vitali Madjar", 5 rue Misalla, Korba, Heliopolis.
Maadi Synagogue Meir Enaim, 55 rue 13, Maadi.
Rav Moshe Maimonides Synagogue, Haret el Yehoud; **Rav Haim Capucci Synagogue,** Haret el Yehoud; **Pashad Ishak Synagogue,** Daher; **Etz Haim Synagogue,** Daher; **Ashkenaz Syn.**, Ataba; **Karaite Synagogue**, Abbassia

ALEXANDRIA

Great Synagogue Eliahu HaNabi, 69 rue Nebi Daniel, Ramla Station. *President* Dr Max Salama.

EL SALVADOR (100)

The small Jewish community of about 100 lives primarily in the capital, San Salvador.

ESTONIA (3,000)
TALLINN
Jewish Community of Estonia. Karu Str. 16. *Contact* Cilja Laud, POB 3576 Tallinn 10507.
☎ /Fax 662 3034. Email community@jewish.ee
Syn., 16 Karu St. (662 3050.
Jewish Cultural Centre. *Exec. Dir.*
WIZO Estonia. *Contact*

ETHIOPIA
The indigenous Jews of Ethiopia, known as Falashas, have probably lived in the country for about 2,000 years. Their origin is obscure but they are believed to be the descendants of members of the Agau tribe who accepted pre-Talmudic Judaism brought into Ethiopia (Abyssinia) from Jewish settlements in Egypt, such as that at Elephantine (Aswan). They were estimated to number half-a-million in the 17th century but by the 1970s the population had shrunk to less than 30,000. In 1975 the Israel Govt. recognised their right to enter under the Law of Return. Towards the end of 1984 the Israel Govt. undertook Operation Moses which entailed transporting about 8,000 Ethiopian Jews from refugee camps in Sudan to Israel. It is estimated that approximately 3,000 died from famine and disease before they could reach Israel. A further dramatic mass emigration to Israel was completed in 1991 and very few remain. A useful book on the subject is David Kessler's The Falashas, the Forgotten Jews of Ethiopia (3rd ed., London 1996), obtainable from Frank Cass Publishers.
Jewish Community, POB 50 Addis Ababa.

FIJI
Many Jews, mostly from Britain and some from Australia, settled in the islands in the 19th and early 20th centuries. About 12 Jewish families now live in Suva. *Corr.* K.R. Fleischman, GPO Box 905, Suva or Cherry Schneider, POB 882, Suva.

FINLAND (1,500)
The settlement of Jews in Finland dates from about 1850. The number living there today is about 1,500, with 1,200 in Helsinki, the rest in Turku and other parts of the country.
*Synagogue and Communal Centre: Malminkatu 26, 00100 Helsinki 10. ☎ (09) 5860310. Fax 6948916. Email srk@jchelsinki.fi.
Synagogue and Communal Centre: Brahenkatu 17, Turku. ☎ (02) 2312557.

FRANCE (650,000)
The first Jewish settlers in France arrived with the Greek founders of Marseilles some 500 years B.C.E. After the destruction of the Second Temple, Jewish exiles established new communities, or reinforced old ones. Rashi and Rabenu Tam are the best known of hundreds of brilliant medieval French rabbis and scholars. In 1791 the emancipation of French Jewry was the signal for the ghetto walls to crumble throughout Europe. During the Second World War, under the German occupation, 120,000 Jews were deported or massacred; but the post-war influx from Central and Eastern Europe and particularly from North Africa has increased the numbers of French Jewry to about 600,000 (the fourth largest in the world), of whom 380,000 are in Paris and Greater Paris. There are Jewish coms. in about 150 other towns.

PARIS
*Consistoire Central: The principal Jewish religious org. in France. It administers the **Union des Communautés Juives de France**, 19 rue St. Georges, 75009. *President* Richard Pasquier; *Dir. Gen.* F. Attali. ☎ 49708800. Fax 42810366.
Association Consistoriale Israélite de Paris, 17 rue St. Georges, 75009. The principal Jewish religious org. for the Paris area. *President* Joel Mergui. ☎ 40 82 26 26.
Alliance Israélite Universelle, 45 rue La Bruyère, 75009. This org. works through its network of schools in France, but also in 7 countries, especially in North Africa, Asia and North America. It houses the 'College des Etudes juives' and a library, which includes more than

120,000 books in the field of Hebraica-Judaica and the Nadir Publishing House. *President* Prof. A. Steg; *Dir.* Joseph Tolédano. ☎ 0153328855. Fax 0148745133. Email info@aiu.org. www.aiu.org.

American Jewish Joint Distribution Committee, 5 Ave. de Matignon, 75008. ☎ 01.56.59.79.79. Fax 01.56.59.79.89. *Dir.* Alberto Senderey.

Appel Unifié Juif de France (A.U.J.F.), Espace Rachi, 39 Rue Broca, 75005. ☎ 01.42.17.11.40. Fax 01.42.17.11.45. *President* David de Rothschild.

Association Culturelle Israélite Agudas Hakehilos, 10 rue Pavée, 75004. ☎ 488721 54.

B'nai B'rith France, 5 Bis, rue de Rochechouart, 75009. ☎ 01.55.07.85.45. Fax 01.42.82.70.63. Email BBFRANCE@wanadoo.Fr; Website http/www-bnaibrith-France.org. *Dir.* Mrs Yaël Simon.

Bureau du Chabbath, 8 Rue Maillard, 75011. ☎ 01.44.64.64.64. Fax 01.44.64.64.60. *Dir.* Mrs Noémie Konopnicki. This service helps unemployed people to find work.

CASIP-COJADOR Fondation, 8 Rue de Pali-kao, 75020. ☎ 01.44.62.13.13. Fax 01.44.62.13.14. The CASIP helps people with social and private problems and gives them money and assistance. The COJASOR takes care of old people and assists them in their everyday lives.

Centre de Documentation Juive Contemporaine, 17 Rue Geoffroy l'Asnier, 75004. (Est. 1943.) This org. has gathered and organised data of Jewish life under the Hitler regime in Europe. *Founder* The late Isaac Schneersohn; *President* Baron Eric de Rothschild; *Dir.* Jacky Fredj.

Communauté Israélite de la Stricte Observance, 10 rue Cadet, 75009. ☎ 42 46 36 47.

*Conseil Représentatif des Institutions Juives de France (CRIF), Espace Rachi, 39 Rue Broca, 75005. ☎ 01.42.17.11.11. Fax 01.42.17.11.13. *President* R. Cukerman; *Dir.* Haïm Musicant. This organisation represents French Judaïsm at a political level.

Conseil Représentatif du Judaisme Traditionaliste, c/o Eric Schieber, 6 rue Albert Camus, le Montigny 75010 Paris. 16¡. Rep. org. of Orthodox Jewry. ☎ 45 04 94 00. *President* I. Frankforter; *Sec. Gen.* E. Schieber.

Fédération des Organisations Sionistes de France (FOSF), 10 Rue Richer, 75009. ☎ 01.48.24.04.23.

Fédération des Sociétés Juives de France (FSJF), 70 Rue de Turbigo, 75003. ☎ 01.44.61.29.15. Fax 01.44.61.29.16.

Fonds Social Juif Unifié (F.S.J.U.), Espace Rachi, 39 Rue Broca, 75005. ☎ 01.42.17.10.10. Fax 01.42.17.10.45.

Jeunesse Loubavitch, 8 Rue Lamartine, 75009. ☎ 01.45.26.87.60. Fax 01.45.26.24.37.

Keren Kayemeth Leisrael, 11 Rue du 4 Septembre, 75002. ☎ 42.86.88.88. Fax 01.42.60.18.13.

Mouvement Juif Libéral de France (MJLF), 11 Rue Gaston de Caillavet, 75015. ☎ 01.44.37.48.48. Fax 01.44.37.48.50. (Affil. to World Union of Progressive Judaism.) *President* Félix Mosbacher; *Rabbis* Daniel and Gabriel Farhi.

Mouvement Loubavitch, 8 rue Lamartine 9°. ☎ 45 26 87 60.

Musée d'Art et d'Histoire du Judaisme, Hôtel de St Aignan, 71 rue du Temple, 75003 ☎ 01.53.01.86.60. Fax 01.42.72.97.47. Email info@mahj.org

ORT, 10 Villa D'Eylau, 75016. ☎ 01.45.00.74.22.

Renouveau Juif, 18 passage du Chantier 12°. ☎ 43 40   40 55. Est. 1979 by Henri Hajdenberg. Advocates stronger pro-Israel stand.

Siona, 52 rue Richer 9°. ☎ 42 46 01 91. Sephardi Z. movement est. by Roger Pinto.

Union des Juifs pour la Résistance et l'Entr'aide, 14 rue de Paradis, 10°. Social, cultural and political org. of extreme Left-wing political views, founded as an armed Resistance group in 1943 under German occupation. *President* Charles Lederman. ☎ 47 70 62 16.

Union Libérale Israélite, 24 rue Copernic, 75116. Org. of Liberal Judaism. *President* C Bloch. ☎ 47 04 37 27. Fax 47 27 81 02.

Union des Sociétés Mutalistes Juives de France, 58 rue du Chateau d'Eau 10°. ☎ 42 06 62 88. East European background.

Wizo, 54 rue de Paradis, 10°. French women Zionists' centre. ☎ 48 01 97 70. *President* Nora Gailland-Hofman.

Chief Rabbi of France: Rabbi Joseph Sitruk, Consistoire Central, 19 rue Saint-Georges, 75009. ☎ 49 70 88 00. Fax 40 16 06 11.

SYNAGOGUES

Synagogues of the Consistoire de Paris, 44 rue de la Victoire, 9°; 15 rue Notre-Dame-de-Nazareth, 3°; 21 bis rue des Tournelles, 4°; 28 rue Buffault, 9°Ñ Sephardi; 14 rue Chasseloup-Laubat, 15°; 18 rue Sainte-Isaure, 18°; 75 rue Julien Lacroix, 20°; 9 rue Vauquelin, 5°; 70 Avenue Secretan, 19°; 13 rue Fondary, 15°; 6 bis rue Michel Ange, 16°; 14 Place des Vosges, 4°; 84 rue de la Roquette; 120 Boulevard de Belleville 20°; 120 rue des Saule, 18°; 19 Blvd. Poissonniére; 18 rue St. Lazare, 9° (Algerian).

Orthodox Synagogues: 10 rue Cadet, 9°; 31 rue de Montévidéo, 16°; 10 rue Pavee, 4°; 6 rue Ambroise Thomas, 9°; 3 rue Saulnier, 9°; 32 rue Basfroi, H°; 25 rue des Rosiers, 4°; 17 rue des Rosiers, 4°; 24 rue de Bourg Tibourg, 4°; 80 rue Doudeauville, 18°; 5 rue Duc, 18°; 18 rue des Ecouffes, 4°.

Conservative Syn., Adath Shalom, 22 bis, rue des Belles Feuilles, 75116 Paris. ☎ 45 53 84 09.

Liberal Synagogues, 24 rue Copernic, 16°; 11 rue Gaston de Caillavet 15°. There are also many syns. in the Paris suburbs and in the Provinces.

GEORGIA (13,000)

The Jews of Georgia are divided into two groups, the native Georgian-speaking Jews, who have a history going back 1,500 years (some claim much longer) and the Ashkenazi Jews who came to Georgia following its annexation by Russia at the beginning of the nineteenth century. The Jewish population of Georgia has declined over the last 35 years due to emigration, mostly to Israel. Once numbering as many as 100,000, today the Georgian Jewish population is approximately 13,000. Tiblisi has the largest Jewish population at 11,000. Jewish communities are also located in Kutaisi, Batumi, Oni. Achaltische, Ahalkalaki, Surami, Kareli, and Gori, and synagogues are located in most of these cities.

GERMANY (108,000)

A large Jewish community has existed continuously in Germany since Roman times. Despite recurring periods of persecution, the Jewish communities contributed much of lasting value to culture and civilisation. Hitler and the Nazi regime destroyed the community, which numbered more than half a million before 1933, 160,000 of whom lived in Berlin. Today there are about 108,000 (incl. 11,000 in Berlin,7,000 in Frankfurt and 9,300 in Munich). There are 100 other coms. in Germany. See Hidden Legacy Foundation, p.???

*Zentralrat der Jüden in Deutschland (Central Council of Jews in Germany), Tucholskystr. 9, D-10117 Berlin. ☎ 030 284 4560. Fax 030 284 5613. Email info@zentralrat derjuden.de. Website www.zentralratderjuden.de

Central Welfare Org. of Jews in Germany, Hebelstr. 6, D-60318 Frankfurt. ☎ 069-944371-0. Fax 069-494817.

Conference of German Rabbis, Landesrabbiner Joel Berger, Hospitalstr. 36, D-70174 Stuttgart 1. ☎ /Fax 0711-22836; Tucholskystr. 910117 Berlin

The Union of Progressive Jews in Germany, Austria & Switzerland, Herman-Hummel-Str. 18, D-82166 Graäfelfing. ☎ 8980 9373. Fax 8980 9374. Email info@liberale-juden.de.

B'nai B'rith Lodges, Berlin, Cologne, Düsseldorf, Frankfurt a.Main Hamburg, Munich and Saarbrücken.

*Bundesverband Jüd. Studenten, Oranienburger Str. 29-31,, D-10117 Berlin ☎ 030 8855304 Email info@bjsd.de, and at Jewish Student Organisations at Aachen, Cologne, Frankfurt, Stuttgart, Hanover, Hamburg, Heidelberg and Munich.

Hochschule Für Jüdische Studien Heidelberg (University for Jewish Studies), Friedrichstr. 9, D-69117 Heidelberg. ☎ 06221-4388510 Fax 06221 4385129 Website www.hfsj.uni-heidelberg.de.

Jewish Agency for Israel, Hebelstr. 6,D- 60318 Frankfurt. ☎ 069-9433340. Fax 069-94333420. Email jafi.frankfurt@t-online.de

Jewish Museum, Lindenstrasse 9-14, D-10969, Berlin. ☎ 030 25993300.
Website www.jmberlin.de.
Jewish National Fund, Liebigstr.2, D-60323 Frankfurt. ☎ 069-9714020. Fax 069-97140225.
Jewish Women's League (Frauenbund), c/o ZWST, Hebelstr. 6, D-60318 Frankfurt.
Jewish Restitution Successor Organisation, Sophienstr. 26, D-60481, Frankfurt.
Jüdische Liberale Gemeinde, Köln, Stammheimer Str. 22, D-50735 Köln.
☎/Fax 221 287 0424. Email jlg.köln@gmx.de.
Keren Hayessod, Vereinigte Israel Aktion e.v., Hauptbüro Berlin, Kurfürstendamm88 D-10707 Berlin. ☎ 030-8871933.
Makkabi, Thusneldastr. 7, Köln D-50679. ☎ 568 04229 . Fax 04229569.**ORT,** Hebelstr. 6, D-60318 Frankfurt. ☎ 069-9449081.
Wizo, Joachimstalerstr. 13, D-10719 Berlin.
Youth Aliyah, Hebelstr. 6, D-60318 Frankfurt.
Zentralarchiv zur Erforschung der Geschichte der Juden in Deutschland, Bienenstr. 5, D-69117 Heidelberg. ☎ 06221-164141. Fax 06221-181049. Website www.zentralarchiv.uni-hd.de
Zionist Organisation in Deutschland e. V. St. -Jacobs-Platz 18 D-80331 München ☎ 0-89-22 80 25 77. Fax 0-89-22 80 25 79. Email anizioni@yahoo.de
Zionist Youth, Falkensteiner St. 1, D-60322 Frankfurt. ☎ 069-556963. Email zjd-habonim@t-online.de

GIBRALTAR (650)

In 1473 there was a suggestion that the promontory should be reserved for Marranos (see D. Lamelas, 'The Sale of Gibraltar in 1474', 1992). The present Jewish community was formed of immigrants from North Africa shortly after the British annexation in 1704, but Jews had no legal right to settle in the city until 1749, by which year however, the Jewish residents numbered about 600, a third of the total number of residents, and possessed two syns.

During the siege of 1779 to 1783 the size of the Jewish population was reduced, a large proportion removing to England. After the siege the numbers rose again, being at their highest in the middle of the nineteenth century, when they rose above two thousand. (For the history of the Jews of Gibraltar, see A. B. M. Serfaty, 'The Jews of Gibraltar under British Rule,' 1933.)

Following the period of stasis and decline, the last ten to fifteen years has seen a marked increase in the Jewish numbers with a large number of Gibraltarians returning from study and residence abroad. This has created a young and vibrant Community

*Managing Board of the Jewish Community, 91 Irish Town. ☎ 72606. Fax 40487*President* H.J.M. Levy. Fax 40487. *Admin.* Mrs S. Levy. Email mbjc@gibtelecom.net
Synagogue Shaar Hashamayim, 47, Engineer Lane. ☎ 78069. Fax 74029. (Est. before 1749; rebuilt 1768.) *H. Sec.* G. Belilo ☎ 48728.
Synagogue Nefusot Yehudah, 65, Line Wall Rd. (Est. 1781.) *H. Sec.* I. Beniso. ☎ 74791. Fax 40907.
Synagogue Es Hayim, Irish Town. (Est. 1759.) *H. M. & Sec.* S. Benaim. ☎ 75563.
Synagogue, Abudarham, 20, Parliament Lane. (Est. 1820.) *H. Sec.* D. J. Abudarham. ☎ 78506. Fax 73249.
Mikveh, Mrs G. Hassan. ☎ 74929; Mrs R. Serfaty ☎ 73090.
Joint Israel Appeal. *H. Sec.* E. Benamor. ☎ 77680. Fax 40493.

GREECE (4,800)

There have been Jewish communities in Greece since the days of antiquity. Before 1939, 77,200 Jews lived in Greece (56,000 in Salonika, now known as Thessaloniki). Today there are fewer than 5,000, all Sephardim, of these about 2,800 live in Athens; some 1,100 in Thessaloniki; and the rest in some 12 provincial towns.

ATHENS
*Central Board of Jewish Communities, 36 Voulis St., GR 105 57. *President* Moissis

Constantinis. ☎ 210 3244315. Fax 210 3313852. Email hhkis@ath.forthnet.gr. Website www.kis.gr.
B'nai B'rith, 15 Paparigopoulou St., 105 61. ☎ 210 3230405.
Jewish Community Office, 8 Melidoni St., 105 53. ☎ 210 3252823. Fax 3220-761.
Synagogue, Beth Shalom, 5 Melidoni St., 105 53. *M.* Rabbi Jakob Arar. ☎ 210 325 2773.
Jewish Museum of Greece, 39 Nikis St., 105 57. ☎ 210 32 25 582. Fax 32 31 577.
Communal Centre, 9 Vissarionos St., 106 72. ☎ 210 36 37 092. Fax 360 8896.

THESSALONIKI
Jewish Community Office, 26 Vasileos Irakliou St., 54624. ☎ 2310 275 701. Fax 2310 229 063.
Monastirioton Synagogue, 35 Sigrou St., 54630. ☎ 2310 524968.
Synagogue Yad Le Zicaron, 24 Vasileos Irakliou St., 54624. ☎ 2310 223231.
Museum, 13 Agiou Mina Str., 54624 ☎ 2310 250406, ☎ Fax/250407.

Other communities:
Corfu Jewish Community, 5 Riz. Voulefton St., 49100. *President* Moisis Velelis. ☎ 26610 47777. Fax 26610 47710
Halkis Jewish Community, *President* M. Maissis. 5 Papingi Str., 34100. ☎ 22210 60111. Fax 22210 83781.
Ioannina Jewish Community, 18 Joseph Eliyia Str. GR 452 21. ☎ 26510 25195. *President* M. Elisaf.
Larissa Jewish Community, Platia Evreon Martiron, 29 Kentavron St.GR 412 22. ☎ 2410 532965. *President* M. Magrizos.
Rodos Jewish Community, 5 Polidorou Str. GR 85100. ☎ 22410 22364. Fax 22410 73039. Email jcrhodes@otenet.gr. *President* Bella Angel-Restis.
Trikala Jewish Community, *President* I. Venouziou, Kondili-Philippou, 42100. ☎ 24310 25-834.
Volos Jewish Community, 51 Hatziargyuri St., GR 383 33. *President* M. Solomon. ☎/Fax 24210 25302. Email jcvol@otenet.gr. Website www.atlantis.gr/kis/volos.html.

GUATEMALA (1,500)
Jews have been resident in Guatemala since 1898. The present population is about 1,500, made up of some 300 families all living in the capital.

GUATEMALA CITY
*Comunidad Judia Guatemalteca, 7a. Av. 13-51 Zona 9, Guatemala City, C.A. ☎ 560 1509. Fax 560 1589. Email comjugua@guaweb.net. *President* T. Rybar.
Centro Hebreo (East European Jews) 7a. Av. 13-51 Zona 9. ☎ 3311975. *President* Boris Barac.
Maguen David (Sephardi), 7a. Avenida 3-80 Zona 2. ☎ 2320932. Fax 360 1589. *President* Moises Beer.
Consejo Central Sionista de la Comunidad Judia de Guatemala, Apto. Postal 502, Guatemala, C.A. *President* Mano Permuth.

HAITI (150)
There has been a Jewish community in Haiti for the past 80 years, and it now numbers about 150 people.

HONDURAS (150)
There has been a Jewish community in Honduras for the past 50 years.
Tegucigalpa Community. *Sec.* H. Seidel.
Israel Embassy S. Cohen, Ambassador; H. Schiftan, Consul. ☎ 32-4232/32-5176. Telex: 1606 Memistra.
San Pedro Sula, Syn. and Com. Centre. *Sec.* M. Weizenblut. ☎ 552 8136. Fax 557 5244.

HUNGARY (100,000)

Jews have lived in this part of Europe since Roman times. Tombstones with Hebrew inscription have been found originating from the 3rd century. Before World War II, Hungary's Jewish population was about 800,000, of whom some 250,000 lived in Budapest. Some 600,000 perished in the Holocaust. The estimated Jewish population now is 100,000 and some 80,000 live in Budapest and the remainder in the provincial Jewish communities, all affiliated to the Central Board of the Federation of the Jewish Communities in Hungary.

BUDAPEST

*Federation of the Jewish Communities in Hungary (Magyarországi Zsidó Hitközségek Szövetsége) and the Budapest Jewish Community, 1075 Budapest VII Sip utca 12. ☎ 413 5569. Fax 342-1790. *Man. Dir.* Gusztav Zoltai; *Dir. Foreign Rel.* Ernö Lazarovits.

Main Synagogue, Budapest VII Dohany utca 2 (Conservative). Chief Rabbi Robert Frölich.

Central Rabbinate, Budapest VII Sip utca 12. *Dir.* Robert Deutsch, Chief Rabbi.

Orthodox Synagogue, Budapest VII Kazinczy utca 27. *President* Herczog, László

Rabbinical Seminary and Jewish University, Budapest VIII, József körut 27. *Dir. Rector* Dr A. Schöner.

There are 20 other syns. and prayer houses in Budapest.

MAZSOK The Jewish Heritage of Hungary Public Endowment, 1054 Budapest, Tūköry u. 3. *President* Gusztáv Zoltai; *Sec.* György Vályi.

The main provincial coms. are at Debrecen, Miskolc, Szeged, Pécs, Györ.

INDIA (5,600)

The settlement of Jews in India goes back at least to the early centuries of the Christian era. The Indian Jews of today may be divided into four groups: (i) those who arrived in this and the last century mainly from Baghdad, Iran, Afghanistan, etc., known as "Yehudim," forming communities in Bombay, Pune and Calcutta; (ii) Bene Israel, who believe that their ancestors arrived in India after the destruction of the First Temple, and who maintained a distinct religious identity while using local language and dress over the centuries; their main centre is the Bombay area; (iii) the Cochin Jews, in Cochin and the neighbouring centres of the Malabar Coast, in Kerala State in South India, who have records dating back to the fourth century, but who believe that there was a Jewish settlement in Craganore as early as 78 C.E.; (iv) European Jews who came within the last 50 years or so. Since 1948 there has been steady emigration to Israel. According to the 1971 census the Jewish pop. was 6,134. Today, it is estimated at 5,618.

The largest com. is in Maharastra State (4,354), mainly in the Bombay area. Smaller coms. are in Calcutta, Madras, New Delhi and Pune Ahmedabad. In Manipur there are 464 and in Gujarat 217. There are 13 Jews in Cochin.

*Council of Indian Jewry, c/o The Jewish Club, Jeroo Bldg., Second Fl., 137 Mahatma Gandhi Rd., Bombay, 400023. ☎ 271628. *President* N. Talkar. ☎ 8515195, 861941; *V. Presidents* A. Talegawkar, A. Samson; *Sec.* Mrs J. Bhattacharya. ☎ 6320589.

INDONESIA

Of the 16 Jews living in Indonesia, 15, made up of five families, live in Surabaya where there is provision for prayers. One lives in Jakarta.

IRAN (24,000)

Jews have lived in the country at least since the time of the Persian King Cyrus in the sixth century BCE. Many of the tombs of Jewish prophets, such as Daniel, Habakuk, Esther and Mordechai, are located in the cities of Iran. These holy places are respected by both Jews and Muslims. From the beginning of the twentieth century, the Iranian Jewish population has been under 70,000. Today it is in the region of 27,000. there are some legal differences between the majority and minority religions in Iran, and in some areas Jewish rights are under threat. Nevertheless, Jews in Iran have been free to maintain their religious affairs and ceremonies, and the cultural training of Jewish students since the Islamic Revolution of 1979. There has been a Jewish representative in every Islamic parliament in the modern period. Iranian Jews live in Tehran, Shiraz, Isfahan, Kerman, and Kermanshah.

TEHRAN
Comité Central de la Communauté Juive de Tehran, 385 Sheikh-Hadi St., Jomhuri Ave., 11397-3-3317. ☎ 66702556. Fax 66716429. Email iranjewish@iranjewish.com; Website www.iranjewish.com.
Synagogues: Yousefabad, 15th Street, Seyed Jamaleddin Assadabadi Ave.; Abrishami, 4th Street, North Felestin Ave. *Chief Rabbi* Hakham Yousef Haim Hamedani Cohen.

IRAQ (75)
The Jewish community in Iraq (anciently known as Babylonia) is the oldest in the Diaspora. Strong hostility exists towards the Jewish remnant of about 200, mainly elderly, that is now left. They mostly live in Baghdad and a few in Basra.

ISRAEL (5,330,000)
Palestine was administered until May 14, 1948, by Gt. Britain under a Mandate approved by the Council of the League of Nations, the preamble to which incorporated the Balfour Declaration. On November 20, 1947, the Assembly of the United Nations recommended that Palestine should be reorganised as two States, one Jewish, the other Arab, together with an internationalised Jerusalem and district combined in an economic union. On the surrender of the Mandate by Britain on May 14, 1948, the Jewish territory, with a Jewish pop. of 655,000, took the name of Israel and set up a Provisional Govt., with Dr Chaim Weizmann as President and David Ben-Gurion as Prime Minister. On July 5, 1950, the 'Law of Return' was proclaimed, conferring on every Jew the right to live in Israel.

The signing of a declaration of a set of principles by Israel and the PLO under the leadership of Yasser Arafat on September 13, 1993, concluded an era of forty-five years of strife between Israel and her Arab neighbours and recognised the aspirations of Palestinian Arabs for territory proposed for them by the UN in 1947. A peace treaty with Jordan was agreed in 1994. Prime Minister Rabin was assassinated in November 1995.

Key events in this history include:
The invasion of the Jewish state by the Arab armies in 1948 concluded by a series of armistices in 1949 and the recognition of Israel by the UN on May 11, 1949; the annexation of Arab Palestine by Jordan in 1950; the absorption by Israel of Jews from Arab lands and the establishment of Palestinian refugee camps in the Arab states; seizure by Egypt of the Suez Canal Zone and the (Franco-British and Israeli) Sinai-Suez campaign of 1956; Egypt's closure of the Straits of Tiran in May 1967 which provoked the Six-Day War of June 1967 and saw the Israeli capture of Jerusalem and occupation of Gaza, Sinai, the Golan and the West Bank and the first National Unity Coalition (1967–70); the Yom Kippur War of October 1973 and the ensuing negotiations leading to partial Israeli withdrawals in Sinai and the Golan; the Likud election victory of 1977 and the visit to Israel by Egyptian President Anwar Sadat in November 1977 which led to the Camp David Agreement of March 26, 1979, the establishment of diplomatic relations between Egypt and Israel, and the Israeli withdrawal from the whole of Sinai in April 1982; Israel's 'Operation peace for Galilee' in Lebanon in June 1982 and withdrawal in 1985, a war which caused great divisions in Israel; the Intifada of the Palestinians in Gaza and the West Bank starting in 1988; the US-inspired five-point peace plan of 1989 and its failure in 1990; the Gulf War (January 1991) following the Iraqi invasion of Kuwait when the PLO supported Iraq and Israel sustained scud missile attacks without retaliation; the launching of negotiations for a comprehensive Middle East 'peace settlement' between Israel, the Arabs, and representatives of the Palestinians at a meeting in Madrid in October 1991.

It is these negotiations, that came to fruition on the eve of the New Year 5754. The continuing 'Peace Process' was repeatedly put in jeopardy through the actions of terrorists intent on destabilizing any progress towards détente and under protest at the consolidation of Israeli settlements. President Clinton endeavoured to broker a new agreement between Prime Minister

Barak and the PLO, but this failed and Mr Barak resigned. Nonetheless Mr Barak's achievement in securing withdrawal of Israeli forces from southern Lebanon indicated positive efforts to reconcile neighbourly relations. The new *Intifada* that broke out in 2000 continues unabated and Israel's predicament has been exacerbated by the aftermath of the terror of September 2001, the American war against the Taliban of Afghanistan and the Anglo-American war of 2003 against Saddam Hussein's Iraq. Interventions by President Bush and the promulgation of a 'Road Map' for reviving the peace process have faltered. Ariel Sharon saw through the construction of a barrier-wall to deflect continuing bombing raids from Gaza into Israel but broke with his Likud government in 2005 when he also forced through the withdrawal from Gaza. With the establishment of his Kadima Party he indicated some prospect of withdrawals also from parts of the West Bank.

The death of Yassir Arafat and the election of Mahmoud Abbas as PLO President were followed by Palestinian elections at the beginning of 2006. These were won by Hamas who, in government, have not rescinded their policy towards the destruction of Israel. Ariel Sharon suffered a stroke ahead of the scheduled elections in Israel and while Kadima secured power at these elections the new government found itself at increased risk from continuing militancy in Gaza and a new embroilment in Lebanon which was provoked by the rise and belligerency of the Hizbollah turning northern Israel into a war-zone. Following UN Resolution 1701 on the ceasefire in southern Lebanon and the monitoring of the withdrawal of Hizbollah under UN control, a tentative measure of peace has been restored. Against this the increasing stridency of Iranian rhetoric and her unabashed pursuit of nuclear power leave Israel exposed to untold dangers while the body politic reviews the outcome of the hostilities and the shortcomings of policies of a new leadership.

Government
The Provisional Government of Israel was replaced by a permanent one after the election of the First **Knesset** (Parliament) in January, 1949.

Israel's Basic Law provides that elections must be 'universal, nationwide, equal, secret and proportional'. A general election must be held at least every four years. The Knesset is elected by a form of proportional representation in which members are selected in strict proportion to the votes cast for each party. Any candidate who obtains one per cent of the total votes cast is assured of a Knesset seat.

Mainly as a result of the voting system, no single party has so far been able to form a government on the basis of its own Knesset majority. Until the election in 1977, the dominant political force was a coalition of the Left, which formed governments with the help of various smaller parties, usually those with a religious programme. In the elections of 1977 and 1981 an alliance of the Right was able to form an administration with the help of religious parties. One feature of the political situation has been that the religious parties, in particular, have been able to exercise an influence out of proportion to their members.

Within recent years, however, there has been a marked polarisation of attitudes among sections of Israeli society and this was reflected by the proliferation of small parties which contested the 1984 election. The 1984 election produced an inconclusive result, with only three seats separating the two big party blocs. The two big parties formed Israel's second National Unity Government to cope with the urgent economic and other problems. The office of Prime Minister was held in rotation, first by Mr Shimon Peres, the Labour Alignment leader, and then by Mr Yitzhak Shamir, the Likud leader. The 1988 election was also inconclusive and was followed by another Coalition Government, with Mr Shamir continuing as Prime Minister and Mr Peres as Vice-Premier. The national unity government broke up in March 1990 when the Likud declined to go along with a U.S. plan to promote peace talks. Mr Shamir constructed a centre-right religious government supported by 66% of the 120 members of the Knesset. The elections of 1992 produced a Labour coalition led by Yitzhak Rabin. Demographic changes brought about by the influx of settlers from Eastern Europe and political and economic pressures contributed in large part to this outcome. The Knesset elections of 1996 were the first at which there was also direct voting for the position of Prime Minister. Following the resignation of Mr Barak in 2001, however, Ariel Sharon was elected Prime Minister while the 15th

Knesset remained in session. While political power rests constitutionally in the Knesset, the President of Israel, essentially a symbolic and representational figure, can in certain circumstances exercise a degree of de facto power based on his prestige. In particular, he can emerge as the voice of the nation's conscience. The President is elected for a five-year period, renewable only once. Moshe Katsav was elected President in 2000, but was obliged to stand down in 2007

Elections to the 17th Knesset were held in March 2006. Party votes were follows:

Kadima	29	(2003: –)	United Arab	10	(2)
Labour	19	(19)	National Union-NRP	9	(6)
Shas	12	(11)	Pensioners	7	(–)
Likud	12	(38)	United Torah	6	(5)
Yisrael Beitenu	11	(–)	Meretz	5	(6)

This outcome gave Mr Olmert the opportunity to form a centrist government with Labour support in a coalition of 73 seats. He resigned in August 2008 and Foreign Minister Tzipi Livni won the Kadima vote to succeed him in negotiations for a new coalition. The new coalition has failed to materialise and elections are called for February 2009.

The Presidents of Israel: Chaim Weizmann 1949–52; Yitzhak Ben Zvi 1952–63; Zalman Shazar 1963–73; Prof. Ephraim Katzir 1973–78; Yitzhak Navon 1978–83; Chaim Herzog 1983–93; Ezer Weizman 1993–2000; Moshe Katsav 2000–07; **Shimon Peres** 2007–

The Prime Ministers of Israel: David Ben-Gurion 1948–53 and Nov. 1955–63; Moshe Sharett Dec. 1953–55; Levi Eshkol 1963–69; Golda Meir 1969–74; Yitzhak Rabin 1974–77 and 1992–95; Menachem Begin 1977–83, Yitzhak Shamir Oct. 1983–Sept. 1984, Oct. 1986–June 1992; Shimon Peres Sept. 1984–Oct. 1986, Nov. 1995–May 1996; Benjamin Netanyahu, May 1996–99; Ehud Barak, May 1999–Feb. 2001; Ariel Sharon, Feb. 2001–06; Ehud Olmert (Apr. 2006–08); **Tzipi Livni** (Sept 2008-)

Judiciary: The *President* appoints judges on the recommendation of an independent committee.

Defence Forces: Unified command of Army, Navy and Air Force. Small regular force; compulsory military service for persons aged between 18 and 29 followed by annual service in the Reserve.

Area: Following 1949 armistice agreements – approx. 20,750 sq. km. Following withdrawal from Sinai in April 1982, approx. 28,161 sq. km. (including Golan Heights, West Bank and Gaza).

Neighbouring countries: Egypt, Jordan, Syria, Lebanon.

Population: Sept. 1998: 4,850,000. These figures include 17,000 Druse on the Golan Heights but not the other territories occupied in the Six-Day War (est. at 1,381,000).

Main Towns: Jerusalem (the capital), Tel Aviv, Haifa, Ramat Gan, Petach Tikvah, Netanya, Holon, Bnei Brak, Rehovot, Hadera, Nazareth, Rishon le-Zion, Beersheba, Ashkelon, Ashdod, Bat Yam, Tiberias, Eilat.

Industry: Main products: Cement, fertilisers, metal products, polished diamonds, ceramics, tyres and tubes, plywood, textiles, clothing and footwear, citrus by-products, electrical and electronic applicances, micro-electronics, chemicals, canned fruit, military equipment.

Agricultural Products: Citrus, fruit, vegetables, eggs, milk, wheat, barley, tobacco, groundnuts, cotton, sugarbeet, beef, fish, flowers, wine.

Minerals: Potash and bromine, magnesium, phosphate, petroleum, salt, glass, sand, clay, gypsum, granite, copper, iron, oil, natural gas.

With the exception of Jerusalem and Haifa, the country's largest port, the main centres of population are concentrated in the flat and fertile western coastal plain. Tel Aviv, the centre of Israel's largest metropolitan area, is the chief commercial and industrial centre.   Beersheba is the capital of the arid northern Negev, while Eilat, the country's southernmost port, has become a bustling Red Sea township linked to the northern centres by a modern highway and giving access now to Jordan as well. In the north lie the largely Arab centre of Nazareth, the popular health resort of Tiberias, and Safad. Round Tel Aviv are clustered a number of towns, including Ramat Gan, Holon and Bnei Brak.

President of State Shimon Peres; *Knesset Speaker* Dalia Itsik.

ISRAELI EMBASSIES AND LEGATIONS
Israel now enjoys diplomatic relations with 160 countries and many of these ties have come into being or have been renewed following the peace agreements of 1993.

Permanent Delegation to U.N. 800 2nd Ave., New York, N.Y. 10017. ☎ (212) 449-5400. Fax (212) 490 5900. Ambassador Dan Gilerman; *Dep.* Ambassador David Peleg. European H.Q. of U.N. Geneva, 153 ave de la Paix, Geneva; Ambassador Y. Levi. ☎ 7980500; Vienna, 20 Anton Frankgasse, 1180 Vienna. ☎ 470-4742. Ambassador Dan Gillerman.

Embassy to European Communities. 40 Ave. de L'Observatoire, Brussels 1180. ☎ 373-55500. Ambassador Oded Eran.

Permanent Delegation to Council of Europe, 3 Rue Rabelais, 75008 Paris. ☎ 4076-5500. Ambassador A. Gabai.

Albania (see Italy).

Andorra (see Spain).

Angola. Emb. Rua Rainha Ngina 34, Luanda. ☎ 395295. Ambassador Mansour Bahigi.

Antigua and Barbuda (see Dominican Republic).

Argentina. Emb.: 701 Mayo Ave., Buenos Aires. ☎ 4338-2500. Ambassador Benjamin Oran.

Armenia (see Georgia).

Australia. Emb.: 6 Turrana St., Yarralumla, Canberra, 2600. 1033, ☎ 6273-1309. Ambassador Yuval Rotem.

Austria. Emb.: Anton Frankgasse, 20, Vienna 1180. (4764-6500. Ambassador Avraham Toledo. ☎ 4764-6510.

Azerbaijan. Emb: Hyatt Tower 3, 7th Floor, Izmir St., 1033, Baku. Ambassador Eitan Nae.

Bahamas. Consulate, PO Box 7776, Nassau NP. ☎ 3264421. Hon. Consul. Raphael Seligman.

Barbados. Consulate, PO Box 256, Bridgetown. Hon. Consul Bernard Gilbert.

Belgium. Emb.: 40 Ave. de l'Observatoire, Brussels 1180. ☎ 373-5500. Ambassador Yehudi Kinar.

Belize (see San Salvador).

Benin (see Côte d'Ivoire).

Bolivia. Emb.: Edificio 'Esperanza', Ave., Mariscal, Santa Cruz; Edificio 'Esperanza', 10 Pizo, Calle 1309, La Paz. (391126. Ambassador Reuven Miron.

Botswana (see Zimbabwe).

Brazil. Emb.: Avenida das Nacoes, Lote 38, Brasilia. ☎ 244-7675. Ambassador Daniel Gazit.

Bulgaria. 1 Bulgaria Sq., NDK Building, 7th Floor. ☎ 9515029. Ambassador Avraham Sharon.

Burkina Faso (see Côte d'Ivoire).

Burundi (see Zaire).

Kingdom of **Cambodia** (see Thailand).

Cameroon. Emb.: P.O. Box 5934, Yaounde. ☎ 201644. Ambassador Yoram Elron.

Canada. Emb.: 50 O'Connor St., Ottawa K1P 672. ☎ 5676450. Ambassador Haim Dibon.

Cape Verde (see Senegal).

Central African Republic (see Cameroon).

Chile. Emb.: Av. Bosque, Las Condes San Sebastian 2812, Santiago De Chile. ☎ 750-0500. Ambassador Yosef Regev.

China. Emb.: No. 17, Tian Ze Lu, Chaoyang District, Beijing 100600. ☎ 6505-2970. Ambassador Yehuda Haim.

Colombia. Emb.: Edificio Caxdac Calle 35, No. 7-25, Bogota. ☎ 288 4637. Ambassador Ehud Itam.

Costa Rica. Emb.: Edificio Centro, Colon, Paseo Colon, Calle 38. ☎ 221-6444. Ambassador Alexander Ben Zvi.

Republic of Côte D'Ivoire. O.1. B.P. 1877, Abidjan 01. ☎ 202 27191. Ambassador Daniel Kedem.

Cyprus. Emb.: 4 Gripari St., POB 25159, W. Nicosia. ☎ 369500. Ambassador Michael Eligal.

Czech Republic. 2 Badeniho St., Prague 7. ☎ 3309 7500. Ambassador Arthur Avnon.

Denmark. Emb.: Lundevangsvej 4, Hellerup, Copenhagen. ☎ 881 85500. Ambassador Carmi Gillon.
Dominica (see Dominican Republic).
Dominican Republic. Emb.: Pedro Henriques Unena 80. ☎ 4720774. Ambassador Eliahu Lopez.
Ecuador. Emb.: 12 De Octubrey Salazar, Edf. Plaza 2000, Quito. ☎ 238055. Ambassador Mansour Rada.
Egypt. Emb.: 6 Shariah Ibn-el Maleck, Giza, Cairo. ☎ 3610 528. Ambassador Gideon Ben-Ami.
El Salvador. Emb.: Centro Financiero Gigante, Torre B Piso 63, Avenida Sury Alameda, San Salvador. ☎ 2113434. Ambassador Yosef Livne.
Eritrea. Emb.: Ogaden St. 32, Asmara. ☎ 185626. Ambassador Hanan Goder-Goldberger.
Estonia (see Latvia).
Ethiopia. PO Box 1266, Addis Ababa. ☎ 460 999. Ambassador .
Fiji (see Australia).
Finland. Emb.: 5a Vironkatu, Helsinki. ☎ 6812020. Ambassador Miryam Shomrat.
France. Emb.: 66 ave Champs Elysées, Paris 75008. ☎ 40765500. Ambassador D. Shek.
Gabon (see Cameroon).
Gambia (see Senegal).
Georgia. Emb.: Agmashenebeli Ave. 61, Tbilisi 380002. ☎ 951 709. Ambassador Rivka Cohen.
Germany. Emb.: Auguste Victoria Str. 74-75, Berlin 14193. ☎ 8904-5500. Ambassador Shimon Stein.
Ghana (see Côte d'Ivoire).
Gibraltar. Con.: 3 City Mill Lane. ☎ 59555956. Hon. Con. M. E. Benaim.
Grenada. Emb.: (see Jamaica).
Greece. Emb.: Marathonodromu No. 1. Paleo Psychico, Athens. ☎ 6719-530. Ambassador David Sason.
Guatemala. Emb.: 13 Ave 14-07, Zona 10, Guatemala City. ☎ 363-5665. Ambassador Yaakov Faran.
Guinea Bissau (see Senegal).
Guyana (see Venezuela).
Equatorial Guinea (see Cameroon).
Haiti (see Panama).
Honduras (see Guatamala).
Hong Kong. Cons.: Admiralty 701, Tower 2, 18 Harcourt Rd., Central. ☎ 25296091. Con.-Gen. Eli Avidar.
Hungary. Fulank, Utca 8, Budapest. ☎ 2000781. Ambassador Yehudit Várnai-Shorer.
Iceland. Emb.: (see Norway.) H. Con.-Gen. Pall Arnor Palsson.
India. Emb: 3 Aurangzeb Rd., New Delhi 10011. ☎ 3013238. Ambassador Yehoyada Haim. Cons.: Bombay: Earnest House, 16th Fl., NCPA Marg 154, 400 021 Nariman Point. ☎ 386 2793. Consul Dov Segev-Steinberg.
Ireland. Emb.: Carrisbrook House, 122 Pembroke Rd, Ballsbridge, Dublin 4. ☎ 6680303. Ambassador Dr Zion Evrony.
Italy. Emb.: Via Michele Mercati 12, Rome. ☎ 36198500. Ambassador Ehud Gol.
Jamaica. Con.: 7-9 Harbour St., Kingston. ☎ 922-5990. Hon. Consul Joseph Mayer-Matalon.
Japan. Emb.: 3 Niban-Cho, Chiyoda-ku, Tokyo. ☎ 3264-0911. Ambassador Yitzhak Lior.
Jordan. Emb.: 47 Maysaloun St., Rabiya, Amman 111195. ☎ 552-4680. Ambassador David Dadon.
Kazakhstan. Emb: Dgeltoxan St. 87, Almaty. ☎ 507215. Ambassador Moshe Kemchi.
Kenya. Emb.: Bishop Rd., Fair View Hotel, P.O. Box 30354, Nairobi. ☎ 722182. Ambassador Yakov Amitai.
Kirghizstan (see Kazakhstan).
Kiribati (Republic of) (see Australia).
Korea (South). Emb.: 823-21 Daekong Building, Yoksam-Dong Kangnam-Ku. ☎ 5643448. Ambassador Ouzi Manor.
Laos (see Vietnam).
Latvia. Emb.: 2 Elizabetes St., LV 1340 Riga. ☎ 732-0739. Ambassador Avraham Benjamin.

Lesotho (see Swaziland).
Liberia. Emb.: Gardiner Avenue, Sinkor, POB 2057, Monrovia. ☎ 262073/ 262861. Fax (977) 4415.
Liechtenstein. Con-Gen. G. Yarden (see Switzerland.)
Lithuania (see Latvia)
Luxembourg (see Belgium). **Macao** (see Hong Kong). **Macedonia** (see Greece). **Madagascar** (see Kenya). **Malawi** (see Zimbabwe). **Malta** (see Italy). **Marshall Islands** (see Australia).
Mauritania. Emb. Ilot-A-516, Tevraghi-Zenia, Nouakchott ☎ 254610. Ambassador Ariel Kerem.
Mauritius (see Kenya).
Mexico. Emb.: Sierra Madre 215, Mexico City 1100 D.F. ☎ 52011500. Ambassador Yosef Amihud.
Micronesia (see Australia). **Moldova** (see Ukraine).
Monaco (see France). Con.-Gen.
Mongolia (see China).
Morocco. (Closed).
Mozambique (see Zimbabwe).
The Union of Mayanmar. Emb.: 49 Pyay Rd., Yangon. ☎ 222290. Fax 22463. Ambassador Gad Natan.
Namibia (see Zimbabwe).
Nauro (see Australia).
Nepal. Emb.: Bishramalaya Hse., Lazimpat, Katmandu. ☎ 413419. Ambassador Avraham Nir.
Netherlands. Emb.: Buitenhof 47, The Hague, 2513 AH. ☎ 3760500. Ambassador Etan Margalit.
Netherlands Antilles. Curaçao Consulate, Blauwduiffweg 5, Willemstad, Curaçao. ☎ 373533. Hon. Consul Paul Ackerman.
New Zealand. Emb.: (Ambassador Naftali Tamir.
Nicaragua (see Guatamala).
Nigeria. Emb.: Plot 1317, A2B UPO Udoma Crescent, Zone 4A, Asokoro, Abuja 2143170. Ambassador Noam Katz.
Norway. Emb.: Parkveien 35, Oslo 0258. ☎ 2101-9500. Ambassador Liora Herzl.
Oman. Israel Trade Representation Office, PO Box 194, Aladhiba, P.C. 130 Muscat. ☎ 604857. Hd. of Mission Oded Ben Haim.
Republic of Palau (see Australia).
Papua, New Guinea (see Australia).
Paraguay. Emb.: Piso 8, Edificion San Rafael, Calle Yergos No. 437 C/25 De Mayo. ☎ 495097. Ambassador Yoav Bar-On.
Peru. Emb.: Sanches 125, 6 Piso, Santa Beatriz, Lima. ☎ 4334431. Ambassador Ouri Noy.
Philippines. Emb.: Trafalgar Plaza 23 Floor, Emb.: Trafalgar Plaza 23 Floor, Makati, Manila. ☎ 892-5330. Fax 894-1027. Ambassador Irit Ben-Abba Vitla.
Poland. Interests Office: Ul. L. Krzywickiego 24, Warsaw. ☎ 825-2897. Ambassador Shevach Weiss.
Portugal. Emb.: Rua Antonio Enes 16-4°, Lisbon. ☎ 355-3640. Ambassador Shmuel Tevet.
Qatar. Israel Trade Representation Office, 15 Al Buhturi St, Doha. ☎ 4689077. Hd. of Mission Yakov Hadas-Hendelsman.
Romania. Emb.: B-Dul Dimitrei Cantemiri, Tronson 2+3 B2, Piata Unir II, Bucharest. ☎ 3204149. Ambassador Sando Mazor.
Russia. Emb.: 56 Bolshaya Ordinka, Moscow. ☎ 2306777. Ambassador Arkadi Mil-Man.
Rwanda (see Zaire).
St. Christopher, St. Kitts and St. Nevis (see Dominican Republic).
St. Lucia (see Jamaica).
St. Vincent and the Grenadines (see Jamaica).
San Marino. Con.-Gen. (see Italy).
Sao Tome and Principe (see Cameroon).
Senegal. Emb.: B.P. 2096, Dakar. ☎ 8233561. Ambassador Shlomo Avital.
Serbia. Emb. 47 Bulevar Mira, Dedinje Belgrade. ☎ 367-2400.

Seychelles (see Kenya).
Singapore. Emb.: 58 Dalvey Rd., Singapore 1025. ☎ 6834 9200. Ambassador Yitzhak Shoham.
Slovakia (see Austria).
Slovenia (see Austria).
Solomon Islands (see Australia).
South Africa. Emb.: 339 Hilda St., Hatfield, Pretoria. ☎ 3422-693. Ambassador Tova Herzl.
Spain. Emb.: Calle Velazques 150, Madrid 28002. ☎ 4111357. Ambassador V. Harel.
Surinam (see Venezuela).
Swaziland. Emb.: Mbabane Hse., Warner St., P.O.B. 146, Mbabane. ☎ 42626. Ambassador.
Sweden. Emb.: Torstenssonsgatan 4, Stockholm. ☎ 6630435. Ambassador Zvi Mazel.
Switzerland. Emb.: Alpenstrasse 32, Berne. ☎ 3511-042. Ambassador Igal Antebi.
Tajikistan (see Uzbekistan).
Tanzania (see Kenya).
Thailand. Emb.: 75 Sukumvit Soi 19, Ocean Tower II 25th Floor, Bangkok 10110. ☎ 2049255. Ambassador Gershon Zohar.
Togo (see Côte d'Ivoire).
Tonga (see Australia).
Trinidad and Tobago (see Venezuela).
Tunisia. Interests Office. ☎ 795-695. Hd. Shalom Cohen.
Turkey. Emb.: Mahatma Gandhi Sok 85, Gaziosmanpasa, Ankara. ☎ 4463605. Ambassador David Sultan.
Turkmenistan. Emb.: (Closed).
Tuvalu (see Australia).
Uganda (see Kenya).
Ukraine. Emb.: GPE - S, Lesi Ukrainki 34, 252195, Kiev, Ukraine. ☎ 296-1731. Ambassador Anna Azari.
United Kingdom. Emb.: 2 Palace Green, Kensington, W8 4QB. ☎ 020-7957 9500. Opening Hours: Mon.-Thur. 09.00-18.00 and Fri. 09.00-14.00. Ambassador Ron Prosor (see also p.17).
United States of America. Emb.: 3514 International Dr, Washington, D.C., 20008. ☎ 364 5500. Ambassador D. Ayalon.
Uruguay. Emb.: Bulevar Artigas 1585/89, Montevideo. ☎ 4004164. Ambassador Yoel Selfek.
Uzbekistan. Emb.: 3A Kahhar Str., Tashkent. ☎ 152-5808. Ambassador Zvika Cohen-Itant.
Vanuata (see Australia).
Vatican, Via Michle Mercati 12, Rome 00197. ☎ 3619-8690. Ambassador Oded Ben-Hur.
Venezuela. Emb.: Avenida Franciso de Miranda, Centro Empresarial, Miranda 4 Piso Oficina 4-D, Los Ruices, Caracas. ☎ 2394-921. Ambassador Arieh Tena.
Vietnam. Emb.: PO Box 003, Thai Hoc, 68 Hguyen, Hanoi. ☎ 8433140. Ambassador Uri Levi.
Western Samoa (see Australia).
Zambia (see Zimbabwe).
Zimbabwe. Emb.: Three Anchor House, 6th floor, 54 Jason Moyo Ave, PO Box CY3191, Causeway. ☎ 756808. Ambassador Gershon Gan.

Main Political Parties

ISRAEL LABOUR PARTY
Est. 1968 by the merger of Mapai, Achdut Avoda and Rafi. Its programme: 'To attain national, social and pioneering aims, in the spirit of the heritage of the Jewish People, the vision of socialist Zionism and the values of the Labour movement'. *Chairman* Amir Peretz. Ad. 1 Urim St., Tel Aviv. ☎ 6899444.

KADIMA ('Forward')
A new party that defines itself as a broad popular movement which works to ensure the future of Israel as a Jewish democratic state. The party, formed by Ariel Sharon in November 2005 following the Israeli withdrawal from Gaza which spilt the Likud alliance, has adopted a 'centrist

and liberal' platform designed to uphold a moderate political agenda. *Chairman* Tsipi Livni. Ad.: Petah Tikva. ☎ 972-3-9788000 extension 157; Fax: 972-3-9788009. Website www.kadimahsharon.co.il.

LIKUD PARTY
Conservative Political Party. Dedicated to the principles of a free-market economy and the attainment of peace with security while preserving Israel's national interests. *Chairman* B. Netanyahu. Ad.: Metsudat Ze'ev, 38 King George St., Tel Aviv. ☎ (03) 621 0666. Email webmaster@likud.org.il

MERETZ-YACHAD
Meretz-Yachad was formed in 1992 by a merger of 'Ratz', 'Mapam' and the then 'Shinui' and was led by Shulamit Aloni. The party disbanded in 2003 and joined Yossi Belin's ' Shahar' party which renamed itself 'Yachad' but the original name re-emerged in 2005 under Belin's chairmanship. Meretz-Yachad defines itself as a Zionist Green left wing social democratic party. It has inherited Meretz's membership in the Socialist International. *Chairman* Yossi Belin. Ad.: Tel Aviv. Website www.meretz.org.il

GIL (Pensioners' Party)
Founded in 2005 by Rafi Eitan to fight the Knesset Elections, committed to support for pensioners.

NATIONAL RELIGIOUS PARTY
Created through the merger of Mizrachi and Hapoel Hamizrachi in 1956. Its motto 'The People of Israel in the Land of Israel, according to the Torah of Israel'. Ad.: Jerusalem. ☎ 02-537727. *Chairman* Binyamin Elon.

SHINUI ('Change' in English)
Est. 1971. A reformist and liberal party. Maintains that the rights of the individual are supreme and that all legislation must be measured against that principle. A democratic, secular, liberal, Zionist, peace-seeking party. *Chairman* Ron Levinthal. Ad.: 100 Hashmona'im Street, PO Box 20533, Tel Aviv 61200. ☎ 972-3-5620118.

AGUDAT ISRAEL
Founded in 1912 in Katowice, Poland. Its principle is that only the Torah unites the Jewish people. *Political Sec.* M. Porush. Central Off.: Haherut Sq., Jerusalem. ☎ 384357, and 5 Bardechefsky St., Tel Aviv. ☎ 5617844).

SHAS
Founded in 1984 as a representing Haredi Sephardi Judaism. Thte party was formed under the leadership of Rabbi Ovadia Yosef (a former Israeli Chief rabbi), who remains its spiritual leader today. *Chairman* Eli Yishai.

YISRAEL BEYTENU
A right-wing party formed by Avigdor Liberman in 1997 to create a platform for Russian immigrants who support a hard line in negotiations with the Palestinian Authority. Ad.: Jerusalem. Website www.beytenu.org.il.

HISTADRUT – GENERAL FEDERATION OF LABOUR IN ISRAEL
93 Arlozoroff St., Tel-Aviv. 62098
☎ 972 3 6921513. Fax 972 3 6921512. Email histint@netvision.net.il.
Chairman Amir Peretz, MK.
Histadrut, the largest labour organisation in Israel, is a democratic organisation which strives to ensure the welfare, social security and rights of working people, to protect them and act for their professional advancement, while endeavouring to reduce the gaps in society to achieve a more

just society. The executive body of Histadrut is separate from the elected body and the legislative body. The legislative and regulatory body, the Histadrut Assembly, represents the relative strengths of the different political groups of Israel.

Membership is voluntary and individual, and open to all men and women of 18 years of age and above who live on the earnings of their own labour without exploiting the work of others. Membership totals over 600,000, including workers from all spheres, housewives, the self-employed and professionals as well as the unemployed, students and pensioners. Workers' interests are protected through a number of occupational and professional unions affiliated to the Histadrut. The Histadrut operates courses for trade unionists and new immigrants and apprenticeship classes. It maintains an Institute for Social and Economic Issues and the International Institute, one of the largest centres of leadership training in Israel for students from Africa, Asia, Latin America and Eastern Europe, which includes the Levinson Centre for Adult Education and the Jewish–Arab Institute for Regional Cooperation. Attached to the Histadrut is a women's organisation, 'Na'amat', which promotes changes in legislation, operates a network of legal service bureaux and vocational training courses, and runs counselling centres for the treatment and prevention of domestic violence, etc.

Selected Educational and Research Institutions

HEBREW UNIVERSITY OF JERUSALEM
Founded in 1918 and opened in 1925 on Mount Scopus. When, contrary to the provisions of the Armistice Agreement after the War of Independence in 1949, access to Mount Scopus was denied by Jordan, the University functioned in scattered temporary quarters until a new campus was built on Givat Ram, and a medical campus in Ein Kerem, both in Jerusalem. After the Six-Day War of June 1967, the Mount Scopus campus was rebuilt and expanded. Today the University serves some 24,000 students in its seven Faculties: Humanities, Social Sciences, Science, Law, Medicine, Dental Medicine and Agricultural, Food and Environmental Quality Sciences (the latter located in Rehovot). There are 11 Schools: Education, Business Administration, Nutritional Sciences, Nursing, Occupational Therapy, Pharmacy, Public Health, Social Work, Veterinary Medicine, Library, Archive and Information Studies, and the Rothberg International School. The Jewish National and University Library is on the Givat Ram campus and there are about 100 research centres. The Magnes Press/Hebrew University publishes scientific and academic works. Five graduates and faculty have received Nobel prizes since 2001. *Ch. Bd. of Govs.* Charles H. Goodman; *President* Prof. Menachem Magidor; *Rector* Prof. Haim Rabinowitch. Ad.: Mount Scopus, Jerusalem, 91905.
☎ (02) 5882811. Fax (02) 5880058. Website www.huji. ac.il

TECHNION-ISRAEL INSTITUTE OF TECHNOLOGY
Established in 1924 as a small technical institute, it now has more than 12,500 students, making it the largest full-service university wholly dedicated to science and technology in Israel. The institute has 19 faculties and departments including: Aerospace, Biomedical, Chemical, Civil, Electrical and Industrial Engineering, and Architecture, Chemistry, Computer Science and Management, Medicine and Physics. The Technion is located on Mount Carmel. The main buildings include the Winston Churchill Auditorium and the Shine Student Union. It also has a graduate school, a school for continuing education and a Research & Development Foundation. *President* Prof. Y. Apeloig. Ad.: Technion City, Mount Carmel, Haifa 32000. ☎ (04) 829 4986. Fax (04) 823 5195. Website www.technion.ac.il

WEIZMANN INSTITUTE OF SCIENCE
The Institute engages in research in Mathematical Sciences, Chemistry, Physics, Biology, Biochemistry and Science Teaching. *President* Prof. D. Zajfman; *V. President* Prof. H. Garty. Ad.: POB 26, Rehovot 76100. ☎ 972-8-9343111. Fax 972-8-934107. Website www.weizmann.ac.il.

BAR-ILAN UNIVERSITY
Since its founding in 1955, Bar-Ilan has grown to become Israel's second-largest university,

comprising a modern 70-acre campus in Ramat Gan, outside Tel Aviv, with five regional colleges across Israel. Over 6,000 courses are taught in the faculties of exact, life and social sciences, humanities, Jewish studies and law, by 1,300 academic faculty to 25,000 students. Today, Israel's largest schools of education and social work and the premier Jewish studies faculty, operate at Bar-Ilan. Additionally, the university is home to world-class scientific research institutes in physics, medicinal chemistry, mathematics, brain reseach, economics, strategic studies, developmental psychology, musicology, archaeology, bible, Jewish law and philosophy, and more. Some 40 prominent universities around the world maintain academic cooperation agreements with Bar-Ilan. Every day, Israelis of widely varying backgrounds and religious beliefs work and study together in harmony at Bar Ilan. *Chancellor* Rabbi Prof. Emanuel Rackman; *President* Prof. Moshe Kaveh; *Rector* Prof. J. Menis. *Cor.* BIU, Ramat Gan, Israel 52900. ☎ 972-3-531-8111. *Student information:* 972-3-531-8274; Fax 972-3-535-1522. Website www.biu.ac.il.

BEN GURION UNIVERSITY OF THE NEGEV, BEERSHEVA
Founded 1969, the university comprises the following faculties: Humanities and Social Sciences, Natural Sciences, Engineering Sciences, Health Sciences, School of Management, the Kreitman School of Advanced Graduate Studies and the Jacob Blaustein Institute for Desert Research. *President* Prof. R. Carmi. Ad.: P.O. Box 653, BeerSheva, 84105. ☎ 08-6461279.

CENTER FOR JEWISH ART
Hebrew University of Jerusalem, Mount Scopus, Humanities Building, Jerusalem 91905. ☎ 972-2-5882281, Fax 972-2-5400105, Email cja@vms.huji.ac.il. Website www.lcja.huji.ac.il. *Dir.* Dr R. Talgam; *Acad. Chairman* Prof. R. Elior.

UNIVERSITY OF HAIFA
Established in 1963, Haifa is one of the seven accredited research universities in Israel. Academic instruction is conducted in the framework of the six Faculties (Humanities, Social Science, Law, Social Welfare and Health, Education, Sciences). Most of the 59 departments and schools offer bachelor, master and Ph.D. degrees. Research activity is carried out in the framework of research institutes and centres. The Research Authority encourages and coordinates research at the University. The total student body in the academic year 2007/8 numbered 16,500. *President* A. Ben-Ze'ev; *Rector* Y. Ben-Artzi. Ad.: Mount Carmel, Haifa 31905. Email webmaster@univhaifa.ac.il; Website www.haifa.ac.il. ☎ 972-4-824011. Fax 972-4-8288110.

ISRAEL NATURE AND PARKS AUTHORITY
3 Am Ve'Olamo Stret, Givat Shaul, Jerusalem 95463. ☎ 972-2-5005444. Fax 972-2-6529232. Website www.parks.org.il
The Authority is the result of a merger in 1968 of two bodies, one of which was in change of the Israeli nature reserves and the other of national parks and heritage sites in Israel

ISRAEL OCEANOGRAPHIC AND LIMNOLOGICAL RESEARCH
(Est. 1967) To develop knowledge and technology for sustainable use of marine and fresh water resources. *Dir.-Gen.* Prof. Barak Herut.Email barak@ocean.org.il. Ad.: Tel Shikmona, POB 8030, Haifa 31080. ☎ 04-8565200. Fax 04-8511911.

JERUSALEM ACADEMY OF JEWISH STUDIES (Yeshivat Dvar Yerushalayim)
53 Katzenellenbogen St., Har Nof, POB 5454, Jerusalem 91053. ☎ 6522817. Fax 652287. Email dvar@dvar.org.il; Website www.dvar.org.il. *Dean* Rabbi B. Horovitz, MA; UK office (Reg. Charity No. 262716), 1007, Finchley Rd., London NW11 7HB; *Chairman* A. Maslo. ☎/Fax 020-8458 8563. *Student Off.* Rabbi Taubman ☎ 020-8905 4930. (See p. 31)

JERUSALEM COLLEGE OF TECHNOLOGY
Est. in 1969 to train engineers and applied scientists within a religious framework. The College has a men's campus in Jerusalem-Machon Lev and Machon Naveh, and 2 campuses for

women-Machon Tal in Jerusalem and Machon Lustig in Ramat Gan, with depts., in Electro-Optics and Applied Physics, Medical Engineering, Electronic Engineering, Computer Sciences, Technology Management and Marketing, Software Engineering,Teacher training and Registered Nursing. The men's Jerusalem complex inculdes a Bet Midrash for Jewish studies; one year yeshiva academic programme for English-speaking student. The women's programmes also include religious studies. *President* Prof. J. Bodenheimer; *Rector* Prof. M. Steiner. Ad.: 21 Havaad Haleumi St., Jerusalem. ☎ 9722-6751111. Fax 9722-6422075. Email pr@mail.jct. ac.il

THE LOUIS GUTTMAN ISRAEL INSTITUTE OF APPLIED SOCIAL RESEARCH
Founded in 1946 to advise governmental, public and private bodies on research in social psychology, sociology, psychology and related disciplines. *Scientific Dir.* Prof. S. Kugelmass. Ad.: ☎ 231421.

MIKVEH ISRAEL AGRICULTURAL SCHOOL
The first agricultural school in Israel, it was founded by Charles Netter of the Alliance Isralite Universelle in 1870. The curriculum, in addition to training in agriculture, comprises instruction in the humanities, Jewish subjects, science, etc. Ad.: Mikveh Israel, Doar Holon, 58910. ☎ 03-842050.

ORT ISRAEL NETWORK
(Est. 1949) ORT Israel manages Scientific and Technological Colleges and schools for around 100,000 young and adult students yearly. *Dir. Gen.* Z. Peleg. Head office: 39 King David Blvd., Tel-Aviv 61160. ☎ 03-5203275. Email zvikap@admin.ort. org.il. Website www.ort.org.il,

TEL AVIV UNIVERSITY
The university sponsors studies and research in all the arts and sciences and includes among its faculties a department of space and planetary sciences, its observatory, at Mitzpe Ramon in the Negev, being the first in Israel. A science based industry utilising the university's manpower and equipment has been established. Its Graduate School of Business Administration was the first established in the country. There is a one year course which prepares new immigrants for entry into Israeli universities. *President* Prof. Itamar Rabinowitch; *Rector* Prof. Nili Cohen. Ad.: Ramat Aviv, Tel Aviv. ☎ 5450111.

WEITZ CENTER FOR DEVELOPMENT STUDIES
Founded in Rehovot in 1963, its main object is interdisciplinary research & training activities related to regional development in Israel and the developing world. Ad.: P.O.B. 12 Rehovot, 76100. ☎ 08-9474111. Fax 08-9475884. Email training@netvision.net.il. Website www.ort.org.il

THE ZINMAN COLLEGE OF PHYSICAL EDUCATION AND SPORTS SCIENCES AT THE WINGATE INSTITUTE
(Est. 1944) Teachers College for Physical Educators. Offers four-year Bachelor of Education course, including Teachers' Diploma. Specializations in early childhood, special education, sports for the disabled, posture cultivation, cardiac rehabilitation, physical activity for the elderly, public health, behaviour analysis, dance and movement, leisure and recreation education, nautical education, scouting education, sports media. Joint M.A. programme with Haifa University. Faculty of 200, student body of 900 full-time students, 1,500 in part-time in-service courses. Ad.: P.E. College at Wingate Institute, Netanya, Israel 42902. ☎ 972-9-863922. Fax 972-9-8650960. Email zinman@wincol.macam98.ac.il. Website www.zin.macam98.ac.il.

Selected Commercial Organisations
BANK OF ISRAEL
Set up by the Knesset in 1954. Its functions include those usually discharged by central banks. It issues the currency and acts as Government banker, and manages the official gold and foreign

reserves. The governor is chief economic adviser to the Government. Ad.: Rechov Eliezer Kaplan, Kiryat Ben-Gurion, Jerusalem, 91007. ☎ (2) 6552211. Fax (2) 6528805. Email webmaster@bankisrael.gov.il

ISRAEL-AMERICA CHAMBER OF COMMERCE AND INDUSTRY
Exec. Dir. Tamar Guy. Ad.: 35 Shaul Hamelech Blvd., Tel Aviv. ☎ (03) 6952341. Fax (03) 6951272. Email amcham@amcham.co.il Website http://amcham.co.il

ISRAEL-BRITISH CHAMBER OF COMMERCE
(Est. 1951.) 29 Hamered St., PO Box 50321, Tel Aviv 61502. ☎ (03) 5109424. Fax (03) 5109540. Email isrbrit@bezeqint.co.il; Website www.ibcc.co.il. *Chairman* L. Judes, *Exec. Dir.* F. Kipper.

MANUFACTURERS' ASSOCIATION OF ISRAEL
29 Hamered Street, Tel Aviv 68125 ☎ (03) 5198787. Fax (03) 5103154. Email trade@industry.org.il. *President* S. Brosh.

Other Selected Organisations

ASSOCIATION FOR THE WELLBEING OF ISRAEL'S SOLDIERS
(Ha'aguda Lemaan Hechayal. Charity No. 580004307) The Association for the Wellbeing of Israel's Soldiers was founded in 1942, during the Second World War, at a time when the young men of pre-state Israel were being drafted into the allied armies and the Jewish Brigade. The slogan back then was 'The Heart of the People is with its Soldiers', and this sentiment continues to guide the Association's activity today. *Head Off.:* P.O. Box 21707, Tel Aviv 61217. *Overseas Dept:* 60 Weizman St., Tel Aviv 62155. ☎ 03 5465135. Fax (03) 5465145. Email awis@awis.co.il

BETH HATEFUTSOTH
The Nahum Goldmann Museum of the Jewish Diaspora, which opened in Tel-Aviv in 1978, tells the story of the Jewish people from the time of their expulsion from the Land of Israel 2,500 years ago to the present. History, tradition and the heritage of Jewish life in all parts of the world are brought to life in murals, reconstructions, dioramas, audio-visual displays, documentary films and interactive multi-media presentation. *Dir.* Hasia Israeli. Ad: Tel-Aviv University Campus, Ramat-Aviv, POB 39359. Tel-Aviv 61392. ☎ 03-7457800. Fax 03-7457891. Email bhwebmas@ post.tau.ac.il. Website www.bh.org.il

CHIEF RABBINATE
The Chief Rabbinate consists of two joint Chief Rabbis and the Chief Rabbinical Council of 16. *Chief Rabbis* Rabbi Israel Yona Metzger (Ashkenazi) and Rabbi Shlomo Amar (Rishon Lezion, Sephardi). Ad.: Beit Yahav, 80 Yirmiyahu St., POB 36016, Jerusalem 91360; ☎ (02) 5313191; 531 3190. Fax (02) 537 7872. There are District Rabbinical Courts (Batei Din) in Jerusalem, Haifa, Petach Tikvah, Rehovot, Tiberias-Safad, Beersheba and Ashkelon.

ISRAEL MOVEMENT FOR PROGRESSIVE JUDAISM
13 King David Street, Jerusalem 94101. ☎ 02-6203448. Email iri@impj.org.il. Website www.reform.org.il.

THE ISRAEL MUSEUM
Ruppin Boulevard, Jerusalem, POBox 71117, Jerusalem 91710. ☎ 02-670-8811. Fax 02-563-1833. Website www.imj.org.il. Israel's leading cultural institution and a museum of world-class status, its 20-acre campus houses an encyclopaedic collection of art and archaeology, with special emphasis on the culture of the Land of Israel and the Jewish people. The Museum has the world's most extensive collections of the archaeology of the Holy Land, Judaica and the ethnography of Diaspora Jewish Communities, as well as significant and extensive hold-

ings in the Fine Arts, ranging from Old Masters to Contemporary Art, and including separate departments for Asian Art, the Arts of Africa and Oceania, Prints and Drawings, Photography, and Architecture and Design. The campus also includes the Shrine of the Book, which houses the Dead Sea Scrolls, the Billy Rose Art Garden and a Youth Wing. *Dir.* James Snyder.

ISRAEL NATURE AND NATIONAL PARKS PROTECTION AUTHORITY

The Authority is the result of a merger in 1998 of two bodies, one of which was in charge of the Israeli nature reserves and the other of national parks and heritage sites in Israel. Ad.: 78 Yirmeyahu St., Jerusalem. ☎ (02) 500 5444. Fax (02) 500 5444; 35 Jabotinsky St., Ramat-Gan 52511. ☎ (03) 576 6888. Fax (03) 751 1858.

JEWISH AGENCY FOR ISRAEL

Founded 1929; Reconstituted 1971. Constitutents are the World Zionist Organisation, United Israel Appeal, Inc. (USA), and Keren Hayesod. By reasons of its record and world-wide org. the Jewish Agency has come to be widely regarded as the representative org. of Jews the world over particularly in regard to the development of Israel and immigration to it. The governing bodies of the Jewish Agency are: the Assembly, which lays down basic policy, the Bd. of Governors, which manages its affairs between annual Assembly meetings, and the Executive, responsible for day-to-day operations. *Ch. Exec.* Ze'ev Bielski; *Ch. Bd.* R. L. Pearlstone; *Dir.-Gen.* M. Vigdor; *Sec.-Gen.* J. Schwarcz. Ad.: P.O. Box 92, Jerusalem 91000. ☎ 972 2 6202080. Fax 972 6252352. Email zeevik@jafi.org. Website www.Jewishagency.org

KEREN KAYEMETH LEISRAEL (Jewish National Fund)

P.O. Box 283, Jerusalem 91002. *World Chairman* Yehiel Leket; *Dir. Division of Resource and Development* Avi Dickstein. (Est. 1901) A non-profit organisation dedicated to the development of Israel through improvement of the quality of life through afforestation, water conservation, ecology and educational activities.

SHAMIR-ASSOCIATION OF JEWISH RELIGIOUS PROFESSIONALS FROM THE FORMER SOVIET UNION AND EASTERN EUROPE

6 David Yellin St., POB 5749, Jerusalem. ☎ 02-5385384. Fax 02-5385118. Email shamirbooks@bezeqint.net. Website www.shamirbooks.org.il. *Sec.* Bayla Granovsky.

WOMEN'S INTERNATIONAL ZIONIST ORGANISATION (Wizo)

(Reg. Charity No.: 580057321). 250,000 women, 100,000 of them in Israel, are members of this org. which maintains 800 institutions and services in Israel. World *President* Mrs M. Modai; *Chairman Exec.* Mrs H. Glaser. Ad.: 38 David Hamelech Blvd., Tel Aviv. 64237. ☎ 03-6923717. Fax 972-3-6958-267.

WORLD ZIONIST ORGANISATION

Founded by Theodor Herzl at the First Zionist Congress in Basle in 1897, it was the moving spirit in the events leading up to the establishment of the State of Israel in 1948. The 'Jerusalem Programme', adopted by the 27th Zionist Congress in Jerusalem in 1968, reformulated the aims of the Zionist Movement as: the unity of the Jewish people and the centrality of the State of Israel in its life, the ingathering of the exiles in the historic Jewish homeland by aliya; the strengthening of the State of Israel, which is founded on the prophetic ideals of justice and peace; preserving the uniqueness of the Jewish people by promoting Jewish and Hebr. educ. and upholding Jewish spiritual and cultural values; defending the rights of Jews wherever they live. The supreme body of the WZO is the Zionist Congress, to which delegates are elected by members of Z. Federations abroad and by the Z. parties in Israel. The two governing bodies elected by the Congress are: the Executive, and the Zionist General Council to which the Executive is responsible and which decides Z. policy between Congresses. *Ch. of Executive* S. Meridor. P.O. Box 92, Jerusalem 91000. ☎ (02) 602 2080. Fax (02) 625 2352. Email sallaim@ jazo.org.il.

YAD VASHEM

Har Hazikaron (Mount of Remembrance), Jerusalem, ☎ (02) 6443400. Fax (02) 6443443. POB 3477, Jerusalem 91034. Email general.information@yadvashem.org.il; www.yadvashem.org. The Holocaust Martyrs' and Heroes' Authority, Archives, Library, International School for Holocaust Studies, International Institute for Holocaust Research, Holocaust Museum, Art Museum, Hall of Remembrance, Hall of Names, Children's Memorial, Memorial to the Deportees, Avenue and Garden of the Righteous Among the Nations, Valley of the Communities, Synagogue.

British Settlements

The following are some of the settlements populated by large groups of immigrants from the United Kingdom and Ireland associated with the UJIA Israel (see below), which represents the Israeli Office of the Zionist Federation of Great Britain and Ireland. In some cases groups from Britain themselves established these settlements; in others, they joined existing settlements as 'reinforcement' groups.

Beit Chever (Kfar Daniel) established in 1951 near Ben Shemen by Machal exServicemen, mainly from Britain and South Africa. The 80 settlers there specialise in mixed farming.

Kfar Blum, established in 1943 north of Lake Hula, in Upper Galilee. Named after the late Leon Blum, it was the first kibbutz of British and American Habonim who joined forces with Latvian immigrants. Specialises in mixed farming and fish-breeding. Population over 700.

Kfar Hanassi was founded in 1948 in an abandoned Arab village called Mansura, located near the Jordan River on the Syrian border. The kibbutz was placed there to halt westward advancement by the Syrian Army in any attempt to cut Northern Gallilee in half. Two years later, the kibbutz was moved two kilometres westward to its present site, six kilometers from Rosh Pina. Until the Six Day War the kibbutz had been a border settlement. The kibbutz was named in honour of Israel's first president, Chaim Weizmann ('Kfar Hanassi' means 'Village of the President'). Most of the first settlers came from the Habonim Youth Movement in Britain, where they had spent the war years on training farms and had then joined the illegal immigration by sea to Israel. Many were refugees from Europe, brought over to Britain by the youth transports. There was also a small- er group from France and Australia among the first settlers. In the late 1950s the kibbutz was reinforced by another group from 'Habonim' Britain and it also absorbed individuals from America, South Africa and Israel. Most of the younger members (30-50) are Israelis, born on kibbutzim, and their spouses.

Affilation United Kibbutz Movement: Takam. Kfar Hanassi is a non-Orthodox kibbutz. There are services on high holy days and all Jewish festivals are celebrated communally, based upon old tradition and new kibbutz tradition (especially agricultural festivals).

Population 600, including 450 adults (250 of whom are members, and 150 children and 200 temporary residents.

Kibbutz institutions Main decisions in the kibbutz are decided in the general assembly and by polls. On a day-to-day basis, the kibbutz is run by committees, such as those for education, health, transport, housing, culture and finance. Members are usually electedn to serve on a committee for a period of two years.

Agriculture Avocado orchards, citrus groves, pears, lichees, field crops juniper nursery, poultry, and a small beef herd.

Industry Foundry for stainless-steel ball valves; guest houses offering bed and breakfast; hydroelectric plant.

Ad. Kibbutz Kfar Hanassi, Upper Galilee 1, 12305. ☎ 972-4-6914901. Fax 972-4-6914017.

Kfar Mordechai, founded near G'dera in 1950, is named after the late Mordechai Eliash, first Israeli Minister to Britain. Sponsored by the British Zionist Federation, Kfar Mordechai was the first middle-class settlement established for immigrants from Britain. Population about 60 families, half of them from Britain. Sugar is produced from locally grown beet. The moshav holds annual summer camps for local children.

Kibbutz Amiad is located in the southern part of Upper Galilee on the Tiberias-Kiryat

Shmona road. It is near the route of the ancient coast road which ran from Syria to Egypt. Amiad was founded in 1946 by a settlement group of Jewish youth who had served togeth-er in the Jewish underground defence force (Palmach) which operated during the British Mandate in Palestine. Upon completion of their military service, they received agricultural training in Kibbutz Geva and in 1946 they founded their own community. The site was cho-sen for its strategic value: it overlooks the main road to Upper Galilee. This strategic impor-tance grew during the War of Independence when the kibbutz housed an Israeli army base. Over the years the founders have been joined by Jewish immigrants from England and Holland. Near the kibbutz are the ruins of a medieval inn which are called 'Joseph's Well'. According the Arab tradition, this is the site of the well into which Joseph was thrown by his brothers. In addition, flint tools from the early Canaanite period have been found near the kibbutz.

Affiliations United Kibbutz Movement; Upper Galilee Regional Council.

Population Approximately 400, including 225 members and 150 children.

Agriculture Admiad farms approximately 15,000 dunams of land (3,750 acres) and has anoth-er 20,000 dunams (5,000 acres) of natural pastureland at its disposal. Major branches are orchards, both deciduous and subtropical, bananas, citrus, field crops, chickens and cattle.

Industry The kibbutz factory manufactures plastic and metal irrigation and waterfiltering equipment for agriculture, industry and municipalities which is marketed world wide. Other commercial initiatives include a winery, graphic design studio, engineering consultants - plastics, and a bed and breakfast motel.

Ad. Kibbutz Amiad, Mobile Post Galil Elyon 1, 12335. ☎ 972-6-6933550. Fax 972-6-6933866.

Kibbutz Bet Rimon is situated in the hills of Lower Galilee. Established in 1980 by members of British Bnei Akiva. Mixed farming with a large dairy herd. Manufacturers of light agri-cultural tools and parchment for Torah scrolls, Mezuzot and other religious items. Guest house and seminar centre on the kibbutz. A new community neighbourhood is being estab-lished beside the kibbutz for non-kibbutz residents. Population about 100.

Ad. Kibbutz Bet Rimon, D.N. Hamovil Natzeret Illit, 17950. ☎ 972-6-6509611. Fax 972-6-6412583.

Kibbutz Belt Ha'emek, established in 1949, near Nahariya, Western Galilee, is the third kib-butz of British Habonim. The original settlers were Hungarian members of the movement and these were later joined by British and Dutch Habonim. The settlement grows avocado, cotton, citrus fruit and bananas. Its activities include poultry, dairy and sheep farming. It has factories involved in the biochemical industry. Kibbutz Kadarim, in central Galilee overlook-ing the Kinneret, is an intimate rural community based on the principles of personal free-dom, social justice and communal participation. Established in 1980 with a core population of Israeli, Australian and New Zealand youth movement members, Kadarim today has a population of 50 adults, and 40 young children under the age of ten. Approximately 25 per cent of current members are Olim from Habonim-Dror Australasia. Kadarim is a unique com-munity, a partnership in which members retain their individual freedom: in particular, the right to make independent choices about their work-lives and finances. At the same time, a sophisticated system of communal services are provided to all members - and their children with particular emphasis on high-quality education and healthcare, communal cultural events and social security. Kadarim is presently absorbing new couples and families, and is currently pursuing the option of home-ownership within the kibbutz framework. Kadarim's businesses at present include manufacturing (Kapro spirit levels and measuring tools), agri-culture (mango and citrus groves, a chicken run and beef cattle), and a newly opened bed and breakfast tourist facility. Many members also pursue their chosen professions outside the kibbutz, in teaching, medicine, alternative therapies, engineering, law, social work and computers. ☎ 06-986222. Fax. 06-986208. E-mail kapro@inter.net.il

Kibbutz Lavi was founded in 1949 by members of 'British Bachad - TheOrganization of Religious Pioneers' and today is one of the 17 Religious Kibbutzim in Israel. It is located in Lower Galilee, ten minutes west of Tiberias. Over 125 families live in Lavi (total population 650) where they share a communal life based on Torah (Judaism) and Avoda (working and settling the Land of Israel).

Kibbutz Lavi is world famous for its two major businesses: the well-known Kibbutz Hotel Lavi, one of the pioneers of the kibbutz hospitality idea 30 years ago, which hosts tens of thousands of guests each year; and Kibbutz Lavi Furniture Industries, the world's largest manufacturer of synagogue furniture. Kibbutz Lavi is also involved in educational tourism through the Kibbutz Lavi Education Center, which offers programmes and seminars for groups interested in enriching their understanding of Judaism, the kibbutz way of life and the Galilee region. In addition, Kibbutz Lavi has a large dairy and poultry farm, orchards and numerous field crops. E-mail lavi@lavi.co.il

Kibbutz Yassu'r was founded in January 1949 in western Galilee, ten kilometres east of Acco. The first kibbutz of British members of Hashomer Hatzair. Population of about 350. Economy based on mixed farming, 'Tree of Knowledge' (educational assembly kits factory), 'Magi' sock factory and tourist services. Ad. D.N., Misgav, ☎ 20150. S04-9960111. Fax 04-9960113.

Kibbutz Zikim, established in 1949 near the northern border of the Gaza Strip by Romanian members of Hashomer Hatzair. British members of the movement have since joined the settlement. The kibbutz concentrates on arable farming and has large vineyards, in addition to citrus groves and banana plantations. Has foam rubber mattress factory. Population about 250.

Massuoth Yitzhak, near Ashkelon, a Hapoel Hamizrachi moshav shitufi established in 1949. Population nearly 300, including 20 families from Britain. Specialises in mixed farming. Moshav Habonim (Kfar Lamm) near Atlit, was set up in 1948 by Machal members from Britain and South Africa. Specialises in mixed farming and has factory making building insulating material. Runs summer camp for children. Population about 200.

Kibbutz Mevo Hama. Founded on Golan Heights overlooking Lake Kinneret by British and Australian Habonim after Six-Day War. In addition to beef cattle, ranching and cotton farming, they run a factory, specialising in plastic products.

Kibbutz Mishmar David. Two British Habonim garinim joined to revive this small kibbutz in Jerusalem corridor. Mixed farming and large offset print shop. Originally founded 1948. Population about 140.

Kibbutz Machanayim. Re-established in early 1950s in Upper Galilee near Rosh Pina with members of British Dror movement. Specialises in fruit orchards and mixed farming, particularly flowers. Has a precision tool factory. About 310 members.

Kibbutz Alumim is situated in the north-western Negev, approximately two miles south of Kibbutz Saad; closest towns are Sederot and Netivot. It is an hour's drive from Tel Aviv, one and a half hour's from Jerusalem, and half an hour from both Ashkelon and Beer Sheva. Alumim was established in 1966, by graduates of Bnei Akiva youth movement, and is a member of the Religious Kibbutz Movement (HaKibbutz HaDati). Initially intended as a border settlement, its status changed when Israel captured the Gaza Strip in the 1967 Six Day War. Alumim's livelihood comes mainly from agriculture: field crops, citrus orchards, avocado plantations, a dairy herd of aproximately 250 milking cows, and rearing chickens for meat. Alumim has no industry but recently opened up several kibbutz branches to outside customers - for example, the garage, carpentry shop, electrical shop and the metalwork shop (now 'Shelah Systems', building computerised automated materials handling systems). There are comfortable, air-conditioned guest rooms and, as a religious kibbutz, all religious facilities are provided. Alumim has a population of approximately 400, with about 80 families and various temporary groups such as Aliyat HaNoar, Nahal Army groups and youth groups visiting from abroad. Kibbutz Alumim had two large influxes of British Bnei Akiva graduates, in the early 1970s and mid-1980s, and they now comprise about 20 per cent of the population, taking on many of the leading communal roles. Kibbutz Alumim, although past its fortieth birthday, is young in spirit, financially and socially stable, and set to face the challenges of the twenty-first century.

Ad. Kibbutz Alumim, D.N. HaNegev 85138. ☎ 08 993711. Fax 07 993 9700. Guest Rooms Office 08 9937300. Correspondence to Sarah Jane Landsman, Kibbutz Secretary.

Kibbutz Adamit. Founded after Yom Kippur War by young members of Hashomer Hatzair from various Western countries. Right on Lebanese border. Farming. Moshav Sde Nitzan was founded in 1973 by a group of immigrants from English-speaking countries including England, US, Canada, New Zealand, Australia and South Africa. We started with 20 families as a small farming community in the western Negev. We are now celebrating our twenty-fifth anniversary having grown to 74 families, 14 of whom joined us during the last three years. About 50 per cent of original families are still here. The original families were joined over the years by Israeli families. Our main occupation is still agriculture, primarily flowers for export. We also have mango orchards and recently planted 1,600 dunam to citrus. The moshav is, in fact, a small village of independent families. In the future we are planning to open a section of up to 100 lots for non-farming families. Our area of the country is entirely kibbutzim and moshavim and very underpopulated. We have a school complex shared by all the moshavim taking children from 18 months through high school. We also have a regional medical centre, including, in addition to medical doctors and visits from specialists, a pharmacy, a dental clinic and a physical therapy wing. Closest city is Beersheva.

Kibbutz Tuval was established in January 1981 by immigrants from British and South African Habonim-Dror as well as graduates of the Israeli Scout Movement. In the course of its history, the kibbutz has maintained a mix of Anglo-Saxons and Israelis, and this has very much shaped the unique quality of the community. The kibbutz today has 35 members and has recently taken a decision to enlarge its ranks by establishing a 'Community Village' which will run in parallel with the kibbutz. The plan is for families from both Israel and abroad to join the community. The primary sources of income are a dairy herd, chicken houses, a kiwifruit plantation and the Tuval Seminar Centre and guest houses, providing educational workshops for both English- and Hebrew-speaking groups.
Ad. Kibbutz Tuval, D.N. Bikat Bet HaKerem, 20136. ☎ 972-9907-907. Fax 972-4-9907-900.

UJIA Israel (incorporating the British Olim Society). Head Office: 76 Ibn Gvirol St., POB 16266, Tel Aviv 61162. ☎ 03-6965244. Fax 03-6968696. Email israel@ujia.org.il. *Man. Dir.* There are branches in Jerusalem and Karmiel. UJIA Israel is the official representative of the United Jewish Israel Appeal of Great Britain & Northern Ireland, formerly known as the British Olim Society (est. 1949 in order to assist and support new immigrants from the UK settling in Israel).

UJIA Israel represents UJIA UK on all campaign and renewal-related activities and aims at strengthening the ties between British Jewry and Israel, through projects, guests, missions and Israel Experience youth programmes.

UJIA Israel provides comprehensive absorption services to immigrants from the UK, Australia and Scandinavia and promotes absorption needs of new immigrants in Israel.

During 1990, the BOS Charitable Trust was established as a funding conduit for new immigrant activities and programmes in Israel, essentially aimed at helping the disadvantaged and less fortunate.

Israel English Speaking Legal Experts P.O.Box 2828, Jerusalem . ☎ 5820126; Fax 6232742. Provides legal advice and representation.

Israel, Britain and the Commonwealth Association (IBCA), Industry House, 29 Hamored St., Tel Aviv 68125. Fax (03) 5104646. Branches in Haifa and Jerusalem. The main aims of the Association are to encourage, develop, and extend social, cultural and economic relations between Israel and the British Commonwealth. *Chairman* L. Harris; *Vice-Chairman* Dr A. Lerner; *Hon. Sec.* Madelaine Mordecai; *Contact* Freida Peled.

ITALY (34,500)

The Jewish community of Italy, whose history goes back to very early times, increased considerably at the time of the Dispersion in C.E. 70. During the Middle Ages and the Renaissance there were newcomers from Spain and Germany. Rich syns. as well as rabbinical schools, yeshivot, and printing houses were set up and became known in many countries. During the first years of fascism Italian Jews did not suffer; only after 1938 (under Nazi pressure) were racial laws introduced and, during the German occupation from 1943 to 1945 nearly 12,000, especially from Rome, were murdered or banished. The number of persons registered as Jews now is around 35,000. The most important communities are those of Rome (15,000), Milan (10,000), and Turin (1,630), followed by Florence, Trieste, Livorno and Venice and other centres.

ROME
*Central organisation: Unione delle Comunità Ebraiche Italiane, 00153 Roma, Lungotevere Sanzio 9. ☎ 5803670. Fax 5899569. *President* R. Gattegna.
Community: Lungotevere Cenci, 00186. ☎ 6840061. Fax 68400684. Rabbinical office. Fax 68400655.
Chief Rabbi, Dr R. di Segni. (6875051/2/3.
Jewish Agency, Corso Vittorio Emanuele 173, 00185. ☎ 68805290. Fax 6789511.
Synagogues, Lungotevere Cenci; Via Catalana; Via Balbo 33.
Syn. of Libyan refugees-Via Padova 92. ☎ 44233334.

MILAN
Community, Via Sally Mayer, 2, 20146. ☎ (02) 48311002. Fax 02/48304660.
Synagogue, Via Guastalla, 19, 10122. ☎ (02) 5512029. Fax (02) 55192699.

JAMAICA (350)
The Jewish settlement here, first composed of fugitives from the Inquisition, goes back before the period of the British occupation in 1655. During the eighteenth century there was an Ashkenazi influx from England. Jewish disabilities were abolished in 1831. There were former-ly congregations at Port Royal, Spanish Town (two syns.) and at Montego Bay (1845-1900). The Ashkenazi and Sephardi communities in Kingston merged into one in 1921, the last of eight which once flourished. Recently published: The Island of one People: an Account of the History of the Jews of Jamaica, M. Delevante & A. Alberga, 2006
*United Congregation of Israelites, Synagogue Shaare Shalom, Duke St. (Syn. built 1885, rebuilt 1911.) *Acting Spiritual Leader* Stephen C. Henriques. ☎ 876-924-2451.
Hillel Academy (Est. 1969).
Home for the Aged (Est. 1864). Managed by the Jewish Ladies Organisation. *Chairman* Mrs Sandra Phillipps.

JAPAN (2,000)
The first Jewish community in Japan (at Yokohama) dates back to 1860 and old Jewish ceme-teries exist in Yokohama, Kobe and Nagasaki. Jews were among the early foreign settlers. In 1940, 5,000 Jewish refugees from Germany and Poland arrived in Kobe, subsequently leaving for the USA and Shanghai. There are now about 2,000 Jews in Japan. About 1,000 live in the Tokyo area. There is a cong. of about 40 families in Kobe.
*Jewish Community of Japan, 8-8 Hiroo 3-chome, Shibuya-Ku, Tokyo 150-0012. ☎ 3400-2559. Fax 03-3400-1827. Emailoffice@jccjapan.or.jp. *M.* Rabbi Henri Noach; *Man.* Kosher meals available on Shabbat and during the week. Advance notification requested.

KAZAKHSTAN (7,000)
The Jews of Kazakhstan are predominately Russian-speaking Ashkenazim and identify with Russian culture, many of whom arrived only in the 1940s, fleeing the Nazis or 'exiled' by Stalin. There a a number of Bukharian Jews and Tat (Caucasion Mountain Jews). Some 7,000 Jews now remain in the country. Almaty is the main Jewish centre. Smaller Jewish communities are spread out across this large country, in Karaganda, Chimkent, Astana, Semiplatinsk, Kokchetav, Dzhambul, Uralsk, Aktyubinsk, Petropavlovsk and several villages.
Association of Jewish Communities of Kazakhstan, 66/120 Buhar-zhirau St., Almaty 480057, ☎/ Fax 7 3272 45-00-43

KENYA (100 families)
Jewish settlement in East Africa dates from 1903, when the British Government offered the Zionist Organisation a territory in the present Kenya for an autonomous Jewish settlement. The offer was refused but not unanimously and shortly afterwards a few Jews settled in the colony. Later, a number of Central European Jewish refugees settled here. The Jewish population today is about 100 families, most of whom are Israelis, together with others employed in the diplo-matic services and NGOs. See 'Jews of Nairobi 1903–1962', by Julius Carlebach. The communi-

ty marked its centenary with a new history by Cynthia Salvadori 'Glimpses of the Jews of Kenya: the Centennial History of the Nairobi Hebrew Congregation 1904–2004, 5664–5764.
*Nairobi Hebrew Congregation, PO Box 40990, 00100. ☎ 2222770.
Email info@nhc.co.ke. Website www.nhc.co.ke(Est. 1904.) *Rosh Kehilla* Dr D. Silverstein; *H.T.* M. Abbema; *H. Sec.* Ms A. Zola.

KIRGHIZSTAN (1,500)

There are around 1,500 Jews in Kirghizstan today, out of a 1979 population of 7,200. Over 80 per cent of the Kirghiz Jews reside in the capital, Frunze, with small communities in the towns of Osh, Kyzyl-Kiya, Kara-Kol, Tokmak and Kant.

LATVIA (10,800)

The current Jewish population is 10,800, with 8,250 Jews living in Riga. Most Jews in Riga speak Russian, although some speak Latvian and a few speak Yiddish. Rezekne, Kraslava, Jurmal, Jelgava, Jekabpils, Ventspils, Liepaja (450), Ludza and Daugavpils (Dvinsk, 550) support smaller Jewish populations. About 25 towns still have Jewish cemeteries (see 'A Guide to Jewish Genealogy in Latvia and Estonia' by Arlene Beare).

REZEKNE
Syn.: Kaleyu St.

RIGA
Jewish Community of Latvia, 141 Lacplesas St, LV-1003. Email latvia@fjc.ru. Community leaders: Arkadi Suharenko (secular), Dovid Kogan (religious), Chief Rabbi of Latvia.
Synagogue, 6/8 Peitavas St. ☎ (371) 721-4507, *M.* Rabbi M. Glazman ☎ 67-22207. *Chairman* D. Kogan ☎ 67-214507
Chabad Lubavitch School and community, 141 Lacplesa St. ☎ 67-2720-4022; Rabbi Sh. Kot.
Jewish Community Centre, Museum and Library (LOEK), 6 Skolas St. 226050. ☎ (371) 67-28-95-80. *Comm. Leader* A, Suharenko
Old Jewish Cemetery, 2/4 Liksnas St is now a park. New Jewish Cemetery, 4 Lizuma St, Shmerli.
Mikva, Mei Menachem, Bruninieku 43/3. ☎ 29506721.

LEBANON (100)

In the civil war which broke out in 1975 most of the 2,000 Jews left the country. About 100 remain in Beirut.

LIBYA (50)

About the time that Libya became an independent State in 1951 there was a mass emigration of most of its 37,000 Jews to Israel, and only very few remain in Tripoli.

LITHUANIA (11,000)

Jewish Community of Lithuania, 4 Pylimo, Vilnius 2001. ☎ 2-613-003. Fax 3705 212 7915. Email jewishcom@post.5ci.lt

KAUNAS
Syn.: 13, Ozheskienes St.
Jewish Community Offices, 26B Gedimino St. ☎ 203-717. Fax 370 7203717.

VILNIUS
Syn.: 39 Pylimo St. ☎ (5) 261-2523.
Vilna Gaon Jewish State Museum, Pamelkalnio Str. 12, Vilnius. ☎ (5) 262-0730.
There are also communities in Druskininkai, Klaipeda, Panevezys and Shiauliai.

LUXEMBOURG (1,000)

There are today about 1,000 Jews in Luxembourg, the majority in Luxembourg City. Since the

French Revolution they have enjoyed the same rights as other citizens. Before 1933 there were 1,800 Jews in the country; by 1940 the influx of German and other refugees had brought the Jewish population to about 5,000. The main syn. was destroyed by the Nazis.

Synagogue: 45 Avenue Monterey, Luxembourg City 2163.
Chief Rabbi, Joseph Sayagh, 45, Ave Montery. *Chairman* M. Bulz, ☎ 452314.
Or Chadash Liberal Jewish Community (affiliated to LJ). *Corr.* 29 rue Leandre Lacoix, 1-1913. ☎ 316 594 Email lljc@liberaljudaism.org. *Chair.* Erica Peresman
Esch/Alzette: Synagogue, 52 Rue du Canal. *Chairman* R. Wolf, 19 rue du Nord 4260 Esch/Alzette.

MACEDONIA (Republic) (250)

The Jewish presence in Macedonia (former Yugoslavia) dates back to the 6th century B.C.E. with a considerable influx during the Roman Second-Temple period. The largest migration of Jews to Macedonia took place in the early Ottoman period following the expulsions from Spain and Portugal. In such cities as Bitola, Shtip, and Skopje Jews came to prosper in medicine, law and trade, as well as more traditionally in agriculture. By 1910 there were more than 90, 000 Jews in Macedonia, mostly in Salonika (now Greek Thessaloniki, q.v.) by which time Ladino was widely spoken in that city, and the Shabbat was widely observed throughout all sectors. When Greece took over the city in 1912, prohibitions on residence were brought in and a mass emigration to other parts of Europe and to North America began. Nonetheless, still by 1941 there were over 100,000 living in Macedonia when the effects of the Nazi-domination of Europe and the pressures of the Holocaust took their toll. Those who survived Auschwitz and Treblinka mostly settled in Israel and few returned to Macedonia. Today perhaps some 250 Jews reside in the country, chiefly in Skopje, Tetova, Shtip and Betola.

SKOPJE

Jewish Community of the Republic of Macedonia, Borka Talevski St., No. 24, 1000 ☎ 3214799 Fax 3214880. ezrm   *President* Mr. Z. Sami; *Gen. See.* Ms Z. Mucheva
Synagogue "Beth Ya'akov", at the same address. Tel 3237543. *Chief Rabbi* Rabbi A.M. Kozma (2008-).
Social Jewish Aid"La Benevolencija" *Rep* Mr. V. Mizrahi.
Holocaust Foundation of the Jews in Macedonia (FHEM). *President* Mrs L. Mizrahi; *Vice-President* Mr. P. Lazarevski: *Sec.* Ms V. Sarkisjan. ☎ 23122697. Email fhem @on.net.mk

MALTA (50)

There have been Jews in Malta since pre-Roman times and, just before the Spanish-directed expulsion in 1492, one-third of the population of the then capital city, Mdina, was Jewish. After the coming of the Knights of St John, the only Jews in Malta became their captives and slaves, held for ransom. This situation persisted until Napoleon overthrew the Knights and released all their prisoners. Following the defeat of the French by the British, a small Jewish community was established early in the nineteenth century which has survived until the present day. There were never more than about 20 families with a normal total of under 100 people, and it was financially unable to build a synagogue. However, following a successful appeal, launched in 1998, local and international donations enabled the acquisition and conversion of premises into a Jewish Centre and Synagogue. The Malta Jewish Community now, once again, owns its own property, after a gap of over 500 years.
Jewish Community of Malta, *President* Abraham C. Ohayon, 1 Enrico Mizzi Street, Ta-Xbiex, MSD 02 ☎ 00356-21237309; Fax 00356-21249410. Email ohayon@digigate.net. *Deputy President* Shelley Tayar, Villa Tayara, Tric ic cawl, Kappara. SGN 06 ☎ 00356-21386266, Fax 00356-21385901, Email shell@onvol.net; *Lay Leader* Reuben Ohayon.
Jewish Foundation of Malta. *President* R. Eder.

MAURITIUS

There is no permanent Jewish community. The Jewish cemetery contains the graves of 125 refugees from Europe. They were part of a group of 1,700 Jews denied entry to Palestine and interned on the island during 1940-1945. *Corr.* P.M. Birger. P.O. Box 209, Port Louis, Mauritius. ☎ 2020200. Fax 2083391.

MEXICO (40,000)

The Jewish presence in Mexico dates back to the Spanish Conquest, although it was not until the final years of the nineteenth century and the beginning of the twentieth that a mass immigration of Jews from Syria, the Balkanic countries and eastern Europe, fleeing from persecution and poverty, laid the foundations of the modern Jewish Mexican community. Today's Jewish population is about 40,000, the majority in Mexico City. The city has twelve Jewish day-schools and several Yeshivot attended by up to 90 per cent of Mexican Jewish children. There are communities in Guadalajara, Monterrey and Tijuana.

MEXICO CITY

*Central Committee of the Jewish Community in Mexico, Cofre de Perote 115, Col. Lomas Barrilaco, 11010 Mexico DF. ☎ 5520-9393. Fax 5540-3050. *Exec. Dir.* Mauricio Lulka, comitecentral@prodigy.net.mx.

Tribuna Israelita (analysis and opinion office of the Jewish Community in Mexico), Cofre de Perote 115, Col. Lomas Barrilaco, 11010 Mexico DF. ☎ 5520-9393. Fax 5540-3050. Email mailto:tribuna@tribuna.org; Website tribuna.org.mx. *Dir.* Renee Dayan-Shabot.

Synagogues: Askenazi, Acapulco 70, Col. Roma, ☎ 5211-0575; Bet El (Conservative) Horacio 1722, Polanco. ☎ 9112-9950; Beth Israel (Conservtive, English speaking), Virreyes 1140, Lomas. ☎ 5540-2642; Sephardic, Av. de los Bosques 292A, Tecamachalco. ☎ 1085-1400; Monte Sinaì (Damascan), Fuente de la Huerta 22, Tecamachalco. ☎ 5596-9966; Maguén David (Aleppo), Bernard Shaw 10, Polanco. ☎ 5814-0600.

Jewish Sport Center, Manuel Avila Camacho 620, Lomas de Sotelo. ☎ 2629-7400.

MOLDOVA (40,000)

Federation of the Jewish Communities of Moldova, ☎ (3732) 541023. Fax (3732) 541020. Email sbf@hotmail.co.il; info@jewishmoldova.org. Website www.moldova.org.

CHISINAU

Syn.: 8 Habad-Lubavici Str., 2012. ☎ (3732) 541 023/052. Fax (3732) 541 020. Website www.kishinev.org.

Towns with Jewish populations include: Tiraspol, Baltsy, Bendery, Soroky, Ribnitsa, Rezina and Orxey.

MOROCCO (5,000)

The Jews of Morocco have a history dating back to the times before it became a Roman province. Under Moslem rule they experienced alternate toleration and persecution. The expulsion from Spain and Portugal brought many newcomers to Morocco. In the nineteenth century many of the oppressed Jews sought the protection of Britain and France. The former French Protectorate removed legal disabilities, but the economic position of most Jews remained very precarious. During the Vichy period of the second World War Sultan Mohamed V protected the community. Before the est. of the independent kingdom of Morocco in 1956 many emigrated to Israel, France, Spain and Canada, and the present Jewish pop. is est. at 7,000 under the protection of King Mohammed VI.

CASABLANCA

*Community Offices, 12 rue Abou Abdallah Al Mahassibi. ☎ 22222861.Fax 22266953.

Synagogues: Temple Beth El, 61 rue Jaber Ben Hayane. ☎ 22267192; Em Habanim, 14, rue Ibn Rochd; Benarroch, 24 rue Ibn Rochd; Tehilla Le David, Blvd. du 11 Janvier; David Hamelekh, rue Khemisset (Anfa).

Casablanca Jewish Meseum, 56 rue Abbou Dhabi. ☎ 22994940.
International Organisations: American Joint Distribution Committee, 3 rue Rouget de
Lisle. ☎ 22274717. Fax 264089; Ittihad-Maroc, 13 rue Addamir Al Kabir. ☎ 222003-72.
Fax 2003-09; OSE, 151 bis, blvd. Ziraoui. ☎ 22267891. Fax 278924; Lubavitch-Maroc, 174
blvd. Ziraoui. ☎ 22269037; Ozar Hatorah (Religious School Organisation), 31 rue Jaber Ben
Hayane. ☎ 22270920; D.E.J.J., 85 Blvd Moulay Youssef. ☎ 22267486; Neve Shalom, 140
Taha Houcine ☎ 022 267676; David Hamelech, rue Khemisset, Anfa, ☎ 061 411033
There are also coms. in Fez, Kenitra, Marrakech, Meknès, Rabat, Tangier, Tetuan, and Agadir.

MOZAMBIQUE
Jewish Community of Mozambique, c/o Israel Consulate, R. Fonseca Levy, PO Box 2972, Maputo.

NETHERLANDS (25,000)
From the sixteenth century onwards the Jews of the provinces of Holland had a distinguished
historical record. Since 1792 they have had the same constitutional and civil rights as all other
citizens. In 1940 there were approximately 140,000 Jews in the country, but as the result of
the Nazi occupation only some 25,000 remain, of whom about half are in Amsterdam.
Rabbinate Ashkenazic Community: **Amsterdam**: Chief Rabbi Aryeh L. Ralbag, Dayan
Eliezer Wolff, Rabbi Shmuel Katz (secr), **The Hague**: Rabbi Shmuel Katzman, **Rotterdam**:
Rabbi Raphael Evers, **Other communities** Rabbi Binyomin Jacobs.
Rabbinate Sephardic Community: Rabbi Dr P. Toledano.
Rabbinate Liberal Jewish Congregations: Rabbi D. Lilienthal (Amsterdam); Rabbi A.
Soetendorp (The Hague); Rabbi Dr E. van Voolen (Arnhem).

AMSTERDAM
***Ashkenazi Community Centre and Offices**: Van der Boechorststraat 26, 1081 BT.
☎ 646 00 46. Fax 646-4357.Email info@nihs.nl
***Sephardi Communal Centre**: Mr Visserplein, 3, 1011 RD. ☎ 624 53 51. Fax 625-4680.
Email info@esnoga.com
Ashkenazi Synagogues: Jacob Obrechtplein; Lekstr 61; Gerard Doustr. 238; Van der
Boechorststraat, 26; Straat van Messina 10, Amstelveen.
East European Jews' Synagogue: G. van der Veenstr. 26-28.
Portuguese Synagogue, Mr Visserplein 3. ☎ 624 5351. Email info@esnoga.com
Liberal Community Centre and Synagogue. J. Soetendorpstraat, 8, 1079.
☎ 6423562. Fax 642-8135. Amsterdam and Dutch Liberal Rabbinate. ☎ 644-2619.Fax 642-
8135. Email ljg@x$4all.nl.

Beit Ha'Chidush Postbus 14613, 1001 Amsterdam ☎ 235 247204 Email info@bei-
thachidush.nt Website www.beithachidush.nt
Zionist Offices: Joh. Vermeerstr. 24. Netzer-Kadima at the Liberal Community Centre.
Jewish Historical Museum: Synagogue Bldg., J. D. Meyerplein.
Anne Frank House, Prinsengracht 267. **Judith Drake Library** at the Liberal Community Centre.
   Other small coms. are in Amersfoort, Arnhem, Bussum, Eindhoven, Groningen, Haarlem, The
Hague, Rotterdam, Utrecht and Zwolle.

NETHERLANDS ANTILLES (West Indies)

CURAÇAO (350)
A Sephardi Jewish settlement was est. in 1651, making it the oldest community in the New
World. The Mikve Israel-Emanuel Syn. building, which dates from 1732, is the oldest in continuous use in the western Hemisphere; there is a small Jewish museum in the synagogue
compound. About 350 Jews live in Curaçao. The cemetery (Bet Hayim) at Blenheim (est. 1659)
is the oldest in the Americas.
Synagogues: Sephardi-Mikve Israel-Emanuel, Hanchi di Snoa 29, P.O. Box 322.
☎ 4611067. Fax 4654141. *M*.

Ashkenazi: Shaarei Tsedek, Magdalenaweg, P.O. Box 498. ☎ 7375738. *M.*
Israel Consulate: Dr P. Ackerman, Blauwduifweg 5. ☎ 7365068. Fax 7370707.

NEW CALEDONIA (120)
There are approximately 120 Jews on this French possession in Pacific

NEW ZEALAND (8,000)
The settlement of Jews in New Zealand dates from the establishment of British sovereignty in 1840. In the first emigrant ships were a number of Jews from England. But still earlier a few Jewish wayfarers had settled in the northern part of New Zealand, including John Israel Montefiore, a cousin of Sir Moses Montefiore, who settled at the Bay of Islands in 1831, Joel Samuel Polack, one of the earliest writers on the country, in which he travelled in 1831-37, and David Nathan, who laid the foundations of the Jewish community in Auckland in the early 1840s.

The Wellington Jewish com. was founded by Abraham Hort, under the authority of the Chief Rabbi, on January 7, 1843, when the first Jewish service was held. Communities were later est. in Christchurch and Dunedin and other parts of the South Island. From the earliest times Jewish settlers have helped to lay the foundation of the commercial and industrial prosperity of the country.

The number of Jews in New Zealand at the cᶜnsus of 2001 was over 8,000. Most live in Auckland and Wellington. There has been recent settlement from the former Soviet Union, South Africa and Israel.

Jews have occupied most important positions in New Zealand including that of Administrator, Prime Minister and Chief Justice. There have been six Jewish mayors of Auckland and two of Wellington. See: History of the Jews in New Zealand by L. M. Goldmann (1959), A Standard for the People: The 150th Anniversary of the Wellington Hebrew Congregation, edited by S. Levine (1994) and Auckland Jewry Past and Present, edited by A. and L. Gluckman (1993).
*New Zealand Jewish Council. *President* S. Goodman PO Box 4315, Auckland 1001. ☎ (09) 523 4297 Fax (09) 523 4238. Email: nzjc@ajc.org.nz.
N.Z. Council of Christians & Jews, PO Box 68-224, Newton, Auckland. ☎ (09) 638-7710.
Council of Jewish Women of N.Z., PO Box 27-156, Wellington. *President:* Mrs S. Payes. ☎ (04) 567-1679.
*Zionist Federation of N.Z. N. Lawrence, P.O. Box 4315 Auckland.
New Zealand Jewish Chronicle. *Ed.* M. Regan
Wizo Federation. *President:* Mrs Clements, 80 Webb St., Wellington.

WELLINGTON (1,000)
Regional Jewish Council. *Chairman* D. Zwartz ☎ 475 7622.
Hebrew Congregration. *President* G. Stone. 80 Webb St. ☎ 3845 081.
Beth-El Synagogue, opened 1870 rebuilt 1929, resited in Jewish Community Centre and opened 1977.
Jewish Community Centre, 80 Webb St. Moriah Kindergarten open daily.
Moriah College. (Primary Day Sch.) (Est. 1987.) P.O. Box 27233. ☎ 3842401.
Progressive Jewish Congregation (Temple Sinai). *President* L. Young, P.O. Box 27 176. ☎ 3850 0720.
New Zealand Jewish Chronicle (monthly), PO Box 27156, Wellington. ☎ (04) 934 6077.
2. *Ed.* M. Regan.
Zionist Society. *President* D. Schnellenberg, 80 Webb Street.

AUCKLAND (1,600)
Hebrew Congregation. *President* J. Barnett. PO Box 68 224. ☎ 373 2908.
Beth Israel Synagogue, 108 Greys Ave. PO Box 68 224. ☎ 373-2908 (Est. 1841).
Beth Shalom, The Auckland Congregation for Progressive Judaism, 180 Manukau Rd., Epsom. *President* L. Lipman.
Email bshalom@ihug.co.nz. Website www.bethshalom.org.nz.
Kadimah College and Kindergarten, Greys Ave.
Zionist Society, (Est. 1904). PO Box 4315.

There are smaller coms. in Christchurch (640), Hamilton (50) and Dunedin (60).

NORWAY (2,000)

The Jewish population of Norway is estimated to be about 2,000. There are two organised communities, Det Mosaiske Trossamfund Oslo (about 1,000 members) and Det Mosaiske Trossamfund Trondheim (about 130 members).

The community in Oslo is very active, with regular synagogue services (Friday night and Saturday as well as all holidays), a kindergarten, afternoon classes for children of school-going age, regular meetings and seminars for members of different age-groups, a home for the elderly as well as a shop which supplies kosher food.

*Det Mosaiske Trossamfund (Jewish Community): *President* A. Sender, Bergstien 13 0172 Oslo ☎ 23205750. Fax 23205781. Email adam@dmt.oslo.no. Website www.dmt.oslo.no.

Synagogue and Community Centre, Bergstien 13, Oslo 0172. Postbooks 2722, St Hanshaugen, 0131.

Synagogue and Community Centre, Ark. Cristiesgt. 1, Trondheim. ☎ 7352 6568. *President* R. Abrahamsen.

PAKISTAN

Two Jewish families remain in Pakistan's port of Karachi. The Magen Shalom Syn. built in 1893, at Jamila St. and Nishta Rd. junction, was reported closed in 1987.

PANAMA (9,250)

The community has been in existence for nearly 150 years and numbers nearly 9,250, with 8,420 in Panama City.

*Consejo Central Comunitario Hebreo de Panama, Apartado 55-0882-Paitilla, Panama City. ☎ (507) 263-8411. Fax (507) 264-7936. Email sion@plazareg.com *Contact* Sion Harari (*President*).

Beth El, (Cons), Apartado 3087, Panama 3, Panama City.

Congregation Shevet Ahim, (Orth.), Apartado 6222, Panama 2, Panama City.

Kol Shearith Israel, (Reform), Apartado 4120, Panama City. (225-4100. Fax 225-6512.

There are smaller coms. in Colon (100) and David (100).

PARAGUAY (900)

The community, which has been in existence since 1912, numbers about 900.

Consejo Representativo Israelita del Paraguay (CRIP), General Diaz 657. Asuncion, POB 756. ☎ 41744.

PERU (3,000)

Marranos were prominent in the early development of Peru. Many Jews suffered martyrdom during the centuries that the Inquisition prevailed. The present Jewish population is about 3,000 nearly all living in Lima. There are an Ashkenazi community and a Sephardi community.

*Synagogue and Communal Centre, Húsares de Junin 163 (Jesus Maria), Lima. ☎ 241-412, 31-2410.

Sociedad de Beneficencia (Sefaradim), Enrique Villar 581, Lima.

Sociedad de Beneficencia Israelita de 1870, Esq Jose Gálvez 282 Miraflores.

PHILIPPINES (250)

Jewish Association of the Philippines, 110 H.V. de la Costa, crn. Tordesillas West, Salcedo Village, Makati, Metro Manila 1227. ☎ 2815 0265; (Rabbi) 2815 0263. Fax 2840-2566. Email jap.manila@gmail.com. *President* P. Rosenberg.

POLAND (6,000)

Jews first settled in Poland in the twelfth century. Casimir the Great, the last Polish King of the Piast dynasty (1303–70), was a staunch protector of the Jews. Periods of Jewish freedom and prosperity have alternated with periods of persecution and, sometimes, expulsion. Jewish learning flourished in the land from the sixteenth century onwards. Mystic Chasidism, based on study of the Cabala, had its wonder rabbis. Famous Talmudic scholars, codifiers of the ritual and other eminent men of learning were produced by Polish Jewry. Of the 3,500,000 Jews in Poland in 1939 about three million were exterminated by Hitler. Many put up an heroic fight, like those of the Warsaw Ghetto in 1943. Under half a million fled to the West and the Soviet Union. Until 1968 the Jewish population was estimated at 50,000. Large-scale emigration followed the anti-Jewish policy pursued from then on under the guise of 'anti-Zionism'. Today's Jewish pop. is estimated at between 6,000 and 8,000.

WARSAW

Synagogue and Religious Organisation: Zwiazek Religijny Wyznania Mojzeszowego (Religious Union of Mosaic Faith),Warsaw 00-105. ul. Twarda 6. ☎ 20-43-24. 20-06-76.

Secular Organisation: Towarzystwo Spoleczno-Kulturalne Zydów w Polsce (Social and Cultural Association of Jews in Poland), Zarzad Glowny (Central Board), Warsaw, 00-104, Plac. Grzybowski 12/16, ☎ 20-05-57, 20-05-54.

CIESZYN

Fundacja Instytut Victora Ullmanna Cieszyn, Office: 1, Gorney Rynek, 43-400 Cieszyn. (Est: 2004) *Fr. & Exec.Dir.* Jacqueline Bowen Cole.
E-mail: office@viktorullmann.freeserve.co.uk; *Hon.vice president* Wojciech Kilar and Sir John Tavener; *Hon.Patrons* Pierre Boulez, James Gibb, George Benjamin, Eva Fox Gal, Daniel Barenboim. Paul Aron Standford, Dr. Yehuda Bauer.

Strange Passenger International Music and Arts Festival Cieszyn Poland, *Artistic Dir.* Jacqueline Bowen Cole, 1 Gorny Rynek, 43-400.
Email: sp@viktorullmann. freeserve.co.uk; www.strangepassengerfestivacieszyn.org. A festival to honour Victor Ullmann and his contemporaries in Cieszyn, Poland.

CRACOW

Religious Organisation: Zwiazek Religijny Wyznania Mojzeszowego, Kongregacja (Religious Union of Mosaic Faith, Congregation) Cracow, 31-066, ☎ 56-23-49. ul. Skawinska 2. Rabbi Avraham Flaks.

Secular Organisation: Towarzystwo Spoleczno-Kulturalne Zydów w Polsce (Social and Cultural Association of Jews in Poland), (Cracow Section), Krakow, 31-014, ☎ 22-98-41.ul. Stawkowska 30.

Jewish organisations also exist in the following 16 towns: Bielsko-Biala, Bytom, Chrzanów, Dzierzoniów, Gliwice, Katowice, Legnica, Lódz, Lublin, Piotrkow, Swindnice, Szczecin Wa³brzych, Wroc³aw, and Zary.

PORTUGAL (1000)

Between the 12th century, date of the founding of the Potuguese nationality, and the 15th century the Jews lived in Portugal in relative peace: and enjoyed religious freedom, Talmudic law prevailed and they were able to carry out all of their economic, scientific and cultural activity in the midst of the Christian society, thus contrbuting greatly to its development.

This coexistence was brutally interrupted with the proclamation by King Dom Manuel I of the Expulsion Edict in 1496, with forced conversions and later, the establishment of the Inquisition. For three centuries, up to the 1800's, ther were officially no Jews in Portugal. However, and in spite of these hardships, a number of marrano groups survived, especially in the Northeast regions of the country.

At the beginning of the 19th century a large number of Jews from Gibraltar and Morocco started settling in Lisbon, Faro and the Azores Islands. Although their presence was well tolerated and they intergrated into Portuguese society with ease, the Community would only be legally recognised after the Republican Revolution of 1910, which seperated the State from the Church.

The implantation of democracy in 1974 reinforced religious freedom and protection forall religious affiliations against doiscrimination.

There exist now three Jewish communities in Portugal: the Jewish Community of Lisbon, founded by Jews from Gibraltar and Morocco in the 19th Century; the Jewish Community of Porto, founded in 1923 by Captain Barros Basto, a marrano who converted to Judsism with the Mekor haim Synagogue, financed by the Kadoorie family of Hong Kong, and the Jewish Community of Belmonte, founded by former marranos, with their own synagogue and cemetery. A small community has also been created in Faro on account of the restoration of the Jewish cemetery of Faro, which dtes from the 19th Century.

LISBON
*Communal Offices, Rua do Monte Olivete, 16 r/c 1200-280 Lisbon. ☎ 213 931130, Fax 213 931139, Email: secretaria@cilisboa.org. Website www.cilisboa.org
Jewish Centre, Rua Rosa Araujo 10. ☎ 357 20 41.
Synagogue: 59 Rua Alexandre Herculano (Sephardi), 1250-010 Lisbon. ☎ 213388 15 92.
Maccabi Country Club, Rua Gonçalves Correia 8, Albarraque 2635-037 Rio de Mouro.
☎ 213 881592

PUERTO RICO (1,500)
Some 1,500 Jews live in Puerto Rico, which is an associated Commonwealth of the USA. A syn. is maintained as well as a pre-school, an afternoon school, adult educ. classes and other organisations.
*Shaare Zedeck Synagogue (Con.) and **Community Centre**, 903 Ponce de León Ave. Santurce, P.R. 00907-3390. ☎ (809)724 4157. Fax (809)722 4157.
Temple Beth Shalom (Reform), 101 San Jorge & Loiza St., Santurce, P.R. 00911. ☎ 721 6333.

ROMANIA (10,000)
Jews have been resident in the territory that now forms Romania since Roman times. Today they number 10,000, of whom some 4,000 live in Bucharest, and the rest in 160 communities. There are 42 syns., three of them in Bucharest, 11 Talmud Torahs and 8 kosher restaurants. A newspaper in Hebrew, Romanian and English, *Realitatea*, with a circulation of 4,500, is published fortnightly. There is a Yiddish theatre in Bucharest, the publishing house Hasefer, a Museum of Jewish History and a Holocaust Exhibit.

BUCHAREST
Chief Rabbi:
*Federation of Jewish Communities, Centre of Romanian Jewish History Research. Mamulari Str., 4, Etaj 1, Apt. 1, Sectorul 3, 4. ☎ /Fax 012-3151045. *Dir.* D. Hîncu.

RUSSIA (440,000) (Russian Federation)
Before World War I, Russian Jewry was the largest Jewish community in the world. For centuries, until the Revolution of 1917, the Jews were cruelly persecuted under the antisemitic policy of the Tsars. The subsequent Soviet regime virtually destroyed the former religious life and organisation of the Jewish communities. According to the official Soviet 1989 census the Jewish population was 1,449,000 but recent mass emigration will have reduced that total. The break up of the Soviet Union following August 1991 is reflected in the new entries under the separate republics, e.g. Belarus, Latvia, Moldova, Ukraine, etc. Population figures are difficult to estimate but some 400,000 Jews have left the country since 1989.

MOSCOW (200,000)
Synagogues: Central ul. Archipova 8; Marina Roshcha, 2nd Vysheslavtsev per.5-A.
World Union for Progressive Judaism - Orosir, 2 Usevolovsky Pereulot, Entrance 1, Moscow 119034. Email wupj-orosir@yandex.ru. Rabbi Gregory Kotlyar.

ST PETERSBURG (100,000)
Synagogue: 2 Lermontovsky Prospekt. (216-11-53.
Jewish Association 'LEA', Ryleeva 29-31, 191123. ☎ 812-2756104. Fax 812-2756103.
Jewish Tourist and Research Center HA-IR), Stachek 212-46, 198262. ☎ (812) 184 12 48. Fax (812) 310 61 48.

Other centres of Jewish population include those of Astrakhan, Berdichev, Beregovo, Birobidjan, Irkutsk, Krasnoyarsk, Kuybyshev, Kursk, Malakhavka, Nalchik, Novosibirsk, Ordzhonikidze, Penza, Perm, Rostov Saratov, Sverdlovsk, Tula.

SERBIA (3,500)
(Republic)
Jews have lived in this territory since Roman times. In 1941 there were about 34,000 Jews in the territory of the former Yugoslavia and some 29,000 perished in the Holocaust.

BELGRADE (BEOGRAD)
*Federation of Jewish Communities of Serbia, Ulica Kralja Petra 71a, III, 11000 Belgrade. POB 512 Belgrade. ☎ 2621837 2910363. Fax 2626 674. *President* A. Nećak; *Sec.* D. Danon.Email office@savezscg.org
Jewish Community of Belgrade, Ulica Kralja Petra 71a/II. ☎ 2622 449. Fax 2624 289*President* Miroslav Herzog. ☎ 2623-535, 3281-468. Email jcb@ikomline.net
Synagogue, Maršala Birjuzova 19. M. Rabbi Y. Asiel (2008-).
Jewish Historical Museum, Ulica Kralja Petra 71a/I. ☎ 2622 634. *Dir* V. Radovanovic Email muzej@eunet.yu
Communities also in Kikinda, Novi Sad, Niš, Panševo, Priština, Sombor, Subotica, Zemun and Zrenjanin.

SINGAPORE (240)
The Jewish community of Singapore dates from about the year 1840. The street in which Jewish divine service was first held in a house is now known as Synagogue Street. The first building to be erected as a syn. was the Maghain Aboth, opened in 1878. This was rebuilt and enlarged in 1925. A second syn., Chesed El, was built in 1905. The Jewish community consists mainly of Sephardim (of Baghdad origin) but with some Ashkenazim. The affairs of the community are managed by the Jewish Welfare Board, which is elected annually.
*Jewish Welfare Board, 24/26 Waterloo Street, 187950. ☎ 337 2189. Fax 336 2127. *President* Jacob Ballas. *H. Sec.* Mrs M. Whelan.
Synagogue Maghain Aboth, 24 Waterloo Street, 187950. ☎ 337 2189. Fax 336 2127. Email jewishwb@singnet.com.sg. Open daily except Monday mornings. Mikvah available. *Community Rabbi* Mordechai Abergel. ☎ 737-9112. Email mordehai@singnet.com.sg.
Synagogue Chesed El, 2 Oxley Rise, 238693. Open Mon. only.
United Hebrew Congregation (Reform), 65 Chulia St., OCBC Centre #31-00 East Lobby, 049513. *Pres.* K. Lewis. ☎ 536-8300.

SLOVAKIA (6,000)
Written evidence of Jewish settlement in Slovakia goes back to the 13th c. but there may have been Jews in the area as far back as Roman times.

BRATISLAVA
Central Union of Jewish Religious Coms. (UZZNO), *H. Chairman* Prof Pavel Traubner, PhD.; *Exec. Chairman* Fero Alexander. Ad.: Kozia 21/II, 81447 Bratislava. (+421-2-54412167. Fax 421-2-54411106. Email uzzno@netax.sk.
Synagogue, Heydukova 11-13, Services: Friday, Saturday.
Bratislava Jewish Com., Kozia 18, 81103 Bratislava. ☎ 421-2-54416949. Email noba@znoba.sk.
Bnai Brith 'Tolerance' in Bratislava. *President* Dr. J. Alner,
Pension Chez David Accommodation and Restaurant, Mikvah. Fax +421-2-54412642. ☎ +421-2-54413824, 54416943. Email recepcia@chezdavid.sk.
Mausoleum of Chatham Sopher, Orthodox and Neological Jewish cemeteries.

KOSICE
Jewish Religious Community, Zvonárska 5, 04001 Kosice. Kosher restaurant, Mitvah.

President Dr P. Sitar. ☎ /Fax +421-55-6221272.
Synagogue: Puskinova St.
There are Jewish coms. in Galanta, Dunajska Streda, Presov, Banska Bystrica, Nove Zamky, Komarno, Zilina, Nitra.

SLOVENIA (78)
Jewish Community of Slovenia, Tr-aška Cesta 2, 1000 Ljubljana; PO Box 37, Ljubljana 1101. ☎/Fax 368-2521836. Email jss@siol.net. Website www. jewishcommunity.si.

LJUBLJANA
Syn.: ☎ 315-884.

SOUTH AFRICA (75,000)
The Jewish Community began as an organised body at Cape Town on the eve of the Day of Atonement, Friday, September 26, 1841. Its first title was 'The Society of the Jewish Community of the Cape of Good Hope', but there had been Jewish residents at the Cape long before the foundation of the Hebrew Congregation. In fact, Jews have been connected with the Cape of Good Hope from the earliest days of South African history.

Jewish pilots accompanied the Portuguese navigators. During the 17th and 18th centuries when the Dutch East India Co. ruled the Cape, there were no professing Jews but it is probable that some individuals were of Jewish origin. After the British occupation in 1806, freedom of religion was extended to all Cape inhabitants and Jews eventually held official positions in the administration.

For further particulars see the 'History of the Jews in South Africa', by Louis Herrman (Victor Gollancz, 1930), The Jews in South Africa: A History, ed. by G. Saron and L. Hotz (Oxford Univ. Press, 1956), The Vision Amazing, by Marcia Gitlin (Johannesburg 1950), South African Jewry, 1976-77, ed. by Leon Feldberg (Alex White, 1977), Jews and Zionism: The South African Experience (Gideon Shimoni, 1980), South African Jewry, ed. by Marcus Arkin (Oxford Univ. Press 1984), Jewish Roots in the S.A. Economy, by Mendel Kaplan (Struik 1986), Chapters from S.A. History, Jewish and General, by Nathan Berger (Kayor, Vol. 1, 1982; Vol. 2, 1986), Jewry and Cape Society, by Milton Shain (Historical Publication Society, 1983), Tiger Tapestry, by Rudy Frankel (Struik, 1988), The Jews of S.A. - What Future? by Hoffman and Fischer (Southern, 1988), Founders and Followers Johannesburg Jewry 1887-1915, Mendel Kaplan (Vlaeberg 1991), The Roots of Antisemitism in South Africa, by M. Shain (Wits U.P. 1994); The Jewish population in South Africa, by A. Dubb (Kaplan Centre, 1994).

The Jews being scattered throughout the territory of the Republic, the organisation of Jewish religious life varies with the density of the Jewish population, which is about 75,000. Over recent years several thousand members of the community have emigrated, especially to Israel, Canada, Australia, the UK and the US, but the com. has been strengthened by the arrival of some Jews from Zimbabwe and Israel. In all, there are about 50 organised Jewish coms.

The largest coms. are in Johannesburg (50,000), Cape Town (16,000), Durban (3,000) and Pretoria (1,500).

The South African Jewish Board of Deputies is the representative institution of South African Jewry. The B.o.D. for the Transvaal and Natal was founded in 1903, and a similar organisation at the Cape in 1904. The two were united in 1912. The headquarters of the Board is in Johannesburg, and there are provincial committees in Cape Town, Pretoria, Durban, Bloemfontein, East London, and Port Elizabeth.

COMMUNAL INSTITUTIONS
*S.A. Jewish Board of Deputies, 2 Elray Street, Raedene, 2192, PO Box 87557, Houghton 2041. ☎ 645-2523. Fax 645-2559. Email infobod@beyachad.co.za. Website www.jewish.org.za. *National Dir.* Mrs W. Kahn.
S.A. Zionist Federation, PO Box 29203, Sandringham 2131. ☎ 485-1020. Fax 640-6758. *Dir. General* Mrs I. Brito-Feldman.
S.A. Board of Jewish Education, PO Box 46204, Orange Grove 2119. ☎ 480-4700. *Gen. Dir.* Rabbi C. Kacev.
S.A. Jewish Ex-Service League. Chairman P. Bailey PO Box 29213, Sandringham 2029 ☎

786-5408.
Union of Orthodox Synagogues of South Africa, 58 Oaklands Rd, Orchards 2192, Johannesburg. ☎ 485-4865. Fax 640-7528. Rabbi Dr. W. Goldstein, Chief Rabbi of S. Africa. **S.A. Rabbinical Association**.

S.A. Union for Progressive Judaism, POB 1190, Houghton 2041. ☎ 646-7903. Fax 646 7904. Email saupj@worldonline.co.za.
Bnai B'rith, PO Box 8425 Johannesburg, 2000. ☎ 648-3804.
Johannesburg Jewish Helping Hand & Burial Society, Private Bag X7, Sandringham 2131. ☎ 532-9600. Email chevragroup@jhbchev.co.za
Kollel Yad Shaul, 5 Water Lane, Orchards 2198. ☎ 728-1308.
Lubavitch Foundation of S.A., 55 Oaklands Rd., Orchards 2192 Johannesburg. ☎ 640-7561.
ORT SA, PO Box 95090, Grant Park, 2051. ☎ 728-7154.
Union of Jewish Women of S.A., PO Box 87556, Houghton 2041. ☎ 011-645 2593 Email ujwexec@beyachad.co.za.
Mizrachi Organisation of S.A., PO Box 29189, Sandringham 2131. ☎ 640 4420.

JOHANNESBURG
United Hebrew Congregation (est. 1915).
Beth Din. ☎ 485-4865.
Main synagogues. Glenhazel Hebrew Cong., Long Ave., Glenhazel, 2192. Tel: 640-5016 (Orth). Sydenham/Highlands North Heb Cong., 24 Main St., Rouxville, 2192 (Orth) ☎ 640-5021. Temple Emanuel, 38 Oxford Road, Parktown, 2193 (Reform). ☎ 646-6170; Great Park, Glenhovse Rd., Houghton. ☎ 728-8531.

CAPE TOWN
Western Province Zionist Council, 87 Hatfield St., 8001. PO Box 4176, 8000. ☎ 021-464-6700. Fax 021-461-5805. Email wpzc@ctjc.co.za. *Dir.* J. Berman.
The Jacob Gitlin Library, Albow Centre, 88 Hatfield St., 8001 ☎ 021-462-5088. Fax 021-465-8671. Email gitlib@netactive.co.za.
Union of Orthodox Synagogues of S.A., and Beth Din, 191, Buitenkant St. ☎ 461-6310. Fax 461-8320. *Exec. Dir.* M. Glass.
Main synagogues. Great Syn. Government Ave. (Orth.), Temple Israel, Upper Portswood Rd., Green Point (Reform).

STEPNEY
Beit Shalom Synagogue, PO Box 47, Stepney SA 5069 ☎ 08 8362 8281. Email: bshalom@bshalomadel.com

SOUTH KOREA
About 25 Jewish families live in Seoul, the capital. Religious services are held on Friday evenings at the 8th U.S. Army Religious Retreat Centre. ☎ 7904-4113.

SPAIN (25,000)
Jews were settled in Spain in Roman times. They made an outstanding contribution to culture and civilisation in medieval times. Persecution by the Church culminated in the Inquisition and the Expulsion in 1492. Today there are about 25,000 Jews in Spain, of whom 8,000 live in Barcelona, 9,000 in Madrid 2,000 in Malaga, and the rest in Valencia, Seville, Alicante, Majorca and the Canary Islands. The Jewish com. in Melilla has 1,500 members and that in Ceuta 1,000. Ancient syns. of pre-Inquisition times (now put to other uses) exist in Cordoba, Seville and Toledo. The first synagogue and community centre in Spain since the Inquisition opened in Barcelona in 1954. The Madrid com. was legally recognised in 1965 and the city's first syn. was consecrated in 1968. Synagogues and Community Centres:

MADRID
Federación de Comunidades Judias de España, Miguel Angel 7, 1°C 28010 Madrid. ☎ 91 700 1208 Fax 91 391 5717 Email fcje@fcje.org. Website www.fcje.org
Comunidad Judía de Madrid, Balmes, 3- 28010. ☎ 91 591 3131. Fax 91 594 1517.Email secretaria@comjudiamadrid.org. Website www.comjudiamadrid.org.

BARCELONA
Barcelona: **Comunidad Israelita de Barcelona**, Avenir, 24 08001. ☎ /Fax 93 2006148. Email info@cibonline.org; Website www.cibonline.org

Benidorm Comunidad Judía de Alicante, C/ Berlín Edificio Parque Loix 3500 Benidorm Contact Harvey Bourne. Email hbourne@telrefonica.net
Alicante Comunidad Judia, C/ Juan de Herrera, 19 – entreplanta Alicante Contact Armando Azubel. Email armandoazubele@ig.com.br.
Mallorca: Comunidad Judía de Baleares, Monsenyor Palmer 3 – 07014 – Palma de Mallorca Contact Mr Abraham Barchilón, Email a.barchilon@wanadoo.es
Malaga: Comunidad Israelita de Malaga, Duquesa de Parcent, 8, 3º 29001 Alameda Principal, 47, 2ºB. *President* Mr Hayon. Email cimalaga@cimalaga.org
Marbella: Comunidad Judía de Marbella, Jazmines 21 (Urb. El Real) – 29600 – Marbella ☎ 952-859 395 Fax 952 765 783. Email cimarbella@yahoo.es *President* Mr. Cohen
Melilla: Comunidad Israelita de Melilla, Duquesa de la Victoria, No19, 52001. ☎ 952-674057.
Seville: Comunidad Israelita de Sevilla, 41003-Bustos Tavera, 8. ☎ 427-5517. Email communidadjudiaesevilla@hotmail.com
Valencia: Comunidad Israelita de Valencia, Ingeniero Joaquin Benlloch 29 2ª⁻46006-Valencia. Email civ@ctv.es.
Aviv Judia: Masorti Community Aviv (Est, 2004) Email cjvaviv@gmail.com. Website www.cjaviv.org *President* W. Teplitsky
Tenerife 38001-Jewish Community, P. Abecasis, Ap. de Correos 939, Villalba Hervas, Santa Cruz de Tenerife.
Torremolinos Comunidad Israelita de Torremolinos, Av. Palma de Mallorca 55, 29620 ☎ 952 602 583. *President* Mr Stern. Email rs@yonah-by.info.
Las Palmas de Gran Canaria, *President* Mr Bendahan, Ap. Correos 2142, Las Palmas 35080.

SRI LANKA
Corr. Mrs A. Ranasinghe, 82 Rosmead Place, Colombo 7. ☎ 9411-2695642.

SURINAM (300)
Surinam is one of the oldest permanent Jewish settlements in the Western Hemisphere. The Sephardi Cong. was est. about 1661, but earlier settlements in 1632, 1639 and 1652 have been reported. Some 225 Jews are members of the two synagogues, where Sephardi services are conducted.
Neve Salom Synagogue, Keizerstr. 82, Paramaribo.
Sedek Ve Salom Synagogue, Herenstr. 20, Paramaribo. The synagogue has been restored but is no longer used for services. *President* René Fernandes, Commewijnestraat 21, Paramaribo. ☎ 400236; PO Box 1834, Paramaribo. ☎ 597-411998; Fax 597-471154; 597-402380 (home).

SWEDEN (20,000)
In 1774, the first Jew was granted the right to live in Sweden. In 1782 Jews were admitted to three Swedish towns, Stockholm, Gothenburg and Norrköping, and the Karlskrona com. was founded soon afterwards. After the emancipation of the Jews in Sweden in 1870, coms. were founded in Malmö and several other towns. Today there are some 20,000 Jews in Sweden, 9–10,000 of them in Stockholm. Others are in Gothenburg, Malmö, Borås and smaller centres.

STOCKHOLM

*Judiska Församlingen (Jewish community), Wahrendorffsgatan 3, Box 7427 103 91 Stockholm. ☎ 08-587-85800. Fax 08-587-85858. Email kansli@jfst.se.Website www.jfst.se
Jewish Centre, Nybrogatan 19. ☎ 08-587-85865.
Synagogues: Wahrendorffsgatan 3 (Great Synagogue, Masorti); Adas Jeshurun, Riddargatan 5 (Orthodox); Adas Jisroel, St. Paulsgatan 13 (Orth.).
Jewish Museum, Hälsingegatan 2. ☎ 08-310143 Email info@judiska-museet.se

MALMÖ

Judiska Församlingen (Jewish Community), Box 4198,203 13 ☎ 46 40 611 8460 Fax 46 40 23 4469 Email jfm@algonet.se

GÖTEBORG

Judiska Församlingen (Jewish Community), Östra Larmgatan 12, 411 07 ☎ 46 31 10 9400 Fax 46 31 711 9360 Email kansli@judiskaforsamlingen.se Website www.judiskaforsamlingen.se

SWITZERLAND (17,600)

The Jews were expelled from Switzerland in the fifteenth century, and it was not until early in the seventeenth century that they received permission to settle in the Lengnau and Endingen coms. In 1856 immigration increased, most of the immigrants coming from Southern Germany, Alsace and Eastern Europe. The Jewish pop. is now about 17,600 The largest coms. are in Zurich (6,252), Basle (2,005) and Geneva (3,901). The Swiss Federation of Jewish Communites comprised in 2005 18 coms. with a total membership of 14,000.

*Swiss Federation of Jewish Communities, PO Box 2105, 8027 Zurich. ☎ (043) 3050777. Fax (043) 3050766. Email info@swissjews.org. Website www.swissjews.org.

American Joint Distribution Committee, European Headquarters, 75 rue de Lyon, 1211 Geneva 13. ☎ (022) 344.90.00.

OSE, rue du Mont-Blanc 11, 1201 Geneva. ☎ (022) 732.33.01.

B'nai B'rith, *President* W. de Botton, c/o CIG, 21 av Dumas 1206 Geneva. ☎ (022) 731.69.80.

Basle Communal Centre, Leimenstrasse 24. ☎ (061) 279.98.50. Email igb@igb.ch. Website www.igb.ch; Synagogues: (Orth. Ashk.) Leimenstrasse 24, Rabbi Arie Folger, Leimenstrasse 45. ☎ (061) 271.60.24; (Orth. Ashk.) Ahornstrasse 14, Rabbi Benzion Snyders, Rudolfstrasse 28. ☎ (061) 302.53.91.

Berne Communal Centre and Synagogue, Kapellenstrasse 2. ☎ (031) 381.49.92, Email info@jgb.ch. Website www.jgb.ch. *M.* Rabbi D. Polaner.

Fribourg Synagogue, 9 rue Joseph-Philler. ☎ (026) 322.16.70.

Geneva Communal Centre, Rue 21av. Dumas 1206. ☎ (022) 317.89.00. Email secretgen@comisra.ch. Synagogues: (Orth. Ashk.) Grande Synagogue Beit Yaakov, Place de la Synagogue; (Orth. Ashk.) Machsike Hadass, 2 Place des Eaux Vives. Rabbi Abraham Schlesinger. ☎ (022) 735.22.98; (Seph.) Hekhal Haness, 54ter, route de Malagnou. ☎ 736.96 ; (Ref.) Liberal Syn., 12 Quai du Seujet. ☎ (022) 732.32.45. Rabbi François Garaï. ☎ (022) 738.19.11.

Lausanne Communal Centre, 3 ave. Georgette. [Case Postale 336, 1001 Lausanne]☎ (021) 341.72.40.
Email secretariat@cilv.ch Website www.cilv.ch. Synagogue: 1 Ave. Juste-Oliver (corner Ave. Florimont). Chief Rabbi Alain Nacache. ☎ (021) 311.71.68.

Zürich Communal Centre, Lavaterstrasse 33, 8002. ☎ (044) 3283.22.99.
Email info@icz.org, Website www.icz.org; Synagogues: (Modern Orth. Ashk.) Nüschelerstrasse 36, 8001. M. Rabbi M. Y. Ebel ☎ 283 22 44
☎ (044) 3283.22.99. Rabbi Dr Zalman Kossowsky. ☎ (044) 283.22.44; (Orth. Ashk.) Freigutstrasse 37, 8002. ☎ (01) 241.80.57, Email irg@bluewin.ch ; (Orth. Ashk.) Erikastrasse 8,8003. ☎ (044) 463.80.33. Rabbi Schoul Breisch. ☎ (044) 61.30.40; Beth Chabad, Rüdigerstrasse 10,8055. ☎ (044) 4289.70.50; Minyan Sikna, Sallenbachstrasse 40. ☎ (044)

455.75.75; Minyan Wollishofen, Etzelstrasse 6.8038 ☎ (044) 482.70.50; (Ref.) Or Chadasch, Hallwylstrass 78,8004. ☎ 043 322 0314. Email info@jlg.ch. Website www.jlg.ch; Rabbi R. Bar-Ephraim.

SYRIA (1,500)
The remnants of this historic Jewish community resident in Damascus, Aleppo and Kamishli, have been estimated at 1,500 following recent aliyah.

DAMASCUS
President of Rabbinical Court Rabbi Ibrahim Hamura, Ecole Ben-Maymoun, Kattatib. Al-Ittihad Al-Ahlieh School (Alliance Israélite), rue El Amine.

TAHITI (FRENCH POLYNESIA) (130)
Some 130 Jews live on the Pacific Island of Tahiti, in French Polynesia.

TAIWAN (180)
More than 30 Jewish families live on the Island, most of them in Taipei, the capital.
Taiwan Jewish Community Centre. Information: F. Chitayat. ☎ 2861-6303. Mailing address: Donald Shapiro, Trade Winds Company, P.O.Box 7-179, Taipei 10602, Taiwan. ☎ 886-2-23960159. Fax 886-2-23964022. Email dshapiro@ topz.ficnet. Services are held at Landis Hotel, 41 Min Chuan East Road, Sec. 2, Taipei. For details contact Rabbi Dr E. Einhorn at ☎(886) 2597-1234. Fax (886) 2596-9223. Email mailto:einhorn@ttn.net.

TAJIKISTAN (1,000)
The Jews of Tajikistan were divided into two groups, the Bukharan Jews and the later arrivals of Ashkenazi origin, many of whom came as refugees from Nazi-occupied areas of the Soviet Union. The Bukharan Jews have a long history in the region and speak *Bukhori* or Judeo-Tajik, a distinct dialect of the Tajiki-Persian language that incorporated a number of Hebrew words. Many of the Jewish community left the country during the violence sparked by civil war of the 1990s between rival Muslim factions. Out of a community of over 20,000, probably less than 1,000 Tajik Jews remain, mostly in the capital, Dushanbe.
Jewish Community of Dushanbe, Nazima Khikmata St., 26, Diushanbe 7340001, ☎ (992 372) 21-76-58

THAILAND (250)
The community consists of approx. 250 persons, including citizens of the country and expatriates.
Jewish Association of Thailand, Beth Elisheva Synagogue, Mikveh, Jewish Centre, 121 Soi Sai Nam Thip 2, Sukhumvit 22, Bangkok. ☎ 663-0244. Fax 663-0245.
Email rabbi@jewishthailand.com
Even-Chen Synagogue, Chao Phya Tower, Shangri a Hotel Weekly classes & activities. Soi Charoengkrung, 42/1 New Road, Bangkok. ☎ 630 6120. Fax 237 3225.
Ohr Menachem-Chabad, 96 Ram Buttri Rd., Kaosarn Rd., Banglampoo. Daily services. *M.* Rabbi Y. Kantor. ☎629-2770. Fax 629 1153 Website www.jewishthailand.com

TRINIDAD AND TOBAGO
Jewish links go back to 1658 when Portuguese Jews from Livorno and Amsterdam settled there. Most of them left by the end of the 17th century. Portuguese Jews from Venezuela and Curaçao settled in Trinidad in the 19th century. The names of many Catholic families are traceable to 'conversos' of the earlier period. In the mid-1930s some 800 Jews sought temporary refuge in Trinidad and Tobago from Nazi persecution in Germany and Austria and later from other parts of Nazi - occupied Europe. Those with German and Austrian passports were subject to internment between 1940 and 1943. Numbers have dropped since with only a few Jews living there now. *Corr.* Hans Stecher, c/o The Tackle Shop, 176A Western Main Rd., Carenago, Trinidad, W.I. (Caribbean). ☎ /Fax (868) 637-3870.

TUNISIA (3,000)

The history of the community goes back to antiquity. After Tunisia became a French protectorate in 1881 Jews obtained equal rights with the Moslems, and the continuance of these rights was promised by the authorities of the independent State established in 1957. The Jewish population fell from nearly 100,000 in 1950 to 25,000 in June 1967, and to some 3,000 today. There are coms. in Tunis, Sfax, Sousse and Jerba island, where the ancient El Ghriba synagogue in Hara Sghire village is a listed building.

TUNIS
Grand Rabbinat de Tunisie, 26 Rue Palestine. Communal Offices, 15 Rue du Cap Vert.
Synagogues: 43 Ave. de la Liberté: 3 Rue Eve Nöelle.
American Joint Distribution Committee, 101 Ave. de la Liberté.

TURKEY (25,000)

During the Spanish Inquisition, the Ottoman Empire was one of the principal lands of refuge. With the proclamation of the Turkish Republic, the Jews were granted full citizenship rights. Today their number is estimated at about 25,000 of whom about 23,000 live in Istanbul, 2,000 in Izmir, and 100 each in Ankara, Adana, Bursa, Edirne and Kirklareli.

ISTANBUL
Chief Rabbinate: Yemenici Sok. No. 23 Tünel, Beyoğlu. ☎ (212) 2938794-95. Fax (212) 244-1980. *Chief Rabbi* Isak Haleva; *Sec. General.*
Communal Centre, Büyük Hendek Sokak No. 61, Galata. ☎ (212) 2441576. Fax (212) 292 0385.
Synagogues: Neve Shalom, 61 Büyük Hendek Sokak, Galata. ☎ (212) 293-7566; Beth Israel, Efe Sok. 4, Þiþli, ☎ (212) 2406599; Etz Ahayim, Muallim Naci Sok. 40/1. ☎ (212) 2601896; (Ashkenazi), 37 Yüksekkaldirim sok, Galata. (243-6909; (Italian), 29, Þair Ziya Paþa Yokusu, Galata. ☎ (212) 2937784; Hemdat Israel, Izzettin Sok 65 Kadiköy ☎ (216) 336 5293; Heset Leavraam, Pancur Sok, 15, Büyükada ☎ (216) 382-5788 (summer); Caddebostan, Taþ Mektep Sokak Göztepe. ☎ (216) 356-5922.
There are ten charitable and social institutions, six youth clubs, a high school and an elementary school in Istanbul. Synagogues also in Izmir, Ankara, Bursa and Adane.

TURKMENISTAN (1,000)

Although some 2,500 Jews lived in Turkmenistan in 1989, many have now emigrated and less than 1,000 remain today, mostly in the capital city, Ashkhabad.

UKRAINE (300,000)

KIEV
Syn.: 29 Shchekovichnaya St., 252071. ☎ (044) 463 7085. Fax 463 7088.
Assoc. of Jewish Organisations, Kurskaya ul. 6, r. 42 03049 ☎ (044) 2483670. Email vaad-ua@ukr.net.
Jewish Historical Society, Iskrovskaya Str., 3, Apt. 6, 252087. ☎ (044) 242-7944.
Makor Centre for Jewish Youth Activities, 10/1 Gorodeskogo St., Apt. 10, 252001. ☎ 044-229-6141. Fax 044-229-8069.
Association of Progressive Jewish Congregations in Ukraine, 01023 Kiev-23, POB 517, 'Hatikva' Congregation, *M.* Rabbi A. Dukhovny. ☎ 0038-044-234-2215, ☎ /Fax 0038-044-234-8482. Email ravdukh@alfacom.net.
Other towns with Jewish centres include Bershad, Chernigor, Chernovtsy, Kharkov, Kremenchug, Lviv, Odessa, Simferopol, Uzhgorod and Zhitomir.

UNITED STATES OF AMERICA (5,280,000)

Though there had been individual Jewish settlers before 1654 in the territory which is now the

United States, it was not until that year that Jewish immigrants arrived in a group at New Amsterdam (renamed New York in 1664) 23 of them, who came from Brazil by way of Cuba and Jamaica. The story of the growth of Jewry in the U.S.A. is the story of successive waves of immigration resulting from persecution in Russia, Poland, Romania, Germany and other countries. Today the Jewish population is est. at 5,950,000, of whom 1,720,000 live in the New York Metropolitan Area.

For general information about the American Jewish Community write to: **UJA - Federation Resource Line**, *130 E 59th St., New York City, 10022. Email resourceline@ujafedny.org; Website www.ujafedny.org.*

REPRESENTATIVE ORGANISATIONS

American Jewish Committee, 165 E. 56th St., New York City, 10022.

American Jewish Congress, Stephen Wise Hse., 15 E. 84th St., New York City, 10028.

Anti-Defamation League of B'nai B'rith, 823 United Nations Plaza, New York City, 10017.

B'nai B'rith International, 1640 Rhode Island Av., N.W. Washington, D.C., 20036.

Conference of Presidents of Major Jewish Organizations, 110 E 59th St., NYC 10022.

Consultative Council of Jewish Organizations, 420 Lexington Av., Suite 1733, NYC 10170. (212-808-5437.

Co-ordinating Board of Jewish Organizations, 1640 Rhode Island Ave., N.W. Washington, D.C., 20036.

Jewish Labour Committee, Atran Centre, 25 E. 21st St., New York City, 10010.

Jewish War Veterans of the United States of America, 1811 R St., N.W. Washington, D.C. 20009.

National Jewish Community Relations Advisory Council, 443 Park Ave. S., I Ith floor, New York City, 10016.

National Council of Jewish Women, 820 Second Avenue, New York City, 10017.

National Conference on Soviet Jewry, 2020 K Street, N.W., Suite 7800, Washington D.C. 20006.

National Council of Young Israel, 3 W. 16th St., New York City, 10011.

North American Jewish Students Network, 501 Madison Ave., 17th Fl., New York City, 10022.

United Jewish Communities Federations of North America, PO Box 30, Old Chelsea Station, New York City, 10113.

World Confederation of Jewish Community Centers, 15 E. 26th St. New York City, 10010.

World Jewish Congress, 501 Madison Ave., 17th Fl., New York City, 10022. ☎ 755 5770.

RELIGIOUS ORGANISATIONS

Agudath Israel of America, 84 William St., New York City, 10038.

Agudath Israel World Organization, 84 William St., New York City, 10038.

Association of Orthodox Jewish Scientists, 1373 Coney Island Ave., Brooklyn, New York, 11219.

Central Conference of American Rabbis, 355 Lexington Ave., New York City, 10017-6603. ☎ 212-972 3636 (Reform).

Jewish Reconstructionist Federation, 101, Greenwood Avenue, Jenkintown, PA 19046. ☎ 215-782 885 5601. Fax 215-8852 56035. Email info@jrf.org.

Lubavitcher Headquarters, 770 Eastem Parkway, Brooklyn, N.Y. 11213. New York Board of Rabbis, 10 E. 73rd St., New York City, 10021.

Rabbinical Alliance of America, 3 W. 16th St., 4th Fl., New York City, 10011. (Orthodox.)

Rabbinical Assembly (Cons.), 3080 Broadway, New York City, 10027.

Rabbinical Council of America, 275 7th Ave., New York City, 10001. (Modern Orthodox).

Reconstructionist Rabbinical Association, 7804 Montgomery Ave., St. No.9, Elkins Park, PA 19027. (215-782 8500. Fax 215-782 8805. Email info@jrf.org

Synagogue Council of America, 327 Lexington Ave., New York City 10016.

Union of American Hebrew Congregations, 633 Third Ave, New York City 10017. ☎(212-650 4000. Email uahc@uahc.org.

Union of Orthodox Jewish Congregations, 333 Seventh Ave., New York City, 10001.
Union of Orthodox Rabbis, 235 E. Broadway, New York City, 10002.
Union of Sephardic Congregations, 8 W 70th St., New York City, 10023.
United Synagogue of America, 155 Fifth Ave., New York City, 10010. (Conservative.)
World Union for Progressive Judaism, 838 Fifth Ave., New York City, 10021.

WELFARE AND REFUGEE ORGANISATIONS
American Association for Ethiopian Jews,
American Federation of Jews from Central Europe, 570 7th Ave., New York City, 10018.
American Jewish Joint Distribution Committee (I.D.C.), 711 Third Ave, New York City, 10017.
American ORT Federation, 817 Broadway, New York City, 10003.
Council of Jewish Federations, 730 Broadway, New York City, 10003.
HIAS, 333 7th Ave., New York City, 1000.
Jewish Conciliation Board, 235 Park Ave. S., New York City, 10003.
JWB, 15 East 26th St., New York City, 10010.
U.J.A. Federation of New York, 130 E. 59th St., New York City, 10022.

ZIONIST ORGANISATIONS and others concerned with Israel
American Associates of Ben-Gurion University of Negev, 342 Madison Ave., Suite 1924, New York City, 10173.
American Committee for Weizmann Institute, 515 Park Ave., New York City, 10022.
American Friends of the Hebrew University, 11 E. 69th St., New York City, 10021.
American Friends of Tel Aviv University,
American Friends of Haifa University, 41 E. 42nd St., 828, New York City, 10017.
American-Israel Cultural Foundation, 485 Madison Ave., New York City, 10022.
American-Israel Public Affairs Committee, 500 N. Capitol St., N.W. Washington, D.C. 20001.
American Jewish League for Israel, 30 E. 60th St., New York City, 10022.
American Red Magen David for Israel, 888 7th Ave., New York City, 10106.
American Technion Society, 271 Madison Ave., New York City, 10016.
American Zionist Federation, 515 Park Ave., New York City, 10022 from whom information on Zionist organisations and activities can be obtained.
American Zionist Youth Foundation, 515 Park Ave., New York City, 10022.
Americans for Progressive Israel, 150 Fifth Ave., Suite 911, New York City, 10011.
Bar-Ilan University in Israel, 853 Seventh Ave., New York City, 10019.
Bnei Akiva of North America, 25 W. 26th St., New York City, 10010.
Betar Zionist Youth Movement, 625 Broadway #7F, New York City, 10012.
Emunah Women of America, 370 7th Ave., New York City, 10001.
Hadassah, Women's Zionist Organization of America, 50 W. 58th St., New York City, 10019.
Theodor Herzl Foundation, 515 Park Ave., New York City, 10022.
Jewish National Fund, 42 E. 69th St., New York City, 10021.
Labor Zionist Alliance (formerly Poale Zion United Labour Org. of America), 275 Seventh Ave., New York City, 10001.
Mercaz, Conservative Zionists, 155 Fifth Ave., New York City, 10010.
Mizrachi-Hapoel Hamizrachi (Religious Zionists of America), 25 W. 26th St., New York City, 10010.
National Committee for Labor Israel–Histadrut, 33 E. 67th St., New York City, 10021.
PEC Israel Economic Corporation, 511 Fifth Ave., New York City, 10017.
Pioneer Women Na'armat, The Women's Labour Zionist Organisation of America,
State of Israel Bonds, 730 Broadway, New York City, 10003
Women's League for Israel, 515 Park Ave., New York City, 10022.
World Confederation of United Zionists, 30 E. 60th St., New York City 10022.
World Zionist Organization, American Section, 515 Park Ave., New York City, 10022.

EDUCATIONAL AND CULTURAL ORGANISATIONS

American Friends of the Alliance Israélite Universelle, 135 William St., New York City, 10038.

Annenberg Research Institute, formerly Dropsie College, 250 N. Highland Ave., Merion. Pa., 19066.

Center for Cultural Judaism, 80 Eighth Ave., Suite 206, New York, N.Y. 10011. ☎ (212) 564-6711 Website www.culturaljudaism.org.

Center for Holocaust Studies, Documentation & Research, 1610 Ave. J., Brooklyn, New York 11230.

Center for Jewish History, 15 West 16th St., New York City, 10011. ☎ (212) 294-6160.

Central Yiddish Culture Organization, 25 E. 21st St., New York City, 10010.

Gratz College, 10th St., & Tabor Rd., Phila., PA 19141.

Theodor Herzl Institute and Foundation, 515 Park Ave., New York City, 10022.

Hebrew Arts School, 129 W. 67th St., New York City, 10023.

Hebrew College, 43 Hawes St., Brookline, MA 02146.

Hebrew Union College-Jewish Institute of Religion, 3101 Clifton Ave., Cincinnati, OH 45220; 1 W. 4th St., New York City, 10012, 3077 University Mall, Los Angeles, CA 90007; 13 King David St., Jerusalem 94101, Israel.

Herzliah Jewish Teachers' Seminary, Touro College, Jewish Peoples, University of the Air, 30 W. 44th St., New York City, 10036.

Histadruth Ivrith of America, 426 W. 58th Street, 4th Floor, New York, 10019.

JWB Jewish Book Council, 15 E. 26th St., New York City, 10010.

Jewish Education Service of North America, 730 Broadway, New York.

Jewish Publication Society, 1930 Chestnut St., Philadelphia, PA 19103.

Jewish Museum, 1109 Fifth Ave., New York City, 10128.

Jewish Theological Seminary of America, 3080 Broadway, New York City, 10027.

Leo Baeck Institute, Brandeis University, Waltham, MA 02254.

Memorial Foundation for Jewish Culture, 50 Broadway, 34th Floor, New York City, 10004.

Mesivta Yeshiva Rabbi Chaim Berlin Rabbinical Academy, 1593 Coney Island Ave., Brooklyn, New York City.

National Foundation for Jewish Culture, 330 7th Ave., 21st Fl., New York City, 10024.

National Yiddish Book Center, Weinberg Building, Amherst, MH 01002-3375. ((800) 535-3595; Fax (413) 256-4700.

Reconstructionist Rabbinical College, Church Road and Greenwood Ave., Wyncote, PA 19095.

Shomrei Adamah Jewish Resource Center for the Environment, Church Road and Greenwood Ave., Wyncote, PA 19095.

Simon Wiesenthal Centre, 9760 W. Pico Blvd., Los Angeles, CA 90035.

Torah Umesorah–National Society for Hebrew Day Schools, 160 Broadway, New York City, 10038.

United Lubavitcher Yeshivoth, 841 Ocean Parkway, Brooklyn, N.Y., 11230.

Yeshiva University, 500 W. 185th St., New York City, 10033; 9760 W. Pico Blvd., Los Angeles, CA 90035.

Yivo Institute for Jewish Research, 555 West 57th St., 11th Floor, New York City, 10019 (Temporary removal) ((212) 535-6700.

URUGUAY (25,000)

Jewish immigration to Uruguay began in the early 20th century, with a large influx in the 1920s. Some 10,000 European Jews fled to Uruguay with Hitler's rise to power and large numbers came after the Second World War. In the 1940s, 50,000 Jews were est. to be living in the country. At present there are about 35,000, mostly in Montevideo, the capital. Some 12,000 emigrated to Israel before the State was established, during the War of Independence and since.

MONTEVIDEO

*Central and representative org.: Comité Central Israelita del Uruguay, Rio Negro 1308

Piso 5 Esc. ☎ 90 06562. Fax 91 6057. Email cciu@cciu.org.uk
Communities: Comunidad Israelita del Uruguay, Canelones 1084 Piso 1º; Comunidad Israelita Sefaradi, 21 de Setiembre 3111 (office), Buenos Aires 234 (syn.); Nueva Congregacion Israelita, Wilson Ferreira Aldunate 1168; Comunidad Israelita Hungara, Durazno 972. Each com. maintains its own syns. There are 3 Jewish schs. and an ORT training centre.
Zionist Organisation of Uruguay, Juan Ma Pérez 2716 Email osuur@adinet.com.uy.
International Council of Jewish Women, PO Box 12130 Local 4, Montevideo 11300, Uruguay. ☎/Fax +598 (0)2 628 5874. Email icjw@montevideo.com.uy. Website www.icjw.org.uk. *President* Sara Winkowski.
There are also communities at Maldonado and Paysandu.

UZBEKISTAN (35,000)
The three principal Jewish centres in Uzbekistan today are Tashkent (13,000), Samarkand (3,000), and Bukhara (2,000). The community includes Ashkenazi Jews who came to the region from other parts of the then Soviet Union, and the Bukharan community, which traces its Uzbek roots back many centuries, and speaks *Bukhori* or Judeo-Tajik, a distinct dialectof the Tajiki-Persian language that incorporated a number of Hebrew words. The Bukharan Jews account for almost the entire community in Samarkand. Nearly all the Ashkenazim live in the capital, Tashkent, as do some 2,000 Bukharan Jews.

VENEZUELA (20,000)
The first community was established in the coastal town of Coro by Sephardi Jews early in the 19th century. Today the Jews in Venezuela number some 21,000, most of whom live in Caracas and the rest mainly in Maracaibo.

CARACAS
*****Confederación de Asociaciones Israelitas de Venezuela** (CAIV), Representative organisation of Venezuelan Jewry, Av. Washington (al lado del Hotel Avila), San Bernardino. ☎ (58-212) 551.0368; 550.2454. Fax (58-212) 551.0377; 550.1721.
Ashkenazi Synagogue and Centre: **Unión Israelita de Caracas**, Av. Washington, San Bernardino. ((58-212) 551.5253. Fax (58-212) 552.7956. *M.* Rabbi Pynchas Brener.
Sephardic Synagogue and Centre: **Asociación Israelita de Venezuela**, Tiferet Yisrael, Av. Maripérez, Frente al Paseo Colón, Los Caobos. ☎ (58-212) 574.4975; 574.8297. Fax 577.0259. *M.* Rabbi Isaac Cohén.
B'nai B'rith, **Fraternidad Hebrea B'nai B'rith de Venezuela**, 9ª. Transversal entre 7ª. Y Av. Avila, Altarmira. ☎ 261.7497, 261.4083. Fax (58-212) 261.4083.
Zionist Federation (**Federación Sionista de Venezuela**), Edif. Bet Am, Av. Washington, San Bernardino. ☎ (58-212) 551 2562; 551.4852. Fax (58-212) 551.3089.
Ladies' organization: **Federación Venezuela de Mujeres Judías**. Unión Israelita de Caracas, Avenida Washington (al lado del Hotel Avila), San Bernardino. P.O.B.: Apartado de Correo 5506, Caracas 1010.. ☎ (58-212) 551 0423. Fax (58-212) 551 7457

VIRGIN ISLANDS (350)
Jews have lived in the Virgin Islands since the eighteenth century and played an important part under Danish rule. Since 1917 the Virgin Islands have been US territory. The congregation was established in 1796. There are some 100 families in the community and the number of affiliated and non-affiliated Jews is about 350. The 150th anniversary of the rebuilding of the synagogue, situated in Crystal Gade, St. Thomas, was celebrated in 1983, and the synagogue was restored in 2000. See: J. Cohen, 'Through the sands of time: a history of the Jewish community of St. Thomas, US Virgin Islands', Brandeis U.P. 2004.
Jewish Community, Crystal Gade, Charlotte Amalie. *M.* Rabbi A. F. Starr.
Hebrew Congretation of St Thomas (Reform), POB 266, St Thomas, 00804-0266. ☎ 1340-774 4312. Fax 1340-774 3249. Email hebrewcong@islands.vi. Website www.onepaper. com/synagogue.

YEMEN

Since 1948 the vast majority of Yemeni Jews (who then numbered about 50,000) have emigrated to Israel. It is est. about 1,200 remain in Sa'ana.The bulk of the Jews of Aden, situated in the south of the country in what was known as South Yemen until 1990, left the country prior to Aden attaining independence from Britain in 1967.

ZAMBIA (35)

*The Council for Zambia Jewry Ltd., PO Box 30020, Lusaka 10101. *Chairman* M. C. Galaun. ☎ 2602-1122 9190 Fax 2602-1122 1428. Email ceo@galaunia.co,zm.
Lusaka Hebrew Congregation, PO Box 30020. (Est. 1941.) *Chairman* M. C. Galaun.

ZIMBABWE (510)

Jews came to Rhodesia (Zimbabwe) even before the British South Africa Company received its charter in 1889. Daniel Montague Kisch arrived in the territory in 1869, becoming chief adviser to King Lobengula.

In the 1880s the number of Jewish pioneers, most of them of East European origin, gradually increased. Among those who took a leading part in the development and admin. of the country was Sir Roy Welensky, Prime Minister of the former Central African Federation (1956-1963).

Most of the Jewish settlers came from Russia or Lithuania but others settled from the Aegean Island of Rhodes. Many came up from the South, some through the east coast Portuguese territory of Beira. Joe van Praagh, who became Mayor of Salisbury, walked from Beira. During the 1930s, a small influx of German refugees settled mainly in Salisbury (now Harare) and Bulawayo. Post World War II, others joined them mostly from the United Kingdom and South Africa.

Today, most of Zimbabwe's Jews live in Harare and Bulawayo with a very few residing in the smaller districts around the country about 392 in Harare, 116 in Bulawayo and 5 in other centres. There are two synagogues in Harare and one in Bulawayo and each city has its own Jewish primary day school.

Zimbabwe Jewish Board of Deputies (Head Office), Jewish Centre, Lezard Ave., Milton Park, POB 1954, Harare..☎ (04) 798683. Email cazo@zol.co.zw. *President* F. Plein; *Sec.* Mrs T. Goldsmith.
Zimbabwe Jewish Board of Deputies (Bulawayo Office), PO Box AC 783, Ascot, Bulawayo.. ☎ (09)-250443. Email cazobyo@gatorzw.com.
Central African Zionist Organisation (Head Office), PO Box AC 783, Ascot, Bulawayo. ☎ (09)-250443. Email cazobyo@gatorzw.com.
Central African Zionist Organisation (Bulawayo Office), PO Box AC 783, Ascot, Bulawayo. ☎ 09-250443. Email cazobyo@gatorzw.com. *President* Mrs C. Bernstein (Southern Region).
Women's Zionist Council of Central Africa, PO Box AC 783, Ascot, Bulawayo. ☎ (09)-250443. *President* Mrs Rhebe Tatz.
*Synagogues. *Harare*: Harare Hebrew Congregation, Lezard Ave., PO Box 342. (Est. 1895.) ☎ (04)-798683. Email hhc@zol.co.zw; Sephardi Hebrew Congregation, 54 Josiah Chinamano Ave., PO Box 1051. (Est. 1932.). ☎ (04)-722899. *Bulawayo*: Bulawayo Hebrew Congregation, (Est. 1894), PO Box 337. ☎ (09)-250443.
There are branches of the Union of Jewish Women in both Bulawayo and Harare.

JEWISH STATISTICS

In view of the large movements of population in recent years and the difficulty of obtaining exact figures, the compilation of Jewish population statistics can only be based on estimates received from a variety of sources. Data from censuses of 2001 in various countries have yet to be digested.

The exodus of Russian Jewry of the 1980s and 1990s has compounded the problem of maintaining reliable figures but for the time being we can only repeat previous figures pending formal revisions from our informants, most notably the IJPR who have furnished the principle figures on Table I (1991), the World Jewish Congress (1998), and the American Jewish Year Book (2006).

Estimates of the present world Jewish population give a total of about 13,000,000. Some 1,600,000 are in Europe, about 6,483,900 in North and South America, some 4,932,900 in Asia, including 4,847,000 in Israel, about 89,800 in Africa and about 101,900 in Oceania. Based on the 1996 census in Australia, W. D. Rubinstein has provided new figures for the state centres. Figures for the USA have been revised in the light of Kosman & Scheckner (AJYB 1993). The number of Jews in Moslem countries is about 71,600.

The number of Jews in the world before the outbreak of war in 1939 was estimated at a figure slightly under 17,000,000, of whom about 10,000,000 lived in Europe, 5,375,000 in North and South America (which seems to have been an overestimate), 830,000 in Asia, 600,000 in Africa, and less than 33,000 in Oceania. The difference between the pre-war and post-war figures is accounted for principally by the enormous losses suffered by the Jewish people between 1939 and 1945. Although estimates of Jews murdered by the Nazis and their collaborators vary, the number is commonly accepted to be 6,000,000.

From the seizure of power by Hitler until the outbreak of war in 1939, 80,000 refugees from Central Europe were admitted to Britain. During the six years of war, a further 70,000 were admitted and since the end of the war about 70,000 displaced persons as well as refugees from a number of other countries. Probably some 80 per cent of these were Jews. Many of these were, however, only temporary residents.

Table III has been revised in the light of new figures from the census of 2001.

Table I
POPULATION OF THE PRINCIPAL COUNTRIES

Albania	50	Croatia	2,500
Algeria	30	Cuba	1,500
Argentina	240,000	Czech Republic	10,000
Armenia	500	Denmark	7,000
Aruba	50	Dominican Rep.	150
Australia	110,000	Ecuador	1,000
Austria	12,000	Egypt	240
Azerbaijan	6,000	El Salvador	100
Bahamas	300	Estonia	3,000
Barbados	55	Ethiopia	100
Belarus	28,000	Fiji	40
Belgium	31,000	Finland	1,500
Bermuda	125	France	650,000
Bolivia	640	Georgia	13,000
Bosnia Hercegovina	1,100	Germany	108,000
Brazil	250,000	Gibraltar	650
Bulgaria	6,500	* Great Britain and	
Canada	348,600	N. Ireland	267,000
Chile	25,000	Greece	4,800
China	3,100	Guatemala	1,500
Colombia	5,000	Haiti	150
Congo	100	Honduras	150
Costa Rica	2,500	Hungary	100,000

(Table I continued)

India	5,600
Iran	24,000
Iraq	75
*Ireland	1,790
¶ Israel	5,330,000
Italy	35,000
Jamaica	350
Japan	2,000
Kazakhstan	7,000
Kenya	330
Kirghizstan	1,500
Latvia	10,800
Lebanon	100
Libya	50
Lithuania	11,000
Luxembourg	1,000
Macedonia	250
Malta	50
Mexico	40,000
Moldova	40,000
Morocco	5,800
Netherlands	25,000
Netherlands Antilles	350
New Caledonia	120
New Zealand	8,000
Norway	2,000
Panama	9,250
Paraguay	900
Peru	3,000
Poland	6,000
Portugal	1,000
Puerto Rico	1,500
Romania	10,000
Russia	440,000
Serbia	3,500
Singapore	300
Slovakia	6,000
South Africa	75,000
Spain	25,000
Surinam	300
Sweden	20,000
Switzerland	17,600
Syria	1,500
Tahiti	130
Taiwan	180
Tajikistan	1,000
Thailand	250
Trinidad	10
Tunisia	3,000
Turkey	25,000
Turkmenistan	1,000
Ukraine	300,000
U.S.A.	5,280,000
Uruguay	25,000
Uzbekistan	35,000
Venezuela	20,000
Virgin Islands	500
Yemen	1,000
Zambia	35
Zimbabwe	510

¶ Israel Statistical Abstract. Including Eastern Jerusalem and West Bank Settlements. Total Israeli population is 7,026,000 [The Jewish pop. is 76.2%, 2005].

* Census 2001.

Table II
MAJOR CENTRES OF JEWISH POPULATION

EUROPE

Amsterdam	15,000	Malaga	1,500
Antwerp	15,000	Malmo	1,950
Athens	2,800	Marseilles	70,000
Barcelona	3,000	Metz	2,500
Basle	2,000	Milan	10,000
Belgrade	1,627	Minsk	45,000
Berlin	11,000	Moscow	200,000
Bordeaux	7,000	Munich	9,300
Brussels	23,000	Nancy	2,000
Bucharest	11,000	Nice	25,000
Budapest	40,000	Odessa	20,000
Cisinau	50,000	Oslo	900
Cologne	1,260	Paris, Greater	350,000
Copenhagen	8,500	Prague	1,400
Dublin	1,500	Riga	15,000
Dusseldorf	1,710	Rome	15,000
Florence	1,290	Rotterdam	1,500
Frankfurt	7,000	St. Petersburg	100,000
Geneva	3,900	Salonika	1,100
Gothenburg	2,500	Sarajevo	1,090
Grenoble	5,000	Sofia	3,200
Hamburg	1,415	Stockholm	9,500
Helsinki	1,200	Strasbourg	18,000
Istanbul	23,000	Sverdlovsk	20,000
Izmir	1,000	The Hague	2,500
Kaunas	5,500	Toulouse	25,000
Kazan	10,000	Turin	1,630
Kharkov	80,000	Vienna	1,000
Kiev	50,000	Vilnius	4,500
Lille	3,000	Warsaw	2,000
Lisbon	300	Wroclaw ´	1,500
Lodz	1,500	Zagreb	1,500
Lvov	25,000	Zhitomir	20,000
Lyons	30,000	Zurich	6,252
Madrid	3,500		

ASIA

Ankara	100	Shiraz	3,000
Bombay	4,354	Tashkent	50,000
Damascus	1,000	Teheran	20,000
Hong Kong	3,000	Tokyo	750
Sa'ana	1,000		

(Table II continued)
ISRAEL

Acco	28,900	Kiryat Gat	27,400
Afula	24,200	Kiryat Motzkin	29,300
Ashdod	72,900	Kiryat Ono	22,000
Askelon	55,700	Kiryat Yam	31,700
Bat Yam	132,800	Lod	33,200
Beersheba	114,600	Nahariya	29,400
Bnei Brak	107,400	Netanya	114,400
Dimona	25,400	Or Yehuda	19,900
Eilat	24,200	Petach Tikva	132,100
Givatayim	45,900	Ramat Gan	115,600
Hadera	43,200	Ramat Hasharon	35,800
Haifa	270,000	Ramle	36,800
Herzlia	70,200	Ra'anana	48,000
Hod Hasharon	23,700	Rehovot	71,900
Holon	143,600	Rishon le Zion	120,100
Jerusalem	346,100	Tel Aviv-Jaffa	380,000
Kfar Saba	52,800	Tiberias	30,800
Kiryat Atta	35,100	Upper Nazareth	21,900
Kiryat Bialik	32,400	West Bank Settlements	140,000

AMERICAS

Alameda (Ca.)	30,000	Miami	535,000
Atlanta	50,000	Middlesex Co. (N.J.)	40,000
Baltimore	94,000	Milwaukee (Wisc.)	29,000
Bergen County (N.J.)	83,700	Minneapolis (Min.)	22,000
Boca Raton-Delray (Florida)	50,000	Montgomery & Prince Georges	105,000
Boston	210,000	Montreal (Que.)	100,000
Buenos Aires	180,000	New Haven (Con.)	26,000
Calgary (Alberta)	5,500	New York (Greater)	1,970,000
Camden (New Jersey)	28,000	Newark & Essex County (N.J.)	79,000
Caracas	18,000	Orange County (Ca.)	75,000
Chicago	248,000	Ottawa (Ont.)	9,000
Cincinnati	22,000	Palm Beach County (Florida)	209,000
Cleveland	70,000	Philadelphia	254,000
Dallas	24,000	Phoenix	50,000
Denver	45,000	Pittsburgh (Pa.)	45,000
Detroit	94,000	Rio de Janeiro	80,000
Edmonton (Alberta)	3,700	Rockland County (N.Y.)	57,000
Elizabeth & Union County (N.J.)	30,000	St. Louis (Mis.)	53,500
Englewood & Bergen Co. (N.J.)	100,000	San Diego	36,400
Fort Lauderdale (Florida)	284,000	San Jose (Ca)	32,000
Halifax (N.S.)	1,500	San Francisco	250,000
Hamilton (Ont.)	4,600	Santiago	21,000
Hartford (Con.)	27,500	Sao Paulo	90,000
Hollywood (Florida)	60,000	Seattle	19,500
Houston	40,000	Toronto (Ont.)	175,000
Kansas City	22,000	Vancouver (B.C.)	18,000
Lima	5,000	Washington (D.C.)	165,000
London (Ont.)	1,900	Windsor (Ont.)	2,500
Los Angeles	620,000	Winnipeg (Man.)	16,000
Mexico City	50,000		

(Table II continued)

AFRICA		OCEANIA	
Alexandria	.100	Adelaide	.1,250
Bulawayo	.116	Auckland	.3,100
Cape Town	.12,000	Brisbane	.1,500
Durban	.2,000	Canberra	.500
Fez	.1,500	Christchurch	.650
Harare	.392	Dunedin	.100
Johannesburg	.45,000	Hamilton	.50
Kinshasa	.300	Hobart	.100
Port Elizabeth	.2,740	Melbourne	.50,000
Pretoria	.3,750	Noumea (New Caledonia)	.100
Rabat	.1,500	Perth	.4,800
Tangier	.1,000	Sydney	.40,000
Tunis	.2,200	Wellington	.1,200

Table III
JEWS IN BRITAIN AND NORTHERN IRELAND

Aberdeen	.30	Hemel Hempstead	.270
Amersham	.70	High Wycombe	.35
Basildon	.10	Hull	.670
Bedford	.30	Leamington (Warwick)	.132
Belfast	.500	Leeds	.8,270
Birmingham	.2,340	Leicester	.417
Blackpool	.302	Liverpool	.2,700
Bognor Regis	.40	Llandudno, Colwyn Bay & Rhyl	.15
Bournemouth	.2,110	London (Greater London Area)	.168,700
Bradford	.356	Luton	.530
Brighton & Hove	.3,360	Maidenhead (Royal Windsor &)	.570
Bristol	.823	Manchester & Salford	.21,730
Cambridge	.850	Margate & Thanet	.200
Canterbury	.210	Middlesbrough	.65
Cardiff	.940	Milton Keynes	.466
Chatham & Rochester	.50	Newcastle upon Tyne	.550
Chelmsford	.145	Newport	.39
Cheltenham	.133	Northampton	.322
Chester	.132	Norwich	.239
Colchester	.100	Nottingham	.630
Coventry	.140	Oxford	.500
Crawley	.50	Peterborough	.147
Darlington	.40	Plymouth	.181
Dundee	.22	Portsmouth	.235
East Grinstead	.35	Radlett	.750
Eastbourne	.63	Reading	.415
Edinburgh	.760	Reigate & Banstead	.45
Exeter	.150	St. Albans	.200
Gateshead	.1,560	St. Anne's (Fylde)	.500
Glasgow	.4,330	Sheffield	.763
Grimsby (Great)	.40	Solihull	.389
Guildford	.383	Southampton & Winchester	.300
Harlow	.190	Southend & Westcliff	.2,720
Harrogate	.327	Southport (Sefton)	.700
Hastings	.33	Staines & Slough	.390

(Table III continued)

HISTORICAL NOTE ON BRITISH JEWRY

There were probably individual Jews in England in Roman and (though less likely) in Anglo-Saxon times, but the historical records of any organised settlement here start after the Norman Conquest of 1066. Jewish immigrants arrived early in the reign of William the Conqueror and important settlements came to be established in London (at a site still known as Old Jewry), Lincoln and many other centres. In 1190 massacres of Jews occurred in many cities, most notably in York. This medieval settlement was ended by Edward I's expulsion of the Jews in 1290, after which date, with rare and temporary exceptions, only converts to Christianity or secret adherents of Judaism could live here. The Domus Conversorum, the House for Converted Jews (on the site of the former Public Record Office in Chancery Lane, London) had been established in 1232. Perhaps the most notable Jews in medieval England were the financier, Aaron of Lincoln (d.c. 1186), and Elijah Menahem of London (d. 1284), financier, physician and Talmudist.

After the expulsion of the Jews from Spain in 1492 a secret Marrano community became established in London, but the present Anglo-Jewish community dates in practice from the period of the Commonwealth. In 1650 Menasseh ben Israel, of Amsterdam, began to champion the cause of Jewish readmission to England, and in 1655 he led a mission to London for this purpose. A conference was convened at Whitehall and a petition was presented to Oliver Cromwell. Though no formal decision was then recorded, in 1656 the Spanish and Portuguese Congregation in London was organised. It was followed towards the end of the seventeenth century by the establishment of an Ashkenazi community, which increased rapidly inside London as well as throwing out offshoots before long to a number of provincial centres and seaports. The London community, has, however, always comprised numerically the preponderant part of British Jewry.

Britain has the distinction of being one of the few countries in Europe where during the course of the past three centuries there have been no serious outbreaks of violence against Jews and in which the ghetto system never obtained a footing, though in 1753 the passage through Parliament of a Bill to facilitate the naturalisation of foreign-born Jews caused such an outcry that it was repealed in the following year. A short-lived outbreak of anti-semitism in 1772, associated with the so-called 'Chelsea murders' is also notable for its rarity.

Although Jews in Britain had achieved a virtual economic and social emancipation by the early nineteenth century they had not yet gained 'political emancipation'. Minor Jewish disabilities were progressively removed and Jews were admitted to municipal rights and began to win distinction in the professions. The movement for the removal of Jewish political disabilities became an issue after the final removal of political disabilities from Protestant dissenters and then Roman Catholics (1829), and a Bill with that object was first introduced into the House of Commons in 1830. Among the advocates of Jewish emancipation were Macaulay, Lord John Russell, Gladstone (from 1847) and Disraeli. The latter, who was a Christian of Jewish birth, entered Parliament in 1837. Jewish MPs were repeatedly elected from 1847 onwards, but were prevented from taking their seats by the nature of the various oaths required from all new members. Owing to the opposition in the House of Lords it was not until 1858 that a Jew (Lionel de Rothschild) was formally admitted to Parliament, this being followed in 1885 by the elevation of his son (Sir Nathaniel de Rothschild) to the Peerage. Meanwhile, in 1835, David Salomons was the first Jew to become Sheriff of London, and in 1855 Lord Mayor of London (Bart. 1869). The first to be a member of the government was Sir George Jessel, who became Solicitor-General in 1871, and the first Jewish Cabinet Minister was Herbert Samuel in 1909.

During the 19th century British Jews spread out from those callings which had hitherto been regarded as characteristic of the Jews. A further mark of the organisational consolidation of the community can be seen in the growth and strength of many of the communal institutions mentioned elsewhere in this book, such as the Board of Deputies (founded 1760), the Board of Guardians (founded 1859), and the United Synagogue (founded 1870), as well as the development of the office of Chief Rabbi and the longevity of the Jewish Chronicle which marked its 150th anniversary in 1991. Equally significant by the middle of the century was the appearance of a number of newer Jewish communities which had been formed in many of the new industrial centres in the North of England and the Midlands, the intellectual activities and the overseas connections of which received thereby a powerful impetus.

There has always been a steady stream of immigration into Britain from Jewish communities in Europe, originally from the Iberian Penninsula and Northern Italy, later from Western and Central Europe. The community was radically transformed by the large influx of refugees which occurred between 1881 and 1914, the result of the intensified persecution of Jews in the Russian Empire. The Jewish population rose from about 25,000 in the middle of the 19th century to nearly 350,000 by 1914. It also became far more dispersed geographically. The last two decades of the nineteenth century saw a substantial growth in the number of communities both in England and in Scotland, and in consequence the 'provinces' became more significant both in numbers and in the influence upon the community as a whole. The impact of this immigration on the Anglo-Jewish community was intensified because very many of the Jews who left Eastern Europe on their way to North America or South Africa passed through Britain. From 1933 a new emigration of Jews commenced, this time from Nazi persecution, and again many settled in this country. Since the end of the Second World War and notably since 1956, smaller numbers of refugees have come from Egypt, Iran, Iraq and Hungary whose fertility is currently giving demographic figures such growth as there is in some localities. There is, also, a large Israeli 'diaspora' in certain areas.

One of the main features of the years after 1914 was the gradual transfer of the leadership of the community from the representatives of the older establishment of Anglo-Jewry to the children and grandchildren of the newer wave of immigrants.

Another feature was the growth of Zionist movements, firstly the Chovevei Zion (Lovers of Zion) and later, under the inspiration of Theodore Herzl, the English Zionist Federation. Under the leadership of Chaim Weizmann and his colleagues in this country, the Zionist Movement obtained, in 1917, the historic Balfour Declaration from the British Government. In 1920 the first British High Commissioner in Mandate Palestine was Sir Herbert Samuel. It was after the withdrawal of the British Government from the Mandate that the State of Israel was proclaimed in 1948.

A mark of British Jewry's full participation in public life is reflected in the number of Jewish signatories to the proclamation of accession of Queen Elizabeth II in 1952 which included seven Jewish Privy Councillors. At the Jubilee there were twenty-one. In the highest offices of the State, in Parliamentary and municipal life, in the Civil and Armed Services, in the judiciary and the universities, in all professions and occupations, the Jewish subjects of the Crown – both at home and overseas – play their full part as inheritors of the political and civic emancipation that was achieved in the mid-nineteenth century. There were 22 Jewish Members in the House of Commons elected in May, 2005. There are, however, no Jews among the hereditary peers in the Reformed House of Lords and no Jewish members of the Scottish Parliament. Five Jews serve as Chancellors of British universities.

The events marking the celebration of the 350th anniversary of Readmission (1656-2006) culminated in public festivities in Trafalgar Square, a royal reception at St James's Palace and an address by the Prime Minister at Bevis Marks.

In its internal life and organisation, British Jewry has constructed the complex fabric of religious, social and philanthropic institutions enumerated in this book. The Jews in Britain are now estimated to number about 267,000 (see the relevant note in the statistical tables) of whom some 168,784 reside in Greater London and the remainder are spread in some 90 regional communities. The census returns of 2001 disclose the fact that there are Jews now resident in all but one (the Scilly Isles) of Britain's areas of registration.

UNITED KINGDOM LEGISLATION
CONCERNING JEWS

(Prepared (1996) by His Honour Judge Aron Owen. Rev. 2003)

HISTORICAL BACKGROUND

In the Middle Ages, hostility towards Jews was a common feature in many European countries. In England, during the reign of Edward I (1272–1307), the *Statutum de Judeismo* was passed in 1275. This statute forbade usury and included an order continuing to oblige Jews to wear a distinguishing badge and imposing upon them an annual poll tax.

In 1290, Edward personally decreed the expulsion of Jews from England. During the reign of Charles I (1625–49) the number of Jews in England steadily increased. Menasseh ben Israel (1604–57) of Amsterdam made a direct appeal to Cromwell to authorize readmission. His 'Humble Addresses' presented to the Lord Protector in October 1655 urged the revocation of the edict of 1290 and entreated that the Jews be accorded the right of public worship and the right to trade freely. No formal announcement was ever made of the Jews' 're-admission' but, from about 1657, the edict of 1290 ceased to have effect.

The Religious Disabilities Act 1846 extended to Jews the provisions of the Toleration Act 1688. Under the 1846 Act, British subjects professing the Jewish religion were to be subject to the same laws in respect of their schools, places for religious worship, education and charitable purposes, and the property held with them, as Protestant dissenters from the Church of England.

PRESENT POSITION

Today, English Law does not regard Jews as a separate nationality or as different from any other British citizen. They have no special status except in so far as they constitute a dissenting religious denomination.

Provision for that special religious position of Jews has, from time to time, been made in legislation (see, for example, the 1846 Act mentioned above). A discussion of the subject will be found in Halsbury's *Laws of England*, fourth edition 1975, Volume 14, paragraphs 1423 to 1432.

Some of the various statutory provisions in force today are set out briefly below. Further information and details can be obtained from the Board of Deputies 6 Bloomsbury Square, London, WC1A 2LP. ☎ 020-7543 5400). Legal advice should be sought by those wishing to know the impact of specific legislation upon their own particular circumstances.

1. The *Representation of the People Act 1983* (which is a consolidation of several previous Acts) enables a voter in a parliamentary or local election, 'who declares that he is a Jew' and objects on religious grounds to marking the ballot paper on the Jewish Sabbath, to have, if the poll is taken on a Saturday, his vote recorded by the presiding officer. This right does not apply to Jewish Holy-days other than the Sabbath. A person unable by reason of 'religious observance' to go in person to the polling station may apply to be treated as an absent voter and to be given a postal vote for a particular parliamentary or local election.

2. The *Education Act 1994* permits Jewish parents to have their children attending state or state-aided voluntary schools withdrawn from any period of religious instruction and/or worship where such   instruction or worship is not in the Jewish faith. In order to take advantage of these provisions of the Act, a written request must be submitted to the head teacher of the school.

3. The *Oaths Act 1978*. A Jew may take an oath (in England, Wales or Northern Ireland) by

holding the Old Testament in his uplifted hand, and saying or repeating after the officer administering the oath the words: 'I swear by Almighty God that ...' followed by the words of the oath prescribed by law. The officer will administer the oath in that form and manner without question, unless the person about to take the oath voluntarily objects thereto or is physically incapable of so taking the oath.

Any person who objects to being sworn (whether in that way or in the form and manner usually administered in Scotland) is at liberty instead to make a *solemn affirmation* which will have the same force and effect as an oath. The form of the affirmation is as follows: 'I ... do solemnly, sincerely and truly declare and affirm that ...' followed by the words of the oath prescribed by law. The form of affirmation omits any words of imprecation or calling to witness.

4. *Marriage Act 1949.* English law expressly recognizes the validity of marriages by Jews in England if the ceremonies of the Jewish religion have been complied with.

The Secretary of a synagogue has statutory powers and duties in regard to keeping the marriage register books, and the due registration of marriages between persons professing the Jewish religion under the provisions of the Marriage Act 1949. He has no authority unless and until he has been certified in writing to be the Secretary of a synagogue in England of persons professing the Jewish religion by the President of the Board of Deputies.

When the West London Synagogue was established, acting on the advice of the Chief Rabbi and other recognized Jewish ecclesiastical authorities, the President of the Board of Deputies refused to certify the secretary of the new congregation. Accordingly, by the Marriage Act 1949, it is enacted that the Secretary of the West London Synagogue of British Jews, if certified in writing to the Registrar-General by twenty householders being members of that synagogue, shall be entitled to the same privileges as if he had been certified by the President of the Board of Deputies. These privileges are also accorded to a person whom the Secretary of the West London Synagogue certifies in writing to be the secretary of some other synagogue of not less than twenty householders professing the Jewish religion, if it is connected with the West London Synagogue and has been established for not less than one year.

The Marriages (Secretaries of Synagogues) Act 1959 gives similar rights to Liberal Jewish synagogues.

5. *Divorce (Religious Marriages) Act 2002.* This Act, which was passed on 24 February 2002, came into operation on 24 January 2003. It is not retrospective. It amends the Matrimonial Causes Act 1973 by the insertion of a new clause 10A which enacts important provisions for orthodox Jewish couples seeking a divorce where a *Get* (Jewish Religious Divorce) is essential.

The relevant wording of the new section 10A reads as follows:

10A Proceedings after decree nisi: religious marriage
(1)   This section applies if the decree of divorce has been granted but not made absolute and the parties to the marriage concerned –
    (a) were married in accordance with
       (i) the usage of the Jews ... And
    (b) must co-operate if the marriage is to be dissolved in accordance with those usages.
(2)   On the application of either party, the court may order that a decree of divorce is not to be made absolute until a declaration made by both parties that they have taken such steps as are required to dissolve the marriage in accordance with those usages is produced to the court.
(3)   An order made under subsection (2) –
    (a) may be made only if the court is satisfied that in all the circumstances of the case it is just and reasonable to do so; and
    (b) may be revoked at any time ...

The effect of the statutory provisions, now in operation, is that where the parties, who have been married in accordance with the usages of Jewish Law (that is *Chuppah* and *Kiddushin*) seek a divorce then, before such a Jewish husband and wife would be granted a civil decree absolute of divorce by the English court, they could be required to declare that there has been a *Get*, that is, the Jewish religious divorce. There would thus be a barrier to such a Jewish husband or wife obtaining a civil divorce and being able to remarry unless and until there has been a prior *Get*.

It is hoped that these new statutory provisions will go some way towards alleviating the plight of an *Agunah*. The usual case of an *Agunah* (literally 'a chained woman') is that of a wife whose husband refuses to give her a *Get* so that she is unable to remarry in accordance with orthodox Jewish law. Under the above provisions of the Divorce (Religious Marriages) Act 2002, such a husband would himself be unable to obtain a civil divorce and remarry.

To invoke the provisions of section 10A, an application, by either wife or husband, has to be made to the Court. This application must be made in accordance with the Family Proceedings (Amendment) Rules 2003. It is advisable to consult a solicitor (practising, *inter alia*, in Family Law) to ensure that the necessary legal proceedings are carried out correctly.

6. *Shechita.* Animals and birds slaughtered by the Jewish method (*shechita*) for the food of Jews by a Jew duly licensed by the Rabbinical Commission constituted for the purpose do not come within the provision of the Slaughterhouses Act 1974 or the Slaughter of Poultry Act 1967 relating to the methods of slaughter of animals and birds. The right to practice *shechita* is thus preserved.

In March 1995 both Acts (the Slaughterhouses Act 1974 and the Slaughter of Poultry Act 1967) were repealed and replaced by secondary legislation in the form of a Statutory Instrument. This implements the European Community's Directive (93/119/EC) on the protection of animals at the time of slaughter. There is specific provision that the requirement for animals and poultry to be stunned before slaughter or killed instantaneously does not apply in the case of animals subject to particular methods of slaughter required by certain religious rites. *Shechita* is accordingly safeguarded.

7. The *Sunday Trading Act*, which came into operation on 26 August 1994, has removed many of the difficulties caused by the Shops Act 1950. All shops with a selling and display area of less than 280 square metres may be open at any time on Sundays. Shops with a selling and display area of 280 square metres or more are still subject to some restriction, with an opening time limited to a continuous period of six hours between 10 a.m. and 6 p.m.

There is, however, a special exemption for 'persons observing the Jewish Sabbath' who are occupiers of these 'large' shops. Provided such an individual (and there are parallel conditions for partnerships and companies) gives a signed notice to the Local Authority that he is a person of the Jewish religion and intends to keep the shop closed for the serving of customers on the Jewish Sabbath, he may open it as and when he wishes on a Sunday.

The notice given to the Local Authority must be accompanied by a statement from the minister of the shopkeeper's synagogue or the secretary for marriages of that synagogue or a person designated by the President of the Board of Deputies, that the shopkeeper is a person of the Jewish religion. There are severe penalties for any false statements made in connection with this intention to trade.

Large shops which were previously registered under Section 53 of the Shops Act 1950 may continue to trade on Sundays without new notification. But occupiers of food stores and kosher meat shops over 280 square metres who, even if closed on Shabbat, did not previously require exemption, may well have formally to notify their Local Authority that their premises will be closed on Shabbat to enable them to open on Sunday.

Jewish shopkeepers who close their premises for the 25 hours of Shabbat may open after Shabbat.

8. Discrimination against a person on account of his being a Jew is unlawful under the *Race Relations Act 1976*.

9. *Friendly Societies Act 1974* (which consolidates the Friendly Societies Acts 1896 to 1971 and certain other enactments). A Friendly Society may be registered for the purpose, *inter alia*, of ensuring that money is paid to persons of the Jewish persuasion during *Shiva* (referred to in the Act as 'the period of confined mourning').

10. By the *Places of Worship Registration Act 1855*, as amended by the *Charities Act 1960*, the Registrar-General may certify a synagogue. The effect of Certification is freedom from uninvited interference by the Charity Commissioners and, if exclusively appropriate to public worship, from general and special rates.

11. By the *Juries Act 1870*, the minister of a synagogue who has been certified, is free from liability to serve on a jury, provided he follows no secular occupation except that of a schoolmaster.

THE SCOTTISH POSITION

(Prepared by Sheriff Sir G. H. Gordon, CBE, QC, LL.D)

Jews do not appear in Scots legislation as a unique group, except in relation to United Kingdom statutes which treat them as such, of which the only one still in force is the Representation of the People Act 1983. European Regulations apply in Scotland as they do in England.

The Education (Scotland) Act 1944 provides by section 9 that every public and grant-aided school shall be open to all denominations, and that any pupil may be withdrawn by his parents from instruction in religious subjects and from any religious observance in any such school.

The oath is administered by the judge in Scots courts, and the witness repeats the words (which begin 'I swear by Almighty God') after him with his right hand upraised. No books are used. A Jewish witness is in practice allowed to cover his head if he wishes to do so. Anyone who indicates a wish to affirm is allowed to do so.

Section 8 of the Marriages (Scotland) Act 1977 provides that a religious marriage may be solemnized by the minister or clergyman of any religious body prescribed by Regulations, or by any person recognized by such a body as entitled to solemnize marriages. The bodies prescribed by the Marriage (Prescription of Religious Bodies) (Scotland) (Regulations) 1977 (S.I.No. 1670) include 'The Hebrew Congregation', whatever that denotes. In practice Orthodox marriages are solemnized by ministers authorized to do so by the Board of Deputies.

The Law Reform (Miscellaneous Provisions) (Scotland) Act 1980 includes regular ministers of any religious denomination among those persons who although eligible for jury service are entitled to be excused therefrom as of right.

The Race Relations Act 1976 applies to Scotland, but the Sunday Trading Act 1994 does not, nor does the Places of Worship Registration Act 1855.

LISTED SYNAGOGUES, FORMER SYNAGOGUES AND OTHER JEWISH SITES IN THE UK

This list is compiled by **Jewish Heritage UK**, P.O. Box 193, Manchester, M13 9PL☎ 0161-275 3611 Email director@jewish-heritage-uk.org. For Regular updates See Website www.jewish-heritage-uk.org/ (see p. 33)

SYNAGOGUES

LONDON
Grade I
Bevis Marks, EC3 (Joseph Avis 1699–1701)
New West End, St Petersburgh Place, W2 (George Audsley in association with N.S. Joseph 1877–79)

Grade II*
In use as synagogue
Hampstead, Dennington Park Road, NW6 (Delissa Joseph 1892–1901)

Former synagogues
Princelet Street, E1 (Former synagogue 1870 behind Huguenot house 1719. Hudson 1870. Remodelled by
    Lewis Solomon 1893)
Spitalfields Great Synagogue, 23 Brick Lane/Fournier Street, E1 (Former French church 1743. Converted
    into synagogue 1897-98. Now London Jamia Mosque)

Grade II
In use as synagogues
Sandys Row, E1 (Former chapel 1766. Converted into synagogue 1867. Remodelled by N.S. Joseph 1870)
West London (Reform), Upper Berkeley Street, W1 (Davis & Emanuel 1870)
Western & Marble Arch Synagogue, 32 Great Cumberland Place, W1 (T. P. Bennett & Son 1962. Listed façade)
Spanish & Portuguese, Lauderdale Road, W9 (Davis & Emanuel 1895-96)
New London, 33 Abbey Road, NW8 (H.H. Collins 1882. Formerly St John's Wood United Synagogue)
Golders Green, 41 Dunstan road, London NW11 (Lewis Solomon & Sons [Digby] 1921-22. Enlarged by
    Messers. Joseph 1927)
Former synagogues
East London Synagogue, Rectory Square, E1 (Davis & Emanuel 1876-77. Flats)
New Synagogue and School, Egerton Road, N16 (Joseph & Smithem 1915. Interior reconstructed from
    Great St Helen's, Bishopsgate, by John Davies 1838. Bobover Talmud Torah)
Dollis Hill, Parkside, NW2 (Sir Owen Williams 1936-38. Torah Temimah Primary School)

ENGLISH REGIONS
Grade I
Liverpool, Old Hebrew Congregation, Princes Road, L8 (W. & G. Audsley 1872-74)

Grade II*
In use as synagogues
Birmingham, Singers Hill, Blucher Street, B1 (Henry R. Yeoville Thomason 1855-56)
Brighton, Middle Street, BN1 (Thomas Lainson 1874-75)
Chatham Memorial Synagogue, High Street, Rochester, ME1 (H.H. Collins 1865-70)
Cheltenham, St James's Square, GL50 (W.H. Knight 1837-39)
Exeter, Mary Arches Street, EX4. (1763-64. Refronted 1835)
Plymouth, Catherine Street, PL1 (1762)
Ramsgate, Montefiore Synagogue, Honeysuckle Road, CT11 (David Mocatta 1831-33)

Former Synagogues
Liverpool, Greenbank Drive, L17 (E. Alfred Shennan 1936-37) Manchester, Spanish & Portuguese, 190
    Cheetham Hill Road, M8 (Edward Salomons 1873-74. Manchester Jewish Museum)
Grade II
In use as synagogues
Blackpool, Leamington Road, FY1 (R.B. Mather 1916)
Bradford Synagogue (Reform), Bowland Street, BD1 (T.H. & F. Healey 1880-81)

Grimsby, Sir Moses Montefiore Synagogue, Heneage Road, DN32 (B.S. Jacobs 1885-88 and *Mikveh* 1915-16)
Leicester Synagogue, Highfield Street, LE2 (Arthur Wakerley 1897-98)
Manchester, Withington Spanish and Portuguese, 8 Queenston Road, West Didsbury, M20 (Delissa Joseph 1925-27)
Manchester, Higher Crumpsall Synagogue, Bury Old Road, Salford, M7 (Pendleton & Dickinson 1928-29)
Manchester, South Manchester, Wilbraham Road, M14 (Joseph Sunlight 1912-13)
Reading, Goldsmid Road, RG1 (W.G. Lewton 1900)

Former synagogues
Grade II
Brighton, 37-39 Devonshire Place, BN2 (Remodelled by David Mocatta 1836-37. Flats)
Brighton, 26 Brunswick Terrace, Hove, BN3 (Rooftop private synagogue of Philip Salomon *ca.* 1850s)
Birmingham, Severn Street, The Athol Masonic Hall, Severn Street 1BI (Richard Tutin 1825-27)
Canterbury, King Street, CT1 (Hezekiah Marshall 1847-48. King's School Recital Room)
Carmel College Synagogue, Mongewell Park, Crowmarsh, Wallingford, Oxfordshire, OX10 (Thomas Hancock 1963)
Falmouth, Smithick Hill, TR11 (1806-8. Studio)
Hull, The Western Synagogue, Linnaeus Street, HU3 (B.S. Jacobs 1902-3).
Leeds, New Synagogue, Louis Street/Chapeltown Road, LS7 (J. Stanley Wright 1929-32. Northern School of Contemporary Dance)
Newcastle-upon-Tyne, Leazes Park, NE1 (John Johnstone 1879-80. Flats)
Sheffield, Wilson Road, S11 (Rawcliffe & Ogden 1929-30. Church)
Sunderland, Ryhope Road, SR2 (Marcus K. Glass 1928)

WALES
Grade II
Former synagogues
Cardiff, Cathedral Road, CF11 (Delissa Joseph 1896-97. Demolished behind façade)
Merthyr Tydfil, Bryntirion Road, Thomastown, CF47 (1877. Gym)

SCOTLAND
Scottish B List
In use as synagogues
Edinburgh, Salisbury Road, Newington, EH16 (James Miller 1929-32)
Glasgow, Garnethill, 127 Hill Street, G3 (John McLeod in association with N.S. Joseph 1877-79)

Former synagogue
Glasgow, Queen's Park, 4 Falloch Road, G42 (Ninian MacWhannel 1925-27)

OTHER LISTED JEWISH BUILDINGS

Grade II
London, Soup Kitchen for the Jewish Poor, Brune Street E1 (Lewis Solomon 1902. Flats)
London, Stepney Jewish Schools, Stepney Green, E1 (Davis & Emanuel 1906)
London, No. 88, Whitechapel High Street, E1: former offices of the Jewish Daily Post, with shop signs by Arthur Szyk (ca.1935)
Carmel College, Mongewell Park, Crowmarsh, Wallingford, Oxfordshire, OX10; Julius Gottlieb Gallery & Boathouse (Sir Basil Spence, Bonnington & Collins 1968-70 Grade II*); Amphitheatre (Thomas Hancock 1965)

Post-war synagogues currently housed in listed buildings
Grade II*
London, Sukkat Shalom Reform Synagogue, 1 Victory Road, Hermon Hill, E11 (Merchant Seaman's Orphan Asylum at Wanstead Hospital Chapel by George Somers Clarke 1861-63. Contains fixtures and fittings from the synagogue at the former Tottenham Jewish Home & Hospital 1924)
Grade II
Nottingham Hebrew Congregation, Shakespeare Street, NG1 (Wesleyan Methodist Chapel by Thomas Simpson 1854. Synagogue 1954. Contains Ark from former Chaucer Street Synagogue 1890)

Medieval sites with possible Jewish associations
Grade I
Bury St Edmunds, Moyses Hall, Cornhill, IP33 (*ca.*1180)
Lincoln: Jews' Court, 2-3 Steep Hill, LN2 (*ca.*1170); Jews' House, 15 The Strait, LN2 (*ca.*1170); Aaron the Jew's House (the Norman House), 47 Steep Hill, LN2 (*ca.*1170)
Norwich, the Music House or Jurnet's House, Wensum Lodge, 167-169 King Street, NR1 (*ca.*1175)

Scheduled Ancient Monuments
Bristol, Jacob's Well, 33 Jacob's Well Road, Bristol BS8 (Possible Medieval *Mikveh ca.*1140)
York, Clifford's Tower, YO1 (Rebuilt)

JEWISH BURIAL GROUNDS, MAUSOLEA AND MEMORIALS

Listed sites (or parts of sites, e.g. boundary walls, screens and gates, buildings or memorials)

LONDON
Grade II
Mile End Velho (Sephardi) 253 Mile End Road, E1 (1657)
Alderney Road, E1 (Ashkenazi) (1696-97)

ENGLISH REGIONS
Grade II*
Ramsgate, Montefiore Mausoleum, Hereson and Honeysuckle Road, CT11 (1862)

Grade II
Birmingham, *Ohel*, Witton New Jewish Cemetery, Warren Road, B44 (Essex & Goodman 1937)
Brighton, Florence Place, Ditchling Road, BN1 (1826, *Ohel* by Lainson & Son 1893)
Brighton, Sassoon Mausoleum, Paston Place, Kemp Town, BN2 (1896)
Bristol, St Philips Cemetery, Barton Road, BS2 (Oldest tombstone 1762)
Exeter, Jews' Burial Ground, Magdalen Street, Bull Meadow, EX2 (1757)
Kings Lynn, Millfleet, Stonegate Street, PE30 (Before 1811)
Liverpool, Jews' Burial Ground, Deane Road, Fairfield, L7 (1836)
Penzance, Jews' Burial Ground, Westinnick Terrace, TR18 (1791)
Southampton,*Ohel*, Southampton Old/Common Cemetery, Cemetery Road, SO15 (1854) (The whole cemetery (1846) is on the *Parks and Gardens Register* – see website)

Scheduled Ancient Monument
Falmouth Jews' Burial Ground, TR11 (*ca.* 1780)

SCOTLAND
Scottish A List
Glasgow, Jews' Enclosure, Glasgow Necropolis, Cathedral Square, G4 (1836)

Scottish B List
Edinburgh, Sciennes House Place (Braid Place), Causewayside, EH9 (1820)
Edinburgh, Jewish Section, Newington Cemetery, Echobank, EH16 (1867)
Glasgow, Janefield Jewish Cemetery, Eastern Necropolis, Gallowgate, G31 (1856)

PRIVY COUNSELLORS, PEERS, MPs, etc

PRIVY COUNSELLORS

Barnett, Lord
Brittan, Lord, QC
Brown, Lord
Burnton, Sir Stanley (Lord Justice)
Clinton-Davis, Lord
Collins, Sir Laurence (Lord Justice)
Cosgrove, Lady, CBE
Cowen, Sir Zelman, AK, GCMG GCVO, QC
Dyson, Sir John (Lord Justice)
Goldsmith, Lord, QC
Hayman, Baroness
Hoffman, Lord
Howard, Michael, MP, QC
Kaufman, Sir Gerald B., MP
Lawson, Lord
Letwin, Oliver, MP
Millett, Lord
Neuberger, Lord David (Lord of Appeal)
Oppenheim-Barnes, Baroness
Rifkind, Sir Malcolm, QC
Rix, Sir Bernard (Lord Justice)
Sedley, Sir Stephen (Lord Justice)
Sheldon, Lord Robert E.
Woolf, Lord
Young, Lord

PEERS

Bearsted of Maidstone, 5th Viscount
Greenhill of Townhead, 3rd Baron, MD
Marks of Broughton, 3rd Baron
Morris of Kenwood, 3rd Baron
Nathan, 3rd Baron
Rothschild, 4th Baron, OM, FBA, MA (Oxon)
Samuel of Mt Carmel & Toxteth, 3rd Viscount
Swaythling, 5th Baron

LIFE PEERS

Alliance, Baron, of Manchester
Barnett, of Heywood & Royton, Baron, PC
Brittan, Baron of Spennithorne PC, QC
Brown, Baron PC (Lord of Appeal)
Carlile, Baron, of Berriew, QC
Clinton-Davis, of Hackney, Baron, PC
Deech, Baroness, of Cumnor, DBE
Dubs, Baron of Battersea
Ezra of Horsham, Baron, MBE
Goldsmith, Baron, of Allerton, PC, QC
Grabiner, Baron, of Aldwych, QC
Greengross, Baroness, of Notting Hill
Hoffman, Baron, of Chedworth PC (Lord of Appeal)
Haskel, of Higher Broughton, Baron
Hayman, of Dartmouth Park, Baroness, PC
Henig, Baroness, of Lancaster

Jacobs, of Belgravia, Baron
Janner, of Braunstone, Baron, QC
Joffe, of Liddington, Baron,
Kalms, of Edgware, Baron,
Lawson, of Blaby, Baron, PC
Lester, of Herne Hill, Baron, QC
Levene, of Portsoken, Baron
Levy, of Mill Hill, Baron
Miller, of Hendon, Baroness
Millett, Baron of St Marylebone, PC (Lord of Appeal)
Moser, Baron of Regent's Park, FBA
Neuberger, Baron, of Abbotsbury PC (Lord of Appeal)
Neuberger, of Primrose Hill, DBE Baroness
Oppenheim-Barnes, of Gloucester, Baroness, PC
Peston, of Mile End, Baron
Puttnam, of Queensgate, CBE, Baron
Saatchi, of Staplefield, Baron
Sheldon, of Ashton-under-Lyne, Baron, PC
Steinberg, of Belfast, Baron
Stern, of Brentford, Baron
Sterling, of Plaistow, Baron, CBE
Stern, of Vauxhall, Baroness,
Stone, of Blackheath, Baron
Triesman, of Tottenham, Baron
Turnberg, Baron of Cheadle
Weidenfeld, of Chelsea, Baron
Winston, of Hammersmith, Baron
Wolfson, of Marylebone, Baron
Wolfson, of Sunningdale, Baron
Woolf, of Barnes, Baron, PC
Young, of Graffham, Baron, PC

MEMBERS OF PARLIAMENT

Bercow, John (C.), Buckingham
Cohen, Harry (Lab.), Leyton
Djanogly, Jonathan S. (C.), Huntingdon
Ellman, Louise (Lab.), Liverpool Riverside
Fabrikant, Michael (C.), Lichfield
Featherstone, Lynne (Lib.), Hornsey & Wood Green
Hamilton, Fabian (Lab.), Leeds North East
Harris, Dr Evan (Lib.), Oxford West & Abingdon
Hodge, Margaret (Lab.), Barking
Howard, Rt. Hon. Michael, PC, QC (C.), Folkestone & Hythe
Kaufman, Rt. Hon. Sir Gerald, PC (Lab.), Manchester, Gorton
Kramer, Susan (Lib.), Richmond
Letwin, Rt Hon. Oliver, PC (C.), Dorset West
Lewis, Ivor (Lab.), Bury South
Lewis, Dr Julian (C.), New Forest East
Merron, Gillian (Lab.), Lincoln

Newmark, Brooks (C.), Braintree
Rifkind, Rt. Hon. Sir Malcolm, PC, (C.),
    Kensington & Chelsea
Shapps, Grant (C.), Welwyn and Hatfield
Scott, Lee (C.) Ilford North
Steen, Anthony (C.), Totnes
Winnick, David (Lab.), Walsall North

MEMBER OF EUROPEAN PARLIAMENT

Sumberg, David (C.) North West England

BARONETS

Cahn, Sir Albert Jonas
Jessel, Sir Charles John
Richardson, Sir Anthony Lewis
Tuck, Sir Bruce A. R.
Waley-Cohen, Sir Stephen

KNIGHTS

Abeles, Sir Peter, AC
Arbib, Sir Martyn
Bean, Sir David (Hon.Mr Justice)
Beecham, Sir Jeremy
Berman, Sir Franklin
Bernstein, Sir Howard
Berry, Sir Michael, FRS
Bindman, Sir Geoffrey
Blank, Sir Victor
Blom-Cooper, Sir Louis
Burgen, Sir Arnold, FRS
Burnton, Sir Stanley (Lord Justice), PC
Burton, Sir Michael (the Hon. Mr Justice)
Calne, Sir Roy, FRS
Caro, Sir Anthony, OM
Chinn, Sir Trevor, CVO
Cohen, Sir Edward
Cohen, Sir Ivor Harold
Cohen, Prof. Sir Philip
Cohen, Sir Ronald
Collins, Sir Laurence (Lord Justice) PC
Colman, Sir Anthony (the Hon. Mr Justice)
Copisarow, Sir Alcon
Cowen, Sir Zelman, AK, CGMC, GCVO
Crewe, Sir Ivor
Djanogly, Sir Harry
Dyson, Sir John (Lord Justice), PC
Elton, Sir Arnold
Epstein, Sir Anthony, FRS
Etherton, Sir Terence (the Hon. Mr Justice)
Falk, Sir Roger Salis
Feldman, Sir Basil
Fersht, Sir Alan, PhD, FRS
Fox, Sir Paul

Freedman, Sir Lawrence
Freud, Sir Clement
Gainsford, Sir Ian
Garrard, Sir David
Gershon, Sir Peter
Gilbert, Sir Martin, CBE
Gillinson, Sir Clive
Goldberg, Prof. Sir David
Golding, Sir John
Goode, Prof. Sir Roy
Gordon, Sir Donald
Gordon, Sir Gerald Henry, CBE, QC
Green, Sir Allan, KCB
Green, Sir Philip
Greengross, Sir Alan
Grierson, Sir Ronald
Halpern, Sir Ralph
Harris, Sir William Woolf, OBE
Hatter, Sir Maurice
Henriques, Sir Richard (the Hon.-Mr Justice)
Hirsch, Sir Peter Bernhard, FRS
Isaacs, Sir Jeremy
Jacobs, Sir Francis Geoffrey KCMG, QC
Japhet, Ernest I., Hon. KBE
Jordan, Sir Gerald
Kaufman, Sir Gerald, PC, MP
Kingsland, Sir Richard, AO, CBE, DFC
Klug, Sir Aaron, FRS, OM
Kornberg, Prof. Sir Hans Leo, FRS
Krusin, Sir Stanley Marks, CB
Lachmann, Prof. Sir Peter, FRS
Laddie, Sir Hugh
Landau, Sir Dennis
Lauterpacht, Prof. Sir Elihu
Lawrence, Sir Ivan, QC
Leigh, Sir Geoffrey, KCB
Leveson, Sir Brian
Levine, Sir Montague
Lewis, Sir Leigh
Lewison, Sir Kim (the Hon-Mr Justice)
Lightman, Sir Gavin (the Hon. Mr Justice),
Lipton, Sir Stuart
Lipworth, Sir Sydney
Marmot, Prof. Sir Michael
Michaels, Sir David
Miller, Sir Jonathan
Milton, Sir Simon
Ognall, Sir Harry Henry (the Hon. Mr Justice)
Oppenheim, Sir Alexander, OBE
Pepper, Sir Michael, FRS
Rieger, Sir Clarence Oscar, CBE
Rifkind, Sir Malcolm, PC, QC, MP
Ritblat, Sir John
Rix, Sir Bernard (Lord Justice), PC
Robinson, Sir Albert EP
Rodley, Prof. Sir Nigel

Rosenthal, Sir Norman
Rothschild, Sir Evelyn de
Sacks, Chief Rabbi Sir Jonathan
Sassoon, Sir James Meyer
Samuelson, Sir Sydney W., CBE
Schreier, Sir Bernard
Sedley, Sir Stephen (Lord Justice), PC
Seligman, Sir Peter Wendel, CBE
Serota, Sir Nicholas
Shaffer, Sir Peter
Sheinwald, Sir Nigel Elton, KCGM Sher, Sir
    Anthony
Sherman, Sir Lou, OBE
Shock, Sir Maurice
Sieff, Sir David
Silber, Sir Stephen (the Hon. Mr Justice)
Smith, Sir David, AK, CVO, AO
Solomon, Sir Harry
Sorrell, Sir Martin
Sternberg, Sir Sigmund
Stoppard, Sir Tom, OM
Sugar, Sir Alan
Wald, Sir Nicholas
Weinberg, Sir Mark
Wesker, Sir Arnold
Winton, Sir Nicholas
Zissman, Sir Bernard
Zunz, Sir Jack

DAMES

Blume, Dame Hilary
Duffield, Dame Vivien
Genn, Dame Hazel
Higgins, Dame Rosalyn, QC
Porter, Dame Shirley
Prendergast, Dame Simone, JP, DL
Robins, Dame Ruth, BA
Ronson, Dame Gail
Waterman, Dame Fanny

FELLOWS OF THE ROYAL SOCIETY

Abramsky, Samson
Berry, Sir Michael
Born, Prof. Gustav Victor Rudolf
Brenner, Prof. Sydney, CH
Burgen, Sir Arnold
Calne, Sir Roy
Cohen, Prof. Sydney, CBE
Domb, Prof. Cyril
Dunitz, Prof. Jack David
Dwek, Raymond
Epstein, Sir Michael Anthony (Vice-President,
    1986–91)
Fersht, Prof. Sir Alan

Glynn, Prof. Ian Michael
Goldstone, Prof. Jeffrey
Grant, Ian Philip
Hirsch, Prof. Sir Peter Bernhard
Horn, Prof. Gabriel
Huppert, Dr Herbert
Ish-Horowicz, David
Josephson, Prof. Brian David
Kalmus, George Ernest
Kennard, Dr Olga, OBE
Klug, Sir Aaron, OM (President 1995–2000)
Kornberg, Prof. Sir Hans Leo
Lachmann, Sir Peter Julius
Levitt, Malcolm
Levitt, Michael
Mahler, Prof. Kurt
Mandelstam, Prof. Joel
Mandelstam, Prof. Stanley
Mestel, Prof. Leon
Neumann, Prof. Bernard H.
Orgel, Prof. L. E.
Orowan, Prof. Egon
Pepper, Dr Sir Michael
Roitt, Prof. Ivan
Sanders, Prof. Jeremy
Segal, Dr Anthony Walter
Sondheimer, Prof. Franz
Wald, Prof. Nicholas
Waldmann, Prof. Herman
Weinberg, Prof. Felix
Weiskrantz, Prof. Lawrence
Woolfson, Prof. Michael Mark
Young, Prof. Alec David, OBE

Foreign Members

Calvin, Prof. Melvin
Katzir, Prof. Ephraim, form. President of Israel
Kornberg, Prof. Arthur

FELLOWS OF THE BRITISH ACADEMY

Bogdanor, Prof. Vernon, CBE
Cohen, Prof. Gerald Allan
Genn, Prof. Hazel, CBE
Goodman, Prof. Martin
Hajnal, Prof. John
Hobsbawm, Prof. Eric John, CH
Israel, Prof. Jonathan Irvine
Josipovici, Prof. Gabriel David
Lewis, Prof. Bernard
Lukes, Prof. Steven
Marks, Prof. Shula
Moser, Lord, KCB, CBE
Prais, Sigbert J.
Prawer, Prof. Siegbert Salomon

Rothschild, Lord OM, MA
Steiner, Prof. George
Stern, Lord
Supple, Prof. Barry, CBE
Ullendorff, Prof. Edward (Vice-President 1980–82)
Vermes, Prof. Geza
Yamey, Prof. Basil Selig, CBE

Corresponding Fellows

Blau, Prof. J.
Levi-Strauss, Prof. Claude
Samuelson, Prof. Paul Antony

VICTORIA CROSS

Lieutenant Frank Alexander De Pass*
Captain Robert Gee, M.C.*
Leonard Keysor*
Acting Corporal Issy Smith*
Jack White*
Lieut.-Cmdr. Thomas William Gould, RNVR*

GEORGE CROSS

Errington, Harry*
Lewin, Sgt. Raymond M., RAF*
Latutin, Capt. Simmon*
Newgass, Lieutenant-Commander Harold Reginald, RNVR*

ORDER OF MERIT

Caro, Sir Anthony
Freud, Lucian, CH
Klug, Sir Aaron, FRS
Rothschild, Lord
Stoppard, Sir Tom

COMPANIONS OF HONOUR

Brenner, Prof. Sydney, FRS
Freud, Lucian, OM
Hobsbawm, Prof. Eric John Ernest, FBA
Pinter, Harold

NOBEL PRIZE WINNERS

Peace

Tobias Asser*; Alfred Fried*; Rene Cassin*; Henry Kissinger; Menachem Begin*; Elie Wiesel; Yitzhak Rabin*; Shimon Peres; Joseph Rotblat*.

Physics

Albert Abraham Michelson*; Gabriel Lippmann*; Albert Einstein*; Niels Bohr*; Enrico Fermi*; James Franck*; Gustav Herts*; Otto Stern*; Isidor Isaac Rabi*; Felix Bloch*; Max Born*; Igor Tamm*; Emilio Segre*; Donald A. Glaser; Robert Hofstadter*; Lev Davidovic Landau*; Richard Feynman*; Julian Schwinger; Hans Bethe*; Murray Gell-Mann; Dennis Gabor*; Brian Josephson; Ben R. Mottelson; Aage Bohr; Burton Richter; Arno Penzias; Sheldon Glashow; Steven Weinberg; Leon Lederman; Melvin Schwartz; Jack Steinberger; Georges Charpak; David Gross.

Chemistry

Adolph Baeyer*; Henri Moissan*; Otto Wallach*; Richard Willstatter*; Fritz Haber*; George de Hevesy*; Melvin Calvin; Max Ferdinand Perutz*; William Stein*; Herbert Brown; Paul Berg; Walter Gilbert; Roald Hoffmann; Aaron Klug; Dudley Herschebach; Herbert Hauptman; Sidney Altman; Rudolf Marcus; Walter Kohn; Aaron Ciechanover, Avraham Hirsko, Irwin Rose; Roger Kornberg

Medicine

Paul Ehrlich*; Elias Metchnikoff*; Robert Barany*; Otto Meyerhoff*; Karl Landsteiner*; Otto Warburg*; Otto Loewi*; Joseph Erlanger*; Sir Ernst B. Chain*; Herbert Gasser*; Hermann Joseph Muller*; Tadeus Reichstein*; Selman Abraham Waksman*; Sir Hans A. Krebs*; Fritz Albert Lipmann*; Joshua Lederberg; Arthur Kornberg*; Konrad Bloch; Francois Jacob-Andre Lwoff*; George Wald*; Marshall W. Nirenberg; Salvador Luria*; Sir Bernard Katz*; Julius Axelrod*; Gerald Maurice Edelman; David Baltimore; Howard Martin Temin; Baruch S. Blumberg; Rosalyn Yalow; David Nathans; Baruj Benacerraf; Cesar Milstein*; Joseph L. Goldstein; Michael Brown; Rita Levi-Montalcini; Stanley Cohen; Gertrude Aeilion; Harold Vermus; Gary Becker; Gunter Blobel; H. Robert Horvitz; Sydney Brenner.

Literature

Paul Heyse*; Henri Bergson*; Boris Pasternak*; Shmuel Yosef Agnon*; Nelly Sachs*; Saul Bellow*; Isaac Bashevis Singer*; Elias Canetti*; Jaroslav Seifert*; Joseph Brodsky*; Nadine Gordimer, Imre Kertész; Harold Pinter

Economics

Paul Samuelson; Simon Kuznets*; Kenneth Arrow; Leonid Kantorovich*; Milton Friedman*; Herbert Simon*; Lawrence Klein*; Franco Modigliani*; Robert Solow; Leonid Hurwicz*; Daniel Kahneman; Robert J. Aumann; Paul Krugman.

* Deceased.

Who's Who

AARON, Martin, MBA, FAIA, FRSM, FRSA; b. London, Jan. 25, 1937; m. Jean née Joseph; Vis. Prof. Univ. Staffordshire; L. Fell. Royal Soc. Medicine; Fdr. and Hon. President, Jewish Assoc. for the Mentally Ill (1989-); Chairman, Nat. Spirituality and Mental Health (inter-faith) Forum (2003-); Mentor, The Prince's Trust (1995–2006); Mem. Adv.C., Three Faiths Forum; Vice President B'nai B'rith First-lodge (2005-). Adv. M., All-Party Parliamentary Group on Mental Health (2001-); Tr., Ravenswood Foundation (1986-90); Fdr. and Hon. President, Jewish Soc. for the Mentally Handicapped (1977-86); form. Memb. Concern for the Mentally Ill (1992-98); form. Adv. C., MENCAP; form. Adv. C. MIND (1976-83). Ad.: c/o JAMI, 16a North End Rd., London NW11 7PH. ☎ 020-8458 2223. Mentalhealthjsmh@aol.com

ABRAHAMSON, Hon. Abraham Eliezer, BA; b. Bulawayo, Oct. 13, 1922, m. Anita née Rabinovitz; MP (Bulawayo East, 1953-64); Min. of Treasury, Local Govt. and Housing (1958), Min. of Labour, Social Welfare and Housing (1958-62); Chairman Bd., South African Jewish Report (2002-); H.L.P. (President 1956-58, 64-79) Central African Jew BoD, Life Member C.A.Z.O. (1989-); Member World Exec. WJC, served on Nat. Exec. S.A. Jewish BoD (1991-); Chairman, S.A.Z. Fed. (1991-94), President (1994-98), Hon. Life P. (1998-); Exec., S.A.Z. Fed (1986); V. Chairman 1988-90. Publ. The Moon Can Wait, (biography by Paul Clingman. 2004) Ad.: 4 Oxford Gdns., 188 Oxford Rd., Illovo 2196, Johannesburg. ☎ 880 1964. Fax 447 2596. Email abita@hixnet.co.za.

ABRAMSKY, Chimen, B.A. (Jerusalem), MA (Oxon); b. Minsk, Mar. 5, 1917; form. President, Jewish Hist. Soc. of England; form. Goldsmid Prof. of Heb. and Jewish Studies; form. Reader in Jewish hist., Univ. Coll., London; Sr. Fel., St. Antony's Coll., Oxford. Publ.: Karl Marx and the Engl. Labour Movement (jt. auth.); Essays in honour of E. H. Carr (ed.), two Prague Haggadot (auth.), First Illustrated Grace After Meals, Jews in Poland (jt ed.), many articles and monographs on modern Jewish hist., etc. Ad: 5 Hillway, N6 6QB. ☎ 020-8340 8302.

ABRAMSON, Glenda (née Melzer), BA, MA, PhD (Rand), Hon. D.Litt (HUC); b. Johannesburg, Nov. 16, 1940; m. David; Academic; Prof. Heb. and Jewish Studies, Univ. Oxford (2006-); form Cowley Lect. Post-Biblical Hebrew, Oxford (1989-2006); form. Schreiber Fell. Modern Jewish Studies, Oxford Centre for Hebrew and Jewish Studies (1981); form. Sen. Lect., Univ. Witwatersrand (1970–78); Edr. Journal of Modern Jewish Studies. Publ.: Modern Hebrew Drama (1979); The Writing of Yehuda Amichai (1989); Hebrew in Three Months (1993, repr. 1998); Drama and Ideology in Modern Israel (1998); Ed.: Essays in Honour of Salo Rappaport (1985); The Blackwell Companion to Jewish Culture (1989); Jewish Education and Learning (1994, with T. Parfitt); Tradition and Trauma (1995, with D. Patterson); The Oxford Book of Hebrew Short Stories (1996); The Experienced Soul: Studies in Amichai (1997); Modern Jewish Mythologies (2000), ed. Encyclopedia of Modern Jewish Culture (2005), ed, with H. Kilpatrick, Religious Perspectives in Modern Hebrew and Islamic Literatures (2005); Ad.: Oriental Institute, Pusey Lane, Oxford OX1 2LE. ☎ 01865-278 093. Fax 01865-278 190. Email glenda.abramson@stx.ox.ac.uk.

ABSE, Dannie, FRSL, MRCS, LRCP; b. Cardiff, Sept. 22, 1923; writer (poems and novels) and physician. Ad.: Green Hollows, Craig-yr-Eos Rd., Ogmore-by-Sea, Glamorgan.

ABULAFIA, David Samuel Harvard, MA, PhD, Litt.D, FRHistS; b. Twickenham, Dec. 12, 1949; m. Anna née Sapir; Historian; Prof., Mediterranean History, Cambridge; Fellow, Gonville & Caius College (1974-); Commendatore dell' Ordine della Stella della Solidarietà Italiana (2003). Publ.: The Two Italies (1977); Italy, Sicily and the Mediterranean (1987); Frederick II (1988); Commerce and Conquest in the Mediterranean (1993); A Mediterranean Emporium (1994); The French Descent into Renaissance Italy (ed.) (1995); En las Costas del Mediterráneo Occidental (ed.) (1998); Cambridge Medieval History, vol. 5, 1198-1300 (ed.) (1999); The Western Mediterranean Kingdoms (1997); Mediterranean Encounters (2000); Medieval Frontiers (ed.) (2002); The Mediterranean in History (2003); Italy in the Central Middle Ages (ed.) (2004); The Discovery of Mankind (2008). Ad.: Gonville & Caius College, Cambridge CB2 1TA. ☎ 01233-332473. Email dsa1000@hermes.cam.ac.uk.

ALDERMAN, Geoffrey, D. Litt (Oxon), MA, D.Phil (Oxon), FRHistS, FRSA, FICPD, MIQA, MCMI; b. Hampton Court, Feb. 10, 1944, m. Marion née Freed; Prof. Politics Contemporary History Univ. Buckingham (2007-); Sen. Vice President American Intercontinental University, London

(2002-06); Visiting Res. Fell., Institute of Historical Research, Univ. London; Sen. Vice President Touro Coll., N.Y. (1999-2002-; Pro.-V.-C. & Prof. Middlesex University (1994-99); form. Prof of Politics & Contemporary History, Royal Holloway Coll. (Lond. Univ.), Senior Associate, Oxford Hebrew Centre; Publ.: British Elections: Myth and Reality, The Railway Interest, The Jewish Vote in Great Britain since 1945, The Jewish Community in British Politics, Pressure Groups and Government in Britain, Modern Britain 1700-1983, The Federation of Synagogues 1887-1987, London Jewry & London Politics, 1889-1986; Modern British Jewry; Controversy and Crisis: Studies in the History of the Jews in Modern Britain (2008). Ad.: 172 Colindeep Lane, London NW9 6EA. Email geoffreyalderman@hotmail.com. www.geoffrey alderman.com.

ALPERT, Michael, MA, PhD; b. London Dec. 24,1935; m. Marie Pradillo Gomez De Acosta; Emeritus Professor. President, JHSE (2008-); Professor of Modern and Contemporary History of Spain, Univ. Westminster (1996-2001, Reader, Senior Lecturer 1976-96). Publ. A New International History of the Spanish Civil War (1994), Crypto-Judaism and the Spanish Inquisition (2nd ed. 2001), Two Spanish Picaresque Novels (repr. 2003), London 1849 (2004), Secret Judaism and the Spanish Inquisition (2008). Ad.: 3, Donaldson Rd., London NW6 6NA. Tel 020-7624 9116 Email malpert@onetel.com.

ALVAREZ, Alfred ('Al'), MA (Oxon), Hon. D.Litt (East London); b. London, Aug. 5, 1929; poet, author and critic; Hon. Fell. Corpus Christi College, Oxford; poetry critic and editor, The Observer (1956-66); Gauss Seminarian, Princeton Univ. (1958); Vis. Prof., Brandeis Univ. (1960-61), State Univ. of NY, Buffalo (1966). Publ.: The Shaping Spirit, The School of Donne, Beyond All This Fiddle, Beckett, The Writer's Voice, Risky Business (lit.crit.); The Savage God, Under Pressure, Life after Marriage, The Biggest Game in Town, Offshore, Feeding the Rat, Rain Forest, Night, Where Did It All Go Right?, Poker: Bets, Bluffs and Bad Beats (non-fiction); Lost, Apparition, Penguin Modern Poets 18, Autumn to Autumn (poems); New and Selected Poems; Hers, Hunt, Day of Atonement (novels); The New Poetry, Faber Book of Modern European Poetry (anthologies). Ad.: c/o Gillon Aitken Associates, 29 Fernshaw Rd., SW10 0TG. ☎ 020-7351 3594. Fax 020-7376 3594.

ANGIER, Carole (née Brainin), MA (Oxon), MLitt (Cantab), FRSL, b. London, Oct. 30, 1943; Writer; Teacher of Life writing, Birkbeck College, London (2005-); Founder & Teacher, Practice of Biography, Univ. Warwick (2002-03); Royal Literary Fund Fellow, Univ. Warwick (1999-2003, 2008-09), Tutor, Open University (1975-85). Publ.: Jean Rhys (1985), Jean Rhys: Life and Work (1990), The Double Bond: Primo Levi, a Biography (2002). Tongue Pie by Fred Russell (ed.), The Story of My Life: Refugees Writing in Oxford (2005). Ad.: 13 High Street, Ascott-u-Wychwood, Oxon OX7 6AW. ☎ 01993-830414/830725. Email carole@cangier.co.uk

APPLE, Rabbi Dr Raymond, AO, RFD, MLitt, BA, LLB; b. Melbourne, Dec. 27, 1935; Emer. Rabbi, Great Syn., Sydney, Senior Rabbi (1972-2005); Sr. Rabbi., Australian Defence Force; Dayan & Reg., Sydney Beth Din (1975-2005); H.V. President, New South Wales Bd. of Jewish Educ.; Jt. Master Mandelbaum House, Sydney Univ.; Lect. in Judaic Studies, Sydney Univ.; Lect., Jewish Law, NSW Univ.; President, Assn. of Rabbis & Mins. of Australia & New Zealand (1980-84; 1988-1992); Jt.P., Australian Council of Christians & Jews (1996-); President, Australian Jewish Hist. Soc.(1985-89); M., Bayswater Syn. (1960-65), Hampstead Syn. (1965-1972); form. Rel. Dir., AJY. Publ.: The Hampstead Syn., 1892-1967; The Jewish Way: Jews & Judaism in Australia (3rd. ed. 2002); Francis Lyon Cohen – the Passionate Patriot (1955); The Big Shule: Essays on the history of the Great Synagogue, Sydney (2006), 'Let's Ask Rabbi Apple' (2006) etc. Ad.: 20/6 Hatekufah Jerusalem ☎ (972) 26794 180. Email rabbiapple@hotmail.com.

ARKUSH, Rabbi Shmuel; b. Birmingham, May 5, 1951; Rabbi, Birmingham Jewish Community Care (2000-); Dir. Lubavitch in the Midlands; Dir. Operation Judaism; H.T. B.J.E.B. Talmud Torah; Chaplain of the Midlands Region Chaplaincy Bd. (1980-85). Ad.: 95 Willows Rd., Birmingham B12 9QF. ☎ 0121-440 6673. Fax 0121-446 4199.

AUERBACH, Mrs Geraldine Yvonne (née Kretzmar), M.B.E., BA(Rand), STC (UCT); b. Kimberly, South Africa; Fd. Dir. Jewish Music Institute, SOAS, Univ. London (1999-); Founding Festival Dir. Bnai Brith Jewish Music Festival (1984); Founding Chairman The Jewish Music Heritage Trust Ltd. (1989); Founder and MD Jewish Music Heritage Recordings (1984); Founder and former MD (1984-1991) Jewish Music Distribution. Ad.: PO Box 232, Harrow, Middx. HA1 2NN. ☎ 020-8909 2445. Fax 020-8909 1030. Email g.auerbach@jmi.org.uk.

AVIDAN, Rabbi Hillel, MA; b. London, July 16, 1933, m. Ruth; M. Durban Progressive J. Cong. (2005-); Chairman Southern African Assoc. Progressive Rabbis (2004-08); M., Bet David Reform Cong., Johannesburg (1992-2003); Chairman Southern African Assoc. Progressive Rabbis (1995-99); F.M., West Central Lib. Syn. (1985-92); M. Ealing Lib. Syn. (1986-92); and Chairman, ULPS Rabbinic Conference (1990-92), form. M., Wimbledon & Distr. Ref Syn. (1974-81), Chairman, RSGB Assembly of Rabbis, (1978-80), Teacher Reali High Sch., Haifa; Libr. Haifa Univ. Publ.: Feasts and Fasts of Israel, (Contrib) Judaism & Ecology; Renewing the vision. Ad.: 28 O'Connor Rd., Durban 3629 RSA. ☎ 266 2792. Email dpjc@sbsa.com.

AZIZ, Alan, BSc., ACCA; b. London, Aug. 1, 1968; Chartered Accountant; Exec. Director, ZF Great Britain and Ireland; Dir. Zionist C. Europe (1998-); Dir. Israel Connect European Training Programme. Ad.: 741 High Road, London N12 0BQ. ☎ 020-8343 9756. Fax 020-8446 0639; Email zion-fed@dircon.co.uk.

BAKER, Adrienne, PhD, BSc; b. Manchester, Feb. 15, 1936; Family Therapist & University Lecturer; Senior Lect: School of Psychotherapy, Regent's College, London; Publ.: The Jewish Woman in Contemporary Society: Transitions and Traditions (1993). Ad.: 16 Sheldon Ave., Highgate, London N6 4JT. ☎ 020-8340 5970 (home), Email adrienne@hotmail.co.uk.

BAKER, William, BA (Hons), M.Phil, PhD, MLS; b. Shipston-on-Stour, Warwicks., July 6, 1944; Form. Housemaster, Polack's House, Clifton Coll., Lect. in English, Ben-Gurion Univ. (1971-77), Hebrew Univ., Jerusalem (1973-75); Vis. Prof., Pitzer Coll., Claremont, Ca. (1981-82); Sr. Lect., West Midlands Coll. (1978-85); Edr., George Eliot-G. H. Lewes Newsletter; Publ.: George Eliot and Judaism, Harold Pinter (co. auth.), Some George Eliot Notebooks, Vols. I-IV, The George Eliot-G. H. Lewes Library, The libraries of G. Eliot and G. Lewes, Antony & Cleopatra. The Merchant of Venice.

BALCOMBE, Andrew David, BA (Com), MBA (Harvard); b. Adlington, Cheshire, Aug. 4, 1942; m. Jean née Steinberg; Chairman, National Council Zionist Fed. UK (2007-); Tr. UK Friends of the Assoc. Welfare of Israeli Soldiers (2002-06); Dir. UJIA Israel (1995-2000); Chief Exec. of Armour Trust plc (1970-98); Chairman M@tchnet plc (1998-99); Chairman NetVest.com plc (1999-2002); Dir. Tecc-1S plc (2000-03); Chairman, National Council for Soviet Jewry (1980-82); Founder member of Conscience interdenominational committee for the release of Soviet Jewry (1973-95); Exec. Ctte. Board of Deputies (1980-82); Tr. Metropolitan Charitable Fd. (1975-2008); Dep. Chairman Ben Uri Art Society (2000). Ad.: Flat 9, 22 Rachel Imenu, Jerusalem 93228 ☎ 2566 5132. Fax 2561 1421. Email andrew@balcombelondon.co.uk.

BARAK, Ehud, MK, BSc (HU), MSc (Stanford), DSM; b. Mishmar Hasharon, 1942; Prime Minister of Israel and Minister of Defence (1999-2002); MK (1996-); Min. Foreign Affairs (1995-96); Chairman Israel Labour Party (1996-); formed One Israel Party (1999); Lt. General, Chief of General Staff, IDF (1991); involved in negotiations with Jordan and Peace Treaty (1994); involved in negotiations with Syria.

BARNETT, Rt. Hon. Baron of Heywood & Royton, (Life Peer) (**Joel Barnett**), PC, JP; b. Manchester, Oct. 14, 1923, m. Lilian née Goldstone; Accountant and Chairman/Dirs. of Companies; form. V. Chairman B.B.C. Govs.; Mem. European Union Select Cttee.; Chairman European Union Sub. Cttee. on Finance, Trade & Industry; Tr. Victoria & Albert Museum; Chairman Educ. Broadcasting Society Tr.; Chairman, Public Accounts Cttee.; House of Commons (1979-83); Chief Sec. to H.M. Treasury (1974-79), Member of Cabinet (1977-79), form. Chairman, form. Mem Public Exp. Cttee., M.P (Lab.) for Heywood & Royton (1964-83); Hon. Fell., Birkbeck Coll., Lond. Univ., Hon. Doctorate, Strathclyde, Member, Halle Cttee. Publ.: Inside the Treasury. Ad.: 7 Hillingdon Rd., Whitefield, Manchester, M45 7QQ; Flat 92, 24 John Islip St., SW1.

BARON COHEN, Gerald, BA, FCA; b. Lond., July 13, 1932, m. Daniella née Weiser; Chartered Acct.; President, First Lodge of England, B'nai B'rith, Nat. T., B'nai B'rith, Distr. 15, V. President Hillel Foundation; V. Chairman, U.J.S.; Edr., Mosaic; Dep. Edr., New Middle East, Chairman Bamah-Forum for Jewish Dialogue (Jewish Unity Working Group). Ad.: 70 Wildwood Rd., NW11 6UJ. ☎ 020-8458 1552.

BAYFIELD, Rabbi Dr Anthony Michael, MA (Cantab) DD (Lambeth); b. Ilford, July 4, 1946; Head, Movement for Reform Judaism; Dir. Reform Foundation Trust; Dir., Sternberg Centre for

Judaism; Dir. Manor House Trust; form. Chairman, C., Ref & Lib. Rabbis; Tr., Michael Goulston Educ. Fnd., Lect., Leo Baeck Coll.; Edr., 'Manna'; Rabbi, North-West Surrey Syn. (1972-82); Chairman, Assembly of Rabbis, RSGB (1980-81). Publ.: Churban, The Murder of the Jews of Europe (1981); Dialogue with a Difference (Ed. with Marcus Braybrooke) (1992); Sinai, Law & Responsible Autonomy (1993); He Kissed Him and They Wept (Ed. with Sidney Brichto and Eugene Fisher) (2001). Ad.: The Sternberg Centre for Judaism, 80, East End Road, N3 2SY. ☎ 020-8349 5645. Fax 020-8349 5699. Email admin@reformjudaism.org.uk.

BEECHAM, Sir Jeremy Hugh, MA, DCL, DL, H. Fellow, Northumbria University; b. Leicester, Nov. 11, 1944; m. Brenda Elizabeth née Woolf; Solicitor; Newcastle City Councillor (1967-); Leader Newcastle City Council (1977-94); Chairman, Assn. Metropolitan Auth. (1991-97); Chairman, Labour Party NEC (2005-06); Chairman, Local Govt. Assn. (1997-04), Vice-Chairman (2004-); Mem. Bd., New Israel Fund (2007-); Mems. Adv. Bd. Harold Hartog School of Govt,. Tel Aviv U; Com., English Heritage (1983-87); President, British Urban Regeneration Assn. (1996-). Ad.: 7 Collingwood Street, Newcastle upon Tyne NE1 1JE.

BELLOS, Vivienne, LRAM, ARCM; b. Southend-on-Sea, Apr. 3, 1951; Musician; Director of Music North Western Reform Synagogue; Musical Director, Alyth Choral Society, Jewish Youth Choir. ☎ 07956 912567. Email vivienne.bellos@btinternet.com.

BENADY, S., CBE, QC, MA (Cantab); b. Gibraltar, May 21, 1905; barrister; Life President (President, 1956-73) Gibraltar Jewish Com.; Fd. & L.President Gibraltar Oxford & Cambridge Assoc.; Leader, Gib. Bar; Sqdn.-Leader; RAF, Second World War. Ad.: 124 Main St., Gibraltar ☎ 78549.

BENARROCH, Rev. Halfon, BA; b. Tangiers, Apr. 12, 1939; m. Delia née Sabah; Minister; M. Bevis Marks; Senior Hazan; Spanish & Portuguese Jews' Cong. Ad.: 23 Lauderdale Tower, Barbican, London EC2Y 8BY ☎ 020-7638 5100. Email broch@talktalk.net

BENEDICTUS, David Henry, BA (Oxon); b. London, Sept. 16, 1938; Author, playwright, theatre dir; Hd. Drama, Putney High School; Royal Literary Fund Fell. (2007-08); Ed. Readings BBC Radio (1989-94) plus Radio 3 Drama from 1992; Commissioning Ed., Channel 4 (1984-86); Judith E. Wilson Vis. Fell., Cambridge Univ. (1981-82); Producer 'Something Understood' (with Mark Tully); Berkoff's Macbeth for BBC Radio 4. Publ.: The Fourth of June, You're a Big Boy Now, This Animal is Mischievous, Hump, or Bone by Bone Alive, The Guru and the Golf Club, A World of Windows, The Rabbi's Wife, Junk, A Twentieth Century Man, The Antique Collector's Guide, Lloyd George, Whose Life is it Anyway?, Who Killed the Prince Consort?, Local Hero, The Essential London Guide, Floating Down to Camelot, The Streets of London, The Absolutely Essential London Guide, Little Sir Nicholas, The Odyssey of a Scientist, Sunny Intervals and Showers, The Stamp Collector, How to Cope when the Money Runs Out, Poets for Pleasure (audio books), Dropping Names (2005). Ad.: 95D Talfourd Rd., London SE15 5NN. Email davidbenedictus@hotmail.com

BENJAMIN, Marc Jonathan (Jon), LLB. (Manchester); b. Croydon, Oct. 31, 1964; m. Suzanne née Taylor; Solicitor; Chief Exec. & Dir-Gen., Board of Deputies (2005-); form. Chief. Exec. British ORT (1999-2004). Adr.: Board of Deputies.

BENZIMRA, Maurice; b. Gibraltar, Feb. 21, 1928; Form. Sec., Spanish and Portuguese Jews. Cong., London. Ad.: 119 Poynter House, St. Anne's Rd., W11 4TB. ☎ 020-8603 3255.

BERCOW, John, BA, MP; b. Edgware, Jan. 19, 1963; Public Affairs Consultant; MP for Buckingham; Lambeth Councillor (1986-90); Special Adviser to Treasury Ministers (1995), to National Heritage Secretary (1995-96). Ad.: House of Commons, SW1A 0AA. ☎ 020-7219 3000.

van den BERGH, Rabbi Martin, B.Ed., M.A.; b. Hilversum, Holland, Dec. 2, 1952; Rabbi, Ohel Leah Syn., Hong Kong; M. Wembley Synagogue (1994-2006); Senior Hospital Chaplain Visitation Cttee (1995-2005); Chairman, Multi-Faith Gp for Health-care Chaplaincy (2005-06); Hon. Sec. Rabbinical Council of the U.S.; Memb. Chief Rabbi's Cabinet; form. M., Withington Cong., Span. & Port. Jews, Manchester; Tr., S. Manch. Teenage Centre; Chairman Manchester Jewish Visitation Board, (1990-94); Asst. M., Withington Cong. (1974-77), Sheffield United Hebrew Cong. (1977-78) Fdr. Chairman & H. President, Span. & Port. Cong., Israel (1981-83). Ad.: Ohel Leah Syn., 70 Robinson Rd., Mid-Levels, Hong Kong. ☎ 852-2589-2621. Email rabbimartin@mvdbergh.com.

BERKOVITCH, Rev. Mordechai, BA (Ed), Dip. Counselling, FIBA; b. Sunderland, Feb. 15, 1934; Dir., Jewish Studies, Carmel Coll. (1984-92); H. Vis. M., Nightingale House (1974-2002); M., Kingston, Surbiton & Distr. Syn. (1972-84); Hon. Dir. Welfare Chief Rabbi's Cabinet (1980-1985), Penylan Syn., Cardiff (1968-72), Central Syn., Birmingham (1956-68). Ad.: 2/2 Harosmarin, Gilo, Jerusalem 93758. ☎ 02676 4341. Fax 02676 8169. Email motisali@012.net.il.

BINDMAN, Sir Geoffrey Lionel, BCL, MA (Oxon), Hon LLD (De Montfort), Hon DLaw (Kingston), Knight Bachelor; b. Newcastle-upon-Tyne, January 3, 1933; m. Dr Lynn Janice née Winton; Solicitor. Ad.: 275, Gray's Inn Road, London WC1X 8QB. ☎ 020 7833 4433.

BINSTOCK, Dayan Ivan Alan, BSc; b. London, Oct. 27, 1950; Dayan London Beth Din; Rabbi, St. Johns Wood Syn. (1996-); form. Rabbi, Golders Green Syn.; Princ. North West London Jewish Day School; M. New Syn. (1978-80), Finsbury Pk Syn. (1974-78), R. South-east London Distr. Syn. (1972-74). Ad.: 2 Vale Close, Maida Vale, London W9 1RR. ☎/Fax 020-7289 6229.

BIRAN, Mrs Jane (née Dillon), JP, BA, MIPM; b. London, Sept. 10, 1938; m. Yoav Biran; Adviser to International Charities; form. Dep. Dir, Overseas Dev. Dept., Dir. UK Desk Jerusalem Fd.; form. Dir., Bipac; form. Edr., Zionist Year Book; V. President, Brit. Na'amat. Publ.: Anglo-Jewry: An Analysis; Effectiveness of Fringe Benefits in Industry; The Violent Society (contrib.). Ad.: 3 Oved Street, Abu Tor, Jerusalem, 93551. ☎ 2-672-5885. Fax 2-671-6550.

BLACK, Gerald David, LLB, PhD, FRHistS; b. Montreal, Jan 9, 1928; m. Anita, née Abrahams; Chairman Balfour Society for Children (1964-); Member of Council of JHSE (1992-), President (1998-2000), Hon. Sec. (2000-05); Tr. of London Museum of Jewish Life and Jewish Museum (1983-). Publ.: Lender to the Lords, Giver to the Poor (1992); Living up West: Jewish Life in London's West End (1994); JFS: The History of the Jews' Free School (1997), Lord Rothschild and the Barber (2000); Jewish London: an Illustrated History (2003). Ad.: 54 St. Johns Ct., Finchley Rd., London NW3 6LE. ☎ 020-7624 8320. Fax 020-7372 9015. Email gblack4455@aol. com.

BLANK, Sir (Maurice) Victor, MA (Oxon), HonFRCOG, CIMgt; b. Manchester, 1942; m. Sylvia Helen née Richford; Company Chairman; Chairman, Lloyds TSB Group plc; Tr. Said Business School, Oxford; Adv. Texas Pacific Group; Chairman Govs, Univ. Coll. School; Chairman, Well Being of women (RCOG Health Research Charity); Mem. Israel Britain Business C.; Gov. Tel Aviv University; Chairman UJS/Hillel; Mem Adv. Bd., UJIA. Publ. Weinberg and Blank on Takeovers and Mergers. Ad.: Lloyds TSB Group plc, 25 Gresham Str., London EC2V 7HN ☎ 020-7356 1010. Fax 020-7356 1705.

BLASHKI, Arnold Roy, OBE, AMM, BA, LLB (Melb); b. St. Kilda, May 26, 1918; Barrister-at-Law, State P. and Nat. President, Australian Legion of Ex-Servicemen; form. H. Sec., Victorian Jewish BoD, H. Sec. Victorian Branch AJA; President, Mt. Scopus Coll. Assn.; form T. Australian Legion of Ex-Service Men and Women; form. H. Sec., Exec. C. of Australian Jewry; Fed P, Victorian Jew Ex-Service Assn.; Chairman Australian Veterans and Services Assoc. (Victims). Ad.: 44A Clendon Rd., Toorak, Vic. 3181. ☎ 03 98221694.

BLOM-COOPER, Sir Louis, QC, Dr. Jur. (Amsterdam), LLB (Lond); Hon. D. Litt. (Loughborough), Hon. D. Litt. (Ulster), Hon. D. Litt. (UEA); b. London, March 27, 1926; Judge, Courts of Appeal, Jersey & Guernsey (1989-96); Chairman, Mental Health Act Commission (1987-94); Independent Commissioner for the Holding Centres (NI) (1993-2000); National Chairman Victim Support (1994-97). Ad.: 1 Southgate Road, London N1 3JP. ☎ 020-7704 1514.

BLUE, Rabbi Lionel, OBE, BA, MA, Dr Univ (Open U.); b. London, Feb. 6, 1930; Broadcaster; Lect., Leo Baeck Coll., form. Convener Beth Din, RSGB; Hon. V. President RSGB; V. Chairman, Standing Conference Jews, Christians, Moslems in Europe, form. Rel. Dir. (Europe) World Union for Progressive Judaism; Chairman Assembly of Rabbis RSGB, M., St George's Settlement Syn., Middlesex New Syn. Templeton Prize 1993. Publ. include: Funeral Service, Forms of Prayer, Vol. I, Daily and Sabbath Prayer Book (co-ed.); Vol. III, Days of Awe Prayer Book (co-ed.); Bright Blue, A Backdoor to Heaven; Kitchen Blues; Blue Heaven; The Blue Guide to the Here and Hereafter (co-auth.); Blue Horizons; Bedside Manna: How to get up when life gets you down (co-auth.); Tales of body and soul; The

Little Book of Blue's Thoughts; My affair with Christianity; Hitchhiking to Heaven. Ad.: c/o Leo Baeck College, Sternberg Centre, 80 East End Rd., London N3 2SY.

BLUMENFELD, Jeffery, OBE, BA (Hons), MA; b. London, Dec. 1949; m. Judith née Freimark. 'Chizuk' mental health organization consultant, co-ord. (2003-) Chair WDSH Community Health Forum (2004-); Hd. Jewish Studies, Deputy Hd. Rosh Pinah Primary School (2002-3); Director, Jewish Marriage C. (1987-2002) Mem. Govt. Adv. Gp., Marriage and Relationship Support (1997-2002); Chairman Chief Rabbi's Steering Group on Social and Moral Education (1994-); Act-Chairman JMC Legal Group (1993-2002); form. Dir. US Youth & Com Services Dept.; Edr., Resources Bulletin, Sch. Assemblies C. (1978-80). Ad.: 41 Holders Hill Crescent, London NW4 1NE. ☎ 020-8203 1458. Email blumen@dircon.co.uk.

BOGDANOR, Vernon, MA, FBA, CBE, FRSA; b. London, July 16, 1943; Academic; Professor of Government, Oxford University; Gresham Prof. of Law, Gresham College; Hon. Fell. Society for Advanced Legal Studies. Sir Isaiah Berlin Prize, 2008; Publ.: Joined-Up Government (2005); The British Constitution in the 20th Century; Devolution in the United Kingdom (1999); The Monarchy and the Constitution (1995); The Devolution in the United Kingdom (1999);People and the Party System (1981). Ad.: Brasenose College, Oxford, OX1 4AD. ☎ 01865 277830. Fax. 01865 277822. Email college.office@bnc.ox.ac.uk

BOLCHOVER, Richard Louis, BA (Hons.), MLitt. (Oxon); b. Manchester, Aug. 15, 1960 m. Josephine née Rosenfelder; Fund Manager; Director, Jewish Chronicle; Publ.: British Jewry and the Holocaust (1993, 2nd. ed. Littman Library 2004). Adr.: Close Fund Management Ltd., 10 Crown Place, London EC2A 4FT.

BOROWSKI, Ephraim, MBE, b. Glasgow, Nov. 19, 1949; m. Margalit. Dir., Scottish Council of Jewish Communities (1999-); Univ. Glasgow: Lecturer in Philosophy (1976-91), Sen. Lect. (1991-99; Hd. Dept. (1993-95), President, Glasgow AUT (1985-90); Tr. AUT (1993-96); Scottish Qualifications Authority: Principal Assessor for Advanced Higher Philosophy (2000-08), Consult. Dev. Officer (2003-06); Glasgow Jewish Rep. Council: H.Sec. (1992-98), Vice-President (1998-2000, 2001-04); Regional Chair, BoD (2000-06); President, Royal Philosophical Society of Glasgow (2000-03); Vice-Chair and Act.. Chair, Forum on Scottish Education (2003-07); General Teaching C. (Minister's nominee (2001-); Vice-Convenor, BEMIS (2004-); Equal Opportunities Commission, Scottish Adv. Cttee (2002-07); Commission for Racial Equality, Scottish Bd. (200507); Race Equality Adv. Forum, Scottish executive (1999-2001); H.T, Scottish Interfaith C. (2001-03). Publ.: Collins Dictionary of Mathematics (UK: 1989; 2nd ed, 2002, rev. ed. 2005, US: 1991, 2nd 2006). Ad.19, Norwood Drive, Glasgow G46 7LS ☎ 0141 638 1214 , 07831-121300. Email ephraim@scojec.org

BOWER, Marcus H., MA, LLM (Cantab); b. Belfast, Aug. 22, 1918; Barrister; Chairman, Leo Baeck College (1992-96); V. Chairman, European Board of World Union for Progressive Judaism (1990-96); Chairman RSGB (1987-90); form. Dir., Northern Engineering Industries plc.; Dir., Port of Tyne Auth. Chairman, Northern Counties Inst. of Dirs., Mem. Gov. Body, Newcastle Univ.; Mem. BBC Regional Adv. Council; Ad.: 14 Camelot Cl., SW19 7EA. ☎ 020-8947 5173.

BRICHTO, Rabbi Sidney, MA, DD; b. Philadelphia, July 21, 1936; Sr. V. President ULPS, Chairman Adv. Com. Israel Diaspora Tr; Hon. Sec. European J. Publ. Soc.; form. Exec. V. President & Dir. ULPS (1964-89); form. Chairman, C. of Ref. and Lib. Rabbis; M., Lib. Jewish Syn. (1961-64). Translator of The People's Bible: Genesis, Exodus, Samuel I & II, etc. Publ.: Funny You Don't Look Jewish: Guide to Jews and Jewish Life (1994); Ritual Slaughter: Growing Up Jewish in America (2001), etc. Ad.: ULPS, 21 Maple Street, London W1T 4BE. ☎ 020-7580 1663.

BRICKMAN, Rev. Stanley Ivan, b. London, March 29, 1939; Cantor, Hampstead Synagogue (1987-2004); Chairman Assn. of Ministers (Chazanim); Freeman, City of London (2002); Asst. Grand Chaplain, United Grand Lodge of England (2003); London Regional V. President, Cantorial Council of America (1994-); Cantor: Gt. Synagogue, Sheffield (1960-65), Ilford Synagogue (1966-69), New London Synagogue (1969-71), Singers Hill Synagogue, Birmingham (1971-83), Great Synagogue, Cape Town (1983-86). Publ.: Friday Evening Service with Zemirot for Children (Birmingham, 1976); Recording: Synagogue Liturgy Music with Singers Hill Choir (1981). Ad.: 3 Chatsworth Close, Borehamwood, Herts. WD6 1UE. ☎ 020-8387 9962. Email belstanchatsworth@ntlworld.com.

BRIER, Norma, BA(Hons), MSc, CQSW; b. London, Dec. 23, 1949; Chief Exec. Norwood (1997-);

Exec. Dir. Ravenswood Foundation (1989-96); Dir. of Com. Services – Ravenswood and Jewish Society for Mental Handicap (1985); Lect. in Soc. and Soc. Work/Counselling (Harrow College) (1982); Psychiatric Soc. Worker (1972); Soc. Worker (Camden) (1968). Ad.: Norwood, Broadway House, 80-82 . The Broadway Stanmore, Middx HA7 4HB ☎ 020-8954 4555. Fax 020-8420 6800.

BRIER, Sam, PhD, MA; b. London, July 19, 1946; Directo/Management Consultant, Cross-Sector Consulting Ltd; Senior Research Associate, Institute for Voluntary Action Research, University of London; form.Chief Exec., KIDS 199-2005; form Exec. Dir. (Resources), Norwood Ravenswood (1996-9) Ad.: IVAR, 26 Russell Square, WC1B 5DQ. ☎ 020-7939 542461. Email sambrier@hotmail.com.

BRITTAN, Baron, PC, QC, MA (Cantab), Hon. DCL, Newcastle, Durham, Hon. LLD, Hull, Edinburgh, Bradford, Bath, D.Econ., Korea; b. London, Sept. 25, 1939; Vice-President Commissioner of the European Communities (1989-); MP (Con) for Cleveland and Whitby (1974-83); MP (Con) for Richmond, North Yorkshire (1983-88); Vice-Chairman, Employment Cttee. of Parl. Conservative Party (1974-76); Minister of State, Home Office (1979-81); Chief Sec. to the T. (1981-83); Home Sec. (1983-85); Sec. of State for Trade and Industry (1985-86); President, Cambridge Union (1960); Chairman, Bow Group (1964-65); Editor of Crossbow (1966-67); Distinguished Visiting Fellow at Policy Studies Instit. (1988); Bencher of the Inner Temple (1983). Publ.: The Conservative Opportunity (contributions), Millstones for the Sixties (jointly), Rough Justice, Infancy and the Law, How to Save your Schools, A New Deal for Health Care (1988), Defence and Arms Control in a Changing Era (1988), Europe: Our Sort of Community (1989 Granada Guildhall Lecture), Discussions on Policy (1989), Monetary Union: the issues and the impact (1989), Hersch Lauterpacht Memorial Lectures, University of Cambridge (1990), European Competition Policy (1992), Europe: the Europe we need (1994), The 1997 Rede Lecture. Ad.:

BROCH, Mrs. Hazel (née Rubinstein); b. Dublin, Jan. 29, 1936; H. Life V. President (form. P.) Leeds Jewish Rep. C.; H.V. President, Tzfia Goren Emunah; Fdr. Chairman, Leeds Ladies Com. Chevra Kadisha (Chairman 1996/7); HLP Leeds Joint Chevra Kadisha; HLP Yorkshire and Humberside Chaplaincy Board; Northern Jewish woman of the year 1989. Ad.: 45/33 Shlomo Hamelach, Netanya 42267. ☎ (09) 8342653.

BRODER, Rabbi Gavin, BA (Hons), MA (Lond.); b. Uitenhage, South Africa, April 17, 1963; Chief Rabbi of Ireland (1996-2000); form. Newbury Park Syn. (1990-96), Staines Hebrew Cong. (1988-90); Governor Avigdor Primary School.

BRODIE, Rev. Gabriel, b. Bratislava, July 7, 1924; Sen. M., Manchester Great & New Syn.; Sec. Manch. Yeshiva; Chairman Jerusalem Academy Study Gps.; Hon. Chaplain Jewish Meals on Wheels, 45 Aid Society. Ad.: 43 Stanley Rd., Salford M7 4FR. ☎ 0161-740 2506.

BRODIE, Jeffrey, BA (Hons); b. Manchester, Oct. 3, 1950; Admin., Manch Kashrus Authority; Registrar, Manch. Beth Din; Tr., Keren L'David Educ. Tr. Ad.: 56 Stanley Rd., Salford, 7.

BROOKES, Kenneth Joseph Alban, Eur.Ing., BSc (Eng) Met., C. Eng., FIMMM, FCIJ; b. London, Aug. 5, 1928; Technical Consultant, Author & Journalist; Past-P., Chartered Inst. of Journalists; Editor, International Journalist; Consultant Edr., Metal Powder Report. Publ.: World Directory and Handbook of Hardmetals and other Hard Materials etc. Ad.: 33 Oakhurst Ave., East Barnet, Herts. EN4 8DN. ☎/Fax 020-8368 4997. Email kenbrookes@interearb.org.

BROWN, Malcolm Denis, FSA, MA; b. Fulwood, March 24, 1936; m. Barbara née Langford; Research historian; Chairman, Exec. Cttee and V. President JHSE (1999-), President (1996-98); form. Asst. Keeper of Manuscripts, British Museum; Archivist, Anglo-Jewish Archives (1965-66); Asst. ed. Jnl of Warburg and Courtauld Insts (1962-64); Lect. Extra-Mural Dept., Univ. of London (1969-81). Publ.: David Salomons House: Catalogues of Mementos, Commemorative Medals and Ballooniana (1968, 1969 and 1970). Ad.: c/o The Jewish Historical Society of England, 33 Seymour Place, London W1H 5AP. ☎ 020-7723 5852. Email jhse@dircon.co.uk.

BURMAN, Michael Alfred, BSc (Hons), PGCE, FRGS; b. Southport Sept. 20, 1944; m. Barbara née Schiltzer; Dir. Admin., Liberal Jewish Synagogue (2007-); form Chairman and Trustee Masorti; Sec. Masorti Europe; Chairman, European Masorti Bet Din Man. Cttee; form. Chair Gov. Clore Shalom School; Tr. and Gov. Akiva School; Tr. Jewish Community Day

School Adv. Bd. Ad.: LJS, 28 St. John's Wood Rd., London NW8 7HA.

BURMAN, Rickie Amanda, MA (Cantab), MPhil; b, Liverpool, July 5, 1955, m. Daniel Miller; Director, Jewish Museum (1995-); Curator London Museum of Jewish Life (1984-95); Res. Fell. in Jewish History; Manchester Polytechnic (1979-84); Museum Co-ord., Manchester Jewish Museum (1981-84). Publ. on history of Jewish women in England, and museum studies. Ad.: The Jewish Museum, Raymond Burton House, 129-131 Albert St., London NW1 7NB. ☎ 020-7284 1997. Fax 020-7267 9008.

BURTON, Raymond Montague, CBE, MA (Cantab), FRSA, D. Univ. York; b. Leeds, 1917; P. Burton Group, p.l.c. (1978-84), Jt. President Jewish Museum; V. President, Weizmann Instit Foundation; C., CCJ; Master Worshiful Comp. of Loriners (1976); Major, R.A. (1945). Ad.: c/o Trustee Management Ltd., 19 Cookridge St., Leeds LS2 3AG.

CALLMAN, His Honour, Clive Vernon, BSc (Econ); b. June 21, 1927; Circuit Judge, South-Eastern Circuit (1973-2000), Dep. High Court Judge, Royal Courts of Justice (1975-2000); Mediator, Court of Appeal (2004); Dir. Vallentine Mitchell & Co. Ltd.; Tr. Jewish Studies Found.; Senator, London Univ. (1978-94), Gov. Council (1994-2001); Member Careers Adv. Bd. (1979-92), Gov., Birkbeck Coll. (1982-2001); Gov. LSE (1990-), C., AJA (1956); BoD (1998); Gov. Hebrew Univ. of Jerusalem (since 1992); Court City Univ. (1991-2001), C., West London Syn. (1981-87); Member, Adv. Cttee. for Magistrates' Courses (1979-); Edr. Bd., Media Law & Practice (1980-95); Professional Negligence (1985); Journal of Child Law (1988-94), Child and Family Law Q. (1995-2002); Exec., Soc. of Labour Lawyers (1958), Chairman, St Marylebone Lab. Party (1960-62). Ad.: 11 Constable Close, NW11 6UA. ☎ 020-8458 3010.

CANNON, Raymond; b. London. Nov. 13, 1933; Solicitor; First Chairman, US Educ. Bd.; form. Chairman, Govs., J.F.S. Comprehensive Sch.; form. T., US Burial Soc.; V.Chairman, Lond. Bd. Jew Rel. Educ., Foundation Chairman, Govs. Michael Sobell Sinai Sch., Chairman, Govs. Solomon Wolfson Jewish Sch; Gov., Ilford Primary Sch. Ad.: 2 Harewood Pl., Hanover Sq. W1R 9HB ☎ 020-7629 7991. Fax 020-7499 6792.

CAPLAN, The Hon. Lord (Philip Isaac), QC, LLD (Hon) (Glasgow), FRPS, AFIAP; b. Glasgow, Feb. 24, 1929, m. Joyce née Stone; Hon. Patron, Scottish Assoc. for the Study of Offenders (2006-); Senator of the College of Justice, Scotland (1989-2000); Sheriff Princ., North Strathclyde (1983-1989); Member, Sheriff Courts Rules C. (1983-1989) Memb. Advi. Coun. on Messengers-At-Arms, and Sheriff Officers (1987-88); Com., Northern Lighthouse Bd. (1983-1989); Hon. V. President, Scottish Assn. for Study of Offenders; Hon. President, Family Mediation Scotland (1994-); Sheriff, Lothian & Borders, Edinburgh (1979-83); V. President, Sheriffs' Assn. (1982-83); Chairman, Plant Variety & Seeds Tribunal (Scotland) (1978-79). Chairman James Powell, U.K. Trust, (1992-2005); Gov. UK College of Family Mediators (1996-99). Ad.: Court of Session, Parliament House, Edinburgh.

CAPLAN, Simon, MA (Oxon), PGCE; b. Hamburg (Brit. Army Hospital), Apr. 28, 1955; Community Development Consultant; Dir., Jews' College (1985-90); Dir., Jewish Educ. Development Tr. (1985-90); Jerusalem Fellow (1990-93); Ad.: Rehov Nahum Lipshitz 27/5, Jerusalem 93622.

CAPLIN, Maxwell, OBE, FRCP; b. Lond., Feb. 6, 1917, Ret. Consultant Physician; Lond Chest Hospital (1983); Consultant in Occupational Health, Royal Brompton Nat. Heart and Lung Hospitals and Nat. Heart & Lung Instit. (1983-1991); Honorary Lecturer, Univ. of Lond. (1979-83); Consultant Member Lond. Medical Appeal Tribunal (1977-89); Medical Referee Dept. of Health (1979-90); Chairman Lond. N E Cttee. for Employment of Disabled People (1980-86); Patron, form. Chairman, later President, Greater Lond. Assn. of Disabled People (1982-89). Other professional and vol. offices. Publs: Medical Writings. Ad: 498 Finchley Rd, NW11 8DE. ☎ 020-8455 3314.

CARLOWE, Melvyn, OBE, B.Soc. Sci. (Hons); b. Abingdon, Oxon., April 13, 1941; form. Chief Exec. Jewish Care (1990-2000); form. Chief Exec. Jewish Welfare Board (1972-89); form. Hon. Sec. Central Council for Jewish Communal Service (1972-2000); Tr. Third Sector Trust, North London Hospice (1975-2006), Institute of Jewish Policy Research

(2000-05), Jewish Community Ombudsman Service (1999-2008), Jewish Chronicle Trust; mem. Beacon Selection Panel for the office of Deputy Prime Minister (2000-04); mem. King's Fund Inquiry on Care Workers (2000-02). ☎/Fax 020-8364 6686. Email karlatsky@aol.com.

CARTER, Emmanuel, B.Com., FCCA, Fel.CTA; b. London, May 18, 1925; Elder US form. V. President, US; Exec., Chief Rabbinate C.; Financial Adv. Chief Rabbi; Fel., Chartered Assn.; Certified Accts., form. Lect., Accounting, LSE. Ad.: 37 Deansway, N2 ONF. ☎ 020-8883 7759.

CESARANI, David, OBE, D.Phil; b. London, Nov. 13, 1956; Research Prof. in Modern History, Royal Holloway, Univ. London (2004-); form. Prof. Modern Jewish History and Dir. AHRB Parkes Centre for the Study of Jewish/non-Jewish Relations, University of Southampton (2000-2004); Dr., Inst. of Contemporary History and Wiener Library (1993-95, 1996-2000); Parkes-Wiener Prof. of 20th Century Jewish History and Culture (1996-2000); Alliance Prof. of Modern J. Studies, Univ. Manchester (1995-96); Montague Burton Fel. in Jewish Studies, Univ. of Leeds, (1983-86); Barnett Shine Senior Res. Fel., Queen Mary College, Univ. of London, (1986-89). Publ.: ed. Making of Modern Anglo-Jewry (1990); Justice Delayed (1992); co-ed. The Internment of Aliens in Twentieth Century Britain (1993); ed. The Final Solution (1994); The Jewish Chronicle and Anglo Jewry, 1841-1991 (1994); co-ed. Citizenship, Nationality and Migration in Europe (1996); ed. 'Lest We Forget', CD-ROM Interactive History of the Holocaust; ed. Genocide and Rescue: the Holocaust in Hungary 1944 (1997); Arthur Koestler: the homeless mind (1998); Bystanders to the Holocaust (co.ed. 2002); Port Jews: Jewish Communities in Cosmopolitan Maritime Trading Centres, 1650-1950 (ed., 2003); Eichmann: His Life and Crimes (2004); ed. Critical Concepts: the Holocaust, 6 volumes, (2004); ed. After Eichmann, Collective Memory and the Holocaust Since 1960, (2005); co.ed. Jews in Port Cities, 1650-1990, (2006). Ad.: History Dept., Royal Holloway, University of London, Egham, Surrey TW2D 0EX.

CHARING, Rabbi Douglas Stephen; b. London, Nov. 16, 1945; Dir., Jewish Educ. Bureau, Leeds; Tutor, Geneva Theological Coll., Adv., Theol. & Rel. Studies Bd., Dir. Concord MultiFaith/Multi-Cultural Res. Centre (Leeds), Inter-Euro. Com. on Church & Sch, form. Gov. Centre for Study of Rel. & Educ. (Salford); Vis. Rabbi, Southport New Syn.; Vis. Lect. Northern Ordination College; M., Sinai Syn., Leeds; Vis. Rabbi, Bradford Syn.; C. for Nat. Academic Awards; Lect., Leeds Univ., Manchester Police Coll. Member Brd. of Dir. British Friends of the Anne Frank Centre; Exec. M. Coun. for Religious Freedom; Publ.: Glimpses of Jewish Leeds; Comparative Religions (co-auth.), The Jewish World Visiting a Synagogue, Modern Judaism (audio-visual), Jewish Contrib., The Junior R.E. Handbook, World Faiths in Education, Praying Their Faith (contributor), Religion in Leeds (contributor), A Dictionary of Religious Education In the Beginning (Audiovisual), The Torah, Eyewitness Judaism, Encyclopedia of Religion (co-author), etc. Ad.: 8 Westcombe Ave., Leeds LS8 2BS. ☎ 0870 800 8532. Fax 0844 873 1046. Email rabbi@jewisheducationbureau.co.uk.

CHERNETT, Jaclyn, ALCM, MPhil; b. St. Neots, June 16, 1941; m. Brian Chernett; Chazan (2006, Acad. for Jewish Religion, NY); Dir. Masorti Assoc. (1984-86); Co-chairman, Assembly of Masorti Synagogues (1992-95); Hon. Life President, Edgware Masorti Synagogue; Vice President Assembly of Masorti Synagogues; Past V. President, World Council of Synagogues. Fd. Dir. European Academy for Jewish Liturgy. Publ.: Conference papers. Ad.: 4 Brockley Close, Stanmore, Middx. HA7 4QL. ☎ 020-8958 5090. Fax 020-8958 7651. Email jaclyn@chazan.org.uk Website www.chazan.org.uk.

CHEYETTE, Bryan, PhD; b. Leicester, Jan. 15, 1959; m. Susan Cooklin; Prof. Twentieth Century Literature, Univ. Southampton (1999-); form. Reader in English Literature, School of English and Drama, Queen Mary and Westfield College, University of London (1992-99); British Academy Postdoctoral Fellow, School of English, University of Leeds (1989-92); Montague Burton Fellow in Jewish Studies, School of English, University of Leeds (1986-89); editorial board, Jewish Quarterly and Patterns of Prejudice. Publ. Constructions of 'the Jew' in English Literature and Society: Racial Representations, 1875-1945 (1993); (editor), Between 'Race' and Culture: Representations of 'the Jew' in English and American Literature (1996); (editor), H. G. Wells, 'Tono-Bungay' (1997); published widely on British-Jewish Literature. Ad.: Dept of English, Univ. Southampton, Highfield, Southampton SO17

1BJ. ☎ 023-80593409. Fax 023-80592859. Email bhc@soton.ac.uk.

CHINN, Sir Trevor, CVO; b. London, July 24, 1935; m. Susan née Speelman; Chairman, AA; P., UJIA; Chairman, Israel Britain Business Council; member Jewish Leadership Council and Exec. Memb. BICOM Exec. Bd., Member Jewish Community Centre Bd; V. Pres., Jewish Assoc. for Business Ethics; Hon. V. Pres., Reform Movement; Hon. V. Pres., Z. Fed..

CLINTON-DAVIS, Baron of Hackney (Life Peer), (**Stanley Clinton Clinton-Davis**), PC, LLB, FRSA; b. London, Dec. 6, 1928; Solicitor; Min. State for Trade (1997-98); Mem. European Commission (1985-89); Pres. British Airline Pilots' Assoc. (BALPA); M.P. (Lab.), Hackney Central (1970-83); Parl. Under Sec. for Companies, Aviation and Shipping, Dept. of Trade (1974-79); Cllr., Hackney Bor. (1959-71); Mayor (1968-69); President, Assoc. of the Metropolitan Authorities (1992); President, UK Pilots (Marine) (1991-98); Honorary Member of the Council of Justice (1989-); Order of Leopold II for Services to EC, 1990; Fel. of Queen Mary and Westfield College and King's College, London Univ.; H. D., Polytechnical Univ. of Bucharest (1993). Publ.: Good Neighbours? Nicaragua, Central America and the United States (jt. auth.). Ad.: House of Lords, London SW1A 1AA. ☎ 020-7533 2222. Fax 020-7533 2000.

COCKS, Lady Valerie (née Davis); b. London, July 10, 1932; Dir., Labour Friends of Israel and Trade Union Friends of Israel (1978-88); Chairman Parliamentary Wives for Soviet Jewry; Exec.Com.Zionist Federation. Ad.: 162 South Block, County Hall, London SE1 7GE. ☎ 020-7787 2539.

COFNAS, Rabbi Mordechai Leib; b. Birmingham, Dec. 9, 1943; Senior Rabbi, Merseyside J. Community, Rabbi, Childwall Syn., Liverpool; Princ. L'pool Yeshiva & Midrasha; Rav, L'pool Kashrut Comm.; Mem. Chief Rabbi's Cabinet; form. Chairman Rabbinical Council of the Provinces; form. Sr. M., Cardiff United Syn.; M., Sunderland Hebrew Cong. Ad.: Childwall Synagogue, Dunbabin Rd., Liverpool, L15 6XL. ☎ 0151-722 2079.

COHEN, Arnold Judah, FCA, ATII; b. London, Dec. 17, 1936; m. Sara née Kaminski; Chartered Accountant; Life President, form. President, Fed. of Synagogues (1989-2001); form. Tr. Fed. of Synagogues. Publ.: An Introduction to Jewish Civil Law (1991). Ad.: 807 Finchley Rd., NW11 8DP. ☎ 020-8458 2720.

COHEN, (Bernard) Martin; b. London, Jan. 31, 1933; Administrator, Lobbyist; Chairman, Jewish Defence & Group Relations Cttee., BoD (1991-94); form. Member, United Synagogue Council; Harrow Councillor (1962-68, 1971-80); Chairman, Public Works & Services Cttee. (1971-74); Gen. Sec., Labour Friends of Israel (1972-80); V. Chairman, Jewish Defence & Group Relations Cttee. (1988-91). Ad.: 486 Kenton Road, Kenton, Harrow, Middlesex HA3 9DL. ☎ 020-8204 6300. Email gilmarco@orchidserve.com.

COHEN, David Mayer, LL B, CA, MBA; b. Glasgow, April 18, 1949; m. Smadar née Karni; Company Director, Private Equity; Chairman REIT India; Chairman UJIA Bd. (2006-), President (2006-); Mem. Bd., BICOM, Mem. Jewish Leadership Council. Ad.: Flat 20, 39 Hyde Park Gate, London SW7 5DS. ☎ 020 7052 9750 Email davidcohen@reit.india.in.

COHEN, Isaac Norman, MBE, BA, BCom, BSc (Econ); b. Cardiff, Oct. 30 1924, m. Naomi née Cohen; Tr. Machzike Hadath Comm.; form. Sr. W., Penylan Syn., Cardiff; Member, Chief Rabbinate C.; Gov. Body, Univ. of Wales; form. Chairman, Cardiff JIA Cttee. Ad.: 17 Riverside Drive, 300 Golders Green Rd., London NW11 9PU. ☎ 020-8381 4305. Fax 020-8381 4302.

COHEN, Rabbi Jeffrey M., BA, MPhil, AJC, PhD; b. Manchester, Feb. 19, 1940; m. Gloria née Goldberg; Chief Examiner, Mod. Hebrew, Jt. Matric Bd. (1973-1987), Lect., Liturg. Studies, Jews' Coll. (1980-1992), Rabbinical Adv. and Gov., Immanuel College; Chaplain to Mayor of Harrow (1994-95); Scholar-in-Residence, U.S.A. (1998); form. M. Kenton Syn.; Sr. M., Newton Mearns Syn., Glasgow; Lect. in Hebrew, Glasg. Univ.; Princ. Glasg. Heb Coll., Dir. Glasg. Bd. of Jewish Educ.; Dir., Jew Educ., King David Schs., Manchester; Member, Rev. Cttee., Singers Prayer Bk; Publ.: Understanding The Synagogue Service, A Samaritan Chronicle, Festival Adventure, Understanding the High Holyday Services, Yizkor, Horizons of Jewish Prayer, Moments of Insight, Blessed Are You, (Contrib. ed., Judaism section) Penguin Encyclopedia of Religions, Prayer & Penitence, Dear Chief Rabbi (ed.); 1001 Questions on Pesach, Following the Synagogue Service, 1001 Questions and Answers on Rosh Hashanah and Yom Kippur, Issues of the Day, Abridged Haggadah for Rusty Readers, Let My People

Go: Insights into Pesach and the Haggadah; The Bedside Companion for Jewish Patients; 500 Questions and Answers on Chanukah, Torah for Teens: Growing up Spiritually with the weekly Sidrah. Ad.: 26 Belvedere Ct., 115 Lyttelton Road, London N2 0AH. ☎ 020-8457 5849. Email jeffreyandgloria@yahoo.co.uk.

COHEN, Joseph, BA; b. London Oct. 1, 1920; Exec. Dir., Brit. Technion Soc. (1957-1986); Chairman Friends of Bikur Cholim Hospital, Jerusalem. Ad.: 10 Leeside Cres., NW11 0DB. ☎ 020-8455 0738.

COHEN, Marion (née Mendelssohn), BA (Hons), MPhil; b. Prestwich, Lancs., May 8, 1945; m. David J. Cohen; form. Chairman, Jewish Book Council (1992-2002); Chairman, Friends of Hillel Lecture Committee (1988-91); Tr. Jewish Literary Trust; Co-admin. Jewish Quarterly/H. H. Wingate Literary Awards; Instigator and Admin. Porjes Award for Hebrew-English Translation. Ad.: Jewish Book Council, PO Box 20513, London NW8 6ZS. ☎/Fax 020-7483 2092. Email info@jewishbookweek.org.uk. Website www.jewishbookweek. com.

COHEN, Michael, BA, MPhil, PGCE.; b. Oxford, Nov. 3, 1941; Teacher Training Co-ord. (London Borough of Hackney); Principal, MST College; Educ. Consultant, Stratford College, Dublin, Tiferes Shlomo School, London, American Endowment School (Budapest), Prague Jewish Community; Consultant to Broughton Jewish Cassel Fox Primary School, Manchester (1996-98); Principal of Leibler Yavneh College, Melbourne (1993-95); form. Exec. Dir. United Synagogue Bd of Religious Education, London (1980-92); form. Headmaster Mount Scopus Memorial College, Melbourne (1975-80); form. Dir. Jewish Studies, North-West London Jewish Day School (1969-75). Ad.: 50 Princes Park Ave., NW11 0JT ☎ 020-8458 4537. Fax 020-8201 9396.

COHEN, Lieut-Colonel Mordaunt, TD, DL, FRSA; b. Sunderland, Aug. 6, 1916; Solicitor; Reg. Chairman, Industrial Tribunals (1976-89); Chairman (1974-76); Dep. Lieut., Tyne & Wear; Chairman, Provincial Cttee., BoD (1985-91); H. Dir., Central Enquiry Desk (1990-2000), BoD (1964-2006); H. Life President, Sunderland Hebrew Cong. (1988-); form. Member, Chief Rabbinate C., Tr. Ajex Charitable Tr.; Tr. AJEX Charitable Foundation; V. President, and Nat. Chairman AJEX (1993-95); Chairman Edgware School (1991-96); H. Life President, Sunderland Ajex; Tr. Colwyn Bay Synagogue Trust, Alderman Sunderland Co. Borough C. (1967-74); Cllr., Tyne & Wear County C. (1973-74), Chairman Sund. Educ. Cttee. (1970-72), Ch. Govs., Sund. Polytechnic (1969-72), Court, Newcastle upon Tyne Univ. (1968-72); Chairman, Mental Health Review Tribunal (1967-76); Dep. Chairman, Northern Traffic Coms. (1972-74), President, Sund. Law Soc. (1970); War service, RA (1940-46) (dispatches, Burma campaign), TA (1947-55), CO 463 (M) HAA Regt. (1954-55); Territorial Decoration (1954). Ad.: 1, Peters Lodge, 2 Stonegrove, Edgware, Middlesex HA8 7TY .

COHEN, Sir Ronald, MA (Oxon), MBA (Harvard); b. London, Aug. 1, 1945; m. Sharon Ruth Harel; Businessman; Dir. NASDAQ Europe (2001-05); Chairman, Tech Stars St. Cttee. DTI (1997-); Social Inv. Task Force (2000-); UK Competitiveness Ctt, DTI (1998-); RIIA Mem. Adv. Bd. InterAction (1986-). Publ. The Second Bounce of the Ball: Turning Risk into Opportunity. Adr.: 42 Portland Place, London W1B 1NB. ☎ 020-7182 7801. Fax 020-7182 7897.

COHEN, Shimon David FRSA; b. Cardiff, May 24, 1960; Chairman The PR Office Ltd.; Mem. IPR; Mem. BAFTA; form. Dir., Bell Pottinger Consultants (1990-2003); form. Exec. Dir. Office of the Chief Rabbi (1983-90); Ad.: 53-79 Highgate Rd., London NW5 1TL ☎ 020-7284 6969. Email scohen@theoffice.com.

COHEN, Sydney, CBE, MD, PhD, FRC Path, FRS; b. Johannesburg, S. Africa, Sept. 18, 1921; Emer. Prof, Chemical Pathology, Guy's Hospital Med. Sch.; H. Consultant, Chemical Pathologist, Guy's Hospital; Chairman, Malaria Immunology Cttee., WHO (1978-83); Med. Res. C. (1974-76); Chairman, Tropical Med. Res. Bd. (1974-76). Publ.: Immunology of Parasitic Infections. Ad.: 11, Knole Wood, Ascot, SL5 9QR.

COHN, Norman, MA (Oxon), D.Litt (Glas), FBA. b. London, Jan. 12, 1915, m. Vera Broido; Prof., Sussex Univ., and Dir., Columbus Centre (1966-80); form. Prof of French, Univ. of Durham. Publ.: The Pursuit of the Millennium, Warrant for Genocide, Europe's Inner Demons, Cosmos, chaos and the world to come, Noah's Flood. Ad.: Orchard Cottage, Wood End, Ardeley, Herts. SG2 7AZ. ☎ 01438 869247.

COHN-SHERBOK, Dan, BA, BHL, MA, MLitt, PhD(Cantab), DD; b. Denver, Col., Feb. 1, 1945; Prof. Judaism, Univ. Wales (Lampeter) (1997-); Form. Rabbi in synagogues in the USA, England, S. Africa, Australia (1971-75); University Lect. in Theology, Univ. of Kent (1975-); Chairman, Dept. of Theology, Univ. of Kent (1980-2); Vis. Prof., Univ. of Essex (1993-94); Vis. Prof. Univ. Middlesex (1994-), Lampeter (1994-96), Vilnius (2000); Chaplain, Trinity College, Carmarthen (2007-), Publ. include: The Jews of Canterbury (1984); The Salman Rushdie Controversy in Interreligious Perspective (ed.) (1990); Tradition and Unity: Essays in Honour of Robert Runcie (ed.) (1991); A Traditional Quest: Essays in Honour of Louis Jacobs (ed.) (1991); Dictionary of Judaism and Christianity (1991); The Blackwell Dictionary of Judaica (1992); The Crucified Jew: Twenty Centuries of Christian Anti-Semitism (1992); Atlas of Jewish History (1993); A Short History of Judaism (1995); Jewish Mysticism (1995); A Popular Dictionary of Judaism (1995); The Hebrew Bible (1996); Fifty Key Jewish Thinkers (1996); The Jewish Messiah (1997); Jews, Christians and Religious Pluralism (1999); The Future of Jewish-Christian Dialogue (ed.); Understanding the Holocaust (1999); Wisdom of Judaism (2000); The Palestine–Israeli Conflict (2001); Interfaith Theology (2001); Holocaust Theology: A Reader (2001); Anti-Semitism (2002); Judaism: History, Belief and Practice (2003); The Vision of Judaism (2004); Pursuing the Dream (2005); Christian Zionism (2006); Kabbalah (2006), The Paradox of Antisemitism (2006); The Politics of Apocalypse (2006) etc. Ad.: Dept. of Theology and Religious Studies, Lampeter SA48 7ED. ☎ 01570 424968.

COLEMAN, Rabbi Dr Shalom, CBE, MA, BLitt, PhD, JP, AM (Order of Australia), Hon. LLD (Univ. W. Australia); b. Liverpool, Dec. 5, 1918; Centenary Medal of Australia (2003); Rabbi Emer., Perth Hebrew Cong.;Hon. Life P. Organisation of Rabbi of Australasia; form. M. South Head Syn., Sydney; United Heb Inst., Bloemfontein. Publ.: Hosea Concepts in Midrash and Talmud, What Every Jew Should Know, What is a Jewish Home? What is a Synagogue?, Life is a Corridor (An Autobiography) (1992), Another Decade (2002), etc. Ad.: Unit 1, 72 Spencer Ave., Yokine, Western Australia 6060. ☎ 618-9375 3222. Email scoleman1@iinet.net.au.

COLLINS, John Morris, MA (Oxon); b. Leeds, June 25, 1931; Barrister; Doyen, Leeds Bar; Head of Chambers (1966-2002); HL V. President, Leeds Jewish Rep. C. (form. P., 1986-89); Crown Courts Recorder (1980-98); Dep. Circuit Judge (1970-80); Called to the Bar, Middle Temple (1956); past P. Leeds Lodge, B'nai B'rith; BoD (1971-93); President, Beth Hamidrash Hagadol Syn., Leeds (1992-95). Publ.: Summary Justice (1963). Ad.: 14 Sandhill Oval, Leeds, LS17 8EA. ☎ 0113 2686008.

COLLINS, Kenneth Edward, Dr MBChB, FRCGP, MPhil, PhD; b. Glasgow, Dec. 23, 1947; Chairman Scottish Council of Jewish Communities (1999-2003; 2007-08); Vis Prof., Faculty of Medicine, Hebrew Univ.; Chairman: Scottish Jewish Archives Cttee., Glasgow Bd. of Jewish Educ. (1989-93); President Glasgow Jewish Rep. C. (2004-07); and 1995-98); Chairman Glasgow Yeshiva. Publ.: Aspects of Scottish Jewry (ed.) (1987); Go and Learn (1988); Second City Jewry (1990); Glasgow Jewry (1994); Scotland's Jews (1999); Be Well: Jewish Immigrant Health and Welfare in Glasgow (2001). Ad.: 3 Glenburn Road, Giffnock, Glasgow G46 6RE. ☎ 0141-638 7462.

CONNICK, (Harold) Ivor, LLB; b. London, Jan. 25, 1927; Consultant, Dir., Land Securities plc (1987-98), and A. Beckman plc (1990-98); V. P. Brit. ORT; Chairman, Central Board World ORT Union (1993-2000); Pres. Westminster Syn. (1990-2000); Board JIA (1985-93); Chairman, Professions Div., JIA (1979-83); Dep. Chairman UDS Group PLC (1983), Director (1975-83). Ad.: 54 Fairacres, Roehampton La., SW15 5LY. ☎ 020-8876 7188. Email cardicon.03@virgin.net.

COPISAROW, Sir Alcon Charles; b. St. Annes-on-Sea, Lancs., June 25, 1920; Council IJPR and AJA; Lieut. Royal Navy (1943-47); Min. of Defence (1947-54), British Embassy, Paris (1954-60); Chief Scientific Officer, Min. of Technology (1964-66), Senior Partner McKinsey and Co Inc. (1966-76); Subsequently: Chairman Tr., The Prince's Youth Business Trust, The Eden Project, Tr., Duke of Edinburgh's Award; C. Royal Jubilee Trusts; Press Council; Gov., Benenden School; Dep. Chairman Gov. English Speaking Union; Patron, Conseil National des Ingénieurs et des Scientifiques de France; Patron, Assoc. MBAs; Chairman & Senior Man. Tr., The Athenaeum; By-Fellow, Churchill Coll., Cambridge; Hon. Fell. Lloyds; form.

Chairman Humanitarian Trust of Hebrew Univ. Ad.: 7 Southwell Gardens, London SW7 4SB.

CORNEY, Hyam, BA (Hons); b. Lond., May 20, 1938; Deputy Edr, Jewish Chronicle (1991-2002); form. Foreign edr. Home News edr. Exec. Dir., Publ. Rel., Israel & Foreign Affairs Cttees., BoD; Lond. Corres 'Jerusalem Post'; Edr., 'Jewish Observer & Middle East Review', Information Dir., JNF Ad.: Netanya, Israel.

COROB, Sidney, CBE DSc Tech (hc); Hon. Fell. UCL; b. London, May 2, 1928; Chairman, Corob Holdings Ltd.; Dir., EJPS; Dir. Jewish Assoc. Business Ethics; Life President Hope Charity; H.V. President, Frs. of the Sick; V. President Magen David Adom in Brit.; V. President CCJ; T., Westmount Housing Assn.; H.T., Westmount Charitable Tr.; V. Chairman Central C for Jewish Soc. Service; Chairman Int. Centre for Learning Potential, Jerusalem. Ad.: 62 Grosvenor St., London W1K 3JF.

CORREN, Asher, MCMI; b. Warsaw, Nov. 2, 1932; form. Director, Central C. Jewish Community Services; Jt. Tr. CCJ; Mem. Exec. Cttee; form. Exec. Dir. Nightingale House; form. Member of Wandsworth Health Authority; form. Member of Exec. Cttee, Alzheimer's Disease Soc.; Member of Adv. Cttee., St Wilfrid's Home for Aged, Chelsea. form. Co-Tr., Council of Christians and Jews,. Email patricia.corren@virgin.net.

COSGROVE, The Rt. Hon. Lady, PC CBE, LLD. (née Hazel Josephine Aronson) b. Glasgow, Jan 12, 1946; m. John A. Cosgrove; Senator of the College of Justice, Scotland (1996-2006); Dep. Chairman Boundary Commission for Scotland (1996-2006); President, Scottish Friends of Alyn Hospital; Hon Fellow, Harris Manchester College, Oxford; Chairman Expert Panel on Sex Offending (1998-2001); Chairman, Mental Welfare Commission for Scotland (1991-96); member, Parole Board for Scotland (1988-91); Sheriff of Lothian & Borders at Edinburgh (1983-96); Sheriff of Glasgow and Strathkelvin at Glasgow (1979-83); Advocate (1968-79); Queens Counsel (1991) Ad.; 4, Avenue Mansions, Finchley Rd., London NW3 7AU; ☎ 079-7065 7157 Fax 087-0133 4568. Email hazelcosgrove@tiscali.co.uk.

COSGROVE, John Allan, BDS (Glasgow); b. Carmarthen, S. Wales, Dec. 5, 1943; m. The Rt. Honourable Lady Cosgrove (Hazel Aronson); Dental Surgeon; Chairman Scottish Council of Jewish Communities; (2003-07) President Edinburgh Hebrew Congregation (1986-90), currently Hon. V. President; Scottish representative Chief Rabbinate selection committee (1989-91). Ad.: 4, Avenue Mansions, Finchley Rd., London NW3 7AU; ☎ 079-7065 7157 Fax 087-0133 4568,. Email jacosgrove@tiscali.co.uk.

COWEN, The Rt Hon. Sir Zelman, PC, AK, GCMG, GCVO KStJ, GCOMRI (Italy); QC, BA, LLM (Melbourne), MA, DCL (Oxon), LLD Hon. (HK, Queensland, Melbourne, Australian Nat Univ, West Australia, Tasmania, Turin, Victoria Univ. Technology, Deakin, Monash), D.Litt Hon. (New England, Sydney, James Cook Univ of N Queensland, Oxford); DHL Hon. (Hebrew Union Coll, Cincinnati, Redlands Univ, Calif), D Univ Hon. (Newcastle, Griffith Univ), Southern Cross (Queensland), PhD Hon. (Hebrew Univ, Jerusalem, Tel Aviv Univ); b. Melbourne, Oct. 7, 1919; m. Anna née Wittner; Chairman Australian National Academy of Music (1995-2000); Nat. President, Australia-Brit. Assn. (1993-95); P. Order of Australia Association (1992-95); Hon. Professor Griffith Univ., Queensland (1991-); Professorial Assoc., Univ. of Melbourne (1990-); Member Bd. of Gov. Weizmann Inst. (1990-); Provost, Oriel Coll., Oxford (1982-90); Pro-V. Chancellor, Univ. of Oxford (1988-90); Tr. Winston Churchill Memorial Tr. (UK) (1987-89); Lee Kuan Yew Distinguished Visitor Singapore (1987); Sir Robert Menzies Memorial Tr. (UK) (1984-); Gov.-Gen. of Australia (1977-82), V. Chancellor Queensland Univ. (1970-77); V. Chancellor, New England Univ., NSW (1967-70); H. Fellowships at Oxford, Dublin, Univ. of New England, Univ. Qld, Australian Nat. Univ.; H. Master of Bench, Gray's Inn; Academic Gov., Bd. of Govs., Hebrew Univ., Tel Aviv Univ.; Chairman, Australian V. Chancellors' Cttee (1977). Publ.: Dicey Conflict of Laws; (with P. B. Carter) Essays in the Law of Evidence; (with L. Zines) Federal Jurisdiction in Australia; (with D. M. da Costa) Matrimonial Causes Jurisdiction; The British Commonwealth of Nations in a Changing World; Isaac Isaacs; Individual Liberty and the Law; The Virginia Lectures, Reflections on Medicine, Biotechnology and the Law; A Touch of Healing; Australia and the United States: Some Legal Comparisons; American-Australian Private International Law; The Private Man (ABC Boyer Lectures); A Public Life: Memoirs (2006), etc. Ad.: 4 Treasury Place, East Melbourne, Victoria 3002, Australia. ☎ 61-3-96500299. Fax 61-3-96500301.

CRAFT, Maurice, BSc (Econ), PhD, D.Litt; b. London, May 4, 1932; Emer. Prof., Univ. Nottingham; Non-Exec. Dir., Greenwich NHS Primary Care Tr.; Visiting Prof. of Education, Goldsmiths Coll., Univ. London (1997-2002); Res. Prof of Education, Univ. Greenwich (1993-97). Foundation Dean of Humanities & Social Science, Hong Kong Univ. of Science and Technology (1989-93); Prof of Educ. Nottingham Univ. (Dean of Faculty of Education, and Pro-Vice-Chancellor) (1980-89); Goldsmiths' Prof of Educ., London Univ. (1976-80); Prof of Educ., La Trobe Univ., Melbourne (1974-75), Sr. Lect. in Educ., Exeter Univ (1967-73); Publ. include: Teacher Education in Plural Societies (Edr.); Ethnic Relations and Schooling (Jt. Edr.); Change in Teacher Education (Jt. Edr.); Education and Cultural Pluralism (Edr.); Teaching in a Multicultural Society: the Task for Teacher Education (Edr.); Linking Home and School (Jt. Edr.); Ad.: 28, Foxes Dale, Blackheath, London SE3 9BQ. ☎ 020-8852 7611. Email almacraft@hotmail.com.

CREEGER, Morton. b. Luton, Beds., Sept 22, 1941; Partner Zangwills Charity and Fundraising Consultants (2000-); Dir. Brit. ORT (1973-85); form. Dir. Ronson Foundation (1985-95); Governor, Charles Kalms Henry Ronson Immanuel College (1990-95); Governor, King Solomon High School, Redbridge (1991-); Dir. King Solomon High School, Redbridge Ltd (1993-97); Vice-Chairman, and Non-Exec. Director, Camden and Islington Community Services NHS Trust (1992-95); Council Member, Association for Research into Stammering in Childhood (1994-97); Fellow, Institute of Charity Fund-raising Managers (1994-). Ad.: Zangwills, 1st Floor, 18 North End Rd., London NW11 7PH. ☎ 020-8958 1917. Fax 020-7935 7257.

CREWE, Sir Ivor Martin, Kt., D.Litt (Salford); b. Manchester, Dec. 15, 1945; Univ. teacher; Master, Univ. College, Oxford (2008-); Mem. High Council, European University Institute, Florence; Mem. C. SOAS; President, Universities UK (2003-5); Vice-Chancellor (1995–2007), Pro V. Chancellor (Academic) (1992-95) Univ. of Essex; Prof. of Government, Univ. of Essex; Hon. Fell. Exeter College, Oxford; Dir. SSRC Data Archive (1974-82); Ed./co-ed. British Journal of Political Science (1977-82, 1984-92); Chairman, Dept. of Government (1985-89). Publ.: Survey of Higher Civil Service (HMSO 1969) (with A. H. Halsey), Decade of Dealignment (CUP 1983) (1995, with Bo Särlvik; SDP: The Birth, Life and Death of the Social Democratic Party (1995), etc. Ad.: Masters Lodge, University College, Oxford OX1. Email ivor.crewe@univ.ox.ac.uk

CUTLER, Rabbi Shlomo, b. Liverpool, Dec. 21, 1927; form. Rav. Kol Yakov, Edgware (1997-2001); M., Mill Hill Syn. (1959-93); form. M., Luton Syn. Ad.: 38 Selvage Lane, NW7. ☎ 020-8959 6131.

DANGOOR, Dr Naim E; OBE, BSc (London); b. Baghdad, 1914; Company Chairman; editor and publisher – The Scribe, Journal of Babylonian Jewry; Fd. Exilarch's Foundation. Ad.: 4 Carlos Place, London W1K 3AW.

DAVID, Dan, PhD; b. Bucarest, May 23, 1929; m. Gabriela née Fleischman; Company Director; Dir. GLG Convertible Investment Fund (1998-) Commander, French Republic, Order of Arts and Letters; Mem. Bd. Gov. Tel Aviv Univ.; Mem. Bd. Dir. Dan David Foundation and Dan David Prize; fellow, World Academy of Arts & Sciences; President, Photome International plc (1992-); Man. Dir. Dedem Automatica Sri, Italy (1962-92); Man. Dir. Fomat, Israel (1961-62); Art/Press Photography (1953-60). Ad.: Photome, Church Road, Bookham, Surrey KT23 3EU. ☎ 01372 453399. Email ddavid@dedem.com. Website www.dandavidprize.com.

DAVIDSON, Lionel, b. Hull, Mar. 31, 1922; author. Publ.: The Night of Wenceslas, The Rose of Tibet, A Long Way to Shiloh, Making Good Again, Smith's Gazelle, The Sun Chemist, The Chelsea Murders, Under Plum Lake, Kolymsky Heights. Ad: c/o Curtis Brown Ltd., 28-29 Haymarket, London SW1Y 4SP.

DEECH, Baroness Ruth Lynn (née Fraenkel), DBE, MA (Oxon), MA (Brandeis), Hon. LLD (Strathclyde, Richmond); Barrister; b. London, April 29, 1943, m. Dr John Deech; Gresham Professor of Law (2008-11); Independent Adjudicator for Higher Educ. (2004-08); Principal, St Anne's College, Oxford (1991-2004); Mem., Jewish Leadership Council, Mem. European Academy of Sciences and the Arts; Gov. BBC (2002-6); Freeman, Drapers' Co. (2003); Chairman, UK Human Fertilisation & Embryology Authority (1994-2002); Pro-Vice Chancellor, Oxford University (2001-04); Lecturer in Law, Oxford University (1970–91); Member, Commission on the Representation of the Interests of the British Jewish

Community (1998-2000); Governor, UJIA (1997-99); Governor, Oxford Centre for Hebrew and Jewish Studies (1994-2000); Chairman, Stuart Young Foundation Academic Panel (1991-); Senior Proctor, Oxford University (1985-86); Vice-Principal, St Anne's College (1988-91); Non-executive Director, Oxon Health Authority (1993-94); Governor, Carmel College (1980-90); Member, Committee of Inquiry into Equal Opportunities on the Bar Vocational Course (1993-94); Hon. Bencher, Inner Temple (1996); Rhodes Trustee (1996-2006). Ad.: House of Lords, London SW1A 0PW. ☎ 020 7219 3000. Email deechr@parliament.uk

DJANOGLY, Jonathan Simon, MP; b. London, June 3, 1965; m. Rebecca, née Silk; Solicitor, SJ Berwin LLP (1990-); MP Huntingdon (2001-); Shadow Solictor General, Minister for Business (2004-); form. Cllr. Westminster LBC (1994-2001). Ad.: House of Commons, London SW1A 0AA.

DOMB, Cyril, MA, PhD (Cantab), MA (Oxon), FRS; b. London, Dec. 9, 1920. Em. Prof. of Physics. Bar-Ilan Univ. (since 1989); Academic President, Jerusalem Coll. of Tech (1985-94); form. Prof. of Theoretical Physics, King's Coll., Lond. Univ. (1954-81); ICI Fel. Clarendon Lab., Oxford; Univ. Lect. in Maths, Cambridge; President, Assn. of Orthodox Jewish Sci. Professionals. Publ.: Scientific writings, Clerk Maxwell and Modern Science (ed.), Phase Transitions and Critical Phenomena Vols. 1-3, 5, 6 (ed. with M. S. Green), Vols. 7-20 (ed. with J. L. Lebowitz), The Critical Point (1996), Memories of Kopul Rosen (ed.), Challenge, Torah Views on Science and its problems (ed. with A. Carmell), Maaser Kesafim, Giving a Tenth to Charity (ed.). Ad.: Physics Dept., Bar-Ilan Univ., Ramat Gan, 52900, Israel. ☎ (03) 5137928. Fax (03) 5353298.

DOVER, Dr Oskar, MB, ChB, MRCGP; b. Danzig, Oct. 31, 1929; m. Marlene née Levinson; Hon. Life Vice President, Merseyside Jewish Rep. C.; Tr., Liverpool Jew Youth & Com. Centre; form. Chairman, Foundation Gov. and Tr. King David High Sch., L'pool; form. Chairman, Harold House C. Ad.: 153 Menlove Ave., Liverpool L18 3EE.

DU PARC BRAHAM, Donald Samuel, FRGS, IRRV, ACIArb, FRSA; b. London, June 29, 1928; Lord Mayor, city of Westminster (1980-81); Master of Guild of Freeman of City of London (1989/90); Master of Worshipful Comp. of Horners (1991/1992); President, Regent's Park & Kensington North Conservative Assoc. (1996-); Chairman, London Central European Constituency C. (1988-93); Chairman, Central London Valuation Trib. (1977-); Chairman, Parkinson's Disease Soc. (1990-1991); Pat., Central London Br. Parkinson's Disease Soc. of UK; Member Nat. Exec., CCJ; Member, Bd. Man. W. Hampstead Syn.; Member, Jewish Cttee for H.M. Forces; Member, Wiener Library Endowment Appeal Cttee., Member, C. of the Anglo-Jewish Assoc.; Nepalese Order of Gorkha Dakshina Bahu. Ad.: 11 Jerusalem Passage, St. John's Sq., London EC1V 4JP.

DUNITZ, Alfred Abraham, JP; b. London, May 15, 1917; form. Tr. of the Burial Soc. (1978-87); Chairman Burial Soc. (US), (1987-88); Member Exec. Hillel House, Exec. Jewish Memorial Council of AJA; Tr. Jewish Cttee. HM Forces; Chairman The Friends of Jewish Servicemen; Worshipful Company of Carmen (Livery Company); The Court of Common Council City of London; (1984-2004); Dep. Warden Ward of Portsoken (2002-04);Gov. Guildhall School of Music and Drama (1990-2001); Gov. City of London School for Girls (1998-2004); Freeman, City of London; Chairman Friends of Ramat Gan (1990-94); Exec. of the JWB (1983-85); restored Exeter Synagogue (fd. 1763) (1980); rest. Aberdeen Syn. (1982); Chairman of the House Committee of the JWB Homes at Hemel Hempstead (1978-85); Eastern Region Council of the C.B.I. (1973-76); restored and maintains disused cemeteries; recipient of Inst. of Waste Management Medal (1999). Ad.: 14 Sherwood Rd., Hendon, NW4 1AD. ☎ 020-8203 0658.

DUNITZ, Prof. Jack David, FRS, BSc, PhD (Glasgow), Hon. DSc (Technion, Haifa), Hon. DSc (Glasgow), Hon. PhD (Weizmann Instit.), b. Glasgow, March 29, 1923; m. Barbara née Steuer; Scientist and teacher; Hon. Fell. Royal Society of Chemistry; Prof. Chemical Crystallography at the Swiss Federal Inst of Technology (ETH), Zurich, Switzerland (1957-90); Member Academia Europaea, Foreign Member Royal Netherlands Acad. of Arts and Sciences, Foreign Associate, US National Academy of Science, Member Leopoldina Academy; Member Academia Scientarium Artium Europaea; Foreign Member American Philosophical Society; Foreign Hon. Member American Academy of Arts and Sciences; numerous visiting professorships. Publ.: X-ray Analysis and the Structure of Organic Molecules (1979), Reflections on Symmetry in Chemistry .. and Elsewhere (with E. Heilbronner) (1993). Ad.: Obere Heslibachstr. 77, CH-8700 Küsnacht, Switzerland.

DUNNER, Abraham Moses, MCIJ; b. Konigsberg, Germany, Nov. 13, 1937; m. Charlotte née Austerlitz; Exec. Dir., Conference of European Rabbis; Spec. Adv., Russian Union of Orthodox Cong. (2005-); Mem. Bd., Euro-Asian Rabbinical Conference (2002-); Exec. Dir. Community Centres for Israel Org. (1958-60); Exec. Dir. European Union of Orthodox Hebrew Cong. (1958-60); Dir. Keren Hatorah Education Cttee (1960-71); Sec. Gen. Agudath Israel Org. of Great Britain (1967-71); Ed. Jewish Tribune (1967-71); Ed. Haderech (1962-70); Chairman, N.W. London Police Liaison Cttee; Tr. Beth Jacobs Schools Israel (1988-); Chairman Lakewood Alumni Assn. (1995-); Bd. of Dirs. Simon Wiesenthal Centre UK (1997-); Special Adviser to the Russian Jews Congress (1998-); Cllr. London Borough of Barnet (1998-2006). Ad.: 87 Hodford Rd., London NW11 8NH. ☎ 020-8455 9960. Fax 020-8455 4968.

DUNNER, Rabbi Pinchas Eliezer (Pini), BA Hons; b. London, Sept. 25, 1970; m. Sabine née Ackerman; M. 'The Saatchi Synagogue', Maida Vale (1998-); Asst. Rabbi, Moscow Choral Synagogue (1991-92); Rabbi, Notting Hill Synagogue (1992-93); Producer/Presenter, 'Jewish Spectrum', Spectrum Radio (1996-98). Ad.: 21 Andover Place, London NW6 5ED. ☎ 020-7625 2266. Fax: 020-7625 2277. Email pini@coolshul.org. Website www.coolshul.org.

DUNNETT, Jack, MA, LLM (Cantab); b. Glasgow, June 24, 1922; Solicitor; MP (Lab.) for Nottingham East (1974-83), Central Nottingham (1964-74); form. PPS, Min. of Transport and Foreign Office; form. Cllr., MCC and GLC, and Ald., Enfield Borough C.; Chairman, Notts. County F.C. (1968-87); Football League Man. Cttee. (1977-89), Football Assn. (1977-89); P. Football League, (1981-86 and 1988-9); V. President Football Assn. (1988-89). Ad.: Whitehall Ct., SW1A 2EP. ☎ 020-7839 6962.

DWEK, Joseph Claude (Joe), CBE, BSc, BA, AMCT, FTI, Hon. DSc UMIST; b. Brussels, May 1, 1940; Bd. Mem. North West Dev. Agency Memb. General Assembly, New Univ. Manchester; past Chairman, Environlink, and Memb, DTI/DEFRA Env. Innovation Adv. Gp.; Exec. Chairman Worthington Gp. (1999-); Chairman Penmarric plc, Dir., Jerome Group plc; past Chairman & CEO Bodycode Int'l plc (1972-99). Ad. Penmarric plc, Suite One, Courthill House, 66 Water Lane, Wilmslow SK9 5AP ☎ 01625 549081; Email penjcdwek@aol.com.

EHRENTREU, Dayan Chanoch; b. Frankfurt-am-Main, Dec. 27, 1932; form. Rosh Beth Din, Lond. Beth Din; Av Beth Din, Manchester Beth Din (1979-84); Princ., Sunderland Kolel (1960-79). Ad.:

EILON, Samuel, DSc (Eng), PhD, DIC, FIMechE, FIEE, FR Eng; b. Tel Aviv, Oct. 13, 1923; Emeritus Prof., Univ. London; form. Chief Ed., Omega, The Int Jl. of Management Science; form. Member, Monopolies and Mergers Comm.; form Prof of Man. Science, and Hd of Dept., Imperial Coll., Lond.; form. Dir. of ARC, Compari Int., Spencer Stuart and Associates; management consultant to many industrial companies; form. Assoc. Prof, Technion, Haifa. Publ.: some 300 scientific papers, 16 books. Ad.: 1 Meadway Close, London NW1 7BA. ☎ 020-8458 6650.

EIMER, Rabbi Colin, BSc (Econ), MA; b. London, March 8, 1945; M., Southgate & Distr. Reform Syn. (1977-2001), Finchley Reform Syn. (2001-05), Chairman, Assembly of Rabbis, RSGB (1981-83, 1999-2001); Lect., Hebrew, Leo Baeck Coll. (1976-2007); form. M., Bushey Ref. Syn., Union Liberale Israelite Syn., Paris. Ad.: Southgate & District Reform Synagogue, 120 Oakleigh Road North, London N20 9EZ. ☎ 020-8445 3400. Email colineimer@aol.com.

EISENBERG, Neville, BCom, LLB (Wits), LLM (LSE); b. Cape Town, April 12, 1962; Solictor; Managing Partner, Berwin Leighton Paisner LLP (1999-) Assoc. Gov. Hebrew University (2004-); Freeman, City of London Solictors Company; Chairman, British Israel Law Assoc. (1996-); Cttee, UK Assoc. J. Lawyers& Jurists. Ad.: Adelaide House, London Bridge, London EC4R 9HA. ☎ 020-7760 1000; Fax 020-7760-1111. Email neville.eisenberg@blplaw.com.

EISENBERG, Paul Chaim, BHL; b. Vienna, June 26, 1950; m. Annette née Liebman; Chief Rabbi of Vienna and of the Federation of Jewish Communities in Austria. Ad.: A-1010 Vienna, Seitenstetteng, 4. ☎ 531-04111. Fax 531-04108. Email rabbinat@ikg-wien.at.

EKER, Mrs Rita (née Shapiro), MBE; b. London, Oct. 15, 1938; Co-Chairman, Women's Campaign for Soviet Jewry (the 35s); Co-Chairman of One to One and One to One Treks in

Israel; Co-founder and Project Dir. One to One Children's Fund. Ad.: Carradine House, 237 Regents Park Road, London N3 3LF. ☎ 020-8343 4156. Fax 020-8343 2119. Email rita@one-to-one.org.

ELLENBOGEN, Myrtle Ruth Franklin (née Sebag-Montefiore), widow of Gershon Ellenbogen; b. London, Oct. 18, 1923; form. Chairman, Children's Central Rescue Fund, Gov. and Hon. Fel. of Hebrew Univ. of Jerusalem, President, Women Frs. (since 1984), Brit. Frs., Hebrew Univ.; form. Gov., now Fel. of the Purcell Sch. for Musically Gifted Children (1968-88); Alice Model Nursery (Chairman 1984-87; 1958-66); Member, ILEA (1967-73); Chairman, Union of Jewish Women's Loan Fund (1966-72), Chairman, Hampstead & St. John's Wood Group, form. Chairman, Imp. Cancer R.F. (1987-89); V. Chairman, AJA Educ. Cttee. (1990-93). Publ.: Sir Moses Montefiore 1784 to 1885 (with Michael Bor). Ad.: Flat 83, Apsley House, 23-29 Finchley Rd., London NW8 0NZ. ☎ 020-7586 0464.

ELLIS, Harold, CBE, MA, DM, MCh, FRCS; b. London, Jan. 13, 1926; Emer. Prof. of Surgery, Lond. Univ.; Prof. & Chairman, Surgery Dept. Charing Cross & Westminster Med. Sch Form. V. President, Royal Coll. of Surgeons; Consultant Surgeon to the Army, resident surgical posts in Oxford, Sheffield & Lond. (1948-62). Publ.: Clinical Anatomy (11th ed.), Maingot's Abdominal Operations (9th ed.), Famous Operations, etc. Ad.: Dept. of Anatomy, King's College London (Guy's Campus), Hodgkin Building, London Bridge, SE1 1UL.

EMANUEL, Aaron, CMG, BSc (Econ); b. London, Feb. 11, 1912; form. Asst. Under-Sec. of State Dept. of the Environment; Chairman, W. Midlands Econ. Planning Bd. (1968-72) Consultant, O.E.C.D. (1972-81). Ad.: 44a Westcliff Rd., Bournemouth, Dorset BH4 8BB.

EMANUEL, Rabbi Dr Charles, BA, MHL, DD (HUC); b. New York, Dec. 15, 1944; Rabbi Emer, North Western Ref. Syn.; form M., Sinai Syn., Leeds. Ad.: North Western Reform Synagogue, Alyth Gdns., NW11 7EN. ☎ 020-8455 6763. Fax 020-8458 2469. Email charles@alyth.org.

EPSTEIN, Trude Scarlett (née Gruenwald), OBE, Dip. Economics and Political Science (Oxon), Dip. Industrial Administration, PhD (Manchester), b. Vienna, July 13, 1922; Social Assessment Consultant; Senior Fel. Research School of Pacific Studies, ANU Canberra (1966-72); Research Prof., Sussex (1972-84). Publ.: Economic Development and Social Change in S. India (1962); Capitalism, Primitive and Modern (1968); South India: Yesterday, Today and Tomorrow (1973); The Paradox of Poverty (1975); The Feasibility of Fertility Planning (1977); The Endless Day: Some Case Material on Asian Rural Women (1981); Urban Food Marketing and Third World Rural Development (1982); Women, Work and Family (1986); A Manual for Culturally Adapted Market Research in the Development Process (1988); A Manual for Development Market Research Investigators (1991); Village Voices – Forty Years of Rural Transformation in S. India (1998); A Manual for Culturally Adapted Social Marketing (1999); Swimming Upstream: Autobiography (2005). Ad.: 5 Viceroy Lodge, Kingsway, Hove BN3 4RA. ☎/Fax 01273-735151. Email scarlett@epstein.nu.

EZRA, Baron of Horsham (Life Peer), **(Sir Derek Ezra)**, MBE; b. Feb. 23, 1919; Chairman, Nat. Coal Bd. (1971-82). Lib-Dem spokesman on energy matters. Ad.: House of Lords, SW1.

FAINLIGHT, Ruth, b. New York City; m. Alan Sillitoe; writer poet, translator, librettist. Poet in Resdence, Vanderbilt Univ. (1985 & 1990); Poetry editor, European Judaism. Publ. Thirteen collections of poems, including Another Full Moon (1976), Fifteen to infinity (1983), The Knot (1990), Selected Poems (1995), Burning Wire (2002), Moon Wheels (2006), Two books of short stories. Sibyls and Others (1980; new ed 2007) Ad.: 14 Ladbroke Terrace, London W11 3PG. ☎ 020-7229 6758 Email ruth.fainlight@googlemail.com.

FAITH, Mrs Sheila (née Book), J.P.; b. Newcastle upon Tyne, June 3, 1928, m. Dennis Faith; Dental Surgeon; Member Parole Bd., (1991-94); MEP (Conservative) for Cumbria and Lancashire North (1984-89) Memb. Euro Parl. Transport Cttee (1984-87), Energy Res. & Technological Cttee (1987-89); MP (C.) for Belper (1979-83) Memb. House of Commons Select Cttee on Health and Social Servs (1979-83), Memb. Exec. Cttee Cons Med. Soc. (1981-84); Sec. Cons Backbench Health and Social Servs Cttee (1982-83); Northumberland C.C. (1970-74); Memb. Health and Social Services Cttees, LEA rep on S. Northumberland Youth Employment Bd; Vice-Ch Jt Consult Cttee on Educ, Newcastle (1973-74); Memb. Newcastle City C. (1975-77), (Memb. Educ Cttee); JP: Northumberland (1972-74), Newcastle (1974-78), Inner London (1978-); President Cumbria and Lancashire N. Cons

Euro Constitutency C. (1989-95); Memb. Newcastle upon Tyne CAB, served as Chairman of several sch. governing bodies and mangr. of community homes. Ad.: 52 Moor Ct., Westfield, Gosforth, Newcastle-upon-Tyne NE3 4YD. ☎ 0191-285 4438.

FARHI, Musa Moris, MBE, FRSL, FRGS; b. Ankara, July 5, 1935; m. Nina Ruth née Gould; Writer; Vice-President, International PEN (2001-); Chairman, International PEN Writers in Prison Cttee (1997-2000); Chairman, English PEN Writers in Prison Cttee (1994-97); M. Edr. Bd., Jewish Quarterly. Publ.: The Pleasure of Your Death (1972); The Last of Days (1983); Journey Through the Wilderness (1989); Children of the Rainbow (1999); Young Turk (2004). Ad.: 16, Heathview Court, 20 Corringway London NW11 7EF. ☎ 020-8455 5329. Email farhi@clara.net.

FASS, Richard Andrew, FCA; b. London, Sept. 24, 1945; Chartered Accountant; form.Man. Dir. Jewish Chronicle Ltd; Ad.: 3 The Lane, Marlborough Place, London NW8 0PN.

FEATHERSTONE, Lynne, (née Ryness), MP; b. London, Dec. 20, 1951; MP for Hornsey & Wood Green (2005-; LibDem); London Assembly (2000-05), Councillor, Haringey (1998-2006). Publ.: Marketing & Communication Techniques for Architects (1992). Ad.: House of Commons, London SW1A 0AA. Email Featherstone@parliament.uk.

FEIGENBAUM, Clive Harold, FBOA, FSMC; b St. Albans, Sept. 6, 1939; Company Dir.; Jt. Chairman, Herut Org., Gt. Brit., BoD. Ad.: St. Margarets, Mount Park Rd., Harrow, Middx. HA1 3JP ☎ 020-8422 1231.

FEINSTEIN, Mrs. Elaine (née Cooklin), MA (Cantab), HonD.Litt (Leic.), FRSL; b. Bootle, Oct. 24, 1930; m. Dr Arnold Feinstein; Writer; Cholmondley Prize for Poetry (1990). Publ.: The Circle; The Amberstone Exit; The Crystal Garden; Children of the Rose; The Ecstasy of Dr. Miriam Garner; Some Unease and Angels (poems); The Shadow Master; The Silent Areas; Selected Poems of Marina Tsvetayeva; The Survivors; The Border; Bessie Smith (biog.); A Captive Lion: a life of Marina Tsvetayeva; Badlands (poems); Mother's Girl; All you need; Loving Brecht (novel); Lawrence's Women (biog.); Gold (poems); Dreamers (novel); Selected poems; Daylight (poems); Pushkin (biography); Ted Hughes: The Life of a Poet; Collected Poems; Anna of All the Russias: a biography of Anna Akhmatova; Talking to the Dead (poems); The Russian Jerusalem (2008); Ad.: c/o Gill Coleridge & White, 20 Powis Mews, W11. ☎ 020-8221 3717.

FELDMAN, David Maurice, MA, PhD; b. Lond., Feb. 16, 1957; Historian; Senior Lecturer in History Birkbeck Coll., (1993-); form. Lecturer in Economic & Social History Univ. of Bristol, form. Lect. & Fell., Christ's Coll., Cambridge (1987-90), Junior Res. Fell., Churchill Coll., Cambridge (1983-87); Publ.: Englishmen and Jews, Social relations and political culture 1840-1914 (1993), Metropolis London (ed. with G. Stedman Jones). Ad.: 44 Victoria Park, Cambridge CB4 3EL. ☎ 01223 312272.

FELSENSTEIN, Denis R., BA (Hons), PGCE (Distinction), Ac. Dip., MA (Ed), ACIArb.; b. London, May 16, 1927; form. Hd. Immanuel Coll., form. Dep. Hd. J.F.S.; Hd.Brooke House, Div. Inspector Camden/Westminster and Senior Staff Inspector (Secondary), ILEA. Publ.: Comprehensive Achievement 1987, part-author Combatting Absenteeism 1986, numerous articles. Ad.: 27 Chessington Court, Charter Way, London N3 3DT. ☎ 020-8346 2096.

FELSENSTEIN, Frank, BA (Hons), PhD; b. Westminster, July 28, 1944; m. Carole; Prof. Humanities, Ball State Univ. (2002-); Dir., Honors Program, Yeshiva College, NY (1998-2002); form. Reader in English, Univ. of Leeds; Vis. Prof., Vanderbilt Univ., USA (1989-90). Publ.: Anti-Semitic Stereotypes: A Paradigm of Otherness in English Popular Culture, 1660-1830 (1995); The Jew as Other: A Century of English Caricature, 1730-1830, exhibition catalogue (Jewish Theological Seminary, New York, 1995); Hebraica and Judaica from the Cecil Roth Collection, exhibition catalogue (Brotherton Library, 1997); English Trader, Indian Maid: Representing Gender, Race and Slavery in the New World (1999). (Co-edit) John Thelwall: Two Plays (2006); Ad.: 8 Manor Drive, Morristown, NJ 07960-2611, USA. ☎ 973-889-1323. Dept. English, Ball State University, Muncie, IN 47306. ☎ (765) 285-8580. Fax (765) 285-3765. Email felsenstein@bsu.edu.

FERSHT, Sir Alan Roy, MA, PhD, FRS; b. Lond., Apr. 21, 1943; m. Marilyn née Persell; Herchel Smith Prof., Organic Chem., Cambridge; Dir., Cambridge C. for Protein Eng.; Fel., Gonville & Caius Coll.; Prof., Biological Chem., Imperial Coll., Lond. and Wolfson Res. Prof. Royal Soc., (1978-88); Scientific Staff, MRC Lab., Molecular Biology, Cambridge (1969-77). Publ.: Enzyme Structure and Mechanism; Structure and Mechanism in Protein Science. Ad.:

University Chemical Laboratory, Lensfield Road, Cambridge, CB2 1EW. ☎ 01223 402137 Fax 01223 402140.

FINE, Rabbi Yisroel, BA; b. Swansea, Nov. 11, 1948; M., Cockfosters and N. Southgate Syn., form. M., Wembley Syn., United Hebrew Cong., Newcastle upon Tyne; form. Chairman of the Rabbinical C. of the United Synagogue; Hon. Princ. Wolfson Hillel Primary Sch.; Educ. Portfolio, Chief Rabbi's Cabinet. Ad.: 274 Chase Side, N14 4PR. ☎ 020-8449 1750.

FINESTEIN, Israel, QC, MA (Cantab); Hon. LLD Hull; b. Hull, April 29, 1921, P. BoD (1991-94), V. President (1988-91), Mem. (1945-72, 1988-); form. Deputy High Court Judge, Chairman Mental Health Review Tribunal, Crown Court Judge (1972-87); Mem, President of Israel's Standing Conference on Israel and Diaspora (1976-90); Hon. Life President, Hillel Foundation, P. (1981-94); Chairman of Hillel-Union of Jewish Students Educ. Cttee. (1981-91); form. Exec. Cttee. of C.C.J. (1980-95); V. President, Central C. for Jewish Soc. Services; Chairman, Kessler Foundation (1985-91); form. Mem. Exec. Cttee Memorial Foundation for Jewish Culture; Council United Synagogue and Jewish Chaplaincy Bd.; Jewish Memorial Council, Fdr. Member of Yad Vashem Cttee.; V. President, AJY; V. President, Jewish Museum, London and form. Chairman (1989-92) and V. President, Jewish Historical Soc. and form. P. (1973-75, 1993-4); V. President, Conference J. Material Claims Against Germany (1991-94); V. President, World Jewish Congress (1991-94); form. V. President, European Jewish Congress; Exec. Cttees. of London Bd. and Central Bd. of Jewish Religious Educ.; Cttee. of British ORT. Publ.: James Picciotto's Sketches of Anglo-Jewish History (edr.); Short History of Anglo-Jewry; Jewish Society in Victorian England; Anglo-Jewry in Changing Times: Studies in Diversity, 1840-1914; Scenes and Personalities in Anglo-Jewry, 1800-2000; Studies and Profiles in Anglo-Jewish History: From Picciotto to Bermant (2008). Ad.: 18 Buttermere Ct., Boundary Rd., NW8 6NR.

FINKELSTEIN, Daniel, OBE; b. London, Aug. 30, 1962; m. Nicola Connor; Journalist; Associate Editor and Chief Leader Writer, *The Times* (2008-); form. Comment Editor, Leader Writer (2001-); Fink Tank column (2002-); form. Dir., Conservative Party Res. Dept. (1995-97), Chief Policy Adv., to William Hague (1997-2001); Conservative Party candidate, Harrow West (2001). Awarded the Chaim Bermant Journalism Prize (2008). Ad.: The Times, 1, Pennington St., London E98 1TT

FINKELSTEIN, Ludwik, OBE, MA, PhD, DSc, Dr. Univ. hc, DCLhc, FREng, FIET, C. Phys, FInstP, Hon. FInstMC; b. Lwow, Dec. 6, 1929; Prof. Emer. of Measurement & Instrumentation, City Univ.; form. Pro-V. Chancellor; form. Prof of Instrument & Control Engineering, City Univ.; form Dean, School of Engineering, City Univ. Scientific Staff NCB; President, Instit. of Measurement & Control (1980), Hartley Medallist; Res. Fel. Jewish History and Thought, Leo Baeck Coll.; Publ.: Works in Mathematical Modelling, Measurement, etc. Ad.: City University, Northampton Sq., EC1V 0HB. ☎ 020-7040-8109. Fax 020-7040 8568.

FINLAY, Alan Stanley, LL.B.; b. London, April 2, 1950; m. Kathryn née Fine; Solicitor; President, Federation of Synagogues (form. Treasurer); Chairman, Jewish Youth Voluntary Service (1974-78): Chairman, AJY (1984-88); Vice-President, World Confederation of Jewish Community Centres (1984-88). Ad.: 4, Orchard Close, Edgware Middx HA8 7RE. ☎ 020-8952 7517. Email asf@federationofsynagogues.com

FISHMAN, William J., BSc (Econ), Dip. Lit.; DSc (Econ) (London); b. London, April 1, 1921; Barnett Shine Sr. Res. Fel. in Labour Studies, Queen Mary and Westfield Coll, London Univ. (1972-86), & Vis. Prof. (1986); Princ., Tower Hamlets Coll. for Further Educ. (1955-69); Vis. Fel., Balliol Coll., Oxford Univ. (1965), Vis. Prof., Columbia Univ. (1967), Wisc Univ. (1969-70). Publ.: The Insurrectionists, East End Jewish Radicals, Streets of East London, East End 1888, East End and Docklands; Into the Abyss: the Life and Works of G.R. Sims (2007); Recordings – CDs. Ad.: 42 Willowcourt Ave., Kenton, Harrow, Middx. HA3 8ES. ☎ 020-8907 5166.

FIXMAN, Sydney; b. Manchester, Apr. 5, 1935; Dir., Instit. for Jewish Music Studies & Performance; Music Lect., Lond. Univ. Instit. of Educ.; Fdr., Conductor, Ben Uri Chamber Orchestra, Jewish Youth Orchestra, Music Dir., West Lond. Syn.; form. Guest Conductor, leading orchestras in Brit. & abroad (seasons in Israel: 1976-89); Conductor, B.B.C. (TV & Radio). Publ.: (ed.) Psaume Tehillim (Markevitch); Recordings, CDs. Ad.: 5 Bradby House, Hamilton Tce., NW8 9XE.

FORSTER, Donald, CBE; b. London, Dec. 18, 1920; President Soc. Jewish Golf Captains (1994-); Man. Dir. & Chairman B. Forster & Co. Ltd. (1946-85); Chairman, Merseyside Development Corp. (1984-87); Chairman Warrington/Runcorn Devel. Corp (1981-85), President, Manchester JIA (1981-83); President, Assn. Jewish Golf Clubs & Socs. (1973-83), HLP Whitefield Golf Club; Pilot (Flt.-Lieut.) RAF (1940-45); Rep. England, 1954 Maccabiah (tennis). Ad.: 72A Elizabeth St., London SW1W 9PD.

FRANKENBERG, Ronald Jonas, AcSS, BA (Hons Cantab), MA (Econ), PhD (Manchester), Hon. DSocSci (Brunel), Hon. D.Litt (Keele); b. Cricklewood, London, Oct. 20, 1929; m. Pauline née Hunt; Founding Academician, Academy of Social Sciences (1999); Fell. Keele University, Emer. Professor of Sociology and Social Anthropology; Hon. Fellow, Centre for Jewish Studies, Univ. Manchester; form. Dir. Centre for Medical Social Anthropology, Keele; Prof.Assoc., Hum. Sci., Brunel; Dean and Prof. Zambia University (1966–68); Reader, Manchester; Education Officer NUMineworkers. Publ.: Village on The Border, Communities in Britain, Custom and Conflict in British Society, Time, Health & Medicine. Ad.: 19 Keele Rd., Newcastle-u-Lyme, Staffs. ST5 2JT. ☎ 01782 628498. Email RFrank1251@aol.com.

FRANKLIN, Andrew Cecil; b. London, Mar. 6, 1957; m. Caroline Sarah née Elton; Publisher; Chairman, Tr. Jewish Community Centre for London; Tr. Jewish Literary Tr. Adr.: Profile Books, 3A, Exmouth House, Pine Street, Exmouth Market, London EC1R 0JH.

FRANSES, Rabbi Simon J.; b. Larissa, Greece, May 25, 1943; m. Ann née Lyons; Rabbi Emeritus, Middlesex New Syn., Chairman of the Assembly of Rabbis RSGB (1989-91); Asst. M., Edgware & Dist. Reform Syn. (1971-74); M., Glasgow New Syn. (1974-87); Member of Children's Panel for Strathclyde Region (1977-87). Ad.: 39 Bessborough Rd., Harrow, Middx. HA1 3BS. ☎ 020-8864 0133. Email rabbi@mns.org.uk.

FREEDLAND, Jonathan; b. London, Feb. 25, 1967; m. Sarah née Peters; Journalist; Columnist, The Guardian (1997-); Monthly Columnist, The Jewish Chronicle (1998-); Washington Correspondent, The Guardian (1993-97). Publ.: Bring Home the Revolution: The Case for a British Republic (1998); Jacob's Gift (2005) Ad.: The Guardian, 119 Farringdon Road, London EC1R 3ER. ☎ 020-7278 2332.

FREEDLAND, Michael Rodney; b. London, Dec. 18, 1934; journalist and broadcaster, contributor to national press; Exec. Ed. & Presenter (BBC and LBC), 'You Don't Have to be Jewish' (1971-94). Publ.: Al Jolson; Irving Berlin; James Cagney; Fred Astaire; Sophie; Jerome Kern; Errol Flynn; Gregory Peck; Maurice Chevalier; Peter O'Toole; The Warner Brothers; Katharine Hepburn; So Let's Hear the Applause – The Story of the Jewish Entertainer; Jack Lemmon; The Secret Life of Danny Kaye; Shirley MacLaine; Leonard Bernstein; The Goldwyn Touch: A Biography of Sam Goldwyn; Jane Fonda; Liza With A Z; Dustin Hoffman; Kenneth Williams: A Biography; Andre Previn: Music Man; Sean Connery: A Biography; All the Way: A Biography of Frank Sinatra; Bob Hope; Bing Crosby; Michael Caine; Doris Day; Some Like it Cool; King of the Road; (with Morecambe and Wise) There's No Answer To That; (with Walter Scharf) Composed and Conducted by Walter Scharf; Confessions of a Serial Biographer; Hollywood on Trial,. Ad.: Bays Hill Lodge, Barnet Lane, Elstree, Herts. WD6 3QU. ☎ 020-8953 3000.

FREEDMAN, Harry, PhD, MA (London), BA; b. London 1950; form. Chief Exec., Assembly of Masorti Synagogues (1994-2000); European Rep., Masorti; Lay minister Exeter Synagogue (1981-87); Dir. & Lecturer Masorti Academy (1994-2001); Editorial Advisory Committee, Jewish Bible Quarterly, Judaism Today. Publ.: The Halacha in Targum Pseudo-Jonathan (1999). Ad.: Career Energy, 4-6 Staple Inn, London WC1V 7QH. ☎ 084 5226 1616. Email harry@careerenergy. co.uk.

FREEDMAN, Jerome David, FCA; b. Brighton, 1935; m. Louise née Hershman; Chartered Accountant; Vice President, Liberal Judaism, form. Chairman (1995-2001); form. Hon. Tr. (1990-95); President, South London Liberal Synagogue; Tr., Chartered Accountants' Benevolent Association (CABA 1973-2008, President 2003-05). Ad.: 5 Thanescroft Gardens, Croydon, Surrey CR0 5JR. ☎ 020-8688 2250. Fax 020-8680 4631. Email jerome@freedman.org.

FRIEDLANDER, Evelyn (née Philipp), ARCM, Order of Merit (Germany); b. London, June 22, 1940; Executive Director, Hidden Legacy Foundation; Tr. and Chairman Czech Memorial

Scrolls Trust. Publ.: Ich Will nach Hause, aber ich war noch nie da (1996); Mappot ... The Band of Jewish Tradition (1997, co-ed.); The Jews of Devon and Cornwall (2000);. Westminster Synagogue: the First 50 Years (2007). Ad.: Kent House, Rutland Gardens, London SW7 1BX. ☎ 020-7584 2754. Fax 020-7581 8012. Email e.friedlander@virgin.net.

FRIEDMAN, (Eve) Rosemary, (Robert Tibber, Rosemary Tibber, Rosemary Friedman) b. London, Feb. 5, 1929; Writer. m. Dennis Friedman; Membership: Royal Society of Literature; Society of Authors; Writers Guild of Great Britain; British Academy of Film and Television Arts; Fellow, English PEN. Publi.: No White Coat, 1957; Love on My List, 1959: We All Fall Down, 1960; Patients of a Saint, 1961; The Fraternity, 1963; The Commonplace Day, 1964; Aristide, 1966; The General Practice, 1967; Practice Makes Perfect 1969; The Life Situation, 1977; The Long Hot Summer, 1980; Proofs of Affection, 1982; A Loving Mistress, 1983; Rose of Jericho, 1984; A Second Wife, 1986; Aristide in Paris, 1987; An Eligible Man, 1989 (as stageplay, 2008); Golden Boy, 1994; Vintage, 1996; The Writing game, 1999; Intensive Care, 2001; Paris Summer, 2004; A Writer's Commonplace Book (2006). Other: Home Truths (stage play) 1997; Change of Heart (stage play) 2004. , Ad.: Apt. 5, 3 Cambridge Gate, London NW1 4JX. Email rosemaryfriedman@hotmail.com. Website www.rosemary. friedman.co.uk.

FRIEND, John, BSc, PhD (Liv), PhD (Cantab), FIBiol; b. Liverpool, May 31, 1931; m. Carol née Loofe; President Hull Jewish Representative Council (1999-2003); Emer. Prof. of Plant Biology, Hull Univ.; Prof. of Plant Biology, Hull Univ. (1969-97); Pro-V. Chancellor, Hull Univ. (1983-87); Vis. Prof. Hebrew Univ. of Jerusalem (1974); Vis. Fel. Wolfson College, Cambridge (1988). Publ.: Biochemical Aspects of Plant-Parasite Relations (with D. R. Threlfall, 1976); Recent Advances in the Biochemistry of Fruit and Vegetables (with MJC Rhodes, 1983). Ad.: 9 Allanhall Way, Kirkella, Hull HU10 7QU. ☎ 01482-658930. Email j.friend@cj2fkaroo.co.uk.

FROSH, Sidney, JP; b. London, Aug. 22, 1923; President, US (1987-92), Chairman, Beth Hamedrash & Beth Din. Man. Bd., Chairman, Chief Rabbinate C. (1987-92); Chairman, Min. Placement Cttee., Chairman, Singer's Prayer Book Publ. Cttee. (1987-92); Gov., JFS (1981-2002); VP Norwood Ravenswood; V. President, Cen. C. for Jewish Comm. Services; Chief Rabbinate C.; V. Chairman & T., Lond. Bd. of Jewish Rel. Educ. (1968-78). Ad.: 4, Whitehorse Dr., Stanmore, Middx HA7 4NQ ☎ 020-8954 9566.

GAFFIN, Jean (née Silver), OBE, JP, Hon. FRCPCH, MSc, BSc (Econ); b. London, Aug. 1, 1936; m. Alexander; Tr., St. Luke's Hospice (2007-); Chair, Brent Primary Care NHS Trust (2002-07); Non. Exec. Dir. Harrow & Hillingdon Healthcare NHS Trust (1998-2002); Memb. Consumer Panel Financial Services Auth. (1999-2003); Exec. Dir. National Hospice Council (1991-98); Chief Exec. Arthritis Care (1988-91); Exec. Sec., British Paediatric Assoc. (1982-87); Organising Sec., Child Accident Prevention Cttee (1979-82); Lecturer II/Senior Lecturer, Social Policy and Administration, Polytechnic of the South Bank (1973-79); Chairman, OFTEL's Advisory Committee on Telecommunications for Disabled and Elderly People – DIEL (1993-99); Hon. Sec. Royal Society of Medicine (1997-2001); Mem. UK Xeno-Transplantation Interim Regulatory Authority (1997-2004); Magistrate, Harrow Bench (1981-2006). Publ. include: (Editor) The Nurse and the Welfare State (1981); with D. Thoms, Caring and Sharing: the Centenary History of the Co-operative Women's Guild (1983, second ed. 1993); Women's Co-operative Guild 1884-1914, in Women in the Labour Movement, ed. L. Middleton (1977). Ad.: 79, Chalet Estate, Hammers Lane, London NW7 4DL ☎ 020-8959 9509. Email jean.gaffin@btopenworld.com.

GAINSFORD, Doreen; b. London, May 9, 1937; Public & Press Relations Off.; form. Chairman, 35's (Women's Campaign for Soviet Jewry). Emigrated to Israel, March, 1978, Coord, JIA Project Renewal, Ashkelon; Founder, 35's Israel Campaign for Soviet Jewry; Founder Israel Action Center (IAC); Dir., TAL Mini Gifts (Israel). Ad.: Yehoshua Ben Nun 2, Herzlia Pituach, Israel 46763. ☎ 09-950234771. Fax 9506542.

GAINSFORD, Sir Ian, BDS, DDS, FDSRCS Eng, FDSRCS Edin., FRCSEd.Hon., FICD, FACD, FKC, DDS (Hons) Toronto; b. Twickenham, June 24, 1930; m. Carmel née Liebster; Dental Surgeon; President, Maccabeans (2000-07); Regent, Royal College of Surgeons, Edinburgh (2002-); President, Western Marble Arch Synagogue (1998-2000); Dean, King's College School of Medicine & Dentistry (1988-97); Vice-Principal, King's College, London (1994-97); Hon. President, British Friends of Magen David Adom (1995-). Ad.: 31 York Terrace

East, London NW1 4PT. ☎ 020-7935 8659.

GALE, Rev. Norman Eric, BA, PhD; b. Leeds, Nov. 9, 1929; m. Vera née Shebson; Mem. Prison Religious Advisory Service Group; Rep Standing Adv. C. for Religious Ed. (Kensington & Chelsea); form. M., Hampstead Syn. (1988-95); M., Ealing Syn. (1968-88); M., Harrogate Hebrew Cong. (1958-68); form. Chairman, US Rabbinical C.; Memb. Chief Rabbi's Cabinet (Welfare Portfolio 1990-93); form. H. Chaplain, Nat. Assn. of Jewish Friendship Clubs; H. Dir., Jewish Prison Chaplaincy (1985-2003); Chaplain, Wormwood Scrubs Prison (1979-2003). Ad.: Flat 6, Orford Ct., Marsh Lane, Stanmore, Middx HA7 4TQ. ☎ 020-8954 3843.

GARBACZ, Bernard, FCA; b. Westcliff, Dec. 30, 1932; W., Kingsbury Syn. (1965-72); President, B'nai B'rith First Lodge of England (1976-78); Fdr. Tr, Jewish Education Development Tr. (1980-91); Receiver and Manager, Jewish Secondary Schools Movement (1979-82); Chairman, Bd. of Govs., Hasmonean Boys' Grammar Sch. (1979-82); Chairman, J. Marriage C. (1989-91), T. then V.-Chairman, Brit-Israel Chamber of Commerce (1980-92); T., Jews Coll. (1971-84); V.Chairman, Hillel Foundation (1980-92); H. President, Univ. Jewish Chaplaincy Bd.; Chairman, London Jewish Chaplaincy Bd. (1997-2000); Chairman, Hendon U.S. (2003-05); Dir., Central Middlesex Hospital N.H.S. Tr. (1991-96); Chairman, Black's Leisure Gp. Plc (1986-90), Dmatek Ltd. (1995-96). Evening Standard City Personality Award, 1987. *Publ.*: Moscow Report (1950); Anglo Jewry Research Project 1985 (Garbacz Report on Communal Funding). Ad.: 2 Beatrice Court, 15 Queens Road, London NW4 2TL. ☎ 020-8203 5807. Fax 020-8203 5824. Email bgarbacz@aol.com.

GELLER, Markham Judah, b. Corpus Christi, Texas, Jan. 2, 1949; University Lecturer; Prof. of Semitic Languages, Dept. of Hebrew and Jewish Studies, University College London; Dir. Institute of Jewish Studies, University College London. Ad.: Dept of Hebrew and Jewish Studies, UCL, Gower St., London WC1E 6BT. ☎ 020-7679 3588. Fax 020-7209 1026. Email m.geller@ucl.ac.uk; 30 Gilling Court, London NW3 4XA. ☎ 020-7586 9693.

GILBERT, Andrew, BSc; b. London, May 31, 1959; Managing Dir., Henry Bertrand Silk Fabrics; Chairman, Limmud International (2006-) Limmud (1990-97); Vice-Chairman, World Reform Zionist Movement (2006-); M. Steering Cttee, London Jewish Forum (2006-); Chairman, RSGB (2002-05); M., Educ Cttee, Bd. Gov, Jewish Agency (2003-); M., Council, Jewish Community Leadership C. (2003-05); Chairman, BoD, Youth & Information Cttee (1994-97), Exec. M., BoD (1994-97); Chair, Jewish Youth Service Partners Gp (1994-98); Chairman, European Hanhallah, CAJE (1996); Chairman Israel Experience Policy Gp., UJIA (1998-2002), Exec. Mem. Jewish renewal (1998-); M., Lay Leadership Task Force, Jewish Continuity (1992-96). Ad.: 52 Holmes Rd., London NW5 3AB. ☎ 020-7424 7002. Fax 020-7424 7001. Email alphasilk@gmail.com

GILBERT, Sir Martin, CBE, D.Litt; b. London, Oct. 25, 1936; historian; Official Biographer of Winston Churchill (since 1968); Fel., Merton Col., Oxford; Vis. Prof, Hebrew Univ. (1980, 1995-98); Vis. Prof., Tel Aviv Univ. (1979); Vis. Prof. UCL (1995-6). Publ.: Winston S. Churchill (6 vols.); Churchill, A Life; The Appeasers (with Richard Gott); Britain and Germany Between the Wars; The European Powers 1900-1945; The Roots of Appeasement; Exile and Return: A Study in the Emergence of Jewish Statehood; The Holocaust – the Jewish Tragedy; Churchill, A Photographic Portrait; In Search of Churchill; Auschwitz and the Allies; The Jews of Hope; The Plight of Soviet Jewry Today; Shcharansky, Portrait of a Hero; Jerusalem – Rebirth of a City; Jerusalem in the Twentieth Century; First World War; Second World War; The Day the War Ended; The Boys – Triumph over Adversity; Israel, A History; A History of the Twentieth Century (3 vols); Letters to Aunt Fori: 5,000 Year History of the Jewish People and Their Faith; The Righteous: The Unsung Heroes of the Holocaust; Kristallnacht: Prelude to Destruction; The Story of Israel; and other historical works; 12 history atlases, including the Jewish History Atlas, Jerusalem Illustrated History Atlas, Atlas of the Arab-Israel Conflict and the Atlas of the Holocaust. Ad.: Merton College, Oxford. Website www.martingilbert.com.

GINSBURG David, MA; b. London, Mar. 18, 1921; Comp. Dir., Economist Market and Marketing Res. Consultant; Broadcaster; Fel., Royal Soc. of Med.; M.P. (Lab. 1959-81, SDP 1981-83 Dewsbury), Sec., Research Dept. Labour Party(1952-59); Sr. Research Off., Govt. Social Survey (1946-52). Ad.: 3 Bell Moor, East Heath Rd., NW3 1DY. ☎ 020-8435 8700.

GINSBURY, Rabbi Mordechai Shlomo; b. London, May 10, 1960; m. Judy née Burns; M., Hendon United Synagogue (1999-); Principal Hasmonean Primary School (2003-); M., Prestwich Hebrew Congregation, Manchester (1985-99); Chairman, Rabbinical Council of the Provinces (1997-98); Chairman (2005-08); Vice-Chairman (2002-05) Rabbinical Council, US. Ad.: Hendon United Synagogue, 18 Raleigh Close, London NW4 2TA. ☎ 020-8202 6924 (main office), 020-8203 7762 (direct line, off.). Fax 020-8202 1720. Email rabbiginsbury@hendonus.org.uk

GINSBURY, Rabbi Philip Norman, MA; b. London, Mar. 26, 1936; form. M., South London Syn.; M., Streatham Distr. Syn., Brixton Syn.; Chairman South London Rabbinical Council. Publ. Jewish Faith in Action (1995); The Phases of Jewish History (2005): Ad.: 146 Downton Ave., SW2 3TT. ☎/Fax 020-8674 7451. Email rabbi@ginsburyp.co.uk.

GLANVILLE, Brian Lester, b. London, Sept. 24, 1931; writer. Publ.: Along the Arno, A Bad Streak, The Bankrupts, Diamond, etc. Ad.: 160 Holland Park Ave., W11.

GLATTER, Robert, FCA; b. Antwerp, Belgium, Mar. 14, 1937; Chartered Accountant, Non-Exec. Director Bank Leumi (UK) plc; Chairman, Bank Leumi Pension Fund; Non-Exec. Director CP Holdings Ltd; V-Pres. Bnai Brith Hillel Foundation; form. Council Mem. Weizmann Institute Foundation; Hon. Life President, Maccabi Union GB; Tr. Maccabi Fd., Tr. Arbib Lucas Charity; V-Pres. Akiva School; Member, Maccabi World Union; Form. Tr. Volcani Fnd.; Gov. Tr. Carmel College; Ch. NW Reform Syn.; Chairman, RSGB Cttee for Ed. and Youth; Ch. RSGB Israel Action Ct.; V-Ch., Ch., Tr., V-Press. Maccabi Union GB; Dep. Ch. Maccabi Europe; Ch. and Dep. Ch. Maccabiah Organ. Cttee; Tr. Bd for Jewish Sport; Tr. Manor House Trustees; Tr. Centre for Jewish-Christian Relations, Cambridge. Ad.: 12 York Gate, London NW1 4QS.

GLINERT, Lewis H., BA (Oxon), PhD; b. London, June 17, 1950; m. Joan née Abraham; University Lecturer; Prof. of Hebraic Studies and Linguistics, Dartmouth College; form. Prof. of Hebrew, Univ. of London (School of Oriental and African Studies, 1979-97); Dir. Centre for Jewish Studies, SOAS; Vis. Prof. of Hebrew Studies, Chicago U. (1987/8); Asst. Prof. of Hebrew Linguistics, Haifa U. (1974-77). Publ.: The Grammar of Modern Hebrew (1989); The Joys of Hebrew (1992); Hebrew in Ashkenaz (1993); Modern Hebrew: An Essential Grammar (1994); Mamma Dear (1997). Ad.: Dartmouth College, 6191 Bartlett Hall, Hanover, N.H. 03755, USA. ☎ 603 646 8238. Fax 617 332 0244. Email Lewis.Glinert@Dartmouth.edu.

GOLD, Sir Arthur Abraham, CBE; b. Lond., Jan. 10, 1917; Engineer; President, European Athletic Assn.; V.President, Commonwealth Games C. for England; Chairman, Drug Abuse Adv. Group, Sports C.; P. Counties Athletic Union; Life V. President (H.Sec., 1962-77) Brit. Amateur Athletic Bd.; President, Amateur Ath. Assn.; V.President Brit. Olympic Assn.; Member, Sports C.; Exec. Central C. of Physical Recreation; Athletics Team Leader, Olympic Games, Mexico 1968, Munich 1972, Montreal 1976; Commandant, C'wealth Games Team Brisbane 1982, Edinburgh 1986, Auckland 1990; British Olympic Team 1988, 1992; President, Lond. Ath. Club (1962-63); President, Middlesex CAAA (1963 and 1993). Ad.: 49 Friern Mount Drive, N20 9DJ. ☎ 020-8445 2848.

GOLD, Rev. Sidney, BA; b. London Dec. 6, 1919; Emer. M (Chief M., 1960-85) Birmingham Hebrew Cong., form. M., Highgate Syn., Regent's Park & Belsize Park Syn., Bayswater Syn., Member Chief Rabbi's Cabinet (1979-83); P. Union of Anglo-Jewish Preachers (1977-78), form. V.Chairman B'ham C.C.J.; Chairman B'ham Inter-Faith C.; President, B'ham JIA Cttee. Publ.: Children's Prayer Book for High Festivals (jt. author). Ad.: 12 Dean Park Mans., 27 Dean Park Rd., Bournemouth BH1 1JA ☎ 01202 551578.

GOLDBERG, Rabbi David J., MA (Oxon), DD (Hons), OBE; b. London, Feb. 25, 1939; Rabbi Emeritus Liberal Jewish Syn.; Interfaith Gold Medallion (1999); Premio Iglesias (1999); M. Wembley & Dist. Lib. Syn. (1971-75); Associate Rabbi L.J.S. (1975-86), Senior Rabbi (1986-2001); Chairman, ULPS Rabbinic Conference (1981-83, 1996-98). Publ.: The Jewish People: Their History and their Religion (with John D. Rayner); To the Promised Land: A History of Zionist Thought; On the Vistula Facing East (ed.); Progressive Judaism Today (gen. ed.).; Aspects of Liberal Judaism (co.ed.). The Divided Self: Israel and the Jewish Psyche Today. Ad.: Liberal Jewish Synagogue, 28 St. John's Wood Rd., NW8 7HA.

☎ 020-7286 5181. Email ljs@lJs.org.

GOLDBERG, David Jonathan, MA (Jewish Communal Service) Brandeis; Cert. Youth and Community Studies, London; b. London, June 27, 1961; Dir. Fundraising UJIA (2006-); Dir. UJIA Israel Experience (1998-2006); Exec. Director, Zionist Fed. of Great Britain & Ireland (1992-98); H. Chair, Association of Jewish Communal Professionals (1992-98); Senior Youth and Community Work, Redbridge JYCC (1983-90). Ad. 18 Chiltern Avenue, Bushey, Herts WD23 4QA. ☎ 020-8950 0080. Email goldberg.david@btinternet.com.

GOLDMAN, Lawrence Neil, MA, PhD (Cantab), FRHistS., b. London June 17 1957; m. Madeleine Jean McDonald; University lecturer; Fellow and Tutor in Modern History, St. Peter's College, Oxford (1990-); Editor, Oxford Dictionary of National Biography (2004-). Publ.; Dons and Workers: Oxford and Adult Education Since 1850 (1995), Science, Reform and Politics in Victorian Britain (2002); Politics and Culture in Victorian Britain: Essays in Memory of Colin Matthew (2006, ed., with P. Ghosh). Ad.: Oxford DNB, OUP, Great Clarendon St., Oxford OX2 6DP. ☎ 01865-355010, Fax 01865-355035 Email lawrence.goldman@oup.com.

GOLDMAN, William; b. London, April 4, 1910; Novelist. Publ.: A Start in Life, A Tent of Blue, East End My Cradle, In England and in English, A Saint in the Making, The Light in the Dust, Some Blind Hand, The Forgotten Word, etc. Ad.: 12 Quintock House, Broomfield Rd., Kew Gdns., Richmond, Surrey TW9 3HT. ☎ 020-8948 4798.

GOLDMEIER, Michael, b. London, Nov. 27, 1946; m. Philippa née Yantian; Solicitor, partner Berlwin Leighton Paisner; Chairman, Jewish Care (2002-); Vice-Chairman, European C. Jewish Communities (1996-2002); Mem. Bd., Claims Conference (1998-2002); Immigration Judge (Asylum & Immigration Tribunal) (2001-). Adr.: High Liuden, 104 Marsh Lane, Mill Hill, London NW7 4PA. Email michael.Goldmeier@blplaw.com.

GOLDREIN, Neville Clive, CBE, MA (Cantab.); b. Hull; m. Sonia née Sumner; Solicitor; Mem. Int. Assoc. Jewish Lawyers and Jurists; Mem. BAJS; Vice-President, Southport. J. Rep.C. (2003-); Mem. Port of Liverpool Police Cttee (2000-); Tr. Southport J. Rep. Council (1999-2006); form. Dep. Circuit Judge; form. Member (Leader, 1980-81, V. Chairman, 1977-80) Merseyside County C. (1973-86); Leader, Conservative Group (1980-86); Lancashire County Council (1965-74); Crosby Borough C. (1957-71); Mayor of Crosby (1966-67); Dep. Mayor (1967-68); North-West Economic Planning C. (1972-74); Gov. Merchant Taylors' Schools, Crosby (1965-74); Area President, St. John Amb., Sefton (1965-87); C., L'pool Univ. (1977-81); Vice-President, Crosby MENCAP (1966-); C. L'pool Chamber of Commerce (1986-); Chairman Environment and Energy Cttee (1993-2006); British Assoc. of Chambers of Commerce, Mem. Local & Regional Aff. Cttee (1994-97); Chairman L'pool Royal Court Theatre Foundation (1994-2005); Chairman, Crosby Conservative Association (1986-89); Chairman (Appeals), Crosby Hall Educ. Trust (1989-91); BoD (1965-85, and 1992-2001); Sr.W., L'pool Old Hebrew Cong. (1968-71). Mem. C. Liverpool Institute of Performing Arts (2005-). Ad.: Torreno, St Andrew's Rd., Blundellsands, Liverpool L23 7UR. ☎/Fax 0151-924 2065. Email goldrein@aol.com. 20/8 Rehov HaPalmach, Jerusalem 92542 ☎ 0563 3085.

GOLDSMITH, Lord (Peter Henry), PC, QC, MA (Cantab), LLM (London); b. Liverpool, Jan. 5, 1950; m. Joy née Elterman; form. H.M. Attorney-General (2001-07); President (2001-), Chairman, Bar Pro Bono Unit (1996-2000); Chairman, Financial Reporting Review Panel (1997-2000); Co-Chairman, Human Rights Institute of International Bar Assoc. (1998-2001); Chairman, Bar of England and Wales (1995). Publ.: contr. to Common Values, Common Law, Common Bond (2000). Ad.: House of Lords, London SW1A.

GOLDSMITH, Walter Kenneth, FCA CiMgt, FRSA; b. London, Jan. 19, 1938; Chairman J. Music Inst. (2003-08), Vice-President (2008); Chairman, 'Simcha on the Square' (2006-); Chairman Estates in Management Ltd. (2006-); M. London Jewish Forum (2006-); Chairman ULPS Centenary Committee 2002 (1999-); Chairman (1987-91), V. President (1992-) Brit Overseas Trade Group for Israel; Dir.-Gen. Inst. of Dirs. (1979-84); Co-founder and Tr. Israel Diaspora Tr. (1982-92); Treasurer Leo Baeck College (1987-89); Dir. Bank Leumi (UK) plc (1984-). Ad.: 21, Ashurst Close, Northwood, Middx. HA6 1EL.

GOLDSTEIN, Rabbi Andrew, PhD; b. Warwick, Aug. 12, 1943; M., Northwood and Pinner Liberal Syn. (1970-2008), Emer. Rabbi (2008-); Chairman, European Region, World Univ. for Progressive Judaism (2007-); Vice-Chair, Hillingdon Branch CCJ (2001-); Exec. Bd., ICCJ.

(2003-); Chairman, ULPS Rabbinic Conf (1979-81); Chairman, ULPS Educ. Cttee. (1970-88); Dir., Kadimah Holiday School, (1970-89); Chairman ULPS Prayerbook Editorial Cttee; Consult. Rabbi Liberal congregations in Prague and Bratislava. Publ.: My Jewish Home, Jerusalem, Tradition Roots, Britain and Israel, Mishnah Kadimah, Exploring the Bible, Parts 1 & 2, Machzor Ruach Chadashah (co-ed., 2003). Ad.: 10 Hallowell Rd., Northwood, Middx. HA6 1DW. ☎ 01923 822818. Fax 01923 824454. Email agoldstein@f2s.com

GOLDSTEIN, Rabbi Henry; b. London, March 10, 1936; Rabbi Emeritus, South-West Essex and Settlement Reform Syn. (2001-), M. (1973-2001); M., Finchley Reform Syn. (1967-73); Ch, RSGB Rabbis' Assembly (1973-75). Ad. 15 Chichester Gardens, Ilford Essex 1GI 3NB. ☎ 020-8554 2297. Email ravhen@aol.com.

GOLDSTEIN, Michael, MBE; b. London, April 5, 1919; form. Gen. Sec., AJY (1951-77); form. Chairman, Greater Lond. Conf of Vol. Youth Orgs. Ad.: Flat 12, Broadway Close, Woodford Green, Essex, IG8 OHD. ☎ 020-8504 2304.

GOLDSTEIN, Michael Howard, FCA; b. London, July 7, 1963; m. Lara née Stanton; Chartered Accountant; Partner BDO Stoy Hayward; Vice Chairman, UJIA (2003-), Chairman, Israel Desk (2005-); Gov. King Solomon High School (1992-2003); Tr., UJS Hillel (2003-); Chairman, Office for Small Communities (2005-). Adr.: 4a Parkmead Gardens, Mill Hill, London NW7 2JW. ☎ 020-8201 0881 (home); 020-7893 5529 (office). Email michael.Goldstein@bdo.co.uk.

GOLDSTEIN, Rabbi Dr. Warren, BA, LLB., PhD.; b. Pretoria, 1971; Chief Rabbi of South Africa, Graduate of the Yeshiva of Johannesburg (1996). Adr.: Union of Orthodox Synagogues of South Africa, 58, Oaklands Rd., Orchards 2192, Johannesburg. ☎ 485-4865/ 640-9669. Fax 485-1497. Email office@chiefrabbi.co.za

GOLDSTONE, Barbara D., ALCM, LLAM, Gold Medal LAM, TC, BA (Eng)., MEd; b. Salford, June 24, 1938; Schoolteacher, Tutor of Public Speaking and Drama; President, Jewish Representative Council of Greater Manchester (2007-10); Past President, Whitefield Bnai Brith (1985), Manchester Bnai Brith (2001, 2003, 2005); Chairman, Prestwich Emunah (1958, 1967), Higher Broughton, Higher Crumpsall Ladies Guild. Ad.: 1, Tower Grange, New Hall road, Salford M7 4EL;. ☎ 0161-792 1305. Email office@jewishmanchester.org

GOLDSTONE, Richard Joseph, BA, LLB (Witwatersrand), Hon.DL (Cape Town, Witwatersrand, Natal, Hebrew University, Notre Dame, Maryland, Wilfred Laurier, Glasgow, Catholic University, Brabant, Calgary, Emory University; b. Boksburg, Oct. 26, 1938; m. Noleen Joy née Behrman; Justice of the Constitutional Court of South Africa (1994-2003); Chair, Int. Task Force on Terrorism (International Bar Association) (2001-02); Chair, Commission of Inquiry, Public Violence and Intimidation (Goldstone Commission) (1991-94); Chief Prosecutor, UN International Criminal Tribunals for the former Yugoslavia and Rwanda (1994-96); Chair, Valencia Declaration (1999-2001); Chancellor University of the Witwatersrand (1995-2007); Gov., Hebrew U. (1980-); President, World ORT (1996-2003); Hon. Bencher, Inner Temple; Hon. Fell., St John's College (Cambridge); Foreign M., US Academy of Arts & Science; M. Assoc. Bars of New York. Publ: For Humanity: Reflections of a War Crimes Investigator. Ad.: P.O. Box 396, Morningside 2057, South Africa. ☎ (011) 803 5472. Email goldstone@iafrica.com.

GOLDWATER, Raymond, LLB; b. Hove, Sept. 28, 1918; Solicitor; Elder, US; V. President, AJY; form. Ch, Rel Adv. Cttee., AJY; form Chairman, London Student Counsellor Bd.; form C., Jews' Coll.; form. Lond. Bd., Jewish Rel. Educ.; form. Chairman, Youth & Com. Services Dept. & Jt. T., Bequests & Tr. Funds, US; Chairman, I.U.J.F. & Lond. Jewish Graduates' Assn. Publ.: Jewish Philosophy and Philosophers (Edr.).; The pioneers of Religion Zionism; Ad.: 451 West End Ave., Apt 5E, New York, NY 10024. ☎ 212-873-8221.

GOLOMBOK, Ezra, BSc, PhD; b. Glasgow, Aug. 22, 1922; Dir. Israel Information Office, Glasgow; Edr., Jewish Echo; form. Convener, Public Relations Cttee., Glasgow Jewish Rep. C. Ad.: 222 Fenwick Rd., Giffnock, Glasgow G46 6UE. ☎ 0141-639 3294. Fax 0870 131 6613. Email ezra@isrinfo.demon.co.uk. Website www.isrinfo.demon.co.uk

GOODMAN, Henry; b. London, April 23, 1950; m. Ingrid Susan née Parker; Actor, Teacher, Director (TV, film, radio); Leading Actor, Royal Shakespeare Co., Royal National Theatre, West End and Broadway; BBC (TV and radio); Visiting Teacher, Guildhall, RADA, BADA;

trained RADA (1969-71). Fax 020-8241 7946.

GOODMAN, Martin David, MA, D.Phil (Oxon) FBA; b. Aug. 1, 1953; m. Sarah Jane née Lock; Professor of Jewish Studies, University of Oxford; Fellow of the Oxford Centre for Hebrew and Jewish Studies and Wolfson College; Lecturer in Ancient History, University of Birmingham (1977-86); Fellow of Oxford Centre for Hebrew and Jewish Studies (1986-); Senior Research Fellow, St Cross College (1986-91); Reader in Jewish Studies, University of Oxford (1991-96); President, British Association for Jewish Studies (1995); Sec. European Association for Jewish Studies (1995-98); Joint Editor of Journal of Jewish Studies (1995-99). Publ.: State and Society in Roman Galilee, A.D. 132-212 (1983, 2nd ed. 2000); Johann Reuchlin, On the Art of the Kabbalah (translation with S.J. Goodman) (1983 and 1993); E. Schürer, The History of the Jewish People in the Age of Jesus Christ, rev. ed. (with G. Vermes and F.G.B. Millar), volume 3 (1986 [part 1], 1987 [part 2]); The Ruling Class of Judaea: the origins of the Jewish Revolt against Rome, A.D. 66-70 (1987); The Essenes according to the Classical Sources (with Geza Vermes) (1989); Mission and Conversion: proselytizing in the religious history of the Roman Empire (1994); The Roman World 44BC-AD180 (1997); Jews in a Graeco-Roman World (ed. 1998); Apologetics in the Roman Empire (jt. ed. 1999); Representations of Empire: Rome and the Mediterranean World (jt. ed., 2002); The Oxford Handbook of Jewish Studies (ed., 2002); Judaism in the Roman World: Collected Essays (2007); Rome and Jerusalem (2007). Ad.: Oriental Institute, Pusey Lane, Oxford, OX1 2LE. ☎ 01865-278208. Fax 01865-278190. Email martin.goodman@orinst.ox.ac.uk.

GOODMAN, Mrs Vera (née Appleberg); b. London; Volunteer, Royal Star & Garter Home, Richmond; Volunteer Award for Distinguished Servce (2004); BoD (1973-94), Exec. Cttee. (1985-91), form Chairman, Publ. Rel. Cttee.; Bd. of Elders, Span. & Port Jews' Cong. (1977-80; 1990-94); Life V. President (Chairman, 1976-79) Richmond Park Conservative Women's Constit. Cttee.; Nat. C. for Soviet Jewry (1977-80); Greater Lond. Conservative Women's Gen. Purposes Cttee. (1979-85); Conservative Rep., Nat. C. of Women (1974-79); form. Central Lond. C., Conservative Frs. of Israel; Rep., Union of Jewish Women at U.N.A.; Central C., Conservative Party; Conservative Women's Nat. Cttee, Exec.; European Union of Women (Brit. Section); Chairman, Sephardi Women's Guild; Brit. C., World Sephardi Fed., V. Chairman, Govs., Russell Sch., Petersham (1974-82). Ad.: 87 Ashburnham Rd., Ham, Richmond, Surrey, TW10 7NN. ☎ 020-8948 1060.

GORDIMER, Nadine; b. Springs, S. Africa, Nov. 20, 1923; Author; Nobel Prize for Literature (1991); W. H. Smith Literary Award (1961), James Tait Black Member Prize (1972), Booker Prize (1974), Grand Aigle d'Or (1975), Premio Maleparte (1985), Nelly Sachs Prize (1985), Bennett Award, New York (1986), Primo Levi Award (2002), Mary McCarthy Award (2003). Publ.: Soft Voice of the Serpent, The Lying Days, Six Feet of the Country, A World of Strangers, Friday's Footprint, Occasion for Loving, Not for Publication, The Late Bourgeois World, A Guest of Honour, Livingstone's Companions, The Conservationist, Burger's Daughter, A Soldier's Embrace, July's People, Something Out There, A Sport of Nature (1990), My Son's Story, Jump (1991), None to Accompany Me (1994), The House Gun (1998), The Essential Gesture (1988 non-fiction), Writing and Being (1995, essays), Living in Hope and History (1999, essays), The Pick Up (2001), Loot (2003), Telling Tales (ed. 2004), Get a life (2005), etc. Ad.: c/o A. P. Watt Ltd, 20 John St., London WC1N 2DR. ☎ 020-7405 6774. Fax 020-7831 2154.

GORDON, Sir Gerald Henry, CBE, QC, MA, LLB, PhD (Glasgow), LLD (Edinburgh), LLD (Hon, Glasgow), Hon. FRSE; b. Glasgow, June 17, 1929; Sheriff of Glasgow and Strathkelvin (1977-99); Temp. Judge Ct. Session and High Ct. of Justiciary (1992-); Memb. Scottish Criminal Cases Review Cttee; Personal Professor of Criminal Law (1969-72), Professor of Scots Law (1972-76), Dean of Faculty of Law (1970-73), all at University of Edinburgh. Publ. Criminal Law of Scotland (1st ed. 1968; 2nd ed. 1978), with Second Cumulative Supplement, 1992; Renton & Brown's Criminal Procedure (ed., 6th ed. 1996).

GORDON, Lionel Lawrence, BSc (Econ); b. London, Aug. 31, 1933; form Market Research Dir.; form. Chairman, Jewish Chronicle Ltd.; Chairman Jewish Renaissance. Ad.: The Hyde, 5 Orchard Gate, Esher, Surrey, KT10 8HY. ☎ 020-8398 5774.

GOULD, Samuel Julius, MA (Oxon); b. Liverpool, Oct. 13, 1924; Prof. of Sociology, Nottingham Univ. (1964-82); form R., Social Instits., Lond. Sch. of Econ. & Pol. Sci.; Chairman, Trs., Social Affairs Unit, Lond. (since 1981); Res. Dir., Instit. for Pol. Res. (1983-85), Bd. of Dirs., Centre for Pol. Studies (1985-97);Res. Bd. & Pol. Planning Group, IJA; BoD (1984-90). Publ.: Dictionary of the Social Sciences (jt edr.), Jewish Life in Modern Britain (jt edr.), The Attack on Higher Education Jewish Commitment: A study in London. Ad.: c/o The Reform Club, Pall Mall, London SW1.

GOULDEN, Simon Charles, BSc (Eng), DMS, CEng, MCMI, MICE; b. London, Mar. 1, 1949; Dir. United Synagogue and Chief Exec. Agency for Jewish Education; form. Exec. Dir., Jews' College; Member, Ecumenical Standing Conference on Disability; Member, DCSF Working Gp. on School Security; National Judging Panel for the Teaching Awards Tr.; Princ. Engineer London Borough Haringey (1976-1986). Publ. Medinatenu: the Israel History Book (2002, with M. Binstock). Ad.: Bet Meir, 44b Albert Road, London NW4 2SG. ☎ 020-8457 9700. Fax 020-8457 9707. Email simon@aje.org.uk.

GOURGEY, Percy Sassoon, MBE, FRSA; b. Bombay, June 2, 1923; Journalist; form. Nat. Chairman, Poale Zion; V. Pres. Z Fed.; Chairman Socialist Societies Section of the Labour Party.; Exec. Cttee., BoD, V. Chairman, Erets Israel Cttee., BoD; Chairman, Jews in Arab Lands Cttee., Z. Fed.; Hon. Fel. WZO (1996); form. ed. Jewish Advocate, Bombay; Co-Fdr. and first ed. The Scribe (London), ex-Lieutenant RINVR; Parl. C.; Member, Royal Instit. of International Affairs, Chatham House, London, Contr. to Encyclopaedia Judaica, etc. Publ.: The Jew and his Mission, Ideals, India, Israel in Asia, Indian Jews and the Indian Freedom Struggle, The Indian Naval Revolt of 1946, etc. Ad.: 4 Poplar Ct., Richmond Rd., E. Twickenham, Middx. TW1 2DS ☎ 020-8892 8498.

GRABINER, Michael, b. St. Alban's, August 21, 1950; m. Jane Olivia née Harris; Chair, Partnership for Schools; Partner, Apax Partners LLP; member, Jewish Leadership Council (2005-2008); Chair Movement for Reform Judaism (2005-2008); Exec. Bd. Mem. World Union for Progressive Judaism (2007-); Governor Leo Baeck College (2005-08); Board member UK Jewish Film Festival (2004-); JCOSS Trustee and Vice-Chair, Temporary Governing Body (2008-); Chair, ResponsAbility (2008-). Ad.: 35 Uphill Rd., London NW7 4RA. Email mike@grabiner.net.

GRAHAM, (Stewart) David, QC, MA, BCL (Oxon), FRSA; b. Leeds, Feb. 27, 1934; Barrister; form. Chairman, Law, Parl. & Gen. Purposes Cttee., BoD; Vis. Prof., Faculty of Business, Kingston Univ. (2004-);form. Member, Insolvency Rules Adv. Cttee.; form. Mem., C. & Exec. Cttee. of Justice; Senior Vis. Fellow, Centre for Commercial Law Studies, QMW College; form. Member C. Insurance Ombudsman Bureau; Assoc. Memb. British & Irish Ombudsman Assoc. Publ.: Works on bankruptcy and insolvency. Ad.: 6 Grosvenor Lodge, Dennis Lane, Stanmore, Middx., HA7 4JE. ☎ 020-8954 3783.

GRANT, Linda, BA, MA; b. Liverpool, Feb. 15, 1951; Writer. Publ.: (fiction) The Cast Iron Shore (1996); When I Lived in Modern Times (2000); Still Here (2002); (non-fiction) Sexing the Millenium: A Political History of the Sexual Revolution (1993); Remind Me Who I Am Again (1998); The People on the Street: a Writer's View of Israel (2006); The Clothes on Their Backs (2008). Ad.: c/o A.P. Watt, Literary Agents, 20 John Street, London WC1N 2DR.

GRAUS, Eric; b. Bratislava, April 22, 1927; President, Likud-Herut Movement of Gt Britain. Ad..

GREEN, Sir Allan David, KCB, QC, (KCB 1991); b. March 1, 1935; Form. Dir. of Pub. Prosecutions, First Sr. Treasury Counsel, Central Criminal Court. (1985-87), Sr. Prosecuting Counsel (1979-85), Jr. Prosecuting Counsel (1977-79); Bencher, Inner Temple (1985); Q.C. (1987), Member, Legal Group Tel Aviv Univ. Tr.; Served RN (1953-55). Ad.: 2, Hare Court, Temple, EC4Y 7BH.

GREENBAT, Alan, OBE, JP, b. London, April 1929; Hon. Consultant, Office of the Chief Rabbi; Sec. Rabbinical Commission for the Licensing of Shochetim; President, Norwood Old Scholars Association; Memb. Inner London Youth Courts (1964-99); Exec. & V.Chairman National Council of Voluntary Youth Services (1981-91); Exec. Dir. Office of the Chief Rabbi (1990-91); Dir. Assoc. for Jewish Youth (1980-89); Dir. Victoria Community Centre (1961-80); V.Pres. AJY (1989-96); V.Pres. London Union of Youth Clubs (1984-94); V.Principal Norwood Home for Jewish Children (1955-61). Ad.: Adler House, 735 High Road, London

N12 0US. ☎ 020-8343 6301. Fax 020-8343 6310.

GREENBERG, Rabbi Philip T., BA, MPhil, FJC; b. Liverpool, June 28, 1937; Emer. Rabbi, Giffnock & Newlands Syn., Glasgow; Rav. Glasgow Shechita Bd. (1993-99); Chairman Va'ad HaRabbonim, Glasgow; H. Chaplain, Calderwood Lodge Jewish Sch., Glasg.; M., Nottingham Syn. (1968-72), Highams Park & Chingford Syn. (1959-68); Head, Mishna Stream, Hasmonean Boys' Sch. (1972-81). Ad.: 72 Bridge Lane, Golders Green, London NW11 0EJ. ☎/Fax 020-8455 5685. Email. philip@philipg.fs.com

GREENGROSS, Dr Wendy, MB, BS (Lond), LRCP, MRCS, DObst, RCOG; Dip. Med. Law & Eth.; b. London, Apr. 29, 1925; Medical Practitioner; Broadcaster; Medical Consultant; Marriage Guidance C.; V. President, AJY Fel., Leo Baeck Coll.; Tr., Leonard Cheshire Foundation; President, Ranulf Assn.; Member Govt. Enquiry into human fertilisation and embryology; Chairman, Ethics Cttee, Wellington Humana Hospital Publ.: Sex in the Middle Years, Sex in Early Marriage; Marriage, Sex and Arthritis; The Health of Women; Entitled to Love; Jewish and Homosexual; Living, Loving and Aging. Ad.: 35, Regency House 269, Regent's Park Rd., London N3 3JZ. ☎ 020-8455 1153.

GREENWOOD, Jeffrey Michael, MA, LLM; b. London, Apr. 21, 1935; Solicitor; Chairman Wigmore Property Investment Tr. plc (1998–2004); Stow Securities plc; Senior Partner Nabarro Nathanson (1987-95); Chairman Central Council for Education and Training in Social Work (1993-98); Chairman, Jewish Welfare Bd. (1985-1990), Jewish Care (1990). V. President Jewish Care; Exec., Anglo-Israel Assn.; Tr & Exec., English Frs., Jerusalem Coll. of Tech (1980-98); Dir., Bank Leumi (UK) plc (1988-2005); Dep. Chairman Jewish Chronicle Ltd (1995-2005); Chairman, Jewish Literary Trust (2001-3); M. Council JHSE. Ad.: 5 Spencer Walk, Hampstead High Street, London NW3 1QZ. ☎ 020-7794 5281. Fax 020-7794 0094. Email jeff@thegreenwoods.org.

GRODZINSKI, Emmanuel, FCA; b. Montreal, Sept. 11, 1940; m. Edwina Keidan; Director; Tr.; Jewish Literary Tr. (1995-), Chairman (2003-) Tr., Jewish Book Council (1991-2002). Ad.: Flat 4, 38-40 Eton Avenue, London NW3 3HL. ☎ 020-7431 1924. Email. emmanuel@gds.com.

GROSBERG, Percy, MSc, PhD; b. Cape Town, Apr. 5, 1925; m. Queenie née Fisch; Sr. Res. Off, S. African Wool Textile Res. Instit.(1949-55); Res. Prof., Chair of Textile Engineering, Leeds Univ., (1960-90); Member Bd. Gov. and currently Marcus Sieff Prof. Shenkar School of Engineering and Design, Ramat Gan; Form. Chairman, Leeds Frs., Bar-Ilan Univ. Publ.: Scientific writings. Ad.: Apt 25, 55 Shlomo Hamelech, Netanya 42267. ☎ 077-8858-189. Fax 09-8871534.

GROSS, Solomon Joseph, CMG; b. London, Sept. 3, 1920; Ret., Dir., British Steel (1978-90), Plc and other comps.; Dir., Reg. Affairs, B.T.G. (1983-84); Under-Sec., Dept. of Industry (1974-80); Min., Brit. Embassy, Pretoria (1969-73); Brit. Dep. High Com. in Ghana (1966-67). Ad.: 38 Barnes Ct., Station Rd., New Barnet, Herts EN5 1QY.

GRUNEWALD, Rabbi Jacob Ezekiel, BA; b. Tel Aviv, Oct. 26, 1945; M., Pinner Syn. Ad.: 65 Cecil Park, Pinner, Middx., HA5 5HL. ☎ 020-8933 7045.

GRUNWALD, Henry Cyril, LLB (Hons); b. London, Aug. 8, 1949; m. Alison née Appleton; Barrister, Queen's Counsel; Bencher, Hon. Society of Gray's Inn (2002-); President BoD (2003-), Sen. Vice President (2000-3), V. President (1997-2000); Warden, Hampstead Synagogue (1997-); Tr. North London Relate (1995-); Chairman, Pikuach Bd. Gov. (2000-); Mem. Hillel Bd. Dir. (2000-). Ad.: 2 Tudor Street, London EC4Y 0AA. ☎ 020-7797 7111. Fax 020-7797 7120. Email h.grunwald@btinternet.com.

GRUNWALD-SPIER, Agnes (née Grunwald), JP, BScEcon. (Hons, Lond), MA; b. Budapest July, 1944; Magistrate (Bromsgrove Bench 1948-91; Sheffield 1992-); Board of Deputies; Chairman Regional Assembly (2006-), M., Defence Div. (2003-), Deputy for Sheffield (1997-); Tr., Holocaust Memorial Day Tr. (2004-); Chairman, Women in the Jewish Community Regional Coord. C. (1997-2003, Act. Chairman, 2006-); Mem. Yorkshire and Humber Faiths Forum (2005-08); President, Sheffield and District J. Rep. C. (1999-2002); M. Nat. C., World Jewish Relief (1998-2001); Lay M., Herbal Medicines Adv. Cttee (2005-); Lay M. Conduct and Registration Commmittees, Gen. Social Care C. (2003-); Lay M. Architects' Registration Bd. (2008-). Ad.: Heath Court, 76 Dore Rd., Sheffield S17 3NE ☎ 0114 2360984; 07816 196517; 30, Kings College Court, Primrose Hill Road, London NW3 3EA.

Email agnesgrunwald-spier@ukonline.co.uk.

GUBBAY, Lucien Ezra, MA (Oxon), MICE, C.Eng.; b. Buenos Aires, 1931, m. Joyce née Shammah; Consulting Engineer; Chairman Montefiore Endowment; Tr., LSJS; President of the Board of Elders, Spanish & Portuguese Jews' Congregation London (1996-2000); form. Mem. Exec. Jewish Memorial Council; form. Warden S & P Synagogue; form. Dir. Industrial Dwellings Society (1885) Ltd; Flg. Off. RAF (1952-54). Publ: Ages of Man (1985), The Jewish Book of Why and What (1987), Origins (1989), Quest for the Messiah (1990), You Can Beat Arthritis (1992), The Sephardim (1992), Sunlight and Shadow: Jewish Experience of Islam (1999), Two Worlds (2004), Our Glorious Tradition (2007). Ad.: 26 Linden Lea, London N2 0RG. ☎ 020-8458 3385. Email lucien@gubbay.co.uk

HALBAN, Martine (née Mizrahi), BA (Hons) Sussex; b. Alexandria, Dec. 29, 1953; m. Peter Francis Halban; Book publisher; Director, Peter Halban Publishers; Director, New Israel Fund. Ad.: Halban Publishers, 22, Golden Square, London W1F 9JW. ☎ 020-7437 9300; Fax 020 7437 9512. Email mh@halbanpublishers.com.

HALBAN, Peter Francis, BA (Princeton); b. New York, June 1 1946; m. Martine neé Mizrahi Book Publisher; Dir., Halban Publishers Ltd. (1986-); M. Exec., Jerusalem Foundation; Tr. The Humanitarian Tr. (1998-); C. European Jewish Publication Soc. (1994-); Memb. Exec. Institute for Jewish Policy Green Research (1994-); Memb. Exec. Jerusalem Foundation; Tr. Woolf Centre for Study of Abrahamic Faiths, Cambridge, (2003-). Ad.: Halban Publishers, 22 Golden Square, London W1F 9JW. ☎ 020-7437 9300. Fax 020-7437 9512. Email books@halbanpublishers.com.

HAMILTON, Fabian, BA, MP; b. April 12, 1955; m. Rosemary née Ratcliffe; MP, Leeds North-East (1997-); Leeds City Councillor (1987-98); Chair Edcu. Cttee. (1996-97); Chair Economic Development Cttee (1994-96); Chair Race Equality Cttee (1988-94). Ad.: House of Commons, SW1A 0AA. ☎ 020-7219 3493. Fax 020-7219 4945.

HANDLER, Arieh L.; b. Brun, May 27, 1915; Financial Consultant; Jewish Agency C. & Member Z. Actions Cttee., Life P. Mizrachi Fed.; Hon. President, Bachad Fellowship (Friends of B'nai Akiva); Chairman, Adv. Body, Torah Dept., Jewish Agency; BoD (form. Chairman, Israel Cttee.); Exec. Jewish Child's Day, Youth Aliyah (form Dir., Y.A.); Exec WZO; V.Chairman, Brit Frs., Boys' Town, Jerusalem; V. President (form. Chairman) Nat. C. for Soviet Jewry; Montefiore Found.; Jewish Colonial Tr. C.; President, Brit. Frs., Israel Aged, Patron, Jerusalem Institute for the Blind; President, Midreshet Eretz Yisrael; Fel., Instit. of Dirs.; form. Dir., Hapoel Hamizrachi World Org; form. Man. Dir., Migdal London, form. Man. Dir. JCB, London. Ad.: 31, Eliezer Halevi St., Jerusalem 96108. ☎ 02-652 3520

HARMATZ, Joseph; b. Rokishkis, Lithuania, Jan. 23, 1925; Dir.-Gen. ORT Israel (1966-79); Dir.-Gen. World ORT (1980-93); Publ.: From the Wings (1998); Life with ORT (2002). Ad.: 36 Yehuda Hanassi Str., Tel Aviv 69206. Fax 972 3 642 5463.

HARRIS, Dr Evan, MP, BA, BM, BS; b. Sheffield, Oct. 21, 1965; Registrar in Public Health Medicine (1994-97); MP (Lib.Dem.) Oxford West and Abingdon (1997-); Science Spokesman (2003-); Hon. Assoc. National Secular Soc. (2000-). Ad.: House of Commons, London SW1A 0AA. ☎ 020-7219 5128; 32a North Hinksey Village, Oxford OX2 8NA. ☎ 01865-245584.

HARRIS, Rabbi Michael Jacob, MA (Cantab), MA (Jerusalem), PhD (SOAS); b. London, Feb. 17, 1964; Rabbi, Hampstead Synagogue (1995-); Jt. Vice-Ch., Rabbinical C. United Synagogue (2008-); Res. Fel, London School of J. Studies; Mem. Chief Rabbi's Cabinet; Lecturer in Jewish Law, Jews' College, London (1995-97); form. Rabbi, Southend and Westcliff Hebrew Cong. (1992-95). Publ.: Divine Command Ethics: Jewish and Christian Perspectives (2003). Ad.: The Hampstead Synagogue, Dennington Park Rd., London NW6 1AX. ☎ 020-7435 1518. Fax 020-7431 8368. Email rabbi.michael@talk21.com.

HASKEL, Lord; b. Kaunas, Oct. 9, 1934; m. Carole Lewis; Life Peer; Deputy Speaker, House of Lords; President, IJPR (2002-). Ad.: House of Lords, London SW1A 0PW. ☎ 020-7219 4076. Email haskel@blueyonder.co.uk.

HASS, Rev. Simon, LLCM; b. Poland, May 2, 1927; Cantor Central Syn. Gt Portland St., London,W.l. (since 1951); Composer Musical Arranger. Publ.: Many Recordings of Jewish liturgical and classical music. Ad.: "Beit Shirah", 2A Allandale Ave., N3 3PJ.

HAYMAN, Baroness Helene of Dartmouth Park (née Middleweek), PC, MA (Cantab);

b. Wolverhampton, March 26, 1949; m. Martin Hayman. Lord Speaker (2006-); Chairman, Cancer Research UK (2001-04); Chairman, Human Tissue Authority (2005-06); Min. State, Agriculture (1999-2001); Parlt Under Sec. of State, Dept. of Environment, Transport and the Regions (1997-98); PPS Dept. of Health (1998-99); Labour Mem. of Parliament (1974-79); Chairman, Whittington Hospital (1992-97). Ad.: House of Lords, SW1A 0PW.

HELFGOTT, Ben, MBE. D. Univ (Southampton); b. Pabianice, Poland, Nov. 22, 1929; Tr. Holocaust Memorial Day Trust; Chairman; '45 Aid Soc. (1963–70, 1975–); Chairman, Yad Vashem Cttee., BoD; Chairman C., Promotion of Yiddish & Yiddish Culture; C., Jewish Youth Fund; Exec., Wiener Libr.; Chairman, Polin-Inst. for Polish Jewish Studies; Vice President, Claims Conference; form. Jt. T., CBF-WJR; Brit. Weightlifting Champion & Record Holder; competed in Olympic Games (1956; 1960); Bronze Medal, Commonwealth Games (1958); Gold Medals, Maccabiah (1950, 1953, 1957). Ad.: 46 Amery Rd., Harrow, Middx. HA1 3UG. ☎ 020-8422 1512.

HELLNER, Rabbi Frank, BA, BHL, MA, DD (Hon); b. Philadelphia, Pa., Jan. 1, 1935; Emer. Rabbi Finchley Progressive Syn.; Exec., Barnet Com. Rel. C.; Gov., Akiva Sch.; Mem. Jewish Community Schools Adv. Board; Tr. Jewish Community Schools Adv. Bd.; V. President, Finchley CCJ, Member Leo Baeck Coll. Comp.; Extra-Mural Lect. Birkbeck Coll. (Pt.-time); Chairman, ULPS Rabbinic Conference (1970-71); Edr., ULPS News (1978-86); Chaplain to Mayor of L. B. Barnet (1993-94). Publ.: I Promise I Will Try not to Kick My Sister and Other Sermons. Ad.: Finchley Progressive Synagogue, 54 Hutton Grove, N12 8DR. ☎/Fax 020-8446 4063.

HENIG, Stanley, MA, (Oxford); Hon. RNCM, (Royal Northern College of Music); b. Leicester, July 7, 1939; Sen. Res. Fell., Federal Trust; Man. Dir. Historic Masters; Prof. (Emeritus) of Politics, University of Central Lancashire; Leader, Lancaster City Council (1991-99); MP (Lancaster) (1966-70) Chairman, RNCM (1986-89); Secretary Labour Group, Local Government Association (1997-99). Publ.: Uniting of Europe (1997, 2nd ed. 2002) and other books on political parties and on European Union; Enrico Caruso: Recollections and Retrospectives; Modernising Britain. Ad.: 10 Yealand Drive, Lancaster LA1 4EW. ☎ 01524 69624.

HILL, Brad Sabin, AB, FRAS; b. New York, Nov. 2, 1953; Curator, Judaica & Hebraica, George Washington U., Washington D.C., form Dean of the Library, Sen. Res. Librarian, Yivo Institute for Jewish Research, NY (2002-07); Sen. Assoc., Oxford Centre for Hebrew and Jewish Studies; form. Librarian and Fel. in Hebrew Bibliography, Oxford Centre for Hebrew and Jewish Studies (1996-2001); form. Hd., Hebrew Section, The British Library (1989-96); Curator of Rare Hebraica, National Library of Canada, Ottawa (1979-89). Publ.: Incunabula, Hebraica & Judaica (1981); Hebraica from the Valmadonna Trust (1989); (ed.) Miscellanea Hebraica Bibliographica (1995). Ad.: 35 Thackley End, 119 Banbury Road, Oxford OX2 6LB.

HILLMAN, Mayer, BA Arch. (London), Dipl. TP., Ph.D Soc Sci (Edin.); b. London, Oct. 30, 1931; m. Heidi, née Krott; Social Scientist; Fd. Partner, Dinerman, Davison & Hillman Chartered Architects (1954-67); Senior Fel., Hd. Environment & Quality of Life Res. Programme, (1970-92), Senior Fellow Emeritus, Policy Studies Institute (1992-). Publ.: Author and co-author of over 50 books and reports, most recently: How we can save the Planet (2004); The Suicidal Planet (2007). Ad.: The Coach House, 7A, Netherhall Gardens, London NW3 5RN. ☎ 020-7794 9661. Email mayer.hillman@blueyonder.co.uk. Website www.mayerhillman.com www.psi.org.uk

HILTON, Rabbi Michael, MA, D.Phil, PGCE; b. London, Feb. 27, 1951; M. Kol Chai Hatch End Jewish Community (2001-); M. North London Progressive Synagogue (1999-2001); M. Cheshire Reform Congregation (1987-98); Hon. Res. Fel. Centre for Jewish Studies, University of Manchester (1998-); Homeless Persons off., L.B. Hammersmith & Fulham (1980-82). Publ.: The Gospels and Rabbinic Judaism (with G. Marshall, 1988.), The Christian Effect on Jewish Life (1994). Ad.: Hatch End Jewish Community, 434 Uxbridge Road, Pinner, Middx HA5 4RG. ☎ 020-8906 8241. Email greystar@zetnet.co.uk.

HOBSBAWM, Eric John Ernest, CH, FBA, MA, PhD; b. Alexandria, Egypt, June 9, 1917; Emer. Prof of Econ. and Soc. Hist., Birkbeck Coll., Lond. Univ.; H. Fel., King's Coll., Cambridge.

Publ.: Primitive Rebels, The Jazz Scene, The Age of Revolution, Labouring Men, Industry and Empire, Nations and Nationalism, The Age of Extremes, 1914-1991, Uncommon People, Interesting Times: A Twentieth-Century Life (2002), etc. Ad.: Birkbeck College, Malet St., WC1E 7HX. ☎ 020-7631 6000.

HOCHHAUSER, Dr Daniel, MA, D.Phil, FRCP; b. London, July 18, 1957; m. Joanne née Garland; Kathleen Ferrier Reader and Consultant in Medical Oncology, Univ. College London; Publ.: articles on treatment of gastrointestinal cancer and new agents for treating cancer. Ad.: Dept. of Oncology, University College London. ☎ 020-7679 9326. Fax 020-7436 2956. Email d.hochhauser@ucl.uk.

HOCHHAUSER, Victor, CBE; b. Kosice, Czechoslovakia, Mar. 27, 1923; Impresario for internat. artists orchestras, ballet companies, etc. Ad.: 4 Oak Hill Way, NW3 7LR. ☎ 020-7794 0987. Fax 020-7431 2531. Email admin@viktorhochhauser.co.uk

HOFFMAN, Eva Alfreda (née Wydra), PhD, FRSL; b. Cracow, July 1, 1945; Writer; editor, New York Times (1980-90); Vis. Prof., MIT (199-2005), Hunter College, CUNY (2006-). Publ.: Lost in Translation (1989), Exit into History (1994), Shtetl (1997), The Secret (2001), After Such Knowledge (2004); Illuminations (2008). Ad.: 18 Goldhurst Terrace, London NW6 3HU ☎ 020 7625 8771.

HOROVITZ, Michael, OBE, MA (Oxon); b. Frankfurt am Main, April 4, 1935; Writer, artist, singer, musician, publsher; creative Britons Award (2000); Poetry Book Society recommendation (1986); Arts Council Translator's Award (1983); Arts Council Writer's Award (1976). Publ. include: Love Poems (1971), A Contemplation (1978), Growing Up: Selected Poems and Pictures, 1951-1979 (1979), A Celebration for Frances Horovitz (1984), Wordsounds and Sightlines: New and Selected Poems (1994). The POW! Anthology (1996), The POP! Anthology (2000), Jeff Nuttall's Wake on Paper (2004), Lost Office Campaign Poem (2005), A New Waste-Land (2007). Ad.: New Departures/Poetry Olympics, PO Box 9819, London W11 2GQ. ☎/Fax 020-7229 7850. Email michael.horovitz@btinternet.com. Website www.poetryolympics.com

HOWARD, Michael, PC, QC, MP; b. Gorseinon, Wales, July 7, 1941; M.P. (Cons) for Folkestone and Hythe; Leader of the Opposition (2003-05); Shadow Chancellor (2001-03); form. Home Secretary (1993-97); Secretary of State for the Environment (1992-93); Chairman, Conservative Bow Group (1970-71); form. President, Cambridge Union. Ad.: House of Commons, SW1A 0AA.

HUBERT, Walter I., FRSA, F. Inst. Dir.; b. Schluechtern, Germany, Aug. 13, 1932; First Chairman, Gateshead Foundation for Torah, IJA; Patron, Didsbury Jewish Primary Sch.; H. Life V. President, Brit. Cttee., Peylim of Israel; Gov., Global Bd., & H. Fel., Bar-Ilan Univ.; Gov., Ben Gurion Univ.; V. President, Cancer Res. Cttee.; Dir. State of Israel Bonds (UK); V.P., British Herut; form. Chairman, Blackburn Rovers F.C.; First Recipient (1981) Bank Hapoalim Silver Rose Award for new Israeli industry; Jerusalem Educ. Medal (1974); Zurich Jewish Secondary Schs., 'Man of Year' Gold Medal (1978); assoc. with many educ. and charitable instit. in Brit., Israel, Switzerland, US and Argentina. Ad.: 24 King David Gdns., 27 King David St., Jerusalem, Israel. ☎ 02 241754.

HURST, Alex; b. Liverpool, Jan. 6, 1935; form. Admin., Merseyside Jewish Welfare C.; form. Sec., L'pool Jewish Housing Assn. Ad.: 440 Allerton Rd., Liverpool L18 3JX. ☎ 0151-427 7377.

HYMAN, Barry S.; b. Scotland, June 24, 1941, m. Judith; Broadcaster, Writer; PR consultant and newsletter editor to Movement for Reform Judaism (1995-2002); Hon. Vice President Radlett and Bushey Reform Syn (2000-); BoD Public Relations Cttee (1988-97); Member of the Institute of Public Relations (1987-2002); Head of Corporate Affairs, Media Relations, Community Affairs and Company Archive, Marks and Spencer (1984-94). Publ.: Young in Herts (1996), a history of the Radlett and Bushey Reform Synagogue; A Job for a Jewish Girl ... or Boy? The Rabbinate as a Career (2000); (Ed.) Reform Judaism News (1996-2002). Ad.: Radlett & Bushey Reform Syn., 118 Watling Street, Radlett, Herts. WD7 7AA. ☎ 01923 856110. Fax 01923 818444. Email bsh@hypeople.co.uk.

HYMAN, Mrs. Marguerite Grete (née De Jongh); b. London, Mar. 26, 1913; V. President (form. Fin. Sec.) Union of Lib. & Progr. Syns. Ad.: 14 The Cedars, St. Stephen's Rd., W13 8JF. ☎ 020-8997 8258.

INGRAM, Rabbi Chaim Nota, BA (Hons); b. London, May 14, 1952; Rabbi in Residence, Sydney Jewish Centre on Aging, itinerant rabbi, Surfers Central Syn. Queensland; form Rabbi Bet Josef Caro Syn., Sydney (2003-06), form Assoc. Rabbi, The Central Syn., Sydney (1992-2003); M., Leicester Hebrew Cong. (1986-92); M./R., United Hebrew Cong., Newcastle Upon Tyne (1982-96); R., Cricklewood Syn, London (1979-82). Publ.: Renana Song Book. Ad: 41 Llandaff St., Bondi Junction, Sydney, NSW 2002. ☎ 02-9386 5710. ☎ 0423-831845. Email judaim@bigpond.net.au. Website www.rchi.vze.com.

ISRAEL, Jonathan Irvine, MA, D.Phil. FRHS, FBA; b. London, Jan. 22, 1946; Prof. Inst. for Advanced Study Princeton (2006-); form Prof. Dutch Hist. & Instits., Lond. Univ., Univ. Coll.; H. Sec., JHSE (1974-79); Wolfson Hist. Prize (1986); Ed. Littman Library of Jewish Civilization (1990-); Hon. Ph.D Erasmus U. (2006), Heinekan Prize (2008); Publ.: European Jewry in the Age of Mercantilism, 1550-1750, The Dutch Republic and the Hispanic World, 1606-61, Race, Class and Politics in Colonial Mexico, 1610-70, Dutch Primacy in World Trade (1585-1740), Empires and Entrepots: the Dutch, the Spanish Monarchy and the Jews, 1585-1713, Anglo-Dutch moment: essays on the Glorious Revolution and its world impact, The Dutch Republic, its rise, greatness and fall, 1477-1806 (1995); Conflicts of Empires: Spain, the Low Countries and the Struggle for World Supremacy, 1585-1713 (1997); Radical Enlightenment: Philosophy and the Making of Modernity, 1658-1750 (2001); Enlightenment Contested: Philosophy, Modernity, and the Emancipation of Man, 1670-1752 (2006) Ad.: Institute for Advanced Study, Einstein Dr., Princeton, N.J. 08940.

JACKSON, Bernard Stuart, LLB (Hons), D.Phil, LLD, DHL (h.c.); b. Liverpool, Nov. 16, 1944; Barrister; Alliance Professor of Modern Jewish Studies, Co-Dir. Centre for Jewish Studies, Univ. Manchester (1997-); President BAJS (1993); Edr., Jewish Law Annual (1978-97); Sec., J. Law Publ. Fund (1980-). Publ.: Theft in Early Jewish Law, Essays in Jewish and Comparative Legal Hist., Semiotics and Legal Theory, Law, Fact and Narrative Coherence, Making Sense in Law, Making Sense in Jurisprudence, Studies in the Semiotics of Biblical Law, Wisdom-Laws: a study of the Mishpatim of Exodus 21:1-22:16, Essays in Halakhah in the New Testament; (edr.) Studies in Jewish Legal Hist. in Hon. of David Daube, Modern Research in Jewish Law, Jewish Law in Legal Hist. and the Modern World, Semiotics, Law and Social Science (with D. Carzo), The Touro Conference Volume (Jew. Law Assn. Studies I), The Jerusalem Conference Volume (Jew. Law Assn. Studies II), The Boston Conference Volume (Jew. Law Assn. Studies IV), The Halakhic Thought of R. Isaac Herzog (Jew. Law Assn. Studies V), The Jerusalem 1990 Conference Volume (Jew. Law Assn. Studies VI) (with S. M. Passamaneck); Legal Visions of the New Europe (with D. McGoldrick); Legal Semiotics and the Sociology of Law; Introduction to the History and Sources of Jewish Law (with N. Hecht and others). Ad.: Centre for Jewish Studies, Dept. of Religions and Theology, Samuel Alexander Building, Univ. Manchester, Oxford Rd., M13 9PL. Fax 0161-275 3613. Email bernard.jackson@man.ac.uk. Website www.mucjs.org.

JACOBI, Rabbi Harry Martin, MBE, BA Hons; b. Berlin, Oct. 19, 1925; form. M. South Bucks Jewish Community, Zurich Lib. Syn., Wembley Lib. Syn., Southgate Progressive Syn.; President, Southgate B'nai B'rith Ben-Gurion Lodge (1974-75). Ad.: 1 Walton Court, Lyonsdown Road, New Barnet, EN5 1JW. ☎ 020-8440 1261.

JACOBI, Rabbi Margaret, MB, PhD; b. London, 1957; m. Dr David Ehrlica; Rabbi, Birmingham Progressive Synagogue (1994-); Hon. Progressive Chaplain, Univ. Birmingham (1994-); Jt. chair, liberal Judaism Rabbinic Conference (2006-); Res. Fell. In Physiology, Washington University , St. Louis (1987-89). Publ.: Essays in 'Hear Our Voice' (1994), 'Aspects of Liberal Judaism' (2004), 'For generations: Jewish Motherhood' 2005); and in the field of physiology. Ad.: 14, Sandy Croft, Birmingham B13 0EP. ☎ 0121 777 0280 Email office@bps-pro-syn-.co.uk.

JACOBS, David; b. Manchester, 1951; m. Hannah Rose née Noorden; Dir. of Synagogue Partnership, Movement for Reform Judaism; Vice President, Jewish Genealogical Society of GB; Mem. C. JHSE; Mem. WP on Jewish Monuments in the UK & Ireland; Co-fdr. Jewish East End Project (1977); Co-fdr. London Museum of Jewish Life (1983); RSGB Youth Development Off. (1975-79); Dir. Victoria Com. Centre (1988-91). Publ. A History of Our

Time; Rabbi and Teachers Buried at Hoop Lane Cemetery (2006, with J. Epstein). Ad.: The Sternberg Centre, 80 East End Road, London, N3 2SY. ☎ 020-8349 5643. Email david.jacobs@reformjudaism.org.uk.

JACOBS, David Lewis, CBE, DL, Hon. D. Kingston Univ.; b. London, May 19, 1926; Broadcaster; host and Chairman of BBC radio and television programmes; Dep. Lieutenant for Greater London; High Steward, Royal Borough of Kingston upon Thames; V. President, Stars Org. for Spastics; form. Chairman, Think British Campaign; V. President, R. Star and Garter Home, Richmond; Past President, Nat. Children's Orchestra; form. V. Chairman, R.S.P.C.A.; President, Kingston Upon Thames Royal British Legion; V. President, Wimbledon Girls Choir; President, Kingston Theatre Trust; Life Governor Imperial Cancer Research Fd.; Jt. Pres. Thames Community Tr.; Pres. S.W. London Area SSAFFA; Chairman Thames FM; Pres. T.S. Steadfast; Patron Age Resource; Patron Kingston Bereavement Tr.; Pres. Kingston Alcohol Service. Publ.: Jacobs' Ladder (autobiog.), Caroline, Any Questions (with Michael Bowen). Ad.: Wyncombe Hill Cottage, Fittleworth, West Sussex, RH20 1HN.

JACOBS, David Michael, b. Bristol, June 4, 1930, m. Marion née Davis; Exec. (form. Gen. Sec.), AJA; form. Exec. Dir. Likud-Herut GB; Chairman Jewish Affiliates of the United Nations Assoc.; Vice-P., form. Chairman Guild of Jewish Journalists; form. Chairman, Beds.-Herts. Progressive Jewish Cong.; form. BoD, Press Officer; Brit. Z. Fed. Publ.: Israel (World in Colour series) 1968, Research & writing for Jewish Communities of the World, (Ed. A. Lerman) 1989. Ad.: 56 Normandy Rd., St. Albans, Herts AL3 5PW. ☎/Fax 01727-858454.

JACOBS, Rabbi Irving, BA, PhD (Lond); b. London, Aug. 2, 1938; Princ. Jews, College (1990-93); Res. Fell, (1966-69), Lect. (1969-84); Dean (1984-90); First Incumbent, Sir Israel Brodie Chair in Bible Studies; Dir., Midrashah Instit. for Israel Studies (1980-82); form. Min., Sutton and District Hebrew Cong. Publ.: The Midrashic Process. Ad.: 28 Elmstead Ave., Wembley, Middx. ☎ 020-8248 5777.

JACOBS, June Ruth (née Caller); b. London, June 1, 1930; Professional Volunteer; Past President, Int. Council of Jewish Women; Patron Jewish Council for Racial Equality and Jewish Black Forum; Co-Chair, International Centre for Peace in Middle East; Life Mem. League, Jewish Women; L. President, Jewish Child's Day; Trustee, Kessler Foundation; Mem. of International Council and UK Board, New Israel Fund; Bd. Mem., IJPR; Hon. Sec., Chair, Nahum Goldmann Fellowship, Memorial Foundation for Jewish Culture; Mem.Exec. European Women's Lobby; Mem. Bd., Paideia, European Institute of Jewish Studies in Sweden, Found. Mem. Jewish Forum for Justice and Human Rights. Ad.: 13 Modbury Gardens, London NW5 3QE. ☎ 020-7485 6027.

JACOBS, Myrna (née Appleton); b. London, Aug. 18, 1940; m. Laurance D. Jacobs; Headteacher of Immanuel College (1995-2000); Head of Languages, Anna Head High, Berkeley, California (1962-66); Lecturer, Univ. of California Extension (Berkeley & San Francisco) (1964-66); Head of Language Faculty in Borough of Brent, consecutively Brondesbury & Kilburn, John Kelly Girls, Preston Manor (1973-89).

JACOBSON, Dan, BA, DLitt (Hons); b. Johannesburg, March 7, 1929; Novelist and univ. Prof. Emer., Univ. Coll. London (1994-); Publ.: A Dance in the Sun, The Beginners, The Rape of Tamar, The Story of Stories: the Chosen People and its God, Her Story, Heshel's Kingdom, etc. Ad.: c/o A. M. Heath & Co., 79 St. Martin's La., WC2N 4AA ☎ 020-7836 4271.

JACOBSON, Howard, MA (Cantab); b. Manchester, Aug. 25, 1942; Novelist and critic; JQ/Wingate Prize for Fiction, 2001, 2007; Senior Lect., Wolverhampton Polytechnic (1974-80); Supervisor in English Studies, Selwyn College (1968-72); Lect., English Literature, University of Sydney (1965-67). Publ.: Shakespeare's Magnanimity (with Wilbur Sanders, 1978); Coming from Behind (1983); Peeping Tom (1984); Redback (1986); In the Land of Oz (1987); The Very Model of a Man (1992); Roots Schmoots (1993); Seriously Funny: An Argument for Comedy (1996); No More Mister Nice Guy (1998); The Mighty Walzer (1999); Who's Sorry Now? (2002); The Making of Henry (2004); Kalooki Nights (2006); The Act of Love (2008). Ad. c/o Curtis Brown, Haymarket House, 28-29 Haymarket, London SW17 4SP. ☎ 020-7393 4400.

JAKOBOVITS, Lady, Amelie (née Munk), PhD (Hon); b. Ansbach, May 31, 1928; Fdr. and President, Assoc. of US Women; V. President, Emunah Women's Org.; President, Jewish

Marriage C., Dir. of Jewish Care; Fdr. and Patron of Chai Cancer Care; Patron British Friends of Assof HaRofeh Medical Centre; Patron, British Friends Hadassah Hospital; President, Carelink; L.P. JIA Women's Division; Life V. President, League of Jewish Women; Patron of Dysautonomia Foundation; V. President, Wizo; P. Ladies, Visitation Cttee., US; V. President, Youth Aliyah; Patron 'J' Link; President, 'Chen'. Ad.: 44a Albert Rd., London NW4 2SJ. Email reich@c24.net.

JANNER, Baron of Braunstone (Life Peer) (Hon., Greville Ewan), MA (Cantab), Hon. PhD (Haifa), Hon. LLD (De Montfort), QC; b. Cardiff, July 11, 1928; Barrister-at-law; form. MP (Lab.) for Leicester West (1970-97); President Parlt. Cttee Against Anti-Semitism; Chairman, Select Cttee. on Employment (1993-96); Dir., Ladbroke plc (1986-95); Chairman, JSB Group Ltd., including Effective Presentational Skills (1984-97); President, BoD (1979-85); form Jt. Fd, Chairman Coexistence Trust (2006-08); P. Commonwealth Jewish C.; Hon. V. President, WJC; Fdr. and V. Chairman, All-Party Parl. Cttee. for Jews from the FSU; V. Chairman, Brit.-Israel Parl. Group, H. Sec., All-Party Parl. War Crimes Group; Chairman, Holocaust Educ. Tr.; form. President, Maimonides Foundation; Member Magic Circle and International Brotherhood of Magicians; Sec., Parl. Cttee. for East European Jewry (1993-97); Chairman, All-Party Parl. Industrial Safety Group (1975-97); P. Ret. Execs. Action Group (REACH); form. President, Jewish Museum; Bd. Dirs., UJIA; Tr., Elsie & Barnett Janner Tr.; Exec., Lab. Frs. of Israel; V. President, AJY, Ajex; Fel., Inst. of Personnel and Development; Member NUJ; H. Member, Nat. Union Mineworkers (Leics. Br.); form. President, WJC (Europe); form. President, Nat. C. for Soviet Jewry; form. Tr., Jewish Chronicle, form. Dir., Jewish Chronicle; President, Camb. Union & Fdr. & Chairman, The Bridge in Britain; Chairman, Camb. Univ. Lab. Club; form. Chairman, Brady Boys, Club. Lect., contrib. and author 70 books. Ad.: House of Lords, London SW1A 0PW.

JAQUE, Sidney, JP; b. Toledo, Ohio, USA, June 23, 1912; Ret. Solicitor; form. Mayor of Holborn (1958), H.L. Patron (form. Chairman), Camden (form. Holborn) Chamber of Commerce; form. Chairman, Camden Commercial Ratepayers Group (since 1979); Past President, now Hon. Life President Western Marble Arch Syn. (form. Western Syn.); Chairman, Western Charitable Foundation; form. Gov., St. Nicholas Montessori Instit.; form. Gov., J.F.S.; form. Dep. Chairman, West Central Magistrates, Div.; V. President (form. President), Holborn & St. Pancras Conservative Assn.; Patron, Vice President form. Frs., Royal Lond. Homoeopathic Hospital, form. Vice-P., London Youth Tr. Publ.: The Western Synagogue, 1961-1991 (1998). Ad.: 56 Sheringham, St. Johns Wood Park, NW8 6RA. ☎ 020-7722 3671. Fax 020-7722 9317.

JEUDA, Basil Simon; b. Manchester, Sept. 17, 1938; m. Laura née Madden; Chartered Accountant; Tr. Manchester Jewish Museum (1998-2004); Chairman, Mersey Regional Ambulance Service, NHS Trust (1999-2003); Chairman, Macclesfield Museums Tr. (2002-05); Chairman NHS Pensions Agency Special Health Authority (2004-06); form. Leader, Cheshire County Council (1981-85). Publ.: History of Churnet Valley Railway, 1849-1999; History of Rudyard Lake, 1797-1997; The Knotty: An Illustrated History of the North Staffordshire Railway. Ad.: 47, Sandringham Rd., Macclesfield SK 10 1QB. ☎ 01625-426740. Email b.jeuda@sky.com

JOFFE, Joel Goodman, Baron Joffe of Liddington, CBE, BCom, LLB (Witwatersrand); b. May 12, 1932; m. Vanetta; Lawyer; Trustee, Joffe Charitable Trust; Chair, Giving Campaign (2000-04); Special Adv., South African Minister of Transport (1997-98); Mem. Royal Commission for the Care of the Elderly (1997-99); Chairman, Swindon and Marlborough NHT (1993-95); Chairman, Swidon Health Authority (1988-93); Chairman, Swindon Private Hospital plc (1982-87); Mem. C. IMPACT (1984-); Mem. Steering Cttee of Per Cent Club, UK; Trustee and Patron of various voluntary organisations: International Alert, Canon Collins Educational trust for South Africa, etc.; Chair, OXFAM (Trustee, Hon. Sec., Chairman, Exec. Cttee 1979-2001); Chairman, Thamesdown Voluntary Services Council (1974-2000); Fd. Director, Jt. Managing Dir., Deputy Chairman, Allied Dunbar Assurance (1971-91); Chairman of the Lyddington Bridge association; Fd. Trustee, Thamesdown Community Trust; Fd. Trustee, Action on Disability and Development; Fd. Trustee, Chairman, Allied Dunbar

Charitable Tr. (1974-1993); Secretary, Admin. Director, Abbey-Life Assurance, London (1965-70); Solicitor, Barrister in Johannesburg as a commercial lawyer, then Human Rights lawyer appearing for the defence in a number of major trials including that of Nelson Mandela (1952-65). Ad.: House of Lords. Email J.joffe@mail.com.

JOSEPH, Dr Anthony Peter, MBBChir (Cantab), MRCGP, FSG; b. Birmingham, April 23, 1937; form. GP; Post-graduate tutor in paediatrics, Univ. of Birmingham (1986-91); form. President JHSE (1994-96); President, Jewish Genealogical Society of Gt. Britain (1997-); Chairman, Birmingham Branch of JHSE (1969-); Corresponding member for Great Britain, Australian Jewish Historical Society (1965-); UK rep. of Society of Australian Genealogists (1965-95); Dir., Int. Assoc. Jewish Genealogical Societies (2000-04); Mem., Bd. Govs. Institute for Jewish Genealogy. Contributor on Jewish Genealogy to Blackwell Companion to Jewish Culture; Author of papers in many different genealogical publications, including JHSE. Ad.: 3 Edgbaston Rd., Smethwick, West Midlands B66 4LA. ☎ 0121-555 6165. Fax 0121-555 5975.

JOSEPH, John Michael; b. London, 11 Feb. 1939; Chairman, Jewish Blind & Disabled. Ad.: 24 Rosslyn Hill, London NW3.

JOSEPH, Peter Michael, MA (Cantab); b. London, March 14, 1945, m. Maureen Linda née Ressler; Solicitor, Bookseller and Publisher; Trustee Jewish Literary Trust. Ad. Joseph's Bookstore, 1257 Finchley Rd., London NW11 0AD. ☎ 020-8731 7575. Fax 020 8731 6699. Email info@josephsbookstore.com.

JOSIPOVICI, Prof. Gabriel David, FRSL, FBA; b. Nice, France, Oct. 8, 1940; Writer; Univ. Teacher; Res. Prof. Graduate School of Humanities, Univ. of Sussex; Asst. Lect. in English, School of European Studies, Univ. of Sussex (1963-5); Lect. in English (1965-73); Reader in English (1973-85); Prof. (1985-98); Lord Weidenfeld Vis. Prof., Oxford (1996-97). Publ.: The Inventory, Words, The Present, Migrations, The Air We Breathe, Conversations in Another Room, Contre-Jour, The Big Glass, In a Hotel Garden, Moo Pak, Now, The World and the Book, The Lessons of Modernism, The Book of God, Text and Voice, Touch, On Trust, A Life, Goldberg Variations, Only Joking, The Singer on the Shore, Everything Passes. Ad.: 60 Prince Edward's Rd., Lewes, Sussex BN7 1BH.

JULIUS, Anthony Robert, MA (Cantab), PhD (London), PhD (Hon., Haifa); b. London, July 16, 1956; Solicitor; Partner, Mishcon de Reya (1984-98); Hd. Litigation (1988-98); Consultant; Vice President, Diana, Princess of Wales Mem. Fd. (2002-), Chairman (1997-99), T. (1997-2002); Chairman, Law Panel, IJPR (1997-), reporting on Holocaust Denial Legislation; Mem. Appeals Cttee., Dermatrust (1999-2004); Chairman, Management Bd., Centre for Cultural Analysis, Theory and History, University of Leeds (2001-05); Chairman, London Consortium; Vis. Prof. Birkbeck Coll. (2005-). Publ.: T.S. Eliot, Anti-semitism and Literary Form (1995, 2nd ed. 2003); Idolizing Pictures (2001); Transgressions: The Offences of Art (2002). Ad.: Mishcon de Reya, Summit House, 12 Red Lion Square, London WC1R 4QD. ☎ 020-7440 7000. Email anthony.julius@mishcon.com.

JUST, Rabbi Mayer; b. Wignitz, Aug. 15, 1912; President Chief Rabbinate of Holland; Ad.: Soetendaal 32, 1081 BP.

KADISH, Sharman, BA (Lond.), D.Phil. (Oxon), FSA, FRHist.S.; b. London, Sept. 21, 1959; m.Sydney Greenberg. Research Fellow and part-time lecturer in the Centre for Jewish Studies, University of Manchester. Project Dir., Survey of the Jewish Built Heritage in the UK & Ireland and Director, Jewish Heritage UK. Publ.: Bolsheviks and British Jews (1992); A Good Jew and A Good Englishman: The Jewish Lads' and Girls' Brigade 1895-1995 (1995);Building Jerusalem: Jewish Architecture in Britain (1996 ed.); Synagogues (in the Heinemann Library Places of Worship series for children 1998); Bevis Marks Synagogue 1701-2001 (2001); Jewish Heritage in England: An Architectural Guide (2006); Jewish Heritage in Gibraltar; An Architectural Guide (2007). Ad.: Centre for Jewish Studies, School of Arts, Histories & Cultures, University of Manchester, Lime Grove, Oxford Road, Manchester, M13 9PL. ☎ 0161-275 3611; Email director@jewish-heritage-uk.org. Website www.jewish-heritage-uk.org

KALMS, Lady Pamela, MBE; b. London, July 29, 1931; form. Vol. Services Co-ordinator, Edgware Gen. Hospital; form. Deputy Chairman, form. NHS Wellhouse Tr. (Barnet and Edgware Gen.

Hospitals); form. Mem. Exec. Jewish Marriage Council; Tr. and Dir., Ravenswood Foundation. Ad.: 84 Brook St., London W1K 5EH ☎ 020-7499 3494. Fax 020-7499 3436.

KALMS, Lord, Hon. FCGI (1991), Hon. DLitt CNAA/ University of London (1991), Hon. D. Univ. North London (1994), Hon. Fellow London Business School (1995), Hon. D. Econ. Richmond (1996), Hon. D.Litt, Sheffield (2002), Hon. Degree, Buckingham (2002); b. London Nov. 21, 1931; m. Pamela née Jimack; Chairman Dixons Group plc (1948-2002); Tr., Conservative Party (2001-03); Dir. Centre for Policy Studies (1991-2002); Vis. Prof., Business Sch., Univ. of North London (1991-); Mem. of Bd. of Funding Agency for Schs – Chairman of the Agency's Finance Cttee (1994-97); Gov., Dixons Bradford City Technology Coll. (1988-2002); Tr. Industry in Educn. Ltd. (1993-2002); Gov. of National Institute of Economic & Social Research (1995-2001); Dir. Business for Sterling (1998-2002); Tr., The Economic Education Tr. (1993); F. and Sponsor of Centre for Applied Jewish Ethics in Business and the Professions, Jerusalem; Fd. of Stanley Kalms Foundation; Co-Fd. and Sponsor of Immanuel College; form. Chairman, Jewish Educational Development Tr. (1978-89) and Jews' College (1983-89); Non-Exec. Dir., British Gas (1987-97); Chairman King's Healthcare NHS Trust (1993-96).; Hon. Fell., Shalom Hartman Inst. (2005). Publ.: A Time for Change (1992). Ad.: 84 Brook St., London W1K 5EH. ☎ 020-7499 3494. Fax 020-7499 3436.

KAPLAN, Harvey, MA; b. Glasgow, Dec. 6, 1955. Civil servant; Dir., Scottish Jewish Archives Centre (1987-). Publ.: The Gorbals Jewish Community in 1901 (2006). Ad.: 1/L 11, Millwood St., Glasgow G41 3JY; Email rvlkaplan@googlemail.com.

KARPF, Anne, BA Oxon, MA Oxon, MSc; b. June 8, 1950; Journalist and writer; Radio critic, The Guardian (1993-2000); columnist, Jewish Chronicle (1999-2006); The Guardian (2006-); Publ.: Doctoring the Media: The Reporting of Health and Medicine (1988); The War After: Living with the Holocaust (1996). The Human Voice: the Story of a Remarkable Talent (2006) Ad.: c/o The Guardian.

KATTEN, Brenda (née Rosenblit), b. London, Sept. 8, 1936; Chair, World WIZO Pub. Rel. Dept. (2008-); Chair, Israel, Britain & Commonwealth Asso. (2006); Chairperson, Public Affairs & NGO Dept. World WIZO (Israel); form. Chairperson Bnai Brith Hillel Fd; (1994-98); Chairperson UK National Cttee Jerusalem 3000 (1995-96); form. Mem. JC Tr. Ltd; H.Vice-Pres. Zionist Fed. of Great Britain & Ireland (Chair 1990-94); Jt. H. Pres. British WIZO (Chair 1981-87). Ad.: c/o World WIZO, 38 David Hamelech Blvd, Tel Aviv 64237. ☎ 00 972 3 6923729. Fax 00 972 3 6958267. Email brendak@wizo.org.

KATZ, Agi (née Rojko); b. Budapest, Oct. 29, 1937; m. Peter Katz; Art curator; Exhibition organiser with special knowledge of Anglo-Jewish artists of the 20th century; Dir. Boundary Gallery (1986-); Curator, Ben Uri Gallery (1979-85); Asst. to Chief Economist, Temple Press (1961-63); Economic Intelligence Off., Monsanto UK (1963-65). Publ.: catalogues on Epstein, Brodzky, Herman, Kestelman and Koenig. Ad.: Boundary Gallery, 98 Boundary Rd., London NW8 0RH. ☎ 020-7624 1126. Email agi@boundarygallery.com. Website www.boundarygallery.com

KATZ, Dovid, BA (Columbia), PhD (London); b. New York, May 9, 1956; Yiddish linguist and author; Awards incl. John Marshall Medal in Comp. Philology (1980), British Academy Research Award (1998), Leverhulme Trust Research Award (1999-2001); Guggenheim Fell. (2001-02); Yiddish culture awards include: Israel Marshak (Montreal, 1979); Sholem Aleichem (Tel Aviv, 1988); Hirsh Rosenfeld (Montreal, 1994), Manger Prize (Tel Aviv, 1997); Y.Y. Sigal (Montreal 1999). Fd. Yiddish Studies at Oxford University; Dir. of Yiddish Studies at Oxford Centre for Postgraduate Hebrew Studies (1978-95); Fellow of St Antony's College Oxford (1986-97); Dir. of Res., Oxford Institute for Yiddish Studies (1994-96); Vis. Prof., Yale University (1998-9); Prof. Yiddish Language, Literature and Culture, Vilnius University (1999-); Fd. Dir., Center for Stateless Cultures, Vilnius U. (1999-2001); Dir. of Res. and co-founder, Vilnius Yiddish Institute (2001-); Publ. incl.: Grammar of the Yiddish Language (1987); Klal-takones fun yidishn oysleyg (1992); Tikney-takones (1993); Lithuanian Jewish Culture (2004); Words on Fire: The Unfinished Story of Yiddish (2004, 2007); Fd. Aleichem Sholem (1972-4); Winter Studies in Yiddish (1987-8), Oxford Yiddish (1990-95), Yiddish Pen (1994-6). Columnist, Yiddish Forward (1991-2002), Algemeyner Zhurnal (1997-). Yiddish fiction under the name Heershadovid Menkes: Includes The Flat Peak (1993), Tales of the Misnagdim of Vilna

Province (1996). Ad.: History Faculty, Vilnius University, Universiteto 7, Vilnius 01513, Lithuania. Email: dovidkatz@vilniusuniversity.net. Website: www.dovidkatz.net

KATZ, Rabbi Steven Anthony, BA (Hons); b. London, Dec. 18, 1948; M., Hendon Ref. Syn., H. Sec. RSGB Assembly of Rabbis; Chaplain, Univ., Coll. Hospital, London. Ad.: Hendon Reform Synagogue, Danescroft Ave., NW4 2NA. ☎ 020-8203 4168.

KATZIR (Katchalski), Professor Ephraim; b. Kiev, May 16, 1916; Fourth President, State of Israel (1973-78); Chief Scientist, Israel Def. Forces (1966-68); Prof, Weizmann Instit. of Science; Prof Emer., Tel Aviv Univ.; Foreign Member, Royal Society Lond.; Hon. Member, The Royal Institution of Great Britain (1989); Foreign Assoc. Nat. Acad. of Sciences USA; Foreign Hon. Member, Amer Acad. of Arts & Sciences. Many honorary doctorates, honours prizes, medals and awards. Publ.: Papers & reviews in scientific journals & books. Ad.: Weizmann Instit., Rehovot 76100, Israel. ☎ 972-8-9343947. Fax 972-8-9468256.

KAUFMAN, Rt. Hon. Sir Gerald Bernard, KB, PC, MA, MP; b. Leeds, June 21, 1930; Journalist; Labour Party Parl. Cttee (1980-92); Opposition Spokesman for Foreign Affairs (1987-92); Member, Nat. Exec. Cttee. of the Labour Party (1991-1992), Chairman, House of Commons Nat. Heritage Cttee (1992-97), HoC Culture, Media and Sport Cttee. (1997-2005); Opp. Spokesman for Home Affairs (1983-87); form. Min. of State, Dept of Industry; Parl. Under-Sec., Industry; Parl. Under-Sec., Environment; MP (Lab.) for Ardwick (1970-83) for Gorton, Manchester (since 1983); Parl. Press Liaison Off, Labour Party (1965-70); Pol. Corr., New Statesman, (1964-65); Pol. Staff, Daily Mirror, (1955-64), Asst. Gen. Sec., Fabian Society (1954-55). Publ.: How to be a Minister, To Build the Promised Land, How to live under Labour (co-author), My Life in the Silver Screen, Inside the Promised Land, Meet me in St Louis, The Left (ed.), Renewal (ed). Ad.: 87 Charlbert Ct., Eamont St., London NW8 7DA. ☎ 020-7219 5145. Fax 020-7219 6825.

KAUFMANN, Flo (née Israel), JP, BA; b. Berkamsted, Aug. 3, 1942, m. Aubrey Kaufmann; Vice Chairman (2006), Magistrates' Assoc. Hon. Tr. (2001-06); Chairman, C., European J. Congress (2007-); Board of Deputies: Vice-President (2003-), Vice-Chairman Israel Cttee. (1989-94), Chairman (1994-97), Chairman, Finance & Organisation Div. (1997-2003), Tr., Hon. Off. (1997-2003); Chairman International Div. (2003-); Chairman, NW West London Valuation Tribunal (1996-). Ad.: Board of Deputies, 6 Bloomsbury Square, London WC1A 2LP.

KAY, Rabbi Sidney, b. Manchester, Oct. 25, 1920; M., Southport New Syn. (1976-84), Emer. Rabbi (since 1985). Ad.: 4 Westhill, Lord St. West, Southport, PR8 2BJ. ☎ 01704 541344.. Email ravkay@aol.com.

KEDOURIE, Sylvia (née Haim), MA, PhD (Edin); b. Baghdad, Iraq; Independent scholar; Ed. Middle Eastern Studies. Publ.: Arab Nationalism: An Anthology (1962, 1967, 1975); Elie Kedourie CBE, FBA (1926-1992): History, Philosophy, Politics (1998); Elie Kedourie's Approach to History and Political Thought (2006).. Ad.: 75 Lawn Rd., London NW3 2XB.

KEMPNER GLASMAN, Mrs. Sheila (née Goldstein); b. London, May 22, 1933; Adv. Young Enterprise (2007); Chairman BoD Women's Issues Action Gp. (1995-99); UK Vice-President. Int. Council of Jewish Women (2001-); Memb. Thames Customer Service Cttee OFWAT (1993-96); form. President, League of Jewish Women; V. Chairman, Hillingdon Com. Health C. (1974-82); Member Hillingdon Dist. Health Auth. (1983-87); Member, Women's Nat. Com. (1990-94). Ad.: 10 Ashurst Close, Northwood, Middx. HA6 1EL.

KERNER, Brian Philip, MRPharms; b. London, Nov. 21, 1934; m. Sylvia Evelyne née Goldstein; Mem., JLC (2007-); Vice Chairman, BICOM (2001-); President, UJIA (2000-);. Ad.: 4 Greenaway Gardens, London NW3 7DJ. ☎ 020-7435 2494; Fax 020-7435 2180. Email bpkerner@googlemail.com

KERSHEN, Anne Jacqueline (née Rothenberg), BA, MPhil, PhD, FRHistS, FRSA; b. London, June 8, 1942; Historian; Barnett Shine Res. Fell. Queen Mary Univ. of London (1990-); Director Centre for the Study of Migration, QMW (1994-); Memb. Faculty Leo Baeck Coll. (1992-); Memb. C. JHSE; Council Memb Jewish Museum. Publ.: A Question of Identity (1998); London, the Promised Land? (1997); Uniting the Tailors (1995); 150 years progressive Judaism (ed.) (1990); Off-the-peg: Story of Women's Wholesale Clothing Industry (ed.) (1988); Trade Unionism amongst Jewish Tailors in London, 1872-1915 (1988); (with Jonathan Romain) Tradition and Change: The History of Reform Judaism in

Britain, 1840-1995 (1995); Language, Labour and Migration (2000); Food in the Migrant Experience (2002); Strangers, Aliens & Asians: Huguenots, Jews and Bangladeshis in Spitalfields, 1660-2000 (2005). Ad.: Dept. of Politics, Queen Mary & Westfield College, Mile End Rd., E1 4NS. ☎ 020-7975 5003. Email a.kershen@qmw.ac.uk.

KESTENBAUM, Jonathan, BA (Hons), MA, MBA; b. Tokyo, Japan, Aug. 5, 1961; Chief Exec. Nesta (2005); form. Chief Exec. The Portland Tr., form. Chief of Staff to Sir Ronald Cohen; form. Chief Exec., UJIA; form. Ex. Dir. Office of the Chief Rabbi; Mazkir, Bnei Akiva London (1982-83); IDF, Outstanding Soldier Award (1983); Jerusalem Fellows Researcher (1985-87).

KHALILI, Nasser David, b. Iran, Dec. 18, 1945; m. Marion née Easton; Professor and Businessman. Publ. include: The Nasser D. Khalili Collection of Islamic Art. Ad.: c/o Sue Bond Public Relations, Hollow Lane Farmhouse, Hollow Lane, Thurston, Bury St. Edmunds, Suffolk IP31 3RQ. Website www.khalili.org.

KING-HAMILTON, His Honour Myer Alan Barry, QC, MA; b. London, Dec. 9, 1904; Hon. Fell. Trinity Hall (2003); Judge, Central Criminal Court (1964-79); Chairman, Jt. Standing Cttee. of RSGB and ULPS; President, West Lond. Syn. (1977-83 and 1965-72), Hon. Life President (1994-); President, Maccabaeans (1967-75); Leader Oxford Circuit (1961-64); Recorder of Wolverhampton (1961-64), Gloucester (1956-61), Hereford (1955-56); Dep. Chairman. Oxford Qrt. Sessions (1956-64); Bencher, Middle Temple (1961); V. President, World Cong. of Faiths (since 1970); President, Co-Founder, Westlon Hsg. Trust (1970-95), Hon. Life President (1995); London J.; Hsg. Cttee. (1975-); President, Birnbeck Hsg. Assoc. (1995-97), and Hon. Life President (1997-); Chairman, Pornography and Violence Research Trust (form. Mary Whitehouse, etc.) (1986-96); Master, Worshipful Comp. of Needlemakers (1969-70); Freeman of the City of London (1945); form. President, Cambridge Union Soc.; Squadron Leader RAF. Publ.: And Nothing But The Truth (autobiog.) Ad.: 33 Seymour Place, W1H 6AP.

KINGSLAND, Sir Richard, AO, CBE, DFC; b. Moree, New South Wales, Australia, Oct. 19, 1916, m. Kathleen J. Adams; Dir. Sir Edward Dunlop Medical Res. Fd. (1995-); President Barnardo's Canberra (1995-2004); Chairman, A.C.T. Health Promotion Fund (1990-94); Tr., Canberra Festival (1988-92); Life Gov. National Gallery of Australia; Life Gov. Sir Moses Montefiore Jewish Home, Sydney; Sec., Australian Veterans Affairs Dept. (1970-81); Chairman, Repatriation Com. (1970-81); Sec., Interior Dept. (1963-70); Nat. Dir., Australian Bicentennial Auth. (1983-89); President, Man. Bd., Goodwin Retirement Villages (1984-88); Nat. C., Australian Opera (1983-96); Chairman, Uranium Adv. C. (1982-84); H. Nat. Sec., Nat. Heart Foundation (1976-90); Member at Large since 1990; form. Chairman, Commonwealth Films Review Bd.; First Chairman, Canberra Sch. of Art (1975-84); First Chairman Canberra School of Music (1972-75); First Chairman, ACT Arts Development Bd. (1981-84); Tr., Australian War Memorial (1966-76); Man. Sydney Airport (1948-49); Dir.-Gen., Org., RAAF Hq. (1946-48); Dir., RAAF Intelligence (1944-45); Cdr., RAAF Base, Rathmines, NSW (1942-43); Cdr., No. 11 Sqdn. RAAF Papua New Guinea (1941-42); No. 10 Sqdn. RAAF, Brit. (1939-41). Ad.: 36 Vasey Cresc., Campbell, ACT 2612, Australia. ☎ (02) 624 78502.

KLAUSNER, Menny; b. Frankfurt, Sept. 19, 1926; Comp. Dir.; Chairman, Mizrachi–Hapoel Hamizrachi Fed., UK & Ireland; Chairman, Israel Cttee., BoD; CoChairman, Nat. Z.C.; President, Hendon Adath Yisroel Cong.; T., N.W. Lond. Com. Mikva, T., Mifal Hatora Med. Aid Fund; Gov., Hasmonean Prep. Sch., Hendon; Chairman, Frs. of Ariel Instits., Israel; Netiv Meir Sch., Jerusalem; Actions Cttee., WZO, Adv. Bd., Torah Dept. Youth Aff. Com., World Mizrachi Exec.; Chairman, Mizrachi Fed. (1972-76); V. Chairman & T., Jewish Review, (1966-71); V.Chairman, Tora Vavoda (1948-52). Ad.: 1 Edgeworth Ave., NW4 4EX. ☎ 020-8202 9220, 020-7286 9141.

KLINER, Stephen Ivor, MA, LLB, NP; b. Glasgow April 15, 1953; m. Barbara née Mitchell; Solicitor (Partner), Vallance Kliner and Associates, Glasgow; Chairman Scottish C. Jewish Communities (2007-); Vice Chairman Cosgrove Care (2006-); President Glasgow Jewish Representative Council (2001-04); V. President National Executive Habonim-Dror (1993-2003); Chairman National Habonim-Dror (2003-); Chairman Habonim-Dror Glasgow (1990-2002); H. Sec. Giffnock and Newlands Hebrew Congregation (1995-98). Ad.: 1

Eglinton Drive, Giffnock, Glasgow, G46 7NQ. ☎ 0141-638 6602. Fax 0141-332 3273. Email stephen.kliner@ntlworld.com.

KLUG, Sir Aaron, OM, ScD, FRS; b. Aug. 11, 1926, m. Liebe née Bobrow; President of the Royal Society (1995-2000); Nobel Prize for chemistry (1982); Med. Res. C. Laboratory of Molecular Biology, Cambridge; Hon. Fel., Peterhouse, Cambridge; form. Nuffield Fel., Birkbeck Col., Lond.; Lect., Cambridge Univ., Cape Town Univ. Publ.: Papers in scientific journals. Ad.: MRC Laboratory of Molecular Biology Cambridge CB2 2QH.

KLUG, Brian, MA (Lond.), PhD (Chicago); b. London, Jan. 15, 1949; University Teacher; Mem. Faculty of Philosophy, University of Oxford (2003-); Sen. Res. Fell., St Benet's Hall, Oxford (2001-); Hon. Fell. Parkes Institute, Univ. Southampton (2002-); Publ.: A Time to Speak Out: Independent Jewish Voices on Israel, Zionism and Jewish Identity (2008, co-ed., with A. Karpf, J. Rose, B. Rosebaum); Children as Equals: Exploring the Rights of the Child (2002, co-ed., with K. Alaimo); Ethics, Value and Reality: Selected Papers of Aurel Kolnai (1977, co-ed., with F. Dunlop). Ad: St. Benet's Hall, 38 St. Giles, Oxford OX1 3LN. Email brian.klug@stb.ox.ac.uk.

KNAPP, Alexander Victor, MA (Hons), MusB, PhD(Cantab), Hon. ARAM, LRAM, ARCM, Churchill Fellow; b. London, May 13, 1945; sometime Joe Loss Lecturer in Jewish Music, SOAS (1999-2006); City Univ. (1992-99); Vis. Scholar Wolfson College, Cambridge (1983-86); Assistant Dir. of Studies, Royal College of Music, London (1977-83). Publ.: Four Sephardi Songs (1993); Anthology of Essays on Jewish Music (in Chinese) (1998). Ad.: Flat J, 101 Westbourne Terrace, London W2 6QT. ☎ 020-7402 6248. Email alexknapp@waitrose.com.

KNOBIL, Henry Eric, FTI; b. Vienna, Nov. 27, 1932; form. V. President British-Israel Chamber of Commerce; form. Bd. Gov. Immanuel Coll.; form. President Western Marble Arch Synagogue; form. Bd. Govs., Carmel Coll. (1980-87). Ad.: Apt. 9, Orchard Court, Portman Square, London W1H 6LE. ☎ 020-7224 4005. Fax 020-7224 0875.

KNORPEL, Henry, CB, QC, BCL, MA (Oxon).; b. London, Aug. 18, 1924, m. Brenda née Sterling; Barrister; Bencher, Inner Temple; Counsel to the Speaker, House of Commons (1985-95); Solicitor to DHSS (1978-85); Princ. Asst. Solicitor (1971-78); form. Chairman Sutton and District Syn.; form. V. President Epsom Syn. Ad.: Conway, 32 Sunnybank, Woodcote Grn., Epsom, Surrey KT18 7DX. ☎ 01372 721394.

KOPELOWITZ, Lionel, MA (Cantab), MRCS, LRCP, MRCGP, JP; b. Newcastle upon Tyne, Dec. 9, 1926; President, BoD (1985-91); Chairman, London Regional Council, BMA (2001-04); Exec. Cttee, Friends of Hebrew Univ. (1998-); C. Initiation Soc. (1993-); V. President, Trades Adv. C.; V. President, Conf J. Material Claims against Germany; Member, Gen. Med. C. (1984-94); C., BMA (1982-94), Fel. (1980); President, WJC Europe (1988-91), World Exec. WJC (1986); C., AJA; President, Nat. C., Soviet Jewry (1985-91); President, Rep. C., Newc. Jewry (1967-73); First President, United Hebrew Cong. Newc. (1973-76); Life President (President 1964-74), Newc. JWB; V. President, British Friends Shaare Zedek Hospital Medical Centre; President, Old Cliftonian Soc. (1991-93); Council, United Synagogue (1991-96); Chairman, St Marylebone Division BMA (1992-); Mem. Bd. Gov., Clifton Coll., Bristol; Mem. C., Royal Coll. General Practitioners (1995-99); Vice President, Assoc. Baltic Jews. Ad.: 10 Cumberland House, Clifton Gardens, W9 1DX. ☎ 020-7289 6375; 145 Barrack Lane, Aldwick, West Sussex PO21 4ED. ☎ 01243 268134.

KOPS, Bernard; b. London, 1926; Writer; C., Day Lewis Fellowship (1980-83). Pub.: Yes; From No Man's Land, The Dissent of Dominick Shapiro, By the Waters of Whitechapel, The Passionate Past of Gloria Gaye, Settle Down Simon Katz, Partners, On Margate Sands (novels), Collected Plays, The Hamlet of Stepney Green, Erica I Want to Read You Something, For the Record (poetry), Barricades In West Hampstead (poetry), This Room in the Sunlight (poetry), The World is a Wedding (autobiography, re-published 2008), Plays One (collection), Plays Two (collection), Plays Three (collection), Shalom Bomb (autobiography continued), Neither Your Honey Nor Your Sting (history), Bernard Kops East-End (collection), Grandchildren and other poems; Plays: Playing Sinatra, Dreams of Anne Frank, Green Rabbi, Cafe Zeitgeist, River change, The Opening, I am Isaac Babel, Returning We Hear the Larks, Knocking on Heaven's Door, Rogues and Vagabonds etc. Ad.: 41B Canfield Gdns., London NW6 3JL. ☎ 020-7624 2940.

KORNBERG, Sir Hans (Leo), MA, DSc (Oxon), ScD (Cantab), Hon. ScD (Cincinnati), Hon. DSc (Warwick, Leicester, Sheffield, Bath, Strathclyde, Leeds, South Bank, London, La Trobe), Hon. DU (Essex), Dr Med, hc (Leipzig), Hon. LLD (Dundee), PhD (Sheffield), FRS, Hon. FRCP, FIBiol, FRSA; b. Herford, Germany, Jan. 14, 1928; Sir W. Dunn Prof of Biochemistry, Cambridge Univ. (1974-95); Master, Christ's Coll. Cambridge (1982-95); H.Fel., Brasenose and Worcester Colls., Oxford, Wolfson Coll., Cambridge; Member, German Acad. Sciences 'Leopoldina', For. Assoc., Nat. Acad. Sci., US; For. H. Member, Amer. Acad. Arts & Sciences; H. Member, Amer. Soc. Biochem. & Mol. Biol.; Japanese Biochem. Soc., German Soc. Biol. Chem. (Warburg Medallist); The Biochem. Soc. (UK), Brit. Assn. Adv. Sci.; Fel., Amer. Acad. Microbiol.; Mem. Academia Europea; Accademia Nazionale dei Lincei; American Philosophical Soc.; Hon. Mem. Phi Beta Kappa; President, Brit. Assn. Adv. Sci. (1984-85); Chairman, Brit. Nat. Cttee. for Problems of Environment (1982-87); P. Internat. Union of Biochem. & Mol. Biol. (1991-1994); President, Biochemical Soc. (1990-95); Ch, Adv. Cttee. on Genetic Modification (1986-95); Dir., UK Nirex Ltd (1986-95); Chairman, Kurt Hahn Trust (U. of Camb.) (1990-95); Acad. Gov., Hebrew U. (1973-97); Scientific Gov., Weizmann Institute (1980-90); Member, Science Res. C. (1967-72) and Chairman, Science Bd. (1969-72). Publ.: Scientific writings. Ad.: The University Professors, Boston University, 745 Commonwealth Ave., Boston, MA 02215. Fax (617) 353-5084.

KOSMIN, Barry A., BA, MA, D.Phil; b. London, 1946; m. Helen; Res. in Public Policy; Professor; Exec. Dir. JPR (2000-05); Exec. Dir. Research Unit, Board of Deputies of British Jews (1974-86); Fellow, Institute for Advanced Studies, Hebrew University (1980-81); Founding Dir., North American Jewish Data Bank, The Graduate School and University Center of The City University of New York (1986-96); Dir. of Research, Council of Jewish Federations, NY (1986-96); Dir. CUNY National Survey of Religious Identification (1989); Dir. CJF 1990 US National Jewish Population Survey (1990). Publ.: Majuta: A History of the Jews in Zimbabwe (1981); Highlights of the CJF 1990 National Jewish Research Population Survey (with S. Goldstein, J. Waksberg, N. Lerer, and A. Keysar) (1991); Contemporary Jewish Philanthropy in America (Jt. Ed. with P. Ritterband (1991); One Nation Under God: Religion in Contemporary American Society (with S. Lachman) (1993); A New Antisemitism: Debating Judeophobia in 21st Century Britain (jt.ed., 2003). Ad.: Trinity College 300 Summit Str., Hartford, Conn. 06106-3100. ☎ (860) 297 2140.

KOSSOWSKY, Rabbi Zalman, MEd, PhD; b. Teheran, Dec. 15, 1940; Rabbi Emer. (2007-) Rabbi Israelitische Cultusgemeinde, Zurich (1992-2006); form. Rabbi, Kenton Syn. (1986-91); Chaplain, US Naval Reserve; Rabbi, Sydenham Highlands N. Hebrew Cong., Johannesburg (1978-86); Admin., Colorado Kosher Meats, Colorado Springs, US (1974-78), Rabbi, Young Israel, Greater Miami Florida (1972-74); Assoc. Dean, Talmudic Res. Instit., Colorado (1967-72). Publ.: Prayer Book for Friday Evening and Festivals, Prayer Book for the House of Mourning, The Modern Kosher Home. Ad.: 10289 Isle Wynd Ct. Boynton Beach, FL 33437 ☎ 561 7338310. Email rabbi@kossowsky.net.

KRAIS, Anthony, JP; b. Lond., May 3, 1938; Assoc. Ch. Exec., Jewish Care (1990-97); Exec. Dir. Jewish Blind Society (1980-89); Ch. British Frs. Israel Guide Dog Centre for the Blind; Dep. Ch. Resources for Autism (1997-2004); Member The Appeals Service (1998-2006); General Commissioner of Taxes. (1997-2008). Ad.: 14 Mayflower Lodge, Regents Park Rd., London N3 3HU ☎ 020-8349 0337. Email ajkrais@gmail.com.

KRAMER, Lotte Karoline (née Wertheimer); b. Mainz, Germany, Oct., 22, 1923; m. Frederic Kramer; Poet. Publ.: Ice Break (1980); Family Arrivals (1981, 1992); A Lifelong House (1983); The Shoemaker's Wife (1987); The Desecration of Trees (1994); Earthquake and Other Poems (1994); Selected and New Poems 1980-1997; Heimweh/Homesick (German/English ed., 1999); The Phantom Lane (2000); Black over Red (2005). Kindertransport, Before and After, Elegy and Celebration (2007). Ad.: 4 Apsley Way, Longthorpe, Peterborough PE3 9NE. ☎ 01733-264378.

KRAUSZ, Ernest, MSc, PhD; b. Romania, Aug. 13, 1931; Prof., School of Behavioural Science, Netanya (2000-); Prof. Emer (1999-), Rector, Bar-Ilan Univ. (1986-89), Prof. of Soc. (Dean, Soc. Sci. Faculty (1973-76) Bar-Ilan Univ.; Reader in Sociology, City Univ. Lond. (1971-72); Vis. Prof, Dept. of Social Studies, Newcastle Univ. (1976-77); LSE (1981-82); C., Higher

Educ, Israel (1979-81), Planning and Grants Cttee. C. Higher Educ. (1990-96); Mem.C. Israel Science Fd. (1994-2001); Mem. British Association for the Advancement of Science (1998-); American Assoc. for the Advancement of Science (2000-); Edr., Studies of Israeli Society (1979-2000); Dir., Sociological Instit. for Community Studies, Bar-Ilan Univ. (1990-99), Senior Res. Fell. (1999-). Publs.: Leeds Jewry, Sociology in Britain, Jews in a London Suburb, Ethnic Minorities in Britain, Key Variables in Social Research, Social Research Design, On Ethnic and Religious Diversity in Israel, Sociological Research - A Philosophy of Science Perspective, The Limits of Science, Co-ed. Sociological Papers (1992-2006), Starting the XXIst Century (2001). Ad.: Dept. of Sociology Bar-Ilan Univ., Ramat Gan 52900, Israel. ☎ (03) 5317892. Fax (03) 6350422.

KRIKLER, Douglas Henry, MA; b. London, Nov. 3, 1965; m. Tali née Zetuni; Chief Exec., UJIA; fd. Dir. British Jewish Yemeni Cultural Soc. (1991-94); fd. Dir. Maimonides Foudation (1994-2000), Exec. Cttee (2000-); Exec. Dir., CST (2000-04); School Gov., Campsbourne School (2003-08); fd. Dir., Jewish Leadership C. (2003-05). Ad.: Balfour House, 741 High Road, London N12 0BQ. ☎ 020-8369 5000. Email doug.krikler@ujia.org.

KUPFERMANN, Jeannette Anne, B.A. (Hons.), M.Phil. Anthropology, (née Weitz); b. Woking, March 28, 1941; Anthropologist, Feature writer for The Sunday Times, Broadcaster Columnist, The Daily Telegraph, TV Critic, Daily Mail, TV writer: The Quest for Beauty (Channel 4); Everyman Film on Edith Stein (BBC). Publ.: The Mistaken Body, When the Crying's Done: A Journey through Widowhood. Ad.: c/o Sunday Times, 1 Pennington St, E1.

KUSHNER, Tony, PhD; b. Manchester, May 30, 1960; Marcus Sieff Professor, Dept of History and Parkes Institute for the Study of Jewish/Non-Jewish Relations, University of Southampton; Trustee, Jewish Heritage UK (2007-); President, BAJS (2002). Historian at Manchester Jewish Museum (1985-86).Publ.: The Persistence of Prejudice: Antisemitism in British Society During the Second World War (1989); (jt. ed.) Traditions of Intolerance (1989); (jt. ed.) The Politics of Marginality (1990); (ed.) Jewish Heritage in British History: Englishness and Jewishness (1992); (jt. ed.) The Internment of Aliens in Twentieth Century Britain (1993); The Holocaust and the Liberal Imagination (1994); (jt. col.) Belsen in History and Memory (1997); (jt. ed.) Cultures of Ambivalence and Contempt (1998); Refugees in an Age of Genocide (1999); Remembering Cable Street (jt. ed., 1999); Disraeli's Jewishness (jt. ed., 2002); (jt. ed) Philosemitism, Antisemitism and the Jews (2004); We Europeans (2004); The Holocaust: Critical Historical Approaches (2005); Remembering Refugees: Then and Now (2006). Ad.: Dept. of History, The University, Southampton SO17 1BJ ☎ 02380-592211.

KUSTOW, Michael David, b. London Nov. 18, 1939; Writer, Theatre Dir.; Literary Dir., Amer. Repertory Theatre (1980-82); Associate Dir., Nat. Theatre (1975-80), Dir., Instit. of Contemporary Arts (1968-71); Member, Ed. Cttee, Jewish Quarterly. Publ.: Tank, an Autobiographical Fiction; Peter Brook: a Biography (2005). Ad.: c/o Tim Corrie, The Chambers, Chelsea Harbour, Lots Rd., London SW10 0XF.

LAMM, Rabbi Norman, PhD; b. Brooklyn, NY, Dec. 19, 1927; Chancellor and Rosh Hayeshiva (2003-); President, Yeshiva Univ. (1976-2003); President, Rabbi Isaac Elchanan Theol. Semin., New York (1976-); Erna and Jakob Michael Prof of Jewish Philosophy, Yeshiva Univ. (1966-); Fdr. Edr., Tradition; Edr., The Library of Jewish Law and Ethics (14 vols.); Rabbi, Cong. Kodimoh, Springfield, Mass. (1954-58); Rabbi, The Jewish Center, New York (1958-76). Publ. A Hedge of Roses, The Royal Reach; Faith and Doubt, Torah Lishmah, The Good Society, Torah Umadda, Halakhot ve'Halikhot, Shema, The Religious Thought of Hasidism; Seventy Faces. Ad.: Yeshiva Univ., 500 W. 185th St., New York, NY 10033. ☎ (212) 960 5280.

LANGDON, Harold S., B.Com; b. Lond. April 22, 1916; Economist; Chairman, Public Rel. Cttee. (1979-85), BoD; Exec., BoD (1974-91); Life Vice-President, Leo Baeck College (2002-), Governor (1978-2001), Chairman (1975-78); Chairman, RSGB (1967-70); North Western Reform Syn. (1960-61). Publ.: Contr., A Genuine Search (ed. Dow Marmur). Ad.: 5 Hazelmere Ct., London NW4 4HL.

de LANGE, Rabbi Nicholas, RM, MA, DPhil, DD; b. Nottingham, Aug. 7, 1944; Professor of Hebrew & Jewish Studies, Cambridge Univ; Fel., Wolfson Coll., Cambridge. Publ.: Judaism,

Apocrypha Jewish Literature of the Hellenistic Age, Atlas of the Jewish World, Illustrated History of the Jewish People, An Introduction to Judaism, various specialised works and literary translations. Ad.: Faculty of Divinity, West Road, Cambridge CB3 9BS. ☎ 01223 763019. Fax 01223 763003.

LAPPIN, Elena, b. Moscow, Dec. 16, 1954; form. Editor, "Jewish Quarterly". Freelance editor & author, New York (1990-94); English (ESL) instructor, Technion, Haifa, Israel (1986-90). Publ.: Jewish Voices, German Words: Growing up Jewish in Postwar Germany and Austria (1994), Daylight in Nightclub Inferno: New Fiction from the Post-Kundera Generation (1997).

LAQUEUR, Walter; b. Breslau, May 26, 1921; Dir., Wiener Library (1964-1992); Edr., Journal of Contemporary History; Chairman, Research C., Centre for Strategic and International Studies, Washington, USA.; Several honorary degrees. Publ.: Communism and Nationalism in the Middle East, Young Germany, Russia and Germany, The Road to War - 1967, Europe since Hitler, A History of Zionism, Holocaust Encyclopedia (Edr. 2001), etc. Email walter@laqueur.net.

LASSERSON, Rachel, BA (Hons); b. London, Dec. 11, 1968; m. James Rossiter; Editor, Jewish Quarterly (2007-); Dir. Contraband Productions Ltd. (1993-2003). Publ.: Editor of Adam International review (2005).Email Editor@jewishquarterly.org

LATCHMAN, David Seymour, MA (Cantab.), PhD, DSc (Lond.), FRCPath, FRSA; b. London, Jan. 22, 1956; m. Hannah née Garson; Master of Birkbeck College (2003-); Professor of Genetics, Univesity of London (1999-); Dean, Inst. Child Health, UCL (1999-2002); Professor of Molecular Biology, UCL (1991-99); President, The Maccabaeans; form Mem. C., United Synagogue; Bd. Man. Golders Green Synagogue; form. Mem. BoD, C. JHSE. Publ. include: Gene Regulation (1990, 5th ed. 2005); Eukaryotic Transcription Factors (1991, 5th ed., 2007); Landmarks in Gene Regulation (1997, ed.); Stress Proteins (1999, ed.); Viral Vectors for Treating Diseases of the Nervous System (2003 ed.). Ad: Birkbeck College, Malet Street, London WC1E 7HX. Email d.latchman@bbk.ac.uk

LAUTERPACHT, Sir Elihu, CBE, QC, MA, LLB; b. London, July 13, 1928; International Lawyer; Fel., Trinity Coll., Cambridge; Hon. Prof. International Law; Reader, Internat. Law (1980-88); Dir., Res. Centre for Internat. Law, Cambridge Univ. (1983-95); Chairman, East African Common Market Tribunal (1972-75); Dir. of Research, Hague Academy of Internat. Law (1959-60); Legal Adv. to Australian Dept. of Foreign Affairs (1975-77); Consultant, Central Policy Review Staff (1978-80; 1972-74); Member, World Bank Admin. Tribunal (1979-98); President (1995-98); Chairman, Asian Development Bank Admin. Tribunal(1993-95); Judge ad hoc, Int. Court of Justice (1993-98); Chairman, Dispute Settlement Panel, US-Canada NAFTA (1996), US-Mexico (1997-99), US-Costa Rica (1997-99), US-Ukraine (1998-99); President Eritrea-Ethiopia Boundary Commission (2002-); Member Institut de Droit International; Bencher, Gray's Inn (1983); H. Fel., Hebrew Univ. of Jerusalem, 1989; H. Member, Amer. Soc. of Internat. Law, (1993); Hudson Medal (2005). Publ.: Aspects of the Administration of International Justice (1991); Jerusalem and the Holy Places (1968), The Development of the Law of International Organisations; Ed. International Law Reports. Ad.: Lauterpacht Centre for Internat. Law, 5 Cranmer Road, Cambridge CB3 9BP. ☎ 01223 335358. Fax 01223 300406.

LAWRENCE, Sir Ivan, MA (Oxon), QC; b. Brighton, Dec. 24, 1936; Barrister; Mem. of BoD (1979-); Tr. Holocaust Educational Trust; Mem. of Commonwealth Jewish Council; form. MP (C.) for Burton (1974-97); Bencher, Inner Temple (1990); Recorder of the Crown Courts (1983-2002); Vis. Prof. of Law, Univ. Buckingham; Exec. Mem. Society of Conservative Lawyers; form. Vice-Chairman Conservative Friends of Israel; form. Mem. of Policy Planning Gp. of IJA; form. Vice Chairman Inter-Parlt. Cttee for the Release of Soviet Jewry. Ad.: Dunally Cottage, Walton Lane, Shepperton, Middx. TW17 8LH.

LAWSON, Arthur Abraham, MBE; b. Glasgow, April 19, 1922; Ret. Consulting Engineer; m. Toby (Sagman [Green]); Vice-President Nat. Chairman (2002-2004) AJEX; Hon. Sec. AJEX Housing Assoc. (1996-2008); Hon. Sec. Monash Branch of Royal British Legion (1997-2007); President Glasgow Jewish Rep. C. (1964-68); form. Chairman Glasgow Branch of AJEX and Glasgow Jewish Branch of Royal British Legion Scotland; form. Hon. T. Glasgow Maccabi; Co-opted Mem. of Univ. Strathclyde Gen. Convocation (1975-89); Mem. Children's Panel for

Glasgow and Strathclyde (1971-82); Jt. Chairman Scottish Cttee for Jewish-Christian Relations (1964-68); form. Nat. Chairman, Combined Heat & Power Assoc. Ad.: 21 Woronzow Rd., London NW8 6BA. ☎ 020-7722 5405. Fax 020-7483 2592. Email arthur.lawson@lineone.net.

LAWTON, Clive Allen, JP, BA, MA, MEd, MSc, Cert. Ed., ADB (Ed); b. London, July 14, 1951; Educ. and organisational consultant; Sen. Consult. Limmud; Faculty, London J. Cultural C., form. Chair North Middlesex University Hospital NHS Trust; form. UJIA Fellow in Jewish Education, SOAS (2001-05); Tr. Jewish Community Centre for London; Faculty, European Centre for Leadership Development; Faculty, LSJS; Chair Tzedek; Patron, Jewish AIDS Tr.; Mem. Home Office Racial Equality Adv. Panel; form. V. Chair Anne Frank Educ. Trust; form. Ch. Exec. Jewish Continuity (1993-96); form. Dep. Dir., Liverpool City Local Educ. Auth.; Member RS Cttee., School's Examination and Assessment Council (SEAC); form. Exec., AJY; Chairman, Shap Working Party on World Rels. in Educ.; Edr., Shap Calendar of World Rel. Festivals; Fdr., Limmud Conf; form. HM, King David High Sch., L'pool; Exec. Dir., Central Jewish Lect. & Information Cttee. & Educ. Off, BoD; Coordinator, Vietnam Working Party; Educ. Off., Yad Vashem Cttee., Exec. C. CCJ; form. V. Chairman, IUJF. Publ.: The Jewish People – Some Questions Answered; The Seder Handbook; I am a Jew; Passport to Israel; Religion Through Festivals; Celebrating Cultures: Islam; Ethics in Six Traditions; The Story of the Holocaust; The Web of Insights; Auschwitz; Hiroshima. Ad.: 363 Alexandra Rd., London N10 2ET. Email clive@clivelawton.co.uk.

LAYTON, Nigel Graham, BSc (Hons); b. London, March 23, 1963; m. Sarah née Nelson; Managing Director Quest Ltd.,; Chairman, World Jewish Relief (2002-); M. Jewish Leadership Council (2005-). Ad.: Email nlayton@quest.co.uk.

LEBRECHT, Norman, b. London, July 11, 1948; m. Elbie née Spivack; Writer; assistant editor, Evening Standard (2002-); Presenter of Lebrecht Live on BBC3' Whitbread First Novel Award 2003 (Song of Names). Publ.: include: The Maestro Myth (1991); When the Music Stops (1996); Covent Garden : the Untold Story : Dispatches from the English Culture War, 1945-2000 (2000); Zsuzsi Roboz : Drawn to Music (2002). Ad.: Website www.norman.lebrecht.

LEE, Arnold, b. London, Aug. 31, 1920; Solicitor; form. Chairman, Jews, Coll. Ad.: 47 Orchard Court, Portman Sq., W1H 9PD. ☎ 020-7486 8918.

LEE, John Robert Louis, b. Manchester, June 2, 1942; MP (Cons.), Pendle, (1983-92) and for Nelson & Colne (1979-83); FCA, Fdn. Dir., Chancery Consolidated Ltd., Investment Bankers; Dir., Paterson Zochonis (UK) Ltd., (1975-76); V. Chairman NW Conciliation Cttee., Race Relations Bd. (1976-77); Political Sec. to Rt. Hon. Robert Carr, (1974); Chairman Council, Nat. Youth Bureau, (1980-83); Jt. Sec., Conservative Back Bench Industry Cttee., (1979-80); PPS to Minister of State for Industry (1981-83); to Sec.of State for Trade & Industry, (1983); Parly. Under Sec. of State MOD, (1983-86); Dept. of Employment, (1986-89); Minister for Tourism, (1987-89); Non-exec.; Chairman, Country Holidays Ltd. (1989); Non-exec. Dir., P. S. Turner (Holdings) Ltd (1989); Non-exec. Dir., Paterson Zochonis, (1990-); Chairman, ALVA (1990-). Ad.:

LEHMAN, Rabbi Israel Otto, MA, BLitt, DPhil, FRAS; b. 1912; Adjunct Prof. of Jewish Studies, Miami Univ.; Assoc. Oxford Centre for PostGraduate Hebrew Studies; Hon. Fel. of the John F. Kennedy Library; form. Lect., Leo Baeck Coll.; Curator of Manuscripts Emer., Hebrew Union Coll., form. Assist. Keeper, Bodleian Library (1947-56); Fdr., Oxford B.B. Lodge, OUJS Library. Publ.: Translation of Chief Rabbi's Pentat. into Germ., 'Moses', (ed.), Handbook of Hebrew and Aramaic Manuscripts. etc. Ad.: 3101 Clifton Ave., Cincinnati, Ohio, USA. ☎ 45220-2488.

LEIBLER, Isi Joseph, AO, CBE, BA (Hons); D.Litt (Hon), Deakin University; b. Antwerp, Belgium, Oct. 9, 1934; m. Naomi née Porush; Chairman and Chief Exec. Leibler Investments Ltd. (1997-); fd. Chairman and Chief Exec., Jetset Tours Pty Ltd. (1965-2000); Chairman Gov. Bd., World Jewish Congress (1997-2001); Senior Vice-President World Jewish Congress (2001-04); Chairman, Diaspora-Israel Relations Cttee, Jerusalem Centre for Public Affairs (2005-); President, Asia Pacific Region, World Jewish Congress (1981-2001); Chairman, Asia Pacific Jewish Assoc. (1980-2001); Chairman, Australian

Institute of Jewish Affairs (1983-2003); President, Exec. Council of Australian Jewry (1978-80, 1982-85, 1987-89, 1992-95); Bd. of Gov., Memorial Foundation for Jewish Culture (1979-95); Board of Gov., Tel Aviv University (1990-); Dir. and Member, Exec. Cttee., Conference on Jewish Claims Against Germany (1979-95). Publ.: Soviet Jewry and Human Rights (1963), Soviet Jewry and the Australian Communist Party (1964), The Case for Israel (1972), The Contemporary Condition of World Jewry (1990), Jewish Religious Extremism: A Threat to the Future of the Jewish People (1991), The Israel-Diaspora Identity Crisis: A Looming Disaster (1994), Is the Dream Ending? Post Zionism and Its Discontents (2001). Weekly columnist: Jerusalem Post, Yisarael HayomAd.: 8 Ahad Ha'am St., 92151 Jerusalem. ☎ (02) 561 2241. Fax (02) 561 2243. Email ileibler@leibler. com.

LEIGH, Howard D., BSc., FCA, ACTI; b. London, Apr. 3, 1959; m. Jennifer née Peach; Investment Banker; Sen. Tr., Conservative Party (2001-); Tr. Jerusalem Foundation (1995-); Exec. BD, Conservative Friends of Israel (2004-); Mem. Exec. Bd., Jewish Care (2004-06); Chairman, Jewish Care Breakfast Gp. (1998-); Chairman, Westminster Synagogue (2000-). Ad.: 40 Portland Place, London W1B 1NB. ☎ 020-7908 6000; Fax 020-7908 6008. Email hleigh@cavendish.com.

LERMAN, Antony, BA Hons; b. London, Mar. 11, 1946; Exec Dir. inst. for Jewish Policy Research (2006-; previously 1991-99) Dir. European Programmes, Yad Hanadiv (1999-2000); Chief Exec. Hanadiv Charitable Fd. (2000-05); Memb. Imperial War Museum Holocaust Exhibition Advisory Cttee; Memb. Runnymede Trust Commission on the Future of Multi-Ethnic Britain (1998-2000); Memb. Jewish Memorial Foundation Think-Tank on the Holocaust (1996-99); Jt. Ed., Patterns of Prejudice (1983-99); Chairman Jewish Council for Com. Relations (1992-94); Assist Ed., Survey of Jewish Affairs (1982-91); form. Ed., Jewish Quarterly (1985-86). Publ.: Ed., The Jewish Communities of the World (1989), Jt. Gen. Ed. Antisemitism World Report (1992-98). Ad.: 14 St. James's Place, London SW1A 1NP. ☎ 020-7493 8111. Email tony.lerman@hanadiv. org.uk.

LETWIN, Rt. Hon. Dr Oliver, PC; b. London, May 19, 1956; m. Isabel Grace née Davidson; MP (Dorset West 1997-); Chairman, Conservative Party Policy Review (2006-); Shadow, Sec. State for Environment (2005-06); Shadow Chancellor (2003-05); Shadow Home Sec. (2001-03); Shadow Financial Sec. (1998-99), Shadow Chief Sec. to the Treasury (1999-2001). Publ.: Ethics, Emotion and the Unity of Self (1987); Privatising the World (1989); The Purpose of Politics (1999). Ad.: House of Commons, London SW1A 0AA.

LEVENBERG, Fayge (née Schwab), BA (Hons), MA; b. Gateshead, Dec. 10, 1949; m. Rabbi Yechiel Levenberg; Teacher; Head of Jewish Studies, Dep. Hd., Naima Jewish Preparatory School (1997-); OFSTED Inspector (1996-); Pikuach Inspector (1997-); Additional Inspector, Independent and Faith Schools (2004-); External assessor, GTP & RTP Students (2001-); form. Lect., Jews College (1984-95); Educ Off., US Bd. Rel. Educ. (1988-93); Inspector/Advisor, US Bd. Rel. Educ. (1990-93). Ad.: 76, Princes Park Ave., London NW11 0JX. ☎ 020-8381 4227. Fax 020-8455 0769. Email levenberg@totalise.co.uk.

LEVENE, Baron of Portsoken (Life Peer), **(Peter)** KBE; b. Pinner, Middlesex, December 8, 1941; Lord Mayor of London (1998–99); Chairman & Chief Exec. Canary Wharf Ltd; Prime Minister's Adviser on Efficiency & Effectiveness; Deputy Chairman & Managing Dir. Wasserstein Perella & Co. Ltd; Alderman, City of London (Portsoken) (1984-); form. Managing Dir. United Scientific Holdings plc (1968-85); Chairman (1981-85); Chief of Defence Procurement, Ministry of Defence (1985-91); Chairman Docklands Light Railway Ltd. (1991-94). Ad.: One Canada Square, Canary Wharf, London E14 5AB. ☎ 020-7418 2250. Fax 020-7418 2082.

LEVY, Rabbi Abraham, Knight Commander (Encomienda) Order of Civil Merit (Spain), OBE, BA, PhD, FJC; b. Gibraltar, July 16, 1939; m. Estelle née Nahum; Com. Rabbi, Spiritual Head, S. & P. Cong., Lond.; M., Lauderdale Rd. Syn.; Jt. Eccl. Auth. BoD; Dep.P., LSJS; Vice Chairman, Rabbinical Commission for the Licensing of Shochtim; Founder and Dir., The Sephardi Centre; form. Dir. Young Jewish Leadership Instit.; Founder and H. Princ., Naima Jewish Preparatory Sch.; Gov., Carmel Coll.; Hon. Chaplain, J. Lads & Girls Brigade; Patron, J. Medical Association (UK); Hon. Chaplain, Lord Mayor of London (1998-9); Mem., St.

Cttee, Conference European Rabbis; Vice President British Friends Hebrew Univ.; Hospital Kosher Meals Service, Jewish Care, Norwood; Hon. President Jewish Childs Day; President, Union Anglo-Jewish Preachers (1973-75); V. President, AJA, JHSE. Publ.: The Sephardim – A Problem of Survival; Ages of Man (jt. auth.); The Sephardim (jt. auth.). Ad.: 2 Ashworth Road, London W9 1JY ☎ 020-7289 2573. Fax 020 Email bridieoak@googlemailmail.com.

LEVY, David, B.A. (Com.), FCA, b. Manchester, June 27, 1942; Chart. Accountant; Chief Exec. Brideoak Associates, Management Consultants; Mem., Worshipful Comp. of Chartered Accountants; Freeman, City of London. Ad.: 6, The Mews, Gatley, Cheadle, Cheshire SK8 4PS. ☎ 0161-428 7708/0161. Email bridieoak@googlemailmail.com

LEVY, Elkan David, BA (Hons), MHL; b. Preston, Lancs, March 29, 1943; m. Celia, née Fisher; Solicitor; Dir. Office of Small Communities (UJIA); Mem. Exec. BoD (2000-03); Dir. President, United Synagogue (1996-99); form. Chairman, Chief Rabbinate Conference; Chairman, Singers Prayer Book Publication Cttee.; form. Minister, Belmont Synagogue (1969-73); Warden, Stanmore Synagogue (1980-90); Chairman US Burial Society (1992-96); Mem. United Synagogue Council (1980-92); Officer, United Grand Lodge of England and Grand Lodge of the State of Israel. Ad.: Balfour House, 741, High Rd., London N12 0BQ ☎ 020-8369 5173. Email elkan.levy@easynet.co.uk.

LEVY, Rabbi Emanuel, BA, b. Manchester, July 31, 1948; m. Myriam née Blum; M., Palmers Grn. & Southgate Syn. form.Vice-Chairman Rabbinical Council of the United Synagogue; Memb. Borough of Enfield Educ. Cttee.; Chaplain to Whittington Hospital; Form. Hon. Principal, Herzlia Jewish Day School, Westcliff-on-Sea; form. Rabbi, Southend & Westcliff Hebrew Cong.; Chief Rabbi's Cabinet, Reg. Affairs, to Chief Rabbi's Cabinet Education Portfolio; J. Rep. to Standing Advisory Council for Religious Education (SACRE) for Borough of Enfield: form. Chaplain to Mayor of Southend (1981-82, 1983-84); form. Rabbi, Langside Hebrew Cong., Glasgow; Rabbi, South Broughton Syn, Manchester; Chairman, Rabbinical Council of the Provinces (1986-88); F.P. Southend Community Relations Council, (1986-88). Publ. Pninei Kahal (2005). Ad.: 11, Morton Crescent, Southgate, London N14 7AH. ☎ 020-8882-2943.

LEVY, John David Ashley, BA (Hon) Sociology; b. Lond., Sept. 10, 1947; Dir. Frs. of Israel Educ. Fd.; Exec. Dir., Academic Study Group on Israel & Middle East; Hon. Co-ord. UK Society for the Protection of Nature in Israel; form. Information Dir., Z. Fed.; Social Worker, Lond. Borough of Lambeth Ad.: POB 42763, London N2 0YJ. ☎ 020-8444 0777. Fax 020-8444 0681. Email info@foi-asg.org.

LEVY, Baron of Mill Hill (Life Peer) (Michael Abraham), FCA, HonD (Middx); b. London, July 11, 1944; Comp. Chairman; President of Jewish Care (1998-); President, Specialist Schools and Academies Trust; Mem. Exec. Cttee., Chai-Lifeline (2001-2); Patron, Simon Marks Jewish Primary School Tr. (2002-); Hon. Patron, Cambridge Univ. J. Soc. (2002-); Chairman Bd. Trustees of New Policy Network Fd. (2000-07); Trustee of the Holocaust Educational Trust (1998-2007); Patron of Friends of Israel Educational Trust (1998-); President of CSV (Community Service Volunteers) (1998-); Patron of the British Music Industry Awards (1995-); Member of the Advisory Council to the Foreign Policy Centre (1997-2006); Patron of the Prostate Cancer Charitable Trust (1997-); Member of the International Board of Governors of the Peres Center for Peace (1997-); Tr., Mem. Exec. Committee of the Jewish Leadership Council; Hon. President UJIA; Chairman Fd. for Education (1993-); Chairman, Chief Rabbinate Awards for Excellence (1992-2007); Hon. President JFS School (1995-2001), President (2001-); V. Chairman Central Council for Jewish Social Services (1994-2006); Member of World Commission on Israel-Diaspora Relations (1995-); Member, National Council for Voluntary Organisations Advisory Cttee; (1998-); Member, Community Legal Service Champions Panel (1999-); Patron, Save a Child's Heart Foundation (2000-); Mem. Hon. Cttee Israel, Britain and the Commonwealth Association (2000-); recipient of B'nai B'rith First Lodge Award (1994); Scopus Award Friends of the Hebrew University (1998), Israel Policy Forum Recognition Award (2003); form. Member of the World Board of Gov. of the Jewish Agency – representing Great Britain; form. Nat. Campaign Chairman JIA (1982-85); form. Chairman, JIA Kol Nidre Appeal; form. V. Chairman British Phonographic Industry; form. V. Chairman Phonographic

Performance Limited. Ad.: House of Lords, London SW1A 0PW.

LEVY, Peter Lawrence, OBE, BSc, FRICS; b. Lond., Nov. 10, 1939; Chartered Surveyor; Chairman Jewish Chronicle; Chairman IJPR; Hon. Vice President Reform Judaism; Tr. "For Dementia"; President, Akiva Sch.; V. President Cystic Fibrosis Tr.; V. President, London Youth; V. Chairman, JIA (1979-81); Chairman, Young Leadership JIA (1973-79); Professional Div. JIA (1977-79). Ad.: 52 Springfield Rd., NW8 0QN. ☎ 020-7328 6109. Fax 020-7372 7424.

LEWIN, Mrs. Sylvia Rose (née Goldschmidt), BA (Log), (Rand), RSA Dip.Sp.L.D.; b. Johannesburg; Speech and Dyslexia Therapist; Chairman, Leadership Training and Development, B'nai B'rith, UK; H. President (Nat. President 1982-86, 1988) Bnai Brith UK; Vice-President, Jewish Music Institute; past Chairman Jewish Music Heritage Trust. Ad.: White Gables, 156 Totteridge Lane, N20 8JJ. ☎ 020-8446 0404. Fax 020-8445 8732. Email sylvialewin@btinternet.com.

LEWIS, Bernard, BA, PhD, FBA, FR Hist. S., Hon. Dr. (Hebrew Univ, Tel Aviv Univ., Northwestern Univ., HUC, Univ. Pennsylvania, SUNY, Univ. Haifa, Yeshiva Univ., Brandeis, Bar-Ilan Univ., Ben Gurion Univ., Ankara Univ., New School Univ. Univ. Judaism, Los Angeles; NY, Princeton Univ.; b. London, May 31, 1916; Cleveland E. Dodge, Prof. of Near Eastern Studies Princeton Univ. (1974-86), now Emer.; Mem. American Philosophical Soc.; American Academy of Arts & Sciences; Corr. Mem. Institut de France, Académie des Inscriptions et Belles-Lettres. Member, Instit. for Advanced Study, Princeton (1974-86); Prof. Near & Middle East Hist., Lond. Univ. (1949-74); Army (1940-41), attached to a Foreign Office dept. (1941-45). Publ. include: The Jews of Islam; The Political Language of Islam; books on Turkish and Arabic Studies; Islam and the West; Cultures in Conflict; The Middle East: Two Thousand Years of History; The Multiple Identities of the Middle East (1998); A Middle East Mosaic: Fragments of Life, Letters and History; Music of a Distant Drum (2001); What Went Wrong? Western Impact and Middle Eastern Response (2002); The Crisis of Islam: Holy War and Unholy Terror (2003); From Babel to Dragomans: Interpreting the Middle East (2004) Ad.: Near Eastern Studies Dept., 110 Jones Hall, Princeton University, Princeton, NJ, 08544, USA. ☎ (609) 258 5489. Fax (609) 258 1242.

LEWIS, D. Jerry, BA (Econ) (Hons, Manchester); b. Surrey, June 12, 1949; Parlt. Lobby Journalist and Broadcaster; Vice-President, Board of Deputies (2000-03), Senior Vice President (2003-06); Chairman, Community Issues Div. (2000–06), M. Defence Dir. Vice-Chairman Law, Parlt. and General Purposes Cttee (1994-97), Constitution Standing Cttee (1981-97), Exec. (1985-2006), etc.; Mem. Exec. Cttee, ZF, Nat. Council for Soviet Jewry; Mem. Foreign Press Assoc.; London correspondent Israel Radio, Yediot Ahronot; Political and diplomatic Corresp: Jewish Telegraph; contr. BBC World TV, BBC News 24, BBC World Service, BBC Radio 5 Live, Sky News, etc. Ad.: 9 Weech Hall, Fortune Green Road, London NW6 1DJ. ☎ 020-7794 0044; Fax 020-7431 6450. Email attnjerrylewis@aol.com.

LEWIS, Ivan, b. Manchester, March 4, 1967; M.P. (Lab.), Bury South (1997); Parlt. Under Sec. for Health (2007-), Adult Skills (2005-07); EConomic Sec. to Treasury (2005-06); PPS Sec. State of Trade and Industry (1999-2001); Tr. of Holocaust Educ. Tr. (1998-); V. Chairman, Inter-Parliamentary Council Against Anti-semitism (1998-2001); V. Chairman, Labour Friends of Israel (1998-2001); member Exec. Cttee of the Commonwealth Jewish Council (1998-2001); Member Health Select Cttee (1998-99); Chairman All-Party Parliamentary Group for Parenting (1999); Chief Exec. Jewish Social Services, Greater Manchester (1992-97); Coordinator, Contact Community Care Group (1986-89). Ad.: House of Commons, London SW1A 0AA. ☎ 0161-773 5500.

LEWIS, Jonathan Malcolm, MA (Law) (Cantab); b. London, Mar. 27, 1946; m. Rosemary Anne née Mays; Solicitor; Freeman of the City of London; authorised insolvency practitioner (1986-2000); Designated Immigration Judge, Deputy District Judge; Chairman, UK Association of Jewish Lawyers and Jurists (2002-07); Mem. BoD (Pinner, 1995-), Chairman, Constitution Cttee, Exec. Cttee (1997-03). Publ.: Insolvency in Jewish Law (1996). Ad.: Taylor House, 88 Rosebery Ave., London EC1R 4QU. ☎ 0845-6000-877; Email lewisjandr2004@yahoo.co.uk.

LEWIS, Dr Julian Murray, b. Swansea, Sept. 26, 1951; MP (Con.), New Forest East (1997-); Historian, researcher and campaigner; Shadow Defence Minister (2002-04, 2005-),

Shadow Min. for the Cabinet Office (2004-05), Opposition Whip (2001-2); Jt. Sec. Cons Parlt. Defence Cttee (1997-2001); Vice Chairman Cons. Parlt. Foreign Affairs and Europe Cttees (2000-1); Member Select Cttee on Defence (2000-1); Member Select Cttee on Welsh Affairs (1998-2001); Dep. Dir. Conservative Research Dept. (1990-96); Dir., Policy Research Associates (1985-); Research Dir. and Dir., Coalition for Peace Through Security (1981-85). Publ.: Changing Direction: British Military Planning for Post-War Strategic Defence, 1942-1947 (1988, 2nd ed., 2003); Who's Left? An Index of Labour MPs and Left-wing Causes, 1985-1992 (1992); What's Liberal? Liberal Democrat Quotations and Facts (1996). Ad.: House of Commons, London SW1A 0AA. ☎ 020-7219 3000. Website www.julianlewis.net.

LEWIS, Leonie Rachelle (née Merkel), BA (Hons), MSc; b. London, Dec. 212, 1955; m. Howard Lewis; Director Jewish Volunteering Network & Community Consultant; M. UJIA JAMS Cttee (2008-); Project Dir., Office of the Chief Rabbi (2007-08); Dir. Communities, US (1995-2007); M. Exec., Faiths Forum (2007-); Advisor to Faith in Leadership (2007-); M. Exec.,London Civic Forum (2006-); Ashdown Fellow (2005); Tr., Faith Based Regen Network (2000-); M. Faith Communities Consult. Cttee (Inner Cities Religious C.), Dept. Communities & Local Gov. (1999-); Tr., AJ6 (1990–). Publ. Ten out of Ten: Perspectives on Community Development. Ad.: 659, Uxbridge Rd., Pinner, Middx HA5 3LW ☎ 020-8866 9239

LIBESKIND, Daniel, BArch, MA, BDA; b. Łodz, May 12, 1946; m. Nina née Lewis; Architect; Principal, Studio Daniel Libeskind (1989-); Prof., Hochschule für Gestaltung, Karlsruhe; Cret Chair of Architecture, Univ. of Pennsylvania; Frank O. Grety Chair, Univ. of Toronto. Architectural projects include: Imperial War Museum North (Manchester, 2002), University of North London Graduate School (2003), The Spiral, Victoria & Albert Museum (London), Felix-Nusbaum-House (Osnabrück, 1998), Jewish Museum (Berlin, 2001), Maurice Wohl Convention Centre (Bar Ilan University, 2003), Jewish Museum (San Francisco), Danish Jewish Museum (Copenhagen, 2003). Publ.: Between Zero and Infinity (1981); Chamber Works (1983); Theatrum Mundi (1985); Line of Fire (1988); Marking City Boundaries (1990); Countersign (1992); El Croquis: Daniel Liberskind (1996); Unfolding (with Cecil Balmond, 1997); Fishing from the Pavement (1997); Radix: Matrix: Works and Writings (1997); The Space of Encounter (2001). Ad.: Studio Daniel Libeskind, Windscheidstr. 18, 10627 Berlin, Germany. ☎ 30-3277820. Fax 30-32778299. Email info@daniel-libeskind.com.

LICHFIELD, Nathaniel, BSc, PhD, DSc, FRICS; b. Lond., Feb. 29, 1916; Emer. Prof. of Economics of Environmental Planning, Lond. Univ.; Fdr. Partner, Nathaniel Lichfield & Part. (1962-92); Partner, Lichfield Planning (1992-); Vis. Prof. Berkeley (1959-60, 1968), Hebrew Univ. (1980-2000); Consultant to Mins., internat. orgs., cities in Britain and overseas. Publ.: Israel's New Towns: A Strategy for their Future (with A. Berler and Samuel Shaked), etc. Ad.: 13 Chalcot Gdns., Englands Lane, NW3 4YB. ☎ 020-7586 0461.

LIGHTMAN, Sir Gavin Anthony, b. London, Dec. 20, 1939; Justice of the High Court, Chancery Division (1994-); Fellow, Univ. College London (2002); QC (1980-94); Bencher of Lincolns Inn (1987); Deputy President of AJA (1986-92); Chairman of Education Cttee of AJA (1988-94); V. President, AJA (1994-); Chairman Education Cttee of Hillel (1992-94), Vice-President (1994-); Chairman, Legal Friends of Univ. Haifa (1986-2002); Chairman Commonwealth J. Assoc. (1999-); Patron, The Hammerson Home (1995-); Chairman, The Bar Adv. Bd. of the College of Law (1996-99); Chairman, Sainer Legal Fd. (1999-). Publ.: (with G. Battersby) Cases and Statutes on the Law of Real Property (1965); (with G. Moss) Law of Receivers of Companies (4th ed. 2007). Ad.: Royal Courts of Justice, Strand, London WC2A 2LL. ☎ 020-7947 6671. Fax 020-7947 6291.

LIGHTMAN, Sidney, FCIL; b. Lond. Apr. 5, 1924; journalist, translator; Sec., British & European Machal Assoc.; form. (1981-89) Asst. Foreign Edr., Jewish Chronicle; form. (1966-89) Edr., Jewish Travel Guide. Ad.: 5 West Heath Ct., North End Rd., NW11 7RE. ☎ 020-8455 1673.

LIND, Eleanor Frances (née Platt), QC, LLB (Lond.); b. May 6, 1938; m. Frederick (Freddy) M. Lind ; Barrister (Gray's Inn 1960, Q.C. (1982); Record Crown Court (1982-2004); Deputy High Court Judge, Family Division (1987-2004); Tr. Family Law Bar Association (1990-95), Act. Chairman (1995); President Medico-Legal Society. (2002-04); Jt. H. 1 Garden Court

Family Law Chambers (1990-2007); Chairman, New London Syn. (1994-99); Vice President, Chairman Defence and Gp Relations, Board of Deputies (2003-06), Member (1984-88), and Chairman Law, Parliamentary Gen. Purposes Cttee (1988-94; Chairman 'Get' Cttee/Working group (1999-). Ad.: 1 Garden Court, Temple, London EC4Y 9BJ.. ☎ 020 7797 7900. Email platt@1gc.com.

LIPMAN, Maureen Diane, CBE, Hon. D.Litt; b. Hull, May 10, 1946; Actress/Writer. Theatre: Re:Joyce; Lost in Yonkers; The Cabinet Minister; See How they Run; Peggy For You; Oklahoma; Aladdin; Glorious. TV: Agony; About Face; The Knowledge: Eskimo Day; In Search of Style - Art Deco; Dr Who; Sensitive Skin; He Kills Coppers; Casualty; Skins. Film: Pianist. 7 books of anecdotes published by Robson Books. Regular column in Guardian, Good Housekeeping. Ad.: c/o Conway Van Gelder, 18/21 Jermyn Street, SW1Y 6HP. ☎ 020-7287 0077.

LITHMAN-IMBER, Mrs. Ethel; b. London; P. (form. Nat. Chairman), Brit. Olim Relatives Assn.; Hadassah Medal for services to Israel (1967-); Staff Off, Brit. Red Cross, Second World War; form. Cttee., Guild Jewish Journs.; form. Member, Norfolk County Council SACRE; President Norwich Hebrew Cong. (1997-2000); V. President Norwich Hebrew Congregation (1996, 2000-); form. Act. Chairman, Norwich CCJ. Publ.: The Man Who Wrote Hatikvah. Ad.: c/o BORA, Balfour House, 741 High Road, N12 0BQ. ☎ 01379-674400.

LIVINGSTON, Edward Colin, MBE, MB, BS (Lond.), JP; b. London, Mar. 22, 1925; Med. Prac.; Barrister; Chairman, Austrian Fund Com. AJR Agudas; Chairman Emergency Fund; Chairman H.S.C. Advisory Cttee. form. Ombudsman, Central C. for Jewish Community Services; Medical Examiner, Medical Fnd. for Care of Victims of Torture; P/T Chairman, Soc Sec. Appeal Trib., Harrow; V. President, Harrow Com. Tr; Liveryman. Soc. of Apothecaries; Freeman, City of Lond.; Flt./Lieut (Med. Br.) RAFVR (1948-50); form. P/T Chairman, Disability Appeal Tribunal, South East Region. Ad.: Wyck Cottage, Barrow Point La., Pinner, Middx. HA5 3DH.

LIVINGSTONE, Rabbi Reuben, BA, LLB, MA, LLM, PgDipCPsych, PgDipLaw, JD; b. Johannesburg, South Africa, July 3, 1959; m. Esther née Koenigsberg; Rabbi, Lecturer (barrister/solicitor, non-practising); Rabbi, Hampstead Garden Suburb Synagogue (1999-); Programme Dir., Jewish Cultural Centre, Manchester (1983-85); Rabbi, Sale and District Hebrew Congregation (1985-88); Rabbi, Ilford Federation Synagogue (1988-99); Lecturer in Jewish and Comparative Law, Jews' College, London (1990-98); Corob Lecturer in Jewish Studies, Jews' College, London (1994-95). Publ: Contract in the Law of Obligations: A Comparative Analysis of Jewish Law and English Common Law (1994). Ad.: Hampstead Garden Suburb Synagogue, Norrice Lea, London N2 0RE.

LOBENSTEIN, Josef H., MBE; b. Hanover, Apr. 27, 1927; Mayor, London Borough of Hackney (1997-2001); Hon. Freeman L. B. Hackney; President, Adath Yisroel Syn. and Burial Soc.; Chairman, N. London Jewish Liaison Cttee.; Vice-President; Union of Orth. Hebrew Cong and Chairman External Affairs Cttee; Exec. Kedassia Kashruth Cttee.; Exec., Agudath Israel World Org.; V. Chairman, Agudath Israel of Great Britain; Mem. Ed. Bd., Jewish Tribune; Vice-President, National Shechita C.; Chairman, Bd. Gov. Yesode Hatorah Senior Girls' School; Gov., Avigdor Primary School, Craven Park Primary School, Bd. Gov, Homerton Univ. Hospital; President Hackney Conservative Assn.; form. Gen. Sec., Agudath Israel of Great Britain; Member, BoD; Tr. Jewish Secondary School Movement; Conservative Opposition Leader L. B. Hackney (1974-97); Councillor Metropolitan Borough of Stoke Newington (1962-65); Hon. President Hackney and Tower Hamlets Chamber of Commerce. Ad.: 27 Fairholt Rd., N16 5EW. ☎ 020-8800 4746. Fax 020-7502 0985.

LOEWE, Raphael James, MC, MA (Cantab), FSA; b. Calcutta, Apr. 16, 1919; m. Chloe née Klatzkin; form. Goldsmid Prof. of Hebrew (form. Dir., Instit. of Jewish Studies), Univ. Coll., Lond.; form. S. A. Cook Fellow, Caius Coll., Cambridge; form. Lect. in Hebrew, Leeds Univ.; Vis. Prof in Judaica, Brown Univ. Providence, R.I. (1963-64); form. P., C., JHSE; C., Soc. for Jew Study; form. P., C., BAJS; Seatonian Prize for Sacred Poem, Cambridge (2000); form. Elder and Warden, Span. & Port. Jews, Cong., London; War service, Suffolk Regt., Royal Armoured Corps. Publ.: Women in Judaism, Omar Khayyam (Hebr.), The Rylands Sephardi Haggadah, Ibn Gabirol, contr.ed., The North French Hebrew Miscellany

(2003), Isaac Ibn Sahula's 'Meshel Haqadmoni' (2004), etc. Ad.: 50 Gurney Dr., N2 0DE. ☎/Fax 020-8455 5379.

LUCAS, Mrs Stella (née Waldman), MBE, JP; b. London, July 30, 1916; V. President Jewish Care; Chairman, Stepney Girls' Club and Settlement; President, First Women's Lodge B'nai B'rith (1975-77), V. President Assn. of US Women; President, Dollis Hill Ladies, Guild; V. President (Chairman, 1978-84); Frs. of Hebrew Univ. (Women's Group); Exec. Off., Internat. C. of Jewish Women (1963-66); Chairman, Union of Jewish Women (1966-72); Chairman, Women Frs. of Jewis, Coll. (1957-66); Central Council for Jewish Soc. Services; BoD; Chairman, Brodie Instit.; Convenor BoD Central Enquiry Desk; Fdr. 'All Aboard Shops'. Ad.: 51 Wellington Ct., Wellington Rd., NW8 9TB. ☎ 020-7586 3030.

LYONS, Edward, QC, LLB, BA (Leeds); b. Glasgow, May 17, 1926, m. Barbara née Katz; Recorder (1972-98); MP (SDP) Bradford West (1981-83); MP (Lab.) Bradford West (1974-81); Bradford East (1966-74); Parl. Pr. Sec. Treasury (1969-70); Bencher Emer. Lincoln's Inn; Nat. Cttee., SDP (1984-89). Ad.: 4 Primley Park Lane, Leeds, LS17 7JR. ☎ 0113 2685351 and 59 Westminster Gardens, Marsham Street, SW1P 4JG. ☎ 020-7834 1960.

MAGONET, Rabbi Professor Dr Jonathan David, MB, BS, PhD (Heid.), FRSA; b. London, Aug. 2, 1942; form. Emeritus Professor of Bible, Princ., Leo Baeck Coll.; V. President, World Union for Progressive Judaism; Schalom Ben Chorim Prof. J. Studies, Univs Würzburg and Augsburg (2008);Guest Prof. Univ. Oldenburg (1999); Chairman, Yth Section, WUPJ (1964-66); Co-Editor European Judaism (1992-). Guest Prof., Univ. Lucerne (2004), Theologische Hochschule Wuppertal (2004). Publ.: Returning: Exercises in Repentance, Forms of Prayer, Vol. I, Daily and Sabbath (co-ed.); Vol. II, Pilgrim Festivals (co-ed.); Vol. III, Days of Awe Prayerbook (co-ed.); Form and Meaning – Studies in Literary Techniques in the Book of Jonah, Guide to the Here and Hereafter (co-ed.); A Rabbi Reads the Bible (2004); Bible Lives (1992); How To Get Up When Life Gets You Down (1993) (co-ed.); The Little Blue Book Of Prayer (1993) (co-ed.) (8th ed., 2008); A Rabbi Reads the Psalms (2004); Kindred Spirits (co-ed. 1995); Jewish Explorations of Sexuality (ed. 1995); The Subversive Bible (1997); The Explorer's Guide to Judaism (1998); Sun, Sand and Soul (co-ed. 1999); Abraham–Jesus–Mohammed: Interreligiöser Dialog aus Jüdischer Perspektiv (2000); From Autumn to Summer: A Biblical Journey through the Jewish Year (2000); Talking to the Other: Interfaith Dialogue with Christians and Muslims (2003); Einführung in Judentum (2004); Ad.: 22 Avenue Mansions, Finchley Road, London, NW3 7AX. ☎ 020-7209-0911.

MALITS, Rabbi Malcolm Henry, MBE, MA, D.Litt; b. Birmingham, Jan. 26, 1919; Emer. R.; M., Allerton Hebrew Cong. Liverpool (1964-90); Chaplain Ajex; (Masonic), Past Prov. Grand Chap. for West Lancashire. Ad.: 12 Glenside, Liverpool L18 9UJ. ☎ 0151-724 1967.

MARCUS, Rabbi Barry, BA (Hons), PGCE; b. Cape Town, Oct. 28, 1949; Rabbi, Central Synagogue (1995-); Tr., Holocaust Memorial Day Trust (2004-); Tr., Yad Vashem UK (2005-); pioneer of the one-day educational visit to Auschwitz-Birkenau scheme. Publ. Father and Son (1986); You Are Witnesses (1999). Ad.: 40 Hallam St., London W1W 6NW. ☎ 020-7580 1355; Fax 020-7636 3831. Email bmarcus@brijnet.org

MARCUS, Daniel, b. London, July 9, 1973; m Deborah née Saville; Chief Executive UJS Hillel (2007-); form. Exec. Director, John Hopkins University Hillel (2005-07), Ad.: 1-2, Endsleigh Street, London WC1H 0DS ☎ 020- 7388 0801, Fax 020-7380 6599, Email danielm@ujshillel.co,uk.

MARCUS, Mark Hyman, BA (Com); b. Manchester, Feb. 22, 1933; Chairman B'nai B'rith London Bureau of Int. Affairs; form. Exec. Dir., B'nai B'rith UK (1984-98); Dir. Provincial & London Divisions, JIA. Ad.: B'nai B'rith UK, ORT House, 126, Albert St., London NW1 7NE.

MARGOLYES, Miriam, BA (Cantab), LGSM&D; b. Oxford, May 18, 1941; Actress. Ad.: c/o Jonathan Altaras Associates Ltd, 2 Goodwins Court, WC2N 4LL. ☎ 020-7497 8878. Fax 020-7497 8876.

MARINER, Rabbi Rodney John, BA (Hons), Dip. Ed.; b. Melbourne, Australia, May 29, 1941; m. Susan; M., Belsize Sq. Syn.; Convener, Beth Din, Reform Judaism; Assoc. M., Edgware & Distr. Ref. Syn. (1979-82); Asst. M., North Western Ref Syn. (1976-79). Publ.: Prayers For All The Year: Part 1, Shabbat; Part 2, Festivals; Part 3, New Year; Part 4, Atonement; Part 5,

Evening Prayers. Ad.: 92 North Road, London N6 4AA.

MARKS, John Henry, MD, FRCGP, DObst, RCOG; b. London, May 30, 1925; m. Shirley, née Nathan; Chairman, C. BMA (1984-90); Chairman, Rep. Body BMA (1981-84); Gen. Med. C. (1979-84, 1989-94); V. President, Lond. Jewish Med. Soc. (1983-84, 1999-2000). Publ.: The Conference of Local Medical Committees and its Executive: An Historical Review; The NHS: Beginning, Middle and End? Ad.: 62 Eyre Court, Finchley Rd., London NW8 9TU. ☎ 0781 350 1711. Email johnhenrymarks@btinternet.com

MARKS, Shula Eta (née Winokur), OBE, FBA, BA (UCT), PhD (London), Hon. DLitt (UCT), Hon. D.Soc.Sci. (Natal), Distinguished Africanist Award, African Studies Assoc. (UK) (2002); Hon. Senior Res. Fell. SAS, London; Hon. Fellow, SOAS (2005-); Hon. Prof., UCT (2005-); b. Cape Town, Oct. 14, 1936; m. Isaac Meyer Marks; Historian; Emer. Prof. History of Southern Africa, SOAS (2001-), Prof. (1993-2001); Dir. Institute of Commonwealth Studies, Univ. of London (1983-93); Lecturer and Reader, History of Southern Africa, Jointly SOAS and ICS (1963-83); Mem. Arts and Humanities Research Bd. (1998-2000); Chair, Council for Assisting Refugee Academics, (CARA) (1993-2004); Chair International Records Management Tr. (1995-2004); Publ.: Reluctant Rebellion: The 1906-1908 Disturbances in Natal (1970); The Ambiguities of Dependence in South Africa (1986); Not Either an Experimental Doll: The Separate Lives of Three South African Women (1987); Divided Sisterhood: Class, Race and Gender in the South African Nursing Profession (1994). Ad.: Email shulamarks@yahoo.co.uk.

MARMUR, Rabbi Dow, b. Sosnowiec, Poland, Feb. 24, 1935; Rabbi-Emer., Holy Blossom Temple, Toronto; form. President, Toronto Board of Rabbis; form. Chairman, C. of Reform and Lib. Rabbis; M., North Western Reform Syn. (1969-83); South-West Essex Reform Syn. (1962-69). Publ.: Beyond Survival; The Star of Return; Walking Toward Elijah; On being a Jew; Six Lives: a Memoir; Reform Judaism (Edr.); A Genuine Search (Edr.); Choose Life. Ad.: 1950 Bathurst St., Toronto, Ontario, M5P 3K9, Canada. ☎ (416) 789 3291. Fax (416) 789 9697.

MASSIL, Stephen W., BA, Dip. Lib, FLA, FRAS; b. Eynsham, Oxon, Sept. 21, 1941; m. Brenda Goldstein; Librarian; posts at the University of Birmingham (1966-77), London University (1977-96), Cambridge (1996-2000), Warburg Institute (1999/2002), University College London (2002-03), Huguenot Society of Great Britain and Ireland (1997-2002); Sir John Soane's Museum (2002-06); National Trust (2006-); Garrick Club (2006-); consultant for Unesco, the British Council and other international organisations; Vice President (2006-), President, JHSE (2004-06), Member of Council (1985-); Editor, Jewish Year Book (JC 1989-93, Vallentine Mitchell, 1994-); Editor, Jewish Travel Guide (1991-94); Convenor, Hebraica Libraries Group (1991-2007); Member, Jewish Book Council, Tr., Jewish Literary Trust, Editor, Jewish Book News & Reviews (1986-); Member, Oxford Food Symposium; Young Jewish Leadership Institute (1978-81). Publ.: Facsimile edition of 'Jewish Year Book, 1896' (ed.); Anglo-Jewish Bibliography, 1971-90 (co-ed.; 1992); articles and conference papers on library history, bibliography, consultancy reports for Unesco and the British Council. Ad.: JHSE, 33 Seymour Place, London W1H 5AP.

MAY, Michael, MSc (econ.); b. Jerusalem, Dec. 16, 1945; Exec. Director, European Council of Jewish Communities; Form. Dir., Institute of Jewish Affairs, London; Dir. Jewish Film Fdn.; form. Assoc. Ed., J. Quarterly; Member BoD Foreign Affairs Cttee.; Member Adv. C., STIBA (Dutch) Foundation for the Fight Against Anti-Semitism; Member Adv. Bd., Intern. Centre for Holocaust Studies, NY; former Dir. Jewish Book Council; Member Gov. Bd., World Jewish Congress (1983-91); Dir., Jewish Literary Trust (1984-91); Co-Fdr. & Tr. Limmud Conf. (1980-84). Ad.: 74 Gloucester Place, W1H 3HN. ☎ 020-7224 3445. Fax 020-7224 3446. Email ecjc@ort.org.

MAYER, Daniel, b. Paris, April 29, 1909; Member (President, 1983) French Constitutional C.; form. M. of Labour, War-time Member of C.N.R. (Resistance Nat. C.); Deputy for Seine; Sec.-Gen.; Socialist Party, S.F.I.O.; President, Internat. Fedn. of Human Rights; Conseil Supérieur de la Magistrature; President, Ligue des Droits de l'Homme. Ad.: Conseil Constitutionnel, 2 rue de Montpensier, Paris, 1e.

MEHDI, Sion, b. Jersualem, July 14, 1932; form. Officer of commmunal organisations. Ad: 3/17 Nitza Boulevard, Netanya 42262. ☎/Fax (09) 8336320. Email sionmehdi@yahoo.co.uk.

MENDELSOHN, Jon, b. London, Dec. 30, 1966; m. Nicola née Clyne; Company Director;

Chairman, Labour Friends of Israel (2002-07). Ad.: LLM Communications, Holborn Gate, 26 Southampton Buildings, London WC2A 1PB.

MICHAELS, Leslie David, FCA, MBA; b. London, July 14, 1943; m. Lesley née Stern; Dir. Time Products Ltd; Tr. Cecil Roth Memorial Tr.; Chairman, NorthWestern Ref. Syn., Israel Support Gp., NWRS Council M.; form. Chairman Ben Uri Art Gallery and Society. Ad.: 34, Dover St., London W15 4NG. ☎ 020-7343 7215. Email lmichaels@timeproducts.co.uk.

MICHAELS, Rabbi Maurice Arnold, MA; b. Woolmer's Park, Herts., Aug. 31, 1941; Sen. Rabbi, South West Essex and Settlement Reform Syn.; Hon. Life Vice-President LBC-CJE; Chair Tr. Ahada Bereavement Counselling. Tr. Empathy Counselling; Dir. Refugee and Migrant Forum of East London; Man. Cttee Redbridge Faith Forum (2002-), Previous: Chairman and V. President, RSGB; Chairman, Leo Baeck Coll.; Chairman, S. W. Essex Reform Syn.; Chairman, Assembly of Reform Rabbis; Chairman, Redbridge Business Educ. Partnership; Gov. of Redbridge Coll.; Gov. of Akiva School; Gov. of Jewish Joint Bur. Soc.; Tr., Redbridge Racial Equality Council; Tr., Limmud; Member, World Union for Progressive Judaism Gov. Body; Chairman Govs, Clore Tikva School; Member, Redbridge Jewish Community Cttee; Council Member, Redbridge Campaign Against Racism and Fascism; Dir., Harlow Enterprise Agency; Man. Cttee., West Essex Business Educ. Partnership; V. Chairman, Harlow & Dist. Employers' Group; Member, BoD; Member, Nat. Council Zionist Fed.; Member, Nat. Council Soviet Jewry. Ad.: 18 Exeter Gardens, Ilford, Essex IG1 3LA. ☎ 020-8554 2812. Email ramaby@ntlworld.com.

MIDDLEBURGH, Rabbi Charles H., BA Hons, PhD, FRSA; b. Hove, Oct. 2, 1956; Rabbi, Cardiff Ref. Syn. (2005-); Dublin Jewish Progressive Cong.(2002-), Progressive Jewish Forum, Copenhagen (2002-05); Minister, Kingston Liberal Synagogue (1977-83); Rabbi, Harrow and Wembley Progressive Synagogue (1983-97); Exec. Dir. Union of Liberal and Progressive Synagogues (1997-2002); Sen. Lect. Rabbinics, Leo Baeck Coll. (2004-); Lect. Aramaic, Practical Rabbinics (2002-); Assoc. Ed. Siddur Lev Chadash (1989-95); Co-Ed., Mahzor Ruach Chadashah (1996-); Chairman, ULPS Rabbinic Conference (1988-90, 1993-95); Lect. and Principal, ULPS Evening Institute (1980-92); Lect. Aramaic, Bible, Practical Rabbinics, Leo Baeck College (1985-2001); Fell. Zoological Soc., London; Publ.: Mishnah Parshanut (2003). Tefillot ve-Tachanunim (with A. Goldstein, 2006). Ad.: Leo Baeck Coll., 80 East End Rd., London N3 2SY. ☎ 020-8349-5615.

MILLER, Jonathan Moss, BSc (Hons), ARCS, PGCE, MA, NPQH; m. Hannah née Babad. Headteacher, JFS (2008-). Ad.: JFS, The Mall, Kenton, Harrow, Middx. HA3 9TE ☎ 020 8206 3100. Fax 020 8206 3101 Email admin@jfs.brent,sch.uk

MILLER, Maurice Solomon, MBChB, JP; b. Glasgow, Aug. 16, 1920; Med. practitioner; MP (Lab.) for East Kilbride (1974-87); MP for Kelvingrove (Glasgow) (1964-74), form. H.Sec., Lab. Frs. of Israel, Parl. Br. Publ.: Window on Russia. Ad.:

MILLETT, The Rt. Hon. The Lord Millett, Baron Millett of St. Marylebone, PC, MA (Cantab), Hon. DLL (Univ. London); b. London, June 23, 1932; Non-Permanent Judge, Court of Final Appeal, Hong Kong (2000-); Lord of Appeal in Ordinary (1998-2004); Member, Court of Appeal (1994-98); Judge of the High Court Chancery Div. (1986-94); QC (1973-86), Member, Insolvency Law Review Cttee. (1976-82); Stndg. Jr. Counsel, Trade & Industry Dept. (1967-73); Bencher, Lincoln's Inn, Called to Bar, Middle Temple; form. Chairman, Lewis Hammerson Home (1981-1991); President, West London Syn. (1991-95); Hon. Fel. Trinity Hall (1994); Tr. Lincoln's Inn (2004); Publ.: (contrib.) Halsbury's Law of England; Ed-in-Chief: Encyclopaedia of Forms and Precedents. Ad.: 18 Portman Cl., W1H 6BR. ☎ 020-7935 1152.

MILSTON, Michael, BA (Lond.); b. June 7, 1949; m. Helen Esther née Moss; Freelance journalist; Radio Producer, Tikkun Spectrum; Lecturer and Principal, Lingua Franca, English as a Foreign Language School; Lecturer, Yakar Kehilla; Chairman, Friends of East London Orthodox Association of Synagogues (2001-). Publ.: A Critical Review (2nd Ed. 2003). Ad.: 6, Elmfield House, 77, Carlton Hill, London NW8 9XB ☎/Fax 020 7624 8183.

MIRVIS, Rabbi Ephraim Yitzchak, BA: b. Johannesburg, Sept. 7, 1956; Rabbi Finchley Synagogue (1996-); Chairman Rabbinical Council of the US (1999-2002); Member, Chief Rabbi's Cabinet; Edr. Daf Hashavua; Member St. Cttee of Conference of European Rabbis; Religious Adv. to the Jewish Marriage Council; Dir. Kinloss Learning Centre. M. Western Marble Arch Syn. (1992-96); form. Chief Rabbi, Jewish Coms. of Ireland (1984-92); M.

Dublin Hebrew Cong. (1982-84); Lect. Machon Meir, Jerusalem (1980-82). Ad.: 69 Lichfield Grove, London N3 2JJ. ☎/Fax 020-8346 3773. Email mirvis@mirvis.homechoice.co.uk.

MITCHELL, Lord Parry Andrew, (Baron Mitchell of Hampstead), B.Sc. (Lond.), MBA (Columbia); b. London, May 6, 1943; m. Hannah née Lowy; Chairman Weizmann UK; Chairman eLearning Foundation; Mem. House of Lords Select Cttee for Science and Technology. Ad.: House of Lords, London SW1A 0PW. ☎ 020-7433 3238. Email parrym@mac.com

MOCKTON, Rev. Leslie, b. Manchester Aug. 5, 1928; retired M., Waltham Forest Hebrew Cong.; Mayor's Chaplain, Lond. Borough Waltham Forest (1981-82); Hospital Chaplain Forest. Health Care Trust (1992-96); Ministered to the communities at Highams Pk. & Chingford Syn., Bradford Hebrew Cong., West End Gt. Synagogue, and Barking & Becontree Hebrew Congregation. Ad.: 36 Halleswelle Rd., London NW11 0DJ. ☎ 020-8458 1204.

MONTAGUE, Lee, b. Bow, London, Oct. 16, 1927; Actor; many leading roles including Shakespeare and Chekhov, title-role Leon in The Workshop, Raymond Chandler in Private Dick, O'Connor in Cause Célèbre (London 1977), Ed in Entertaining Mr. Sloane (New York 1965); Court in the Act (London 1987); films include Moulin Rouge, Mahler, Brass Target, London Affair, Silver Dream Racer, Lady Jane, Madame Sousatzka, Enigma; Television appearances include Holocaust, Thank You Comrades, Tussy Marx, Parsons Pleasure, The Workshop, Passing Through, Sharing Time, Kim, Dr. Sakharov, Bird of Prey, Much Ado About Nothing, Countdown to War, Incident in Judaea, House of Elliott, Casualty, Waking the Dead. Best TV Actor of the Year 1960. Ad.: c/o Joyce Edwards, 4, Turner Close, London SW9 6UQ.

MONTEFIORE, Alan Claude Robin Goldsmid, MA (Oxon); b. London Dec. 29, 1926; Emer. Fellow, form. Fellow and Tutor in Philosophy, Balliol College, Oxford; Vis. Prof. Middlesex Univ.; form. Sr. Lect. in Moral & Political Philosophy, Keele Univ.; Jt. President, Wiener Libr.; President Forum for European Philosophy. Publ.: A Modern Introduction to Moral Philosophy, British Analytic Philosophy (co-ed.), Neutrality and Impartiality, The University and Political Commitment (ed.), French Philosophy Today (ed.), Goals, No-Goals and Own Goals: A Debate on Goal Directed and Intentional Behaviour (co-ed.), The Political Responsibility of Intellectuals (co-ed.), Integrity in the Public and Private Domains (co-ed.), etc. Ad.: 34 Scarsdale Villas, W8 6PR. ☎ 020-7937 7708. Fax 020-7938 4257.

MONTY, Mrs Regina Joy (née Dixon); b. London, Sept. 19, 1935; Hon. President Wizo.UK (FWZ); form. Chairman, V. Chairman and Membership Chairman, WIZO UK. Ad.: c/o 107 Gloucester Pl., W1U 6BY, Please Forward

MOONMAN, Eric, OBE; b. Liverpool, Apr. 29, 1929; m. Gillian Louise née Mayer; Adv. ITN/IRN Counter-Terrorism; President Zionist Federation (2001-); M.P. (Lab.) for Basildon (1974-79), for Billericay (1966-70); Chair, Friends Natural History Museum (2007-); Chair, ERG Group of Radio Stations (1991-2002); V. President, BoD (1994-2000); Sr. V. President, BoD (1985-91); Chairman, Media Network; Chairman City of Liverpool Continuing Care Cttee (1996-); Prof Health Management, City Univ., London; Chairman, Academic Response to Racism & Antisemitism (1994-); Bd. Memb. IRC, Potomac Inst. for Policy Studies; Consultant, ICRC (Africa) (1992-95); Director Natural History Museum Development Trust (1989-91); (seconded) Chairman, WJC Europe Br. Cttee. on Antisemitism (1985-92, 1998-2002); Chairman Community Research Unit, (1985-96); Chairman, Z. Fed. (1975-80); President, Friends of Union of Jewish Students; Co.-Chairman, Nat. Jewish Solidarity Cttee. (1975-79); form. Parl. Pte. Sec. to Sec. of State for Educ. and Science; form. Sr. Res. Fel., Manch. Univ.; form. Leader, Stepney Borough C.; Sr. Adv., Brit. Instit. of Management (1956-62); European Adv. WJC (1973-76); Chairman, Nat. Aliyah and Volunteers C. (1975-99); Chairman, P.R. Cttee., Z.F. (1983-85, 1972-75); Trustee, Balfour Tr.; CRE Award for Multi - Racial Service (1996). Publ.: Learning to Live with the Violent Society (2004), The Alternative Government, The Manager and the Organisation, Reluctant Partnership, European Science and Technology, etc. Ad.:1 Beacon Hill, N7 9LY.

MORGAN, Rabbi Fred; b. New York City, March 18, 1948, m. Susan Sinclair; Sen. M. Temple Beth Israel, Melbourne, Australia; Chairman, C. Progressive Rabbis of Australia & N.Z. (2000-03); Hon. Assoc. Rabbi Sim Shalom Jewish Community Budapest; M. North West Surrey Synagogue (1984-97); Lect. in Midrash and Jewish Thought Leo Baeck Rabbinical

College (1987-97); V.-Chairman Assembly of Reform Rabbis (1996-97); Lect. in Judaism, Roehampton Institute (1989-92); Lect. in Religious Studies, Univ. of Bristol (1973-79); Vis. Prof. Eotvos Lorand Univ., Budapest (1992-94). Ad.: Temple Beth Israel, 76-82 Alma Road, St Kilda 3182, Victoria, Australia. ☎ 61-3-9510 1488. Fax 61-3-9521 1229. Email rabbi.fred.morgan@tbi.org.au.

MORRIS, Henry, b. London Mar. 5, 1921; Curator, Jewish Military Museum; form. Chairman, Jewish Defence & Group Rel Cttee., J. BoD; V. President (Nat.Chairman 1979-81) Ajex. Publ.: We Will Remember Them (1989 and Addendum 1994); The AJEX Chronicles: A History of the Association (2000). Ad.: 4 Ashbrook, Stonegrove, Edgware, Middx HA8 7SU. ☎ 020-8958 7154.

MORRIS, Simon, BA Hons Sociology and Applied Social Studies, MBA (Henley/Brunel) b. June 4, 1960; m. Lucille née Balcombe; Chief Exec. Jewish Care; form. Dir. of Community Services, Jewish Care (1999-2003); Assist. Dir. Community Services, Jewish Care (1996-99); London Borough of Hounslow; (1996-98); Commissions Manager Adult Services (1994-96). Team Manager Community (1988-94). Ad: Jewish Care, Merit House, The Hyde, 508 Edgware Rd., London NW9 5AB ☎ 020 8922 2000. Fax 020 8922 1998. Email: smorris @jcare.org.

MORRIS OF KENWOOD, Lady Ruth (née Janner); b. London, Sept. 21, 1932; Solicitor; President, Nat. Cttee., Va'ad Lema'an Habonim; Dir. Connaught Brown plc., H. Solicitor, various youth orgs.; form. Dir., WOYL; Tr. Jewish Youth Fund; Tr. Brady Maccabi; Tr. Elsie & Barnett Janner Charitable Tr.; form. Man., Brady Girls' Club; form. exec. Member, Victoria Boys' and Girls' Club; form. Tr. Victim Support, London. Ad.: 35 Fitzjohn's Ave., London NW3 5JY. ☎ 020-7431 6332.

MOSER, Lord, KCB, CBE, FBA, BSc (Econ), Hon. D. (Southampton, Leeds, Surrey, Sussex, York, Keele, City, Wales, Edinburgh, Liverpool London, Brunel, Brighton, Hull, Heriot-Watt, Northumbria, South Bank Univs); b. Berlin, Nov. 24, 1922; Chancellor, Keele Univ. (1986-2002); Tr. British Museum (1988-2002); Chairman British Museum Dev. Trust (1994-2004); Chancellor Open University Israel (1994-2004), Hon. Fellow; Warden, Wadham Coll., Oxford (1984-93); Chairman, Askones Holt Ltd. (1990-2002); Chairman Basic Skills Agency (1998-2002); Dir., V. Chairman, CBF-WJR. Publ.: Writings on statistics. Ad.: 3 Regent's Park Tce., NW1 7EE. ☎ 020-7485 1619.

NAGLER, Neville Anthony, MA (Cantab); b. London, Jan. 2, 1945; m. Judy née Mordant; Dir. Sternberg Fd.; Interfaith Consult., Vice-Chairman Inter Faith Network; form. Dir. Gen. BoD (1991-2005); Exec. Cttee, form. Certificate in Public Services Management (2000); form. Asst. Sec. Home Office (1980-91); UK Representative to UN Narcotics Comm., (1983-88); Chairman, Council of Europe Drug Co-op Group (1984-88); Haldane Essay Prize (1979); Princ. H.M. Treasury; Pte. Sec. Chancellor of Exchequer (1971); Fin. Rep. and Warden, Pinner Syn. (1979-91). Ad.: Star House, 124, Grafton Rd., London NW5 4BA. ☎ 020 -7485 2538. Email nnagler@sternberg-foundation.co.uk.

NATHAN, Clemens Neumann, CTexFTI, FRAI, Officers' Cross, Austria; Cavalieri, al Merito della Repub. Italiana; b. Hamburg, Aug. 24, 1933; Comp. Dir., P. (T., 1965-71) Anglo-Jewish Assn.; V. President (President 1983-89); Jt. Chairman Consultant C. of Jewish Orgs. (Non-Govt. Org. at United Nations); form. Chairman, Centre for Christian–Jewish Studies, Cambridge (1998-2004), Hon. Fell., Member of the Bd.; Claims Conf, Memorial Foundation for Jewish Culture; Mem, Jewish Memorial C.; Hon. Fell. Shenkar Coll., Israel; V. President, Centre for German-Jewish Studies, Sussex; Hon. Fell. SSEES, Univ. London; Director Sephardi Centre; CCJ, Fdr. Member, Internat. Cttee. for Human Rights in Soviet Union (1966); BoD (1979-85); Soc. of Heshaim, Span. & Port. Jews, Cong., Lond. (1979-), Bd. of Elders (1977-83); Chairman, Sha'are Tikva Cttee. (1975-81); form. V. President, Textile Instit.; Textile Institute Medal for services to the Industry and Institute; Companionship of the Textile Inst. (2007). Publ.: Technological and marketing works. Ad.: Flat 10, 3 Cambridge Terrace, London NW1 4JL. ☎ 020-7034 1980.

NAVON, Yitzhak, b. Jerusalem, April 9, 1921; form. Israeli Dep. Prime Min. and Educ & Culture Min.; Fifth President, State of Israel (1978-83); Member, Knesset (1965-78; since 1984); Chairman, Neot Kedumim; Chairman, Jerusalem Academy for Music and Dance;

Chairman, Nat. Authority for Ladino Culture; form. Chairman, Knesset Foreign Affairs and Defence Cttee.; Dir., Office of Prime Minister (Ben-Gurion) (1952-63); form. Chairman, World Zionist Council. Publ.: Bustan Sephardi, Six Days and Seven Gates. Ad.: 31 Haneviim St., Jerusalem.

NETANYAHU, Binyamin, BSc, MBA; b. Tel Aviv, Oct. 21, 1949; m. Sarah; Businessman, Diplomat; Ambassador to the UN (1984-88); entered the Knesset in 1988; Leader of Likud (1993-99); Prime Minister (1996-99); Foreign Minister (2002-03); Finance Minister (2003-05); Leader of Likud (2005-) and Leader of the Opposition (2006-). Publ.: A Durable Peace: Israel and Its Place Among the Nations (2000). Ad.: Knesset.

NEUBERGER, Rabbi Dame Julia Babette Sarah (née Schwab), Baroness, DBE, MA (Cantab), Hon. Doctorates Univ. Humberside, Ulster, City, Stirling, Oxford Brookes, Teesside, Nottingham, Open U., Queens Belfast, Sheffield Hallam, Aberdeen, Liverpool, London; b. London, Feb. 27, 1950, m. Anthony; Tr. Imperial War Museum (1999-2006); Civil Service Commissioner (2001-2); Hon. Fell. Royal Coll. Phys. (2004); Hon. Fell City & Guilds, FRC Psych, FRCGPs (2006-); Tr. Jewish Care (2005-07); Tr. Booker Prize Foundation (2003-); Vis. Prof. Bloomberg Chair, Harvard (2006); Mem., Cttee on Standards in Public Life (Wicks Committee 2001-04); Mem. Cttee to Review Funding of the BBC (1999); Chancellor Univ. Ulster (1994-2000); Chief Exec. The King's Fund (1997-2004); Council Mem. Save the Children Fund (1994-98); Mem. General Medical Council (1993-2000); Mem. Medical Res. C. (1995-2000); Lect., Leo Baeck Coll.; Harkness Fel. Harvard University (1991-92); Mem. Human Fertilisation and Embryology Authority (1990-95); T., Runnymede Trust (1990-97); Rabbi, S. Lond. Lib. Syn. (1977-89); Presenter, Choices, BBC-1 (1986-87); Hon. Fellow, Roy Coll. Physicians; Hon. Fell. Royal College GPs, Royal College Psychiatrists. Publ.: Women in Judaism: The Fact and the Fiction (in Women's Religious Experience, ed. Pat Holden); The Story of Judaism (for children); Judaism (in Spiritual Care in Nursing, ed. McGilloway and Myco); Days of Decision, Vols. I-IV (ed.); Women's Policy, Defence and Disarmament; Bill of Rights and Freedom of Information; Privatisation; Caring for Dying Patients of Different Faiths (3rd ed. 2004); ed. (with Canon John White), A Necessary End (1991); Whatever's Happening to Women (1991); Ethics and Healthcare: The role of research ethics committees in the UK (Kings's Fund 1992); (ed.) The Things that Matter (1993); On Being Jewish (1995); Dying Well: A Guide to Enabling a Good Death (2nd ed. 2004); Hidden Assets: Decision Making in the NHS (jt. ed., 2002); The Moral State We're In (2005); Not Dead Yet: a Manifesto for Old Age (2008). Ad.: House of Lords, London SW1. ☎/Fax 01206 503130.

NEWMAN, Aubrey Norris, MA (Glasgow), MA, D.Phil (Oxon), FRHistS; b. London, Dec. 14, 1927; m. Bernice Freda née Gould; Prof. (Emeritus) of History, Leicester Univ.; President, Jewish Hist. Soc. (1977-79, 1992-93). Publ.: The United Synagogue, 1870-1970 (1977); The History of the Board of Deputies (1985); The Stanhopes of Chevening (1970); The Parliamentary Diary of Sir Edward Knatchbull (1966); The Holocaust (2002); (ed.) Migration and Settlement (1971); (ed.) Provincial Jewry in Victorian Britain (1975); (ed.) The Jewish East End, 1840-1939 (1981); (joint ed.) Patterns of Migration, 1850-1914 (1996). Ad.: 33 Stanley Road, Stoneygate, Leicester, LE2 1RF. ☎ (0116) 270 4065 (home), (0116) 252 2802 (university). Fax. (0116) 252 3986. Email new@leicester.ac.uk.

NEWMAN, Eddy, b. Liverpool, May 14, 1953. Manchester City Councillor (1979-85, 2002-); Chair, Willow Park Housing Tr.; Labour MEP for Greater Manchester Central (1984-99); Member of the European Parliament's Delegation for Relations with Israel and the Knesset (1994-99); V. Chairman, European Parliament Regional Policy ad Regional Planning Cttee (1984-87); Chairman, European Parliament Cttee on Petitions (1994-97); V. Chairman, Cttee on Petitions (1997-99). Publ.: Respect for Human Rights in the European Union', a report of the European Parliament Committee on Civil Liberties, 1994; Contributor to 'The European Ombudsmen' (2005). Ad.: 234 Ryebank Rd., Manchester M21 9LU. ☎ 0161-881 9641.

NEWMAN, Rabbi Isaac, MPhil, PGCE, Dip. Counselling; b. London, Apr. 3, 1924; form. Chairman, Rabbis for Human Rights (Israel); M. Retd., Barnet Syn.; Sr. Lect., Judaica, & Chaplain, Middlesex Polytechnic, Trent Park; form. H.Sec., Rabbinical C., United Synagogue; Chaplain to

RAF Publ.: Talmudic Discipleship. Ad.: 90 Sderot Herzl, Jerusalem. ☎ 02 6525763.

NEWMAN, Rabbi Jeffrey, MA (Oxon.); b. Reading, Dec. 26 1941; m. Bracha; Rabbinic Adv. to Rabbinic Dev. Fd.; Emeritus, form Rabbi, Finchley Reform Synagogue (1973-2001); Dir. Eaith Charter UK; form. Chairman Rabbinic In-service training, Leo Baeck Rabbinical College (LBC); form. Chairman, Pastoral Skills and Counselling Department LBC; Chairman of Tr. Israel Palestine Centre for Research and Information; Ed. Living Judaism (1969-73); Lect. in Heimler Training; contributor to various journals on Judaism, psychology and spirituality. Ad.: 46, Torrington Park, London N12 9TP. Email jeffrey@jnewman.org.uk.

NEWMAN, Dr Joanna Frances, BA (Hons), MA in Jewish History (UCL), PhD (Southampton); b. London; m. Uwe Westphal; Civil servant; Higher Ed., Strategic Partnerships Hd., British Library (2007-); Hon. Sec., JHSE (2007-); Board Mem. Artsdepot; Bd, Dir JPR; Exec. Director, Arts & Education, London Jewish Cultural Centre (2002-2006); Vice Chair, Centre for German-Jewish Studies, Univ. Sussex; Hon. Fell., Univ. Southampton; Postdoctoral Fellowship, Insitute of Commonwealth Studies; Mem. C., Wiener Library; Parkes Fellowship (Southampton). Mem. Editorial Bd., Jewish Renaissance. Publ.: (Ed., with Toby Haggith) Holocaust and the Moving Image: Representation in Film and Television Since 1993 (2005). Ad.: The British Library, 96 Euston Rd., London NW1 2DB. Email joanna.newman@bl.uk.

NEWMAN, Lotte Therese, CBE, MB, BS, LRCP, MRCS, FRCGP FRNZCGP; b. Frankfurt am Main, Jan. 22, 1929; m. Norman Aronsohn; General practitioner; Mem. GMC (1984-98); Chairman, Registration Committee, General Medical Council (1997-98); Gov. PPP Medical Trust (1996-99); President, London Jewish Medical Society (1998-99); President Royal College General Practitioners (1994-97); Freeman, City of London; Mem. Hampstead Synagogue Bd of Management (1999-2005); Mem. BoD (1999-05); Mem. Defence Group Relations Cttee and Chairman of Circumcision Working Group (1999-2005); Medical Adv. St John Ambulance (1999-2003). Publ.: Papers on Medicine, health and medical training issues especially relating to women doctors, and 'medicine and the Jews'. Ad.: The White House, 1 Ardwick Rd., London NW2 2BX. ☎ 020-7436 6630. Fax 020-7435 6672. Email JH44@dial.pipex.com.

NEWMARK, Brooks Philip Victor, MP, b. Norwalk, Ct., May 8, 1958; m. Lucy née Keegan; Businessman; Partner, Apollo LP; MP (Cons.), for Braintree (2005-); M. Science and Technology Sect Cttee (2005-), M. Treasury Sect Cttee (2006-); Co-Chairman, Conservative Party 'Women2Win' (2005-); Chairman, Southwark and Bermondsey Conservative Assoc. (1990-93). Publ.: Direct Democracy: an Agenda for a New Model Party (2005). Ad.; House of Commons, London SW1A 0AA;. Email newmarkb@parliament.uk. Website www.brooksnewmark.com

NEWMARK, Jeremy, MCIPR; b. Hertfordshire, Sept. 19, 1972; m. Hilary née Cawson; Chief Executive, Jewish Leadership Council (2006-); Man. C. Fair Play Campaign Gp.; Jt. Head, Stop the Boycott; Chair 'Salute to Israel' Group (2008-); Mem. Bd. Directors, European Institute for the Study of Antisemitism (2007-); Dir. Antisemitism Coordination Unit (2004-06); Director of Communications, Office of the Chief Rabbi (1999-2004); International Affairs Officer, BoD (1997-99); Chief Media Officer, Israel 50 (UK) (1999); Campaign Organiser, UJS (1995-96) Former Trustee, Anglo-Israel Assoc.; Former Man. C., Searchlight Education Tr. Ad.: JLC, 6, Bloomsbury Square, London WC1A 2LP. ☎ 020-7242 9734; Fax 020-7099 5897; Email jn@thejlc.org.

OLMERT, Ehud, BA, LL.B.; b. Binyamina, Sept. 30, 1945; m. Alisa; Lawyer; entered Knesset 1973; former treasurer of Likud; Mayor of Jerusalem (1993-2003); Chairman of Kadima, Acting Prime-Minister, Jan-April 2006; Prime Minister (2006-08). Ad.: Knesset.

OPPENHEIM, Jeremy, b. June 6, 1955; m. Karen née Tanner; form. Chief Exec. Jewish Care (2000-03); form. Dir. Social Services, London Borough of Hackney (1997-99); Hd. Children's Services, London Borough of Barking and Dagenham (1993-97); London Borough of Haringey: Service Man., Child Care (1989-93), Team Man. (1986-89), Social Worker (1983-86); Senior Social Worker, Jewish Welfare Board (1980-83); Social Worker, Jewish Welfare Board (1977-79). Ad.:

OPPENHEIM-BARNES, Baroness of Gloucester (Life Peer) (Sally), PC; b. Dublin, July 1930; Mem. Shadow Cabinet (1974-79); MP (Conservative) for Gloucester (1970-87);

form. Chairman, Conservative Party Parl. Prices and Consumer Protection Cttee.; form Nat. V. President, Nat. Union of Townswomen's Guilds; form. Nat. V. President, ROSPA; Chairman, Nat. Consumer C. (1987-89); Dir. (non-exec.) Robert Fleming (1989-97); Non-Exec. Director. HFC Bank (1989-98); Minister of State, Consumer Affairs (1979-83); Non-Exec. Dir. Boots (1983-94). Ad.: House of Lords.

OPPENHEIMER, Peter Morris, MA; b. London, Apr 16, 1938; President, Oxford Centre for Hebrew and Jewish Studies (2000-08); Student (Fel.) Emer, Christ Church Oxford; Director, Jewish Chronicle Ltd (1986-2006), Chairman (2001-04); Dir. Dixons plc (1987-93); Delbanco, Meyer & Co. Ltd. (1987-2001); Chief Economist, Shell Internat. Petroleum Co. (1985-86). Ad.: Christ Church, Oxford OX1 1DP. ☎ 01865 558226. Fax 01865-516834.

ORGEL, Leslie Eleazer, DPhil, FRS; b. London, Jan 12, 1927; m. Hassia Alice née Levinson; Sr. Fellow & Res. Prof., Salk Instit. and Adjunct Prof., Univ. of California, San Diego; Member Nat Acad. Sci., form. Fellow of Peterhouse, Cambridge Univ. Publ.: Scientific work. Ad.: The Salk Institute, 10010 North Torrey Pines Road, La Jolla, CA 92037-1099, USA. ☎ 858-453 4100, ext 1321. Fax 858-550 9959. Email orgel@salk.edu.

ORLINSKY, Harry M., BA, PhD; b. Owen Sound, Ont., Can, Mar 14, 1908; Prof. of Bible. HUC-JIR, New York (since 1943); Ed., Library of Biblical Studies, President, Soc. of Biblical Lit. (1969-70); Centennial Award for Biblical Scholarship; President, Amer. Friends of Israel Exploration Soc. (1951-79); President, Internat. Org. for Masoretic Studies; President, Internat. Org. for Septuagint and Cognate Studies (1969-75), President, Amer. Acad. for Jewish Res.; Fel. Guggenheim Form. Soc. of Scholars, Johns Hopkins Univ. (1982); form. Vis. Prof., Hebrew Univ.; Acad. Cttee., Annenberg Res. Instit. (since 1987). Publ.: Works of Bible, lit. and hist., The Pentateuch A Linear Translation, 5 vols.; Revised Standard Version, Old Testament; The Torah, Edr.-in-chief of J.P.S. trans. (1963); The Prophets; The Writings; The So-called Servant of the Lord and Suffering Servant in Second Isaiah; Ancient Israel; Understanding the Bible; The Bible as Law; Tanakh; Essays in Biblical Culture and Bible Translation, etc. Ad.: 1 West 4th St., New York 10012. ☎ 212-674 5300.

OWEN, His Honour Judge Aron, BA, PhD (Wales); b. Tredegar, Gwent, Feb. 16, 1919, m. Rose née Fishman; Circuit Judge, South-East Circuit (1980-94); Dep. High Court Judge, Family Division; Freeman, City of Lond; C. JHSE; Patron, Jewish Marriage Co. Publ.: Social History of Jews in Thirteenth-Century Europe, Amos and Hosea, Rashi. Ad.: 44 Brampton Grove, NW4 4AQ. ☎ 020-8202 8151.

OZIN, Malcolm John; b. London, Nov. 14, 1934; President Jewish Blind & Disabled; Tr. Cecil Rosen Found.; Hon. Sec. Cavendish Housing Trust Ltd. Ad.: 22, Lisson Grove, London NW1 6TT. ☎ 020-7258 2070. Email mjo@manninggroup.co.uk.

PAISNER, Harold Michael, BA (Oxon); b. London, June 4, 1939; m. Judith née Rechtman; Solicitor, Senior Partner of Berwin Leighton Paisner LLP; Member of the Paris Bar pursuant to European Directive 98/5/CE; Hon. member of the Lithuanian Bar; UK National Vice President, Union Internationale des Avocats – Mem. International Cttee, the Law Society, the International Baz\r Association, the British Baltic Lawyers Association and the American Bar Association; Directorships; FIBI Bank (UK) plc, Think London, interface, Inc, The Institute of Jewish Policy Research and Ben Gurion University Foundation; Gov., Ben Gurion Univ. Negev. Ad.: 16 Ilchester Place, London W14 8AA. Email Harold.paisner@blplaw,.com

PAISNER, Martin David, CBE, MA (Oxon), LLM (Ann Arbor, Michigan) H.D. (Glasgow); b. Windsor, Berks., Sept. 1, 1943; m. Susan Sarah née Spence; Solicitor; Partner, Berwin Leighton Paisner Solicitors; Chairman, The Jerusalem Foundation (1997-); Vice Chairman, Weizmann Institute Foundation; Board Member – The American Jewish Joint Distribution Committee Inc, Oxford Centre for Hebrew and Jewish Studies, Holocaust Educational Trust, European Jewish Publication Society, Share Zedek UK, Pincus Fund, Ovarian Cancer Action, The Royal Free Cancerkin Breat Cancer Trust; Governor, Weizmann Institute of Science. Hon. Fellow, Queen Mary, University of London; Hon. Doctorate University of Glasgow and Hon. Fellow, IDC Herzliya. Ad.: 4 Heath Drive, Hampstead, London NW3 7SY.

PASCAL, Julia, BA (Hons) (Lond.); b. Manchester, Nov. 15, 1949; m. Alain Carpentier;

Playwright/Theatre director; Dir. Pascal Theatre Co.; Leverhulme Writer-in-Residence, Wiener Library (2007-);Theatre Dir., National Theatre (1978); Assoc. Dir., Orange Tree Theatre (1979); Artistic Dir., Pascal Theatre Co. (1983-2009); Prima Ballerina Assoluta in Virago's 'Truth, Dare or Promise' and Boxtree's 'Memoirs of a Jewish Childhood'; Edr. Bd. Jewish Quarterly. Plays include Theresa (1990), The Dybbuk (1992), Year Zero (1995), The Yiddish Queen Lear (1999), London Continental (2000), 20/20 for Amici Dance Theatre (2000), Woman in the Moon (2001); Radio Plays: The Road to Paradise (1997), The Golem (2002), Crossing Jerusalem (2003); Elegy for Amici Dance Theatre Co., The Merchant of Venice (2007). Publ.: The Holocaust Trilogy; The Yiddish Queen Lear and Woman in the Moon; The Golem and Crossing Jerusalem; The Shylock Play, Nesta Dream Time Fellowship (2006). Ad.: c/o United Agents, 130, Shaftesbury Ave., London W1D 5EU. ☎ 020-7166 5266. Fax 020-7166 5282. Email pascal7038@aol.com.

PAUL, Geoffrey D., OBE, FRSA; b. Liverpool, March 26, 1929; Director, Anglo-Israel Assoc. (2001-3); Ed. (1977-1990) Jewish Chronicle, American Affairs Ed. (1991-96). Ad.: 1 Carlton Close, West Heath Rd., NW3 7UA. ☎/Fax 020-8458 6948. Email infoman@btinternet.com.

PEPPER, Sir Michael, Kt., BSc, MA, PhD, ScD, FRS; b. London, Aug. 10, 1942, m. Jeannette; Prof. Nanoeletronics Univ. Coll. London; Emer. Physics Prof, Cambridge Univ., Fel., Trinity Coll.; Warren Res. Fel., Royal Soc. (1978-86); Vis. Prof Bar-Ilan Univ. (1984). Ad.: London Centre for Nanotechnology, 17, Gordon St., London WC1H 0AH. ☎ 020-7679 0604. Email m.pepper@e.e.ucl.ac.uk

PERES, Shimon, Nobel Peace Laureate; b. Vishniev, Belarus, Aug. 16, 1923; m. Sonia née Gelman; President, State of Israel (2007-); form. Deputy Prime Minister of Israel and Minister of Foreign Affairs (2001-05); Minister for Regional Cooperation (1999-2001); Fd. Peres Center for Peace (1997); Prime Minister and Minister of Defense (1995-96); Minister of Foreign Affairs (1992-95); Chairman of the Labour Party (1977-92, 1995-97); M.K. (1959-2007); Publ.: In Between Hatred and Neighbourhood (1961), The Next Phase (1965), David's Sling (1970), Entebbe Diary (1991), The New Middle East (1993), Battling for Peace (1995), For the Future of Israel (1997), New Genesis (1998), The Imaginary Voyage (1999), A Time for War, a Time for Peace? Ad. The Presidency.

PERETZ, Amir, b. Boujad, Morocco, March 9, 1952; m. Ahlama; Farmer; Mayor of Sderot (1983-88); entered Knesset in 1988; Chairman, Histadrut (1995-2005); formed Am Ehad in 1999, merged with the Labour Party in 2004; leader of the Labour Party (2005-); Deputy Prime-Minister and Minister of Defense (2006-). Ad.: Knesset.

PERSOFF, Meir, JP, MA (Lond), FRSA; b. Letchworth, Aug. 25, 1941; Judaism Edr., Saleroom Edr. (1981-2000), News Edr. (1974-76), Arts Edr. (1980-85), Features Edr. (1976-90), Jewish Chronicle; President, Israel-Judaica Philatelic Soc.; form. Cttee, Jewish Book C.; form. Publ. Cttee., Jewish Marriage C.; Silver Medallist, internat. philatelic exhibitions, Jerusalem, London, Stockholm, Pretoria, Paris, Madrid. Publ.: The Hasmonean (1970), The Running Stag: The Stamps and Postal History of Israel (1973), Jewish Living (1982), Immanuel Jakobovits: a Prophet in Israel (2002), Faith Against Reason: Religious Reform and the British Chief Rabbinate, 1840-1990 (2008), etc. Ad.: 17/9, Shmuel Hanagid Str., Jerusalem. 94592 ☎ 02-6235834. Email meir-per@013.net

PINNICK, Jeffrey, FCA; b. London Dec. 6, 1935; T., BoD; Chairman, Fin. Cttee., BoD (V. Chairman, 1982-85); V.Chairman, Frs., Boys Town, Jerusalem, Ad.: 5th Floor, Commonwealth House, 1-19 Oxford St., London WC1A 1NF.

PINTER, Harold, CH, CBE; b. London, Oct. 10, 1930; Playwright. Nobel Prize for Literature (2005). Publ.: The Birthday Party, The Caretaker, The Homecoming, Old Times, No Man's Land, Moonlight, Betrayal, and other plays. Ad.: Judy Daish Associates Ltd., 2 St Charles Place, W10 6EG. ☎ 020-8964 8811. Fax 020-8964 8966.

PLANCEY, Rabbi Alan; b. Edinburgh, Oct. 30, 1941; M., Northwood United Synagogue (2007-); Borehamwood & Elstree Syn. (1976-2007); Chairman, Rabbin. C. US (1987-94); Member Chief Rabbi's Cabinet; H. V.-President & Rel Adv., Jewish Care; Area Chaplain Herts. Police; Hon. Chaplain JLGB; Hon. Chaplain Jewish Scouting Adv. Cttee.; Freeman of the City of London; M., Luton Syn. (1965-69); Youth M., Hampstead Garden Sub. Syn. (1970-76). Ad.: 98 Anthony Rd., Borehamwood, Herts., WD6 4NB. ☎ 020-8207 3759. Fax

020-8207 0568.

PLASKOW, Rev. Michael Lionel, MBE, LTSC, ALCM; b. Palestine, July 8, 1936; form. Chairman, Hard of Hearing Assoc., Netanya; Emer. R., Woodside Park Syn.; Chaplain to the Mayor of Barnet (1999-2000); Life Pres. Central Found. School, Jewish Old Boys Group; Norman B. Spencer award 1992 for research into Freemasonry; Freeman City of London (1994). Publ. The Story of a Community: Woodside Park 1937-1987. Ad.: 4/4 Nitza Boulevard, 42262 Netanya. ☎ (09) 832-9592.

POLONSKY, Antony, BA (Rand), MA, D.Phil (Oxon), Knight's Cross of the Order of Merit, Poland; b. Johannesburg, Sept. 23, 1940, m. Arlene née Glickman; Albert Abramson Professor of Holocaust Studies at the United States Holocaust Memorial Museum and Brandeis University; Vice-president, Institute for Polish-Jewish Studies, Oxford; Vice-president, American Association for Polish-Jewish Studies, Cambridge, MA; Member Exec Ctte, National Polish American-Jewish American Council; Ed., Polin: A Journal of Polish-Jewish Studies. Publ. Politics in Independent Poland (1972), The Little Dictators (1973), The Great Powers and the Polish Question (1976), The Beginnings of Communist Rule in Poland (1981), (ed.) The Jews in Poland (1986), (ed.) A Cup of Tears (1989), (ed.) Recent Polish Debates about the Holocaust (1990), (ed.) Polish Paradoxes (1990), (ed.) The Jews of Warsaw (1991), (ed.) The Jews in Old Poland (1992), Contemporary Jewish Writing in Poland (ed.) (2001), The Neighbours Respond: the Controversy Over the Jedwabne Massacre (2004). Ad.: 322 Harvard Street, Cambridge, MA 02139. ☎ (617) 492 9788, 736 2980, Fax (617) 736 2070 Email polonsky@brandeis.edu.

PORTER, Dame Shirley (née Cohen), DBE, FRSA, HonPhD (Tel Aviv); b. Nov. 29, 1930; Form. Leader, Westminster City C. (1983-91); Lord Mayor (1991); V. President London Union of Youth Clubs; Past Master Worshipful Co. Environmental Cleaners; Freeman of the City of London; form. Dep. Ch., London Festival Ballet. Publ.: A Minister for London, Efficiency in Local Government. Ad.: 9, Savoy St., London WC2E 7ER. ☎ 020-7240 3222.

POSEN, Felix, BA (John Hopkins Univ.), D.Phil. (Hon., Hebrew Univ., Hon, Tel Aviv); b. Berlin, Oct. 24, 1928; m. Jane née Levy; Gov. Emer. and Hon. Fellow Oxford Centre for Hebrew and Jewish Studies; Chairman, Posen Foundation, Lucerne; Gov. Hebrew University; Tr. Institute of Archaeo-metallurgical Studies University of London; Member of the Bd of the College of Pluralistic Judaism, Jerusalem; Member Cttee Interfaith Mission for Christians, Muslims and Jews. Ad.: 24 Kensington Gate, London W8 5NA. ☎ 020-7584 0915. Fax 020-7584 0904. Email nesop@dircon.co.uk.

PRAG, Derek Nathan, MA (Cantab), HD.Litt (Univ. Herts), Hon. MEP; b. Merthyr Tydfil, Aug. 6, 1923; m. Dora née Weiner; President Herts. Assoc. local councils (2003-); form MEP (Cons), for Hertfordshire (1979-94); Mem. European Parl. Delegation for Relations with Israel (1989-94); Chairman, All-Party Disablement Group (1980-94); President (2001-),Chairman, London Europe Society (1973-2001); V. Chairman, European Parl.-Israel Intergroup (1990-94); Commander of the Order of Leopold II, Belgium (1996); Silver Medal of European Merit, Luxembourg (1974); H. Dir., EU Com. (1974). Publ.: Businessman's Guide to the Common Market (1973), Europe's International Strategy (1978), Democracy in the European Union (1998), etc. Ad.: Pine Hill, 47 New Rd., Digswell, Herts., AL6 0AQ. ☎ 01438-715686. Fax 01438-840422.

PRAIS, Sigbert J., M.Com, PhD, ScD (Cantab), Hon. D.Litt (City), FBA, Hon D.Sc (Birm); b. Frankfurt am Main, Dec. 19, 1928; Economist; Sr. Res. Fel., Nat. Instit. of Econ. and Social Res., London; form. Edr. Adv. Bd., Jewish Journal of Soc.; Vis. Prof. of Econometrics, City Univ.; form. H. Consultant, BoD Statistical and Demographic Res. Unit; Economist, Internat. Monetary Fund; Adv. on Statistics, Govt. of Israel; Lect., Cambridge Univ. Publ.: Productivity and Industrial Structure; The Evolution of Giant Firms; Analysis of Family Budgets; Productivity, Education and Training, etc. Ad.: 83 West Heath Rd., NW3 7TN. ☎ 020-8458 4428.

PRAWER, Siegbert Salomon, MA, D.Litt (Oxon.), MA, LittD (Cantab), PhD, Hon D.Litt (Birmingham), D.Phil hc. (Cologne), FBA; b. Cologne, Feb. 15, 1925; Member of the German Academy of Languages and Literature; Taylor Prof of German, Emer., Oxford Univ.; Hon.

Fel. Jesus College, Cambridge; Hon. Fel. Queen's Coll. Oxford; Hon. Fel., form. President, Brit. Comparative Lit. Assn.; H.Fel., form. H. Dir., Lond. Univ. Instit. of Germanic Studies; Hon. Member of the Modern Language Association of America; V. President of the English Goethe Soc. (1994-), President (1991-94); Memb. of the London Bd. of the Leo Baeck Inst. (1969-96); form. Prof of German, Lond. Univ. and Head of German Dept., Westfield Coll.; Sr. Lect. Birmingham Univ.; Vis. Prof, City Coll., New York, Chicago, Harvard, Hamburg, California, Pittsburgh, Otago (New Zealand), Australian Nat. Univ., Canberra, Brandeis; C., Leo Baeck Instit.; Goethe Medal (1973); Isaac Deutscher Prize (1977); Friedrich Gundolf Prize (1986); Gold Medal of the Goethe Gesellschaft 1995. Publ.: Writings on German, English, Jewish and Comparative Literature. Visual Arts & Film. Ad.: The Queen's Coll., Oxford OX1 4AW.

PRENDERGAST, Dame Simone Ruth (née Laski), DBE, JP, DL, OStJ; b. Manchester, July 2, 1930;, President CBF World Jewish Relief; Solicitors' Disciplinary Tribunal (1986-2002); Vice-Chairman, Age Concern Westminster (1989-2004); Chairman, Jewish Refugees Cttee. (1981-1991); Pt. time Commissioner for Commission for Racial Equality (1996-98); Commandant JLGB (1986-2000); Co. Patron Fed. Women Zionists; Chairman East Grinstead Med. Res. Tr.; Tr. Kennedy Int. Rheumatology (2002-); Chairman, Westminster Children's Soc. (1980-90); Court of Patrons, Royal Coll. of Surgeons; Chairman, Greater London Area Conservative & Unionist Assns. (1984-87), Solicitors Disciplinary Tribunal (1986-2002); Lord Chancellors Advisory Cttee. (Inner London) (1981-91); Member East London & Bethnal Green Housing Assoc. (1990-); Tr., Camperdown House Trust (1990-2004). Ad.: 52 Warwick Sq., SW1V 2AJ.

PRESTON, Rosalind (née Morris), OBE; b. London, Dec. 29, 1935; Professional Volunteer; Tr. Jewish Volunteering Network (2008-); Tr., Olive Tree Tr. (2001-); Tr. Jewish Chronicle (2000-); Chair, Nightingale House (1999-2007); Hon. Vice-President British WIZO (1993-); Jt. Hon. Sec. CCJ (1997-2005); form. Co-Chair Interfaith Network, UK; form. V. President, BoD; form. President, The National Council of Women of G.B. (1988-90). Ad.: 7 Woodside Close, Stanmore, Middx. HA7 3AJ. ☎ 020-8954 1411. Fax 020-8954 6898. Email rpreston@f2s.com.

PULZER, Peter George Julius, MA, B.Sc.(Econ.), PhD; b. Vienna, May 20, 1929; Gladstone Prof, Government & Publ. Admin., Fel. All Souls, Oxford (1985-96); Official Student (Fel.) in Politics, Christ Church, Oxford (1962-84); Grosses Silbernes Ehrenzeichen, Rep. Austria (2008); Bundesverdienst Kreuz, Rep. of Germany (2004). Publ.: The Rise of Political Antisemitism in Germany and Austria, Political Representation and Elections in Britain, Jews and the German State: The Political History of a Minority (1848-1933); German Politics 1945-1995; Germany 1870-1945: Politics, State Formation and War; contr. German Jewish History in Modern Times (ed. M. Meyer). Ad.: All Souls College, Oxford, OX1 4AL. ☎ 01865 559347. Fax 01865 279299. Email peter.pulzer@ntlworld.com.

RABINOVITCH, Rabbi Nachum L., BSc, MA, PhD, b. Montreal, Apr 30, 1928; Rosh Yeshiva, Maale Adumim; form. Princ., Jews, College; Rab., Clanton Park Syn., Toronto. Publ.: Hadar Itamar, Probability and Statistical Inference in Ancient and Medieval Jewish Literature; Critical Edn. of Rambam's Mishneh Torah with comprehensive commentary, Yad P'shutah, 17 vols. Ad.: 72 Mizpe Nevo St., Maale Adumim, Israel 98410. ☎ (02) 5353655. Fax (02) 535 3947. Email y-bm@moreshet.co.il.

RABINOWITZ, Rabbi Benjamin, BA, M.Phil, AJC; b. Newcastle upon Tyne June 21, 1945; M., Edgware Syn.; Tr., Co-Chairman Edgware CCJ (1982-); form. M. Yeshurun Heb Cong., Gatley; Blackpool Hebrew Cong. Ad.: 14 Ashcombe Gdns., Edgware, Middx. HA8 8HS. ☎ 020-8958 5320/6126 (Synagogue office). Fax 020-8958 7684. Email benrab@shalombayyit.demon.co.uk.

RABINOWITZ, Rabbi Lippa, b. Manchester, Nov. 15, 1930; Rav, Vine St Syn., Manch.; Princ., Manch. Jewish Grammar Sch., form. Princ. Judith Lady Montefiore Coll., Ramsgate; Lect., Etz Haim Yeshiva, Tangier. Publ.: Eleph Lamateh Chidushim on Sugioth (Israel). Ad.: 57 Waterpark Rd., Salford.

RABSON, Ronald Jeffery, MA; Dipl. Arch. FRIBA; b. Lond, March 3, 1928; Chartered Architect; form. Chairman & Jt. H. Sec., Lond. Bd. Jewish Rel. Educ.; form. Chairman &

Gov., JFS Comp. Sch.; form. Chairman, Instit. of Jewish Educ.; form. Gov., Michael Sobell Sinai Sch.; Life M., C., US. Ad.: 16 Broadfields Ave., Edgware, Middx, HA8 8PG. ☎ 020-8958 9035. Fax 020-8905 4035.

RADOMSKY, Rabbi David, BA, MA, NPQH; b. East London, South Africa, Sept. 4, 1956; Educational Consultant; form. H.T. Hasmonean High School (2000-06); form. Deputy H.T. and Head of Jewish Studies at Immanuel Coll.; Lect., Jews, Coll., (1991-93); form. M., Wembley Syn.; Com. M. Jewish Com. in Eire (1985-88); Talmud Lect., Midrashiat Noam Yeshiva High Sch. Pardes Hanna, Israel (1982-85). Ad.: 27 Windsor Ave, Edgware, Middx. HA8 8SR. ☎ 020-8958 3879.

RAJAK, Tessa, née Goldsmith, MA, D.Phil; b. London, Aug. 2, 1946, m. Harry; Scholar and University Teacher; Prof. Ancient History, Univ. Reading; Horace W. Goldsmith Visiting Prof., Programme in Judaic Studies Yale Univ., Grinfeld Lect. in the Septuagint, Oxford (1994-96). Publ.: Josephus, the Historian and his Society, The Jews among Pagans and Christians in the Roman Empire (jt. ed); The Jewish Dialogue with Greece and Rome; Philosophers and Power (jt.ed.). Ad.: 64 Talbot Rd., London, N6 4RA.

RAPHAEL, David Daiches, D.Phil, MA, Hon. FIC; b. Liverpool, Jan. 25, 1916; Emer. Prof of Philosophy, Lond. Univ.; Chairman, Westminster Syn. (1987-89); form. Head Humanities Dept., Imperial Coll.; Prof. Phil., Reading Univ.; Prof. Pol. & Soc. Phil., Glasgow Univ.; Sr. Lect., Moral Phil., Glasgow Univ.; Prof., Phil., Otago Univ., Dunedin; form. Princ. Off M. of Lab. and Nat. Service. Publ.: The Moral Sense, Richard Price's Review of Morals, Moral Judgement, The Paradox of Tragedy, Political Theory and the Rights of Man, British Moralists 1650-1800, Problems of Political Philosophy, Adam Smith's Theory of Moral Sentiments (Jt. Edr.), Hobbes: Morals and Politics, Adam Smith's Lectures on Jurisprudence (Jt. Edr.), Adam Smith's Essays on Philosophical Subjects, (Jt. Edr.), Justice and Liberty, Moral Philosophy, Adam Smith, Concepts of Justice, The Impartial Spectator etc. Ad.: 54 Sandy Lane, Petersham, Richmond TW10 7EL.

RAPHAEL, Frederic Michael, MA (Cantab), FRSL; b. Chicago, Aug. 14, 1931; Writer. Publ. Novels, Obbligato, The Earlsdon Way, The Limits of Love, The Graduate Wife, The Trouble with England, Lindmann, Darling, Orchestra and Beginners, Who Were You With Last Night?, Like Men Betrayed, April June and November, California Time, The Glittering Prizes, Heaven and Earth, After The War, The Hidden I, A Double Life, Old Scores, Coast to Coast; Short stories, Sleeps Six, Oxbridge Blues, Think of England, The Latin Lover, All His Sons, Fame and Fortune; Non-fiction: Byron, Somerset Maugham, Cracks in the Ice, Of Gods and Men, France: the Four Seasons, The Necessity of Anti-Semitism, Popper: Historicism and its Poverty, Eyes Wide Open. The Benefits of Doubt (essays), A Spoilt Boy (autobiography); Some Talk of Alexander. Published Screenplays and Drama: Two for the Road, Darling, Oxbridge Blues, Eyes Wide Shut (with Stanley Kubrick); Notebooks: Personal Terms, Rough Copy, Cuts and Bruises. Translations: The Satyrica of Petronius, The Poems of Catullus (with Kenneth McLeish), The Plays of Aeschylus, Sophocles' Aias, Euripides' Medea, Bacchae and Hippolytus. Ad.: Ed. Victor Ltd., 6, Bayley St, London WC1B.

RAPOPORT-ALBERT, Ada, BA, PhD; b. Tel Aviv; Hd. Dept. Hebrew & Jewish Studies, Reader in Jewish History and Hd. of Department, University College London. Publ.: Hasidism Reappraised (ed., 1996); Essays in Jewish Historiography (1988/1991). Ad.: Dept. of Hebrew & Jewish Studies, University College, Gower Street, London WC1E 6BT. ☎ 020-7679 3591. Email uclhara@ucl.ac.uk.

RASMINSKY, Louis, CC, CBE, LLD, DCL, DHL; b. Montreal, Feb. 1, 1908; Gov., Bank of Canada (1961-73); President, Industrial Development Bank (1961-73); H. Fel., Lond. Sch. of Economics. Ad.: 1006-20 Driveway, Ottawa, Ontario, K2P 1C8, Canada. ☎ 613-594-0150.

REIF, Stefan, BA, PhD (Lond.), LittD (Cantab); b. Edinburgh, Jan. 21, 1944; m. Shulamit née; Founder Dir., Taylor-Schechter Genizah Research Unit, Cambridge Univ. Library; Emer. Professor of Medieval Hebrew Studies Cambridge Univ.; Fellow St John's College, Cambridge; President JHSE (1991-92); President Brit. Assoc. for Jewish Studies (1992); President, Cambridge Theological Society (2002-04); Hon. Fel., Mekize Nirdamim Society, Jerusalem; Adv. Panel, International Soc. for the Study of Deuteronomical and Cognate Literature; T., Cambridge Traditional Jewish Cong.; Lect., Hebrew and Semitics, Glasgow

Univ. (1968-72); Princ., Glasgow Hebrew Coll. (1970-72); Asst. Prof., Hebrew Language and Lit., Dropsie Coll. (1972-73). Publ.: Shabbethai Sofer and His Prayer Book; Judaism and Hebrew Prayer; Hebrew Manuscripts at Cambridge University Library; A Jewish Archive from Old Cairo, Why Medieval Hebrew Studies?; Problems with Prayers; (ed.) Interpreting the Hebrew Bible, Genizah Research after Ninety Years, The Cambridge Genizah Collections, Cambridge Univ. Library Genizah Series, etc. Ad.: Cambridge University Library, CB3 9DR. ☎ 01223 766 370. Fax 01223 333160. Email scr3@cam.ac.uk.

REISS, Simon, b. Berlin, Dec. 31, 1923; Comp. Dir.; V. President Zionist Fed.; Hon. Life and form. President Western Marble Arch Syn.; Mem. BoD; Chairman Jt. Cttee., Youth Aff; Co-Chairman and Tr. Balfour Diamond Jubilee Trust; Vice-Chairman and Tr., Yad Vashem Cttee., BoD; Hon. President Int. Fur Trade Fed. Ad.: Fax 020-7409 7410.

REISZ, Matthew Joseph; b. London, Oct. 29, 1954; m. Françoise née Delais; Journalist; Editor, Jewish Quarterly (1998-). Publ. Europe's Jewish Quarters (1991), A. Booklover's Companion (2006). ☎ 020-8830 5367.

RICHARDS, Ivor Bryan, BSc (Econ), FCA, FBRP; b. London, Jan. 22, 1937; m. Jill née Da Costa; Chartered Accountant (Retired); V. President Brighton & Hove Jewish Rep. C. (2001-04). Ad.: Flat 30, 15 Grand Avenue, Hove, E. Sussex BN3 2NG. ☎ 01273 720366. Fax 01273 323125.

RICKAYZEN, Gerald, BSc, PhD, FInstP, CPhys; b. London, Oct. 16, 1929; Physicist; Vis. Prof., Univ. Surrey (2004-); Chairman, Canterbury Jewish Community (1998-2000); Prof. of Theoretical Physics, Univ. of Kent (1965-98), Emeritus (1998-); Pro-Vice-Chancellor (1980-90), Deputy V. Chancellor (1984-90). Publ.: Theory of Superconductivity (1965); Green's Functions and Condensed Matter Physics (1980). Ad: The Physics Laboratory, The University, Canterbury CT2 7NR. ☎ 020- 020-8866 5589. Email gerald.rickayzen@physics.org.

RIETTI, Robert, Cavaliere Ufficiale, OMRI, Officer-Knight of the Italian Republic; b. London, Feb. 8, 1923; Actor, broadcaster, writer, director, editor of Drama Quarterly GAMBIT; BAFTA nomination for Special Award (1993). Publ.: English translations of the entire dramatic works of Luigi Pirandello (John Calder); Look up and dream (1999); A Rose for Reuben (2007). Ad.: 6, Hythe End Rd., Wraysbury, Berks. TW9 5AR. ☎ 01784-482154. Fax 01784 481761.

RIFKIND, Rt. Hon. Sir Malcolm, MP, QC, PC; b. Edinburgh, June 21, 1946; MP, Kensington & Chelsea (Con.) (2005-); form. M.P. for Edinburgh, Pentlands (Con.) (1974-97); Foreign Secretary (1995-97), Min. of Defence (1992-95), Min. of Transport (1990-92); Sec. of State for Scotland (1986-90), Min. of State Foreign & Commonwealth Office (1983-86); Parl. Under-Sec. of State, FCO (1982-83); Parl. Under-Sec. of State, Scottish Office (1979-82); H. President, Scottish Young Conservatives (1976-77); H.Sec., Conservative Frs. of Israel Parl. Group (1974-79); Sec. Conservative Parl. Foreign & Commonwealth Affairs Group (1977-79); Opposition Spokesman on Scottish Affairs (1975-76); Select Cttee. on Overseas Development (1978-79); Edinburgh Town C. (1970-74). Ad.: House of Commons. ☎ 020-7219 5683. Fax 020-7219 4213.

RIGAL, Mrs Margaret H. (née Lazarus); b. London, Nov. 28, 1932; Co-Chairman, Women's Campaign for Soviet Jewry (the 35s); H.Sec., Jewish Aged Needy Pension Soc.; Chairman Jewish Aid Cttee; Hon. Sec. London Society of Jews and Christians. Ad.: 31, St. John's Wood Ct., St. John's Wood Rd., London, NW8 8QR. Tel: 020-7286 4404. MargaretrRigal@gmail.com

ROBERG, Rabbi Meir, BA (Hons), MPhil, DipEd; b. Wurzburg Germany, June 25, 1937;Dean Lauder Midrasha, Berlin; Educ. Consultant to Jewish Schools and Colleges in the CIS and England; Reg. Inspector of Schools in Pikuach; President, Assoc., Hd. Teachers of Orthodox Schools; form. HM Hasmonean; Chairman, Acad. Cttee Massoret Inst.; Dep. HM, Yavneh Grammar Sch. Ad.: 19 Sorotzkin St. Jerusalem ☎ 020- 5386020.

ROBINS, Dame Ruth, DBE, BA, TTHD; form. Headteacher JFS School. Ad.: ☎ 020- 020-8206 3100. Fax 020-8206 3101.

ROBSON, Jeremy, b. Llandudno, Sept. 5, 1939; Publisher, J. R. Books Ltd. Publ.: 33 Poems, In Focus (poetry), Poetry anthologies, incl. The Young British Poets (ed.), Poems from Poetry

and Jazz in Concert (ed.). Ad.: J.R. Books, 10 Greenland Street, London NW1 0NO.
ROITT, Ivan Maurice, MA, DSc (Oxon), FRCPath, FRS, Hon. FRCP; b. Lond., Sept. 30, 1927;
Emer. Prof. Immunology UCL. Publ.: Essential Immunology. Ad.: Windeyer Institute, UCL.,
Cleveland Street, W1T 4JF. ☎ 020-7679 9360. Fax 020-7679 9400. Email i.roitt@ucl.ac.uk
ROMAIN, Rabbi Jonathan Anidjar, MBE, BA; PhD; b. London, Aug. 24, 1954; m. Sybil
Sheridan; M., Maidenhead Syn.; Chairman, Assembly of Rabbis (2007-); Director, Jewish
Information and Media Service; Chaplain, J. Police Assoc.; Chairman, Youth Assn. of Syns. in
Gt. Brit. (1972-74); form. M., Barkingside Progressive Syn. Publ.: The Open and Closed
Paragraphs of the Pentateuch, In a Strange Land, Signs and Wonders, The Jews of England,
Faith and Practice, I'm Jewish, My Partner Isn't, Tradition and Change, Till Faith Us Do Part,
Renewing the Vision, Your God Shall Be My God, Reform Judaism and Modernity; God,
Doubt, and Dawkins. Ad.: Grenfell Lodge, Ray Park Road, Maidenhead, Berks. SL6 8QX. ☎
01628 671058. Fax 01628 625536.
RONSON, Gerald Maurice, b. London, May 27, 1939; m. Dame Gail née Cohen; Property
Developer; Chief Exec. Heron Group; Chairman, Snax 24 Corporation Ltd.; Fd. Mem.
Cancer Research Campaign; Fund Mem., CRC/ICRF Appeal Cabinet (2001-); Chairman,
liaison Cttee, Office of the Chief Rabbi (2001-); Vice-President UJIA (1998-); Mem., Adv. C.,
Prince's Tr. (1986-); Friend, Roy. Coll. Physicians (1985-); Mem Gov. C., Business in the
Community (1986-); Mem. UMIST Millenium Project Exec. Cttee (1988-); Fd. Chairman,
Group Rel. Educ. Tr. (1978-); Ambassador of the Carmel Druse; Property Awards:
Personality of the Year, 2000, 2001/2; Variety Club of GB: Entrepreneur of the Year(2000);
Inaugural Estates Gazette Architecture Award; Hambros Businessman of the Year (1984);
Director Magazine Award for Excellence (1984). Adr.: Heron House, 19 Marylebone Rd.,
London NW1 5JL.
ROSE, Rabbi Abraham Maurice, MA; b. Birmingham, Sept. 7, 1925; Exec. Dir., C. of
Young Israel Syn. (Israel) (1975-90); Adm. Dir. & Lect., Jerusalem Academy of Jewish
Studies (1973-74); Exec. Dir., Office of the Chief Rabbi (1962-73); form. Exec. Dir.,
Conf. of Europ. Rabbis (1962-2004); form. M., Sutton Syn. (1952-62), Derby Syn.
(1948-52). Ad.: Rechov Machal 30/2, Jerusalem 97763. ☎ 5812859. Fax 5810080.
Email rose-nm@netvision. net.il.
ROSE, Aubrey, OBE, CBE, D. Univ. (Hon), FRSA; b. London, Nov. 1, 1926; Solicitor; President,
Indian Jewish Association UK; Senior V. President, BoD (1991, 1994); Commissioner &
Dep. Chairman Commission for Racial Equality (CRE); Dep. Chairman British Caribbean
Assoc.; Tr. Project Fullemploy; Tr. Commonwealth Human Rights Initiative; Member,
Working Group Commonwealth Jewish Coun.; form. Chairman, Defence and Group Rel.
Cttee. BoD; Chairman, Working Group on Environment BoD, Publ.: Jewish Communities
in the Commonwealth (CJT); Judaism and Ecology (1992); Journey into Immortality, the
Story of David Rose (1997); Brief Encounters of a Legal Kind (1997), The Story of Vera
(ed.). From Bitter Came Sweet (2004, ed.). The Rainbow Never Ends (2005), Letters to
my Wife (2007). Ad.: 14 Pagitts Grove, Hadley Wood, Herts EN4 0NT. ☎ 020-8449 2166.
Fax 020-8449 1469. Email as.rose@virgin.net.
ROSE, Jeffery Samuel, BDS, FDS, D.Orth. RCS; b. Harrow, Middx., Dec. 22, 1924; Ret.
Consultant Orthodontist, Royal London Hospital (1967-90); Hon. L. President European
Region, World Union of Progressive Judaism; President, North Western Reform Syn.
(2004); Hon. Vice-President RSGB (1999-); Chairman Reform Foundation Tr. (1996-99);
President Brit. Orthodontic Soc. (1994-95); V. President World Union Progressive Judaism
(1995-99); form. Chairman, Leo Baeck Coll. (1985-88); Life Gov. (1986); Hon. Fellow
(1988); Chairman, Euro. Region, World Union Prog Judaism (1990-95); form. V. President
& Chairman RSGB; form. V. President & Chairman, North Western Reform Syn.; President,
Brit. Paedontic Soc. (1964-65); President, Brit. Soc. for the Study of Orthodontics (1972-
73). President, British Assoc. of Orthodontists (1991-94). Ad.: 17 Broadlands Lodge, 18
Broadlands Road, London N6 4AW. ☎ 020-8340 8836. Fax 020-8374 4355.
ROSE, Mrs Joyce Dora Hester (née Woolf), CBE, JP, DL (Herts); b. London, August 14, 1929;
m. Cyril Rose; Hertfordshire Family Mediation Service(1996-2002); S.W. Hertfordshire

Hospice Charitable Trust (The Peace Hospice) (1996-2003); Chairman, Nat. Exec. and Council, Magistrates Assn. (1990-93); Mem. Bd. Dir. Apex Tr. (1994-2004); Herts Care Tr. (1995-99); V. President Magistrates Assn. and V. President Hertfordshire Branch; H. D. Laws, Univ. of Hertfordshire (1992); form. P. (1979-80), Chairman (1982-83), Lib. Party; President, S.W. Herts Const. L.D.; form. Chairman, Watford (Herts.) Bench (1990-94); form. Chairman, Family Proceedings Panel; P. & Chairman, Women's Liberal Fed. (1972-73); V. Chairman, UK Cttee. for Unicef (1968-70). Ad.: 2 Oak House, 101 Ducks Hill Road, Northwood, Middx HA6 2WQ. ☎ 020- 01923 821385. Fax 01923 840515.

ROSEN, Clive H., FCOptom. Dip. Sports Vision, UMIST (1997); b. London Apr. 15, 1938;); Freeman, City of London 1964; Dir. David Elliott (Opticians) Ltd. (1965-2003); Hon. Tr. East London and City Health Authority LOC (1994-2002); Cttee Mem., Sports Vision Assoc. (1997-2006); Hon. Sports Vision Consult to Leyton Orient FC (1997-2003); Hon. Pres. Broomfield House-owners and Residents Assn. (2002-); ChairmanMenorah JNF Committee (1974-1985); Hon. Off. JNF (1979-1981, 1983-1990); Mem Zionist Federation National Council, (1989-); Hon. Tr. ZF (1994-1996); Chairman ZF Fund-RaisingCttee. (1996-1998); Hon Sec. ZF (2002-2004); Asst. Hon. Sec ZF (2004-2006); Asst. Hon Tr. ZF (2006-); Fdg. Mem. Israel-Judaica Stamp Club (1980); Chairman, I-JSc (1990-); Ed., The Israel-Judaica Collector Journal. Ad.: 152 Morton Way, London N14 7AL. ☎ 020-8886 9331. Fax 020-8886 5116. Email clive@cliverosen.co.uk. Website www. israeljudaica.co.uk.

ROSEN, Rabbi Jeremy, MA (Cantab), PhD; b. Sept. 11, 1942; Dir. Yakar Foundation (1999-); Rabbi Western Syn. (1985-91); Rabbi, Western Marble Arch Syn. (1991-92); Chief Rabbi's Cabinet advisor Interfaith (1987-90); Prof., Jewish Studies F.V.G. Antwerp. (1991-); Tr., Yakar Foundation; Princ., Carmel Coll. (1971-84); Rabbi, Giffnock & Newlands Syn., Glasgow (1968-71). Publ.: Exploding Myths that Jews Believe (2001); Understanding Judaism (2003); Kabbalah Inspirations (2005). Ad.: 28 Johns Av., London NW4 4EN. ☎ 020-8202 4528. Email jeremyrosen@msn. com. Website www.jeremyrosen.com

ROSENBERG, Mrs. Rosita (née Gould); b. London, Sept. 2, 1933; V. President, form. Exec. Dir., Liberal Judaism; President, Liberal Synagogue, Elstree.. Publ. Liberal Judaism: the First Hundred Years (jt. author, 2004). Ad.: The Montagu Centre, 21, Maple St., W1T 4BE. ☎ 020-7580 1663. Fax 020-7631 9838.

ROTHSCHILD, Edmund Leopold de, CBE, VMH,TD, Hon. DSc (Salford Univ.); b. London, Jan. 2, 1916; Hon. LLD (Univ. of Newfoundland); Hon. V. President, CBF, World Jewish Relief; V. President, CCJ; President, Ajex; Bd. Govs., Technical Univ., Nova Scotia; form. Major, Royal Artillery, 1939-46, (Commanded P. Battery, Jewish Field Regt.). Publ.: Window on the World; A gilt-edged life: a memoir. Ad.: New Court, St. Swithin's Lane, EC4P 4DU; Exbury House, Exbury, Southampton, Hampshire SO45 1AF

ROTHSCHILD, Sir Evelyn de; b. Aug. 29, 1931; Merchant Banker; Dir., E.L. Rothchild Limited; Life President, Norwood; form President, JBS. Ad.: 31, Tite St., London SW3 4JP. ☎ 020-7376 5271.

ROTHSCHILD, Leopold David de, CBE; b. London, May 12, 1927; Dir., N. M. Rothschild & Sons; Investment Adv. Cttee., JWB; Jt. President Jewish Music Institute. Ad.: New Court, St. Swithin's Lane, EC4P 4DU. ☎ 020-7280 5000.

ROTHSCHILD, Nathaniel Charles Jacob, Lord, OM, GBE, FBA, MA (Oxon) Hon. PhD, Heb. Univ; b. Cambridge, Apr. 29, 1936; Chairman RIT Capital Partners plc, J. Rothschild Capital Management plc and Five Arrows Ltd; President IJPR (1992-2002); Chairman, Trustees of the National Gallery (1985-91); Chairman, Trustees of the National Heritage Memorial Fund (1992-98); Chairman Yad Hanadiv; Chairman Rothschild Foundation; Tr. Weizmann Institute; Weizmann Award (1977); Commonwealth Council Award (2001); Sir Winston Churchill Award, Technion (2004); Hon. Fell. City of Jerusalem; Hon Fell. Israel Museum. Ad.: 14 St James's Place, SW1A 1NP. ☎ 020-7493 8111. Fax 020-7408 2140.

ROTHSCHILD, Rabbi Sylvia Helen Fay, BSc; b. Bradford, West Yorkshire, Nov. 21, 1957; m. Martin Fischer; M. Wimbledon Syn. (2002-); M. Bromley and District Reform Synagogue (1987-2002); Co-Chair Assembly of Rabbis (1998-2000), Chair (2000-3). Publ.: co-ed., Taking up the Timbrel (2000). Ad.: c/o Wimbledon Synagogue, 1 Queensmere Rd., Parkside, London SW19 5QD.

ROZENBERG, Joshua Rufus, MA (Oxon), Hon. LLD (Herts); b. London, May, 30, 1950; m. Melanie Phillips; Solicitor, Journalist; Freelance legal columnist (2007-); Legal Ed., *Daily Telegraph* (2000-); BBC News (Legal Affairs Corr. 1985-97; Legal and Constitutional Affairs Corr. 1997-2000); Hon Bencher, Gray's Inn (2003), Publ. Your Rights and the Law (with N. Watkins, 1986), The Case for the Crown (1987); The Search for Justice (1994); Trial of Strength (1997); Privacy and the Press (2004). Ad.: C/o Noel Gay, 19 Denmark St., London WC2H 8NA Email joshua@rozenberg.net

RUBEN, David-Hillel, BA, PhD; b. Chicago, July 25, 1943; Prof. Philosophy, Dir J. Studies Birkbeck College (2004-); Dir., New York Univ. in London (2000-08); form. Dir., London School of Jewish Studies (1998-99); Professor of Philosophy, London School of Economics (1984-97); University of Glasgow, Lecturer in Philosophy (1970-75); University of Essex, Lecturer in Philosophy (1975-79); The City University, London, Senior Lecturer in Philosophy (1979-84). Publ.: Marxism and Materialism (1979); The Metaphysics of the Social World (1985); Explaining Explanation (1990); Action and Its Explanation (2003). 29, Sunny Gardens Rd., London NW4 1SL ☎ 020-7907 3201.

RUBENS, Kenneth David, OBE, FRICS, FRSA; b. Lond., Oct. 10, 1929; Chartered Surveyor; Vice President, Jewish Museum, London., L. Elder Span. & Port. Jews, Cong.; Past Chairman, C. World Jewish Relief; Past Master, Worshipful Company, Painter-Stainers.; Hon. Life Mem., Brit. Property Fed. Ad.: 5 Clarke's Mews, London W1G 6QN. ☎ 020-7486 1884. Email kenneth@rubens.org.

RUBINSTEIN, William David, BA, PhD, FAHA, FASSA, FRHistS; b. New York, Aug. 12, 1946; m. Hilary L. Rubinstein; Prof. of History, The University of Wales, Aberystwyth (1995-); President, JHSE (2002-04), Mem. Council (1996-); Prof. of Social and Economic History, Deakin University, Australia (1987-95); Ed., Journal of the Australian Jewish Historical Society (1988-95); President, Australian Association for Jewish Studies (1989-91); Member, Committee of Management, Executive Council of Australian Jewry (1983-95). Publ.: Men of Property: The Very Wealthy in Britain Since the Industrial Revolution (1981); The Jews in Australia: A Thematic History (with Hilary L. Rubinstein) (1991); Capitalism, Culture, and Decline in Britain, 1750-1990 (1993); A History of the Jews in the English-Speaking World: Great Britain (1996); The Myth of Rescue (1997); Britain's Century: A Political and Social History 1815-1905 (1998); Philosemitism: Admiration and Support in the English-speaking World for Jews 1840-1939 (with Hilary L. Rubinstein, 1999); The Jews in the Modern World: A History since 1750 (co-author, 2002); Twentieth Century Britain: A Political History (2003); Genocide: a History (2004); Shadow Pasts (2008). Ad.: Department of History, University of Wales, Aberystwyth, Penglais, Ceredigion SY23 3DY. ☎ 01970 622661. Fax 01970 622676. Email wdr@aber. ac.uk.

RUDMAN, Michael Edward, MA (Oxon), BA (Oberlin Coll.); b. Tyler, Texas, USA, Feb. 14, 1939; Artistic Director, Sheffield Theatres (1992-94); Dir. Chichester Festival Theatre (1989-90); Assoc. Dir., Nat. Theatre, (1979-88); Dir. Lyttelton Theatre (1979-81), Bd. Dirs. Art. Dir.; Hampstead Theatre (1973-78); Art. Dir., Traverse Theatre Club (1970-73). Ad.: c/o Peter Murphy, Curtis Brown Group, 4th Floor, 28/29 Haymarket, SW1Y 4SP. ☎ 020-7396 6600. Fax 020-7396 0110.

RUDOLF, Anthony, BA (Cantab), Chevalier de l'Ordre des Arts et des Lettres, FRSL; b. London, Sept. 6, 1942; Writer, Publisher, Translator. Royal Literary Fund Fell, Univ. Hertfordshire & Westminster (2002-08); Publ.: Kitaj (2001); The Arithmetic of Memory (1999); Piotr Rawicz and Blood from the Sky (1996, and 2007); The Diary of Jerzy Urman (1991); Primo Levi's War against Oblivion (1990); After the Dream (1979). Ad.: 8 The Oaks, Woodside Av., N12 8AR. Email anthony.rudolf@ virgin.net.

RUDOLF, Mary, MBBS, BSc, DCH, FAAP, FRCPCH, b. London, July 15, 1951; m. Michael Krom; Consultant Paediatrician, Leeds PCT; Professor of Child Health, Univ. Leeds (2004-); form. Paediatric Clinical and Res. Fellow, Brown Univ. (1989-91); form. Consult., Paediatrician, Child Development Centre, Haifa (1986-90). Publ. include: Paediatrics and Child Health (with M. Levene, 2007, BMA Book Award; 2nd ed.); At a Glance Paediatrics (with M. Levene, 2004, trans Japanese). Ad.: Community Paediatrics, 3-5 Belmont Grove, Leeds LS2

9DE. ☎ 0113-392 6352; Fax 0113-392 5169. Email mary.rudolf@leedsth.nhs.uk

SACERDOTI, Cesare David Salomone; b. Florence, Feb. 24, 1938; m. Judith née Margulies; Publisher, Company Director; Man. Dir. H. Karnac (Books) Ltd (1984-99); Publications Dir. Int. Psychoanalytical Assoc. (2002-08); Tr. Winnicott Clinic of Psychotherapy Charitable Tr. (1999-); President, Bd. of Elders, Spanish & Portuguese Jews' Cong. (2000-04), Thesoureiro (2000-3), V. President (1996-2000); Parnas Heshaim (1995-2000); Dir. Sephardi Centre Ltd (1997-). Ad.: 25 Manor House Drive, London NW6 7DE. ☎ 020-8459 2012. Fax 020-8451 8829. Email cesare@sacerdoti.com.

SACKER, Anthony (Tony); b. London, March 2, 1940; Solicitor; V. President BoD (2000-03); Chairman, City of London Law Society (1998-2001); Chairperson, Union of Lib. and Prog. Syns. (1990-95); T. ULPS (1988-90); Vice-Chairman, LBC-CJE (2001-05); Freeman of City of London. Publ.: Practical Partnership Agreements (1995). Ad.: ☎ 01923 842225. Email tony@sacker.co.uk.

SACKS, Chief Rabbi Sir Jonathan Henry, MA (Cantab), PhD, DD (Lambeth), Hon. DD (Camb), Hon. DD (King's Coll., Lond.), Hon. D. Univ. (Middx.), Hon. D. Univ (Glasgow); b. London, March 8, 1948; m. Elaine née Taylor; Chief Rabbi of the United Hebrew Congregations of the Commonwealth (1991-); Assoc. President, Conf. European Rabbis (1999-); Vis. Prof. Philosophy Hebrew Univ.; Vis. Prof. Theology and Religious Studies, King's College, London; Vis. Prof. Philosophy, Univ. Essex (1989-90); form. Princ., Jews College and holder of the Lord Jakobovits Chair (1984-1990); M. Marble Arch Syn. (1983-1990); M., Golders Green Syn. (1978-1982); BBC Reith Lect. (1990); Ed. L'Eylah (1984-1990); Hon. Fell. Gonville and Caius Coll. Cambridge (1993-). Publ.: Torah Studies (1986); Tradition and Transition (1986); Traditional Alternatives (1989); Tradition in an Untraditional Age (1990); The Persistence of Faith (1991); Arguments for the Sake of Heaven (1991); Orthodoxy Confronts Modernity (1991); Crisis and Covenant (1992); One People: Tradition Modernity and Jewish Unity (1993); Will We Have Jewish Grandchildren? (1994); Faith in the Future (1995); Community of Faith (1995); The Politics of Hope (1997); Morals and Markets (1999); Radical Then, Radical Now (2000); A Letter in the Scroll (2000); Celebrating Life (2000); The Dignity of Difference (2002); The Passover Haggadah (2003; From Optimism to Hope (2004); To Heal a Fractured World (2005); Authorised Daily Prayer Book (4th ed. New translation and commentary, 2007) Ad.: Office of the Chief Rabbi, 735 High Road, London N12 0US. ☎ 020-8343 6301. Fax 020-8343 6310. Email info@chiefrabbi.org. Website www.chiefrabbi.org.

SAIDEMAN, Seymour Geoffrey, FCA; b. London, April 5, 1939; Senior Vice President of B'nai B'rith International; Mem. B'nai B'rith International Councilon United Nations Affairs;Hon. Life President, B'nai B'rith Europe; form. President, B'nai B'rith Europe (1999-2003); form. National President, B'nai B'rith District 15 of Great Britain and Ireland (1997-99); form. President, United Syn. (1992-96); form. Chairman, Chief Rabbinate Council (1992-96); form. Chairman, London Board of Jewish Rel. Educ. (1984-87); form. Chairman, Governors JFS Comprehensive Sch. (1984-87). Ad.: 19 Rees Drive, Stanmore, HA7 4YN.

SALAMON, Rabbi Thomas; b. Kosice, May 10, 1948; Rabbi/Solicitor; m. Renée née Heffes; M., Westminster Syn. (1997-); M., Hampstead Ref. Jewish Com. (1988-90); M., Hertsmere Progressive Syn. (1980-88); Assoc. M., West London Syn. (1972-75); Exec. Dir., Norwood Child Care (1975-80). Ad.: Westminster Synagogue, Kent House, Rutland Gardens, London SW7 1BX. ☎ 020-7584 3953. Fax 020-7581 8012.

SALASNIK, Rabbi Eli; b. Old City of Jerusalem; Rav. in London since 1950 Chairman, Rabbin. C., East Lond. and West Essex; District Rav Lond. Bd. for Shechita. Ad.: 8 The Lindens, Prospect Hill, Waltham Forest, London E17 3EJ.

SALASNIK, Rabbi Zorach Meir, BA, FJC; b. Lond., July 29, 1951; M., Bushey & Distr. Syn. (1979-); Sec., Chief Rabbi's Cabinet; Chairman Rabbin. C., US (2002-05); Senior Hospital Chaplin; Hertfordshire SACRE; Chaplain, Rishon Multiple Sclerosis Aid Gp.; Gov., Agency for Jewish Education; form. M., Notting Hill Syn., Leytonstone & Wanstead Syn.; Ad.: 8 Richfield Rd., Bushey Heath, Herts., WD23 4LQ. ☎ 020-8950-6453. Email rabbi.salasnik@busheyus.org.

SAMUEL, David Herbert, 3rd Viscount, of Mount Carmel and Toxteth, OBE, MA (Oxon), PhD

(Jerusalem), CChem, FRSC (UK); b. Jerusalem, July 8, 1922; Scientist, Prof. Emeritus, Weizmann Inst. of Science, Rehovot; President, Shenkar Coll. of Textile Tech. and Fashion, Ramat Gan (1987-94); Dir., Centre for Neurosciences and Behavioural Res., Weizmann Inst. of Science (1978-87); Dean, Faculty of Chemistry (1971-73); Dep. Chairman, Scientific C. (1963-65); Postdoctoral Fel., Chemistry Depts, Univ. Coll., London (1956); Harvard Univ. (1957-58); Biodynamics Lab., Univ. of California at Berkeley (1965-66); Visiting Royal Society Prof. MRC Neuroimmunology Unit, Univ. Coll. London (1974-75); Dept of Pharmacology, Yale University Medical School (1983-84); McLaughlin Visiting Prof. Life Sciences, McMaster Univ., Canada (1984); Visiting Prof. Chem. Dept, Univ. of York (1996-97); served in British Army (UK, India, Burma, Sumatra) (mentioned in Despatches) (1942-46); IDF (1948-49); Scopus Award, Hebrew University (2000), Tercentenary Medal, Yale University (2001); Hon. Fellowship, Shenkar College (2002). Publ.: The Aging of the Brain (D. Samuel et al, edrs, 1983); Memory: how we use it, lose it and can improve it (1999), and over 300 scientific articles. Ad.: Weizmann Institute, Rehovot, Israel. ☎ (972)-89344229; 36023507. Fax (972)-36054917. Email dhsamuel@gmail.com.

SAMUEL, Edgar Roy, BA (Hons), M.Phil, FRHistS, FSMC, DCLP; b. Hampstead, 1928; m. Louise Hillman née Shalom; Chairman Publ. Cttee JHSE; Past Dir., Jewish Museum (1983-95); Past President, JHSE (1988-90), Records & Treasures Cttee., Span. & Port Jews. Cong., Lond. Publ.: At the End of the Earth: Essays in the History of the Jews of England and Portugal (2004). Ad.: 5 Hollyview Close, Hendon, NW4 3SZ. ☎ 020-8203 7712.

SAMUELSON, Sir Sydney Wylie, CBE, Hon. D. Sheffield Hallam U.; b. Paddington, London, Dec. 7, 1925, m. Doris née Magen; British Film Commissioner (1991-97); Fel. British Film Institute (1997); Fd., Chairman & Chief Exec., Samuelson Group PLC (1954-1990); Trustee (1973-2008) and Fellow (1993), British Academy of Film and Television Arts, Chairman of Council (1973-76), F. Tr. (1977-2008); Guild of British camera Technicians; Hon. Fell (1970) and Patron (1997), British Kinematograph Sound and Television Society; President (2002-) Projected Picture Tr. Member of Cinema and Television Veterans (1970), President (1980-81), Member of President's Council (2002-); President (1985-), Israel Association for the Mentally Handicapped (AKIM); Mem., Exec. Cttee, Inter-Parliamentary Council Against Antisemitism; Mem., Beth Hatefutsoth. Ad.: 31 West Heath Ave., NW11 7QJ. ☎ 020-8455 6696.

SANDERS, Jeremy Keith Morris, ScD., FRS, FRSC, CChem; b. London, May 3, 1948; m. Louise Sanders née Applebaum; Research Chemist and Academic; University of Cambridge: Lecturer in chemistry (1973-92), Reader (1992-96). Professor (1996-), Head of Dept. (2000-06), Deputy Vice-Chancellor (2006-); Head of School of Physical Sciences (2009). Publ.: Modern NMR Spectroscopy (with B.K. Hunter, 1987, 2nd ed. 1993). Ad.: University Chemical Laboratory, Lensfield Rd., Cambridge CB2 1EW ☎ 01223 336411. Fax 01223 336017 Email jkms@cam.ac.uk

SANDLER, Merton, MD, FRCP, FRCPath, FRCPsych, b. Salford, Mar. 28, 1926; m. Lorna née Grenby; Emeritus Prof. of Chemical Pathology, Royal Postgraduate Med. Sch., Instit. of Obstetrics & Gynaecology, London Univ.; H. Consultant Chemical Pathologist, Queen Charlotte's and Chelsea Hospital. Publ.: Scientific writings. Ad.: 33 Park Rd., East Twickenham, Middx. TW1 2QD. ☎ 020-8892 9085. Fax 020-8891 5370. Email m.sandler@imperial.ac.uk.

SAPERSTEIN, Marc Eli, Professor, AB (Harvard), MA (H.U.), MA (Hebrew Union C.), PhD (Harvard); b. Brooklyn, NY, Sept. 5, 1944; m. Tamar de Vries Winter; Academic; Principal, Leo Baeck College, London (2006-); Chair, Jewish History, George Washigton Univ. (1997-2006); Chair, Jewish History and Thought, Washington Univ., St. Louis (1986-97); Assoc. Prof., Jewish St., Harvard Divinity School (1983-86); Asst. Prof. (1979-83), Lect. Hebrew Lit., Harvard (1977-79). Publ. include edited volumes and contributed articles in Jewish history, literature and thought. Books: Decoding the Rabbis: a Thirteenth- Century Commentary on the Aggadah (1980); Jewish Preaching 1200-1800 (1980); Moments of Crisis in Jewish-Christian relations (1989); 'Your Voice Like a Ram's Horn': Themes and Texts in Traditional Jewish Preaching (1996); Exile in Amsterdam: Saul Levi Morteira's Sermons to a Congregation of 'New Jews' (2005); Jewish Preaching in Times of War 1800-2001 (2007). Ad.: Leo Baeck College, Sternberg Centre, 80 East End Road, London N3 2SY. ☎ 020-8349 5601; Fax 020-8349 5619; Email marc.Saperstein@lbc.ac.uk.

SARAH, Rabbi Elizabeth Tikvah, BSc (Soc.); b. 1955; Semichah Leo Baeck Coll. (1989); Rabbi, Brighton and Hove Progressive Synagogue (2001-); Rabbi, Leicester Progressive J. Cong. (1998-2000); Buckhurst Hill Reform Syn. (1989-94); Assoc. J. Chaplain Brighton Univ. (2003-); Univ. Sussex (2008); Dir. Programmes RSGB, Dep. Dir. Sternberg Centre (1994-97); Chair, Rabbinic In-Service Training, Leo Baeck Coll. (1996-2002); Pt. time Lect. Leo Baeck College (1997-2002). Publ. include: Co-ed., Learning to Lose – Sexism and Education (1980); On the Problem of Men (1982); Jewish Explorations of Sexuality (1995); Renewing the Vision (1996); Taking up the Timbrel (2000); Lesbian Rabbis - the First Generation (2001); Machzor Ruach Chadashah (2003); Aspects of Liberal Judaism (2004). Mem. Edr. Bd., Manna (1994-); Ad.: Brighton & Hove Progressive Syn., 6 Lansdowne Rd, BN3 1FF.

SAXTON, Robert Louis Alfred, MA (Cantab), DMus (Oxon), FGSM; b. London, Oct. 10, 1953; Composer and Univ. Lect.; Fel. and Tutor in Music, Worcester College, Oxford (1999-); Hd. Composition, RAM (1998-99); Hd. Composition, GSMD (1991-97). Publ.: Over 50 compositions; 20 commercial recordings; articles. Ad.: Worcester College, Oxford OX1 2HB. Email robert.saxton@music.ox.ac.uk.

SCHAMA, Simon Michael, CBE, PhD; b. London, Feb. 13, 1945; m. Virginia Papaioannou; Writer and Broadcaster; Univ. Prof., Columbia University. Presented BBC TV series: History of Britain. Publ.: Patriots and Liberators: Revolution in the Netherlands, 1780-1813; Two Rothschilds in the Land of Israel; The Embarrassment of Riches: An Interpretation of Dutch Culture in the Golden Age; Citizens: A Chronicle of the French Revolution; Dead Certainties (Unwarranted Speculations); Landscape and Memory; Rembrandt's Eyes; A History of Britain (3 vols). Ad.: Columbia University, 1180 Amsterdam Avenue, MC 2533, New York, NY 10027.

SCHMOOL, Marlena (née Lee), BSoc. Sc; b. Leeds, 1941; Social Res. Consultant; Dir. Community Issues Divison, BoD (1999-2003); Publ.: Women in the Jewish Community (with S.H. Miller) (1994); A Profile of British Jewry (with F. Cohen) (1998); The Relaxation of Community? (2003) Jewish Britain a Snapshot from the 2001 Census;(with D. Graham and S. Waterman, 2007); various statistical publications. Email marlena.@f-ire.com.

SCHONFIELD, Jeremy Joseph, BA (East Anglia), PhD (Cantab); b. London, July 11, 1951; m. Tamar née Rahmani; Mason Lecturer, Oxford Centre for Hebrew and Jewish Studies (1989-); Lecturer, Leo Baeck College (1995-) Rabbi John Rayner Lecturer in Liturgy (2006); Editor of Publications, Jewish Historical Society of England (1981-); Transactions, Vols 27-41; Joint Founding Editor, Bulletin of the Anglo-Israel Archaeological Society (1982), editorial team (1982-99); Assistant Director, Israel Diaspora Trust (1988-2002); Thesoureiro do Heshaim (2004-). Publ. (jt. ed.) Film, History and the Jewish Experience a Reader (1986); (ed.) The Barcelona Haggadah (1991); (ed.) La Biblia de Alba (1992); (ed.) Me'ah Berakhot (1994); (ed.) Perek Shirah (1996); (ed.) The Rothschild Haggadah (2000); (ed.)The North French Miscellany (2003); Undercurrents of Jewish Prayer (2006); Megillat Esther (ed., 2007). Ad.: 71 Woodland Rise, London N10 3UN. ☎ 020-8365 3226. Email jjschon@globalnet.co.uk.

SCOTT, Lee, M.P.; b. London, Apr. 6, 1956; m. Estelle née Dombey; Consultant; MP (Con.) for Ilford North (2005-); C. Redbridge (1998-06); Scott Associates Consultancy on Regeneration. Adr.: House of Commons, London SW1A 0AA. Email scottle@parliament.uk

SEAL, Gail (née Lew), b. London, Oct. 29, 1948; m. Michael Seal; Member, Jewish Leadership Council; Adv. Bd. LJCC; Tr. Tel Aviv Found.; Bd. Latrun, Israel; Tr. UK Friends of OR; JNF (Educ. Officer, 1987; Deputy President, 1993, President, 1995-2007); Founder Mem., & Co-Chair, Communal Liaison group; Vice-President, Zionist Federation; Bd. Mem, BICOM. Ad.: c/o JLC. Email gail@gbseal,co,uk..

SEBAG-MONTEFIORE, Harold, MA (Cantab); b. Dec. 5, 1924; m. Harriet née Paley; Barrister at Law, President, AJA (1965-71), Dep. Circuit Judge (1973-83); Tr., Royal Nat. Theatre Fdn.; Jt. President, Barkingside Jewish Youth Centre (1988-94); Freeman City of London, Chevalier Legion d'Honneur. Ad.: 4 Breams Buildings, London EC4. ☎ 020-7353 5835.

SECHER, Paul, LLB; b. Whitehaven, March 1, 1951; Man. Dir., JSB Group (Training, Consultancy and Publishing); Mem. Employment Tribunal; Vice-President Commonwealth Jewish C. Author/contributor, books and articles on employment law, communication and management; Ed., Employment Lawletter. Ad.: Dove House, Arcadia Avenue, London N3 2JU. ☎ 020-8371 7000. Fax 020-8371 7001. Email paul.secher@jsbonline.com.

SEGAL, Anthony Walter, MB, ChB, MD, MSc, PhD, DSc, FRCP, FMedSci, FRS; b. Johannesburg, Feb. 24, 1944; Charles Dent Prof. of Med. Lond. Univ., attached Univ. Coll. & Middlesex Hospital Med. Sch. Ad.: 48B Regents Park Rd., NW1 7SX. ☎ 020-7586 8745.

SHAERF, Paul Simon, MA (Cantab); b. London, March 4, 1950; m. Judith née Tunkel; Judicial officeholder; Ombudsman (2001-). Ad.: Board of Deputies, 6 Bloomsbury Square, London WC1A 2LP. Messages ☎ 020-7543 0105. Fax 020-7543 0010. Email ombudsman@bod.org.uk.

SHAHAR, Tovia, BA (Hebrew Univ.); b. Lond., Sept. 14, 1927; form. Sr. Educ. Officer, London Bd. of Jewish Religious Education; Registrar, Central Exam. Bd., Jews' Coll.; Dir., Faculty for Training of Teachers; Lect., Hebrew Grammar, Jerusalem Teachers Coll.; HM, Moriah Coll., Sydney; Dir., Jewish Studies, Mt. Scopus Coll., Melbourne. Publ.: Medinatenu. Ad.: 16/6 Rehov Kfar Ivri, Nevei Ya'akov, Jerusalem 97472. ☎ 02-656-5734.

SHAMIR, Yitzhak; b. Ruzinoy, Poland, 1915; form. Prime Min., State of Israel (June 1990-June 1992; Oct. 1983-Sept 1984; Oct. 1986-Mar. 1990); Vice-Premier (1984-86), Foreign Min. (1980-86); Herut Leader; M. K. (1973-96); Member, Betar in Poland emigrated Palestine 1935; joined Irgun Zvai Leumi (1937); later helped reorganise Central Cttee., Lohamei Herut Yisrael. Publ.: Summing Up (1994). Ad.: Beit Amot Misphat, 8 Shaul HaMelech Blvd., Tel Aviv. ☎ Tel Aviv 695-1166.

SHARON, Ariel, LLB (HU); b. Kfar Malal, 1928; Prime Minister of Israel (2001-06); Career officer in the IDF (1948-72); M.K. (1974-2006); Minister of Agriculture (1977-81); Minister of Defence (1981-83); Minister of Industry and Trade (1984-90); Minister of National Infrastructure (1996-98); Minister of Foreign Affairs (1998-99); Chairman of Likud Party (1999-2001). Publ.: Warrior. Ad.: POB 187, Kiryat Ben Gurion, Jerusalem 91919.

SHATZKES, Pamela Joy, BA, MA, PhD; b. New York, June 12, 1949; m. Jerry Shatzkes; Historian; Lecturer, Dept., International History, LSE (1998-2002); Lect., Holocaust Studies, LSJS (2001); Chair, International Orthodox Forum, LSJS (1999-2000); Lect., Spiro Institute (1989-1992). Publ.: Holocaust and Rescue: Impotent or Indifferent? Anglo-Jewry, 1938-1945 (2004). Ad.: 13 Danescroft Gardens, London NW4 2ND. ☎ 020-8203 2166. Fax 020-8201 5252. Email p.j.shatzkes@lse.ac.uk.

SHAW, Rabbi Andrew Clive, BEng. (Hons), MA; b. London, Sept. 18,1971; m. Gila née Zamir; Community Rabbi, Stanmore & Canons Park Synagogue; Exec. Dir., Tribe; form. Nat. Education Coord., UJS (1994-95); Dir., Youth New Hempstead Syn., NY (1998-2000)(; Consult., Facilitator, Jewish Assoc.,Business Ethics (2000-); Chaplain, Mayor of Harrow (2006-07). Publ.: 50 Days for 50 Years (ed., 1995); 60 Days for 60 Years (ed., 2005); 60 Days for 60 Years: Israel (gen. ed., 2008). Ad.: 25, Wychwood Close, Edgware, Middx HA8 6TE. ☎ 020-8343 5656 rabbishaw@tribeuk.com

SHAW, Martin, BA; b. London, Aug. 16, 1949; Fundraising and Management Consult. (2002-); Gen. Man. Variety Club, GB (2001-2); Chairman, Jubilee Waterside Centre (1998-2008); Chairman, Haringey Shed (2001-); Senior Consult, Charity Recruitment (1999-2001); Ind. Consult, Action Planning (1995-99); Exec. Dir. of the Assoc. for Jewish Youth (1989-95), Senior Youth Off., London Borough of Ealing (1986-89); Sen. Youth Off., ILEA (1983-86); Project Dir. Nat. C. for Voluntary Youth Services (1979-82). Publ.: Young People and Decision; Putting the Fun into Fund raising. Ad.: 64 The Grove, Edgware, Middx. HA8 9QB. ☎ 020-8958 6885. Email mshaw@dircon.co.uk.

SHAW, Peter; b. London, Dec. 17, 1935, m. Leila; Sec., Jewish Youth Fund (1984-2008); Exec. Dir., Jewish Child's Day (1987-2006); Clerk, Finnart House School Trust; Bd. Memb. (1977-2005); Chief Exec. 1971-77) Redbridge Jewish Youth & Com. Centre; Exec. C., Bernhard Baron St. George's Jewish Settlement (1990-98, 2008); Tr., The Duveen Trust Org. (1990-96, 2008); Sec., Stamford Hill Assoc. Clubs (1959-71); Dep. Dir., Youth & Hechalutz Dept., WZO (1977-80); Exec. Dir., Norwood Child Care (1980-84); form. Chairman, Jewish Assn. of Professionals in Soc. Work, Chairman, Assn. of Execs. of Jewish Com. Orgs. (1982-84); Chairman, Jewish Programme Materials Project (1980-84). Ad.: 2 Lodge Close, Canons

Drive, Edgware, Middx HA8 7RL. ☎ 020-8381 2894. Email peter@landps.co.uk.

SHEFF, Mrs Sylvia Claire (née Glickman), MBE, JP, BA; b. Manchester, Nov. 9, 1935; Ret. Teacher; Concert and events promoter (2002-); Asst. Nat. Dir. (Nat. Projects Dir., 1974-85), Conservative Frs. of Israel (1985-89); Fdr. & Dir., Friendship with Israel, Group (European Parl.) (1979-90); P. (Fdr. Chairman, 1972-80), Manch. 35 Group Women's Campaign for Soviet Jewry (1980-); H. Sec., Nat. C. for Soviet Jewry (1987-89); Assoc. Dir. Jewish Cultural & Leisure Centre (1990-93); Del. BoD (1987-). Int. Co-ord. Yeled Yafeh Fellowship of Children of Chernobyl (1990-93). Magistrate (1976). Ad.: 6, The Meadows, Old Hall La., Whitefield, Manchester M45 7RZ. ☎/Fax 0161-766 4391.

SHEK, Daniel, b. Israel, June 16, 1955; m. Marie Memmi; Diplomat; Chief Exec., BICOM (2004-); Dir. European Div, Israel Ministry of Foreign Affairs; Consul Gen., USA Pacific North West; Chief Spokesman, Dir. Press Divi, MFA. Adr.: BICOM 5708, London WC1N 3XX. ☎ 020-7636 5500. Fax 020-7636 5600. Email daniels@bicom.org.uk.

SHELDON, Peter, JP, FCA; b. Chesterfield, June 11, 1941; m. Judith Marion née Grunberger; International Business Consultant; Chairman BATM Advanced Communications Ltd; M., BoD (2006-); Chairman, N. W. London Eruv Cttee (2001-); Tr. Finchley Jewish Primary School Tr (2007-); President United Synagogue (1999-2005); Hon. Officer (1996-99); Tr. Hadassah Medical Relief Assoc. UK (2006-), British Israel Chamber of Commerce (2006-), Tr. Chief Rabbinate Tr. (2005-), Chairman (2003-05); Chairman Kashrut Division London Beth Din (1996-99); Chairman Kerem Schools (1976-88); Council Mem. Friends of Bnei Akivah (1985-92). Ad.: 34 Fairholme Gardens, London N3 3EB. ☎ 020-8349 9462. Email sheldp@btinternet.com.

SHELDON, Rt. Hon. Lord Robert Edward, PC; b. Sept. 13, 1923; M.P. (Lab.) for Ashton-under-Lyne (1964–2001); form. Chairman, Public Accounts Cttee; form. Fin. Sec., Treasury. Ad.: 27 Darley Ave., West Didsbury, Manchester M20 8ZD.

SHELLEY, Ronald Charles, MBE, FCA; b. London, March 27, 1929; Chairman Jewish Military Museum; Nat. Chairman AJEX (2004-06; also 1975-77); Chairman AJEX Housing Assoc. (1987-91); T., BoD (1991-97); Tr., Jewish Museum. Ad.: 1st Floor, 7-10 Chandos St., London W1G 9DQ. ☎ 020-7323 6626. Fax 020-7255 1203.

SHERIDAN, Rabbi Sybil Ann, MA (Cantab); b. Bolton, Lancs., Sept. 27, 1953; m. Rabbi Dr. Jonathan Romain; M., Wimbledon & District Reform Synagogue; Chaplain, Roehampton Univ.. Publ. include: Stories from the Jewish World (1987, 1998), Creating the Old Testament (contr. 1994), Hear Our Voice (1994, ed.), Renewing the Vision (1996, contr.); Abraham's Children: Jews, Christians and Muslims in Conversation (2006; contr.)Taking up the Timbrel (ed., 2000), Feminist Perspectives on History and Religion (2001, contr.). Ad.: 1 Queensmere Rd., Wimbledon, London SW19 5QD. ☎ 020-8946 4836. Fax 020-8944 7790. Email rabbisheridan@wimshul.org.

SHINDLER, Colin, BSc, MSc DipEd (Further Education), PhD; b. Hackney, London, Sept. 3, 1946; Prof. Israeli Studies, Chairman, Centre for Jewish Studies, SOAS; Assoc. Lect. in Chemistry, Open U.; Ed., Judaism Today (1994-2000); Political Affairs Sec., World Union of Jewish Students (1970-72); Ed., Jews in the USSR, (1972-75). Ed. Jewish Quarterly (1985-94); Dir. European Jewish Publication Soc. (1995-). Publ.: All Party Parl. Exhibition on Soviet Jewry (1974), Exit Visa: Detente, Human Rights and the Jewish Emigration Movement in the USSR (1978), The Raoul Wallenburg Exhibition (1982), Ploughshares into Swords? Israelis and Jews in the Shadow of the Intifada (1991), Israel, Likud and the Zionist Dream (1995), The Land Beyond Promise (2002), The Triumph of Military Zionism (2005); Nationalism and the Origins of the Israeli Right (2005); The Triumph of Military Zionism: Nationalism and the Origin of the Israeli Right (2006); What do Zionists Believe? (2007); History of Modern Israel (2008). Ad.: SOAS, Thornhaugh St., Russell Sq., London WC1H 0XG ☎ 020-7898 4358.

SHIRE, Michael, BA (Hons), MA, PhD (Hebrew Union Coll. LA); Rabbinic ordination at Leo Baeck Coll. (1996); b. 1957; Vice-Principal Leo Baeck College; Assoc. Memb. Int. Seminar on Religon and Values; Dir. of Education, Temple Beth Hillel, Hollywood (1983-88). Publ.: Ed. Cons. Illustrated Atlas of Jewish Civilization, The Illuminated Haggadah (1998), L'Chaim!

(2000), The Jewish Prophet (2002), Mazal Tov (2003). Ad.: Leo Baeck College, 80 East End Road, Finchley N3 2SY.

SHOMBROT, Jeffrey, OBE, BSc (Eng), FICE; b. London, Apr. 30, 1915; Ret. Consult, form. Supt. Eng. Admiralty and Environment Dept. Ad. Holly Lodge, 7 Aylmer Dr., Stanmore HA7 3EJ. ☎ 020-8954 4316.

SHUKMAN, Harold, BA (Nottingham), MA, D.Phil (Oxon); b. London, March 23, 1931; Emer. Fel., St. Antony's Coll., Oxford; Chairman Edr. Bd., East European Jewish Affairs. Publ.: Lenin and the Russian Revolution; Ed. Blackwell's Encyclopedia of the Russian Revolution; trans. Children of the Arbat, by A. Rybakov; Ed. & trans. Memories by Andrey Gromyko; Ed. & trans. Stalin: Triumph & Tragedy by Dmitri Volkogonov; Ed. Stalin's Generals; trans. Lenin (D. Volkogonov); Ed. & trans. Trotsky, The Rise and Fall of the Soviet Empire; Rasputin; The Russian Revolution; Stalin; (Ed.) Agents for Change: Intelligence Services in the 21st Century; Stalin and the Soviet–Finnish War (ed.); Secret Classrooms (with G. Elliot); Redefining Stalinism (ed.). War or Revolution: Russian Jews and Conscription in Britain 1917; Railways and the Russo-Japanese War (with F. Patrikeef) Ad.: St. Antony's Coll., Oxford, OX2 6JF. ☎ 01865 554147.

SHULMAN, Rabbi Nisson E., BA, MA, DHL; Capt. CHC, USNR, Ret.; b. New York, Dec. 12, 1931; m. Rywka née Kossowsky; Faculty, Yeshiva Univ. (1999-); Rabbi St John's Wood Syn., London (1988-94); Rabbi, Fifth Ave. Syn., New York (1978-85); Chaplain, US Naval Reserve, Ready (1956-88); Edr., Yearbook of Med. Ethics, Jews College, London (1993). Publ.: Authority and Community: 16th Century Polish Jewry (1986); Jewish Answers to Medical Ethics Questions (1988). Ad.: 383 Grand St., Apt. 207, New York City 10002. USA. ☎/Fax 212 505-3432.

SILK, Donald, MA (Oxon); b. Lond., 1928; Solicitor; H.V. President, Z. Fed.; Chairman, Fed. Z. Youth (1953-55), Tr. Chichester Festival Theatre. Ad.: 69 Charlbury Rd., Oxford OX2 6UX. ☎ 01865 513881.

SILVERMAN, Rabbi Robert (Reuven), BA, PhD, DD, MBACP, Adv. Dip. Counselling; b. Oxford, July 26, 1947; m. Dr Isobel Braidman; M., Manchester Reform Syn.; Hon. Fel., Middle Eastern Studies Dept. and Centre for Jewish Studies, Univ. Manchester; Chairman, Assembly of Rabbis, RSGB (1991-93); Anglo-Israel Friendship League, Manch.; Chaplain, Progressive Jew. Students, Manch.; form. Second M., Edgware Reform Syn.; M., Mikve Israel Emanuel, Curacao. Publ: Baruch Spinoza. Ad.: 26 Daylesford Rd., Cheadle, Cheshire, SK8 1LF. Fax 0161-834 0415 or 0161-839 4865.

SINCLAIR, Clive John, BA, PhD (East Anglia Univ.), FRSL; b. Lond., Feb 19, 1948; British Library Penguin Writers Fellow (1996); form. Lit. Edr., Jewish Chronicle; Writer-in-Residence Uppsala Univ., 1988; Prizes: Somerset Maugham Award (1981); Jewish Quarterly Award for Fiction (1997); PEN Silver Pen for Fiction (1997). Publ.: The Brothers Singer, Bedbugs, Hearts of Gold, Bibliosexuality, Blood Libels, Diaspora Blues, Cosmetic Effects, Augustus Rex, The Lady with the Laptop, A Soap Opera from Hell, Meet the Wife, Clive Sinclair's True Tales of the Wild West. Ad.: 22 Church St., St Albans, Herts. AL3 5NQ.

SINCLAIR, Rabbi Dr Daniel Bernard, LLB, LLM, LLD; b. London, June 30, 1950; Prof. Jewish Law and Comparative Biomedical Law, Tel Aviv College of Management Law School; Prof in Jewish Law, Fordham Univ., N.Y., Principal, Jews' College (1994-97); Lect. in Jewish Law, Gold College, Jerusalem (1978-84); Research Fellow, Institute for Research in Jewish Law, Hebrew University, Jerusalem (1978-84); Tutor in Jewish Law, Hebrew University, Jerusalem (1980-84); Visiting Research Associate, Centre for Criminology and the Social and Philosophical Study of Law, Edinburgh University (1984-87); M. of the Edinburgh Hebrew Congregation, Edinburgh (1984-87); Tutor in Jurisprudence, Faculty of Law, Edinburgh University, Edinburgh (1985-87); Senior Research Fellow, Institute for Research in Jewish Law, Jerusalem (1987-); Lect. in Jewish Law and Comparative Biomedical Law, Tel Aviv University (1988-); Lect. in Jewish Law and Philosophy of Halakhah, Pardes Institute, Jerusalem (1988-90); Lecturer in Jewish and Comparative Bioethics, Hebrew University, Jerusalem (1991); Jacob Herzog Memorial Prize, 1980; Asst. Ed. Jewish Law Annual (1990). Publ: Selected Topics in Jewish Law, vols. 4-5 (1994), Law, Judicial Policy and Jewish Identity in the State of Israel (2000); Jewish Biomedical Law: Legal and Extra-

Legal Dimensions (2003). Ad.: 3/21 Ben Tabbai St., Jerusalem 93591. ☎ (02) 6784268.

SINCLAIR, Dr Michael J.; b. London, Dec. 20, 1942, m. Penny; Chairman, Sinclair Montrose Trust Ltd.; Chairman, Laniado UK; Chairman Exec. Bd. World Council of Torah Education; Chairman of Management Cttee, Sidney and Ruza Last Foundation Home; Vice-Chairman, JNF; Bd. Mem British Friends of Arad; Tr. Jewish Outreach Network. Ad.: 6th Floor, 54 Baker St., London W14 7BU. ☎ 020-7034 1949. Fax 020-7034 1941 Email msinclair@carecapital.co.uk.

SINGER, Malcolm John, b. London, July 13, 1953; m. Sara née Nathan; Composer and Conductor; Director of Music, Yehudi Menuhin School (1998-). Ad.: Yehudi Menuhin School, Stoke D'Abernon, Cobham, Surrey KT11 3QQ.

SINGER, Norbert, CBE, BSc, PhD, Hon. DSc (Greenwich), C.Chem., FRSC; b. Vienna May 3, 1931; Physical Chemist; Fellow Queen Mary & Westfield College; Fellow Nene College; Vis. Prof. Univ. Westminster (1996-2001); Chairman Gov. St. Peter's CE Primary School (2004-); Chairman, Bexley Dist. Health Auth. (1993-94); Chairman Oxleas NHS Tr. (1994-2001); Chairman Rose Bruford College Gov. Body (1994-99); V. Chanc., Univ. Greenwich [form. Thames Polytechnic] (1978-92); Res. Chemist, Morgan Crucibles Co. Ltd. (1954-57); Lect. and eventually Dep. Hd. of Dept. of Chemistry Northern Polytechnic (1958-70); Hd. of Dept. of Life Sciences & Prof., Polytechnic of Central London (1971-1974); Assist. then Dep. Dir., Polytechnic of North London (1974-78); Member of C.N.A.A. & Cttees. (1982-93). Ad.: Croft Lodge, Bayhall Rd.; Tunbridge Wells, Kent TN2 4TP ☎ 01892 523821.

SITRUK, Rabbi Joseph, b. Tunis, 1944; Chief Rabbi of France; Chief Rabbi Marseilles (1975-87); Rabbi, Strassbourg (1970-75). Ad.: 19 rue St. Georges, 75009 Paris. ☎ 14970 8800.

SKEAPING, Lucie (née Finch), b. London, Dec. 30, 1951; m. Rodrick Mursell Skeaping; Musician; BBC Broadcaster; writer on early music; columnist for BBC Music Magazine (2005-); Presenter, BBC Early Music Show (1999-); Director, The Burning Bush (1990-). Publ.: Let's Make Tudor Music (2000); Broadside Ballads (2005); CDs include: Raisins and Almonds (1990)., Best of Yiddish, Klezmer and Sephardic Music (1996), Music of the Old Jewish World (2003). Penny Merriments (2005). Lusty Songs and Country Dances (2007). Ad.: 19, Patshull Rd., London NW5 2JX. ☎ 020-7485 3957; Email lucieskeaping@hotmail.com Website www.lucieskeaping.co.uk, and www.theburningbush.co.uk.

SKELKER, Philip David, MA (Oxon), FRSA; b. Sept. 7, 1946; H.M. Immanuel College (2000-); Educational Leadership Dir., UJIA (1998-2000); English master, Eton College (1997-98); form. HM, Carmel Coll. (1984-97), HM, King David High Sch., Liverpool (1981-84). Ad.: 4 Broadhurst Ave., Edgware, Middx. HA8 8TR. ☎ 020-8950 0604 Fax 020-8950 8687. Email pdskelker@immanuelhrts.sch.uk.

SKLAN, Alexander, BSc, Soc. Sci, MSc Econ, CQSW; b. London Jan. 13, 1947; Chief Exec. Jewish Care, Dir. of Quality Assurance; Dir. of Social Services Jewish Welfare Board (1979-90); Dir. of Social Services Jewish Care (1990-96); Jt. Chairman, Assembly of Masorti Synagogues (1996-2000); Dir. of Clinical Services, Medical Foundation for Care of Victims of Torture (1997-). Ad.: 111, Isledon Road, London N7 7JW. ☎ 020-7697 7777. Fax 020-7697 7799. Email asklan@torturecare.org.uk.

SMITH, Rabbi Amnon Daniel, MA; b. Hadera, Israel, Oct. 10, 1949; Sr. M., Edgware & Dist. Reform Syn.; form. Chairman RSGB Assembly of Rabbis; form. M., Wimbledon & Dist. Syn.; form. Assoc. M., West Lond. Syn.; Fdr. Chairman, Raphael Centre – a Jewish counselling service. Ad.: 118 Stonegrove, Edgware, HA8 8AB.

SOBER, Phillip, FCA, FRSA; b. London, April 1, 1931; m. Vivien; Chartered Accountant; form. Dir. Liberty International plc Mem. C. Univ. London (1998); Mem. Finance Cttee Univ. London (1999); form. Dir. Capital & Counties plc (1993-); form. Dir. Capital Shopping Centres plc (Chairman Audit Cttee.) (1994-); Consultant, BDO Stoy Hayward, Chartered Accountants (1990); form Gov. and Chairman of Audit Cttee., London Institute Higher Education Corporation (1994); form. Tr. Jewish Assoc. of Business Ethics; form. Chairman, Central Council for Jewish Community Services; form. Jt. Tr., Ravenswood; Partner, Stoy Hayward, Chartered Accountants (1958-90); Fell. of the Inst. of Chartered Accountants (1963-); International Partner and Member of Management Cttee., Stoy Hayward,

Chartered Accountants (1974-90); Chairman, Accounting Standards Cttee., British Property Federation (1976-83); Member Council, UK Central Council for Nursing, Midwifery and Health Visiting (1980-83); Crown Estate Commissioner (1983-94); Senior Partner, Stoy Hayward, Chartered Accountants (1985-90); Tr., Royal Opera House Tr. (1985-91); President, Norwood Child Care (1989-94); European Regional Dir., Horwath International (1990-94); Consult. Hunting Gate Group Ltd. (1992-95). Publ.: Articles in professional press on various subjects but primarily on property company accounting. Ad.: 67B, Clarendon Rd., London NW11 4JE ☎ 020-7221 8545

SOETENDORP, Rabbi David Menachem Baruch, DMB, FPC, MBACP; b. Amsterdam, July 1, 1945; M., Hatch End Masorti; form. Rabbi, Bournemouth Reform Syn; V. President, B'mouth Br., CCJ; Chairman Exodus 2000; J.; Psychodynamic Counsellor, Headway House Day Centre, Poole; Contrib., local radio, TV; Contr. 'Renewing the Vision', SPC London; fd. AFET; ; Counsellor; form. Rabbi, South Hants Reform Cong. Publ.: Op Weg Naar Het Verleden. Ad.: 25 De Lisle Rd., Bournemouth, BH3 7NF ☎ 01202 514788. Email soetendorp@ntlworld.com.

SOFER, Mark, b. London, Sept. 29, 1954; m. Sara née Giladi; Diplomat; Ambassador of Israel to Dublin (1999-); Policy adviser to the Ministry of Foreign Affairs, Jerusalem (1993-96); form. Dep. Consul-General, Israeli Consulate, New York (1991-93). Ad.: 121 Pembroke Road, Ballsbridge, Dublin 4, Ireland. ☎ 230-9400. Fax 230-9446.

SOLOMON, Sir Harry, KB, FRCP (Hon); b. Middlesbrough, March 20, 1937; Company Chairman; Hillsdown Holdings plc (1975-1993): Chairman (1987-1993); Non-Exec. Dir. (1993-97); Fel. of the Royal Coll. of Physicians (Hon.). Ad.: Hillsdown House, 32 Hampstead High St., London NW3 1QD. ☎ 020-7431 7739.

SOLOMON, Rabbi Norman, PhD (Manc), MA (Cantab.), BMus (Lond.); b. Cardiff, May 31, 1933; Fellow, Oxford Centre for Hebrew and Jewish Studies (1995-2001); form. Lect. Faculty of Theology, Univ. Oxford; form. Dir., Centre for Study of Judaism & Jewish Christian Relations, Selly Oak Colls.; President BAJS (1994); Edr., Christian Jewish Relations (1986-91); form. M., Birmingham Central Syn., Hampstead Syn., Lond., Greenbank Drive Syn., Liverpool, Whitefield Hebrew Cong., Manchester. Publ: Judaism and World Religion (1991); The Analytic Movement (1993); A Very Short Introduction to Judaism (1996); Historical Dictionary of Judaism (1998); Edr. Abraham's Children (2006). Ad.: 58 Thames Str., Oxford OX1 1SU. ☎ 01865-243424.

SPENCER, Charles Samuel, b. Lond. Aug. 26, 1920; Fine Art and Theatre Lect.; Exhibition organiser; Lond. correspondent art publ. in Italy, Germany, Greece, etc.; form. Sec., AJA, Maccabi Union, Brady Clubs, Edr., Art and Artists; Member Jewish Relief Unit (1944-48). Publ.: Erté; The Aesthetic Movement: A Decade of Print Making, Leon Bakst and the Ballets Russes, The World of Serge Diaghilev, Cecil Beaton, Film and Stage Designs, 'Dear Charliko': Memoirs of a British Art Critic in Greece; Bakst in Greece. Ad.: 24A Ashworth Rd., W9 1JY. ☎ 020-7286 9396.

SPIRO, Nitza (née Lieberman), M.Phil. (Oxon); b. Jerusalem, Nov. 1937; m. Robin; Dir. The Spiro Ark, an educational, languages and cultural institute for adults (1978-98); Org. national and international Jewish tours and cultural events; Deputy Dir. Ulpan Akiva Netanya, Israel (1959-68); Lect. in Hebrew and Hebrew Literature, Univ. Oxford (1976-83); Exec. Dir. Spiro Inst. (1983-98); teaching of Hebrew on radio. Publ.: Hebrew Correspondence Course (1987); Hebrew Accelerated Learning Course (Suggestopedia course co-author); weekly Hebrew column London Jewish News. Ad.: 43 St John's Wood Ct., St John's Wood Rd., London NW8 8QR. ☎ 020-7723 9991. Fax 020-7289 6825. Email spiroark@aol.com. Website www.spiroark.org.

SPIRO, Robin Myer, MA, M.Phil (Oxon), FCA; b. London, Feb. 9, 1931; m. Nitza née Lieberman; Dir. Property Companies (1961-78); Creator and developer of St Christopher's Place, off London's Oxford St. (W1); Founding Dir. and part-time lecturer in Jewish History at Spiro Institute (1978-98); Jt. Founding Dir., Spiro Ark (1999-); Develope, Anglo - Jewish Heritage Trail (2006-); regular lecturer in Jewish History at Florida Atlantic University, Boca Raton, USA; org., contributor, The Jewish Enigma (Open Univ., BBC). Ad.: 43/44 St. John's Wood Court, St. John's Wood Rd., London NW8 8QR.

STEEN, Anthony, MP; b. London, July 22, 1939; Barrister, social worker, youth ldr., law lect;

MP (Con.) for Totnes (1997-), South Hams (1983-97), Liverpool, Wavertree (1974-83); V. Chairman All-Party Fisheries Gp; Party Cttees: Sec. to 1922 Cttee (2001-), Public Admin. (2001-2); Chairman, Urban & Inner City Cttee (1987-93); Chairman Deregulation Cttee (1994-97); European Scrutiny (1997-); Chairman Sane Planning; V. Chairman, Health & Soc. Services (1979-80);Vice-Chairman Parl. Brit. Caribbean Gp; (2006-). Publ.: New Life for Old Cities (1981), Tested Ideas for Political Success (rev. 1993), Public Land Utilisation Management Schemes (PLUMS) (1988). Ad.: House of Commons, SW1A 0AA. ☎ 020-7219 5045. Email steena@parliament.uk.

STEINER, Prof. George, FBA, MA, D.Phil; Hon. D.Litt: East Anglia, 1976; Louvain, 1980; Mount Holyoke Coll., USA, 1983; Bristol, 1989; Glasgow, 1990; Liège, 1990; Ulster, 1993; Kenyon College, 1995; Trinity College, Dublin, 1995; b. Apr. 23, 1929; m. Zara née Shakow; Member, staff of the Economist, in London (1952-56); Extraordinary Fellow, Churchill College, Cambridge (1969); RA (Hon); Weidenfeld Professor of Comparative Literature, and Hon. Fellow of Balliol College, Oxford (1995-); Hon. Fellow St. Anne's College, Oxford; Inst. for Advanced Study, Princeton (1956-58); Gauss Lect., Princeton Univ. (1959-60); Fellow of Churchill Coll., Cambridge (1961-); Prof. of English and Comparative Literature, Univ. of Geneva (1974-94). Lectures: Massey (1974); Leslie Stephen, Cambridge (1986); W. P. Ker (1986), Gifford (1990), Univ. of Glasgow; Page-Barbour, Univ. of Viriginia (1987). Fulbright Professorship (1959-69); Vis. Prof., Collège de France (1992). O. Henry Short Story Award (1958); Guggenheim Fellowship (1971-72); Zabel Award of Nat. Inst. of Arts and Letters of the US (1970); Faulkner Stipend for Fiction, PEN (1983); Pres., English Assoc., 1975; Corresp. Mem., (Federal) German Acad. of Literature (1981); Hon. Mem., Amer. Acad. of Arts and Sciences (1989); FRSL (1964). PEN Macmillan Fiction Prize, 1993. Chevalier de la Légion d'Honneur (1984); Ludwig Börne Prize (2003). Publ: Tolstoy or Dostoevsky, 1958; The Death of Tragedy, 1960; Anno Domini, 1964; Language and Silence, 1967; Extraterritorial, 1971; In Bluebeard's Castle, 1971; The Sporting Scene: White Knights in Reykjavik, 1973; After Babel, 1975 (adapted for TV as The Tongues of Men, 1977); Heidegger, 1978; On Difficulty and Other Essays, 1978; The Portage to San Cristobel of A.H., 1981; Antigones, 1984; George Steiner: a reader, 1984; Real Presences: is there anything in what we say?, 1989; Proofs and Three Parables, 1992; No Passion Spent, 1996; The Deeps of the Sea, 1996; Homer in English (ed.), 1996; Errata: an Examined Life, 1997. Ad: 32 Barrow Rd., Cambridge CB2 2AS. ☎ 01223 61200.

STEPHENS, Judge Martin, QC, MA (Oxon); b. Swansea, June 26, 1939; Circuit Judge (since 1986); Recorder (1979-86); form. Chairman, Cardiff Jewish Rep. C. (1986-95). Member Parole Bd (1995-2000); Member Main Bd., Judicial St. Bd. (1997-2000); Bencher, Middle Temple (2004); Ad.: c/o Central Criminal Court, City of London, London EC4M 7EH.

STERLING, Baron of Plaistow (Life Peer) (Jeffrey Maurice), GCVO, CBE; Hon. DBA (Nottingham Trent Univ.); Hon. DCL (Durham), Kt., Order of St John; b. Dec. 27, 1934; m. Dorothy Ann née Smith; Paul Schweder and Co. (Stock Exchange (1955-57); G. Eberstadt & Co. (1957-62); Fin. Dir. Gen. Guarantee Corp. (1962-64); Mng. Dir., Gula Investments Ltd. (1964-69); Chairman Sterling Guarantee Trust plc (1969-) (merging with P&O 1985); The Peninsular and Oriental Steam Navigation Company Chairman, 19832005); Chairman, orgn. cttee. World ORT Union (1969-93), Mem. Exec. (1966-), Tech. svcs. (1974-), V. President Brit. ORT (1978-); Dep. Chairman and Hon. Tr. London Celebrations Cttee. Queen's Silver Jubilee (1975-83); Chairman Young Vic Co. (1975-83); V. Chairman and Chairman of the Exec. Motability (1977-); Bd. Dirs. British Airways (1979-82); Spl Adv. Sec. of State for Industry (1982-83) and to Sec. of State for Trade & Industry (1983-90); Chairman Govs. Royal Ballet Sch. (1983-99); Gov. Royal Ballet (1986-99); Chairman P&O Princess Cruises (2000); President of the General Council of British Shipping (1990-91); President, European Community Shipowners' Associations (1992-94); Freeman of the City of London; Hon. Captain Royal Naval Reserve (1991); Elder Brother Trinity House (1991); Hon. Fellow Institute of Marine Engineers (1991); Hon. Fellow Institute of Chartered Shipbrokers (1992); Hon. Member Institute of Chartered Surveyors (1993); Fellow of the ISVA (1995); Hon. Fellow R. Institute of Naval Architects (1997); Chairman, Queen's Golden Jubilee Weekend Tr. (2002). Ad. Office: 15, St. James's Place, London SW1A 1NP. ☎ 020-7409 2345.

STERNBERG, Sir Sigmund, KCSG, JP, DU, Essex, Open, Hebrew Union Coll., Leg. Hon.; b. Hungary, June 2, 1921; m. Hazel née Everett Jones; Chairman Martin Slowe Estates (1971-); Patron, Bd of Deputies (2005); Paul Harris Fell., Rotary Internat.; Life V. President, Keston Institute; Award of Honour; Officer Brother of the Order of St. John; Patron International Council of Christians and Jews; Mem. Board of Deputies of British Jews; Gov. Hebrew Univ. of Jerusalem; Life President Sternberg Centre for Judaism (1996-); Pres. RSGB, Movement for Reform (1998-); Founder Three Faiths Forum; Fell. Leo Baeck College;LL.D. (Leic, 2007); Order Pentru Merit (Romania, 2007); Templeton Prize for Progress in Religion (1998); Comdr., Order of Honour (Greece); Commander's Cross Order of Merit (Germany); Cmdr., Royal Order of Polar Star (Sweden) (1997); Wilhelm Leuschner Medal (Wiesbaden) (1998); Order of Commandatore of the Italian Republic (Italy) (1999); The Commander's Cross with a Star of the Order of Merit (Poland) (1999); Order of Bernardo O'Higgins Gran Cruz (Chile, 1999); Order of Ukraine for Public Services (2001); Order of Merit (Portugal, 2002); Madora Horseman (Bulgaria 2003);Off. Legion d' Honneur (2003); Hungarian Jewry Award (2004); Miranda Award (Venezuela 2004) Knight Grand Cross, Royal Order of francis I (2005) Order of Merit (Hungary, 2004); Co-ord. Religious Comp. World Economic Forum (2002-); Sen. Life V. President Royal College Speech & Language Therapists (2002-). Ad.: 80 East End Rd., N3 2SY. Fax 020-7485 4512.

STONE, Baron of Blackheath (Andrew Zelig), Hon. LLD (Oxford Brookes), Hon. D. Design (Kingston); b. Sept. 9, 1942; m. Vivienne née Lee; Company Director; N. Brown Group plc; Chairman Dipex; Deputy Chairman Sindication Capital; Patron Gauchers Assoc.; Cllr, Israel British Business Council; form. Jt. Man. Dir. Marks and Spencer plc (1994-2000); Gov. Weizmann Institute; Gov. British University of Egypt; Tr. Olive Tree Tr.; Tr. Israel Diaspora Tr.; Mem. Labour Friends of Israel; Ad.: House of Lords, London SW1A 0PW.

SUDAK, Rabbi Nachman, OBE; b. Feb. 3, 1936; Princ., Lubavitch Foundation (1959-); Lubavitcher Rebbe's Emissary in Britain. Ad.: 37 Portland Ave., N16 6HD. ☎ (H.) 020-8800 6432; ☎ (O.) 020-8800 0022.

SUMBERG, David Anthony Gerald, MEP; b. Stoke-on-Trent, June 2, 1941, m. Carolyn née Franks; Solicitor; Dir. Anglo-Israel Association (1997-2001); MEP, North West England (1999-); form. M.P. (Cons) for Bury South (1983-97); Parl. Pte. Sec., Attorney Gen. (1986-90); Jt. H.Sec., Parl. Group, Conservative Frs. of Israel, V.Chairman, All-Party Cttee., Release of Soviet Jewry; V. Chairman, All-Party War Crimes Group; Memb. Home Affairs Select Cttee. of the House of Commons, (1991-92); Memb. Foreign Affairs Select Cttee. House of Commons (1992-97); Mem. Lord Chancellor's Adv. Cttee. on Public Records (1992); Ad.: 42 Camden Sq., London NW1 9XA. ☎ 020-7267 9590.

SUMRAY, Monty, CBE, FINSTD, FCFI, FRSA; b. London, Oct. 12, 1918; m. Kitty née); Dir. of FIBI Bank (UK) Plc; V.-P., British-Israel Chamber of Commerce; Chairman, British Footwear Manufacturers Federation Project Survival Cttee.; V. President, Jewish Care; V -P., Stamford Hill branch of AJEX; Member of the Anti-Boycott Co-ordination Cttee.; Fel. of the Clothing & Footwear Instit.; Fel. of the Instit. of Dir.; Pres. London Footwear Manufacturers Assoc; Member of the Footwear Industry Study Steering Group, and Chairman of its Home Working Cttee.; President, British Footwear Manufacturers Federation (1976-77); Mem., Footwear Economic Development Cttee. Chairman, British-Israel Chamber of Commerce; Captain Royal Berkshire Regiment (1939-46); Served in Burma. Ad.: 6 Inverforth House, North End Way, London NW3 7EU. ☎ 020-8458 2788.

SUZMAN, Janet; b. Johannesburg, Feb. 9, 1939; Actress/Director; V. President C. of LAMDA; Hon. MA (Open University); Hon. D.Litt (Warwick, Leicester, QMW, London, Southampton, Middlesex, Kingston); Hon. Assoc. Artist, RSC. Publ.: Acting with Shakespeare (1996); Commentary on Antony and Cleopatra (2001); Free State: A South African Response to the Cherry Orchard (2000). Ad.: c/o Steve Kenis & Co, Royalty House, 72-74 Dean Street, London W1D 3SG. ☎ 020-7354 6001. Fax 020-7287 6328.

TABACHNIK, Eldred, QC, BA, LLB (Cape Town), LLM (London); b. Cape Town, Nov. 5, 1943; m. Jennifer; President Board of Deputies (1994–2000); President European Jewish Congress (1994-98); Hon. Officer (Warden), Richmond Syn. (1980-94); Chairman, British Friends of Boys Town, Jerusalem. Ad.:

TABICK, Rabbi Jacqueline Hazel (née Acker), BA (Hons.), Dip. Ed.; b. Dublin, Oct. 8, 1948; Rabbi North West Surrey Syngogue; Chairman, World Congress of Faiths; Patron, JCORE; V. President RSGB; Past Chairman, Assembly of Rabbis, RSGB; Past Chairman, Central Educ Cttee., R.S.G.B; Council of Reform & Liberal Rabbis. Ad.: Horvath Close, Weybridge, Surrey KT13 9QZ. ☎ 01932-855400.

TABICK, Rabbi Larry Alan, BA, MA, FLBC; b. Brooklyn, NY, Nov. 24, 1947; Rabbi, Hampstead Ref. Jewish Com. (1976-81, 1990-); Rabbi Leicester Progressive Jewish Community (1994-98); Assoc. Rabbi, Edgware & Dist. Ref. Syn. (1986-90); Asst. Rabbi, Middlesex New Syn. (1981-86). Publ. Growing into your Soul (2005). Ad.: 1 Ashbourne Grove, Mill Hill, NW7 3RS. ☎ 020-8959 3129. Email rabtab@tabick.abel.co.uk. Website www.tabick.abel.co.uk.

TAHAN, Ilana Antoinette (née Mates), BA (HU), MPhil (Aston) Dip. Lib., CILIP; b. Bucharest, Dec. 6, 1946; m. Dr Menashe Tahan; Librarian; Hebraica Curator (1989-) & Head of Hebrew Section, British Library (1997-); Convenor, Hebraica Libraries Group (2007-). Publ.: Memorial volumes to Jews and communities destroyed in the Holocaust: a bibliography of BL holdings (2007); Hebrew Manuscripts: the power of script and image (2007). Ad.: APAC, The British Library, 96 Euston Road, London NW1 2DB ☎ 020-7412 7646. Fax 020-7412 7641 Email ilana.tahan@bl.uk

TANKEL, Henry Isidore, OBE, MD, FRCS; b. Glasgow, Jan. 14, 1926; surgeon; Non-Exec. Dir., Southern Gen. Hosp. NHS Trust (1993-97); Chairman W. of Scotland Branch CCJ (1998-2001); Chairman, Glasgow J. Hsng. Assoc. (1996-2001); H.V. President Glasgow Jew. Rep. C.; Sec. Glasgow and West of Scotland Kashruth Commission; Chairman, Scottish Joint Consultants Cttee. (1989-92); Member Scottish Health Service Advisory Cttee. (1989-92); Jt. Con. Cttee. (UK) (1989-92); Chairman, Youth Liaison Cttee.- Glasgow Hospital Med. Services Cttee; Scottish Hospital Med. Services Cttee. Books: Gastroenterology – an intergrated course (contrib 1983); Cancer in the Elderly (contrib 1990). Ad.: 26 Dalziel Drive, Glasgow, G41 4PI . ☎ 0141-423 5830.

TANNENBAUM, Mrs. Bernice Salpeter; b. New York City; Liaison Hadassah Foundation; form. Chairman Hadassah Magazine; Sec. Jewish Telegraphic Agency; form. Chairman, Amer. Section, WZO; Fd, Hadassah International; Nat. President, Hadassah (1976-80); Life Tr., United Israel Appeal; form. M, WJC Amer. Section and Jewish Agency; Hon. President, World Confed., United Zionists; Gov. Bd., Hebrew Univ.; Bd., U.I.A. Publ.: It Takes a Dream, The Story of Hadassah; The Hadassah Idea (co.-ed.). Ad.: Hadassah, 50 W 58 Street, N.Y., 10019. ☎ (212) 303-8081.

TEMERLIES, Marc Stephen, ACA, BSc, ALCM; b. Hove; m. Idit née Herstik; Chartered Accountant & Investment Banker; Conductor, Choirmaster, Arranger and Pianist; Fd and Conductor, Ne'imah Singers (1993-); Choirmaster, St John's Wood Syn. (1996-); Chazan, Hove Hebrew Congregation (1991-92). Ad.: 4, 7 Rehov Ha Chayil, Ra'anana, 43316. ☎ 972-9772 4857. Email marc.temerlies@citigroup.com.

TEMKO, Edward J.; b. Washington, DC, USA, Nov. 5, 1952; Journalist, Ed. Jewish Chronicle (1990-2004); Foreign Corr. United Press International (1976); Associated Press (1977-78), The Christian Science Monitor (1978-1988); World Monitor Television (1984-90). Publ.: To Win or To Die (Biography of Menachem Begin, 1987). Ad.:

TERRET, Norman Harold, JP; Compagnon d'Europe; FInstD, MBA; b. Ayr, Scotland, Jan. 10, 1951; President, CITS Group Hounslow, Middx.; SITA V. President, Marketing; Tr., British Israel Educ. Tr. Ad.: SITA, Lampton House, Lampton Road, Hounslow, Middx. TW3 4ED.

TIBBER, His Honour Anthony Harris; b. London, June 23, 1926; ret. Circuit Judge. Ad: 22 Holmwood Gardens, London N3 3NS. ☎ 020-8349 1287.

TILSON THOMAS, Michael; b. Dec. 21, 1944; Conductor; Musical Director, San Francisco S.; Artistic Director, New World S.; Princ. Guest Conductor, London Symphony Orchestra; Ad: c/o Columbia Artists Management Inc., 165 W. 57th Street, New York, NY 10019.

TOLEDANO, Dayan Pinchas, BA, PhD; b. Meknes, Morocco, Oct. 12, 1940; form. Rabbi, Wembley Sephardi Cong.; Eccl. Auth., Lond. Bd. of Shechita; V. President, Mizrachi Fed.; V. President, Herut, Gt. Brit., Patron, Mentally Handicapped Soc., Patron, Massoret; Edr., SRIDIM (Standing Cttee., Conf of European Rabbis). Publ.: Rinah-oo-Tefillah (co-Edr), Fountain of Blessings, Code of Jewish Law, Everlasting life-Laws of Mourning, Home Ceremonies, Sha'alou - Le Baruch, Rabbinic response (co-ed.). Ad.:

TOWNSLEY, Barry Stephen, CBE; b. London, Oct. 14, 1946; m. Laura Helen née Wolfson; Stockbroker; Chairman, Dawnay, Day Capital Markets (2005-); Company Director, Caprice Holdings Ltd. (2005-), Wentworth Group Holdings Ltd.(2004-) United Trust Bank Ltd. (2004-); chairman, Oxford Children's Hospital Campaign (2004-); Vice-President, Weizmanmn Inst. (2004-); Bd. Mem., Nat. Gallery East Wing Dev. Project (2002-); Principal Sponsor, Stockley Acad., Hillingdon (2000-); Vice Chairman, Serpentine Gallery. Adr.: Dawnay, Day Capital Markets. Email barry.townsley @dawnayday.com.

TRAVIS, Anthony Selwyn; b. Cardiff, June 9, 1932; m. Philippa née Brostoff; Emeritus Prof. of Planning, Prof. Urban Reg. Studies, Univ. of Birmingham; late Visiting Prof. in Tourism, Glasgow Caledonian Univ.; Director, East-West Tourism Consultancy; form. Programme Co-ordinator EEC PHARE. Tourism Programme for Poland; Dir. Research, Newcastle City Planning Dept. (1962-64); Prof. of Planning, Heriot Watt Univ., Edinburgh (1967-73); Prof and Dir., Centre for Urban and Regional Studies, Univ. of Birmingham; Past Mem. Birmingham and West Midland J. Rep. C.; Past Chairman 'Grads' ORT, FHU etc. Lecturer on synagogue design, history and Israel. Publ.: 300, including Recreation Planning for the Clyde (1970), Realising Tourism Potential of the S. Wales Valleys (1985), Report on 'Synagogue Design & Siting (for BoD). Ad.: 20 Mead Rise, Birmingham B15 3SD. ☎/Fax 0121-454 1215. Email tony@e-w-tourism.demon.co.uk.

TROPP, Asher, BSc (Econ), MA, PhD; b. Johannesburg, Jan. 2, 1925; Prof. of Sociology, University of Surrey (1967-87). Publ.: The School Teachers (1957); Jews in the Professions in Great Britain 1891-1991 (1991). Ad.: 162 Goldhurst Terrace, NW6 3HP. ☎ 020-7372 6662.

TUCKMAN, Fred, OBE; b. Magdeburg, June 9, 1922; Management Consultant; President, AJA (1989-95); MEP (1979-89), Conservative Spokesman, Soc. & Employment Affairs (1984-89); Cllr., Lond. Borough of Camden (1965-71); H.Sec., Conservative Bow Group (1958-9); Commanders Cross of the German Order of Merit 1990. Ad.: 6 Cumberland Rd., London SW13 9LY ☎ 020-8748 2392. Fax 020-8746 3918.

TURNER, Rev. Reuben; b. Karlsruhe, Jan. 8, 1924; Min., Finsbury Park Syn. (1948-50); Reader, Brixton Syn. (1950-68), Dir. Zion. Fed Syn C. (1967-70); Gen. Sec., Mizrachi-Hapoel Hamizrachi Fed. of Gt. Britain (1970-73). Director JNF Educ. Dept. (1973-91). Publ.: Jewish Living, The Popular Jewish Bible Atlas; Producer, The Four Brothers Kusevitsky (CD), Selections from the Seder service (CD), The Master Chazanim Collection. Ad.: 13 St Peter's Court, NW4 2HG. ☎ 020-8202 7023.

ULLENDORFF, Edward, MA (Jerusalem), D.Phil (Oxford), Hon. D.Litt (St Andrews), Hon. Dr Phil (Hamburg); Hon. Fell. SOAS, Hon. Fellow Oxford Hebrew Centre, FBA; b. Jan. 25, 1920; Prof Emer., Semitic Languages Lond. Univ. (since 1982); Prof. of Ethiopian Studies (1964-79); form. Prof. of Semitic Languages and Literatures, Manchester Univ. (1959-64); Jt. Edr., Journal of Semitic Studies; V. President, Brit. Academy (1980-82), Schweich Lect. (1967); V. President, Royal Asiatic Soc. (1975-79; 1981-85); Foreign Fell. Accademia Lincei, Rome; served in Brit. Mil. Govt , Eritrea and Ethiopia (1942-46); Asst. Sec. Palestine Govt (1947-48); Res. officer, Inst. Colonial Studies Oxford (1948-49); Reader in Semitic Languages, St. Andrews Univ. (1950-59); Chairman, Assn. of Brit. Orientalists (1963-64); Chairman, Anglo-Ethiopian Soc. (1965-68); Haile Selassie intern. prize for Ethiopian studies (1972). Publ.: The Semitic Languages of Ethiopia, The Ethiopians, Comp. Grammar of the Semitic Languages, Ethiopia and the Bible, Studies in Semitic Languages & Civilizations, The Hebrew Letters of Prester John, The Two Zions, From the Bible to Enrico Cerulli, H. J. Polotsky 1905-91, From Emperor Haile Selassie to H. J. Polotsky, 1995, Contributor to ODNB, etc. Ad.: 4 Bladon Close, Oxford, OX2 8AD.

UNTERMAN, Rev. Alan, BA, B.Phil, PhD; b. Bushey, Herts., May 31, 1942; form. M., Yeshurun Syn., Gatley, Cheshire; form. Lect., Comparative Rel. & Chaplain to Jewish Students, Manchester Univ.; Lect., Jerusalem Academy of Jewish Studies; Hillel Dir., Victoria, Australia. Publ: Encyclopaedia Judaica (Contribs), Wisdom of the Jewish Mystics, Jews their Religious Beliefs and Practices, Judaism, Penguin Dictionary of Religion (Contribs. on Judaism and Hinduism), Penguin Handbook of Living Religions (Contrib. Judaism), Dictionary of Jewish Lore and Legend. Ad.: 13 South Park Rd., Gatley, Cheshire, SK8 4AL. ☎ 0161-428 8469. Email unterman_alan@hotmail.com.

VEIL, Mme. Simone (née Jacob), Hon. DBE; b. Nice, July 13, 1927; deported to Auschwitz and Bergen-Belsen Nazi concentration camps (1944-45); m. 1946 Antoine Veil, Inspecteur des Finances. Educ.: Lycée de Nice; Lic. en Droit, dipl. de l'Institut d'Etudes Politiques, Paris; qualified as Magistrate, 1956; Sec. Gen. Superior Council of the Magistrature (1970-74); Cons. Adm. ORTF (1972-74); French Health Min. (1974-76), Health and Social Security Min. (1976-79); Member Europ. Parliament (1979-93), President (1979-82); Chairman Liberal Group (1984-89); State Min. Social Affairs, Health and Urban (1993-95); President Haut Conseil à l'Intégration (1997); Memb. Constitutional Council (1998); Chevalier de l'Ordre National du Mérite; Médaille Pénitentiaire; Médaille de l'Education surveillée. Dr (h.c.) Universities: Princeton, USA; Weizman Institute, Israel; Bar Ilan, Israel; Yale, USA; Cambridge, GB; Edinburgh, GB; Georgetown, USA; Urbino, Italy; Yeshiva Univ., NY, USA; Sussex, GB; Université Libre de Bruxelles, Belgium; Brandeis, USA; Glasgow, GB; Pennsylvania, USA. Recipient of honours and prizes from many countries including France, Israel, Germany, Spain, Brazil, Luxembourg, Greece, Ivory Coast, Morocco, Senegal, Venezuela, Sweden, USA, Italy. Publ.: Les Données Psycho-sociologiques de l'Adoption (with Prof. Launay and Dr Soule, Les Hommes Aussi S'en Souviennent (with Annie Cojean), Une Vie. Ad.: 10 rue de Rome, 75008 Paris. ☎ 01 42 93 00 60.

VERMES, Geza, MA, D.Litt (Oxon), Hon. DD (Edinburgh, Durham), Hon. D.Litt (Sheffield), FBA, W. Bacher Medallist, Hungarian Academy of Sciences, Fellow, European Academy of Arts, Sciences and Humanities; b. Mako, June 22, 1924; Prof. of Jew. Studies, Oxford Univ. (1989-91), now Emeritus; Dir. Forum for Qumran Research, Oxford Centre for Hebrew and Jewish Studies (1991-); R. in Jew. Studies, Oxford (1965-91), Fel. of Wolfson Coll. (1965-91), now Emer.; President, British Assn. for Jew. Studies (1975, 1988); President, European Assn. for Jew. Studies (1981-84); Edr. Journal of Jew. Studies (1971-); Vis. Prof. Rel. Studies, San Diego (1995),Brown Univ. (1971); Riddell Memorial Lect., Newcastle Univ. (1981). Publ. include: Discovery in the Judean Desert, The Dead Sea Scrolls in English, Jesus the Jew, The Gospel of Jesus the Jew, History of the Jewish People in the Age of Jesus Christ by E. Schürer (co-ed. and reviser), The Essenes According to the Classical Sources (co-author), The Religion of Jesus the Jew, The Complete Dead Sea Scrolls in English, Providential Accidents: An Autobiography; (co-ed.) Discovery in the Judean Desert XXVI: An Introduction to the Complete Dead Sea Scrolls; The Dead Sea Scrolls; The Authentic Gospel of Jesus, Jesus in his Jewish Context, The Passion, Who's Who in the Age of Jesus, The Nativity, The Resurrection, etc. Ad.: West Wood Cottage, Foxcombe Lane, Boars Hill, Oxford, OX1 5DH. ☎ 01865 735384. Fax 01865 735 034. Email geza.vermes@orinst.ox.ac.uk

VOGEL, Rabbi Shraga Faivish; b. Salford, Lancs, April 22, 1936; Chairman, Centre for Jewish Life; form. Dir., Lubavitch Foundation (1960-2007). Ad.: 15 Paget Rd, N16. ☎ 020-8800 7355.

WAGERMAN, Mrs. Josephine Miriam (née Barbanel), OBE, BA (Hons.), PGCE, Ac. Dip., MA (Ed); b. London, Sept. 17, 1933, m. Peter; Cttee. Women's Interfaith Network (2004-); form. President BoD (2000-3), Senior Vice-President (1997-2000), Vice-President (1994-97); Inner Cities Religious C. (Dept. of the Environment) (1994-); Mem. Academic Panel, Stuart Young Awards (1990-); Advisor to the Trustees, Pierre and Maniusia Gildesgame Trust (1996-99); Trustee of the Central Foundation Schools London (1996); Jewish Care Woman of Distinction (1996); Hadassah Intl Volunteer of Distinction (2003); Mem. Adv. Bd., UJIA (1997-); Gov. Naima J. Prep. School (1996-); Chief Exec. Lennox Lewis College (1994-96); Memb.C. Centre for Study of Jewish Christian Relations Selly Oak Colleges (1995-98); form. Headteacher, JFS (1985-93); President, London AMMA (1982-83); form. Member, ILEA Standing Jt. Adv. Cttee., Working Party on Teachers Service Conditions, Hist. & Soc. Studies Adv. Cttee; Independent Assessor NHS Non-Exec. Appointments Panel

(1998-). Ad.: 38 Crespigny Rd., London NW4 3DX. ☎/Fax 020-8203 7471.

WAGNER, Leslie, CBE, MA (Econ.) D. Univ. Middx, D. Univ. Leeds Metropolitan, D. Civil Laws, Huddersfield, D. Univ, Open; b. Manchester, Feb. 21, 1943, m. Jennifer; Chancellor, University of Derby (2003-08); Chairman, Higher Educ. Academy (2004-07); Chairman, Educ. Leeds (2004-07); Vice-Chancellor, Leeds Metropolitan Univ. (1994-2003); Chairman, University Vocational Awards C. (2001-03); V. Chanc. & Chief Exec. University of North London (1987-93); Dep. Sec., Nat. Adv. Body, Publ. Sector Higher Educ. (1982-87); Prof. & Dean, Sch. of Soc. Sciences & Business Studies Central Lond. Poly. (1976-82); Lect. The Open Univ. (1970-76); V. President, United Syn., (1992-93); Member, C., US; Tr. Chief Rabbinate Trust; Chairman, Society for Research into Higher Education (1994-96); Chairman, Higher Education for Capability (1994-98); Chairman, Yorkshire and Humberside Universities Association (1996-99); Mem. Leeds Cares Leadership Gp (2000-1); Dir. Leeds TEC Ltd (1997-2001); Mem. National Skills Task Force (1998-2000); Chairman Jewish Community Allocation Bd. (1994-96); Tr. Jewish Chronicle. Publ.: Choosing to Learn: Mature Students in Education (with others), The Economics of Educational Media, Agenda for Institutional Change in Higher Education (Edr.), Readings in Applied Microeconomics (Edr.). Ad.: 3 Lakeland Drive, Leeds LS17 7PJ. ☎ 0113-268 7355.

WALSH, David, LLB (Hons); b. Leeds, May 21, 1937; m. Jenny, née Cronin, Solicitor, Director, Peek Plc, Carlisle Group Plc; Mem. Bd. of J.I.A.; form. Chairman, RSGB, now Vice President; form. Chairman, West London Synagogue (1981-85); President, West London Synagogue (1988-91). Ad.: 82 North Gate, Prince Albert Road, London NW8 7EJ. ☎ 020-7586 1118. Fax 020-7483 2598.

WASSERSTEIN, Bernard Mano Julius, MA, DPhil, DLitt, FRHistS; b. London, Jan. 22, 1948; Meyer Prof. Modern J. History, Univ. Chicago (2003-); Guggenheim Fellow, (2007-08); Prof. History, Univ. Glasgow (2000-3); President JHSE (2000-2); President Oxford Centre for Hebrew & Jewish Studies (1996-2000); form. Prof. of Hist., Brandeis Univ. (Dean of Graduate Sch. of Arts and Sciences, 1990-92) (1982-96); Lect., Modern Hist., Sheffield Univ. (1976-80); Vis. Lect., Hist. Hebrew Univ. (1979-80); form. Res. Fel., Nuffield Coll., Oxford. Publ.: The British in Palestine, Britain and the Jews of Europe 1939-1945, The Secret Lives of Trebitsch Lincoln, Herbert Samuel, Vanishing Diaspora, Secret War in Shanghai, Divided Jerusalem, Israel and Palestine, Barbarism and Civilization. Ad.: History Dept., Univ. of Chicago, 1126 East 59th Street, Chicago, IL 60637. ☎ 773-702 3637.

WASSERSTEIN, David John, MA, DPhil, FRHistS, FRAS; b. London, Sept. 21, 1951; Academic; Prof., History and J. Studies, Vanderbilt Univ. (2004-) Dir. Program in Jewish Studies (2005); Asst. Lecturer (later College Lecturer) Semitic Languages Dept., University College, Dublin (1978-90), Assoc. Professor (1990-94), Professor (1994-2004), Islamic History, Tel Aviv University; Fellow, Wissenschaftskolleg zu Berlin (1999-2000); Fellow, Institute for Advanced Studies, Jerusalem (2002-3). Publ.: The Rise and Fall of the Party-Kings: Politics and Society in Islamic Spain 1002-1086 (1985); The Caliphate in the West: An Islamic Political Institution in the Iberian Peninsula (1993); Madrasa: Education, Religion and State in the Middle East (ed., with A. Ayalon, 2004); Mamluks and Ottomans (ed., with A. Ayalon, 2006); The Legend of the Septuagint, from Classical Antiquity to Today (with A. Wasserstein, 2006); Language of Religion, Language of People: Medieval Judaism, Christianity and Islam (co. ed., 2006). Ad.: Dept. of History, Vanderbilt Univ., VU Station B# 351802, 2301 Vanderbilt Place, Nashville, TN37235-1802. ☎ (615) 343-5692, Fax (615) 343-6002. Emaildavid.wasserstein@vanderbilt.edu.

WATERMAN, Stanley, PhD; b. Dublin, Jan. 27, 1945; m. Vivien née Lee; Professor Dept. of Geography, Univ. Haifa (1972-); form. Dir. Research, JPR; Vis. Assoc. Prof., University of Toronto (1977-78); Acad. Vis. LSE (1984-86), Queen Mary College (1995-97). Publ.: Pluralism and Political Geography (with N. Kliot, 1983); The Political Geography of Conflict and Peace (with N. Kliot, 1990); British Jewry in the Eighties (with Barry Kosmin, 1986); Jews in an Outer London Borough: Barnet (1989); Cultural Politics and European Jewry (1999). Ad.: 79 Wimpole Street, London W1G 9RY. ☎ 020-7935 8266. Fax 020-7935 3252. Email swaterman@jpr.org.uk.

WEBBER, Alan, MSc, PhD, FRICS; b. London, Sept. 5, 1933; m. Roseruth Freedman; Hon. Tr., Israel, Britain & Commonwealth Assoc.; Deputy Chairman, B'nai B'rith Hillel Foundation Executive (2001-05); Chairman, B'nai B'rith Hillel Foundation (1998-2001); Chairman of Governors, St. Margaret's School, Hampstead (1990-2001); form. Hon. Sec. B'nai B'rith Hillel Foundation (1990-98); President First Lodge, B'nai B'rith (1995-97); Chairman, Jewish Community Information (1994-97); Hon. Officer Hampstead Synagogue (1970-76); Hon. Officer St. John's Wood Synagogue (1990-91); Jt. Ed. (with Sylvia Webber) of Hampstead (1960-70) and St. John's Wood (1986-97) synagogue magazines. Publ.: The B'nai B'rith Hillel Foundation – 1953-1993; B'nai B'rith – 150 years of service to the community. Ad.: 14/1 Ha M'Apilim, Netanya, 42264. Email alanwebber@012.net.il.

WEBBER, Anne, BSc (Hons.); b. Manchester; Fd. & Co.-Chair, Commission for Looted Art in Europe (1999-); Dir., Central Registry, Information on Looted Cultural Property, 1933-1945 (2001-); Chair, Jewish Book Council (2002-05); Bd. Memb., European Council of Jewish Communities (2004-); Documentary film-maker: Dir., Legend Films (1994-) Producer Documentary and Director. BBC TV Documentaries & Features Depts (1980-94). Ad.: 76 Gloucester Place, London W1U 6HJ. ☎ 020-7487-3401. Fax 020-7487 4211. Email Annewebber@lootedartcommission.com.

WEIDENFELD, Baron of Chelsea (Life Peer) (Sir George Weidenfeld), Hon. MA (Oxon), Hon. PhD, Ben Gurion Univ., D.Litt, Exeter; Holder of the Knight Commander's Cross (Badge & Star) of the German Order of Merit; Holder of the Golden Knight's Cross with Star of the Austrian Order of Merit, Austrian Cross of Honour for Arts and Science; Order of Merit of Italian republic; Chevalier de l'Ordre National de la Légion d'Honneur, France, Charlemagne Medal for European Media, Italian Order of Merit, Fell. King's Coll. London; b. Vienna, Sept. 13, 1919; Publisher; Chairman, Weidenfeld & Nicolson, Lond.; Fd. President, Inst.. for Strategic Dialogues, Weidenfeld Scholarships and Leadership Programme, Oxford; Hon. Fell. St. Peter's College, Oxford (1992), St. Anne's College, Oxford (1993); Member Bd. Gov Institute of Human Science, Vienna; Political adv. to President Weizmann of Israel (1949-50); Chairman, Bd of Govs, Ben Gurion Univ. of Negev (1995-2004), Hon. Chairman (2005); Gov., Weizmann Instit. of Science; Gov., Tel Aviv Univ.; Tr., Jerusalem Foundation; Hon. Senator, Univ. Bonn (1996); Freeman City of London, etc. Publ.: The Goebbels Experiment, Remembering My Good Friends (auto). Ad.: 9 Chelsea Embankment, SW3 4LE. ☎ 020-7351 0042.

WEIL (Breuer-Weil), George; b. Vienna July 7, 1938; Sculptor, painter, jeweller, exhibited UK, US, Israel, Tokyo, Switzerland, South Africa etc.; portrait busts Ben-Gurion, Churchill, General de Gaulle, etc., Specialist in Judaica, including Bar-Ilan collection shown in Mann Auditorium, Tel Aviv; collections in Brit. Museum, Antwerp Museum, Royal Museum of Scotland, etc. H. Mem., Japanese Art Carvers Soc. (1986), only Western Artist so honoured. Ad.: 93 Ha Eshel Street, Herzlia Pituach, Israel.

WEINBERG, Joanna, BA, PhD (London); b. London, Nov. 11, 1949; Catherine Lewis Fellow in Rabbinics, Oxford Centre for Hebrew and Jewish Studies (2001-); James Mew lecturer in Rabbinic texts, University of Oxford (1999-); Reader in Rabbinics, Leo Baeck College, London (1982-2001). Publ.: The Light of the Eyes of Azariah de' Rossi: An English translation with introduction and notes (2001); Azariah de' Rossi's Observations on the Syriac New Testament. Ad.: The Oriental Institute, Pusey Lane, Oxford, OX1 2LE. ☎ 01865 288213. Email joanna.weinberg@oriental-institute.ox.ac.uk.

WEINER, Rabbi Chaim, BA (Hebrew Univ. of Jerusalem), M.A. (Hebrew Univ. of Jerusalem), Rabbinical Ordination (Seminary of Judaic Studies Jerusalem (Masorti); b. Sydney, Nova Scotia, Nov. 11, 1958; m. Judy; Rabbi New London Synagogue (2000-07); form. M. Edgware Masorti Synagogue (1991-98); Jerusalem Fellow (1998-2000); National Dir. of Noam, Masorti Youth Movement, Israel (1987-91); Dir. Gesher, Masorti Teenage Centre, London (1991-96). Ad.: c/o Masorti Bet Din, 3, Shakespeare Rd., London N3 1XE

WEISMAN, Malcolm, OBE, MA (Oxon), OCF; Barrister-at-Law; Recorder, S.E. Circuit; Vice President, Commonwealth J. trust; Special Adjudicator, Immigration Appeals (1998-); US Rabbi of the Year Award (2006); Award for Outstanding Leadership, Rabbinical C.,

US (2005); Chaplin, Mayor of Montgomery (2006-07); Tr. Intl. Chaplaincy, Univ. Derby; Chief Rabbi's Award for Excellence (1993); B'nai B'rith Award for Community Service (1980); Asst. Com., Parl. Boundaries (1976-85), Rel. Adv. to Small Coms; Member, Chief Rabbi's Cabinet; Chaplain, Oxford Univ. & new univs., Mayor of Redbridge (2005-06); Fell. Centre for the Study of Theology, Univ. of Essex; Hon. Fell., Lancaster Univ.; Patron JNF; Hillel Nat. Student Cllr.; Patron, Davar; Sr. Jew. Chaplain to H.M. Forces; Hon. V. President, Monash Branch of Roy. Brit. Legion; Tr. Jewish Music Institute; Tr. International Multi-Faith Centre, Univ. Derby; ICCJ Gold Medallion (2001); National Hon. Chaplain AJEX (2000-); form. Gov. Carmel College (1996-98); Edr. Menorah; Chairman and Sec.Gen., Sr. Allied Air Force Chaplains (1980-) President (1993-); Special Award US Airforce Jewish Chaplain Council (2000); Sec. Allied Air Forces Chaplain Cttee.; Member, Council of Selly Oak Coll. Birmingham (1992), Chaplain to Lord Mayor of Westminster (1992-93), Mayor of Barnet (1994-95), Mayor of Montgomery (2006-07); Hon. President Birmingham J. Graduates Assoc. (1995-96); Member, Min. of Def. Advisory Cttee on Chaplaincy; Chaplain RAF Univs. Jew Chaplaincy Bd., Progr. Jewish Students Chaplaincy; Nat. Exec., Mizrachi Fed.; Nat. Exec. Council of Christians and Jews; Cttee, Three Faiths Forum; Ct., Lancaster, East Anglia, Kent, Warwick, Sussex and Essex Univs.; Exec. United States Military Chaplains Assoc.; form. JWB, Ajex Exec.; Jewish Youth Fund; President, Univ. Coll. Jew. Soc.; form. President Birmingham J. Graduates Assoc.; form. H. Sec., IUJF; form. V. President, Torah V'avodah Org., Provincial Exec., JIA. Ad.: JMC, 25 Enford St., W1H 1DW. ☎ 020-8459 4372. Email chaplainsclerkwb@btconnect.com

WEISSBORT, Daniel, MA (Cantab); b. London, April 30,1935; m. Valentina Polukhina; Professor; Hon. Prof., Centre for Translation and Comparative Cultural Studies, Univ. Warwick (2002); Research Fellow, Dept. of English, King's College, London (2001-); Emer. Professor of English & Comparative Literature, University of Iowa (2001); Fd. Editor (with Ted Hughes) Modern Poetry in Translation (1965-2004). Publ.: Selected Poems of Nikolai Zabolotsky (1999); Selected Poems of Yehuda Amichai (2000); What was all the Fuss About (2002); Letters to Ted (2003); From Russian with Love: A Translation Memoir of Joseph Brdosky (2003); Contemporary Russian Women's Poetry (with Valentina Polukhina, 2004), etc. Ad.: 3, Powis Gardens, London NW11 8HH. Email danielweissbort@ntlworld.com.

WEISSER, Jacques, b. Antwerp, Feb. 7, 1942; m. Judy née Blitz; Journalist; Gen. Sec AJEX (1994-); Gen. Sec. Int. Council of Jewish War Veterans (1998-); Radlett US: Bd. Man, (2002-); Vice Chairman, (2006-07), Chairman (2007-); Dep. Tr., Zionist Fed. (2004-); Dir. Yad Vashem Tr. (2004-); M., and Tr., Jewish Lads and Girls Brigade; Bd. Man. Wembley US (1983-2001); Tr., and Chairman, North West London teenage Centre (1985-94); Bd. Man, Croydon Fed. Syn. (1973-82); Mem. Guild of Jewish Journalists. Ad.: Email Jacques@ajex.org.uk.

WEITZMAN, Peter David Jacob, MA, MSc, D.Phil (Oxon), DSc (Bath), FIBiol, FRSC; b. London, Sept. 22, 1935; m. Avis née Galinski; Higher Education consultant; Emer. Prof. Univ. Wales; Dir. of Academic Affairs, Univ. Wales Inst., Cardiff (1988-93); Prof. of Biochemistry, Univ. Bath (1979-88); President, Penylan House Jewish Retirement Home, Cardiff (1991-99); Chairman, South Wales Jewish Representative Council (1997-2003); Chairman Bournemouth Branch, Friends Israel Sport Centre. Publ.: Scientific writings. Ad.: 28 Albany, Manor Rd., Bournemouth BH1 3EN. Email pdjw@btinternet.com.

WEIZMAN, Ezer; b. Tel Aviv, 1924; Seventh President of Israel (1993-2000); Science and Technology Min., State of Israel, Defence Min. (1977-80); Transport Min. (1969-70); Served as fighter pilot in World War II and Israel War of Independence Commander of Israel Air Force 1958-66; Head of General Staff Branch/GHQ (1966-69). Publ.: On Eagles' Wings (autobiog.), The Battle for Peace. Ad.:

WESKER, Sir Arnold, Kt., FRSL, D.Litt (Hon. UEA), DHL (Denison Univ.), Hon. Fell. Queen Mary & Westfield Coll., London; b. London, May 24, 1932, m. Dusty Bicker; CoP, Internat. Playwrights Cttee. (1980-83); Chairman, Brit. Section, Internat. Theatre Instit. (1978-83); Dir.

Centre 42 (1960-70). Publ. include: Chicken Soup with Barley (1959); I'm Talking about Jerusalem (1960); The Wesker Trilogy (1960); The Kitchen (1961); Chips with Everything (1962); The Four Seasons (1966); Their Very Own and Golden City (1966); The Friends (1970); Fears of Fragmentation (essays) (1971); Six Sundays in January (1971); The Old Ones (1972); The Journalists (1974) (in Dialog; repr. 1975); Love Letters on Blue Paper (stories) (1974), 2nd edn 1990; (with John Allin) Say Goodbye! You May Never See Them Again (1974); Words – as definitions of experience (1976); The Wedding Feast (1977); Journey into Journalism (1977); Said the Old Man to the Young Man (stories) (1978); The Merchant (1978); Fatlips (for young people) (1978); The Journalists, a triptych (with Journey into Journalism and A Diary of the Writing of The Journalists) (1979); Caritas (1981); Shylock (form. The Merchant) (1983); Distinctions (1985); Yardsale (1987); Whatever Happened to Betty Lemon (1987); Little Old Lady (1988); Shoeshine (1989); Collected Plays (vols. 1 and 5, 1989, vols. 2, 3, 4 and 6, 1990, vol. 7), As Much As I Dare (autobiog.) (1994); Circles of Perception (1996); Denial (1997); Break, My Heart (1997); The Birth of Shylock and the Death of Zero Mostel (1997); The King's Daughters (1998); Letter to a Daughter (1998). Film scripts: Lady Othello (1980); Homage to Catalonia (1990). Letter to Myself (2003) Television: (first play) Menace (1963); Breakfast (1981); (adapted) Thieves in the Night, by A. Koestler (1984); (adapted) Diary of Jane Somers, by Doris Lessing (1989); Maudie (1995); Barabbas (2000). Radio: Yardsdale (1984); Bluey (Eur. Radio Commn.) (Cologne Radio, 1984, BBC Radio 3, 1985), Groupie (2001). Longitude (2002); Libretto: Grief (2003); Honey: a Novel (2005); Amazed and Surprised (radio/stage 2006), Phoenix, Phoenix Burning Bright (2006); The Rocking Horse (BBC World Service 75th Anniversary Commission, 2007); Wesker's Love Plays (2008); Wesker's Monologutes (2008); All Things Tire Themselves (2008).'Catching up with Wesker', available from David Higham Associates, 5 Lower John St., Golden Square, London W1F 4HA. Ad.: Hay-on-Wye, Hereford HR3 5RJ. ☎ 01497 820473. Website www. arnoldwesker.com.

WHINE, Michael David, BA(Hons), FCIM; b. London, Apr. 4,1947; m. Ester née Kamenetzki; Director, Defence and GROUP Relations Division, BoD; Director, Government and International Affairs, Community Security Trust (1986-); Consult., Defence & Security, European J. Congress (1998-); EJC Rep., Organisation for Security and Cooperation in Europe (2003-); Metropolitan Police Authority, Hate Crime Forum (2003-); Adv. Gp., London Criminal Justice Bd. (2006-); Adv. Gp., Race for Justice, Office of Criminal Justice Reform (2007-). Publ. include: The Far Right on the Internet (1997); Islamism and Totalitarianism: Similarities and Differences (2001); Antisemitism on the Streets (2003); Holocaust Denial in the United Kingdom (2006); An Unholy Alliance: Nazi Links with Arab Totalitarianism (2006); The Homegrown Terrorist Threat in Europe (2008). Ad.: POBox 35501, London NW4 2FZ ☎ 020-8457 9999

WHITESON, Adrian Leon, OBE, MBBS (Hons.), MRCS, LRCP; b. London, Dec. 12, 1934, m. Myrna; Med. Practitioner; Vice-President of the Brit. Paralympic Assoc., form. Chairman, World Boxing Council and European Boxing Union Med. Commission; form. Chief Med. Off., Brit. Boxing Board of Control; Chairman, The Teenage Cancer Tr.; Member, Govt. Review Body for Sport for People with Disabilities. Ad.: Pender Lodge, 6 Oakleigh Park North, Whetstone, London, N20 9AR. ☎ 020-7580 3637. 58a Wimpole St., W1G 8YR. ☎ 020-7935 3351. Fax 020-7487 2504.

WIESEL, Elie, D.Lett (hc), D.Hum.Lett (hc), D.Hebrew.Lett. (hc), PhD (hc), DL (hc), etc.; b. Sighet, Sept. 30, 1928; m. Marion; Survivor of Auschwitz and Buchenwald; Fd. Elie Wiesel Foundation for Humanity; Andrew W. Mellon Prof. in the Humanities, Boston Univ.; Dist. Prof., Judaic Studies, City Univ , N.Y. (1972-76); Chairman, US President's Com. on Holocaust (1979-80); Chairman, US Holocaust Memorial C. (1980-86); Bd. Dirs., Internat. Rescue Cttee., Grand-Croix, Legion of Honour; US Congress Gold Medal (1986); Presidential Medal of Freedom (1992); Nobel Peace Prize (1986); Internat. Peace Prize Royal Belgian Acad. Publ.: Night, (new translation 2006), Dawn, The Jews of Silence, etc.; Ani Maamin, a cantata (music by D. Milhaud), Zalmen, or the Madness of God, A Jew Today, Messengers of God,

Souls on Fire, The Trial of God (play), The Testament (novel), Five Biblical Portraits, Somewhere a Master, Paroles d'Etranger, The Golem, Signes D'Exode, Twilight, L'oublié, From the Kingdom of Memory, Reminiscences, The Forgotten, Memoirs: All Rivers Run to the Sea; Vol.II: And the Sea is Never Full (1999), Wise Men and Their Tales (2003) Time of the Uprooted (2005), Un désir fou de danser (2006), Confronting Anti-Semitism: essays (with Kofi Annan 2006) etc. Ad.: Boston University, 147 Bay State Rd., Boston, Mass., 02215. ☎ (617) 353 4561.

WINE, Judge Hubert, MA, LLB, TCD; b. Dublin, April 3, 1922; Dublin district judge (1976-), H. President, Jewish Rep. C. of Ireland; Act. President Dublin Hebrew Cong.; Cllr., HLP, Dublin Hebrew Cong.; H. President, C. of Ireland for Soviet Jewry; Patron, Criminal Lawyers, Assn., Gt. Brit. & Ireland; Patron, Jewish Adoption Soc., Great Britain & Ireland, H. L. P. Dublin Maccabi Assn., Patron, Irish Frs. of Hebrew Univ.; Patron Israel-Ireland Friendship League; Patron Irish Penal Reform Tr.; Patron Irish Rape Crisis Centre; Tr. Irish Legal Research and Education Tr.; form. Irish Internat. Table Tennis player & Irish champion; form. Capt., Edmondstown Golf Club. Ad.: 19 Merrion Village, Merrion Rd., Dublin, 4. ☎ Dublin 269 5895.

WINEMAN, Vivian, MA (Cantab); b. London, Feb. 14,1950; m. Naomi Helen née Greenberg; Solicitor; Senior Partner, David Wineman; Senior Vice-President, BoD (2006-); Chairman, New Israel Fund (1992-94). Publ. Contracts (Rights of Third Parties) Act, 1999 (2001). Ad.: 76, Meadway, London NW11 6QH.

WINER, Rabbi Dr Mark L., PhD, DD; b. Logan, Utah, Dec. 12, 1942; m. Suellen née Mark; Senior Rabbi West London Synagogue (1998-); Chairman, Int. Interfaith Task Force (1998-) Vice-Chairman, WUPj (2005-) President National C. of Synagogues (1995-98); V. President, Synagogue C. of America (1993-94); Mem., International Jewish Committee for Interreligious Consultations (1987-98). Publ.: Articles in Manna, European Judaism, etc. Ad.: West London Synagogue, 33 Seymour Place, London W1H 5AU. ☎ 020-7723 4404. Fax 020-7224 8258.

WINNICK, David, MP; b. Brighton, June, 1933; MP (Lab.), for Walsall North (1979-), Croydon South (1966-70). Ad.: House of Commons, SW1A 0AA.

WINSTON, Clive Noel, BA (Cantab); b. London, April 20, 1925; m. Beatrice Jeannette née Lawton; V. President (form. Chairman) Liberal Judaism; form. Tr., European Bd. of WUPJ; form., Dep. Solicitor, Metropolitan Police. Ad.: 2 Bournwell Cl., Cockfosters, Herts. EN4 0JX. ☎ 020-8449 5963.

WINSTON, Baron of Hammersmith (Life Peer) (Robert Maurice Lipson), MB, BS, DSc., FRCP, FMed Sci, LRCP, MRCS, FRCOG; b. London, July 15, 1940; form. Prof., Fertility Studies, Imperial Coll., London; Chairman Science & Technology Select Cttee, House of Lords (1999-); Chairman, Royal College of Music (2007-); Chancellor, Sheffield Hallam University (2001-); Dean, Institute of Obstetrics & Gynaecology (1995-); Consultant Obstetrician & Gynaecologist, Hammersmith Hospital, Lond., Prof. of Gynaecology, Texas Univ. (1980-81); Vis. Prof., Leuven Univ., Belgium (1976-77); Chief Rabbi's Open Award for Contribution to Society (1993). Publ.: Reversibility of Female Sterilization, Tubal Infertility, Infertility: a Sympathetic Approach; Scientific writings on aspects of reproduction; The Story of God (2005). Ad.: 11 Denman Dr., London NW11. ☎ 020-8455 7475.

WISTRICH, Robert Solomon, BA, MA (Cantab, 1970), PhD (London, 1974); b. Lenger (USSR), April 7, 1945; Univ Prof.; First Holder of the Jewish Chronicle Chair in Jewish Studies, University Coll., London; Neuberger Chair of Modern Jewish History, Hebrew University of Jerusalem (1985-); Dir., Vidal Sassoon International Centre for the Study of Antisemitism (2002-). Awards: James Parkes Prize (1984); H.H. Wingate/Jewish Quarterly Prize for Non-Fiction (1992); Austrian State Prize for Danubian History (1992). Publ.: Revolutionary Jews from Marx to Trotsky (1976); Trotsky (1979); Socialism and the Jews (1982), Who's Who in Nazi Germany (1982), Hitler's Apocalypse (1985); The Jews of Vienna in the Age of Franz Joseph (1989); Between Redemption and Perdition (1990); Antisemitism: The Longest Hatred (1991); Weekend in Munich (1995); Co-maker, Understanding the Holocaust (film, 1997); Demonizing the Other: Antisemitism, Racism and Xenophobia (1999); Hitler and the Holocaust (2001). Nietzsche: Godfather of Fascism (2002); Blaming the Jews (film, 2003); Obsession: Radical Islamic War Against the West (film, 2006); Laboratory of World Destruction: Germans and Jews in Central Europe (2007). Ad.: 63 Woodstock Road, NW11. ☎ 020-8455 6949.

WITTENBERG, Rabbi Jonathan, MA, PGCE; b. Glasgow, Sept. 17, 1957; m. Nicola Solomon; Senior Rabbi, Assembly of Masorti Synagogue (2008-); Rabbi, New North London Masorti Synagogue (1987-). Publ.: The Three Pillars of Judaism: A Search for Faith and Values (1996); The Laws of Life: A Guide to Traditional Jewish Practice in Times of Bereavement (1997); A High Holiday Companion (ed. and co-auth., 1996); A Pesach Companion (ed. and co-auth., 1997); The Eternal Journey: Meditations on the Jewish Year (2001). Ad.: 10 Amberden Ave., London N3 3BJ. ☎ 20-8343 3927. Fax 020-8346 1914. Email wittenberg@masorti.org.uk.

WOLFF, Rabbi William, b. Berlin; Landersrabbiner Mecklenburg-Vorpommern (2002-); M. Wimbledon Reform Syn. (1997-2002); M. Brighton & Hove Progressive Syn. (1993-97); form. rabbi West London, Newcastle Reform, Milton Keynes Syn.; Chairman, C. Reform and Liberal Rabbis (1994-97); form. Journalist, Daily Mirror (1963-75), Evening News (1976-80), Glasgow Sunday Mail (1980-89). Ad.: c/o Montagu Centre, 21 Maple St., London W1P 6DS. ☎ 0049 385550 7345. Fax 0049 385593 60989.

WOLFSON, Dianna (née Sherry), BA, DCE; b. Birmingham, June 29, 1938; Head Teacher (retd.); Head Teacher, Calderwood Lodge Jewish Primary School (1976-98); Conv. Scottish Interfaith C. (2004-); President, Glasgow Jewish Representative Council (1998-2001), Hon. President (2001-); Chairman, West of Scotland Council of Christians and Jews (1992-95). Ad.: 22 Park Court, Giffnock, Glasgow G46 7PB. ☎/Fax 0141-620 0650. Email d.wolfson@tinyworld.co.uk.

WOLFSON, Baron of Marylebone in the City of Westminster (Life Peer) (Leonard Gordon Wolfson), 2nd Bart, Hon. Fel. St. Catherine's Coll. Oxford; Wolfson Coll., Cambridge, Wolfson Coll., Oxford; Worcester Coll., Somerville College, Oxon; UCL; LSHTM, 1985; Queen Mary Coll., 1985; Poly. of Central London, 1991; Imperial CoD., 1985, Royal Academy of Music (2003); Patron Royal College of Surgeons, 1976; Hon. FRCP, 1977; Hon. FRCS, 1988; Hon. FBA, 1986; Hon. DCL, Oxon, 1972; East Anglia, 1986; Hon. LLD, Strathclyde, 1972; Dundee, 1979; Cantab, 1982; London, 1982; Hon. DSC, Hull, 1977; Wales, 1984; D. Univ. Surrey, 1990; Hon. D. Medicine, Birmingham, 1992; Hon. DSc. Cape Town, 2008; Hon. D. Litt. Loughborough 2003; Hon. DSC. Sheffield (2005); Hon. PhD, Tel Aviv, 1971; Hebrew Univ., 1978; Weitzmann Inst., 1988; Hon. DHL, Bar-Ilan Univ., 1983; Winston Churchill award British Technion Society, 1989; b. London, Nov. 11, 1927; m. Estelle Jackson; Chairman, Wolfson Fdn (1972-); Chairman, Great Universal Stores (1981-96) (Man. Dir., 1962, Dir., 1952); Burberrys Ltd. (1978-96); Tr. Imperial War Museum (1988-94); Pr. of Jewish Welfare Bd. (1972-82); Fellow, Birkbeck College; President's Award, Hebrew Univ. (2005); Hon. President British Technion Society (2006-); President Shaare Zedek (2006-); Fellow, Israel Museum (2001); Hon. Fellow, Institute of Education, U. London (2001); Hon. Fell. Royal Academy of Music; Hon. Fellow, City of Jerusalem (2002); Hon. Fellow, Royal Institution (2002); Sheldon Medal, Oxford (2003); Fell. Royal Albert Hall (2003); Hon. Fell. Royal Society (2005); Companion, Royal Coll. Surgeons of Edinburgh (2006). Ad.: 8 Queen Anne St., London W1G 9LD.

WOOLF, The Lord, The Rt. Hon. Harry, PC, LLB, Hon. FBA, DLL (Hon.), Buckingham 1992, Bristol 1992, London 1993, Anglia 1994, Manchester Metropolitan 1995, LLD Hon., Cranfield 2001, Hull 2001, Richmond 2001, Cambridge 2002, Exeter 2002, Birmingham 2002, Wolverhampton 2002; b. Newcastle-upon-Tyne, May 2, 1933; Chartered Arbitrator/Mediator (2006-); President, Qatar Financial Services Court (2006-); Chairman, Bank of England's Financial Markets Law Committee (2005-); Chairman of the Council, University College London (2005-); Chancellor, Open University of Israel (2005-); Lord Chief Justice (2000-05); Master of the Rolls (1996-2000); Lord of Appeal in Ordinary (1992-96); Lord Justice (1985-92); High Court Judge (1979-85); Presiding Judge S.E. Circuit (1981-85), Member, Senate Bench & Bar; Master of the Bench, Inner Temple; Pro-Chancellor, Univ.

London (1994-); Tr. Jewish Chronicle Trust (1994-, Chairman 2000-); Tr. Jewish Continuity (1994-2000); Fel. Univ. Coll., Lond.; First Counsel to Treasury (Common Law) (1974-79); Jnr. Counsel to Inland Revenue (1973-74), Recorder of the Crown Court (1972-9); Chairman, Bd. of Man., Instit. of Advanced Legal Studies (1987-94), H. President, Assn. of Law Teachers, (1985-89); Instit. of Jewish Affairs Legal Section; Int. Jewish Lawyers Assoc. (1993-); Anglo-Jewish Archives (1985-89), Tel Aviv Univ. Tr. (Legal Section) (1995); Chairman, Lord Chancellor's Adv. Cttee. on Legal Educ. (1987-90); President, UK Frs., Magen David Adam (1987-); President, Central C. for Jewish Soc. Services (1987-99); Gov. of the Oxford Centre for Hebrew & Jewish Studies (1989-93); Chairman, Bar & Bench Cttee., J.P.A. (1974-76); 15/19th Hussars (1954-56) Captain (1955). Publ.: Protecting the Public: The New Challenge (Hamlyn Lectures, 1989), Zamir and Woolf, Declaring Judgement (3rd edn, 2002), Appointed to Inquire into Prison Disturbances (1990), Civil Procedure of Access to Justice (1996); Judicial Review of Administration, 6th ed (2008, jt. ed.); Pursuit of Justice (2008). Ad.: House of Lords, London SW1A 0PW.

WOOLFSON, Michael Mark, MA, PhD, DSc, FRS, FRAS, FInstP; b. London, Jan. 9, 1927; Emer. Prof., Theoretical Physics York Univ., form. Reader in Physics, Manchester Instit. of Sci. & Tech. Publ.: Direct Methods in Crystallography; An Introduction to X-Ray Crystallography; The Origin of the Solar System; Physical and Non-physical Methods of Solving Crystal Structures; An Introduction to Computer Simulation, The Origin and Evolution of the Solar System, Planetary Science, Mathematics for Physics, The Formation of the Solar System, Everyday Probability and Statistics. Ad.: Physics Dept., Univ. York, York, YO10 5DD. ☎ 01904-432230.

WORMS, Fred Simon, OBE, Hon. PhD, Heb. Univ; b. Frankfurt, Nov. 21, 1920; Hon. Fell. Israel Museum; Hon. Fell. Hebrew University; President, B'nai B'rith Hillel Foundation; Hon. Vice-President UJIA, Jewish Care; C. Member Israel Museum; form Gov. North London Collegiate School; Chairman, B'nai B'rith Foundation; Found-Chairman, European Jewish Publication Society; Chairman, B'nai B'rith Housing Tr.; Hon. President, B'nai B'rith Gt. Britain & N.I.; Life President, Union of Jewish Students; President, Jewish Community Housing Assoc.; Hon. President, formerly President, Maccabi World Union; Gov. Hebrew University; Council, Tel Aviv Museum; Chairman of Tr. B'nai B'rith World Centre; Founder Gov., Immanuel College; form. Dir. Bank Leumi (UK) PLC and Union Bank of Israel. Awards: B'nai B'rith International Award for Communal Services; The Jerusalem Medal (builder of Jerusalem); The Samuel Rothberg Prize in Jewish Education (Hebrew University); Int. Jewish Sports Hall of Fame, Lifetime Achievement Award. Publ.: Worms Report on Jewish Education in the UK (1992); A Life in Three Cities (1996). Ad.: 23 Highpoint, North Hill, Highgate, N6 4BA. ☎ 020-8342 5360. Fax 020-8342 5359.

WOUK, Herman, BA, Columbia U., 1934; LHD (Hon.), Yeshiva Univ.; LLD (Hon.), Clark U.; DLitt (Hon.), American International College; PhD (Hon.), Bar-Ilan Univ., Hebrew Univ.; DLitt (Hon.) Trinity College; DLitt George Washington Univ.; b. New York, May 27, 1915; Writer. Publ.: Non-fiction: This is My God; The Will to Live On; Novels: Aurora Dawn, Marjorie Morningstar, The Winds of War, War and Remembrance, Youngblood Hawke, Don't Stop the Carnival, The Caine Mutiny, Inside, Outside, City Boy, The Hope, The Glory; A Hole in Texas. Plays: The Caine Mutiny Court-Martial, etc. TV Screenplays: The Winds of War, War and Remembrance. Ad.: c/o B.S.W. Literary Agency, 303 Crestview Dr., Palm Springs CA 92264.

WRIGHT, Rabbi Alexandra (née Levitt), BA, PGCE; b. London, Dec. 10, 1956; m. Roderick Wright; Senior Rabbi, Liberal Jewish Synagogue (Assoc. M. 1986-89); Jewish Chaplain, North London Hospice (1997-2005) M. Radlett & Bushey Ref. Syn. (1990-2003); Lect. in Classical Hebrew Leo Baeck College (1987-97). Publ.: 'An approach to feminist theology' in Hear Our Voice (1994); 'Judaism' in Women in Religion (1994). Ad.: 90 The Ridgeway, London NW11 9RU. ☎ 020-8455 5305.

WRIGHT, Rosalind (née Kerstein), QC, CB, LLB (Hons) (London); b. London, Nov. 2, 1942; m. Dr David J.M. Wright; Barrister; Chairman Fraud Advisory Panel (2003-); Non-Exec. Dir. Office of Fair Trading (2003-07); Mem. Supervisory Committee of OLAF (European anti-Fraud Office) (2005-); Non-Exec. Dir. Insolvency Service Steering Board (2006-); Non-Exc. Dir. DTI Legal Services Group (2001-); Director, Serious Fraud Office (1997-2003); Head,

Prosecutions, Exec. Director, Securities and Futures Authority (1987-97); Asst. Director, Head of Fraud Investigation Group, DPP (1985-87); V. Chairman Jewish Association for Business Ethics. Ad.: Fraud Advisory Panel, PO Box 433, Chartered Accountan ts Hall, Moorgate Place, London EC2P 2BJ. ☎ 020-7920 8721. Email info@fraudadvisorypanel.org.

WURZBURGER, Rabbi Walter S.; b. Munich Mar. 29, 1920; m. Naomi née Rabinowitz; form. President, Syn. C. of Amer.; form President, Rab. C. of Amer. Rabbi, Emer. Cong. Shaaray Tefila, Lawrence N.Y., Adjunct Prof. of Philosophy Yeshiva Univ.; Edr., Tradition, (1962-87), Co-Edr., A Treasury of Tradition. Publ.: Ethics of responsibility (1994); God is Proof Enough (2000). Ad.: 138 Hards La., Lawrence, New York, NY 11559, USA. ☎ 516-2397181. Fax 516-239 7413.

YAMEY, Basil Selig, CBE, BCom, FBA; b. Cape Town, May 4, 1919, m. Demetra Georgakopoulou; Emer. Prof., Lond. Univ.; form. Economics Prof., Lond. Sch. of Economics; Member, Monopolies and Mergers Com. (1966-78); Tr., National Gallery (1974-81); Tr., Tate Gallery (1978-81), Museums & Galleries Com (1983-85); Tr., Instit. of Econ. Aff (1986-91). Publ.: Economics of Resale Price Maintenance, Economics of Underdeveloped Countries (part auth.), The Restrictive Practices Court (part auth.), Economics of Futures Trading (part auth.), Essays on the History of Accounting, Arte e Contabilità, Art & Accounting. Ad.: London Sch. of Economics, Houghton Street, London WC2A 2AE. ☎ 020-7405 7686.

YOUNG, Rt. Hon. Baron of Graffham (Life Peer) (David Ivor Young), PC, LLB (Hons.); b. London, Feb. 27, 1932; Solicitor; Dep. Chairman, Conservative Party (1989-90); President, Jewish Care (1990-); Chairman Oxford Centre for Hebrew and Jewish Studies (1989-92); Exec. Chairman, Cable & Wireless plc (1990-); Dir. Salomon Inc. (1990-); Sec. of State for Trade and Industry (1987-89); Sec. of State for Employment (1985-87), Min. without Portfolio, Min. in Cabinet (1984-85); Chairman, Manpower Services Com. (1982-84), Nat. Economic Development Org (1982-89); Chairman, Admin. Cttee., World ORT Union (1980-84), Gov., Oxford Centre for Post-Graduate Heb Studies; form. President, Brit. ORT; Dir., Centre for Policy Studies (1979-82), Chairman Internat. C., Jewish Soc. & Welfare Services (1982-83). Publ.: The Enterprise Years: A Businessman in the Cabinet (1990). Ad.: Young Associates, Harcourt House, 19 Cavendish Sq., London W1G 0PL.

YOUNG, Emanuel, ARCM; b. Brighton, Feb. 12, 1918; Conductor, Royal Ballet, Royal Opera House Lond. Guest Conductor, concerts, TV recordings, etc.; form. Cond., Royal Opera House, New Lond. Opera Company. Ad.: 16 Selborne Rd., N14 7DH. ☎ 020-8886 1144.

YUDKIN, Leon Israel, D.Litt (Lond); b. Northampton, Sept. 8, 1939; m. Meirah (Mickey) née Goss; University Lecturer, Hebrew Dept., UCL (1996-) and Author; Vis. Prof. Univ. Paris VIII (2000-); Univ. Lect., University of Manchester (1966-96). Publ.: Isaac Lamdan: A Study in Twentieth-Century Hebrew Poetry (1971); Escape into Siege: A Survey of Israeli Literature Today (1974); Jewish Writing and Identity in the Twentieth Century (1982); 1984 and After: Aspects of Israeli Fiction (1984); On the Poetry of Uri Zvi Greenberg (in Hebrew, 1987); Else Lasker-Schueler: A Study in German Jewish Literature (1991); Beyond Sequence: Current Israeli Fiction and its Context (1992); A Home Within: Varieties of Jewish Expression in Modern Fiction (1996); Public Crisis and Literary Response: The Adjustment of Modern Jewish Literature (2001); Literature in the Wake of the Holocaust (2003); Israel: the Vision of a State and its Literature (2005). Ed. Modern Hebrew Literature in English Translation (1987); Agnon: Texts and Contexts in English Translation (1988); Hebrew Literature in the Wake of the Holocaust (1993); Israeli Writers Consider the 'Outsider' (1993); Co-edited (with Benjamin Tammuz) Meetings with the Angel: Seven Stories from Israel (1973); Israel: the Vision of a State, and its Literature (2005); Ed. of the monograph series 'Jews in Modern Culture'. Ad.: 51 Hillside Court, 409 Finchley Rd., London NW3 6HQ. ☎ 020-7435 5777. Fax 020-7209 1026. Email yudle4@aol.com.

ZALUD, Rabbi Norman, APhS, FRSA; b. Liverpool, Oct. 5, 1932; Rabbi Emer Liverpool Reform Syn.; also Minister at Sha'arei Shalom Syn., Manchester, and Blackpool Reform Jewish Cong.; Jewish Chaplain to H.M. Prisons. Ad.: 265 Woolton Rd., L16 8NB. ☎ 0151-722 4389; 0151-733 5871.

ZEIDMAN, His Honour Judge Martyn, QC, LLB; b. Cardiff May 30, 1952; m. Verity née Owen; Circuit Judge (2001-); Recorder (1995); President of Mental Health Tribunal (1999-); Jewish Marriage Council, Chairman. (2004). Publ.: A Short Guide to the Landlord & Tenant Act 1987 (1987); A Short Guide to the Housing Act 1988 (1988); Steps to Possession (1989); A Short Guide to the Courts & Legal Services Act 1990 (1990); A Short Guide to the Road Traffic Act 1991 (1991); Making Sense of the Leasehold Reform Housing & Urban Development Act 1993 (1994). Ad.: The Crown Court at Snaresbrook, The Court House, Hollybush Hill, London E11 1QW ☎ 020-8530 0000. Fax 020-8530 0073.

ZELLICK, Graham John., MA, PhD (Cantab), Hon. LHD (NYU), AcSS, CCMI, FRSA, Hon. LLD (Richmond, Birm), Hon. FSALS, Hon.FRAM Hon. FBS; b. London, Aug. 12, 1948; Barrister; Assoc. Mem. Chambers (Gray's Inn); Hon. Prof. Law, Univ. Birmingham (2004-); Chairman, Criminal Cases Review Comm. (2003-08); Vice-Chancellor and President Univ. London (1997-2003), Dep. V. Chancellor (1994-97); Princ., Queen Mary & Westfield Coll., Univ. of London (1991-98); Prof. of Law, Univ. of London (1982-98), Emer. Prof. (1998-); Hon. Fellow Gonville & Caius Coll., Cambridge (2001-); Chairman, Bd. Gov., Leo Baeck Coll. (2005-06); Gov. Tel Aviv Univ. (2000-); Mem. Criminal Injuries Compensation Appeals Panel (2000-3); Electoral Commissioner (2001-04); Fell. Heythrop Coll. (2005); Master of the Bench, Middle Temple (2001); Mem. Competition Appeal Tribunal (2000-3); Master Warden, Drapers' Company (200708); Patron, London Jewish Cultural Centre (2001-); Freeman, City of London; President West London Syn. (2000-06); Member of Council Cttee. of Vice-Chancellors & Principals (1993-97); Hd. of Law Dept., Queen Mary Coll , Lond. (1984-90); Dean of Laws Faculty, Lond. Univ. (1986-88); Chairman Cttee. of Heads of Univ. Law Schs. (1988-90); V. Chairman Nat. Adv. Council, Acad. Study Group for Israel & The Middle East. (1995-2003). Ad.: 63, Hampstead Way, London NW11 7DN; Welard House, Barrowden, Rutland LE15 8EQ.

ZERMANSKY, Victor David, LLB (Hon.); b. Leeds, Dec. 28, 1931, m. Anita née Levison; Solicitor; Past P. Leeds Law Soc. (1988-9), form. Asst. Recorder; H. L. V-P (President, 1974-77), Leeds Jewish Rep. C.; Life President, Leeds Z.C.; form. Chairman Leeds Kashrut Auth., Beth Din Admin. Cttee., form. Immigration Appeals Adjudicator (1970-78). Ad.: 52 Alwoodley Lane, Leeds, LS17 7PT ☎/Fax 0113 267 3523. Email victor.zermansky@virgin.net

ZIPPERSTEIN, Steven J., BA, MA, PhD (UCLA); b. Los Angeles, Dec. 11, 1950; Daniel E. Koshland Prof. in Jewish Culture and History, Stanford University; Co.-Dir. Taube Centre for Jewish Studies; Faculty Director, Undergraduate Advising, Stanford; Vice-President, Assoc. Jewish Social Studies; Fellow, Academy Jewish Research; Ed. Jewish Social Studies; Prof. Stanford University (1991-); Assoc. Prof. UCLA (1987-91); Frank Green Fellow in Modern Jewish History, Oxford Centre for Postgraduate Hebrew Studies (1981-87); Research Fellow, Wolfson College, Oxford (1983-87). Publ.: Imagining Russian Jewry: Memory, History, Identity (1999); Elusive Prophet: Ahad Ha'am and the Origins of Zionism (1993), awarded National Jewish Book Award; Assimilation and Community: The Jews in Nineteenth-Century Europe, jnt. ed. (1992); The Jews of Odessa: A Cultural History (1985), awarded Smilen Prize in Jewish History. Ad.: Dept. of History, Stanford University, Building 200, Room 11, Stanford, CA 94305. ☎ (650) 725-5660. Fax (650) 725-0597.

ZISSMAN, Sir Bernard Philip, Hon. LLD (B'ham), Hon. D. (UCE), FRSA; b. Birmingham, Dec. 11, 1934; Chairman, Good Hope Hospital NHS Tr. (1998-2003); Dir. BRMB (1995-2000); C. Mem. Birmingham, Chamber of Commerce & Industry; Lord Mayor, City of Birmingham (1990-91); Freeman of the City of London (1991); Leader, Conservative Group, Birmingham City Council (1992-95); Hon. Alderman, City of Birmingham (1995); Tr. City of Birmingham Symphony Orchestra (1992-); President, Representative Council of Birmingham & Midland Jewry (2005-); Chairman, Alexandra Theatre (Birmingham) Ltd (1986-93); Chairman, Cttee to establish Birmingham International Convention Centre/Symphony Hall (1982-86); Mem. Birmingham City Council (1965-95); Chairman, Millennium Point Trust (2006-); President Council Birmingham Hebrew Congregation (1999-2004). Publ. Knight out with Chamberlain (2002); Herzl's Journey (2008). Ad.: 4 Petersham Place, Richmond Hill Rd., Birmingham B15 3RY. ☎/Fax 0121-454 1751.

ZNEIMER, Rabbi Saul, MA (Oxon); b. Wokingham, Berkshire, Oct. 12, 1960; m. Elizabeth née Colman; Chief Executive of the United Synagogue (2001-07); Dir. of Youth Programme, Yakar (1984-86); Dir. Informal Education, United Synagogue Board of Religious Education (1992); Rabbinic Liaison Officer, Office of the Chief Rabbi (1993-94); Chief Rabbi's Cabinet (1994-); Rabbi, Kenton United Synagogue (1994-2000); Dir. Jewish Outreach Network (1999-2001). Ad.: United Synagogue, Adler House, 735 High Road, North Finchley, London N12 0US. ☎ 020-8343 8989. Website www.unitedsynagogue.org.uk

Obituaries, October 2007–October 2008

Full obituary notices may be found in the pages of the Jewish Chronicle, The Times, The Guardian, and The Independent, and selective journals in music and the arts

Abse, Leo, Politician, 22 April 1917-19 August 2008
Asher, Aaron Moses, Editor and publisher, 26 August 1929-18 March 2008
Balcon, Raphael, Cardiologist, 26 August 1936-15 January 2008
Baum, Derek, Communal leader, 1 September 1927-19 January 2008
Bernadt, Himan 'Himie', Lawyer, 21 December 1909-25 December 2007
Beyer, Ralph Alexander, Letter-cutter, sculptor, 6 April 1921-13 February 2008
Blacker, Jacob, Architect, 13 October 1933-14 May 2008
Blond, Anthony, Publisher and writer, 20 March 1928-27 February 2008
Bock, Claus, Germanist, 7 May 1926-5 January 2008
Boxer, Betty (née Sklan), Marriage Counsellor, 29 March 1914-9 March 2008
Bruegel, Irene, Academic and activist, 7 November 1945-6 October 2008
Brown, Rabbi Solomon, 25 August 1921-4 January 2008
Brumberg, Abraham, Editor and writer, 7 November 1926-26 January 2008
Caminer, David, Businessman, 26 June 1915-18 June 2008
Cansino, Manuel, Communal leader, 12 July 1914-26 February 2008
Carlebach, Rabbi Felix, 15 April 1911-23 January 2008
Cohen, Rabbi Isaac, 26 July 1914-30 November 30, 2007
Coleman, Blanche (née Soester), Band leader, 28 February 1910-22 April 2008
Coren, Alan, Writer, journalist and broadcaster, 27 June 1938-18 October 2007
Ehrlich, Ernst Ludwig, Historian and philosopher, 27 March 1921-21 October 2007
Ehrlich, Eugene, Scholar, lexicographer and teacher, 21 May 1922-5 April 2008
Emanuel, Aaron, Civil servant, 11 February 1912-13 March 2008
Falk, Gertrude (Mrs Fatt), Cellular biophysicist, 24 August 1925-9 March 2008
Fogel, Alf, Comedian, 14 July 1926-4 October2008
Frankel, Jonathan, Historian, 15 July 1935-7 May 2008
Frankel, William, Writer and editor, 3 February 1917-18 April 2008
Gee, George Maxwell, Communal leader, 12 January 1921-21 July 2008
Geremek, Bronislaw, Academic and politician, 6 March 1932-13 July 2008
Goldstone, Rebecca (née Lederer), Nurse, 30 October 1915-12 December 2007
Gourgey, Percy, Communal leader, 2 June 1923-19 September 2008
Grant, Marianne (née Hermann), Artist, 19 September 1921-11 December 2007
Greenman, Leon, Campaigner, 18 December 1910-6 March 2008
Gruenberg, Karl Walter, Mathematician: 3 June 1928-10 October 2007
Hacker, Rose, Charitable volunteer, journalist, 3 March 1906-4 February 2008
Hardman, Rev. Leslie, 18 February 1913-7 October 2008
Harel, Yossi, Israeli soldier, 4 January 1918-26 April 2008
Heilpern, Rev. Chaim, Mohel, 8 April 1914-17 April 2008
Hollander, Rabbi Ben, Campaigner, 3 March 1936-11 February 2008
Houthakker, Hendrik Samuel, Economist, 1924-15 April 2008
Houthakker, Lodewijk, Art-dealer, 16 January 1926-2 October 2008
Hurwicz, Leonid, Nobel economist, 21 August 21, 1917-24 June 24 2008
Jackson, Freda (née Jacobson), Social worker, 20 August 1930-4 July 2008
Kagel, Mauricio, Composer, 24 December 1931-19 September 2008
Kaplanov, Rashid Muradovich, Historian, 19 January 1949- 27 November 2007
Karlin, Samuel, Mathematician, 8 June 924-18 December 2007
Katz, Samuel, Zionist, 9 December 1914-9 May 2008
Kay, Tom, Architect and teacher, 17 October 1935-9 December 2007
Kaye, Michael, Arts administrator, 27 February 1925-3 May 2008
Kitaj, R. B., Painter, 29 October 29, 1932-21 October 2007

Kornberg, Arthur, Nobel Biochemist, 3 March 1918-26 October 2007
Kosky, Mark, Communal leader, 5 January 1923-28 August 2008
Lambert, Verity, Television producer, 27 November 1935-22 November 2007
Lantos, Thomas (Tamas) Peter, Politician, 1 February 1928-11 February 2008
Lapid, Josef "Tommy", Journalist, 27 December 1931- 1 June 2008
Lederberg, Joshua, Nobel scientist, 23 May 1925-2 February 2008
Levi, Moshe, Soldier, 18 April 1936-January 8, 2008
Levi, Peta, Design campaigner and journalist, 6 December 1938- 24 April 2008
Levin, Ira, Novelist, 27 August 1929-12 November 2007
Lewis, Geoffrey, Turkish scholar, 19 June 1920-12 February 2008
Lipton, Peter, Philosopher, 9 October 1954-25 November 2007
Lyons, Bernard, Philanthropist, 30 March 1911-12 April 2008
Lyons, Sir Isidore Jack, Industrialist, 1 February 1916-18 February 2008
Mailer, Norman, Writer, 31 January 1923-10 November 2007
Mann, Abby, Scriptwriter, 1 December 1927- 25 March 2008
Mandelbaum, Henryk, Auschwitz survivor, 15 December 1922-17 June 2008
Meyer, Ilse (née Gottheimer), Teacher, 10-October 1906-21 July 2008
Mezei, András, Poet, writer and editor, 23 December 1930- 30 May 2008
Milhaud, Madeleine, Actress, 22 March 1902-17 January 2008
Miller, Jack Elius, Physician, 7 March 1918-1 July 2008
Narkiss, Bezalel, Historian of Jewish art, 14 December 1926-30 June 30 2008
Nathan, Abie, Philanthropist and broadcaster, 29 April 1927-27 August 2008
Nissel, Siegmund, Violinist, 3 January 1922-21 May 2008
Olsberg, Revd. Leslie, 13 May 1922-26 July 2008
Osheroff, Abraham, Political activist, 15 October 1915-6 April 2008
Pinner, Hayim, Zionist, 25 May 1925-5 November 2007
Podro, Michael, Art historian, 13 March 1931-28 March 2008
Pravda, Hana (née Beck), Actor and director, 29 January 29 1918-22 May 2008
Rabinovitch, Dina (Mrs Julius), Journalist, 9 June 1963-30 October, 2007
Rabinowitz, Victor, Lawyer, 2 July 2 1911-16 November 2007
Redhouse, Diana (née Behr), Activist, 6 April 1923-19 October 2007
Robins, David Nathan, Writer and sociologist, 17 November 1944-6 October 2007
Rosenthal, Maud (née Levy), Scholar, 22 April 1909-18 December 2007
Rabinowitsch, Paul (Paul Sandfort), Musician, 12 July 1930-29 December 2007
Rosen, Harold, Educationist, 25 June 1919-31 July 2008
Sacks, Mark, Philosopher, 29 December 1953-17 June 2008
Samuel, Lady (née Edna Nedas), 1919-14 April 2008
Shenton, Ernest (né Schneck), Businessman, 19 December 1930-7 March 2008
Shipton, Sidney, Interfaith activist, 25 July 1929-12 January 2008
Shomron, Dan, Soldier, 5 August 1937-26 February 2008
Silver, Eric, Writer and journalist, 8 July 1935-15 July 2008
Simons, Charles, Chemist, 28 March 1916-26 March 2008
Solman, Joseph, Painter, 25 January 1909-16 April 2008
Sonin, David, Music critic, 14 November 1935-13 May 2008
Sopel, Miriam (née Lazarus), Club leader, 11 April 1927-14 April 2008
Sumray, Monty, Industrialist, 12 October 1929-2 June 2008
Tann, Rabbi Leonard, 20 August 1945-12 November 2007
Temple, Nat, Band leader, 18 July 1913-30 May 2008
Volosky, Valentín Teitelboim, Politician and writer, 17 March 1916-January 2008
Winston-Fox, Ruth (née Lipson), Adoption Officer, 12 September 1912-23 November 2007
Yefimov, Boris (né Boris Fridland), Cartoonist, 28 September 1900-1 October 2008
Yodaikin, Arnold, Teacher, 27 June 1922-11 January 2008
Yoseloff, Thomas, Publisher, 8 September 1913-24 December 2007

Events of 2008

Events of the Year

Anniversaries
150th Lionel de Rothschild's entry into Parliament
150th Jewish Care Scotland
120th JPSA
100th Croydon Synagogue
90th 1918 Armistice
90th WIZO
90th Habonim
75th Danby's Mishnah
70th Greenbank Drive (and closure)
70th Anschluss
70th Kristallnacht
70th Kindertransport
60th Dead Sea Scrolls
60th "Exodus"
60th State of Israel
60th Harry Morgan's
50th First AJY and Zemel Choir visits to Israel
50th Pinter's 'Birthday Party'

January
President Bush in Israel and the West Bank
Publication of Winograd Report
Closure of Greenbank Drive Synagogue
National Holocaust Memorial Day in Liverpool
"Israel" Debates at the Oxford Union and at the LSE

February
Suicide bombers at Dimona
Barenboim's Beethoven cycle at the Royal Festival Hall
Archbishop's Intervention on Shariah Law
'Open-Letter' from Muslim Organisations

March
Attack at Merkaz Harav Yeshivah
Bipartisan motion in support of Israel in the Australian Parliament
Goldie Hawn guest speaker at KKL Scotland Gala Dinner
Orphaned Art: Looted Art From the Holocaust exhibition in Jerusalem and Paris
Daniel Finkelstein awarded inaugural Chaim Bermant Prize for Journalism

April
UJIA Dinner at Windsor Castle
Israel Cinema Festival
Prince Charles opened Communal Centre in Krakow

May
Talks between Israel and Syria
Israel 60th Gala at Wembley
President Peres's 'Facing Tomorrow' Conference

June
Launch of 'Jewish Way of Life' CD
BBC TV "Jews" series
Exhibition on Scots Jewry at Garnethill
R.B. Kitaj late paintings at the RA
Jewish Community Secondary School Approved
Ceasefire in Gaza
Justice for Jews from Arab Countries Congress inaugurated in London

July
Exchange of prisoners with Lebanon
Gordon Brown addressed the Knesset
Barack Obama in the Middle East
Hadrian Exhibition at the British Museum
Mor Karbari performing Ladino songs
Chief Rabbi addressed the Lambeth Conference

August
European Union of Jewish Students 'Summer University' held in Turkey
Hannah Frank centenarian exhibition in Glasgow

September
British-Jewish Visit to Berlin
Resignation of Ehud Olmert
Tzipi Livni won the Kadima leadership primaries
'Statement on Communal Collaboration'

October
Rothko murals exhibition at Tate Modern
New synagogue opened in North Rhine-Westphalia
Batsheva Dance Company in London
Riots in Akko

November
Presidential Election in the USA
Archbishop of Canterbury's visit to Auschwitz
Mayoral Election in Jerusalem

Publications and Booksellers

The following is a list of notable British and Irish publications of 2006–2007 with paperback reprints, available from Jewish and general bookshops and the internet

Antisemitism

All-Party Inquiry into Anti-Semitism: Report: Government response, 29th March 2007: presented to Parliament by the Secretary of State for Communities and Local Government, 29th March 2007, Stationery Office, 2007
Robert S. Wistrich: Laboratory for world destruction : Germans and Jews in Central Europe, University of Nebraska Press for the Vidal Sassoon International Center for the Study of Antisemitism (SICSA), the Hebrew University of Jerusalem, 2007

Biblical and Hebrew Studies
Robert Alter: The Book of Psalms : a translation with commentary, Norton 2007

Biography and Autobiography
Daniel Barenboim: Everything is connected : the power of music, Weidenfeld & Nicolson, 2008
Steven Berkoff: My life in food, ACDC Publishing, 2007
Kai Bird and Martin J Sherwin: American Prometheus : the triumph and tragedy of J. Robert Oppenheimer, Atlantic Books, 2007
Gerry Black: Frank's way : Frank Cass and fifty years of publishing, Vallentine Mitchell, 2008
David M. Crowe: Oskar Schindler : the untold account of his life, wartime activities, and the true story behind the list, Basic Books, 2007
Philip Davis: Bernard Malamud : a writer's life, Oxford University Press, 2007
Georgina Ferry: Max Perutz and the secret of life, Chatto and Windus, 2007
Edward Gelles: An ancient lineage : European roots of a Jewish family, Vallentine Mitchell, 2007
Roman Halter: Roman's journey; preface by Sir Martin Gilbert, Portobello Books, 2007
Walter Isaacson: Einstein : his life and universe, Simon & Schuster, 2007
Ramin Jahanbegloo: Conversations with Isaiah Berlin, Peter Halban, 2007
Miriam Karlin: Some sort of a life, edited by Jan Sargent, Oberon Books, 2007
Lucette Lagnado: The man in the white sharkskin suit : my family's exodus from Old Cairo to the New World, Ecco, 2007
Lord Levy: A question of honour, Simon & Schuster, 2008
Emanuel Litvinoff: Journey through a small planet . Introduction by Patrick Wright, Penguin, 2008
Alasdair MacIntyre: Edith Stein : the philosophical background, Hambledon Continuum, 2007
Norman Mailer: On God : an uncommon conversation, with Michael Lennon, Continuum 2008
Mike Marqusee: If I am not for myself : journey of an anti-Zionist Jew, Verso, 2008
Braham Murray: The worst it can be is a disaster, Methuen Drama, 2007
Neil Pearson: Obelisk : a history of Jack Kahane and the Obelisk Press, Liverpool University Press, 2007
Penny Perrick: Something to hide : the life of Sheila Wingfield, Viscountess Powerscourt, Lilliput Press, 2007
Amy Raphael: Mike Leigh on Mike Leigh, Faber and Faber, 2008
David Rieff: Swimming in a sea of death : a son's memoir, Granta, 2008
Miriam Rothschild: Walter Rothschild : the man, the museum and the menagerie, Natural History Museum, 2008
Sadia Shepard: Footpaths in the painted city : an Indian journey, Atlantic Books, 2008

W. Paul Strassmann: The Strassmanns : science, politics and migration in turbulent times (1793-1993), Berghahn Books, 2008
Jean Moorcroft Wilson: Isaac Rosenberg : the making of a great war poet : a new life, Weidenfeld & Nicolson, 2008

Current Affairs and Sociological
Nathan Abrams, ed: Jews and sex, Five Leaves Publications, 2008
Danny Ben-Moshe and Zohar Segev, eds.: Israel, the diaspora and Jewish identity. Sussex Academic Press, 2007
Simon J. Bronner, ed.: Jewish cultural studies, volume 1: Jewishness, expression, identity, and representation, Littman Library of Jewish Civilization, 2008
Kenneth Collins: Scotland's Jews : a guide to the history and community of the Jews in Scotland, 2nd. ed, Scottish Council of Jewish Communities, 2008
J. Thomas Cook: Spinoza's Ethics, Continuum, 2007
Ruth Deech and Anna Smajdor: From IVF to immortality : controversy in the era of reproductive technology, Oxford University Press, 2007
Irene Eber: Chinese and Jews : encounters between cultures, Vallentine Mitchell, 2008
Abraham H. Foxman: The deadliest lies : the Israel Lobby and the myth of Jewish control, foreword by George Shultz, Palgrave Macmillan, 2007
Eric Hobsbawm: Globalisation, democracy and terrorism, Little Brown, 2007
David B. Goldstein: Jacob's legacy : a genetic view of Jewish history, Yale University Press, 2008
Tony Judt: Reappraisals : reflections on the forgotten twentieth century, Penguin, 2008
Daniel Levy: The fox, the foetus and the fatal injection : a thought-provoking Torah approach addressing the contemporary issues of abortion, assisted dying & euthanasia & their implications for the Jewish community, foreword by Jonathan Sacks, 2007
George Makari: Revolution in mind : the creation of psychoanalysis, Duckworth, 2008
Nadia Malinovich: French and Jewish : culture and politics of identity in early twentieth-century France, Littman Library, 2007
Julia Neuberger: Not dead yet : a manifesto for old age, HarperCollins, 2008
Laurence Rees: Their darkest hour: people tested to the extreme in WWII, Ebury Press, 2007
Jonathan Sacks: The home we build together : recreating society, Continuum, 2007
Bernard Wasserstein: Barbarism and civilization : a history of Europe in our time, Oxford University Press, 2007

Arts
Tim Barringer Gillian Forrester, Barbaro Martinez-Ruiz, eds.: Art and emancipation in Jamaica : Isaac Mendes Belisario and his worlds, Yale University Press, 2007
Rodney Greenberg: George Gershwin, Phaidon, 2008.
Jackie Ranston: Belisario Sketches of character : a historical biography of a Jamaican artist, Kingston: The Mill Press, 2008
Philip Vann and Jackie Wullschlager: Landscapes: Joash Woodrow, foreword by Christopher Bailey, introduction by Andrew Stewart, Leeds Metropolitan University Gallery, 2007

Reference and Bibliography
J.A.S. Grenville and Raphael Gross, eds.: Leo Baeck Institute yearbook, LII, 2007, Berghahn Books, published for the Institute, London, Jerusalem, New York, 2008
Zeev Gries: The book in the Jewish world, 1700-1900, Littman Library, 2007
Alana Newhouse, ed.: A living lens : photographs of Jewish life from the pages of "The Forward", Norton, 2008.
Fred Skolnik, ed.: Encyclopedia Judaica, 2nd, executive editor: Michael Berenbaum,

Macmillan Reference USA in association with the Keter Publishing House, 2007
Rosemary Wenzerul: Tracing your Jewish ancestors, a guide for family historians, Pen and Sword, 2008

Cookery, Travel and Humour
Alan Coren: Chocolate and cuckoo clocks : the essential Alan Coren, Canongate, 2008
Denise Phillips: New flavours of the Jewish table, Ebury Press, 2008
Marlena Spieler: Kosher cooking, Apple Press, 2008

History
Michael Alpert: Secret Judaism and the Spanish Inquisition, Five Leaves Publications, 2008
Yom Tov Assis: The golden age of Aragonese Jewry : community and society in the Crown of Aragon, 1213-1327, Littman Library of Jewish Civilization, 2008
Sharon Barron: A caring community ... 150 years of Jewish Care Scotland, Glasgow Jewish Care, 2008
Morris Beckman: The Jewish Brigade : an army with two masters 1944-45. Foreword by Edmund de Rothschild, The History Press, 2008
Asher Benson: Jewish Dublin : portraits of life by the Liffey, A. & A. Farmar, 2007
Gerry Black: The joys of friendship. A history of the Association of Jewish Friendship Clubs, 1950-2008, Tymsder Publishing, 2008
Jeremy Cohen and Richard I. Cohen, eds.: The Jewish contribution to civilization, Library, 2007
Matthew Dimmock and Andrew Hadfield eds.: Religions of the Book : co-existence and conflict 1400-1600, Palgrave Macmillan, 2008
Edna Fernandes: The last Jews of Kerala : the two thousand year history of India's forgotten Jewish community, Portobello, 2008
Israel Finestein: Studies and profiles in Anglo-Jewish history : from Picciotto to Bermant, Vallentine Mitchell, 2008
William J Fishman: East End Jewish Radicals 1875-1914, Five Leaves Publications, 2008
Helen Fry: The King's Most Loyal Enemy Aliens : Germans who fought for Britain in the Second World War, Sutton Books, 2007
Martin Goodman: Rome and Jerusalem : the clash of ancient civilizations, Penguin Books, 2008
Lester L. Grabbe: Ancient Israel : what do we know and how do we know it?, T.&T. Clarke International, 2007
David J. Halperin: Sabbatai Zevi : testimonies to a fallen messiah, Littman Library, 2007
Heritage No. 6: an historical series of the Jewish inhabitants of North London, Jewish Research Group of the Edmonton Hundred Historical Society, 2007
Jonathan Karp: The politics of Jewish commerce : economic thought and emancipation in Europe, 1638-1848, Cambridge University Press, 2008
Michel S. Laguerre: Global neighborhoods : Jewish quarters in Paris, London, and Berlin, SUNY, 2008
Dan Levene and Beno Rothenberg: A metallurgical Gemara : metals in Jewish sources, Institute for Archaeo-Metallurgical Studies, 2007
Tamar Morad, Dennis Shasha, and Robert Shasha, eds.:Iraq's last Jews: stories of daily life, upheaval, and escape from modern Babylon, Palgrave Macmillan, 2008
Joy L. Oakley, ed.: Lists of the Portuguese Inquisition. Vol. I: Lisbon, 1540-1778. Vol. II: Evora, 1542-1763; Goa, 1650-1653, transcription and index, Jewish Historical Society of England, 2007
Tudor Parfitt: The lost Ark of the Covenant : the remarkable quest for the legendary Ark, HarperElement, 2008
Meir Persoff: Faith against reason : religious reform and the British Chief Rabbinate, 1840-

1990, Vallentine Mitchell, 2008

David Rechter: The Jews of Vienna and the First World War, Littman Library of Jewish Civilization, 2008

Moshe Roseman: How Jewish is Jewish history?, Littman Library, 2007

Minna Rozen, ed.: Homelands and their diasporas : Greeks, Jews and their migrations, Palgrave Macmillan, 2008

Marc Saperstein: Jewish preaching in time of war, 1800-2001, Littman Library of Jewish Civilization, 2007

Violetta Shamash: Memories of Eden : a journey through Jewish Baghdad, edited by Mira Shamash and Tony Rocca, Forum Books, 2008

Susan Sorek: The Jews against Rome : war in Palestine AD 66-73, Hambledon Continuum, 2008

Kenneth Stow: Jewish life in early modern Rome : challenge, conversion, and private life, Ashgate Variorum, 2007

Derek Taylor: Don Pacifico : the acceptable face of gunboat diplomacy, Vallentine Mitchell, 2008

Derek Taylor and Greville Janner: Jewish parliamentarians, Vallentine Mitchell, 2008

Bill Williams: Jewish Manchester : an illustrated history, Breedon Books, 2008

Holocaust

Judith Buber Agassi: Jewish women prisoners of Ravensbruck, Oneworld Publications, 2007

David Bathrick, Brad Prager, and Michael Richardson, eds.: Visualizing the holocaust : documents, aesthetics, memory, Woodbridge: Camden House, 2008

Avraham Burg: The holocaust is over : we must rise from its ashes, Palgrave Macmillan, 2008

Jackie Feldman: Above the death pits, beneath the flag : youth voyages to Poland and the performance of Israeli national identity, Berghahn Books, 2008

Saul Friedlander: The years of extermination : Nazi Germany and the Jews 1939-1945, Weidenfeld & Nicolson, 2007

Nancy Kohner: My father's roses, Hodder & Stoughton, 2008

Mark Kurzem : The mascot : the extraordinary story of a Jewish boy and an SS Extermination Squad, Rider & Co., 2007

Ernest Levy: The single light, Vallentine Mitchell, 2007

Ladislaus Lob: Dealing with Satan : Rezso Kasztner's daring rescue of Hungarian Jews, Jonathan Cape, 2008

Melissa Muller and Reinhard Piechocki: A garden of Eden in Hell : the life of Alice Herz-Sommer, Pan Macmillan, 2007

Jules Schelvis: Sobibor : a history of a Nazi death camp, edited by Bob Moore, Berg

Richard Vinen: The unfree French : life under the Occupation, Penguin Books, 2007

Elie Wiesel: Night, translated by Marion Wiesel, Penguin Books, 2008

Israel

Guy Ben-Porat: Israel since 1980, withYagil Levy, Shlomo Mizrahi, Arye Naor, Erez Tzfadia, Cambridge University Press, 2008

Elinor Burkett: Golda Meir : the Iron Lady of the Middle East : the first woman Prime Minister in the West, Gibson Square Books Ltd., 2008

Martin Gilbert: The story of Israel : from Theodor Herzl to the roadmap for peace, André Deutsch, 2008

Henry Near: The Kibbutz Movement : a history, Littman Library of Jewish Civilization, 2007

Colin Shindler: A history of modern Israel, Cambridge University Press, 2008

Judaism

David Berger: The Rebbe, the Messiah, and the scandal of orthodox indifference, with a new introduction, Littman Library of Jewish Civilization, 2008

Maureen Bloom: Jewish mysticism and magic : an anthropological perspective, Routledge, 2007

Charlotte E. Fonrobert, Martin S. Jaffee, eds.: The Cambridge companion to the Talmud and Rabbinic literature, Cambridge University Press, 2007

Robert Goldenberg: The origins of Judaism : from Canaan to the rise of Islam, Cambridge University Press, 2007

Lenn E. Goodman: On justice : an essay in Jewish philosophy, Littman Library of Jewish Civilization, 2007

Moshe Halbertal and Donniel Hartman, eds.: Judaism and the challenges of modern life, Continuum, 2007

Mitchell B. Har: The healthy Jew : the symbiosis of Judaism and modern medicine, Cambridge University Press, 2007

Donniel Hartman: The boundaries of Judaism, Continuum, 2007

Moshe Idel: Ben : sonship and Jewish mysticism, Continuum, 2008

Joel L. Kraemer, ed.: Perspectives on Maimonides : philosophical and historical studies, Littman Library of Jewish Civilization, 2008

Emmanuel Levinas: Beyond the verse : Talmudic readings and lectures, translated by Gary D. Mole, Continuum, 2008

Emmanuel Levinas: In the time of the nations, translated by Michael B. Smith, Continuum, 2007

Jonathan Magonet, ed.: Seder Hatefillot: Forms of Prayer, Reform Synagogues of Great Britain, 2008

Avi Sagi: The open canon : on the meaning of halakhic Judaism, Continuum, 2008

Avi Sagi and Zvi Zohar: Transforming identity : the ritual transition from gentile to Jew, Continuum, 2007

Isaiah Tishby: Messianic mysticism : Moses Hayim Luzzatto and the Padua School, translated from the Hebrew by Morris Hoffman; introduction by Joseph Dan, Littman Library of Jewish Civilization, 2007

Literature

Glenda Abramson: Hebrew writing of the First World War, Vallentine Mitchell, 2008

S.Y. Agnon: To this day, translated by Hillel Halkin, Toby Press. 2008

Woody Allen: Mere anarchy, Ebury Press, 2007

Hannah Arendt: The Jewish writings, Schocken Books, 2007

Shalom Auslander: Foreskin's lament, Picador, 2008

Paul Auster: Man in the dark : a novel, Faber and Faber, 2008

Paul Auster: Travels in the scriptorium / by. – London: Faber and Faber, 2007

Anthony Bale: The Jew in the medieval book : English antisemitisms 1350-1500, Cambridge University Press, 2007

Chaim Bermant: On the other hand, foreword by David Rowan, Vallentine Mitchell, 2008

Amy Bloom: Away : a novel, Allen and Unwin, 2007

Ruth Borchardt: We are strangers here : an enemy alien in prison in 1940, with an introduction by Charmian Brinson, Vallentine Mitchell, 2008

Sam Bourne: Last testament, HarperCollins, 2007

Sam Bourne: The final reckoning, HarperCollins, 2008

Geraldine Brooks: People of the Book, Fourth Estate, 2008

Justin Cartwright: The song before it is sung, Bloomsbury, 2007

Paul Celan: Snow part/Schneepart, translated by Ian Fairley, Carcanet, 2007

George Clare: Last waltz in Vienna, Pan Books, 2008

George Crowder, Henry Hardy, eds.: The one and the many : reading Isaiah Berlin, Prometheus Books, 2007

Nathan Englander: The Ministry of Special Cases, Faber and Faber, 2007

Eshkol Nevo: Homesick, translated by Sondra Silverston, Chatto & Windus, 2008

Elaine Feinstein: The Russian Jerusalem : a novel, Carcanet, 2008

Elaine Feinstein: Talking to the dead, Carcanet, 2007

Danny Fingeroth: Disguised as Clark Kent : Jews, comics, and the creation, foreword by Stan Lee, Continuum, 2007

Michael Frayn: Afterlife, Methuen Drama, 2008

Deborah Garrison: The second child, Bloodaxe Books, 2008

Markham J. Geller and Mineke Schipper, eds.: Imagining creation, with an introduction by Mary Douglas, E.J. Brill, 2007

David Goldstein, ed.: Hebrew poems from Spain, Littman Library, 2007

Nadine Gordimer: Beethoven was one-sixteenth black : and other stories, Bloomsbury, 2007

Robert S. C. Gordon, ed.: The Cambridge companion to Primo Levi, Cambridge University Press, 2007

Linda Grant: The clothes on their backs, Virago, 2008

Zoe Heller: The believers, Fig Tree, 2008

Eva Hoffman: Illuminations, Harvill Secker, 2008

Howard Jacobson: Kalooki nights, Vintage Books, 2007

Howard Jacobson: The act of love, Jonathan Cape, 2008

Sayed Kashua: Let it be morning, translated by Miriam Shlesinger, Atlantic Books, 2007

Etgar Keret: Missing Kissinger, Chatto & Windus, 2007

Imre Kertesz: Detective story, translated by Tim Wilkinson, Harvill Secker, 2008

Imre Kertesz: The pathseeker, translated by Tim Wilkinson, Melville House Publishing, 2008

Bernard Kops: The world is a wedding, Five Leaves Publications, 2008

Lotte Kramer: Kindertransport, before and after: elegy and celebration : sixty poems 1980-2007, Centre for German-Jewish Studies, University of Sussex, 2007

Anne Landsman: The rowing lesson, Granta Books, 2008

Jennifer Langered: If salt has memory : Jewish exiled writers from Africa, Latin America, Europe and the Middle East, Five Leaves Publications, 2008

Ron Leshem: Beaufort, translation by Evan Fallenber, Harvill Secker, 2008

Sidura Ludwig: Holding my breath : a novel, Tindal Street Press, 2008

Heather McRobie: Psalm 119, Maia Press, Ltd., 2008

Aharon Megged: The flying camel and the golden hump, Toby Books, 2007

Irene Nemirovsky: All our worldly good, Chatto & Windus, 2008

Irene Nemirovsky: The Courilof affair, Vintage, 2008

Irene Nemirovsky: David Golder, The Ball, Snow in autumn, The Courilof affair, translated by Sandra Smith., introduction by Claire Messud, J.M. Dent & Son, 2008

Irene Nemirovsky: Fire in the blood, translated by Sandra Smith, Chatto and Windus, 2007

Eshkol Nevo: Homesick, translated by Sondra Silverston, Chatto & Windus, 2008

Gedalyah Nigal: The Hasidic tale, translated from the Hebrew by Edward Levin, Littman Library of Jewish Civilization, 2008

Naomi Ragen: The Saturday wife, Hodder & Stoughton, 2007

Frederic Raphael: Fame and fortune, JR Books, 2007

Frederic Raphael: The glittering prizes, JR Books, 2007

Frederic Raphael: Lindmann, Five Leaves Publications, 2008

Philip Roth: Exit ghost, Jonathan Cape, 2007

Philip Roth: Indignation, Jonathan Cape, 2008

Diane Samuels, Tracy-Ann Oberman Three sisters on Hope Street, Nick Hern Books, 2008

Danny Scheinmann: Random acts of heroic love, Black Swan, 2008

Bruno Schulz: The Street of Crocodiles and other stories, translated by Celina Wieniewska;

with a foreword by Jonathan Safran Foer, Penguin Books, 2008
J. David Simons: The credit draper, Two Ravens Press, 2008
Julian Sinclair: Let's schmooze : Jewish words today, Continuum International, 2007
Dalia Sofer: The Septembers of Shiraz, Ecco, 2007
George Steiner: My unwritten books, Weidenfeld & Nicolson, 2008
Susanna Tamaro: Listen to my voice, Harvill Secker, 2008
Adam Thirlwell: Miss Herbert, Jonathan Cape, 2007
Kati Tonkin: Marching into history : from the early novels of Joseph Roth to 'Radetzkymarsch' and 'Die Kapuzinergruft', Camden House, 2008
Juan Gabriel Vasquez: The informers, translated from the Spanish by Anne McLean, Bloomsbury, 2008
Fred Wander: The seventh well : a novel, translated by Michael Hofmann, Granta, 2008
Jonathan Wilson: An ambulance is on its way : stories of men in trouble, Five Leaves Publications, 2008
Jonathan Wilson: The hiding room, Five Leaves Publications, 2008
Richard Zimler: The seventh gate, Constable and Robinson, 2007

Middle East
Gilbert Achcar and Michel Warschawski: 33-day war : Israel's war on Hezbollah in Lebanon and its consequences, Saqi Books, 2007
Joel Berkowitz, ed.: Yiddish theatre : new approaches, Littman Library of Jewish Civilization, 2008
Barbara Board: Reporting from Palestine (1943-44), Five Leaves Publications, 2008
Simon Dunstan: The Yom Kippur War: the Arab-Israeli War of 1973, Osprey, 2007
Lawrence Freedman: A choice of enemies : America confronts the Middle East, Weidenfeld & Nicolson, 2008
Gershom Gorenberg: Occupied territories : the untold stories of Israel's settlements, I.B. Tauris, 2007
Jonathan Garfinkel: Ambivalence, Viking, 2007
Simon Goldhill: Jerusalem : city of longing, Belknap Press of Harvard University, 2008
Raja Halwani and Tomis Kapitan: The Israeli-Palestinian conflict : philosophical essays on self-determination, terrorism and the One-State solution, edited by Yaacov Bar-Siman-Tov, Palgrave Macmillan, 2007
Ghada Karmi: Married to another man : Israel's dilemma in Palestine, Pluto Press, 2007
Etgar Keret and Samir El-Youssef, eds.: Shattered dreams : Israel and the Palestinians, photographs by Judah Passow, Peter Halban, 2008
Stephen Law: Israel, Palestine and terror, Continuum, 2008
Neil Lochery: Loaded dice : the Foreign Office and Israel, Continuum, 2007
Nur Masalha: The Bible and Zionism : invented traditions, archaeology and post-colonialism in Palestine-Israel, Zed Books, 2007
Avi Shlaim: Lion of Jordan : the life of King Hussein in war and peace, Penguin Books, 2008
Sandy Tolan: The lemon tree : an Arab, a Jew, and the heart of the Middle East, Bloomsbury, 2008
Eyal Weizman: Hollow land : Israel's architecture of Occupation, Verso, 2007
Robin Wright: Dreams and shadows : the future of the Middle East, Penguin books, 2008

Zionism
Michael Makovsky: Churchill's Promised Land: Zionism and statecraft, Yale University Press, 2007.
Arno J. Mayer: Ploughshares into swords : from Zionism to Israel, Verso Books, 2008
James Renton: The Zionist masquerade : the birth of the Anglo-Zionist alliance, 1914-1918,

Palgrave Macmillan, 2007
Colin Shindler: What do Zionists believe?, Granta Books, 2007
Bernard Zissman: Herzl's journey : conversations with a Zionist legend, Devora Publishing, 2008.

Children's and Educational

Jeffrey M. Cohen: Torah for teens : growing up spiritually with the weekly Sidrah, with a preface by Jonathan Sacks, Vallentine Mitchell, 2007

Booksellers

The booksellers listed below specialise in Jewish books. Many also supply religious requisites.

GREATER LONDON

Aubrey Goldstein, 7 Windsor Court, Chase Side, N14 5HT. ☎ 020-8886 4075
Books Etc, Unit 5 The O2 Centre, 255 Finchley Road, London NW3 6LU. ☎ 020-7433 3299
Borders, Brent Cross Shopping Park, Tilling Road, NW2 1LJ. ☎ 020-8452 9245
Carmel Gifts, 62 Edgware Way, Middx. ☎ 020-8958 7632. Fax 020-8958 6226. Email carmelgifts@aol.com
Daunt Books, 193 Haverstock Hill, NW3 4QL. ☎ 020-7794 4006
Divrei Kodesh, 13 Edgwarebury La, Edgware HA8 8LH. ☎ 020-8958 1133
Hebrew Book & Gift Centre (M.E. Hochhauser), 24 Amhurst Parade, N16 5AA. ☎/Fax 020-8802 0609
J. Aisenthal, 11 Ashbourne Pde., Finchley Rd., NW11. ☎ 020-8455 0501. Fax 020-8455 0501. Email info@aisenthal.co.uk. Website www.aisenthal.co.uk
Jerusalem the Golden Ltd, 146-148 Golders Green Rd., NW11 8HE. ☎ 020-8455 4960 or 8458 7011. Fax 020-8458 3593
Joseph's Bookstore and Café Also, 1255-1257 Finchley Rd., NW11 0AD. ☎ 020-8731 7575. Fax 020-8731 6699. Email info@josephsbookstore.com. Website www.josephsbookstore.com. **Cafe Also** ☎ 020-8455 6890
Kuperard, 59 Hutton Grove, N12 8DS. ☎ 020-8446 2440. Fax 020-8446 2441. Email books@kuperard.co.uk. Website www.kuperard.co.uk (publishers and distributors, mail order, educational suppliers, book fairs, book launches).
Manor House Books, John Trotter Books, Sternberg Centre, 80 East End Road, London N3 2SY. ☎ 20-8349 9484. New, used and rare Jewish and Hebrew books Email jtrotter@freenetname.co.uk. Website www.ukbookworld.com/members/trotter
Menorah Book Centre, 16 Russell Parade, Golders Green Rd., NW11 9NN. ☎ 020-8458 8289. Fax 020-8731 8403
Mesorah Bookstore, 61 Old Hill St., N16 6LU. ☎ 020-8809 4310
M. Rogosnitzky, 20 The Drive, NW11 9SR. ☎ 020-8455 7645 or 4112
Muswell Hill Bookshop, 72 Fortis Green Rd., N10 3HN. ☎ 020-8444 7588
On Your Doorstep, Jewish Books & Gifts (Sandra E. Breger), 1 Rosecroft Walk, Pinner, Middlesex HA5 1LJ. ☎ 020-8866 6236
Steimatzky Hasifria, 46 Golders Green Road, NW11 8LL. ☎ 020-8458 9774. Fax 020-8458 3449. Email info@steimatzky.co.uk. Website www.steimatzky.co.uk
Torah Treasures, 4 Sentinel Sq., NW4 2EL. ☎ 020-8202 3134. Fax 020-8202 3161. Email torahtreasures@btinternet.com.
Waterstone's, 68 Hampstead High St., NW3 1QP. ☎ 020-7794 1098.
Waterstone's, 82 Gower St., WC1E 6EG. ☎ 020-7636 1577.

REGIONS

BIRMINGHAM Lubavitch Bookshop, 95 Willows Rd., B12 9QF. ☎ 0121-440 6673. Fax 0121-446 4199.

GATESHEAD Lehmann's Retail: 28-30 Grasmere St. West, NE8 1TS. ☎ 0191-477 3523; Mail order and wholesale: Unit E, Viking Industrial Park, Rolling Mill Road, Jarrow, Tyne & Wear NE32 3DP. ☎ 0191-430 0333. Fax 0191-430 0555. Email info@lehmanns.co.uk.

GLASGOW J. & E. Levingstone, 47 & 55 Sinclair Dr., G42 9PT. ☎ 0141-649 2962. Fax 0141-649 2962.

LIVERPOOL Jewish Book & Gift Centre, Harold House, Dunbabin Rd., L15 6XL. Sun. only, 11 a.m. to 1 p.m. Orders ☎ 0151-722 3303.

MANCHESTER & SALFORD
B. Horwitz (wholesale & retail Judaica), 2 Kings Rd., Prestwich, M25 0LE. ☎/Fax 0161-773 4956. Email boaz76@aol.com.
Hasefer, 18 Merrybower Rd., Salford M7 4HE. ☎ 0161-740 3013. Fax 0161-721 4649.
J. Goldberg, 11 Parkside Ave., Salford, M7 0HB. ☎ 0161-740 0732.
Jewish Book Centre (Mr Klein), 25 Ashbourne Gr., Salford, M7 4DB. ☎ 0161-792 1253. Fax 0161-661 5505.

OXFORD B. H. Blackwell Ltd., 48-51 Broad St., OX1 3BQ. ☎ 01865 792792. Fax 01865 261 355. Email blackwells.extra@blackwell.co.uk. Has a Jewish book section.

SOUTHEND Dorothy Young, 21 Colchester Rd., SS2 6HW. ☎ 01702 331218 for appointment. Email dorothy@dorothyyoung.co.uk. Website www.dorothyyoung. co.uk.

PRINCIPAL FESTIVALS AND FASTS 2008–2016 (5769–5776)

Festival or Fast	Hebrew Date	5769 2008-09	5770 2009-10	5771 2010-11	5772 2011-12	5773 2012-13	5774 2013-14	5775 2014-15	5776 2015-16
New Year	Tishri 1	Sept. 30	Sept. 19	Sept. 9	Sept. 29	Sept. 17	Sept. 5	Sept. 25	Sept. 14
Day of Atonement	Tishri 10	Oct. 9	Sept. 28	Sept. 18	Oct. 8	Sept. 26	Sept. 14	Oct. 4	Sept. 23
Tabernacles, 1st Day	Tishri 15	Oct.14	Oct. 3	Sept. 23	Oct. 13	Oct. 1	Sept. 19	Oct. 9	Sept. 28
Tabernacles, 8th Day	Tishri 22	Oct. 21	Oct. 10	Sept. 30	Oct. 20	Oct. 8	Sept. 26	Oct. 16	Oct. 5
Rejoicing of the Law	Tishri 23	Oct. 22	Oct. 11	Oct. 1	Oct. 21	Oct. 9	Sept. 27	Oct. 17	Oct. 6
Chanucah	Kislev 25	Dec. 22	Dec. 12	Dec. 2	Dec. 21	Dec. 9	Nov. 28	Dec. 17	Dec. 7
Purim	Adar[1] 14	Mar. 10	Feb. 28	Mar. 20	Mar. 8	Feb. 24	Mar. 16	Mar. 5	Mar. 24
Passover, 1st Day	Nisan 15	Apr. 9	Mar. 30	Apr. 19	Apr. 7	Mar. 26	Apr. 15	Apr. 4	Apr. 23
Passover, 7th Day	Nisan 21	Apr.15	Apr. 5	Apr. 25	Apr. 13	Apr. 1	Apr. 21	Apr. 10	Apr. 29
Israel Indep. Day	Iyar 5[2]	Apr. 29	Apr. 20	May 10	Apr. 26	Apr. 16	May 6	Apr. 23	May 12
Feast of Weeks	Sivan 6	May 29	May 19	June 8	May 27	May 15	June 4	May 24	June 12
Fast of Ab	Ab 9	July 30	July 20	Aug. 9	July 29[3]	July 16	Aug. 5	July 26[3]	Aug. 14[3]

1. Ve-Adar 14 in Leap Years.
2. When this date occurs on Friday or Sabbath, Israel Independence Day is observed on the previous Thursday, and when it occurs on Monday, Independence Day is postponed to Tuesday (to avoid Remembrance Day beginning when Sabbath ends).
3. Ab 10 (Ab 9 being Sabbath).

THE JEWISH CALENDAR

The Jewish Calendar is a lunar one, adapted to the solar year by various expedients. The hour is divided into 1,080 portions or *minims*, and the month between one new moon and the next is reckoned as 29 days, 12 hours, 793 minims. The years are grouped in cycles of 19. The present calendar was fixed by the Palestinian Jewish Patriarch, Hillel II, in 358 C.E. In early Talmudic times the new moons were fixed by the actual observation, and were announced from Jerusalem to the surrounding districts and countries by messenger or beacon.

If the time elapsing between one new moon and another were *exactly* 29½ days, the length of the months could be fixed at alternately 29 and 30 days. But there are three corrections to make which disturb this regularity: (1) The excess of 793 minims over the half day, (2) the adjustment to the solar year, (3) the requirement that the incidence of certain Jewish festivals shall not conflict with the Sabbath. To overcome these difficulties the Jewish Calendar recognises six different classes of years; three of them common and three leap. The leap years, which are the 3rd, 6th, 8th, 11th, 14th, 17th, and 19th of the Metyonic cycle of 19 years, are composed of thirteen months, an additional month being added. It is usually stated that this intercalary month is inserted after the month of Adar which in the ordinary year is of 29 days, but in a leap year has 30 days, but in reality the inserted month precedes the ordinary Adar and always has 30 days. Both the common and the leap years may be either regular, "minimal" , or full. The regular year has an alternation of 30 and 29 days. The "minimal" year gives Kislev only 29 days instead of 30, while in a full year Marcheshvan has 30 instead of 29 days.

Besides the lunar cycle of 19 years there is a solar cycle of 28 years, at the beginning of which the *Tekufah* of Nisan (the vernal equinox) returns to the same day and the same hour.

The chief disturbing influence in the arrangement of the Jewish Calendar is to prevent the Day of Atonement (Tishri 10th) from either immediately preceding or immediately succeeding the Sabbath, and Hoshana Rabba (Tishri 21st) from falling on the Sabbath. Consequently the New Year (Tishri Ist) cannot fall upon Sunday, Wednesday or Friday. A further complication of a purely astronomical character is introduced by the consideration that the Jewish day formally commences six hours before midnight. Hence, if the Molad or lunar conjunction for the month of Tishri occurs at noon or later, the new moon will be seen only after 6 p.m. and the Festival is postponed to the next day. When, after paying regard to these and certain other considerations, the days upon which two successive New Year Festivals fall are determined, the number of days in the intervening year is known and the length of Marcheshvan and Kislev is fixed accordingly.

It is customary to describe the character of a Jewish Year by a "Determinative" consisting of three Hebrew letters. The first of these indicates the day of the week upon which the New Year Festival falls, the second whether the year is regular, "minimal", or full, and the third the day of the week upon which Passover occurs. To this "Determinative" is added the Hebrew word for "ordinary" or "leap".

Authorities differ regarding the manner in which the figure employed for the Jewish Era (this year 5769) is arrived at. It is sufficient to describe it as the "Mundane Era" (dating from the Creation of the World) or the "Adamic Era" (dating from the Creation of Man). The chronology is based on Biblical data.

For the beginning of Sabbaths and Festivals, rules were laid down for the latitude of London by David Nieto, Haham of the Sephardi Community (1702-1728). The hours for nightfall given here are based on those fixed by Nathan Marcus Adler, Chief Rabbi, in accordance with the formula of Michael Friedlander, Principal of Jews' College, but adjusted to take account of the movement of the Jewish population within the Metropolis since their day.

THE JEWISH YEAR

The times in this calendar for the beginning and ending of Sabbaths, Festivals and Fasts are given in Greenwich Mean Time from January 1 to March 28 and October 25 to the end, and in British Summer Time from March 29 to October 24, 2009.

5769

is known as **769** on the short system, and is a regular common year of 12 months, 50 Sabbaths and 354 days. Its first of Tishri is on a Tuesday, and the first day of Passover on a Thursday.

It is the twelfth year of the 304th minor or lunar cycle (of 19 years each) since the Era of Creation, and the first of the 207th major or solar cycle (of 28 years each) since the same epoch.

The year began on Monday evening, September 29, 2008, and concludes on Friday, September 18, 2009.

5770

is known as **770** on the short system, and is a full common year of 12 months, 51 Sabbaths and 355 days. Its first of Tishri is on a Sabbath, and the first day of Passover on a Tuesday.

It is the thirteenth year of the 304th minor or lunar cycle (of 19 years each) since the Era of Creation, and the second of the 207th major or solar cycle (of 28 years each) since the same epoch.

The year begins on Friday evening, September 18, 2009, and concludes on Wednesday September 8, 2010.

CALENDAR NOTES

Pent. denotes Pentateuchal readings; **Proph**. denotes Prophetical readings.
Parentheses in either of the above denote Sephardi ritual.
Times for the commencement of the Sabbath during the summer months are, as is the tradition in Britain, given as 20.00. The actual times are given in parentheses.

ABRIDGED JEWISH CALENDAR FOR 2009
(5769-5770)

Fast of Tebet, 5769	Tuesday	2009 January	6
New Moon Shebat	Monday		26
New Year for Trees	Monday	February	9
New Moon Adar, 1st day	Tuesday		24
Fast of Esther	Monday	March	9
Purim	Tuesday		10
Shushan Purim	Wednesday		11
New Moon Nisan	Thursday		26
Fast of Firstborn	Wednesday	April	8
First Day Passover	Thursday		9
Second Day Passover	Friday		10
Seventh Day Passover	Wednesday		15
Eighth Day Passover	Thursday		16
Holocaust Memorial Day	Tuesday		21
New Moon Iyar, 1st Day	Friday		24
Israel Independence Day	Wednesday		29
Minor Passover	Friday	May	8
Thirty-third day of the (Lag Ba') Omer	Tuesday		12
Jerusalem Day	Friday		22
New Moon Sivan	Sunday		24
First Day Feast of Weeks	Friday		29
Second Day Feast of Weeks	Saturday		30
New Moon Tammuz, 1st day	Monday	June	22
Fast of Tammuz	Thursday	July	9
New Moon Ab	Wednesday		22
Fast of Ab	Thursday		30
Festival of 15th Ab	Wednesday	August	5
New Moon Elul, 1st day	Thursday		20
First Day New Year, 5770	Saturday	September	19
Second Day New Year	Sunday		20
Fast of Gedaliah	Monday		21
Day of Atonement	Monday		28
First Day Tabernacles	Saturday	October	3
Second Day Tabernacles	Sunday		4
Hoshana Rabba	Friday		9
Eighth day of Solemn Assembly	Saturday		10
Rejoicing of the Law	Sunday		11
New Moon Marcheshvan, 1st day	Sunday		18
New Moon Kislev 1st day	Tuesday	November	17
First Day Chanucah	Saturday	December	12
New Moon Tebet, 1st day	Thursday		17
Fast of Tebet	Sunday		27

ABRIDGED JEWISH CALENDAR FOR 2010
(5770-5771)

New Moon Shebat, 5770	Saturday	2010 January 16
New Year for Trees	Saturday	30
New Moon Adar, 1st day	Sunday	February 14
Fast of Esther	Thursday	25
Purim	Sunday	28
Shushan Purim	Monday	March 1
New Moon Nisan	Tuesday	16
Fast of Firstborn	Monday	29
First Day Passover	Tuesday	30
Second Day Passover	Wednesday	31
Seventh Day Passover	Monday	April 5
Eighth Day Passover	Tuesday	6
Holocaust Memorial Day	Sunday	11
New Moon Iyar, 1st day	Wednesday	14
Israel Independence Day	Tuesday	20
Minor Passover	Wednesday	28
Thirty-third day of the (Lag Ba') Omer	Sunday	May 2
Jerusalem Day	Wednesday	12
New Moon Sivan	Friday	14
First Day Feast of Weeks	Wednesday	19
Second Day Feast of Weeks	Thursday	20
New Moon Tammuz, 1st day	Saturday	June 12
Fast of Tammuz	Tuesday	29
New Moon Ab	Monday	July 12
Fast of Ab	Tuesday	20
Festival of 15th Ab	Monday	26
New Moon Elul, 1st day	Tuesday	August 10
First Day New Year, 5771	Thursday	September 9
Second Day New Year	Friday	10
Fast of Gedaliah	Sunday	12
Day of Atonement	Saturday	18
First Day Tabernacles	Thursday	23
Second Day Tabernacles	Friday	24
Hoshana Rabba	Wednesday	29
Eighth Day of Solemn Assembly	Thursday	30
Rejoicing of the Law	Friday	October 1
New Moon Marcheshvan, 1st day	Friday	8
New Moon Kislev, 1st day	Sunday	November 7
First Day Chanucah	Thursday	December 2
New Moon Tebet, 1st day	Tuesday	7
Fast of Tebet	Friday	17

JANUARY, 2009
Tekufah Tues Jan 6 10.30

TEBET 5–SHEBAT 6, 5769
Molad Mon Jan 26 4h 54m 57s

Tebet

1	Th		5
2	F	Sabbath commences 15.48	6
3	S	Sabbath ends 16.58. **Pent** Vayiggash, Gen **44**, 18-**47**, 27. **Proph** Ezek **37**, 15-28	7
4	S		8
5	M		9
6	T	**Fast of Tebet** ends 16.55. **Pent** morning and afternoon Ex **32**, 11-14 and **34**, 1-10. **Proph** afternoon only Is **55**, 6-**56**, 8 (none)	10
7	W		11
8	Th		12
9	F	Sabbath commences 15.57	13
10	S	Sabbath ends 17.06. **Pent** Vay'chi, Gen **47**, 28 to end of book. **Proph** I Kings **2**, 1-12	14
11	S		15
12	M		16
13	T		17
14	W		18
15	Th		19
16	F	Sabbath commences 16.07	20
17	S	Sabbath ends 17.16. **Pent** Shemot, Ex **1-6**, 1. **Proph** Is **27**, 6-28, 13; **29**, 22-23 (Jer **1-2**, 3)	21
18	S		22
19	M		23
20	T		24
21	W		25
22	Th		26
23	F	Sabbath commences 16.19.	27
24	S	Sabbath ends 17.26. **Pent** Va'era, Ex **6**, 2-**9**. **Proph** Ezek **28**, 25-**29**, 21 Benediction of Shebat	28
25	S	Yom Kippur Katan	29

Shebat

26	M	Rosh Chodesh. **Pent** Num **28**, 1-15	1
27	T	Holocaust Day (National)	2
28	W		3
29	Th		4
30	F	Sabbath commences 16.31	5
31	S	Sabbath ends 17.38. **Pent** Bo, Ex **10-13**, 16,. **Proph** Jer **46**, 13-28	6

Liturgical notes – Jan 6, Selichot, Aneinu. – Jan 25, omit Tachanun in Minchah. –Jan 26 , Half-Hallel

FEBRUARY, 2009

SHEBAT 7–ADAR 4, 5769

Molad Tues Feb 24 17h 39m 0s

Shebat

1	S		7
2	M		8
3	T		9
4	W		10
5	Th		11
6	F	Sabbath commences 16.44	12
7	S	Sabbath ends 17.49. **Pent** Beshallach, Shabbat Shirah, Ex **13**, 17-**17**. **Proph** Judges **4**, 4-**5**, 31, (**5**, 1-31)	**13**

8	S		14
9	**M**	**New Year for Trees**	**15**
10	T		16
11	W		17
12	Th		18
13	F	Sabbath commences 16.57	19
14	S	Sabbath ends 18.01. **Pent** Yitro, Ex **18-20**. **Proph** Is **6-7**, 6; **9**, 5-6 (**6**, 1-13)	**20**

15	S		21
16	M		22
17	T		23
18	W		24
19	Th		25
20	F	Sabbath commences 17.09	26
21	S	Sabbath ends 18.13. **Pent** Mishpatim, Parshat Shekalim, Ex **21-24** and **30**, 11-16. **Proph** II Kings **12**, 1-17 (**11**, 17-**12**, 17). Benediction of Adar	**27**

22	S		28
23	M	Yom Kippur Katan	29
24	T	Rosh Chodesh first day. **Pent** Num **28**, 1-15	30
			Adar
25	W	Rosh Chodesh second day. **Pent** Num **28**, 1-15	1
26	Th		2
27	F	Sabbath commences 17.22	3
28	S	Sabbath ends 18.25. **Pent** Terumah, Ex **25**, 1-**27**, 19. **Proph** I Kings **5**, 26-**6**, 13	**4**

Liturgical notes – Feb 8, omit Tachanun in Minchah. – Feb 9, omit Tachanun. – Feb 23, omit Tachanun in Minchah. – Feb 24 and 25, Half-Hallel

MARCH, 2009

ADAR 5–NISAN 6, 5769
Molad Thurs Mar 26 6h 23m 3s

			Adar
1	S		5
2	M		6
3	T		7
4	W		8
5	Th		9
6	F	Sabbath commences 17.35	10
7	S	Sabbath ends 18.38. **Pent** Tetsaveh, Parshat Zachor, Ex **27**, 20-**30**, 10 and Deut **25**, 17-19	**11**
		Proph I Sam **15**, 2-34 (**15**, 1-34)	
8	S		12
9	**M**	**Fast of Esther** ends 18.35. **Pent** morning and afternoon Ex **32**, 11-14 and **34**, 1-10	**13**
		Proph afternoon only Is **55**, 6-**56**, 8 (none)	
10	T	**Purim.** **Pent** Ex **17**, 8-16	**14**
11	W	**Shushan Purim**	**15**
12	Th		16
13	F	Sabbath commences 17.47	17
14	S	Sabbath ends 18.50. **Pent** Ki Tissa, Parshat Parah, Ex **30**, 11-**34** and Num **19**	**18**
		Proph Ezek **36**, 16-38 (16-36)	
15	S		19
16	M		20
17	T		21
18	W		22
19	Th		23
20	F	Sabbath commences 17.59	24
21	S	Sabbath ends 19.02. **Pent** Vayakhel-Pekudei, Parshat Hachodesh. Ex **35** to end of Book and Ex **12**, 1-20,	**25**
		Proph Ezek **45**, 16-**46**, 18 (**45**, 18-**46**, 15). Benediction of Nisan	
22	S		26
23	M		27
24	T		28
25	W	Yom Kippur Katan	29
			Nisan
26	Th	Rosh Chodesh. **Pent** Num **28**, 1-15	1
27	F	Sabbath commences 18.11	2
28	S	Sabbath ends 19.14. **Pent** Vayikra, Lev **1-5**, **Proph** Is **43**, 21-**44**, 23	**3**
29	S		4
30	M		5
31	T		6

Liturgical notes – March 9, Selichot, Aneinu; omit Tachanun in Minchah; Al Hannissim is said in Maariv: Book of Esther is read; Half- Shekel is given. – March 10, Al Hannissim said; Book of Esther read in morning; omit Tachanun and Lamenatse'ach. – March 11, omit Tachanun and Lamenatse'ach. – March 25, omit Tachanun in Minchah. – March 26, Half-Hallel. – March 27 to 31, omit Tachanun, – March 28, omit Tsidkatcha Tsedek in Minchah.

APRIL, 2009
Tekufah Tues Apr 7 18.00

NISAN 7–IYAR 6, 5769
Molad Fri Apr 24 19h 7m 7s

			Nisan
1	W		7
2	Th		8
3	F	Sabbath commences 19.22	9
4	S	Sabbath ends 20.27. **Pent** Tsav, Shabbat Haggadol, Lev **6-8**. **Proph** Mal **3**, 4-24	**10**

5	S		11
6	M		12
7	T		13
8	W	**Fast of Firstborn**. Eruv Tavshilin. Blessing of the sun. Festival commences 19.31. **First Seder** in evening	14
9	Th	**Passover first day** ends 20.36. **Second Seder** in evening. **Pent** Ex **12**, 21-51; Num **28**, 16-25. **Proph** Josh 5, 2-6, 1 (and **6**, 27).	**15** / Omer days
10	F	**Passover second day**. Sabbath commences 19.34. **Pent** Lev 22, 26-23, 44; Num **28**, 16-25. **Proph** II Kings **23**, 1-9 and 21-25	1 / **16**
11	S	**Sabbath ends** 20.40. **Pent** Ex **33**, 12-**34**, 26; Num **28**, 19-25. **Proph** Ezek **37**, 1-14.	2 / **17**

12	S	**Pent** Ex **13**, 1-16; Num **28**, 19-25.	3 / 18
13	M	**Pent** Ex **22**, 24-**23**, 19; Num **28**,19-25	4 / 19
14	T	Festival commences 19.41. **Pent** Num **9**, 1-14 and **28**, 19-25	5 / 20
15	W	**Passover seventh day** ends 20.47. **Pent** Ex **13**, 17-**15**, 26; Num **28**, 19-25; **Proph** II Samuel **22**	6 / **21**
16	Th	**Passover eighth day** ends 20.49. **Pent** Deut **15**, 19-**16**, 17; Num **28**, 19-25; **Proph** Is **10**, 32-**12**, 6	7 / **22**
17	F	Issru Chag. Sabbath commences 19.46	8 / 23
18	S	Sabbath ends 20.53. **Pent** Shemini, Lev **9-11**, 47. **Proph** II Samuel **6-7**, 17 (**6**, 1-19) Benediction of Iyar. Ethics 1.	9 / **24**

19	S		10 / 25
20	M		11 / 26
21	T	**Holocaust Memorial Day**	12 / 27
22	W		13 / 28
23	Th		14 / 29
24	F	Rosh Chodesh first day. Sabbath commences 19.58. **Pent** Num **28**, 1-15	15 / 30
25	S	Rosh Chodesh second day. Sabbath ends 21.06 **Pent** Tazria-Metsora, Lev **12-15** and Num **28**, 9-15. **Proph** Is **66**. Ethics 2.	16 / **1** Iyar

26	S		17 / 2
27	M		18 / 3
28	T		19 / 4
29	W	**Yom Ha'atsma'ut – Israel Independence Day**	20 / **5**
30	Th		21 / 6

Liturgical notes – April 1 to 8, omit Tachanun. – April 4, omit Tsidkatcha Tsedek in Minchah; read from Haggadah and discontinue Barachi Nafshi; omit Vihi Noam in Maariv. –April 7, Bedikat Chamets in evening. – April 8, omit Mizmor Letodah and Lamenatse'ach; abstain from Chamets by 10.49; Biur Chamets; discontinue Tal Umatar after Minchah. –April 9, discontinue Mashiv Haruach in Mussaf; in the evening commence counting the Omer.– April 9 and 10, Whole-Hallel. – April 11 to 16, Half-Hallel. – April 11, read Song of Songs; omit Tsidkatcha Tsedek in Minchah and Vihi Noam in Maariv.– April 12 to 14, omit Mizmor Letodah.

Continued on page 312

MAY, 2009

IYAR 7–SIVAN 8, 5769

Molad Sun May 24 7h 51m 10s

			Omer days	Iyar
1	F	Sabbath commences 20.00 (20.09)	22	7
2	S	Sabbath ends 21.19 **Pent** Acharei Mot-Kedoshim, Lev **16-20**, 27. **Proph** Amos **9**, 7-15 (Ezek **20**, 2-20). Ethics 3	23	**8**
3	S		24	9
4	M	First fast day ends 21.17	25	10
5	T		26	11
6	W		27	12
7	Th	Second fast day ends 21.23	28	13
8	F	**Minor Passover.** Sabbath commences 20.00 (20.21)	29	14
9	S	Sabbath ends 21.33. **Pent** Emor, Lev **21-24**. **Proph** Ezek **44**, 15-31. Ethics 4.	30	**15**
10	S		31	16
11	M	Third fast day ends 21.31	32	17
12	**T**	**Lag b'Omer–Scholars' festival**	33	**18**
13	W	.	34	19
14	Th		35	20
15	F	Sabbath commences 20.00 (20.32)	36	21
16	S	Sabbath ends 21.46. **Pent** Behar-Bechukkotai, Lev **25-27**. **Proph** Jer **16**, 19-**17**, 14. Ethics 5.	37	**22**
17	S		38	23
18	M		39	24
19	T		40	25
20	W		41	26
21	Th	Yom Kippur Katan	42	27
22	F	Sabbath commences 20.00 (20.42). **Yom Yerushalayim– Jerusalem Day**	43	28
23	S	Sabbath ends 21.58. **Pent** Bemidbar, Num **1-4**, 20. **Proph** Machar Chodesh, I Sam **20**, 18-42. Benediction of Sivan. Ethics 6.	44	**29**

				Sivan
24	S	Rosh Chodesh. **Pent** Num **28**, 1-15.	45	1
25	M		46	2
26	T		47	3
27	W		48	4
28	Th	Festival commences 20.00 (20.49). Eruv Tavshilin	49	5
29	F	**Feast of Weeks** first day. Sabbath commences 20.00 (20.51) **Pent** Ex **19-20**. Num **28**, 26-31. **Proph** Ezek **1** and **3**, 12		6
30	S	**Feast of Weeks** second day. Sabbath and Festival end 22.09 **Pent** Deut **14**, 22-**16**, 17; Num **28**, 26-31 **Proph** Habak **2**. 20-**3**, 19		7
31	S	Issru Chag		8

Liturgical notes - May 4, 7 & 11, Selichot are said in some communities and, if there be a Minyan who fast, Vay'chal is read. – May 11, omit Tachanun in Minchah. – May 12, omit Tachanun. – May 23, say Av Harachamim in morning service; omit Tsidkatcha Tsedek in Minchah and Vihi Noam in Maariv. – May 24, Half-Hallel. – May 25 to 31, omit Tachanun. – May 29 and 30, Whole – Hallel. – May 30, Book of Ruth is read.

Continued from previous page
– April 17 to 23, omit Tachanun.– April 18, omit Tsidkatcha Tsedek in Minchah. –April 24 and 25, Half Hallel. – April 25, omit Tsidkatcha Tsedek in Minchah. – April 29, see Order of Service and Customs for Israel Independence Day (pubd. Routledge & Kegan Paul, 1964).

JUNE, 2009

SIVAN 9–TAMMUZ 8, 5769

Molad Mon June 22 20h 35m 13s

			Sivan
1	M		9
2	T		10
3	W		11
4	Th		12
5	F	Sabbath commences 20.00 (20.58)	13
6	S	Sabbath ends 22.18. **Pent** Naso, Num **4**, 21-**7**. **Proph** Judges **13**, 2-25. Ethics 1	**14**
7	S		15
8	M		16
9	T		17
10	W		18
11	Th		19
12	F	Sabbath commences 20.00 (21.04)	20
13	S	Sabbath ends 22.24. **Pent** Beha'alotecha, Num **8-12**. **Proph** Zech **2**, 14-**4**, 7. Ethics 2	**21**
14	S		22
15	M		23
16	T		24
17	W		25
18	Th		26
19	F	Sabbath commences 20.00 (21.07).	27
20	S	Sabbath ends 22.28. **Pent** Shelach Lecha, Num **13-15**. **Proph** Joshua **2**	**28**
		Benediction of Tammuz. Ethics 3	
21	S	Yom Kippur Katan	29
22	M	Rosh Chodesh first day. **Pent** Num **28**, 1-15	30
			Tammuz
23	T	Rosh Chodesh second day. **Pent** Num **28**, 1-15	1
24	W		2
25	Th		3
26	F	Sabbath commences 20.00 (21.08)	4
27	S	Sabbath ends 22.28. **Pent** Korach, Num **16-18**. **Proph** I Sam **11**, 14-**12**, 22, Ethics 4.	**5**
28	S		6
29	M		7
30	T		8

Liturgical notes – June 21, omit Tachanun in Minchah. –June 22 and 23, Half-Hallel

JULY, 2009
Tekufah Wed July 8 01.30

TAMMUZ 9–AB 10, 5769
Molad Wed July 22 9h 19m 17s

			Tammuz
1	W		9
2	Th		10
3	F	Sabbath commences 20.00 (21.06)	11
4	**S**	Sabbath ends 22.24. **Pent** Chukkat-Balak, Num **19-25**, 9. **Proph** Micah **5**, 6-**6**, 8. Ethics 5.	**12**
5	S		13
6	M		14
7	T		15
8	W		16
9	**Th**	**Fast of Tammuz** ends 22.14. **Pent** Morning and afternoon. Ex **32**, 11-14 and **34**, 1-10. **Proph** Afternoon only Is. **55**, 6-**56**, 8 (none).	**17**
10	F	Sabbath commences 20.00 (21.02).	18
11	**S**	Sabbath ends 22.18. **Pent** Pinchas, Num **25**, 10-**30**, 1. **Proph** Jer **1-2**, 3. Ethics 6	**19**
12	S		20
13	M		21
14	T		22
15	W		23
16	Th		24
17	F	Sabbath commences 20.00 (20.55)	25
18	**S**	Sabbath ends 22.09. **Pent** Mattot-Massei, Num **30**, 2-end of book. **Proph** Jer **2**, 4-28; **3**, 4 (Jer **2**, 4-28; **4**, 1-2) Benediction of Ab. Ethics 1	**26**
19	S		27
20	M		28
21	T	Yom Kippur Katan	29
			Ab
22	W	Rosh Chodesh.**Pent** Num **28**, 1-15	1
23	Th		2
24	F	Sabbath commences 20.00 (20.47).	3
25	**S**	Sabbath ends 21.58. **Pent** Devarim, Shabbat Chazon, Deut **1**, 1-**3**, 22. **Proph** Is **1**, 1-27. Ethics 2	**4**
26	S		5
27	M		6
28	T		7
29	W	Fast commences 20.53	8
30	**Th**	**Fast of Ab** ends 21.43. **Pent** Morning Deut **4**, 25-40; afternoon: Ex **32**, 11-14 and **34**, 1-10 **Proph** Morning Jer **8**, 13-**9**, 23; afternoon Is **55**, 6 -**56**, 8 (Hosea **14**, 2-10 and Micah **7**, 18-20)	9
31	F	Sabbath commences 20.00 (20.36)	10

Liturgical notes – July 9, Selichot, Aneinu. – July 21, omit Tachanun in Minchah. – July 22, Half-Hallel. – July 25, say Av Harachamim in morning service. – July 29, omit Tachanun in Minchah; Book of Lamentations is read in Maariv. - July 30, read Kinot; omit Tachanun, El Erech Appayim and Lamenatse'ach; say Aneinu and insert Nachem in Minchah.

AUGUST, 2009

AB 11–ELUL 11, 5769

Molad Thurs Aug 20 22h 3m 20s

			Ab
1	S	Sabbath ends 21.45. **Pent** Va'etchanan, Shabbat Nachamu, Deut **3**, 23-**7**, 11. **Proph** Is **40**, 1-26. Ethics 3	**11**
2	S		12
3	M		13
4	T		14
5	W	**Festival of Ab**	15
6	Th		16
7	F	Sabbath commences 20.00 (20.24).	17
8	S	Sabbath ends 21.31. **Pent** Ekev, Deut **7**, 12-**11**, 25. **Proph** Is **49**, 14-**51**, 3. Ethics 4.	**18**
9	S		19
10	M		20
11	T		21
12	W		22
13	Th		23
14	F	Sabbath commences 20.00 (20.11)	24
15	S	Sabbath ends 21.16. **Pent** Re'eh, Deut **11**, 26-**16**, 17. **Proph** Is **54**, 11-**55**, 5. Benediction of Elul. Ethics 5	**25**
16	S		26
17	M		27
18	T		28
19	W	Yom Kippur Katan	29
20	Th	Rosh Chodesh first day. **Pent** Num **28**, 1-15	30
			Elul
21	F	Rosh Chodesh second day. Sabbath commences 19.57. **Pent** Num **28**, 1-15	1
22	S	Sabbath ends 21.00. **Pent** Shof'tim, Deut **16**, 18-**21**, 9. **Proph** Is **51**, 12-**52**, 12. Ethics 6	**2**
23	S		3
24	M		4
25	T		5
26	W		6
27	Th		7
28	F	Sabbath commences 19.42	8
29	S	Sabbath ends 20.43. **Pent** Ki-Tetsei, Deut **21**, 10-**25**. **Proph** Is **54**, 1-10, Ethics 1 and 2.	**9**
30	S		10
31	M		11

Liturgical notes – Aug 4, omit Tachanun in Minchah. – Aug 5, omit Tachanun. – Aug 19, omit Tachanun in Minchah. – Aug 20 and 21, Half-Hallel. – Aug 21 to 31, the Shofar is blown on weekdays.

SEPTEMBER, 2009   ELUL 12, 5769–TISHRI 12, 5770

Molad Sat Sept 19 10h 47m 23s

			Elul
1	T		12
2	W		13
3	Th		14
4	F	Sabbath commences 19.26.	15
5	S	Sabbath ends 20.27. **Pent** Ki-Tavo, Deut **26-29**, 8.**Proph** Is **60**. Ethics 3 and 4	**16**
6	S		17
7	M		18
8	T		19
9	W		20
10	Th		21
11	F	Sabbath commences 19.10	22
12	S	Sabbath ends 20.10. **Pent** Nitsavim-Vayelech. Deut **29**, 9-**31**. **Proph** Is **61**, 10-**63**, 9. Ethics 5 and 6	**23**
13	S		24
14	M		25
15	T		26
16	W		27
17	Th		28
18	F	Sabbath and Festival commence 18.54	29
			Tishri
19	S	**New Year 5770 first day**. Sabbath ends 19.53 **Pent** Gen **21**; Num **29**, 1-6. **Proph** I Sam **1**, 1-**2**, 10	**1**
20	S	**New Year second day** ends 19.51. **Pent** Gen **22**; Num **29**, 1-6. **Proph** Jer **31**, 2-20	**2**
21	M	**Fast of Gedaliah** ends 19.42. **Pent** Morning and afternoon Ex **32**, 11-14; **34**, 1-10. **Proph** Afternoon only Is **55**, 6-**56**, 8 (none)	**3**
22	T		4
23	W		5
24	Th		6
25	F	Sabbath commences 18.38	7
26	S	Sabbath ends 19.37. **Pent** Ha'azinu, Shabbat Shuvah, Deut **32**. **Proph** Hosea **14**, 2-10; Joel **2**, 15-27 (Hosea **14**, 2-10 and Micah **7**, 18-20)	**8**
27	S	**Fast of Atonement** commences 18.33, service at 18.45	9
28	M	**Day of Atonement** ends 19.32. **Pent** Morning Lev **16**; Num **29**, 7-11. Afternoon Lev **18**. **Proph** Morning Is **57**, 14-**58**, 14; Afternoon Book of Jonah and Micah **7**, 18-20	**10**
29	T		11
30	W		12

Liturgical notes – Sept 1 to 17, the Shofar is blown on weekdays. – Sept 13 to 18, Selichot. – Sept 18, omit Tachanun. – Sept 20, Tashlich. – Sept 21 to 27, Selichot said on weekdays. –Sept 21, Aneinu. – Sept 26, omit Vihi Noam in Maariv. – Sept 27, omit Mizmor Letodah, Tachanun and Lamenatse'ach; Vidduy said in Minchah. –Sept 29 and 30, omit Tachanun.

OCTOBER, 2009
Tekufah Wed Oct 7 09.00

TISHRI 13–MARCHESHVAN 13, 5770
Molad Sun Oct 18 23h 31m 27s

			Tishri
1	Th		13
2	F	Sabbath and Festival commence 18.22	14
3	S	**Tabernacles first day**. Sabbath ends 19.21 **Pent** Lev **22**, 26-**23**, 44; Num **29**, 12-16. **Proph** Zech **14**	**15**
4	S	**Tabernacles second day** ends 19.18. **Pent** Lev **22**, 26-**23**, 44; Num **29**, 12-16 **Proph** I Kings **8**, 2-21	**16**
5	M	**Pent** Num **29**, 17-25	17
6	T	**Pent** Num **29**, 20-28	18
7	W	**Pent** Num **29**, 23-31	19
8	Th	**Pent** Num **29**, 26-34	20
9	F	**Hoshana Rabba,** Sabbath and Festival commence 18.06. **Pent** Num **29**, 26-34	21
10	S	**Eighth day of Solemn Assembly.** Sabbath ends 19.05 **Pent** Deut **14**, 22-**16**, 17; Num **29**, 35-**30**, 1. **Proph** I Kings **8**, 54-66	**22**
11	S	**Rejoicing of the Law** ends 19.03. **Pent** Deut **33-34**; Gen **1-2**, 3; Num **29**, 35-**30**, 1. **Proph** Joshua **1** (**1**, 1-9)	**23**
12	M	Issru Chag	24
13	T		25
14	W		26
15	Th		27
16	F	Sabbath commences 17.51	28
17	S	Sabbath ends 18.50. **Pent** Bereshit, Gen **1-6**, 8. **Proph** Machar Chodesh, I Sam **20**, 18-42. Benediction of Marcheshvan	**29**

			Tishri / Marcheshvan
18	S	Rosh Chodesh first day. **Pent** Num **28**, 1-15	30
			Marcheshvan
19	M	Rosh Chodesh second day. **Pent** Num **28**, 1-15	1
20	T		2
21	W		3
22	Th		4
23	F	Sabbath commences 17.36	5
24	S	Sabbath ends 18.37. **Pent** Noach, Gen **6**, 9-**11**. **Proph** Is **54**, 1-**55**, 5 (**54**, 1-10)	**6**

			Marcheshvan
25	S		7
26	M		8
27	T		9
28	W		10
29	Th		11
30	F	Sabbath commences 16.23	12
31	S	Sabbath ends 17.24. **Pent** Lech Lecha, Gen **12-17**. **Proph** Is **40**. 27-**41**, 16	**13**

Liturgical notes – Oct 1 and 2, omit Tachanun. – Oct 3 to 11, Whole Hallel. – Hoshanot: Oct 3, Om Netsurah; Oct 4, Lema'an Amitach; Oct 5, E'eroch Shu'i; Oct 6, Even Shetiyah; Oct 7, El Lemoshaot; Oct 8, Adon Hammoshia. – Oct 10, Ecclesiastes is read and Mashiv Haruach commenced in Mussaf. – Oct 12, omit Tachanun. – Oct 17, Barachi Nafshi commenced in Minchah and Tsidkatcha Tsedek omitted therein. – Oct 18 and 19, Half-Hallel.

NOVEMBER, 2009   MARCHESHVAN 14—KISLEV 13, 5770

Molad Tues Nov 17 12h 15m 30s

			Marcheshvan
1	S		14
2	M		15
3	T		16
4	W		17
5	Th		18
6	F	Sabbath commences 16.10	19
7	**S**	Sabbath ends 17.13. **Pent** Vayera, Gen **18-22**. **Proph** II Kings **4**, 1-37 (**4**, 1-23)	**20**
8	S		21
9	M	First Fast day ends 17.04	22
10	T		23
11	W		24
12	Th	Second Fast day ends 17.00	25
13	F	Sabbath commences 15.59	26
14	**S**	Sabbath ends 17.03. **Pent** Chayei Sarah, Gen **23-25**, 18. **Proph** I Kings **1**, 1-31. Benediction of Kislev	**27**
15	S		28
16	M	Third Fast Day ends 16.55. Yom Kippur Katan	29
17	T	Rosh Chodesh first day. **Pent** Num **28**, 1-15	30
			Kislev
18	W	Rosh Chodesh second day. **Pent** Num **28**, 1-15	1
19	Th		2
20	F	Sabbath commences 15.50	3
21	**S**	Sabbath ends 16.55. **Pent** Tol'dot. Gen **25**, 19-**28**, 9. **Proph** Malachi **1**, 1-**2**, 7	**4**
22	S		5
23	M		6
24	T		7
25	W		8
26	Th		9
27	F	Sabbath commences 15.43	10
28	**S**	Sabbath ends 16.50. **Pent** Vayetsei, Gen **28**, 10-**32**, 3. **Proph** Hosea **12**, 13-**14**, 10 (**11**, 7-**12**, 12).	**11**
29	S		12
30	M		13

Liturgical notes – Nov 9, 12 and 16, Selichot are said in some communities and, if there be a Minyan who fast, Vay'chal is read. – Nov 16, omit Tachanun in Minchah. – Nov 17 and 18, Half-Hallel

DECEMBER, 2009

KISLEV 14—TEBET 14, 5770

Molad Thurs Dec 17 0h 59m 33s

			Kislev
1	T		14
2	W		15
3	Th		16
4	F	Sabbath commences 15.38	17
5	**S**	Sabbath ends 16.46. **Pent** Vayishlach, Gen **32**, 4-**36. Proph** Hosea **11**, 7-**12**, 12 (Others, Book of Obadiah)	**18**
6	S		19
7	M		20
8	T		21
9	W		22
10	Th		23
11	F	First Chanucah Light. Sabbath commences 15.36	24
12	**S**	**Chanucah first day**. Sabbath ends 16.45. **Pent** Vayeshev, Gen **37-40**; Num **7**, 1-17	**25**
		Proph Zech **2**, 14-**4**, 7. Benediction of Tebet	
13	**S**	**Chanucah second day**. **Pent** Num **7**, 18-29	**26**
14	**M**	**Chanucah third day**. **Pent** Num **7**, 24-35	**27**
15	**T**	**Chanucah fourth day**. **Pent** Num **7**, 30-41	**28**
16	**W**	**Chanucah fifth day**. **Pent** Num **7**, 36-47	**29**
17	**Th**	Rosh Chodesh. **Chanucah sixth day**. **Pent** Num **28**, 1-15 and **7**, 42-47	**30**
			Tebet
18	F	Rosh Chodesh. **Chanucah seventh day**. Sabbath commences 15.37	**1**
		Pent Num **28**, 1-15 and **7**, 48-53	
19	**S**	**Chanucah eighth day**. Sabbath ends 16.47	**2**
		Pent Mikkets, Gen **41-44**, 17: Num **7**, 54-**8**, 4. **Proph** I Kings **7**, 40-50	
20	S		3
21	M		4
22	T		5
23	W		6
24	Th		7
25	F	Sabbath commences 15.41	8
26	**S**	Sabbath ends 16.51. **Pent** Vayiggash, Gen **44**, 18-**47**, 27. **Proph** Ezek **37**, 15-28	**9**
27	**S**	**Fast of Tebet** ends 16.46. **Pent** Morning and afternoon Ex **32**, 11-14 and **34**, 1-10	**10**
		Proph Afternoon only Is **55**, 6-**56**, 8 (none)	
28	M		11
29	T		12
30	W		13
31	Th		14

Liturgical notes – Dec 5, Tal Umatar commenced in Maariv. – During Chanucah say Al Hannissim and Whole-Hallel; omit Tachanun, El Erech Appayim and Lamenatse'ach, and on Sabbath Tsidkatcha Tsedek in Minchah. – Dec 27, Selichot, Aneinu.

JANUARY, 2010
Tekufah Wed Jan 6 16.30

TEBET 15–SHEBAT 16, 5770
Molad Fri Jan 15 13h 43m 37s

			Tebet
1	F	Sabbath commences 15.47	15
2	S	Sabbath ends 16.57. **Pent** Vay'chi, Gen **47**, 28 to end of Book. **Proph** I Kings **2**, 1-12	**16**
3	S		17
4	M		18
5	T		19
6	W		20
7	Th		21
8	F	Sabbath commences 15.55	22
9	S	Sabbath ends 17.05. **Pent** Shemot, Ex **1-6**, 1. **Proph** Is 27, 6-**28**, 13; **29**, 22-23 (Jer **1**, 1-**2**, 3) Benediction of Shebat	**23**
10	S		24
11	M		25
12	T		26
13	W		27
14	Th	Yom Kippur Katan	28
15	F	Sabbath commences 16.05	29
			Shebat
16	S	Rosh Chodesh. Sabbath ends 17.14. **Pent** Va'era, Ex **6**, 2-9 and Num **28**, 9-15. **Proph** Is 66	**1**
17	S		2
18	M		3
19	T		4
20	W		5
21	Th		6
22	F	Sabbath commences 16.17	7
23	S	Sabbath ends 17.25. **Pent** Bo, Ex **10**, 1-**13**, 16. **Proph** Jer **46**, 13-28.	**8**
24	S		9
25	M		10
26	T		11
27	W	Holocaust Day (National)	12
28	Th		13
29	F	Sabbath commences 16.29	14
30	S	**New Year for Trees.** Sabbath ends 17.36. **Pent** Beshallach, Shabbat Shirah, Ex **13**, 17-**17**. **Proph** Judges **4**, 4-**5** (**5**, 1-31)	**15**
31	S		16

Liturgical notes – Jan 16, Half-Hallel; omit Tsidkatcha Tsedek in Minchah.– Jan 30, omit Tsidkatcha Tsedek in Minchah.

FEBRUARY, 2010

SHEBAT 17–ADAR 14, 5770

Molad Sun Feb 14 2h 27m 40s

			Shebat
1	M		17
2	T		18
3	W		19
4	Th		20
5	F	Sabbath commences 16.42.	21
6	S	Sabbath ends 17.48. **Pent** Yitro, Ex **18-20**. **Proph** Is **6**, 1-7,6 and **9**, 5-6 (**6**, 1-13)	**22**

7	S		23
8	M		24
9	T		25
10	W		26
11	Th	Yom Kippur Katan	27
12	F	Sabbath commences 16. 55	28
13	S	Sabbath ends 18.00. **Pent** Mishpatim, Parshat Shekalim, Ex **21-24** and **30**, 11-16 **Proph** II Kings **12**, 1-17 (**11**, 17-**12**, 17; I Sam **20**, 18 and 42). Benediction of Adar	**29**

14	S	Rosh Chodesh first day. **Pent** Num **28**, 1-15	30
			Adar
15	M	Rosh Chodesh second day. **Pent** Num **28**, 1-15	1
16	T		2
17	W		3
18	Th		4
19	F	Sabbath commences 17.07	5
20	S	Sabbath ends 18.12. **Pent** Terumah, Ex **25**, 1-**27**, 19. **Proph** I Kings **5**, 26-**6**, 13	**6**

21	S		7
22	M		8
23	T		9
24	W		10
25	Th	**Fast of Esther** ends 18.14. **Pent** morning and afternoon Ex **32**, 11-14 and **34**, 1-10. **Proph** afternoon only Is **55**, 6-**56**,8 (none)	**11**
26	F	Sabbath commences 17.20	12
27	S	Sabbath ends 18.24. **Pent** Tetsaveh, Parshat Zachor, Ex **27**, 20-**30**, 10 and Deut **25**, 17-19. **Proph** I Sam **15**, 2-34 (**15**, 1-34)	**13**

28	S	**Purim**, **Pent** Ex **17**, 8-16	**14**

Liturgical notes – Feb 13, omit Tsidkatcha Tsedek in Minchah. – Feb 14 and 15, Half-Hallel. – Feb 25, Selichot, Aneinu. – Feb 27, omit Tsidkatcha Tsedek in Minchah; Al Hannissim is said in Maariv; Book of Esther is read. – Feb 28, Half Shekel is given; say Al Hannissim; Book of Esther is read in morning; omit Tachanun and Lamenatse'ach.

EVENING TWILIGHT VARIATION FOR REGIONS

This table shows the number of minutes required to be added to, or substracted from, the times for London, in order to determine the time of the termination of Sabbath, Festival, or Fast. For dates between those indicated here, an approximate calculation must be made.
Acknowledgement is made to the Royal Greenwich Observatory for valued co-operation in the compilation of this table.

		BIRMINGHAM	BOURNEMOUTH	GLASGOW	LEEDS	LIVERPOOL	MANCHESTER	NEWCASTLE
Jan.	1	+ 9	+15	0	+ 4	+11	+ 8	0
	11	+ 9	+14	+ 1	+ 4	+11	+ 8	0
	21	+ 9	+14	+ 3	+ 5	+12	+ 9	+ 2
	31	+ 9	+13	+ 6	+ 6	+12	+ 9	+ 3
Feb.	10	+ 9	+12	+ 9	+ 7	+13	+10	+ 5
	20	+ 9	+11	+12	+ 8	+14	+11	+ 7
Mar.	2	+10	+10	+16	+10	+16	+13	+10
	12	+10	+ 9	+20	+12	+18	+15	+13
	22	+10	+ 7	+22	+12	+18	+15	+14
Apr.	1	+11	+ 7	+27	+15	+20	+17	+18
	11	+12	+ 7	+31	+17	+22	+19	+22
	21	+13	+ 7	+35	+20	+24	+21	+26
May	1	+16	+ 7	+40	+23	+27	+24	+30
	11	+18	+ 7	+46	+26	+30	+27	+35
	21	+20	+ 7	+52	+30	+34	+31	+42
	31	+23	+ 7	+57	+34	+37	+34	+48
June	10	+25	+ 7	+63	+38	+40	+38	+55
	20	+26	+ 7	+64	+40	+41	+39	+58
	30	+26	+ 7	+62	+38	+40	+38	+55
July	10	+23	+ 7	+57	+35	+38	+35	+50
	20	+21	+ 7	+51	+31	+34	+31	+43
	30	+19	+ 8	+46	+27	+30	+27	+38
Aug.	9	+17	+ 8	+40	+24	+27	+24	+32
	19	+16	+ 8	+35	+20	+25	+22	+27
	29	+16	+ 8	+30	+18	+23	+20	+23
Sept.	8	+14	+ 8	+26	+15	+20	+17	+18
	18	+13	+ 8	+23	+12	+18	+15	+15
	28	+13	+10	+20	+12	+18	+15	+14
Oct.	8	+12	+10	+16	+10	+16	+13	+10
	18	+11	+12	+13	+ 9	+15	+12	+9
	28	+11	+12	+10	+ 8	+14	+11	+6
Nov.	7	+10	+13	+ 7	+ 6	+13	+10	+4
	17	+10	+14	+ 4	+ 5	+12	+ 9	+3
	27	+10	+14	+ 2	+ 4	+11	+ 8	+1
Dec.	7	+10	+15	0	+ 4	+11	+ 8	0
	17	+ 9	+15	0	+ 3	+11	+ 7	- 1
	27	+ 9	+15	0	+ 3	+11	+ 8	- 1
	31	+ 9	+15	0	+ 4	+11	+ 8	0

SIDROT AND HAFTAROT FOR 2010
(5770-5771)

Haftara parentheses indicate Sephardi ritual.

2010		5770		HAFTARA	SIDRA
Jan.	2	Tebet	16	I Kings **2**, 1-12	*Vay'chi*
	9		23	Isaiah **27**, 6-**28**, 13 and	
				29, 22-23 (Jer **1**, 1-**2**, 3)	*Shemot*
	16	Shebat	1	Isaiah **66**, 1-24	*Va'era (Rosh Chodesh)*
	23		8	Jeremiah **46**, 13-28	*Bo*
	30		15	Judges **4**, 4-**5**, 31 (**5**, 1-31)	*Beshallach (Shirah)*
Feb.	6		22	Isaiah **6**, 1-**7**, 6; **9**, 5-6 (**6**, 1-13)	*Yitro*
	13		29	II Kings **12**, 1-17 (**11**, 17-**12**, 17;	
				I Sam **20**, 18 and 42)	*Mishpatim (Shekalim)*
	20	Adar	6	I Kings **5**, 26-**6**, 13	*Terumah*
	27		13	I Samuel **15**, 2-34 (**15**, 1-34)	*Tetsaveh (Zachor)*
Mar.	6		20	Ezekiel **36**, 16-38 (16-36)	*Ki Tissa (Parah)*
	13		27	Ezek **45**, 16-**46**, 18 (**45**, 18-	
				46,15).........................	*Vayakhel-Pekudei*
					(Hachodesh)
	20	Nisan	5	Isaiah **43**, 21-**44**, 23	*Vayikra*
	27		12	Malachi **3**, 4-24	*Tsav (Haggadol)*
Apr.	3		19	Ezekiel **37**, 1-14	*Chol Hamo'ed Pesach*
	10		26	II Samuel **6**, 1-**7**, 17 (**6**, 1-19)	*Shemini*
	17	Iyar	3	II Kings **7**, 3-20	*Tazria-Metsora*
	24		10	Amos **9**, 7-15 (Ezekiel **20**, 2-20)	*Acharei Mot-Kedoshim*
May	1		17	Ezekiel **44**, 15-31	*Emor*
	8		24	Jeremiah **16**, 19-**17**, 14	*Behar-Bechukkotai*
	15	Sivan	2	Hosea **2**, 1-22	*Bemidbar*
	22		9	Judges **13**, 2-25	*Naso*
	29		16	Zechariah **2**, 14-**4**, 7	*Beha'alotecha*
June	5		23	Joshua **2**, 1-24	*Shelach Lecha*
	12		30	Isaiah **66**, 1-24 (and I Sam **20**, 18	*Korach*
				and 42)	*(Rosh Chodesh)*
	19	Tammuz	7	Judges **11**, 1-33	*Chukkat*
	26		14	Micah **5**, 6-**6**, 8	*Balak*
July	3		21	Jeremiah **1**, 1-**2**, 3	*Pinchas*
	10		28	Jeremiah **2**, 4-28 and **3**, 4	
				(**2**, 4-28 and **4**, 1-2)	*Mattot-Massei*
	17	Ab	6	Isaiah **1**, 1-27	*Devarim (Chazon)*
	24		13	Isaiah **40**, 1-26	*Va'etchanan (Nachamu)*
	31		20	Isaiah **49**, 14-**51**, 3	*Ekev*

Sidrot and Haftarot

2010		5770	HAFTARA	SIDRA
Aug. 7	Ab	27	Isaiah **54**, 11-**55**, 5	*Re'eh*
14	Elul	4	Isaiah **51**, 12-**52**, 12	*Shof'tim*
21		11	Isaiah **54**, 1-10	*Ki Tetsei*
28		18	Isaiah **60**, 1-22	*Ki Tavo*
Sept. 4		25	Isaiah **61**, 10-**63**, 9	*Nitsavim-Vayelech*
		5771		
11	Tishri	3	Hosea **14**, 2-10 and Joel **2**, 15-27 (Hosea **14**, 2-10 and Micah **7**, 18-20)	*Ha'azinu (Shuvah)*
18		10	Isaiah **57**, 14-**58**, 14	*Yom Kippur*
25		17	Ezekiel **38**, 18-**39**, 16	*Chol Hamoed Succot*
Oct. 2		24	Isaiah **42**, 5-**43**, 10 (**42**, 5-21)	*Bereshit*
9	Cheshvan	1	Isaiah **66**, 1-24	*Noach (Rosh Chodesh)*
16		8	Isaiah **40**, 27-**41**, 16	*Lech Lecha*
23		15	II Kings **4**, 1-37, (**4**, 1-23)	*Vayera*
30		22	I Kings **1**, 1-31	*Chayei Sarah*
Nov. 6		29	I Samuel **20**, 18-42	*Tol'dot (Machar Chodesh)*
13	Kislev	6	Hosea **12**, 13-**14**, 10 (**11**, 7-**12**, 12)	*Vayetsei*
20		13	Hosea **11**, 7-**12**, 12 (Obadiah)	*Vayishlach*
27		20	Amos **2**, 6-**3**, 8	*Vayeshev*
Dec. 4		27	Zechariah **2**, 14-**4**, 7	*Mikkets (Chanucah)*
11	Tebet	4	Ezekiel **37**, 15-28	*Vayiggash*
18		11	I Kings **2**, 1-12	*Vay'chi*
25		18	Isaiah **27**, 6-**28**, 13 and **29**, 22-23 (Jer **1**, 1-**2**, 3)	*Shemot*

MARRIAGE REGULATIONS (General)

Marriages may be contracted according to the usage of the Jews between persons *both* professing the Jewish religion, provided that due notice has been given to the Superintendent Registrar and that his certificate (or licence and certificate) has been obtained. There is no restriction regarding the hours within which the marriage may be solemnised, nor the place of marriage, which may be a synagogue, private house, or any other building.

The date and place of the intended marriage having been decided, the parties should consult the Minister or Secretary for Marriages of the synagogue through which the marriage is to be solemnised. He will advise of the necessary preliminary steps and the suitability of the proposed date.

Notice of the intended marriage must be given to the local Superintendent Registrar, and the document or documents obtained from him must be handed to the Synagogue Marriage Secretary in advance of the date appointed. In the case of a marriage in a building other than a synagogue, care should be taken that these documents contain the words *"both* parties being of the Jewish persuasion" following the description of the building.

If the marriage is to be solemnised at or through a synagogue under the jurisdiction of the Chief Rabbi, his Authorisation of Marriage must be presented. The minister of the synagogue will explain how this may be obtained.

No marriage is valid if solemnised between persons who are within the degrees of kindred of affinity (e.g., between uncle and niece) prohibited by English law, even though such a marriage is permissible by Jewish law.

A marriage between Jews must be registered immediately after the ceremony by the Secretary of Marriages of the synagogue of which the husband is a member. If he is not already a member he may become one by paying a membership fee in addition to the marriage charges.

The belief that marriage by licence may be solemnised only by civil ceremony at a Registry Office is erroneous. It may take place in a synagogue, or any other building, provided that the place of solemnisation is stated to the Superintendent Registrar when application is made for his licence.

No marriage between Jews should take place without due notice being given to the Superintendent Registrar, and without being registered in the Marriage Register of a synagogue. Marriages in such circumstances are not necessarily valid in English law. (Outside England and Wales other regulations apply and the Minister of the synagogue should be consulted.)

According to the regulations valid among Orthodox Jews, marriages may not be solemnised on the following dates:

2009		2010
6 January	Fast of Tebet	——
9 March	Fast of Esther	25 February
10 March	Purim	28 February
8 April	Day before Pesach	29 March
9-16 April	Pesach	30 March-6 April
26 April- 11 May	Sephirah	16-30 April
13 -22 May	Sephirah	3-13 May
28 May	Day before Shavuot	18 May
29-30 May	Shavuot	19-20 May
9-30 July	Three Weeks	29 June-20 July
18 September	Day before Rosh Hashana	8 September
19-20 September	Rosh Hashana	9-10 September
21 September	Fast of Gedaliah	12 September
27 September	Day before Yom Kippur	17 September
28 September	Yom Kippur	18 September
2 October	Day before Succot	22 September
3-11 October	Succot	23 September-1 October
27 December	Fast of Tebet	17 December

Nor on any Sabbath

Among Reform Jews, marriages are solemnised during the Sephirah, from the Fast of Tammuz until the Fast of Ab (but not on the Fast of Ab itself), on the days that precede Festivals, on the Second days of Festivals, and on Purim, but not on the other prohibited days mentioned above.

5754–5783

(1993–2023)

INSTRUCTIONS FOR USE

The following Table shows on one line the civil date and the day of the week on which every date of the Jewish year falls during the thirty years which it covers; those dates which occur on Sabbath are printed in *heavier* type. Thus, Tishri 10, 5759, coincided with September 30, 1998, and this was a Wednesday, since September 26 is marked as being Sabbath. The civil dates on which the festivals and fasts (or any other occasion of the Jewish Calendar) occur in any particular year may be ascertained in the same manner. The Table is arranged according to the months of the Hebrew Year, the day of the month being shown in the left-hand column.

YAHRZEIT. – This is always observed on the Jewish date on which the parent died. It has never been customary under the jurisdiction of the Chief Rabbi of the United Hebrew Congregations of the British Commonwealth to observe the Yahrzeit after the death on the anniversary of the burial as is enjoined, in certain circumstances, by some authorities. If the death took place after dark, it must be dated from the next civil day, as the day is reckoned among Jews from sunset to sunset. This date must be located in the Table, according to the month and day, and the civil date of the Yahrzeit in any particular year will be found on the same line in the column beneath the year in question. It should be noted, however, that if a parent died during Adar in an ordinary year, the Yahrzeit is observed in a leap year in the First Adar. (Some people observe it in both Adars.) If the death took place in a leap year the Yahrzeit is observed in a leap year in the same Adar (whether First or Second) during which the death happened. The Yahrzeit begins and the memorial light is kindled on the evening before the civil date thus ascertained.

BARMITZVAH. – A boy attains his Barmitzvah (religious majority) when he reaches his thirteenth birthday, i.e., on the first day of his fourteenth year, this being computed according to the Jewish date on which he was born. The date and year of birth being located in the Table, the corresponding civil date of the first day of his fourteenth year will be found on the same line in the 13th column. If this be a Sabbath, he reads his *Parsha* on that day; if a week-day, he reads it on the following Sabbath. By consulting the Calendar the scriptural portion of the week may be ascertained. It should be noted, however, that if a boy be born in Adar of an ordinary year and become Barmitzvah in a leap year, the celebration falls in the Second Adar. If he were born in a leap year and becomes Barmitzvah in a leap year it is celebrated in that Adar (whether First or Second) during which his birth occurred. If he were born in a leap year and the Barmitzvah is in an ordinary year, it is observed in Adar.

TISHRI (30 days)

Tish	5754	55	56	57	58	59	60	61	62	63	64	65	66	67	68	69	70	71	72	73	74	75	76	77	78	79	80	81	82	83
	1993	94	95	96	97	98	99	2000	01	02	03	04	05	06	07	08	09	10	11	12	13	14	15	16	17	18	19	20	21	22
	Sept-Oct	Sept-Oct	Sept-Oct	Sept-Oct	October	Sept-Oct	Sept-Oct	Sept-Oct	Sept-Oct	Sept-Oct	Sept-Oct	Sept-Oct	Oct-Nov	Sept-Oct	Sept-Oct	Sept-Oct	Sept-Oct	Sept-Oct	Sept-Oct	Sept-Oct	Sept-Oct	Sept-Oct	Sept-Oct	Oct-Nov	Sept-Oct	Sept-Oct	Sept-Oct	Sept-Oct	Sept-Oct	Sept-Oct
1	16	6	25	14	2	21	11	30	18	7	27	16	4	23	13	30	19	9	29	17	5	25	14	3	21	10	30	19	7	26
2	17	7	26	15	3	22	12	1	19	8	28	17	5	24	14	1	20	10	30	18	6	26	15	4	22	11	1	20	8	27
3	18	8	27	16	4	23	13	2	20	9	29	18	6	25	15	2	21	11	1	19	7	27	16	5	23	12	2	21	9	28
4	19	9	28	17	5	24	14	3	21	10	30	19	7	26	16	3	22	12	2	20	8	28	17	6	24	13	3	22	10	29
5	20	10	29	18	6	25	15	4	22	11	1	20	8	27	17	4	23	13	3	21	9	29	18	7	25	14	4	23	11	30
6	21	11	30	19	7	26	16	5	23	12	2	21	9	28	18	5	24	14	4	22	10	30	19	8	26	15	5	24	12	1
7	22	12	1	20	8	27	17	6	24	13	3	22	10	29	19	6	25	15	5	23	11	1	20	9	27	16	6	25	13	2
8	23	13	2	21	9	28	18	7	25	14	4	23	11	30	20	7	26	16	6	24	12	2	21	10	28	17	7	26	14	3
9	24	14	3	22	10	29	19	8	26	15	5	24	12	1	21	8	27	17	7	25	13	3	22	11	29	18	8	27	15	4
10	25	15	4	23	11	30	20	9	27	16	6	25	13	2	22	9	28	18	8	26	14	4	23	12	30	19	9	28	16	5
11	26	16	5	24	12	1	21	10	28	17	7	26	14	3	23	10	29	19	9	27	15	5	24	13	1	20	10	29	17	6
12	27	17	6	25	13	2	22	11	29	18	8	27	15	4	24	11	30	20	10	28	16	6	25	14	2	21	11	30	18	7
13	28	18	7	26	14	3	23	12	30	19	9	28	16	5	25	12	1	21	11	29	17	7	26	15	3	22	12	1	19	8
14	29	19	8	27	15	4	24	13	1	20	10	29	17	6	26	13	2	22	12	30	18	8	27	16	4	23	13	2	20	9
15	30	20	9	28	16	5	25	14	2	21	11	30	18	7	27	14	3	23	13	1	19	9	28	17	5	24	14	3	21	10
16	1	21	10	29	17	6	26	15	3	22	12	1	19	8	28	15	4	24	14	2	20	10	29	18	6	25	15	4	22	11
17	2	22	11	30	18	7	27	16	4	23	13	2	20	9	29	16	5	25	15	3	21	11	30	19	7	26	16	5	23	12
18	3	23	12	1	19	8	28	17	5	24	14	3	21	10	30	17	6	26	16	4	22	12	1	20	8	27	17	6	24	13
19	4	24	13	2	20	9	29	18	6	25	15	4	22	11	1	18	7	27	17	5	23	13	2	21	9	28	18	7	25	14
20	5	25	14	3	21	10	30	19	7	26	16	5	23	12	2	19	8	28	18	6	24	14	3	22	10	29	19	8	26	15
21	6	26	15	4	22	11	1	20	8	27	17	6	24	13	3	20	9	29	19	7	25	15	4	23	11	30	20	9	27	16
22	7	27	16	5	23	12	2	21	9	28	18	7	25	14	4	21	10	30	20	8	26	16	5	24	12	1	21	10	28	17
23	8	28	17	6	24	13	3	22	10	29	19	8	26	15	5	22	11	1	21	9	27	17	6	25	13	2	22	11	29	18
24	9	29	18	7	25	14	4	23	11	30	20	9	27	16	6	23	12	2	22	10	28	18	7	26	14	3	23	12	30	19
25	10	30	19	8	26	15	5	24	12	1	21	10	28	17	7	24	13	3	23	11	29	19	8	27	15	4	24	13	1	20
26	11	1	20	9	27	16	6	25	13	2	22	11	29	18	8	25	14	4	24	12	30	20	9	28	16	5	25	14	2	21
27	12	2	21	10	28	17	7	26	14	3	23	12	30	19	9	26	15	5	25	13	1	21	10	29	17	6	26	15	3	22
28	13	3	22	11	29	18	8	27	15	4	24	13	31	20	10	27	16	6	26	14	2	22	11	30	18	7	27	16	4	23
29	14	4	23	12	30	19	9	28	16	5	25	14	1	21	11	28	17	7	27	15	3	23	12	31	19	8	28	17	5	24
30	15	5	24	13	31	20	10	29	17	6	26	15	2	22	12	29	18	8	28	16	4	24	13	1	20	9	29	18	6	25

In the left-hand margin figures in **black type** denote major Holy-days; elsewhere they denote Sabbaths.
1st and 2nd, New Year; 3rd, Fast of Gedaliah, postponed to Sunday if on Sabbath); 10th, Day of Atonement; 15th to 23rd, Tabernacles, etc.; 30th, First day of New Moon of Marcheshvan.

CHESHVAN or MARCHESHVAN (29 or 30 days)

Chesh	5754 / 1993	55 / 94	56 / 95	57 / 96	58 / 97	59 / 98	60 / 99	61 / 2000	62 / 01	63 / 02	64 / 03	65 / 04	66 / 05	67 / 06	68 / 07	69 / 08	70 / 09	71 / 10	72 / 11	73 / 12	74 / 13	75 / 14	76 / 15	77 / 16	78 / 17	79 / 18	80 / 19	81 / 20	82 / 21	83 / 22
	Oct-Nov	Oct-Nov	Oct-Nov	Oct-Nov	November	Oct-Nov	Oct-Nov	Oct-Nov	Oct-Nov	Oct-Nov	Oct-Nov	Oct-Nov	Nov-Dec	Oct-Nov	Oct-Nov	Oct-Nov	Oct-Nov	Oct-Nov	Oct-Nov	Oct-Nov	Oct-Nov	Oct-Nov	Oct-Nov	November	Oct-Nov	Oct-Nov	Oct-Nov	Oct-Nov	Oct-Nov	Oct-Nov
1	**16**	6	**25**	14	1	21	11	30	18	7	27	**16**	3	23	**13**	30	19	9	**29**	17	**5**	**25**	14	2	**21**	10	30	19	7	26
2	17	7	26	15	2	22	12	31	19	8	28	17	4	24	14	31	20	10	30	18	6	26	15	3	22	11	31	20	8	27
3	18	**8**	27	16	3	23	13	1	**20**	9	29	18	**5**	25	15	1	21	11	31	**19**	7	27	16	4	23	12	1	21	**9**	28
4	19	9	**28**	17	4	**24**	14	2	21	10	30	19	6	26	16	2	22	12	1	20	8	28	**17**	**5**	24	**13**	**2**	22	10	**29**
5	20	10	29	18	5	25	15	3	22	11	31	20	7	27	17	3	23	13	2	21	9	29	18	6	25	14	3	23	11	30
6	**6**	10	30	19	6	26	**16**	**4**	23	**12**	1	21	8	28	18	4	**24**	14	3	22	10	30	19	7	26	15	4	**24**	12	31
7	7	12	31	20	7	27	17	5	24	13	2	22	9	29	19	5	25	15	4	23	11	31	20	8	27	16	5	25	13	1
8	**8**	13	1	21	**8**	28	17	6	25	14	3	**23**	10	30	**20**	6	26	**16**	**5**	24	**12**	**1**	21	9	**28**	17	6	26	14	2
9	9	14	2	22	9	29	18	7	26	15	4	24	11	31	21	7	27	17	6	25	13	2	22	**10**	29	18	7	27	15	3
10	10	**15**	3	23	10	30	19	8	27	16	5	25	12	1	22	**8**	28	18	7	26	14	3	23	11	30	19	8	28	**16**	4
11	11	16	**4**	24	11	21	21	9	28	17	6	26	13	2	23	9	29	19	8	**27**	15	4	**24**	**12**	31	**20**	**9**	29	17	**5**
12	12	17	5	25	12	22	22	10	29	18	7	26	14	3	24	10	30	20	9	28	16	5	25	13	1	21	10	30	18	6
13	**13**	18	6	**26**	13	23	23	11	30	**19**	8	27	15	4	25	11	31	21	10	29	17	6	26	14	2	22	11	**31**	19	7
14	14	19	7	27	**14**	**24**	24	12	31	20	9	28	16	5	26	12	1	22	11	30	18	7	27	15	3	23	12	1	20	8
15	14	20	8	28	**15**	25	25	13	1	21	10	29	17	6	27	13	2	23	**12**	31	**19**	8	28	16	4	24	13	2	21	9
16	**30**	21	9	29	16	26	26	14	2	22	11	30	18	7	28	14	3	24	13	1	20	9	29	17	5	25	14	3	22	10
17	31	**22**	10	30	17	27	27	15	3	23	12	31	**19**	8	29	**15**	4	25	14	2	21	10	30	**18**	6	**26**	15	4	**23**	11
18	1	23	**11**	31	18	28	28	16	4	24	13	1	20	9	30	16	**15**	26	15	**3**	22	11	**31**	19	7	27	16	5	24	**12**
19	2	24	12	1	19	29	29	17	5	25	14	2	21	10	31	17	16	27	16	4	23	12	1	20	8	28	17	6	25	13
20	3	25	13	**2**	20	30	**30**	**18**	6	26	**15**	3	22	11	1	18	17	28	17	5	24	13	2	21	9	29	18	7	26	14
21	5	26	14	3	21	10	31	19	7	27	16	5	23	12	2	19	8	29	18	6	25	14	3	22	10	30	19	8	27	15
22	6	27	15	4	**22**	11	1	20	8	28	17	6	24	13	3	20	9	**30**	**19**	7	26	**15**	4	23	11	31	20	9	28	16
23	7	28	16	5	23	12	2	21	9	29	18	7	25	14	4	21	10	31	20	8	27	16	5	24	12	1	21	10	29	17
24	8	**29**	17	6	24	13	3	22	**10**	30	19	8	26	15	5	**22**	11	1	21	9	28	17	6	25	13	2	22	11	30	18
25	9	30	**18**	7	25	14	4	23	11	31	20	9	27	16	6	23	12	2	22	**10**	29	18	7	26	14	3	**23**	12	31	**19**
26	10	31	19	**8**	26	**14**	5	24	12	1	21	10	28	17	7	24	13	3	23	11	30	19	8	27	15	4	24	13	1	20
27	11	1	20	9	27	15	**6**	25	13	2	22	10	29	18	8	25	14	4	24	12	31	20	9	28	16	5	25	14	2	21
28	12	2	21	10	28	16	7	26	14	3	23	11	30	19	9	26	15	5	25	13	1	21	10	29	17	6	26	15	3	22
29	**13**	3	22	11	**29**	17	8	27	15	4	24	12	1	20	**10**	27	16	**6**	26	14	**2**	**22**	11	30	**18**	7	27	16	4	23
30	14	—	23	—	—	18	9	—	—	5	25	**13**	—	21	—	—	17	7	—	—	3	—	12	—	—	8	28	—	—	24

Figures in **black type** denote Sabbaths.
30th, First day of New Moon of Kislev.

KISLEV (29 or 30 days)

Kis	5754	55	56	57	58	59	60	61	62	63	64	65	66	67	68	69	70	71	72	73	74	75	76	77	78	79	80	81	82	83
	1993	94	95	96	97	98	99	2000	01	02	03	04	05	06	07	08	09	10	11	12	13	14	15	16	17	18	19	20	21	22
	Nov-Dec	Nov-Dec	Nov-Dec	Nov-Dec	Nov-Dec	Nov-Dec	Nov-Dec	Nov-Dec	Nov-Dec	Nov-Dec	Nov-Dec	Nov-Dec	Dec	Nov-Dec	Nov-Dec	Nov-Dec	Nov-Dec	Nov-Dec	Nov-Dec	Nov-Dec	Nov-Dec	Nov-Dec	Nov-Dec	Dec	Nov-Dec	Nov-Dec	Nov-Dec	Nov-Dec	Nov-Dec	Nov-Dec
1	15	4	24	12	30	20	10	28	16	6	26	14	2	22	11	28	18	8	27	15	4	23	13	1	19	9	29	17	5	25
2	16	**5**	**25**	13	1	**21**	11	29	**17**	7	27	15	**3**	23	12	**29**	19	9	28	16	5	24	**14**	2	20	**10**	**30**	18	**6**	**26**
3	17	6	26	14	2	22	12	30	18	8	28	16	4	24	13	30	20	10	29	**17**	6	25	15	**3**	21	11	1	19	7	27
4	18	7	27	15	3	23	**13**	1	19	**9**	**29**	17	5	**25**	14	1	**21**	11	30	18	7	26	16	4	22	12	2	20	8	28
5	19	8	28	**16**	4	24	14	**2**	20	10	30	18	6	26	15	2	22	12	1	19	8	27	17	5	23	13	3	**21**	9	29
6	**20**	9	29	17	5	25	15	3	21	11	1	19	7	27	16	3	23	**13**	2	20	**9**	28	18	6	24	14	4	22	10	30
7	21	10	30	18	**6**	26	16	4	22	12	2	**20**	8	28	**17**	4	24	14	**3**	21	10	**29**	19	7	**25**	15	5	23	11	1
8	22	11	1	19	7	27	17	5	23	13	3	21	9	29	18	5	25	15	4	22	11	30	20	8	26	16	6	24	12	2
9	23	**12**	**2**	20	8	**28**	18	6	**24**	14	4	22	**10**	30	19	**6**	26	16	5	23	12	1	**21**	9	27	**17**	**7**	25	**13**	**3**
10	24	13	3	21	9	29	19	7	25	15	5	23	11	1	20	7	27	17	6	**24**	13	2	22	**10**	28	18	8	26	14	4
11	25	14	4	22	10	30	**20**	8	26	**16**	**6**	24	12	**2**	21	8	**28**	18	7	25	14	3	23	11	29	19	9	27	15	5
12	26	15	5	**23**	11	1	21	**9**	27	17	7	25	13	3	22	9	29	19	8	26	15	4	24	12	30	20	10	**28**	16	6
13	**27**	16	6	24	**12**	2	22	10	28	18	8	26	14	4	23	10	30	**20**	9	27	**16**	5	25	13	1	21	11	29	17	7
14	28	17	7	25	13	3	23	11	29	19	9	**27**	15	5	**24**	11	1	21	**10**	28	17	**6**	26	14	**2**	22	12	30	18	8
15	29	18	8	26	14	4	24	12	30	20	10	28	16	6	25	12	2	22	11	29	18	7	27	15	3	23	13	1	19	9
16	30	**19**	**9**	27	15	**5**	25	13	**1**	21	11	29	**17**	7	26	**13**	3	23	12	1	19	8	**28**	16	4	**24**	**14**	2	**20**	**10**
17	1	20	10	28	16	6	26	14	2	22	12	30	18	8	27	14	4	24	13	**1**	20	9	29	**17**	5	25	15	3	21	11
18	2	21	11	29	17	7	**27**	15	3	**23**	**13**	1	19	**9**	28	15	**5**	25	14	2	21	10	30	18	6	26	16	4	22	12
19	3	22	12	**30**	18	8	28	**16**	4	24	14	2	20	10	29	16	6	26	15	3	22	11	1	19	7	27	17	**5**	23	13
20	4	23	13	1	19	9	29	17	5	25	15	3	21	11	30	17	7	27	16	4	23	12	2	20	8	28	18	6	24	14
21	5	**24**	**14**	2	20	**10**	30	18	**6**	26	16	4	**22**	12	1	**18**	8	28	17	5	24	13	**3**	21	9	**29**	**19**	7	**25**	**15**
22	6	25	15	3	21	11	1	19	7	27	17	5	23	13	2	19	9	29	18	6	25	14	4	22	10	30	20	8	26	16
23	7	**26**	**16**	4	22	**12**	2	20	**8**	28	18	6	**24**	14	3	**20**	10	30	19	7	26	15	**5**	23	11	1	**21**	9	**27**	**17**
24	8	27	17	5	23	13	3	21	9	29	19	7	25	15	4	21	11	1	20	**8**	27	16	6	**24**	12	2	22	10	28	18
25	9	28	18	6	24	14	**4**	22	10	**30**	**20**	8	26	**16**	5	22	**12**	2	21	9	28	17	7	25	13	3	23	11	29	19
26	10	29	19	**7**	25	15	5	**23**	11	1	21	9	27	17	6	23	13	3	22	10	29	18	8	26	14	4	24	**12**	30	20
27	**11**	30	20	8	**26**	16	6	24	12	2	22	10	28	18	7	24	14	4	23	11	30	19	9	27	15	5	25	13	1	21
28	12	1	21	9	27	17	7	25	13	3	23	11	29	19	8	25	15	5	**24**	12	1	**20**	10	28	**16**	6	26	14	2	22
29	13	2	22	10	28	18	8	26	14	4	24	12	30	20	9	26	16	6	25	13	2	21	11	29	17	7	27	15	3	23
30	14	**3**	**23**	—	29	**19**	9	—	**15**	5	25	—	**31**	21	—	**27**	17	7	26	—	3	22	**12**	—	18	**8**	**28**	—	**4**	**24**

Figures in **black type** denote Sabbaths.

25th to 29th or 30th, Chanucah (opening days); 30th, First day of New Moon of Tebet.

TEBET (29 days)

83	82	81	80	79	78	77	76	75	74	73	72	71	70	69	68	67	66	65	64	63	62	61	60	59	58	57	56	55	5754	
22 23	21 22	20 21	19 20	18 19	17 18	16 17	15 16	14 15	13 14	12 13	11 12	10 11	09 10	08 09	07 08	06 07	06	04 05	03 04	02 03	01 02	2000 01	99 2000	98 99	97 98	96 97	95 96	94 95	1993 1994	Teb
Dec-Jan	Dec-Jan	Dec-Jan	Dec-Jan	Dec-Jan	Dec-Jan	Dec-Jan	Dec-Jan	Dec-Jan	Dec-Jan	Dec-Jan	Dec-Jan	Dec-Jan	Dec-Jan	Dec-Jan	Dec-Jan	Dec-Jan	January	Dec-Jan	Dec-Jan	Dec-Jan	Dec-Jan	Dec-Jan	Dec-Jan	Dec-Jan	Dec-Jan	Dec-Jan	Dec-Jan	Dec-Jan	Dec-Jan	
25	5	16	29	9	19	30	13	23	4	14	27	8	18	28	10	22	1	13	26	6	16	27	10	20	30	11	24	4	15	1
26	6	17	30	10	20	31	14	24	5	15	28	9	19	29	11	23	2	14	27	7	17	28	11	21	31	12	25	5	16	2
27	7	18	31	11	21	1	15	25	6	16	29	10	20	30	12	24	3	15	28	8	18	29	12	22	1	13	26	6	17	3
28	8	19	1	12	22	2	16	26	7	17	30	11	21	31	13	25	4	16	29	9	19	30	13	23	2	14	27	7	18	4
29	9	20	2	13	23	3	17	27	8	18	31	12	22	1	14	26	5	17	30	10	20	31	14	24	3	15	28	8	19	5
30	10	21	3	14	24	4	18	28	9	19	1	13	23	2	15	27	6	18	31	11	21	1	15	25	4	16	29	9	20	6
31	11	22	4	15	25	5	19	29	10	20	2	14	24	3	16	28	7	19	1	12	22	2	16	26	5	17	30	10	21	7
1	12	23	5	16	26	6	20	30	11	21	3	15	25	4	17	29	8	20	2	13	23	3	17	27	6	18	31	11	22	8
2	13	24	6	17	27	7	21	31	12	22	4	16	26	5	18	30	9	21	3	14	24	4	18	28	7	19	1	12	23	9
3	14	25	7	18	28	8	22	1	13	23	5	17	27	6	19	31	10	22	4	15	25	5	19	29	8	20	2	13	24	10
4	15	26	8	19	29	9	23	2	14	24	6	18	28	7	20	1	11	23	5	16	26	6	20	30	9	21	3	14	25	11
5	16	27	9	20	30	10	24	3	15	25	7	19	29	8	21	2	12	24	6	17	27	7	21	31	10	22	4	15	26	12
6	17	28	10	21	31	11	25	4	16	26	8	20	30	9	22	3	13	25	7	18	28	8	22	1	11	23	5	16	27	13
7	18	29	11	22	1	12	26	5	17	27	9	21	31	10	23	4	14	26	8	19	29	9	23	2	12	24	6	17	28	14
8	19	30	12	23	2	13	27	6	18	28	10	22	1	11	24	5	15	27	9	20	30	10	24	3	13	25	7	18	29	15
9	20	31	13	24	3	14	28	7	19	29	11	23	2	12	25	6	16	28	10	21	31	11	25	4	14	26	8	19	30	16
10	21	1	14	25	4	15	29	8	20	30	12	24	3	13	26	7	17	29	11	22	1	12	26	5	15	27	9	20	31	17
11	22	2	15	26	5	16	30	9	21	31	13	25	4	14	27	8	18	30	12	23	2	13	27	6	16	28	10	21	1	18
12	23	3	15	27	6	17	31	10	22	1	14	26	5	15	28	9	19	31	13	24	3	14	28	7	17	29	11	22	2	19
13	24	4	17	28	7	18	1	11	23	2	15	27	6	16	29	10	20	1	14	25	4	15	29	8	18	30	12	23	3	20
14	15	5	18	29	8	19	2	12	24	3	16	28	7	17	30	11	21	2	15	26	5	16	30	9	19	31	13	24	4	21
15	16	6	19	30	9	20	3	13	25	4	17	29	8	18	31	12	22	3	16	27	6	17	31	10	20	1	14	25	5	22
16	17	7	20	31	10	21	4	14	26	5	18	30	9	19	1	13	23	4	17	28	7	18	1	11	21	2	15	26	6	23
17	18	8	21	1	11	22	5	15	27	6	19	31	10	20	2	14	24	5	18	29	8	19	2	12	22	3	16	27	7	24
18	19	9	22	2	12	23	6	16	28	7	20	1	11	21	3	15	25	6	19	30	9	20	3	13	23	4	17	28	8	25
19	20	10	23	3	13	24	7	17	29	8	21	2	12	22	4	16	26	7	20	31	10	21	4	14	24	5	18	29	9	26
20	21	11	24	4	14	25	8	18	30	9	22	3	13	23	5	17	27	8	21	1	11	22	5	15	25	6	19	30	10	27
21	31	12	25	5	15	26	9	19	31	10	23	4	14	24	6	18	28	9	22	2	12	23	6	16	26	7	20	31	11	28
22	2	13	26	6	16	27	10	20	1	11	24	5	15	25	7	19	29	10	23	3	13	24	7	17	27	8	21	1	12	29

Figures in **black type** denote Sabbaths.
1st to 2nd or 3rd, Chanucah (final days); 10th, Fast of Tebet.

SHEBAT (30 days)

Sheb	83	82	81	80	79	78	77	76	75	74	73	72	71	70	69	68	67	66	65	64	63	62	61	60	59	58	57	56	55	5754
	23	22	21	20	19	18	17	16	15	14	13	12	11	10	09	08	07	06	05	04	03	02	01	2000	99	98	97	96	95	1994
	Jan-Feb	Jan-Feb	Jan-Feb	Jan-Feb	Jan-Feb	Jan-Feb	Jan-Feb	Jan-Feb	Jan-Feb	January	Jan-Feb	Jan-Feb	Jan-Feb	Jan-Feb	Jan-Feb	Jan-Feb	Jan-Feb	Jan-Feb	Jan-Feb	Jan-Feb	Jan-Feb	Jan-Feb	Jan-Feb	Jan-Feb	Jan-Feb	Jan-Feb	Jan-Feb	Jan-Feb	January	Jan-Feb
1	23	3	14	27	7	17	28	11	21	2	**12**	25	6	**16**	26	8	**20**	30	11	**24**	**4**	14	25	**8**	18	28	9	22	2	13
2	24	4	15	28	8	18	29	12	22	3	13	26	7	17	27	9	21	31	12	25	5	15	26	9	19	29	10	23	3	14
3	25	5	**16**	29	9	19	30	13	23	**4**	14	27	**8**	18	28	10	22	1	13	26	6	16	**27**	10	20	30	**11**	24	4	**15**
4	26	6	17	30	10	**20**	31	14	**24**	5	15	**28**	9	19	29	11	23	2	14	27	7	17	28	11	21	**31**	12	25	5	16
5	27	7	18	31	11	21	1	15	25	6	16	29	10	20	30	**12**	24	3	**15**	28	8	18	29	12	22	1	13	26	6	17
6	**28**	**8**	19	**1**	**12**	22	2	**16**	26	7	17	30	11	21	**31**	13	25	**4**	16	29	9	**19**	30	13	**23**	2	14	**27**	**7**	18
7	29	9	20	2	13	23	3	17	27	8	18	31	12	22	1	14	26	5	17	30	10	20	31	14	24	3	15	28	8	19
8	30	10	21	3	14	24	4	18	28	9	**19**	1	13	**23**	2	15	**27**	6	18	**31**	**11**	21	1	**15**	25	4	16	29	9	20
9	31	11	22	4	15	25	5	19	29	10	20	2	14	24	3	16	28	7	19	1	12	22	2	16	26	5	17	30	10	21
10	1	12	**23**	5	16	26	6	20	30	**11**	21	3	**15**	25	4	17	29	8	20	2	13	23	**3**	17	27	6	**18**	31	11	**22**
11	2	13	24	6	17	**27**	7	21	**31**	12	22	**4**	16	26	5	18	30	9	21	3	14	24	4	18	28	**7**	19	1	12	23
12	3	14	25	7	18	28	8	22	1	13	23	5	17	27	6	**19**	31	10	**22**	4	15	25	5	19	29	8	20	2	13	24
13	**4**	**15**	26	**8**	**19**	29	9	**23**	2	14	24	6	18	28	**7**	20	1	**11**	23	5	16	**26**	6	20	**30**	9	21	**3**	**14**	25
14	5	16	27	9	20	30	10	24	3	15	25	7	19	29	8	21	2	12	24	6	17	27	7	21	31	10	22	4	15	26
15	6	17	28	10	21	31	**11**	25	4	16	**26**	8	20	**30**	9	22	**3**	13	25	**7**	**18**	28	8	**22**	1	11	23	5	16	27
16	7	18	29	11	22	1	12	26	5	17	27	9	21	31	10	23	4	14	26	8	19	29	9	23	2	12	24	6	17	28
17	8	19	**30**	12	23	2	13	27	6	**18**	28	10	**22**	1	11	24	5	15	27	9	20	30	**10**	24	3	13	**25**	7	18	**29**
18	9	20	31	13	24	**3**	14	28	**7**	19	29	**11**	23	2	12	25	6	16	28	10	21	31	11	25	4	**14**	26	8	19	30
19	10	21	1	14	25	4	15	29	8	20	30	12	24	3	13	**26**	7	17	**29**	11	22	1	12	26	5	15	27	9	20	31
20	**11**	**22**	2	**15**	**26**	5	16	**30**	9	21	31	13	25	4	**14**	27	8	**18**	30	12	23	**2**	13	27	**6**	16	28	**10**	**21**	1
21	12	23	3	16	27	6	17	31	10	22	1	14	26	5	15	28	9	19	31	13	24	3	14	28	7	17	29	11	22	2
22	13	24	4	17	28	7	18	1	11	23	**2**	15	27	**6**	16	29	**10**	20	1	**14**	**25**	4	15	**29**	8	18	30	12	23	3
23	14	25	5	18	29	8	19	2	12	24	3	16	28	7	17	30	11	21	2	15	26	5	16	30	9	19	31	13	24	4
24	15	26	**6**	19	30	9	20	3	13	**25**	4	17	**29**	8	18	31	12	22	3	16	27	6	**17**	31	10	20	**1**	14	25	**5**
25	16	27	7	20	31	**10**	21	4	**14**	26	5	**18**	30	9	19	1	13	23	4	17	28	7	18	1	11	**21**	2	15	26	6
26	17	28	8	21	1	11	22	5	15	27	6	19	31	10	20	**2**	14	24	**5**	18	29	8	19	2	12	22	3	16	27	7
27	**18**	**29**	9	**22**	**2**	12	23	**6**	16	28	7	20	1	11	**21**	3	15	**25**	6	19	30	**9**	20	3	**13**	23	4	**17**	**28**	8
28	19	30	10	23	3	13	24	7	17	29	8	21	2	12	22	4	16	26	7	20	31	10	21	4	14	24	5	18	29	9
29	20	31	11	24	4	14	**25**	8	18	30	**9**	22	3	**13**	23	5	**17**	27	8	**21**	**1**	11	22	**5**	15	25	6	19	30	10
30	21	1	12	25	5	15	26	9	19	31	10	23	4	14	24	6	18	28	9	22	2	12	23	6	16	26	7	20	31	11

Figures in **black type** denote Sabbaths. 15th, New Year for Trees; 30th, First day of New Moon of Adar.

ADAR (29 days); in Leap Year, known as ADAR RISHON — 1st ADAR (30 days)

Adar	83	82	81	80	79	78	77	76	75	74	73	72	71	70	69	68	67	66	65	64	63	62	61	60	59	58	57	56	55	5754
	23	22	21	20	19	18	17	16	15	14	13	12	11	10	09	08	07	06	05	04	03	02	01	2000	99	98	97	96	95	1994
	Feb-Mar	Feb-Mar	Feb-Mar	Feb-Mar	Feb-Mar	Feb-Mar	Feb-Mar	Feb-Mar	Feb-Mar	Feb-Mar	Feb-Mar	Feb-Mar	Feb-Mar	Feb-Mar	Feb-Mar	Feb-Mar	Feb-Mar	March	Feb-Mar	Feb-Mar	Feb-Mar	Feb-Mar	Feb-Mar	Feb-Mar	Feb-Mar	Feb-Mar	Feb-Mar	Feb-Mar	Feb-Mar	Feb-Mar
1	22	2	**13**	26	6	16	27	10	20	**1**	11	24	**5**	15	25	7	19	1	10	23	3	13	**24**	7	17	27	**8**	21	1	**12**
2	23	3	14	27	7	**17**	28	11	**21**	2	12	**25**	6	16	26	8	20	2	11	24	4	14	25	8	18	**28**	9	22	2	13
3	24	4	15	28	8	18	1	**12**	22	3	13	26	7	17	27	**9**	21	3	**12**	25	5	15	26	9	19	1	10	23	3	14
4	**25**	**5**	16	29	**9**	19	2	17	23	4	14	27	8	18	**28**	10	22	**4**	13	26	6	**16**	27	10	**20**	2	11	**24**	**4**	15
5	26	6	17	1	10	20	3	14	24	5	15	28	9	19	1	11	23	5	14	27	7	17	28	11	21	3	12	25	5	16
6	27	7	18	2	11	21	**4**	15	25	6	**16**	29	10	**20**	2	12	**24**	6	15	**28**	**8**	18	1	**12**	22	4	13	26	6	17
7	28	8	19	3	12	22	5	16	26	7	17	1	11	21	3	13	25	7	16	29	9	19	2	13	23	5	14	27	7	18
8	1	9	**20**	4	13	23	6	17	27	**8**	18	2	**12**	22	4	14	26	8	17	1	10	20	**3**	14	24	6	**15**	28	8	**19**
9	2	10	21	5	14	**24**	7	18	**28**	9	19	**3**	13	23	5	15	27	9	18	2	11	21	4	15	25	**7**	16	29	9	20
10	3	11	22	6	15	25	8	19	1	10	20	4	14	24	6	**16**	28	10	**19**	3	12	22	5	16	26	8	17	1	10	21
11	**4**	**12**	23	7	**16**	26	9	**20**	2	11	21	5	15	25	**7**	17	1	**11**	20	4	13	**23**	6	17	**27**	9	18	**2**	**11**	22
12	5	13	24	8	17	27	10	21	3	12	22	6	16	26	8	18	2	12	21	5	14	24	7	18	28	10	19	3	12	23
13	**6**	14	**25**	**9**	18	**28**	**11**	22	**4**	13	**23**	**7**	17	**27**	**9**	19	**3**	**13**	22	**6**	**15**	**25**	**8**	**19**	**1**	**11**	20	**4**	13	**24**
14	**7**	15	**26**	**10**	19	**1**	**12**	23	**5**	14	**24**	**8**	18	**28**	**10**	20	**4**	**14**	23	**7**	16	**26**	**9**	20	**2**	**12**	21	**5**	14	**25**
15	**8**	16	**27**	**11**	20	**2**	**13**	24	**6**	**15**	**25**	**9**	**19**	**1**	**11**	21	**5**	**15**	24	**8**	17	**27**	**10**	21	**3**	**13**	**22**	**6**	15	**26**
16	9	17	28	12	21	**3**	14	25	**7**	16	26	**10**	20	2	12	22	6	16	25	9	18	28	11	22	4	**14**	23	7	16	27
17	10	18	1	13	22	4	15	26	8	17	27	11	21	3	13	**23**	7	17	**26**	10	19	1	12	23	5	15	24	8	17	28
18	**11**	**19**	2	14	**23**	5	16	**27**	9	18	28	12	22	4	**14**	24	8	**18**	27	11	20	**2**	13	24	**6**	16	25	**9**	**18**	1
19	12	20	3	15	24	6	17	28	10	19	1	13	23	5	15	25	9	19	28	12	21	3	14	25	7	17	26	10	19	2
20	13	21	4	16	25	7	**18**	29	11	20	**2**	14	24	**6**	16	26	**10**	20	1	**13**	**22**	4	15	**26**	8	18	27	11	20	3
21	14	22	5	17	26	8	19	1	12	21	3	15	25	7	17	27	11	21	2	14	23	5	16	27	9	19	28	12	21	4
22	15	23	**6**	18	27	9	20	2	13	**22**	4	16	**26**	8	18	28	12	22	3	15	24	6	**17**	28	10	20	1	13	22	**5**
23	16	24	7	19	28	**10**	21	3	**14**	23	5	**17**	27	9	19	29	13	23	4	16	25	7	18	29	11	21	2	14	23	6
24	17	25	8	20	1	11	22	4	15	24	6	18	28	10	20	**1**	14	24	**5**	17	26	8	19	1	12	22	3	15	24	7
25	**18**	**26**	9	21	**2**	12	23	**5**	16	25	7	19	1	11	**21**	2	15	**25**	6	18	27	**9**	20	2	**13**	23	4	**16**	**25**	8
26	19	27	10	22	3	13	24	6	17	26	8	20	2	12	22	3	16	26	7	19	28	10	21	3	14	24	5	17	26	9
27	20	28	11	23	4	14	**25**	7	18	27	**9**	21	3	**13**	23	4	**17**	27	8	**20**	1	11	22	**4**	15	25	6	18	27	10
28	21	1	12	24	5	15	26	8	19	28	10	22	4	14	24	5	18	28	9	21	2	12	23	5	16	26	7	19	28	11
29	22	2	**13**	25	6	16	27	9	20	**1**	11	23	**5**	15	25	6	19	29	10	22	3	13	**24**	6	17	27	**8**	20	1	**12**
30	—	**R**	—	—	**R**	—	—	**R**	—	**R**	—	—	**R**	—	—	**R**	—	—	**R**	—	**R**	—	—	**R**	—	—	**R**	—	**R**	—

Figures in **black type** denote Sabbaths.

13th, Fast of Esther (if on Sabbath, observed the preceding Thursday); 14th, Purim; 15th, Shushan Purim.

NOTE. — In a Jewish leap year, indicated by the letter R (for Adar Rishon) at the foot of a column, the above days are observed in 2nd Adar.
In a leap year, 30th day is First day of New Moon of the 2nd Adar.

2nd ADAR — ADAR SHENI, also known as VE-ADAR (29 days)

	5754	55	56	57	58	59	60	61	62	63	64	65	66	67	68	69	70	71	72	73	74	75	76	77	78	79	80	81	82	83
2nd Adar	1994	95	96	97	98	99	2000	01	02	03	04	05	06	07	08	09	10	11	12	13	14	15	16	17	18	19	20	21	22	23
	March			Mar-Apr			Mar-Apr			Mar-Apr		Mar-Apr			Mar-Apr			Mar-Apr			March		Mar-Apr			Mar-Apr			Mar-Apr	
1	3			10			8			5		**12**			**8**			7			3		11			8			4	
2	**4**			11			9			6		13			9			8			4		**12**			**9**			**5**	
3	5			12			10			7		14			10			9			5		13			10			6	
4	6			13			**11**			**8**		15			11			10			6		14			11			7	
5	7			14			12			9		16			12			11			7		15			12			8	
6	8			**15**			13			10		17			13			**12**			**8**		16			13			9	
7	9			16			14			11		18			14			13			9		17			14			10	
8	10			17			15			12		**19**			**15**			14			10		18			15			11	
9	**11**			18			16			13		20			16			15			11		**19**			**16**			**12**	
10	12			19			17			14		21			17			16			12		20			17			13	
11	13			20			**18**			**15**		22			18			17			13		21			18			14	
12	14			21			19			16		23			19			18			14		22			19			15	
13	15			**22**			20			17		24			20			**19**			**15**		23			20			16	
14	16			23			21			18		25			21			20			16		24			21			17	
15	17			24			22			19		**26**			**22**			21			17		25			22			18	
16	**18**			25			23			20		27			23			22			18		**26**			**23**			**19**	
17	19			26			24			21		28			24			23			19		27			24			20	
18	20			27			**25**			**22**		29			25			24			20		28			25			21	
19	21			28			26			23		30			26			25			21		29			26			22	
20	22			**29**			27			24		31			27			**26**			**22**		30			27			23	
21	23			30			28			25		1			28			27			23		31			28			24	
22	24			31			29			26		**2**			**29**			28			24		1			29			25	
23	**25**			1			30			27		3			30			29			25		**2**			**30**			**26**	
24	26			2			31			28		4			31			30			26		3			31			27	
25	27			3			**1**			29		5			1			31			27		4			1			28	
26	28			4			2			30		6			2			1			28		5			2			29	
27	29			**5**			3			31		7			3			**2**			**29**		6			3			30	
28	30			6			4			1		8			4			3			30		7			4			31	
29	31			7			5			2		**9**			**5**			4			31		8			5			1	

Figures in **black type** denote Sabbaths.

13th, Fast of Esther (if on Sabbath, observed on the preceding Thurday); 14th, Purim; 15th Shushan Purim.

NISAN (30 days)

Nis	83 / 23 / Mar-Apr	82 / 22 / Apr-May	81 / 21 / Mar-Apr	80 / 20 / Mar-Apr	79 / 19 / Apr-May	78 / 18 / Mar-Apr	77 / 17 / Mar-Apr	76 / 16 / Apr-May	75 / 15 / Mar-Apr	74 / 14 / April	73 / 13 / Mar-Apr	72 / 12 / Mar-Apr	71 / 11 / Apr-May	70 / 10 / Mar-Apr	69 / 09 / Mar-Apr	68 / 08 / Apr-May	67 / 07 / Mar-Apr	66 / 06 / Mar-Apr	65 / 05 / Apr-May	64 / 04 / Mar-Apr	63 / 03 / Apr-May	62 / 02 / Mar-Apr	61 / 01 / Mar-Apr	60 / 2000 / Apr-May	59 / 99 / Mar-Apr	58 / 98 / Mar-Apr	57 / 97 / Apr-May	56 / 96 / Mar-Apr	55 / 95 / April	5754 / 1994 / Mar-Apr
1	23	**2**	14	26	6	**17**	28	**9**	**21**	1	12	**24**	5	16	26	6	20	30	10	23	3	14	25	6	18	**28**	8	21	**1**	13
2	24	3	15	27	7	18	29	10	22	2	13	25	6	17	27	7	21	31	11	24	4	15	26	7	19	29	9	22	2	14
3	**25**	4	16	**28**	8	19	30	11	23	3	14	26	7	18	28	8	22	1	12	25	**5**	**16**	27	8	**20**	30	10	**23**	3	15
4	26	5	17	29	9	20	31	12	24	4	15	27	8	19	29	9	23	2	13	26	6	17	28	9	21	31	11	24	4	16
5	27	6	18	30	10	21	**1**	13	25	**5**	**16**	28	**9**	**20**	30	10	**24**	3	14	**27**	7	18	29	10	22	1	**12**	25	5	17
6	28	7	19	31	11	22	2	14	26	6	17	29	10	21	31	11	25	4	15	28	8	19	30	11	23	2	13	26	6	18
7	29	8	**20**	1	12	23	3	15	27	7	18	30	11	22	1	12	26	5	**16**	29	9	20	**31**	12	24	3	14	27	7	**19**
8	30	**9**	21	2	**13**	**24**	4	**16**	**28**	8	19	**31**	12	23	2	**13**	27	6	17	30	10	21	1	13	25	**4**	15	28	**8**	20
9	31	10	22	3	14	25	5	17	29	9	20	1	13	24	3	14	28	7	18	31	11	22	2	14	26	5	16	29	9	21
10	**1**	11	23	**4**	15	26	6	18	30	10	21	2	14	25	**4**	15	29	**8**	19	1	**12**	**23**	3	**15**	**27**	6	17	**30**	10	22
11	2	12	24	5	16	27	7	19	31	11	22	3	15	26	5	16	30	9	20	2	13	24	4	16	28	7	18	31	11	23
12	3	13	25	6	17	28	**8**	20	1	**12**	**23**	4	**16**	**27**	6	17	31	10	21	**3**	14	25	5	17	29	8	**19**	1	12	24
13	4	14	26	7	18	29	9	21	2	13	24	5	17	28	7	18	1	11	22	4	15	26	6	18	30	9	20	2	13	25
14	5	15	**27**	8	19	30	10	22	3	14	25	6	18	29	8	**19**	2	12	**23**	5	16	27	**7**	19	31	10	21	3	14	**26**
15	6	**16**	28	9	**20**	**31**	11	**23**	**4**	15	26	**7**	19	30	9	20	3	13	24	6	17	28	8	20	1	**11**	22	4	**15**	27
16	7	17	29	10	21	1	12	24	5	16	27	8	20	31	10	21	4	14	25	7	18	29	9	21	2	12	23	5	16	28
17	**8**	18	30	11	22	2	13	25	6	17	28	9	21	1	**11**	22	5	**15**	26	8	**19**	**30**	10	**22**	**3**	13	24	**6**	17	29
18	9	19	31	12	23	3	14	26	7	18	29	10	22	2	12	23	6	16	27	9	20	31	11	23	4	14	25	7	18	30
19	10	20	1	13	**20**	4	**15**	27	8	**19**	**30**	11	**23**	3	13	24	**7**	17	28	10	21	1	12	24	5	15	**26**	8	19	31
20	11	21	2	14	25	5	16	28	9	20	31	12	24	4	14	25	8	18	29	11	22	2	13	25	6	16	27	9	20	1
21	12	22	**3**	15	26	6	17	29	10	21	1	13	25	5	15	**26**	9	19	**30**	12	23	3	**14**	26	7	17	28	10	21	**2**
22	13	**23**	4	16	**27**	**7**	18	**30**	**11**	22	2	**14**	26	6	16	27	10	20	1	13	24	4	15	27	8	**18**	29	11	**22**	3
23	14	24	5	17	28	8	19	1	12	23	3	15	27	7	17	28	11	21	2	14	25	5	16	28	9	19	30	12	23	4
24	**15**	25	6	**18**	29	9	20	2	13	24	4	16	28	8	**18**	29	12	**22**	3	15	**26**	**6**	17	**29**	**10**	20	1	**13**	24	5
25	16	26	7	19	30	10	21	3	14	25	5	17	29	9	19	30	13	23	4	16	27	7	18	30	11	21	2	14	25	6
26	17	27	8	20	1	11	**22**	4	15	**26**	**6**	18	**30**	**10**	20	1	**14**	24	5	**17**	28	8	19	1	12	22	**3**	15	26	7
27	18	28	9	21	2	12	23	5	16	27	7	19	1	11	21	2	15	25	6	18	29	9	20	2	13	23	4	16	27	8
28	19	29	**10**	22	3	13	24	6	17	28	8	20	2	12	22	**3**	16	26	**7**	19	30	10	**21**	3	14	24	5	17	28	**9**
29	20	**30**	11	23	**4**	**14**	25	**7**	**18**	29	9	**21**	3	13	23	4	17	27	8	20	1	11	22	4	15	**25**	6	18	**29**	10
30	21	1	12	24	5	15	26	8	19	30	10	22	4	14	24	5	18	28	9	21	2	12	23	5	16	26	7	19	30	11

In the left-hand margin figures in **black type** denote major Holy-days; elsewhere they denote Sabbaths. 14th, Fast of the Firstborn (if on Sabbath, observed on the preceding Thursday); 15th to 22nd, Passover; 30th, First day of New Moon of Iyar.

IYAR (29 days)

Iyar	83 / 23 Apr-May	82 / 22 May	81 / 21 Apr-May	80 / 20 Apr-May	79 / 19 May-Jn	78 / 18 Apr-May	77 / 17 Apr-May	76 / 16 May-Jn	75 / 15 Apr-May	74 / 14 May	73 / 13 Apr-May	72 / 12 Apr-May	71 / 11 May-Jn	70 / 10 Apr-May	69 / 09 Apr-May	68 / 08 May-Jn	67 / 07 Apr-May	66 / 06 Apr-May	65 / 05 May-Jn	64 / 04 Apr-May	63 / 03 May	62 / 02 Apr-May	61 / 01 Apr-May	60 / 2000 May-Jn	59 / 99 Apr-May	58 / 98 Apr-May	57 / 97 May-Jn	56 / 96 Apr-May	55 / 95 May	5754 / 1994 Apr-May
1	**22**	2	13	**25**	6	16	27	9	20	1	11	23	5	15	**25**	6	19	**29**	10	22	**3**	**13**	24	**6**	**17**	27	8	**20**	1	12
2	23	3	14	26	7	17	28	10	21	2	12	24	6	16	26	7	20	30	11	23	4	14	25	7	18	28	9	21	2	13
3	24	4	15	27	8	18	**29**	11	22	**3**	**13**	25	**7**	**17**	27	8	**21**	1	12	**24**	5	15	26	8	19	29	**10**	22	3	14
4	25	5	16	28	9	19	30	12	23	4	14	26	8	18	28	9	22	2	13	25	6	16	27	9	20	30	11	23	4	15
5	26	6	**17**	29	10	20	1	13	24	5	15	27	9	19	29	**10**	23	3	**14**	26	7	17	**28**	10	21	1	12	24	5	**16**
6	**27**	**7**	18	30	**11**	**21**	2	**14**	**25**	6	16	**28**	10	20	30	11	24	4	15	27	8	18	29	11	22	**2**	13	25	**6**	17
7	28	8	19	1	12	22	3	15	26	7	17	29	11	21	1	12	25	5	16	28	9	19	30	12	23	3	14	26	7	18
8	**29**	9	20	**2**	13	23	4	16	27	8	18	30	12	22	**2**	13	26	**6**	17	29	**10**	**20**	1	**13**	**24**	4	15	**27**	8	19
9	30	10	21	3	14	24	5	17	28	9	19	1	13	23	3	14	27	7	18	30	11	21	2	14	25	5	16	28	9	20
10	1	11	22	4	15	25	**6**	18	29	**10**	**20**	2	**14**	**24**	4	15	**28**	8	19	**1**	12	22	3	15	26	6	**17**	29	10	21
11	2	12	23	5	16	26	7	19	30	11	21	3	15	25	5	16	29	9	20	2	13	23	4	16	27	7	18	30	11	22
12	3	13	**24**	6	17	27	8	20	1	12	22	4	16	26	6	**17**	30	10	**21**	3	14	24	**5**	17	28	8	19	1	12	**23**
13	**4**	**14**	25	7	**18**	**28**	9	**21**	**2**	13	23	**5**	17	27	7	18	1	**13**	22	4	15	25	6	18	29	**9**	20	2	**13**	24
14	5	15	26	8	19	29	10	22	3	14	24	6	18	28	8	19	2	14	23	5	16	26	7	19	30	10	21	3	14	25
15	**6**	16	27	**9**	20	30	11	23	4	15	25	7	19	29	**9**	20	3	**15**	24	6	**17**	**27**	8	**20**	**1**	11	22	**4**	15	26
16	7	17	28	10	21	1	12	24	5	16	26	8	20	30	10	21	4	16	25	7	18	28	9	21	2	12	23	5	16	27
17	8	18	29	11	22	2	**13**	25	6	**17**	**27**	9	**21**	**1**	11	22	**5**	17	26	**8**	19	29	10	22	3	13	**24**	6	17	28
18	**9**	**19**	**30**	**12**	**23**	**3**	**14**	**26**	**7**	**18**	**28**	**10**	**22**	**2**	**12**	**23**	**6**	**16**	**27**	**9**	**20**	**30**	**11**	**23**	**4**	**14**	**25**	**7**	**18**	**29**
19	10	20	**1**	13	24	4	15	27	8	19	29	11	23	3	13	**24**	7	17	**28**	10	21	1	**12**	24	5	15	26	8	19	**30**
20	11	**21**	2	14	**25**	**5**	16	**28**	**9**	20	30	**12**	24	4	14	25	8	18	29	11	22	2	13	25	6	**16**	27	9	**20**	1
21	12	22	3	15	26	6	17	29	10	21	1	13	25	5	15	26	9	19	30	12	23	3	14	26	7	17	28	10	21	2
22	**13**	23	4	**16**	27	7	18	30	11	22	2	14	26	6	**16**	27	10	**20**	31	13	**24**	**4**	15	**27**	**8**	18	29	**11**	22	3
23	14	24	5	17	28	8	19	31	12	23	3	15	27	7	17	28	11	21	1	14	25	5	16	28	9	19	30	12	23	4
24	15	25	6	18	29	9	**20**	1	13	**24**	**4**	16	**28**	**8**	18	29	**12**	22	2	**15**	26	6	17	29	10	20	**31**	13	24	5
25	16	26	7	19	30	10	21	2	14	25	5	17	29	9	19	30	13	23	3	16	27	7	18	30	11	21	1	14	25	6
26	17	27	**8**	20	31	11	22	3	15	26	6	18	30	10	20	**31**	14	24	**4**	17	28	8	**19**	31	12	22	2	15	26	**7**
27	18	**28**	9	21	**1**	**12**	23	**4**	**16**	27	7	**19**	31	11	21	1	15	25	5	18	29	9	20	1	13	**23**	3	16	**27**	8
28	19	29	10	22	2	13	24	5	17	28	8	20	1	12	22	2	16	26	6	19	30	10	21	2	14	24	4	17	28	9
29	**20**	30	11	**23**	3	14	25	6	18	29	9	21	2	13	**23**	3	17	**27**	7	20	**31**	**11**	22	**3**	**15**	25	5	**18**	29	10

Figures in **black type** denote Sabbaths.
18th, 33rd Day Omer, Scholars' Festival.

SIVAN (30 days)

Sivan	5754 1994 May-Jn	55 95 May-Jn	56 96 May-Jn	57 97 Jn-July	58 98 May-Jn	59 99 May-Jn	60 2000 Jn-July	61 01 May-Jn	62 02 May-Jn	63 03 June	64 04 May-Jn	65 05 Jn-July	66 06 May-Jn	67 07 May-Jn	68 08 Jn-July	69 09 May-Jn	70 10 May-Jn	71 11 Jn-July	72 12 May-Jn	73 13 May-Jn	74 14 May-Jn	75 15 May-Jn	76 16 Jn-July	77 17 May-Jn	78 18 May-Jn	79 19 Jn-July	80 20 May-Jn	81 21 May-Jn	82 22 May-Jn	83 23 May-Jn
1	11	30	19	6	26	16	4	23	12	1	21	8	28	18	4	24	14	3	22	10	30	19	7	26	15	4	24	12	31	21
2	12	31	20	**7**	27	17	5	24	13	2	**22**	9	29	**19**	5	25	**15**	**4**	23	**11**	**31**	20	8	**27**	16	5	25	13	1	22
3	13	1	21	8	28	18	6	25	14	3	23	10	30	20	6	26	16	5	24	12	1	21	9	28	17	6	26	14	2	23
4	**14**	2	22	9	29	19	7	**26**	15	4	24	**11**	31	21	**7**	27	17	6	25	13	2	22	10	29	18	7	27	**15**	3	24
5	15	**3**	23	10	**30**	20	8	27	16	5	25	12	1	22	8	28	18	7	**26**	14	3	**23**	**11**	30	**19**	**8**	28	16	**4**	25
6	**16**	**4**	**24**	**11**	**31**	**21**	**9**	**28**	**17**	**6**	**26**	**13**	**2**	**23**	**9**	**29**	**19**	**8**	**27**	**15**	**4**	**24**	**12**	**31**	**20**	**9**	**29**	**17**	**5**	**26**
7	**17**	**5**	**25**	**12**	**1**	**22**	**10**	**29**	**18**	**7**	**27**	**14**	**3**	**24**	**10**	**30**	**20**	**9**	**28**	**16**	**5**	**25**	**13**	**1**	**21**	**10**	**30**	**18**	**6**	**27**
8	18	6	26	13	2	23	11	30	19	8	28	15	4	25	11	31	21	10	29	17	6	26	14	2	22	11	31	19	7	28
9	19	7	27	**14**	3	24	12	31	20	9	**29**	16	5	**26**	12	1	**22**	**11**	30	**18**	**7**	27	15	**3**	23	12	1	20	8	29
10	20	8	28	15	4	25	13	1	21	10	30	17	6	27	13	2	23	12	31	19	8	28	16	4	24	13	2	21	9	30
11	**21**	9	29	16	5	26	14	**2**	22	11	31	**18**	7	28	**14**	3	24	13	1	20	9	29	17	5	25	14	3	**22**	10	31
12	22	**10**	30	17	**6**	27	15	3	23	12	1	19	8	29	15	4	25	14	**2**	21	10	**30**	**18**	6	**26**	**15**	4	23	**11**	1
13	23	11	31	18	7	28	16	4	24	13	2	20	9	30	16	5	26	15	3	22	11	31	19	7	27	16	5	24	12	2
14	24	12	**1**	19	8	**29**	**17**	5	**25**	**14**	3	21	**10**	31	17	**6**	27	16	4	23	12	1	20	8	28	17	**6**	25	13	**3**
15	25	13	2	20	9	30	18	6	26	15	4	22	11	1	18	7	28	17	5	24	13	2	21	9	29	18	7	26	14	4
16	26	14	3	**21**	10	31	19	7	27	16	**5**	23	12	**2**	19	8	**29**	**18**	6	**25**	**14**	3	22	**10**	30	19	8	27	15	5
17	27	15	4	22	11	1	20	8	28	17	6	24	13	3	20	9	30	19	7	26	15	4	23	11	31	20	9	28	16	6
18	**28**	16	5	23	12	2	21	**9**	29	18	7	**25**	14	4	**21**	10	31	20	8	27	16	5	24	12	1	21	10	**29**	17	7
19	29	**17**	6	24	**13**	3	22	10	30	19	8	26	15	5	22	11	1	21	**9**	28	17	**6**	**25**	13	**2**	**22**	11	30	**18**	8
20	30	18	7	25	14	4	23	11	31	20	9	27	16	6	23	12	2	22	10	29	18	7	26	14	3	23	12	31	19	9
21	31	19	**8**	26	15	**5**	**24**	12	**1**	**21**	10	28	**17**	7	24	**13**	3	23	11	30	19	8	27	15	4	24	**13**	1	20	**10**
22	1	20	9	27	16	6	25	13	2	22	11	29	18	8	25	14	4	24	12	31	20	9	28	16	5	25	14	2	21	11
23	2	21	10	**28**	17	7	26	14	3	23	**12**	30	19	**9**	26	15	**5**	**25**	13	**1**	**21**	10	29	**17**	6	26	15	3	22	12
24	3	22	11	29	18	8	27	15	4	24	13	1	20	10	27	16	6	26	14	2	22	11	30	18	7	27	16	4	23	13
25	**4**	23	12	30	19	9	28	**16**	5	25	14	**2**	21	11	**28**	17	7	27	15	3	23	12	1	19	8	28	17	**5**	24	14
26	5	**24**	13	1	**20**	10	29	17	6	26	15	3	22	12	29	18	8	28	**16**	4	24	**13**	**2**	20	**9**	**29**	18	6	**25**	15
27	6	25	14	2	21	11	30	18	7	27	16	4	23	13	30	19	9	29	17	5	25	14	3	21	10	30	19	7	26	16
28	7	26	**15**	3	22	**12**	**1**	19	**8**	**28**	17	5	**24**	14	1	**20**	10	30	18	6	26	15	4	22	11	1	**20**	8	27	**17**
29	8	27	16	4	23	13	2	20	9	29	18	6	25	15	2	21	11	1	19	7	27	16	5	23	12	2	21	9	28	18
30	**9**	**28**	**17**	**5**	**24**	**14**	**3**	**21**	**10**	**30**	**19**	**7**	**26**	**16**	**3**	**22**	**12**	**2**	**20**	**8**	**28**	**17**	**6**	**24**	**13**	**3**	**22**	**10**	**29**	**19**

In the left-hand margin figures in **black type** denote major Holy-days; elsewhere they denote Sabbaths. 6th and 7th, Pentecost; 30th, First day of New Moon of Tammuz.

TAMMUZ (29 days)

Tam	83	82	81	80	79	78	77	76	75	74	73	72	71	70	69	68	67	66	65	64	63	62	61	60	59	58	57	56	55	5754
	23	22	21	20	19	18	17	16	15	14	13	12	11	10	09	08	07	06	05	04	03	02	01	2000	99	98	97	96	95	1994
	Jn-July	Jn-July	Jn-July	Jn-July	July-Au	Jn-July	Jn-July	July-Au	Jn-July	Jn-July	Jn-July	Jn-July	July	Jn-July	Jn-July	July-Au	Jn-July	Jn-July	July-Au	Jn-July	July	Jn-July	Jn-July	July-Au	Jn-July	Jn-July	July-Au	Jn-July	Jn-July	Jn-July
1	20	30	11	23	4	14	25	7	18	29	9	21	3	13	23	4	17	27	8	20	1	11	22	4	15	25	6	18	29	10
2	21	1	**12**	24	5	15	26	8	19	30	10	22	4	14	24	**5**	18	28	**9**	21	2	12	**23**	5	16	26	7	19	30	**11**
3	22	**2**	13	25	**6**	**16**	27	**9**	**20**	1	11	**23**	5	15	25	6	19	29	10	22	3	13	24	6	17	**27**	8	20	**1**	12
4	23	3	14	26	7	17	28	10	21	2	12	24	6	16	26	7	20	30	11	23	4	14	25	7	18	28	9	21	2	13
5	**24**	4	15	**27**	8	18	29	11	22	3	13	25	7	17	**27**	8	21	**1**	12	24	**5**	**15**	26	**8**	**19**	29	10	**22**	3	14
6	25	5	16	28	9	19	30	12	23	4	14	26	8	18	28	9	22	2	13	25	6	16	27	9	20	30	11	23	4	15
7	26	6	17	29	10	20	**1**	13	24	**5**	**15**	27	**9**	**19**	29	10	**23**	3	14	**26**	7	17	28	10	21	1	**12**	24	5	16
8	27	7	18	30	11	21	2	14	25	6	16	28	10	20	30	11	24	4	15	27	8	18	29	11	22	2	13	25	6	17
9	28	8	**19**	1	12	22	3	15	26	7	17	29	11	21	1	**12**	25	5	**16**	28	9	19	**30**	12	23	3	14	26	7	**18**
10	29	**9**	20	2	**13**	**23**	4	**16**	**27**	8	18	**30**	12	22	2	13	26	6	17	29	10	20	1	13	24	**4**	15	27	**8**	19
11	30	10	21	3	14	24	5	17	28	9	19	1	13	23	3	14	27	7	18	30	11	21	2	14	25	5	16	28	9	20
12	**1**	11	22	**4**	15	25	6	18	29	10	20	2	14	24	**4**	15	28	**8**	19	1	**12**	**22**	3	**15**	**26**	6	17	**29**	10	21
13	2	12	23	5	16	26	7	19	30	11	21	3	15	25	5	16	29	9	20	2	13	23	4	16	27	7	18	30	11	22
14	3	13	24	6	17	27	**8**	20	1	**12**	**22**	4	**16**	**26**	6	17	**30**	10	21	**3**	14	24	5	17	28	8	**19**	1	12	23
15	4	14	25	7	18	28	9	21	2	13	23	5	17	27	7	18	1	11	22	4	15	25	6	18	29	9	20	2	13	24
16	5	15	**26**	8	19	29	10	22	3	14	24	6	18	28	8	**19**	2	12	**23**	5	16	26	**7**	19	30	10	21	3	14	**25**
17	6	**16**	27	9	**20**	**30**	11	**23**	**4**	15	25	**7**	19	29	9	20	3	13	24	6	17	27	8	20	1	**11**	22	4	**15**	26
18	7	17	28	10	21	1	12	24	5	16	26	8	20	30	10	21	4	14	25	7	18	28	9	21	2	12	23	5	16	27
19	**8**	18	29	**11**	22	2	13	25	6	17	27	9	21	1	**11**	22	5	**15**	26	8	**19**	**29**	10	**22**	**3**	13	24	**6**	17	28
20	9	19	30	12	23	3	14	26	7	18	28	10	22	2	12	23	6	16	27	9	20	30	11	23	4	14	25	7	18	29
21	10	20	1	13	24	4	**15**	27	8	**19**	**29**	11	**23**	**3**	13	24	**7**	17	28	**10**	21	1	12	24	5	15	**26**	7	19	30
22	11	21	2	14	25	5	16	28	9	20	30	12	24	4	14	25	8	18	29	11	22	2	13	25	6	16	27	9	20	1
23	12	22	**3**	15	26	6	17	29	10	21	1	13	25	5	15	**26**	9	19	**30**	12	23	3	**14**	26	7	17	28	10	21	**2**
24	13	**23**	4	16	**27**	**7**	18	**30**	**11**	22	2	**14**	26	6	16	27	10	20	31	13	24	4	15	27	8	**18**	29	11	**22**	3
25	14	24	5	17	28	8	19	31	12	23	3	15	27	7	17	28	11	21	1	14	25	5	16	28	9	19	30	12	23	4
26	**15**	25	6	**18**	29	9	20	1	13	24	4	16	28	8	**18**	29	12	**22**	2	15	**26**	**6**	17	**28**	**10**	20	31	**13**	24	5
27	16	26	7	19	30	10	21	2	14	25	5	17	29	9	19	30	13	23	3	16	27	7	18	29	11	21	1	14	25	6
28	17	27	8	20	31	11	**22**	3	15	**26**	**6**	18	**30**	**10**	20	31	**14**	24	4	**17**	28	8	19	31	12	22	**2**	14	26	7
29	18	28	9	21	1	12	23	4	16	27	7	19	31	11	21	1	15	25	5	18	29	9	20	1	13	23	3	16	27	8

Figures in **black type** denote Sabbaths.
17th, Fast of Tammuz (if on Sabbath, postponed to Sunday).

AB (30 days)

Ab	83	82	81	80	79	78	77	76	75	74	73	72	71	70	69	68	67	66	65	64	63	62	61	60	59	58	57	56	55	5754
	23	22	21	20	19	18	17	16	15	14	13	12	11	10	09	08	07	06	05	04	03	02	01	2000	99	98	97	96	95	1994
	July-Au	July-Au	July-Au	July-Au	August	July-Au	July-Au	Au-Sep	July-Au	July-Au	July-Au	July-Au	August	July-Au	July-Au	August	July-Au	July-Au	Au-Sep	July-Au	July-Au	July-Au	July-Au	August	July-Au	July-Au	Au-Sep	July-Au	July-Au	July-Au
1	19	29	10	22	2	13	24	5	17	28	8	20	1	12	22	2	16	26	6	19	30	10	21	2	14	24	4	17	28	9
2	20	30	11	23	3	14	25	6	18	29	9	21	2	13	23	3	17	27	7	20	31	11	22	3	15	25	5	18	29	10
3	21	31	12	24	4	15	26	7	19	30	10	22	3	14	24	4	18	28	8	21	1	12	23	4	16	26	6	19	30	11
4	22	1	13	25	5	16	27	8	20	31	11	23	4	15	25	5	19	29	9	22	2	13	24	5	17	27	7	20	31	12
5	23	2	14	26	6	17	28	9	21	1	12	24	5	16	26	6	20	30	10	23	3	14	25	6	18	28	8	21	1	13
6	24	3	15	27	7	18	29	10	22	2	13	25	6	17	27	7	21	31	11	24	4	15	26	7	19	29	9	22	2	14
7	25	4	16	28	8	19	30	11	23	3	14	26	7	18	28	8	22	1	12	25	5	16	27	8	20	30	10	23	3	15
8	26	5	17	29	9	20	31	12	24	4	15	27	8	19	29	9	23	2	13	26	6	17	28	9	21	31	11	24	4	16
9	27	6	18	30	10	21	1	13	25	5	16	28	9	20	30	10	24	3	14	27	7	18	29	10	22	1	12	25	5	17
10	28	7	19	31	11	22	2	14	26	6	17	29	10	21	31	11	25	4	15	28	8	19	30	11	23	2	13	26	6	18
11	29	8	20	1	12	23	3	15	27	7	18	30	11	22	1	12	26	5	16	29	9	20	31	12	24	3	14	27	7	19
12	30	9	21	2	13	24	4	16	28	8	19	31	12	23	2	13	27	6	17	30	10	21	1	13	25	4	15	28	8	20
13	31	10	22	3	14	25	5	17	29	9	20	1	13	24	3	14	28	7	18	31	11	22	2	14	26	5	16	29	9	21
14	1	11	23	4	15	26	6	18	30	10	21	2	14	25	4	15	29	8	19	1	12	23	3	15	27	6	17	30	10	22
15	2	12	24	5	16	27	7	19	31	11	22	3	15	26	5	16	30	9	20	2	13	24	4	16	28	7	18	31	11	23
16	3	13	25	6	17	28	8	20	1	12	23	4	16	27	6	17	31	10	21	3	14	25	5	17	29	8	19	1	12	24
17	4	14	26	7	18	29	9	21	2	13	24	5	17	28	7	18	1	11	22	4	15	26	6	18	30	9	20	2	13	25
18	5	15	27	8	19	30	10	22	3	14	25	6	18	29	8	19	2	12	23	5	16	27	7	19	31	10	21	3	14	26
19	6	16	28	9	20	31	11	23	4	15	26	7	19	30	9	20	3	13	24	6	17	28	8	20	1	11	22	4	15	27
20	7	17	29	10	21	1	12	24	5	16	27	8	20	31	10	21	4	14	25	7	18	29	9	21	2	12	23	5	16	28
21	8	18	30	11	22	2	13	25	6	17	28	9	21	1	11	22	5	15	26	8	19	30	10	22	3	13	24	6	17	29
22	9	19	31	12	23	3	14	26	7	18	29	10	22	2	12	23	6	16	27	9	20	31	11	23	4	14	25	7	18	30
23	10	20	1	13	24	4	15	27	8	19	30	11	23	3	13	24	7	17	28	10	21	1	12	24	5	15	26	8	19	31
24	11	21	2	14	25	5	16	28	9	20	31	12	24	4	14	25	8	18	29	11	22	2	13	25	6	16	27	9	20	1
25	12	22	3	15	26	6	17	29	10	21	1	13	25	5	15	26	9	19	30	12	23	3	14	26	7	17	28	10	21	2
26	13	23	4	16	27	7	18	30	11	22	2	14	26	6	16	27	10	20	31	13	24	4	15	27	8	18	29	11	22	3
27	14	24	5	17	28	8	19	31	12	23	3	15	27	7	17	28	11	21	1	14	25	5	16	28	9	19	30	12	23	4
28	15	25	6	18	29	9	20	1	13	24	4	16	28	8	18	29	12	22	2	15	26	6	17	29	10	20	31	13	24	5
29	16	26	7	19	30	10	21	2	14	25	5	17	29	9	19	30	13	23	3	16	27	7	18	30	11	21	1	14	25	6
30	17	27	8	20	31	11	22	3	15	26	6	18	30	10	20	31	14	24	4	17	28	8	19	31	12	22	2	15	26	7

Figures in **black type** denote Sabbaths.

9th, Fast of Ab (if on Sabbath, postponed to Sunday); 30th, First Day of New Moon of Elul.

ELUL (29 days)

83	82	81	80	79	78	77	76	75	74	73	72	71	70	69	68	67	66	65	64	63	62	61	60	59	58	57	56	55	5754	Elul
23	22	21	20	19	18	17	16	15	14	13	12	11	10	09	08	07	06	05	04	03	02	01	2000	99	98	97	96	95	1994	
Au-Sep	Au-Sep	Au-Sep	Au-Sep	Sept	Au-Sep	Au-Sep	Sep-Oct	Au-Sep	Au-Sep	Au-Sep	Au-Sep	Au-Sep	Au-Sep	Au-Sep	Sept	Au-Sep	Au-Sep	Sep-Oct	Au-Sep	Au-Sep	Au-Sep	Au-Sep	Sept	Au-Sep	Au-Sep	Sep-Oct	Au-Sep	Au-Sep	Au-Sep	
18	28	9	21	1	12	23	4	16	27	7	19	31	11	21	1	15	25	5	18	29	9	20	1	13	23	3	16	27	8	1
19	29	10	**22**	2	13	24	5	17	28	8	20	1	12	**22**	2	16	**26**	6	19	**30**	**10**	21	**2**	**14**	24	4	**17**	28	9	2
20	30	11	23	3	14	25	6	18	29	9	21	2	13	23	3	17	27	7	20	31	11	22	3	15	25	5	18	29	10	3
21	31	12	24	4	15	**26**	7	19	**30**	**10**	22	**3**	**14**	24	4	**18**	28	8	**21**	1	12	23	4	16	26	**6**	19	30	11	4
22	1	13	25	5	16	27	8	20	31	11	23	4	15	25	5	19	29	9	22	2	13	24	5	17	27	7	20	31	12	5
23	2	**14**	26	6	17	28	9	21	1	12	24	5	16	26	**6**	20	30	**10**	23	3	14	**25**	6	18	28	8	21	1	**13**	6
24	**3**	15	27	**7**	**18**	29	**10**	**22**	2	13	**25**	6	17	27	7	21	31	11	24	4	15	26	7	19	**29**	9	22	**2**	14	7
25	4	16	28	8	19	30	11	23	3	14	26	7	18	28	8	22	1	12	25	5	16	27	8	20	30	10	23	3	15	8
26	5	17	**29**	9	20	31	12	24	4	15	27	8	19	**29**	9	23	**2**	13	26	**6**	**17**	28	**9**	**21**	31	11	**24**	4	16	9
27	6	18	30	10	21	1	13	25	5	16	28	9	20	30	10	24	3	14	27	7	18	29	10	22	1	12	25	5	17	10
28	7	19	31	11	22	**2**	14	26	**6**	**17**	29	**10**	**21**	31	11	**25**	4	15	**28**	8	19	30	11	23	2	**13**	26	6	18	11
29	8	20	1	12	23	3	15	27	7	18	30	11	22	1	12	26	5	16	29	9	20	31	12	24	3	14	27	7	19	12
30	9	**21**	2	13	24	4	16	28	8	19	31	12	23	2	**13**	27	6	**17**	30	10	21	**1**	13	25	4	15	28	8	**20**	13
31	**10**	22	3	**14**	**25**	5	**17**	**29**	9	20	**1**	13	24	3	14	28	7	18	31	11	22	2	14	26	**5**	16	29	9	21	14
1	11	23	4	15	26	6	18	30	10	21	2	14	25	4	15	29	8	19	1	12	23	3	15	27	6	17	30	10	22	15
2	12	24	**5**	16	27	7	19	31	11	22	3	15	26	**5**	16	30	**9**	20	2	**13**	**24**	4	**16**	**28**	7	18	**31**	11	23	16
3	13	25	6	17	28	8	20	1	12	23	4	16	27	6	17	31	10	21	3	14	25	5	17	29	8	19	1	12	24	17
4	14	26	7	18	29	**9**	21	2	**13**	**24**	5	17	28	7	18	1	11	22	**4**	15	26	6	18	30	9	**20**	2	13	25	18
5	15	27	8	19	30	10	22	3	14	25	6	18	29	8	19	2	12	23	5	16	27	7	19	31	10	21	3	14	26	19
6	16	28	9	20	31	11	23	4	15	26	7	19	30	9	**20**	3	13	24	6	17	28	**8**	20	1	11	22	4	15	**27**	20
7	**17**	29	10	**21**	**1**	12	**24**	**5**	16	27	**8**	20	31	10	21	4	14	**24**	7	18	29	9	21	2	**12**	23	5	**16**	28	21
8	18	30	11	22	2	13	25	6	17	28	9	21	1	11	22	5	15	25	8	19	30	10	22	3	13	24	6	17	29	22
9	19	31	**12**	23	3	14	26	7	18	29	10	22	2	**12**	23	6	**16**	26	9	**20**	**31**	11	**23**	**4**	14	25	**7**	18	30	23
10	20	1	13	24	4	15	27	8	19	30	11	23	3	13	24	7	17	27	10	21	1	12	24	5	15	26	8	19	31	24
11	21	2	14	25	5	**16**	28	9	**20**	**31**	12	24	4	14	25	**8**	18	28	**11**	22	2	13	25	6	16	**27**	9	20	1	25
12	22	3	15	26	6	17	29	10	21	1	13	25	5	15	26	9	19	29	12	23	3	14	26	7	17	28	10	21	2	26
13	23	**4**	16	27	7	18	30	11	22	2	14	26	6	16	**27**	10	20	30	13	24	4	15	27	8	18	29	11	22	**3**	27
14	**24**	5	17	**28**	**8**	19	**1**	**12**	23	3	**15**	27	7	17	28	11	21	**1**	14	25	5	16	28	9	**19**	30	12	**23**	4	28
15	25	6	18	29	9	20	2	13	24	4	16	28	8	18	29	12	22	2	15	26	6	17	29	10	20	1	13	24	5	29

Figures in **black type** denote Sabbaths.

INDEX

Update for Jewish Year Book 2010

Readers are asked kindly to draw attention to any omissions or errors. If errors are discovered, it would be appreciated if you could give up-to-date information, referring to the appropriate page, and send this form to the Editor at the address given below before 31st July 2009. Alternatively, you can email us: info@vmbooks.com giving a full postal address

With reference to the following entry:

Page:

Country:

Entry should read:

Kindly list on separate sheet if preferred.

Signed: _____   Date: _____ .

Name (BLOCK CAPITALS)

_____ .

Address:

_____

_____ .

Telephone:

_____ .

The Editor
Jewish Year Book
Vallentine Mitchell & Co. Ltd.
Suite 314, Premier House, 112-114 Station Road,
Edgware, Middlesex HA8 7BJ
Tel: + 44(0)20 8952 9526   Fax: + 44(0)20 8952 9242.
www.vmbooks.com

Please complete and return the Jewish Year Book form to us by 1 September 2009

Please reserve the following advertising space in

The Jewish Year Book 2010:

FULL COLOUR AVAILABLE

☐ Full Page £675 182 x 115 mm

☐ Half Page £395 90 x 115 mm

☐ Quarter Page £225 45.5 x 115 mm

(UK advertisers please note that the above rates are subject to VAT)

Special positions by arrangement

☐ **Please insert the attached copy (If setting is required a 10% setting charge will be made.)**

☐ **Copy will be forwarded from our Advertising Agents (*see below*)**

Contact Name: _____

Advertisers Name:_____

Address for invoicing: _____

_____

Tel:_____ Fax: _____

Signed: _____ Title: _____

VAT No: _____

Date: _____

Agency Name (if applicable):_____

Address: _____

_____

Tel: _____ Fax: _____

All advertisements set by the publisher will only be included if they have been signed and approved by the advertiser.

To the Advertising Department
The Jewish Year Book
Vallentine Mitchell

Suite 314, Premier House, 112-114 Station Road, Edgware, Middlesex HA8 7BJ

Tel: +44 (0)20 8952 9526 Fax: + 44(0)20 8952 9242

www.vmbooks.com

JEWISH CARE

The difference is *Jewish* care

We promote and celebrate our clients' Jewish identity in every area of our work. Through our Jewish values of warmth, kindness, honesty, respect and dignity we provide more than just care, we provide outstanding *Jewish* care.

Care homes • Community centres
Connect@centres • Day care centres
Dementia care centres • Disability services
Family carers' support • Home care
Holocaust survivors' services • Mental health services
Social work service • Support groups
Talking books and newspapers • Volunteering opportunities

All this on one number!

To find out more about any of our services call our helpline on
020 8922 2222

Visit our website
www.jewishcare.org

or email us at
jewishcaredirect@jcare.org

JEWISH CARE

Charity Registration Number 802559